THE KATHERINE GROUP:
MS BODLEY 34

Religious Writings for Women
in Medieval England

MIDDLE ENGLISH TEXTS SERIES

The Middle English Texts Series is designed for classroom use. Its goal is to make available to teachers, scholars, and students texts that occupy an important place in the literary and cultural canon but have not been readily available in student editions. The series does not include those authors, such as Chaucer, Langland, or Malory, whose English works are normally in print in good student editions. The focus is, instead, upon Middle English literature adjacent to those authors that teachers need in compiling the syllabuses they wish to teach. The editions maintain the linguistic integrity of the original work but within the parameters of modern reading conventions. The texts are printed in the modern alphabet and follow the practices of modern capitalization, word formation, and punctuation. Manuscript abbreviations are silently expanded, and *u/v* and *j/i* spellings are regularized according to modern orthography. Yogh (ʒ) is transcribed as *g, gh, y,* or *s,* according to the sound in Modern English spelling to which it corresponds; thorn (þ) and eth (ð) are transcribed as *th.* Distinction between the second person pronoun and the definite article is made by spelling the one *thee* and the other *the,* and final *-e* that receives full syllabic value is accented (e.g., *charité*). Hard words, difficult phrases, and unusual idioms are glossed either in the right margin or at the foot of the page. Explanatory and textual notes appear at the end of the text, often along with a glossary. The editions include short introductions on the history of the work, its merits and points of topical interest, and brief working bibliographies.

This series is published in association with the University of Rochester.

Medieval Institute Publications is a program of
The Medieval Institute, College of Arts and Sciences

WESTERN MICHIGAN UNIVERSITY

THE KATHERINE GROUP:
MS BODLEY 34

Religious Writings for Women in Medieval England

Edited by
Emily Rebekah Huber and Elizabeth Robertson

TEAMS • Middle English Texts Series • University of Rochester

MEDIEVAL INSTITUTE PUBLICATIONS
Western Michigan University
Kalamazoo

Copyright © 2016 by the Board of Trustees of Western Michigan University

Printed and bound in Great Britain by CPI Group (UK) Ltd, Croydon, CR0 4YY

Library of Congress Cataloging-in-Publication Data
are available at the Library of Congress.

ISBN 978-1-58044-248-0
eISBN 978-1-58044-249-7

 # Contents

ACKNOWLEDGMENTS

Thanks are due to several people without whose time and effort this volume would not have seen the light of day. In the early stages of the project, John Sutton lent his philological expertise and read through and checked our translations of the difficult Middle English; likewise, Bob Hasenfratz offered helpful feedback on several stubborn *cruces* in the translation and notes. A warm thank you to Ralph Hanna for crucial suggestions on the latest developments in the study of the AB Group manuscripts. Thank you to Donald C. Baker for his advice of the transcription of the manuscript early on in the process. Staff editor Sharon E. Rhodes read our text against the Bodleian manuscript, and checked our emendations against the other manuscript sources. We would like to thank Jeremy Smith for some helpful last minute suggestions. We are especially grateful to Joyce Coleman for a thorough and generous response to the entire introduction. John H. Chandler and Alan Lupack read through our volume and offered feedback at several stages of the process. Declan Mollan helped us update our bibliography. Richard Dance provided invaluable advice on our glossary. We are also grateful to Patricia Hollahan and the staff at Medieval Institute Publications. Most importantly, Martha M. Johnson-Olin, former Assistant Editor, Pamela M. Yee, current Assistant Editor; Alison Harper, Jenny Boyar, and Kyle Huskin, staff editors; and Russell A. Peck, General Editor, have our gratitude for their tireless work, eagle eyes, and generous patience. Martha undertook the arduous task of formatting the book and doing multiple read-throughs of the texts and notes at various stages of the editorial process. And, as always, Russell has been there every step of the way with his support, advice, and wisdom as we brought this project from beginning to end.

We would also like to thank the Bodleian Library at Oxford University for allowing us to examine the original manuscript during work on this edition, and the National Endowment for the Humanities for its continuous support of Middle English Texts Series.

INTRODUCTION TO THE KATHERINE GROUP

Since 1929, when J. R. R. Tolkien brought our attention to Oxford, Bodleian Library MS Bodley 34, the importance of this manuscript has been widely recognized.[1] For philologists, it preserves evidence of the linguistic transition between Anglo-Saxon and fourteenth-century Middle English. For literary scholars, it offers some of the few innovative pieces of literature written in English in the first centuries after the Norman Conquest. For cultural studies critics and feminist scholars, it provides rare insight into the history of female literacy and the nature of the female spiritual life in late twelfth and early thirteenth-century England.

Measuring roughly five by seven inches, Bodley 34 is a modest, unadorned manuscript that could easily be held in one's hand. Its eighty folios contain: *The Martyrdom of Sancte Katerine* (The Martyrdom of Saint Katherine); *The Liflade ant te Passiun of Seinte Margarete* (The Life and Passion of Saint Margaret); *The Liflade ant te Passiun of Seinte Juliene* (The Life and Passion of Saint Juliana); *Hali Meithhad* (Holy Maidenhood); and a sermon on the soul called *Sawles Warde* (The Guardianship of the Soul).[2] Collectively, these texts are known as the Katherine Group, after the first of its texts.[3] The manuscript was created in the first quarter of the thirteenth-century (according to E. J. Dobson, roughly 1225).

Produced in an area of Scandinavian settlement on the Welsh marches, far from metropolitan and regal centers, the Katherine Group texts mark a borderland that is not only geographical, but also intellectual and temporal. They were designed to cater to the needs of a predominantly English-reading audience, yet the authors' proximity to prominent religious establishments such as Hereford Cathedral and Wigmore Abbey allowed them to draw on the latest theological developments. In their use of a strong two-beat alliterative rhythm, the texts hearken back to great Anglo-Saxon prose writers such as Ælfric, Wulfstan, and the anonymous homilists. Yet they also drew heavily on the rhetorical resources of the continental Latin tradition. A density of startlingly quotidian detail, some taken from and some added to these sources, enlivens these heterogeneous texts.

---

[1] Tolkien, "*Ancrene Wisse* and *Hali Meiðhad*." Tolkien was not the first to notice Bodley 34 or to connect its existence to the then better-known *Ancrene Wisse*. Hall first published two Bodley 34 texts (*Sawles Warde* and *Þe Liflade ant te Passiun of Seinte Juliene*) in his two-volume *Selections of Early Middle English* in 1920.

[2] With the exception of *Hali Meiðhad*, we follow the titles as they appear in the manuscript itself. However, in the interest of brevity in the explanatory and textual notes, we have abbreviated the titles to, respectively, *SK*, *SM*, *SJ*, *HM*, and *SW*.

[3] See Dobson's discussion of the Katherine Group in *Origins of Ancrene Wisse*, especially pp. 163–66, as well as his edition with d'Ardenne, *Seinte Katerine: Re-Edited from MS Bodley 34 and the other Manuscripts*.

Although all of Bodley 34's texts are closely related to a Latin source or sources, each was chosen and recast in its own distinctive way to highlight the virtues of the virgin life for women. Tolkien established the Katherine Group's close relationship to another work also important as a witness to female spirituality, the *Ancrene Wisse* or *Guide for Anchoresses*. (Anchoresses were female recluses who, having chosen to devote their lives to the contemplation of Christ, allowed themselves to be bricked into a small room or a few rooms, usually on the side of a church.) The Katherine Group and the *Ancrene Wisse*, along with a set of prayers known as the Wooing Group, share not only their interest in female spiritual experience but also closely related dialects and a common geographical region of origin, for both original texts and surviving manuscripts. Collectively, these texts are known, following Bella Millett's recent appellation, as the AB Group.[4] This set of mutually reinforcing and influential compositions apparently derived from what in ideological and linguistic terms might be called a discourse community.

In what follows, we review the contents of Bodley 34 and assess its affinity to the *Ancrene Wisse* and the Wooing Group. We then discuss the possible audience of the AB Group and situate them within their cultural, linguistic, and codicological context. We close with comments on the manuscript and on this edition.

THE SAINTS' LIVES

Bodley 34 begins with the three saints' lives, all of which affirm the triumph of virginity over the enticements and threats of material wealth and power. The stories are particularly appealing for the passion, fortitude, and intelligence of their heroines. One of the most popular forms of writing during the medieval period, saints' lives were composed in Latin and Greek, as well as in every European vernacular. Cults of the saints sprang up throughout Europe. The saints interested medieval people both as exemplary Christians, after whom they might model their own lives, and as remarkable individuals. The popularity of the genre for the purposes of both edification and entertainment is attested by the many surviving copies of collections such as Jacobus de Voragine's *Legenda aurea* (Golden legends; c. 1258) and the *South English Legendary* (late thirteenth century).

Saints could be hermits, soldiers, ascetics, or martyrs (often young women or men, determined to make their Christian way apart from the demands of their pagan parents), and their stories served many discursive and social uses. However, as one scholar has claimed, martyrdom was "the most popular type of saintly achievement," despite the fact that (or perhaps even *because*) the prospect of dying for the faith became increasingly rare for most medieval readers.[5] The most common martyrdom stories concerned early Christian saints who were persecuted, tortured, and killed for their beliefs. However, beginning with the lives of the desert fathers a new kind of martyrdom emerged: spiritual martyrdom, whereby a Christian could, through dedication to a life of asceticism, deprivation, and solitude, achieve a higher form of Christ-like living than if he or she were living in a community. These two types of martyrdom are crucial in a reading of the Bodley 34 saints'

---

[4] See Millett's introduction to her edition of *Ancrene Wisse*, Vol. 2, pp. ix–lvii.

[5] Cazelles, "Introduction," p. 2. See this anthology, *Images of Sainthood*, edited by Blumenfeld-Kosinski and Szell, for studies of some of the varied ways saints might be understood in high and late-medieval Europe.

lives. These stories were written *about* literal martyrs (Katherine, Margaret, and Juliana were all tortured and killed for their faith) but most likely *for* spiritual martyrs, that is, for female contemplatives such as anchoresses.

The function of saints' lives in specific times and places has yet to be explored fully. Karen A. Winstead has helped to identify shifting thematic trends as the genre changed from texts directed primarily at monastic or devotional religious audiences (Anglo-Saxon period to the thirteenth century), to texts expressing clerical anxiety about an educated lay public (from c. 1250 on), and finally to texts addressing lay concerns about estates, property, and possessions (fifteenth century).[6] More detailed work on the function of saints' lives during specific periods in the Middle Ages, however, remains to be done.

Englishmen and women of the thirteenth century enjoyed reading the lives of both male and female saints, whether the protagonists were of local origin (e.g., the early English saints Cuthbert and Aethelthryth) or historically and geographically remote (e.g., the fourth-century Juliana of Nicomedia), or even of doubtful historical existence. In their depictions of young, female virgins choosing to remain faithful to Jesus as their beloved, despite increasingly vicious tortures, Bodley 34's saints' lives clearly had specific resonance for young female readers. Each life offers a different view of female achievement: St. Katherine's celebrates her intellectual skills; St. Margaret's, her physical endurance; and St. Juliana's, her spiritual discernment.[7]

One striking feature of all three of the Katherine Group's saints' lives is that the women undergo extreme torture. The function of torture in the articulation of a female saint's piety has been the subject of some critical debate.[8] Elizabeth Robertson, Carolyn Walker Bynum, and Karma Lochrie agree that the association of women with the body or with flesh that must be tamed governs female piety.[9] Sarah Salih develops that scholarly consensus by arguing that although female sanctity was especially associated with corporeality, the "performance" of virginity allowed the female saints to "successfully redefine their bodies and identities as not feminine but virgin."[10] Virginity, in Salih's view, effectively creates a third gender.

---

[6] See Winstead, *Virgin Martyrs*, as well as Simpson's discussion of some of the motives of the authors of late medieval and early modern saints' lives in "Moving Images." For a discussion of the model of virginity provided by the lives in the Katherine Group, see Wogan-Browne's "Chaste Bodies" and *Saints' Lives and Women's Literary Culture*.

[7] See Robertson's discussion of the Bodley 34 saints' lives in *Early English Devotional Prose*, pp. 94–125.

[8] An early dynamic presentation on the topic was given by Szell at the Modern Language Association Meetings in the early 1990s, but unfortunately that presentation which was far ahead of its time in its detailed analysis of the functions of torture was never developed for publication. See the more recent essay by Lewis, "'Lete me suffer.'"

[9] See Robertson, *Early English Devotional Prose*; Bynum, *Holy Feast and Holy Fast*; and Lochrie, *Margery Kempe and Translations of the Flesh*.

[10] See Salih, "Performing Virginity," p. 97, as well as Chewning's discussion of the fluidity of gender in the Wooing Group in her "The Paradox of Virginity." Virginity is a complex term in the early periods and will be addressed in Margaret Ferguson's forthcoming book on the hymen, *Hymens: Sites of Fantasy and Doubt*. One of the earliest book-length treatments of the topic on these works is Bugge's still useful study, *Virginitas: An Essay on the History of a Medieval Idea*. For two general discussions of virginity in the Middle Ages, see Wogan-Browne, "Chaste Bodies," and her "Virgin's Tale." For a discussion of the ambiguity of virginity as both "mark" and "seal," see Bernau, "Virginal

THE MARTYRDOM OF SANCTE KATERINE

The story of St. Katherine of Alexandria is legendary rather than historical. Nonetheless, she was one of the most popular saints of the Middle Ages. Supposedly martyred in the fourth-century, she is not mentioned until the ninth, when her cult developed and spread widely.[11] Sixty-two churches were dedicated to her in England alone. Versions of her story appeared in many languages, and the story of her torture on a wheel inspired innumerable artistic representations, even though it seems to have been a late addition to the legend. Katherine's feast was on 25 November, but because the historical evidence for her existence is doubtful, her cult was suppressed in 1969.

The legend occurs in two parts: the life, which tells of Katherine's youthful training and early saintly exploits; and the passion, the story of her martyrdom. Bodley 34's account gives only the passion. Some scholars claim that the English text is based on the Latin "Shorter Vulgate" version, which was written in the late eleventh or early twelfth century. Simone d'Ardenne and E. J. Dobson, however, feel that Bodley 34 and the Shorter Vulgate both derived from a common source, an abbreviated version of the longer and very popular Latin *passio*.[12]

After briefly identifying Katherine as the daughter of King Cost, and explaining that she was born and raised in Alexandria, Bodley 34 cuts to the story of her life as an adult. Maxence becomes emperor of Alexandria and demands that all the people sacrifice to heathen idols. Katherine objects and urges Maxence to convert. Enraged, he calls together fifty philosophers to argue with her. She explains to them the mystery of the simultaneous divinity and humanity of Christ, and both her speech and her example inspire them to convert. This intense dispute, which involves matters of Christological detail established in some of the earliest Christian councils and reasserted in Anselm's influential twelfth-century *Cur Deus Homo* (Why God became Man), emphasizes Katherine's remarkable powers of intellect. The argument with the fifty philosophers also echoes the scholastic method of *disputatio* then emerging in the universities — even though women were excluded from academic education.

Maxence's queen, Augusta, and his chief knight, Porphirius, also convert. Maxence inflicts vicious tortures on Augusta and has her beheaded. After Porphirius admits to burying Augusta, he and a large retinue of his knights who have also converted are beheaded. Katherine is tortured on a wheel, which bursts apart after she prays for help. The wheel fails to destroy or intimidate the saint who is, finally, beheaded. Blood and milk flow from her wounds, and angels miraculously carry her body away to Mount Sion and bury it.

Effects." For a full-length study of virginity, see Kelly, *Performing Virginity* and Salih, *Versions of Virginity*. See also the collection of essays on virginity in a variety of medieval works, *Medieval Virginities*, edited by Bernau, Evans and Salih.

[11] Several recent works of scholarship attest to the enormous cultural importance of the St. Katherine legend throughout Europe, and especially in England. See, for example, Walsh, *The Cult of St. Katherine of Alexandria in Early Medieval Europe*; and Lewis, *The Cult of St. Katherine of Alexandria in Late Medieval England*. A later medieval English account of her life, which emphasizes the story of her youth, is John Capgrave's *Life of St. Katherine*, translated by Winstead.

[12] d'Ardenne and Dobson, eds., *Seinte Katerine*, pp. xxvi–xxxiv.

THE LIFLADE ANT TE PASSIUN OF SEINTE MARGARETE

Although all three of the saints whose legends appear in Bodley 34 were well known throughout the Middle Ages, the story of St. Margaret (called St. Marina in the Greek church) may be the most popular.[13] Her *vita* is preserved in various forms throughout Europe. If Margaret was a historical person — which is not definite, although she remains on the Catholic calendar — she and her martyrdom date from fourth-century Antioch (near the modern city of Antakya in Turkey), during the persecutions of Emperors Diocletian and Maximian. One of the earliest references to her occurs in a ninth-century Latin martyrology.

Churches throughout Europe and England are dedicated to Margaret, in particular the Church of St. Margaret of Westminster, reputed to have been founded by Edward the Confessor. Her popularity in England is further attested by the existence of at least three Anglo-Saxon lives, two of which are still extant.[14] Frances Mack asserts that these versions are "the oldest renderings in the vernacular in any European literature."[15] Given that there were many Latin and Anglo-Norman versions in England as well, it is difficult to specify the basis of the Katherine Group's *Margaret*.

This story is told as an eyewitness account by Teochimus, a fictional narrator who observes Margaret's persecutions, feeds her in prison, and later buries her body.[16] Fostered in Antioch, Margaret as a young woman attracts the attention of Olibrius, the town's governor or reeve (manorial supervisor), who desires her as a lover or wife. When she refuses him and scorns his heathen idols, he demands that she pay homage to them. She defies his command, and he has her thrown into a dark dungeon. There she prays that she might meet the devil face to face, and soon is confronted with the devil in the form of a dragon. The dragon swallows her whole, but when she makes the sign of the Cross, she bursts from the dragon's belly unharmed.

Margaret then sees the dragon's brother, another devil, bound in a corner of her prison. She interrogates him, and he confesses in psychologically rich detail his methods for tempting even the seemingly most spotless men and women.[17] Fetched from prison and still refusing to pray to Olibrius' idols, Margaret is first burned, and then thrown into a vat of water, from which she emerges unscathed. Finally, after promising to aid anyone who prays in her name — especially women in labor — she is beheaded.

---

[13] For a discussion of the relationship between the cults of St. Margaret and St. Marina, see Larson, "The Role of Patronage."

[14] The surviving English versions of her life are in London, British Library MS Cotton Tiberius A III and Cambridge, Corpus Christi College MS 303. A third version of her life existed in British Library MS Cotton Otho B X, which was mostly destroyed in the Cotton library fire of 1731. See Clayton and Magennis, *The Old English Lives of St. Margaret*, pp. 84–96.

[15] Mack, *Seinte Marherete*, p. ix.

[16] In the Old English lives, Teochimus not only observes Margaret's passion, but also fosters her earlier on in the story. On Teochimus's role in Margaret's narrative, see Mack, *Seinte Marherete*, pp. 58–59n4/4.

[17] Dendle ("Pain and Saint-Making," pp. 48–49) points out that Margaret's encounters with the dragon and the fiend suggest "a two-stage process of spiritual initiation in which Margaret confronts the untamed forces of both her body and her mind, of *soma* and *psyche*."

Margaret's encounter with the dragon was considered by some hagiographers too fanciful to include in her legend. Jacobus de Voragine, in introducing the story of Margaret, wrote: "istud autem quod dicitur de draconis devoratione et ipsius crepatione, apocryphum et frivolum reputantur" (moreover that which is said about the dragon's devouring and about his explosion is thought to be apocryphal and frivolous).[18] The *South English Legendary* also expresses some skepticism:

> Ac þis ne telle ich noȝt to soþe • for it nis noȝt to soþe iwrite
> Ac weþer it is soþ oþer it nis • I not no man þat wite
> Ac aȝen kunde it were • þat þe deuel were to deþe ibroȝt
> For he ne mai þolie nanne deþ • I ne mai it leue noȝt

> (But I do not tell this as truth, for it is not written as truth,
> But whether or not it is true, I don't know any man who knows,
> But it would be against nature if the devil were put to death,
> For he may not suffer any death; I cannot believe it at all.)[19]

The episode's appeal endured, however, and it appeared often in artistic portrayals of the saint.[20] Moreover, it was this aspect of the *passio* that made it so pertinent to women who were or might become pregnant: swallowed by the dragon, Margaret was safely "reborn" by means of the sign of the Cross.[21] Some pregnant women wore amulets containing versions of the story. Others believed that Margaret would help a woman in labor if a written copy of the legend were placed under her bed.[22] Perhaps in response to such concerns, Bodley 34's account intensifies the physicality of Margaret's encounter with the dragon, turning that episode, along with her subsequent interrogation of the second devil, into its central drama.

THE LIFLADE ANT TE PASSIUN OF SEINTE JULIENE

According to the earliest surviving martyrology (the *Martyrologium Hieronymianum*), Juliana, born of an aristocratic family in Cumae, was martyred during the persecutions under Diocletian in 306 CE.[23] Juliana's legend appears in Latin and in many vernaculars. It was particularly popular among the English, as demonstrated by the existence of a version by the Anglo-Saxon poet Cynewulf, as well as two Anglo-Norman and several Middle English

---

[18]   Quoted by Mack, *Seinte Marherete*, p. xi; translation ours.

[19]   *The South English Legendary*, ed. D'Evelyn and Mill, p. 297, lines 165–68; translation ours.

[20]   See Celletti, "Marina (Margherita), santa, martire," and Weitzmann-Fiedler, "Zur Illustration der Margaretenlegende," cited in Winstead, *Virgin Martyrs*, p. 33 n.32.

[21]   See Mack, *Seinte Marherete*, p. xi and p. xi n1.

[22]   See Millett and Wogan-Browne's discussion of the popularity of the legend in their *Medieval English Prose for Women*, pp. xxi–xxii.

[23]   The *Martyrologium Hieronymianum* was falsely ascribed to St. Jerome. See *Martyrologium Vetustissimum PL* 30.443na.

versions.[24] Although the Latin source for the Middle English text is lost, Bodley 285 contains a Latin version close to that original and from around the same date.[25]

Like the other two Bodley lives, Juliana's legend tells the story of a young woman who attracts the attention of a local governor, here named Eleusius, and like Olibrius in *Seinte Margarete*, described as a reeve.[26] Eleusius is a friend of Juliana's father, Africanus, who urges her to accept the reeve's hand in marriage and to worship his idols. Eleusius' supplications, and his offers of marriage and wealth, are cast in the terms of courtly romance. When Juliana refuses the proposal, Africanus has her stripped and tortured, and then sent to Eleusius. Still infatuated with her, Eleusius tries to convince Juliana to worship his idols so that they can marry. When she refuses, he grows enraged and orders that she be hung by her hair while molten brass is poured on her. Juliana emerges triumphant and unharmed, and a frustrated Eleusius throws her into prison. There she unmasks a devil, Belial, who appears disguised as an angel and demands that he recount the history of his temptations from Adam and Eve on. Eventually she beats the devil Belial and casts him in a pit of filth.

The next day Juliana is brought forth again to be tried by Eleusius, who has by this point completed his transformation from attractive courtly lover to monstrous pagan persecutor. When she still refuses to sacrifice to his gods, he orders her to be tortured on a wheel similar to that of St. Katherine (perhaps a contamination from the Katherine legend.) Finally, she is beheaded and her body is taken away by sea and buried in Campagna by a woman named Sophia. Eleusius and his men follow but are drowned in a storm at sea.

HALI MEITHHAD

Following the saints' lives in Bodley 34 comes a tract on virginity. This "epistel," as it is called in the manuscript, derives from Hildebert of Lavardin's early twelfth-century Latin letter to the recluse Athalisa, along with a rich assortment of commentary on virginity by the Church Fathers, especially St. Jerome.[27] Yet despite being a patchwork of motifs common to the literature of praise for virginity, *Hali Meithhad* (Holy Maidenhood) is widely considered a literary *tour de force*. The originality of the work stems not only from the author's skill in weaving his sources together but also from his recasting of the material to reflect the choices availabl'e to women of middle to upper social status in thirteenth-century England.

Like the lives, *Hali Meithhad* celebrates the choice of a virgin life "married" to Christ. The text begins by comparing the virgin to a tower, praising her for being above those

---

[24] For a complete list of the existing vernacular versions, see d'Ardenne, ed., *Liflade ant te Passiun of Seinte Iuliene*, pp. xx–xxii.

[25] See d'Ardenne, *Liflade ant te Passiun of Seinte Iuliene*, pp. xvi–xviii. This edition includes the first edited text of this Latin *Juliana*.

[26] The pressure an amorous reeve places on an aspiring anchoress is dramatized in Chris Newby's 1993 film *Anchoress,* a work that reflects a number of details about the anchoritic life found in the AB Group.

[27] Millett provides a thorough discussion of these sources in her edition of *Hali Meithhad*, pp. xxiv–xxv. See also Millett's *Ancrene Wisse, the Katherine Group, and the Wooing Group.*

around her and for her protected status. Drawing on a motif known as the *vita angelica*, which ranks virginity above widowhood and marriage, the author commends the life the virgin leads as like the life of the angels. Marriage, though the less desirable of the states, is nonetheless recognized as a "bed" that catches the sinful from falling into hell. The author next compares the life of a virgin to secular marriage, childbirth, and child rearing. His portrait of marriage paints a dark picture of its trials and tribulations, from husbands who are physically and emotionally abusive to the dangers of childbirth and the demands of child-rearing in a time when children might die young or be born with deformities.

Although the portrait of life as a wife and mother seems intensely realistic, it is nonetheless drawn from a tradition known as the *molestiae nuptiarum* (tribulations of marriage). The motif originated with St. Paul (I Corinthians 7:32–34), and continued through the writings of the Church Fathers.[28] In *Hali Meithhad*, the tradition is switched around to recount the problems of marriage from a woman's point of view as imagined by the male author. The author also used some more contemporary commentaries on the virgin life, including Ælred of Rievaulx's letter to his recluse sister, Aldhelm's tract on virginity, and Bernard of Clairvaux's *Sermones super Cantica canticorum* (Sermons on the Song of Songs).[29]

The author punctuates his text with vitriolic attacks on sexual encounters of any kind. Much more fulfilling than a sexual relationship with a man is the marriage to Christ that the virgin has chosen. This *sponsa Christi*, or bride of Christ, motif derives from Mark 2:19–20, where Christ describes himself as the bridegroom. The idea that the virgin has a special status as the bride of Christ was developed by Tertullian. In his account, as in the saints' lives, the author of *Hali Meithhad* literalizes the idea of marriage to Christ.[30] To intensify his description of the virgin's desire for Christ, the writer draws extensively on Bernard's interpretation of the biblical Song of Songs as a celebration of the marriage of the contemplative to God. The text concludes with a warning that the contemplative be vigilant against the dangers of complacency and pride, and by urging the virgin to satisfy her desire for children by having spiritual children — i.e., virtues.

Some readers find *Hali Meithhad*'s attack on earthly marriage distasteful. In its bold contrasts between the woes of earthly marriage and the joys of marriage to Christ, and especially in its energetic descriptions of these woes, *Hali Meithhad* may also seem excessively involved with the secular rather than the religious sphere. This interest in secular life, however, may have derived from the author's conception of the needs of his audience, who were perhaps women who had only lately left secular life for a non-monastic form of religious life.

---

[28] See Millett's introduction to *Hali Meithhad*, pp. xxx–xxxviii. St. Jerome writes about the tribulations of marriage in his *Adversus Jovinianum* (which Chaucer's Wife of Bath so vituperously attacks), and the tradition is extremely popular in eleventh- and twelfth-century writing (see, for example, the *Speculum virginum*). Millett (p. xxxvii) also points to the work of Hildebert of Lavardin, Osbert of Clare, Alan of Lille, and Peter of Blois.

[29] Ælred of Rievaulx, *De Institutione Inclusarum*, ed. Ayto and Barrett; Aldhelm, *De Virginitate*; and Bernard of Clairvaux, *On the Song of Songs*, trans. Walsh. Ayto and Barrett identify two Middle English translations of Ælred's *De Institutione*, preserved in the Vernon manuscript and Bodley 423. They also discuss *De institutione*'s well-attested relationship with *Ancrene Wisse*, but do not mention *Hali Meithhad* (pp. xxxviii–xliii).

[30] For discussions of the significance of this literalization, see Bugge, *Virginitas*, pp. 87–88; and Robertson, *Early English Devotional Prose*, pp. 77–93.

Despite its rhetorical extravagance, *Hali Meithhad* shares with the *Ancrene Wisse* an intense focus on the emotional life of the reader, ventriloquizing the female reader's concerns and providing answers for them. For example, the author writes "'Nai,' thu wult seggen, '. . . Ah monnes elne is muche wurth'" ('No,' you will say, '. . . But a man's strength is worth much'; 20.1–2). He then goes on to answer the objections by showing that these hypothetical goods are difficult to acquire and fragile even if attained. The work grants us insight into the thoughts of a young, aristocratic virgin, untutored in the monastic life, potentially wavering between marrying a local nobleman and following a more difficult and solitary life as a bride of Christ.

SAWLES WARDE

Sawles Warde, or the *Guardianship of the Soul*, seems at first, in its focus on the protection of the soul of any gender, to be the most remote of the Bodley 34 texts from the specific concerns of female contemplatives.[31] In form it is a homily (that is, a sermon) on how an individual should best guard and see to the health of his or her soul. It begins with a quotation from the Gospels: "if the goodman of the house knew at what hour the thief would come, he would certainly watch, and would not suffer his house to be broken open" (Matthew 24:43).[32] Building on the passage's allegory, the author describes the soul as the precious treasure within a castle.[33] The head of the household is Wit (Reason), whose unruly wife, Will, refuses to amend her ways and better supervise the guardians of the household, the five senses. These guardians are monitored by God's four daughters: Vigilance, Strength, Moderation, and Righteousness.[34] Vigilance allows the entrance of a messenger, Fear or Remembrance of Death, who describes hell to the assembled members of the household in order to encourage them to be more alert. Because the household is threatened with despair after Fear's description, Vigilance calls Love of Eternal Life to cheer them with a description of heaven.

Although the allegory provides lessons for any Christian, an analysis of the author's adaptations of his source material, as Anne Eggebroten first observed, reveals the text's

---

[31] In "The Order of the Texts," Mockridge argues that, far from being the most remote of the Bodley 34 texts, *Sawles Warde* represents "the climactic and key work of the group" (p. 212). She continues: "it seems likely that the compiler realized that by placing *Sawles Warde* at the end of the manuscript, the other four works in the manuscript would be recalled in the audience's minds as they heard the lessons imparted by each of the four daughters of God [see footnote 38]. In other words, these cardinal virtues (Vigilance, Strength, Moderation, and Righteousness) can be seen as symbols of the quality that predominates in each of the preceding works" (pp. 213–14). Mockridge's interesting argument sees Bodley 34 not as a collection of individual works but as a compilation with a single aim: to convince possibly reluctant nuns (daughters of noble families who may have been bequeathed against their will to Wigmore Abbey) to retain their virginity.

[32] For a discussion of sermon conventions in Anglo-Saxon England, see Gatch, *Preaching and Theology*, and more generally for medieval England, Owst, *Literature and Pulpit*.

[33] Cannon notes that while the allegory of the body as fortified castle goes back to Plato's *Timaeus*, the extensive use of this imagery in the Katherine Group reflects the authors' knowledge of Norman and Welsh fortification in the marches; see his *Grounds of English Literature*, pp. 150–53.

[34] We decided to translate *Warschipe* as "Vigilance," as opposed to "Prudence," because the text (as well as its biblical source) emphasizes a specific need for watchfulness against the fiend.

particular relevance for women in the contemplative life.[35] First of all, the description of heaven includes an unusually long account of the privileged position accorded there to virgins. Secondly, the allegory as a whole is psychologically astute: it encourages its readers to achieve emotional balance in their earthly life (by avoiding the sins of pride and despair) rather than to worry about the joys or terrors awaiting them in the afterlife. Emotional equanimity, while desirable for anyone pursuing a contemplative life, would be of particular relevance to anchoresses whose daily lives were especially demanding emotionally.

The source of the allegory was thought for a long time to be Hugh of St. Victor's *De anima* (On the soul) but has recently been identified as *De custodia interioris hominis* (On the keeping of the inner self), a work associated with St. Anselm of Canterbury, although the text also draws on motifs common in vernacular sermon literature.[36] Vivid, sensory descriptions of heaven and hell were popular in such literature, as was the portrayal of the soul as a treasure within the building of the body.[37] Among the many other English poems that discuss the castle of the soul, the *Ancrene Wisse* describes the anchoress's soul as a lady besieged in a castle and rescued by Christ the lover-knight. Finally, the author weaves into his allegory another conventional homiletic motif, the allegory of the Four Daughters of God. This motif is of special importance in later medieval English texts such as the *Abbey of the Holy Ghost*, *Piers Plowman*, the Annunciation Play in the *N-Town Cycle*, and the *Castle of Perseverance*.[38]

---

[35] Eggebroten, "*Sawles Warde*: A Retelling of *De Anima*."

[36] For the Latin text of *De custodia*, see Southern and Schmitt, eds., *Memorials of St. Anselm*, pp. 354–60. Savage and Watson point out the likely cause of the mistaken attribution: *De custodia* was sometimes circulated as the work of Hugh of St. Victor (*Anchoritic Spirituality*, p. 210). *De custodia* is now referred to as a "pseudo-Anselmian" work. The identification of the text as the source for *Sawles Warde* was first made by Dobson, who argued that, most likely, an adaptation of *De custodia* served as the source both for Hugh's *De anima* as well as *Sawles Warde* (*Origins of Ancrene Wisse*, pp. 146–54). Wolfgang Becker ("The Source Text of *Sawles Warde*," pp. 44–48) expands on Dobson's argument. It is worth noting that a manuscript containing *De custodia*, as well as other Anselmian works, resides in Hereford Cathedral Library (Hereford Cathedral MS P.I.1), one of the large religious centers close to where the author of *Sawles Warde* was most likely writing (Southern and Schmitt, eds., *Memorials of St. Anselm*, p. 16). In addition to *De custodia*, P.I.1 contains several well-known texts by Anselm (including *Cur Deus homo* and *De humanis moribus*) as well as the *De arca Noe* by Hugh of St. Victor, and numerous texts by Bernard of Clairvaux. Though the manuscript is dated to the second half of the twelfth century, it is possible that the *Sawles Warde* author may have had access to either an exemplar of this manuscript or a similar compilation. See Mynors and Thomson, *Catalogue of the Manuscripts of Hereford Cathedral Library*, pp. 64–65.

[37] For an excellent selection of some of the best-known visions, see Gardiner, *Medieval Visions of Heaven and Hell*. According to Gardiner, the *Vision of Saint Paul* was especially well known and survived in many Latin versions as well as vernaculars (pp. 179–94). Bede's account of the vision of Drythelm in *Bede's Ecclesiastical History of the English People* was another influential early version (pp. 284–89). Of particular note is how many of the staple accounts of the torments of Hell are adapted into visions of Purgatory; see Foster, ed., *Three Purgatory Poems*.

[38] In later Middle English texts the daughters are Mercy, Truth, Justice, and Peace, rather than Vigilance, Strength, Moderation, and Righteousness. Their function differs, as well: in William Langland's *Piers Plowman*, N-Town's "Annunciation Play," and the *Castle of Perseverance*, the daughters debate the morality of redeeming humankind. In *Sawles Warde*, they assist Wit in governing and guarding his household. See Traver's *Four Daughters of God* (1907), as well as her later piece "The Four Daughters of God: A Mirror of Changing Doctrine" (1925).

Sawles Warde, however, is notable for its particularly streamlined and focused use of these allegorical motifs.

Sawles Warde can be seen as a culmination of all the Bodley 34 texts, as they move from historical to contemporary secular contexts and finally to the daily struggle of the female religious to maintain her commitment to the protection of her soul. It is remarkable that this manuscript, so clearly addressed to women readers, has survived. Whether or not it was intended for the anchoresses for whom the *Ancrene Wisse* was written, for a larger group of female contemplatives, or even for religious lay readers, it is hard not to imagine the Katherine Group as a small, well-thumbed compendium of literature, lovingly contemplated by women in pursuit of the highest religious goals.

TEXTUAL MODES: POETRY OR PROSE?

Because of the paucity of Middle English texts surviving from the period between the Norman Conquest and the fourteenth century, some scholars have treated the Katherine Group as a crucial link between Old English and Middle English literature. The Group's texts are written in a rhythmical, alliterative style, although the use of alliteration varies from text to text. *Margaret* seems to conform to a rhythmical alliterative prose style whereas *Juliana* seems to make use of rather clumsily wrought alliterative half-lines that might be said to approximate verse. Since the oldest (and most densely alliterative) ones are the saints' lives, these stories have come under particular scrutiny for their role in transmitting alliterative poetic practice from the Anglo-Saxons to the fourteenth century. Both R. W. Chambers and Dorothy Bethurum praised the rhythmical prose of the texts found in Bodley 34 as a continuation of the Old English alliterative prose style established by King Alfred, which reached its heights in the work of Ælfric.[39] Elaine Treharne has shown that English texts continued to be produced well after the conquest from 1100–1220.[40] The exact relationship between the style of these works, the alliterative prose of the Ælfrician works that continued to be copied in the West Midlands, and the anonymous homilies that continued to be produced after the conquest, as well as their place in the trilingual culture of early thirteenth-century England, needs further investigation.

The representation of the texts on the manuscript page itself contributes to the difficulty we have today in identifying its original identity as either poetry or prose. Anglo-Saxon and early Middle English scribes commonly wrote their English texts out across the full width of the parchment page, whether they were recording verse or prose; when they transcribed Latin verse, however, they allowed the poem to indicate line breaks on the page.[41] Bodley 34's scribe copied his English texts across the full width of the parchment page. And, as

---

[39] For a discussion of the Katherine Group's relationship to Anglo-Saxon prose writers (especially Ælfric), see Chambers, *On the Continuity of English Prose*, and Bethurum, "The Connection of the Katherine Group." Blake, in "Rhythmical Alliteration," argues that early Middle English texts marked by loose alliterative patterns (as opposed to dense and rhythmically strict Old English poetic alliterative patterns), such as the *Ancrene Wisse* and Layamon's *Brut*, represent a direct link between, respectively, Old English poetry, Old English alliterative prose (such as that of Ælfric and Wulfstan), early Middle English texts, and the poetry of the later so-called Alliterative Revival.

[40] See Treharne, *Living Through Conquest*.

[41] See O'Keefe, *Visible Song*.

Julia Boffey and A. S. G. Edwards point out, "the emergence of Middle English did not lead immediately to a new sense of verse as a distinctive form. Indeed, regional pressures (such as those relating to the Worcester area), continued to determine that verse was often transcribed as prose during this period."[42] Three passages in the texts contain rhyme and are thus clearly meant to be read as poetry (these have been indicated in our edition).[43] However, the irregular alliteration, as well as the punctuation used in the manuscript, suggests that the texts were primarily conceived of as prose rather than poetry. The texts clearly draw upon the resources of alliterative poetry, and could be described as poetic prose. Although many early editors of these works printed them as poetry,[44] the editors of the present volume have decided to present them as prose.

It is wise to remember Millett's advice that the "temptation to treat the Katherine Group *Lives* as a kind of master key to all problems of alliterative transmission needs to be resisted."[45] Much early Middle English literature has undoubtedly not survived to the twenty-first century, thus rendering theories about the relationship between the Katherine Group and later Middle English writing highly speculative.

ANCRENE WISSE

As noted above, the Katherine Group has been understood to be closely related to the guide for anchoresses most commonly known as the *Ancrene Wisse*,[46] which even seems to contain an explicit reference, if not to the Katherine Group itself, at least to one of the texts in Bodley 34. In Book 4 of *Ancrene Wisse* the author asks, "Nabbe ye alswa of Ruffin the deovel, Beliales brother, in ower Englische boc of Seinte Margarete?" (Do not you also have [the story] of Ruffin the devil, Belial's brother, in your English book of Saint Margaret?)[47] This reference could well indicate that the intended audience of *Ancrene Wisse* was expected to be familiar with the Katherine Group's version of *Margaret*. Another shared feature is an opening phrase — "I the Feaderes ant i the sunes ant i the Hali Gastes nome her biginneth" (In the name of the Father and of the Son and of the Holy Ghost, here begins) — that occurs in the exact same form in Bodley 34's *Seinte Margarete*, and with a slight variation in *Seinte Juliene, Sancte Katerine,* and in the Cambridge, Corpus Christi College MS 402 manuscript of the *Ancrene Wisse*.[48]

---

[42] "Middle English Literary Writings," p. 383. See Robertson's discussion of the influence of the anonymous homilies on the Bodley 34 texts in *Early English Devotional Prose*. For a discussion of the copying of Old English texts in Worcester see "Middle English Literary Writings," pp. 382–83.

[43] See *Seinte Margarete* 75.1–4, *Seinte Juliene* 76.1, and *Sawles Warde*, 51–59.

[44] Early editions that printed the Katherine Group texts as poetry include Morton's 1841 edition of *The Legend of St. Katherine of Alexandria*, Einenkel's 1884 edition of *The Life of St. Katherine*, and Wagner's 1908 edition of *Sawles Warde*.

[45] Millett, "The Saints' Lives of the Katherine Group," p. 32.

[46] For the *Ancrene Wisse*, see Millett's 2005 EETS edition of the text. This edition draws on the uncompleted edition by Dobson, with a glossary and additional notes by Richard Dance. See also Hasenfratz's 2000 edition of *Ancrene Wisse*.

[47] *Ancrene Wisse*, ed. Hasenfratz, p. 261, lines 795–96.

[48] Stevens, "Titles of 'MSS AB,'" p. 443.

The *Ancrene Wisse* was written as a guide for women undertaking the anchoritic life. In the late twelfth through the thirteenth centuries, English women who were attracted by the religious fervor of reformers such as the Cistercians were impeded from inventing their own new forms of religious life by Canon 14 of the highly influential Fourth Lateran Council of 1215. This decree forbade the establishment of new religious orders, at the same time that religious orders for women in England were in decline. Therefore, women wishing to emulate their religiously inspired sisters on the Continent turned to this exceptionally demanding form of religious asceticism as a way to pursue their vocations.[49]

The number of surviving manuscripts of the *Ancrene Wisse* suggests that this text was by far more influential and widely read than the Katherine Group. Much of what scholars have deduced about the cultural milieu of the latter, therefore, has been based on the greater information available about the former. Originally written for three sisters of high social status who became anchoresses, the *Ancrene Wisse* was copied, adapted, and translated for a wide variety of audiences, including larger groups of anchoresses (twenty or more), nuns, male religious, and even aristocratic secular women readers.[50] The manuscript tradition indicates that readers were invested in the *Ancrene Wisse* not only as an instructional guide to life as a solitary recluse but also as a devotional text applicable to secular and active religious life.

Given the insights that the *Ancrene Wisse* offers into the devotional practices that were probably followed by the readers of Bodley 34 as well, it is worth summarizing here. In eight sections, the author sets out two rules. The primary one is "eaver in-with ant rihteth the heorte" (ever within and directs the heart); the secondary one is "al withuten ant riwleth the licome ant licomliche deden" (completely external and governs the body and bodily deeds).[51] These internal and external rules structure the conception of the work. Books 1 and 8 address the outer rule, advising the anchoress(es) on matters such as prayer schedules, proper dress, and diet, and advising against activities such as conducting business, maintaining close relationships with family, and keeping pets (except for, perhaps, one cat). The six internal books (2–7) present the inner rule, advising the anchoresses on ways to cultivate a contemplative state of mind; they address, respectively, the physical senses, the inner feelings, temptations, confession, penance, and love.[52] The work reaches an emotional climax in the story of the Christ-Knight, an allegory of Christ's love for the human soul presented to its female readers in the form of an erotic, chivalric romance.

THE WOOING GROUP

The Katherine Group has also been associated with a group of prayers and meditations closely related in dialect and theme, known as the Wooing Group. It consists of four poems:

---

[49] See Millett's discussion of the dissemination of the text in her edition of the *Ancrene Wisse* (2006), 2:ix–lvii.

[50] On the fairly extensive lay audience of the *Ancrene Wisse*, see Robertson, "This Living Hand," especially pp. 5–6.

[51] *Ancrene Wisse*, ed. Hasenfratz, p. 60, lines 12–13 and lines 23–24.

[52] These are the titles Savage and Watson, *Anchoritic Spirituality*, give to Books 2–7. Books 1 and 8 are labeled, respectively, "Devotions" and "The Outer Rule." See pp. 43–44, for further discussion of the *Ancrene Wisse*'s structure.

On Ureisun of Ure Louerde (A Prayer to Our Lord), *On Lofsong of Ure Louerde* (A Praise-Song for Our Lord), *The Wohunge of Ure Lauerd* (The Wooing of Our Lord), and *On Lofsong of Ure Lefdi* (A Praise-Song for Our Lady).[53] The phrasing, symbolism, and emotional content of the Wooing Group and the other texts discussed above reflect new trends in theology from the Continent, many of them inspired by the work of Bernard of Clairvaux. However, unlike the Katherine Group and the *Ancrene Wisse*, the Wooing texts, as W. Meredith Thompson has noted, show very little concern with domestic issues, infernal enemies, the terrors of hell, or more generally "the loathsomeness of human life and functions." Instead, these intimate texts are "meditative and emotional."[54] The prayers to Christ request forgiveness and praise Him as lover and spouse, while that to Mary asks for her intercession.

Although several of the Wooing Group prayers are included in manuscripts that also contain the *Ancrene Wisse* or some of the Katherine Group texts,[55] there is little internal evidence that suggests they were composed exclusively for, or by, female contemplatives. Eugen Einenkel, in 1882, proposed that one of the anchoresses for whom the *Ancrene Wisse* was written was the author of some or all of the Wooing Group texts.[56] The proposal that these texts were written by women, which has proven extraordinarily tenacious in discussions of the Wooing Group, perhaps reveals more about nineteenth- and twentieth-century expectations of gender than it does about medieval authors and audiences. Bernard of Clairvaux, it might be remembered, wrote equally emotional and erotic commentaries on the Song of Songs. Even Thompson goes as far as to make the claim that

> She [that is, the author of *Wohunge*] would later have passed it on to some *leue suster* for the latter's comfort and edification. Did she then try to repeat herself with less success? Or did one or more sisters, with less art, try to imitate her? Either conjecture might account for the

---

[53] For an edition of the full Wooing Group, see *Þe Wohunge of Ure Lauerd*, ed. Thompson. For a recent collection of essays on the Wooing Group, see Chewning, ed., *The Milieu and Context of the Wooing Group*.

[54] *Wohunge*, ed. Thompson, p. xix.

[55] See p. 34 of Hasenfratz's introduction to his edition of *Ancrene Wisse* for a chart illustrating the overlapping texts in the AB manuscript tradition. See also Millett's *Ancrene Wisse, the Katherine Group, and the Wooing Group*, pp. 49–61, for an extensive description and history of scholarship of each of the manuscripts.

[56] See Einenkel, "Eine Englische Schriftstellerin." Dobson strongly rebuts Einenkel's claim: "I cannot accept the suggestion, made by Einenkel and supported by Professor Thompson . . . that this group was written by a woman. I do not know how one distinguishes a woman's writing from a man's unless there is some specific reference; allowing for the special stylistic demands of this prose-poetry *genre* and of this type of perfervid devotion, I cannot see any essential difference between the prose meditations and passages of comparable theme in *Ancrene Wisse*. And it seems perverse to me to suppose that 'my dear sister' is a form of address from a man to a woman in *Ancrene Wisse*, but from one woman to another in *Þe Wohunge of Ure Lauerd*; of course it could be, but there is no evidence that it is. The hypothesis seems merely fanciful" (*Origins of Ancrene Wisse*, p. 154). It is extremely difficult to identify the gender of authors when their names are hidden under the cloud of anonymity. While no one has yet suggested that the *Ancrene Wisse* was written by a woman, Anne Savage has recently suggested the three women to whom the *Ancrene Wisse* was addressed co-authored the work. See Savage, "The Communal Authorship of the *Ancrene Wisse*."

Ureisun and *Lofsong* addressed to *ure Louerde*. The *Lofsong of ure Lefdi* is less strongly marked by feminine authorship and might have been written, though not necessarily, by a man.[57]

While it would not be safe to assume female authorship, the gender of the author or authors of these works still remains an open question.

Regardless of who authored the pieces, the important aspect of this discussion is their similarity in point of view and emotional content to the *Ancrene Wisse* and the Katherine Group. In her edition of *Juliana*, d'Ardenne remarks on the similarities between Juliana's impassioned prayers in her Bodley 34 life and those articulated in *Wohunge*. d'Ardenne describes the *Wohunge* as "the thoughts and prayers of Juliene written out at large."[58] These recurrent, overlapping themes, which develop, dramatize, expand, and contextualize the theological and emotional content of the Katherine Group, speak to the consistent presence of a vibrant community, rich in literary and devotional understanding.

AUDIENCE

While the close connections to *Ancrene Wisse* suggest that the texts of Bodley 34 may have been compiled for a similar (if not identical) group of female contemplatives, the Katherine Group contains no specific references to recluses. In her recent study, *Choosing Not to Marry*, Julie Hassel suggests that the Katherine Group was intended for lay spiritual readers. Much of the texts' internal evidence, however, indicates that the audience was deeply religious, if not necessarily anchoritic, and that the texts' readers either were avowed virgins or were contemplating making such vows. For instance, the Bodley 34 scribe entitles *Hali Meithhad* as "Epistel of meidenhad meidene frovre" (A letter on virginity for the encouragement of virgins), suggesting that this text was intended for a female contemplative, or perhaps even a nun.

Hali Meithhad further suggests that its readers came from the gentry, since the author uses the plight of gentlewomen struggling to attain a socially acceptable marriage as a likely familiar basis of comparison to the even worse situation faced by poor women: "the beoth wacliche iyeven . . . as gentile wummen" (who are unworthily given in marriage . . . like . . . gentle women; 6.1). The author recommends that its readers consult saints' lives, including those found in Bodley 34: "Thench o Seinte Katerrine, o Seinte Margarete, Seinte Enneis, Seinte Juliene, ant Seinte Cecille, ant o the othre hali meidnes in Heovene" (Think of Saint Katherine, of Saint Margaret, Saint Agnes, Saint Juliana, and Saint Cecilia, and of the other holy maidens in Heaven; 40.4).

Margaret opens with an address to the widowed, the married, and virgins: "Hercneth! Alle the earen ant herunge habbeth, widewen with tha iweddede, ant te meidnes nomeliche" (Listen! All who have ears and hearing, widows with the wedded, and the maidens especially; 3.1–2). The reference to ears and hearing suggests that the text may have been intended for reading aloud to a group of listeners. The legend concludes: "Alle theo the this iherd heorteliche habbeth: in ower beoden blitheluker munneth this meiden" (All those who have devotedly listened to this: remember in your prayers this maiden more happily; 75.1). Both of these addresses may have been adopted from the Latin source but, as Millett points out,

---

[57] *Wohunge*, ed. Thompson, p. xxiv.

[58] *Seinte Iuliene*, ed. d'Ardenne, p. xliii.

the translator's use of the present tense suggests that he considered the text appropriate to its new audience.[59]

Juliana includes an address to "alle leawede men the understonden ne mahen Latines ledene, litheth ant lusteth the liflade of a meiden" (all unlearned people who cannot understand the language of Latin, hear and listen to the life of a maiden; 1.1), indicating that the intended audience was: (1) expected to listen to, rather than read, the text; and (2) was "lewd," that is, unable to read or write in Latin. Although *Sawles Warde* is addressed to any devout Christian, it expanded its sources' references to the joys that virgins experience in heaven.

The internal evidence from the Katherine Group thus suggests that the texts address a variety of audiences yet may have been compiled for an audience of female readers who possibly were the daughters of provincial gentry families, who may or may not have been considering a monastic or anchoritic life, and who, though they may have been educated in other ways, were not literate in Latin. This portrait accords with our current knowledge of the situation of religious women in the West Midlands in post-Conquest England.[60] As with the other texts, its lessons could potentially apply to anyone.

The audience's lack of literacy, in addition to the doctrinal rules of the Catholic Church, mandated a literate and educated spiritual advisor, who may or may not have been the same person as the author of these texts. Thus, as Robertson notes, readers of the Katherine Group (and of the *Ancrene Wisse*) participate in a "triangulated reading process" that includes the author(s) of the Katherine Group; the male advisor or reader (who may or may not have been the same person as the author) mediating the text; and the woman reading or listening to the text being read. In this way, attempts to reconstruct the original female audience of the Katherine Group will always, to a certain extent, be shaped by the way that the author of the texts imagined them. Robertson's analysis of the audience of the *Ancrene Wisse* can also apply to that of the Katherine Group. "[T]o some degree," she notes, "the audience of the *Ancrene Wisse* will always be a fiction, both a historical fiction, one that is inevitably unstable, and a literary fiction found within the text itself."[61] It is possible that these texts were intended for anyone interested in the spiritual life, or even for lay readers, although they clearly have specific resonance for women in pursuit of a rigorous form of contemplative life. And even if originally written with a specialized audience in mind, such as the three anchoresses for whom *Ancrene Wisse* was originally composed, all five works clearly also have an appeal for larger groups of the spiritually inclined — lay and religious, male and female.

---

[59] Millett, "The Audience of the Saints' Lives," p. 133.

[60] On female literacy in the post-Conquest period, see Millett, "Woman in No Man's Land," and Robertson, "This Living Hand." It is important to note that while the audience of the Katherine Group probably did not know Latin, they may very well have been able to read and/or write in English and French. Robertson points out that "unlike preconquest England, where men and women apparently had similar direct access to texts that articulated the intellectual life, there was a hierarchy of languages in this period, one shaped by the different needs and circumstances of male and female readers" ("This Living Hand," p. 23). For the relationship between women and their male advisors, see Bartlett, *Male Authors, Female Readers*.

[61] "This Living Hand," p. 3. On the triangulated reading process, see pp. 26 ff.

PROVENANCE: MANUSCRIPTS, DIALECT, AND TEXTS

Despite their considerable differences, the sense of unity, in theme and address among the texts discussed above has a basis in possible historical reality. Bodley 34 was one of a group of manuscripts produced in the early thirteenth century, all of which are compendia of what Savage and Watson have called "anchoritic spirituality."[62] The texts were all written in a roughly similar variety of Middle English. Tolkien first identified what he called the "AB dialect" in Corpus 402 and in Bodley 34 (the name derived from the sigla of the two manuscripts). "In no other extant manuscript of middle English," Tolkien wrote, "does precisely the same idiom with all its special peculiarities of grammar and spelling reappear."[63] However, later scholars have aligned several other manuscripts with this dialect or variations on it.[64] Indeed, it might be more accurate to describe the AB Group as texts written in various West Midland dialects linked as part of what might be termed a flourishing regional vernacular culture.[65]

The works associated with the AB Group appear in the following manuscripts:

- Oxford, Bodleian Library MS Bodley 34: Lives of Sts. Katherine, Margaret, and Juliana; *Hali Meithhad*, *Sawles Warde*.
- Cambridge, Corpus Christi College MS 402: *Ancrene Wisse*.
- London, British Library MS Royal 17 A XXVII: a sermon on Matthew; *Sawles Warde*; lives of Sts. Katherine, Margaret, and Juliana; *On Lofsong of Ure Lefdi*; some fifteenth-century hymns.
- London, British Library MS Cotton Titus D XVIII: *Ancrene Riwle* (defective at the beginning), *Sawles Warde*, *Hali Meithhad*, *The Wohunge of Ure Lauerd*, and *The Life of St. Katherine*.[66]
- London, British Library MS Cotton Nero A XIV: *Ancrene Riwle*, *On Lofsong of Ure Lefdi*; *On Ureisun of Ure Lefdi*; *On Ureisun of Ure Louerde*; *On Lofsong of Ure Louerde*.

---

[62] See Savage and Watson, *Anchoritic Spirituality*.

[63] See d'Ardenne's summary of Tolkien's important argument in *Liflade ant te Passiun of Seinte Iuliene*, p. xxvii.

[64] Numerous studies have examined the phonological and orthographic differences (subtle as they are) between the manuscripts of the *Ancrene Wisse* as well as the Wooing Group. See in particular Thompson's helpful discussion of language, phonology, and dialect, particularly as it is distinguished among the AB manuscripts (*Wohunge of Ure Lauerde*, pp. xxx–lxi). Laing and McIntosh, Black, and Smith have urged caution about the designation of AB, persuasively arguing that the language of B is neither uniformly orthographically consistent with A, nor in relationship to A exhibiting the four characteristics that indicate the existence of a standard language. See Laing and McIntosh, "The Language of *Ancrene Riwle*"; Black, "AB or Simply A?"; and J. Smith, "Standard Language."

[65] Dobson provides the fullest argument for the existence of such a center in *Origins*. For a succinct reassertion of the argument see Blake, *History of the English Language*, pp. 129–31. Today's scholars prefer to assert a wider geographical locale of origin in the West Midlands and keep open the possibility of numerous locations of literary production in the area and are wary of the idea of a single center of literary production.

[66] The Titus D XVIII scribe is thought to have worked in a West Midland religious house influenced by the AB dialect; his dialect is close to but distinct from the AB dialect found in Bodley 34's texts. See d'Ardenne and Dobson's introduction to their edition of *Seinte Katerine*, pp. xl–xli.

The dialects that bear a close relationship to one another in the AB Group have been identified generally as West Midlands dialects. Because the grammar and lexicography of the AB Group's texts draw on Welsh and Scandinavian, the AB dialects have been further narrowed to an area on the border between England and Wales. The texts' heavy use of alliterative rhetoric suggests a direct ancestry in Anglo-Saxon prose and poetry, congruent with a western origin. But as noted above, the texts also draw heavily upon the rhetorical resources of the continental Latin tradition. The closely related AB dialects are thus the product of a language community of four if not five languages: English, French, Scandinavian, Welsh, and Latin.[67]

More recently, philologists such as Merja Black, Margaret Laing, Angus McIntosh and Jeremy Smith have argued that the language of Bodley 34 and Corpus 402 is neither linguistically nor orthographically as consistent as Tolkien claimed. Although Bodley 34's texts and the *Ancrene Wisse* share dialectal features, some now believe that the two manuscripts do not indicate the presence of an established standard language in the west Midlands.[68] Paleographer Ralph Hanna adds that a closer look at the compilation of Bodley 34 in relation to other AB Group manuscripts might lead one to question Dobson's view of the texts "as a concerted local canon, the designed product of an 'AB community'."[69] However, while such critiques add more detail to our picture of the AB context, the scholarly consensus still holds in general to the sense that the AB Group reflects an attempt of some sort by a set of authors to write a body of works on female spirituality, using a distinctive literary language that evolved over time.

Tolkien argued further that the dialect found in the surviving manuscripts was closely related to the original language of composition of the Katherine Group, the *Ancrene Wisse*, and the Wooing Group, although recent critics have suggested that this claim should be received with caution.[70] According to Tolkien, none of Bodley 34's works could have been composed earlier than 1190. But they were not contemporary with the manuscript itself: d'Ardenne and Dobson write that "in every case the Bodleian MS is separated by at least one intervening copy from the author's original."[71] The unity of style and subject found in Bodley 34 could suggest that one author wrote all of the works, but most scholars agree that

---

[67] While many of the words in the Katherine Group originate from just one of these languages, de Caluwé-Dor also suggests the possibility of "etymological convergence" in the texts. Some words, that is, may possibly have derived simultaneously from several languages. De Caluwé-Dor's example is *tevelin* (from *Katherine*), meaning "to argue." *Tevelin* is rooted in Old English *tæfl(i)an*, Old Norse *tefla*, and Old French *tables/taubles* ("Etymological Convergence," p. 212).

[68] See Black, "AB or Simply A?," Smith, "Standard Language," and Laing and McIntosh, "The Language of *Ancrene Riwle*."

[69] Hanna, "Lambeth Palace Library MS 487," p. 87.

[70] Scholars less sure that the original texts used the AB dialect include Benskin and Laing, "Translations and *Mischsprachen*"; Hornero Corisco, "An Analysis of the Object Position"; and, much earlier, James R. Hulbert, "A Thirteenth-Century English Literary Standard." Hulbert developed Tolkien's original claim, arguing that "the best explanation of the language of A and B is that it is a standard form, accurately followed by A and B, approximately by a number of other scribes" (p. 414). It is worth noting that Tolkien described AB only in reference to the manuscripts Bodley 34 and the Corpus manuscript of *Ancrene Wisse*.

[71] *Seinte Katerine*, ed. d'Ardenne and Dobson, p. xxxviii.

Hali Meithhad is lexigraphically and linguistically distinct. It has been proposed that the texts fall into three subgroups: *Margarete* and *Juliene*, composed in the last decade of the twelfth century; *Katerine* and *Sawles Warde*, in the first decade of the thirteenth century; and *Hali Meithhad*, a decade later.

Some scholars suggest that, because of its similarity in tone and purpose, *Hali Meithhad* might have been an early composition by the author of the *Ancrene Wisse*.[72] The texts of Bodley 34 do share a number of alliterative phrases and distinctive vocabulary with the *Ancrene Wisse*. Overlap occurs also in the *Ancrene Wisse* author's mention of "ower Englische boc of Seinte Margarete."[73] The general view is that authorship of the Bodley 34 texts and the *Ancrene Wisse* was split between several authors, some of whom may have written more than one work. d'Ardenne's suggestion is that "we are in the presence of a tradition with one specially active and influential centre or school rather than with one busy author and universal provider of devotional literature."[74]

That "centre or school" was probably, like the dialects of the AB Group, located in the West Midlands. In his study of the *Ancrene Wisse*, Dobson, following an idea first articulated by D. S. Brewer, argued that all the texts of the AB Group must have originated from an Augustinian house. Dobson proposed the abbey at Wigmore as a possible center of literary production: located in Herefordshire close to the Welsh border, Wigmore was the only major Augustinian house in the area that suited the linguistic character of the AB Group texts. He further suggested that the *Ancrene Wisse* was written for a small group of anchoresses located at the Deerfold near Limebrook Priory. However, that claim turns out to have been based on a misreading of the scribal abbreviation for "fratribus" (to the brothers) as "sororibus" (to the sisters).[75] Relying on a more fanciful and even more discredited assumption that one manuscript contained an authorial acrostic, Dobson then proposed a possible author of the text, Brian of Lingen.[76]

Since Dobson's time, Millett (among others) has ruled out the Deerfold as the location of the center of AB composition and Brian as author of the *Ancrene Wisse*. On the basis of the devotional practices advocated in the text, Millett proposes a Dominican rather than an

---

[72] *Hali Meithhad* and the *Ancrene Wisse* are comparable on a lexical level as well. Clark's 1966 study of French-derived vocabulary in the Katherine Group found that *Hali Meithhad*, of all the texts in the group, has the highest percentage of French-derived words (6.3%), closest to that of the *Ancrene Wisse* (10.7%); see Clark, "*Ancrene Wisse* and the *Katherine Group*." For a discussion of the French-derived vocabulary of the Katherine Group, see Bately, "On Some Aspects of the Vocabulary of the West Midlands," especially pp. 66–77. Bately notes that, of the Katherine Group, *Hali Meithhad* and *Sawles Warde* have a significantly higher percentage of French-derived words than the saints' lives, although the latter include many vocabulary words not present in *Hali Meithhad* and *Sawles Warde* (p. 77).

[73] *Ancrene Wisse*, ed. Hasenfratz, p. 261, line 796. See also the more detailed discussion above (p. 12) of the *Ancrene Wisse*'s relationship to the Katherine Group.

[74] See d'Ardenne's introduction to her edition *Liflade ant te Passiun of Seinte Iuliene*, p. xliii.

[75] Thompson, *Women Religious*, p. 34 n126.

[76] Dobson, *Origins of Ancrene Wisse*, pp. 174–368. Although he made the most elaborate and best-researched case for the Herefordshire provenance of the AB Group, Dobson was not the first to investigate the issue. For an overview of readings prior to *Origins*, see Dahood, "*Ancrene Wisse*, the Katherine Group, and the *Wohunge* Group," pp. 8–11. For a succinct summary of arguments for the existence of such a center, see Blake, *History of the English Language*, pp. 129–31.

Augustinian origin for the *Ancrene Wisse*. "The importance of Dobson's study," Millett has concluded, "now seems to lie less in the specific answers he offered than in his precise definition of the problems involved, and of the kind of evidence which would be needed to solve them."[77] Recently, Christopher Cannon has argued that the Welsh marches were a particularly appropriate setting for the Katherine Group and the *Ancrene Wisse*. They were, he says, "a place where the anxieties about bodily boundaries and their penetration which fill the AB texts was not only a practical consideration but a function of geography, the general condition of life in a borderland so constantly subject to war."[78]

While it is unlikely that any scholar will conclusively identify the exact location of the composition of the Katherine Group, most scholars have concurred to some degree with Tolkien's (1929) original conclusion, as well as more generally with Dobson's (1976), that the texts and the manuscripts that preserve them were created somewhere near Hereford Cathedral.[79] An important piece of supporting evidence comes from Bodley 34 itself, thanks to one or more mid-sixteenth-century readers who used the manuscript's pages to test pens, jot down names, and practice letter forms. Insignificant as these scribbles may seem, they have proven tantalizing scraps of evidence that contribute to scholars' guesses about the origins of the AB Group, as the names are all of lesser Hereford gentry. Nonetheless, the fact that we know that manuscripts of the *Ancrene Wisse* traveled widely in the West Midlands over many decades reminds us that Bodley 34 may well have traveled widely as well; the scribbled names tell us finally only that the manuscript was in Herefordshire in the sixteenth century.

The fact that Bodley 34 shares some philological similarities with another obscure Middle English religious prose text, and more generally with an assortment of similar texts, might seem of concern only to paleographers and linguists. However, the discovery of the AB Group has been extremely important to our understanding of medieval English literary history. The texts that comprise the AB Group represent some of the few extant examples of literature composed in early Middle English, and as such partially illuminate a period in English literary history from which relatively few texts survive. The Battle of Hastings (1066), when William the Conqueror defeated Harold Godwinson, ushered in a new era of linguistic and literary development in England's history. Previously, literature was written mainly in Latin and Anglo-Saxon. With the Norman Conquest, however, the Norman French dominance in politics and language dictated that secular literature aimed primarily at the upper classes was written in French, while religious writing continued to be composed in Latin.

As Millett has pointed out, literary works in French, such as Hue de Roteland's *Ipomedon* and Simund de Freine's *Vie de Saint Georges* were produced for the local aristocracy in Herefordshire. However, for the provincial gentry far from the cosmopolitan centers of power, who were less familiar with both Latin and French, some religious writing continued to be composed in Anglo-Saxon or in the vernacular it became under the influence of

---

[77] Millett, "New Answers, New Questions," p. 220.

[78] Cannon, *Grounds of English Literature*, p. 143; see especially Chapter 5 (pp. 139–71) for a rich discussion of castles, warfare, and defensive imagery throughout the AB Group texts (particularly on notions of the body as fortification against violence, both physical and psychological).

[79] Millett quotes a private letter she received from Jeremy Smith in 1991 ("New Answers, New Questions," p. 224n15). On the basis of preliminary philological analysis, Smith supported a localization for the AB language in Herefordshire "or the southern tip of Salop [Shropshire]."

French and Latin: early Middle English.[80] This particular audience, lay but devout, gentry but not aristocratic, familiar with both Latin and French but not fully comfortable with either, may well have comprised an unusually distinctive and influential audience in need of literature in English. As Millett observes, anchoresses "seem to have been significant for the development of vernacular literature mainly because of their intermediate position between *laici* and *clerici*, illiterates and *literati*."[81] The Katherine Group and the *Ancrene Wisse* carried over the Latin continental tradition into English, possibly for just such an audience.

Although the Katherine Group has begun to receive some critical attention in recent years, the texts in and of themselves and as a collection deserve much more scrutiny.[82] Among the issues still to be fully addressed are the precise nature of the ideal of virginity in thirteenth-century England; the function of the three saints' lives within the political and historical context of thirteenth-century England; the purposes and meanings of graphic representations of violence against women; and the exact relationship of Bodley 34 to the AB Group of manuscripts, as a measure of female literacy in this period. By making these texts available in full, we hope to stimulate future research on this manuscript, and on the fascinating early Middle English works it contains.

THE MANUSCRIPT

A small, undecorated manuscript measuring 154 by 108 millimeters, Bodley 34 consists of eighty surviving parchment leaves, gathered in eleven quires. Its outer leaves have suffered a fair amount of wear, indicating that the manuscript survived for some time without the protection of a cover. Three folios are missing from *Katerine* (between folios 7 and 8), one from *Juliana* (between folios 40 and 41), and at least one in *Sawles Warde* (following folio 80, which is itself heavily damaged). All five texts in the manuscript were copied in a single hand. For some reason, the scribe began in a regular and neat hand, became increasingly careless in the middle of the manuscript (especially in *Juliana* and *Hali Meithhad*), and returned to careful copying at the end. Based on the orthography and morphology in the manuscript, most scholars have agreed on an approximate copy date of c. 1240. The manuscript preserves not only ð (eth, capital form Ð), ȝ (yogh, capital form Ȝ), and þ (thorn, capital form Þ), Middle English letter forms familiar from fourteenth-century literature, but also the runic letter wynn, a form that according to Hanna went out of fashion after 1270 and may have last been used c. 1320.[83]

Along with the primary hand in Bodley 34, two or more later hands appear. Shortly after the manuscript had been completed (most likely still during the first quarter of the thirteenth century), a second scribe substantially revised folios 18v through 21v of *Margaret*.

---

[80] For a recent discussion of the impact of the Norman Conquest on literature in England, see Cannon, *Grounds of English Literature*, pp. 17–49. For a discussion of the relationship between French, Latin, and English literary production in this period and locale, see Millett, "The Audience of the Saints' Lives," pp. 146–47. On the relationship between the Scandinavian vocabulary of the Katherine Group and the development of early Middle English, see De Caluwé–Dor, "The Chronology of the Scandinavian Loan-Verbs."

[81] Millett, "Woman in No Man's Land," p. 99.

[82] The first book-length study of the Katherine Group alone is Hassel's 2002 *Choosing Not to Marry*.

[83] Hanna in private correspondence.

Much of the revised wording resembles the version of the text in Royal 17 A XXVII (a member of the AB Group; see p. 17 above). Mack suggests that the revising scribe may have based his revisions not on the Royal manuscript itself but on a lost common source for both the Royal and Bodley versions of Margaret's legend.[84]

In the mid-sixteenth century, as noted above, a writer (or possibly a series of writers) adorned Bodley 34's pages with various scribbles, including names. Someone also inscribed five lines of poetry, in a difficult secretary hand, at the end of *Juliana*.[85] The added lines paraphrase *Juliana's* conclusion — indicating that, three hundred years or more after Bodley 34 was written, people were still reading it, understanding the language, and thinking about the text.

NOTE ON THIS EDITION

As noted above, it is difficult sometimes to tell whether Bodley 34's texts were considered in their own time to be prose or poetry. See above, pp. 11–12. The present editors agree with N. F. Blake (1969) that the texts' rhythmical alliterative style bears some affinity to poetry but should be printed as prose. The lines that contain rhyme words and are thus clearly meant to be read as poetry have been indicated as such in our edition. We have used Royal 17 A XXVII to supply the passages missing from Bodley 34.

In editing these texts, we have followed the principles of the Middle English Texts Series regarding *u/v*, *i/j*, capitalization, and the updating of medieval letter forms such as ð, Ð, þ, and Þ into their modern equivalents. Aside from the normal practices of the Series, however, this volume faces a few unique issues, most notably in the difficulty of the early Middle English dialect. Because of this difficulty, we have composed a translation of the five texts, albeit one that adheres as closely as possible to the sense of the original. In creating this translation we have endeavored to match punctuation and syntax with the early Middle English to the fullest extent possible. In addition, our edition generally follows the formatting practices of the scribes in the manuscript with regard to paragraph breaks; where appropriate, we have adjusted the format to improve clarity and have followed modern practices regarding dialogue. We have included a glossary for readers who wish to work in a detailed manner with the Middle English.

A second notable issue in editing these texts is the scribe's confusion between the letterforms *ð* and *d*, which we have made every attempt to regularize over the course of the volume. These emendations are listed without comment in the textual notes that accompany each work. Lastly, we have tried to facilitate cross-referencing not only by maintaining consistency with the treatment of these works in previous editions but also by noting the original text's foliation by means of a singular vertical line (|) accompanied by marginal

---

[84] *Seinte Marherete*, ed. Mack, pp. xiv–xvi. Readers interested in a comprehensive examination of these revisions should consult Furuskog's "A Collation of the Katherine Group," especially pp. 134–43 on *Margaret*.

[85] For details on these sixteenth-century additions, especially about the Herefordshire families that may be related to the men mentioned in Bodley 34, see Ker, *Facsimile of MS Bodley 34*, pp. xiii–xv. He speculates that the additions were most likely made when the manuscript was located in a lawyer's office in northern Herefordshire. For the sixteenth-century poem, see the explanatory note to *Seinte Juliene*, 76.1.

notation specifying the folio that begins at that point. These tools will, we hope, both enable and encourage readers to move with ease among the various editions and critical discussions of these texts.

The Martyrdom of Sancte Katerine

I thes Feaderes ant i thes Sunes ant i the almihti Gastes nome, her biginneth the martyrdom of Sancte Katerine.

(1) Costentin ant Maxence were on a time as i keiseres stude, hehest i Rome. (2) Ah Costentin ferde thurh the burhmenne read into Franclonde ant wunede summe hwile thear for the burhes neode, ant Maxence steorede the refschipe i Rome. (3) Weox umbe-hwile wreathe ham bitweonen, ant comen to fehte. (4) Wes Maxence overcumen ant fleah into Alixandre. (5) Costentin walde efter ant warpen him theonne, ah se wide him weox weorre on euche halve (ant nomeliche in a lont Ylirie hatte) thet ter he etstutte. (6) Tha Maxence iherde this, thet he wes of him siker ant of his cume carles, warth king of thet lont the lei into Rome as duden meast alle the othre of the weorlde. (7) Bigon anan ase wed wulf to weorrin Hali Chirche ant dreaien Cristene men (the lut thet ter weren) alle to heathendom, heathene as he wes, summe thurh muchele yeoven ant misliche meden, summe thurh fearlac of eisfule threates, o least with stronge tintreohen ant licomliche pinen. (8) I the fif ant thrittuthe yer of his rixlinge he set o kine

---

In the name of the Father and of the Son and of the almighty Ghost, here begins the martyrdom of Saint Katherine.

1.

(1) Constantine and Maxence were at one time in the position of emperors, the highest in Rome. (2) But Constantine went, through the citizens' advice, into France and dwelled there for a while because of the city's need, and Maxence guided the government in Rome. (3) There grew, after a time, anger between them, and they came to fight. (4) Maxence was overcome and fled into Alexandria. (5) Constantine wanted to go after and cast him out, but war spread around him so widely on every side (and especially in a land called Illyria) that there he stopped. (6) When Maxence heard this, so that he was sure of him and fearless at his coming, he became king of that land, which was subject to Rome, as were most of the others in the world. (7) He began at once like a mad wolf to wage war on Holy Church and to draw Christian men (the few that there were) all to heathendom, since he was a heathen, some through great gifts and various rewards, some through terror of his fearful threats, and at last with fierce torments and bodily tortures. (8) In the thirty-fifth year of his reign he sat on his royal seat

seotle i the moder-burh of Alixandres riche, ant sende heaste ant bode, se wid se thet lont wes, thet poure ba ant riche comen ther bivoren him to the temple i the tun of his heathene godes, euchan with his lac forte wurthgin ham with. (9) Comen alle to his bode, ant euchan bi his evene bivore Maxence seolf wurdgede

his maumez. (10) The riche reo|theren ant schep ant bule (hwa se mahte), brohte to lake; the poure, cwike briddes.

2.　　　(1) I this burh wes wuniende a meiden swithe yung of yeres, twa wone of twenti, feier ant freolich o wlite ant o westum ant yet (thet is mare wurth), steathelvest withinnen of treowe bileave, anes kinges Cost hehte anlepi dohter, icuret cleargesse Katerine inempnet. (2) Theos meiden wes bathe feaderles ant moderles of hire childhade; ah thah ha yung were, ha heold hire ealdrene hird wisliche ant warliche i the eritage ant i the eard thet com hire of burde, nawt forthi thet hire thuhte god in hire heorte to habbe monie under hire ant beon icleopet leafdi (thet feole telleth wel to) ah ba ha wes offearet of scheome ant of sunne yef theo weren todreavet other misferden thet hire forthfeadres hefden ivostret. (3) For hireseolf, ne kepte ha nawt of the worlde. (4) Thus lo, for hare sake ane dale ha etheold of hire ealdrene god ant spende al thet other i neodfule ant i nakede.

3.　　　(1) Theos milde meoke meiden, theos lufsume leafdi with leastelese lates, ne luvede ha nane lihte plohen ne nane sotte songes, nalde ha nane ronnes ne nane luve-runes leornin ne lusten, ah ever ha hefde on Hali Writ ehnen other heorte, oftest ba togederes. (2) Hire feader hefde iset hire earliche to lare ant heo,

---

in the mother-city of the kingdom of Alexandria, and sent an order and command, as wide as that land was, that both poor and rich should come there before him to the temple of his heathen gods in the town, each with his offering with which to worship them. (9) They all came at his command, and everyone according to his means before Maxence himself worshiped his idols. (10) The rich brought cattle and sheep and bulls (those who could) as offerings; the poor, live birds.

2.　　　(1) In this city was dwelling a maiden very young in years, two less than twenty, fair and lovely in face and form and yet (what is worth more), steadfast within of true belief, the only daughter of a king called Cost, a well-known scholar named Katherine. (2) This maiden was both fatherless and motherless from her childhood; but though she was young, she looked after her parents' household wisely and prudently in the inheritance and in the land which came to her by birth, not because that seemed to her good in her heart to have many under her and to be called lady (which many consider a good) but she was afraid both of shame and of sin if those whom her forefathers had fostered were driven away or came to harm. (3) For herself, she cared nothing for the world. (4) Thus lo, for their sake only she kept a part of her parents' goods, and spent all the rest on the needy and on the naked.

3.　　　(1) This mild meek maiden, this lovely lady with blameless behavior, did not love any frivolous games or any stupid songs, nor did she wish to learn or listen to any love-songs or love-stories, but ever on Holy Writ she had eyes or heart, most often both together. (2) Her father had set her early to learning and she,

thurh the Hali Gast, undernom hit se wel thet nan nes hire evening. (3) Modi
meistres ant feole fondeden ofte hire o swithe feole halve forte underneomen

fol. 2r hire, ah nes thear nan thet mahte neaver eanes | wrenchen hire with al his crefti
crokes ut of the weie, ah se sone ha yeald ham swucche yeincleappes, ant wende
hare wiheles upon hamseolven thet al ha icneowen ham cravant ant overcumen,
ant cwethen hire the meistrie ant te menske al up.

4.   (1) Thus hwil ha wiste hire — ant thohte áá to witen hire — meiden i
meithhad, as ha set in a bur of hire burdeboldes, ha iherde a swuch nurth towart
te aweariede maumetes temple: lowinde of thet ahte, ludinge of the men,
gleowinde of euch gleo to herien ant hersumin hare heathene godes. (2) As ha
this iherde ant nuste yet hwet hit wes, ha sende swithe forte witen hwet wunder hit
were. (3) Sone se hire sonde com agein ant seide hire thet sothe, heo wes swa
itend of wreaththe thet wod ha walde iwurthen. (4) Het up of hire hird hwuch as ha
walde ant wende hire thiderwart. (5) Ifont ter swithe feole yeinde ant yurinde ant
theotinde unthuldeliche with reowthfule reames: the Cristene weren ant leaffule
i Godes lei, ah for dred of death duden thet deofles lac as the heathene duden.
(6) Hwa wes wurse thene heo, heorte iwundet inwith, for the wrecches thet ha seh
se wrathe werkes wurchen agein Godes wille? (7) Thohte, thah (as ha wes thuldi
ant tholemod) se yung thing as ha wes hwet hit mahte yeinen, thah heo hire ane
were, agein se kene keiser ant al his kineriche. (8) Stot stille ane hwile ant hef hire
heorte up to the hehe Healant the iheret is in Heovene. (9) Bisohte Him help ant

---

through the Holy Ghost, undertook it so well that no one was her equal. (3)
Numerous and proud scholars tested her often from very many different sides to
trick her, but there was not one there, with all his crafty tricks, who could ever
once wrench her out of the way, but so soon she repaid them such counter-strokes,
and turned their wiles upon them that they all knew themselves defeated and
overcome, and granted her the victory and the honor completely.

4.   (1) Thus while she kept herself — and thought always to keep herself — a
maiden in maidenhood, as she sat in a room of her family house, she heard a great
noise in the direction of the accursed idols' temple: the lowing of the cattle, the
shouting of the people, the merry-making of each musical instrument to praise and
worship their heathen gods. (2) As she heard this and did not know yet what it was,
she sent quickly to find out what strange thing it could be. (3) As soon as her
messenger came back and told her the truth, she was so inflamed with wrath that
she would have gone mad. (4) She called up from her company of servants
whichever ones as she wanted and went in that direction. (5) She found there a great
many people howling and yelling and crying querulously in pitiable laments: those
who were Christians and faithful to God's law, but for dread of death they did that
devil's sacrifice as the heathen did. (6) Who was worse off than she, her heart
wounded within, for the wretches that she saw work such evil works against God's
will? (7) She thought, though (as she was patient and long-suffering) what it might
gain so young a creature as she was to strive, although she was alone by herself,
against so cruel a king and all his kingdom. (8) She stood still for a moment and
heaved her heart up to the high Savior who is praised in Heaven. (9) She asked Him

fol. 2v hap ant wisdom, ase wisliche as | al the world is iweld thurh His wissunge. (10)
Threfter wepnede hire with sothe bileave ant wrat on hire breoste ant bivoren hire
teth ant te tunge of hire muth the hali Rode-taken. (11) Ant com leapinde forth
as al itent of the lei of the Hali Gast, as the keiser stot bimong thet sunfule slaht
of thet islein ahte — deovele to lake, thet euch waried weoved of the mix maumez
ron of thet balefule blod al biblodeget — ant bigon to yeien ludere steavene:

5.   (1) "Gretunge, keiser! (2) Walde wel bicume the for thin hehnesse yef thu this
ilke yeld thet tu dest to deovelen — thet fordeth the bathe i licome ant i sawle, ant
alle the hit driveth — yef thu hit yulde ant yeve to His wurthemunt the scheop the
ant al the world, ant welt thurh His wisdom al thet ischapen is. (3) Ich walde, king,
greten the yef thu understode thet He ane is to herien, thurh hwam ant under
hwam alle kinges rixlith, ne ne mei nathing withstonden His wille, thah He muche
tholie. (4) Thes heovenliche Lauerd luveth treowe bileave, ant nowther blod ne
ban of unforgult ahte ah thet me halde ant heie His halewinde heastes. (5) Ne nis
nathing hwerthurh monnes muchele meadschipe wreatheth Him mare then the
schafte of mon — thet He schop ant yef schad ba of god ant of ufel thurh wit ant
thurh wisdom — schal wurthe se vorth ut of his witte thur the awariede gast thet
he yelt the wurthemunt to unwitelese thing thet te feont wuneth in thet he ahte
fol. 3r to Gode, ant herieth ant hersumeth | seheliche schaftes — blodles ant banles ant
leomen bute live — as he sculde his ant heoren ant alre thinge Schupent: thet is,
God unsehelich.

---

for help and luck and wisdom, as wisely as all the world is ruled by His guidance.
(10) After that she armed herself with true belief and traced the holy Rood-token
on her breast and before her teeth and the tongue of her mouth. (11) And she came
leaping forth as if all inflamed with the flame of the Holy Ghost, as the emperor
stood among that sinful slaughter of those slain beasts — sacrifices to the devil,
so that each accursed altar of the filthy idols ran bloodied by that foul blood —
and began to cry out in a loud voice:

5.   (1) "Greetings, emperor! (2) It would well become you for your high rank if
you offered this same sacrifice that you do to devils — who destroy you both in
body and in soul, and all who practice it — if you yielded and gave it to His honor
who made you and all the world, and rules through His wisdom all that is made.
(3) I would, king, greet you if you understood that He alone must be praised,
through whom and under whom all kings rule, nor can anything withstand His
will, although He endures much. (4) This heavenly Lord loves true belief, and
neither the blood nor bone of guiltless beasts but one who keeps to and carries
out His sanctifying commandments. (5) Nor is there anything through which the
great madness of men angers Him more than that the creature man — whom He
shaped and to whom He gave discernment both of good and of evil through wit
and through wisdom — should go so far out of his mind through the accursed
spirit that he gives the honor that he ought to give to God to non-sentient things
which the devil dwells in, and praises and worships visible creatures — bloodless
and boneless and limbs without life — as he should the Maker of him and them
and all things: that is, God invisible.

6.   (1) "The feont (the findeth euch uvel), bimong alle hise crokinde creftes, with
neaver an ne kecheth he creftiluker cang men, ne leadeth to unbileave then thet
he maketh men — thet ahten to wite wel thet ha beoth biyetene ant iborene ant
ibroht forth thurh the heovenliche Feader — to makie swucche maumez of treo
other of stan other (thurh mare meadschipe) of gold other of seolver, ant yeoven
ham misliche nomen, of sunne other of mone, of wind ant wude ant weattres, ant
hersumeth ant wurthgith as thah ha godes weren. (2) Ne naveth he thurh other thing
i this bileave ibroht ow bute thet ow thuncheth thet ha schulen leasten áá forthi
thet ye ne sehen ham neaver biginnen. (3) Ah ther nis buten an Godd thur hwam
witerliche ha alle weren iwrahte ant of nawiht, ant i this weorlde iset us forto
frovrin ant to fremien. (4) Ant alswa as euch thing hefde biginnunge of His
godlec, alswa schulden alle habben endunge yef He thet walde. (5) Engles ant
sawlen, thurh thet ha bigunnen, ahten ant mahten endin thurh cunde; ah He
thurh His milce ant godlec of His grace maked ham thet ha beoth in eche buten
ende. (6) Ant thervore nis nathing evening ne eche with Godd — thet ye gremieth
— for He is hare alre schupent ant schop ham i sum time, ant na time nes,
neaver, thet He bigon to beon in."

fol. 3v   (1) The keiser bistearede hire with swithe steape | ehnen hwil thet ha spec
7.   thus. (2) Swithe he awundrede him of hire wliti westum ant swither of hire wordes,
ant feng on thus to speokene: "Thi leor is, meiden, lufsum ant ti muth murie, ant
witti ant wise weordes hit weren yef ha neren false! (3) Ah we witen wel thet ure
laghen, ure bileave, ant ure lei hefde lahe sprung. (4) Ah al thet ye seggeth is se

---

6.   (1) "The fiend (who invents every evil), among all his crooked crafts, with none
does he ever more craftily catch foolish men, nor leads them into unbelief, than when
he makes men — who ought to know well that they are begotten and born and
brought forth through the heavenly Father — to make such idols of tree or of stone
or (through more madness) of gold or of silver, and to give them various names, of
sun or of moon, of wind and wood and waters, and praise and worship them as
though they were gods. (2) Nor has he for another reason brought you into this belief
except that you think that these things will last forever because you never saw them
made. (3) But there is nothing except one God, through whom certainly they all were
wrought and from nothing, and set in this world to comfort and to help us. (4) And
also as each thing had a beginning from His goodness, so must they all have an
ending if He wished it. (5) Angels and souls, because they began, ought and must end
through nature; but He through His mercy and the goodness of His grace makes
them so that they are in eternity without end. (6) And therefore there is nothing equal
to nor eternal with God — whom you anger — for He is the maker of them all and
made them at some time, and there was no time, ever, during which he began to
exist."

7.   (1) The emperor stared at her with very bright eyes while she spoke thus. (2) He
was very surprised by her lovely form and more by her words, and began in this way
to speak: "Your face is, maiden, lovely and your mouth pleasant, and witty and wise
words they would be if they were not false! (3) But we know well that our laws, our
belief, and our religion have a lawful origin. (4) But all that you say is such

sutel sotschipe thet hit na wis mon ah wittlese hit weneth. (5) Me hwet is mare
meadschipe then forte leven on him ant seggen he is Godes sune — the the Giws
demden ant heathene ahongeden — ant thet he wes akennet of Marie, a meiden,
buten monnes man, ant iboren of hire bute bruche of hire bodi, deide ant wes
iburiet, ant herhede helle, ant aras of death, ant steah into Heovene, ant schal eft
o Domesdei cumen ba te demen the cwike ant te deade? (6) Hwa walde ileve this
thet is ase noht wurth, thet alle ower leasunges beoth unlefliche? (7) Ah yet ne
thuncheth ow nawt inoh to forleosen ow thus i thulli misbileave; ah gath yet ant
seggeth scheome bi ure undeaddeliche godes the sunne ant te mone, thet euch
mon ahte hersumin ant herien in eorthe."

8.   (1) Theos meiden lette lutel of thet he seide, ant, smirkinde smetheliche, yef
him thullich onswere: "Al ich iseo thine sahen sottliche isette. (2) Cleopest theo
thing godes the nowther sturien ne mahen ne steoren hamseolven bute as the
hehe King hat ham i Heovene. (3) Ant heo buheth to Him as schafte to his
Schuppent. (4) Nis buten an Godd (as ich ear seide) thet al the world wrahte ant

fol. 4r   al worldliche thing, ant al wurcheth His wil bute mon | ane. (5) Stille beo thu
thenne, ant stew swuche wordes, for ha beoth al witlese ant windi of wisdom."

9.   (1) The keiser wundrede him swithe of hire wordes ant wedinde cweth: "Meiden,
ich iseo wel — for sutel is ant etsene o thine sulliche sahen — thet tu were iset
yung to leaf ant to lare. (2) Ah of swuch larspel thu havest leave ileornet thet tu
art theronont al to deope ilearet hwen thu forcwethest for thi Crist ure undedliche
godes ant seist ha beoth idele ant empti of gode. (3) Ah wastu nu hwet is?

---

clear foolishness that no wise man but a witless one would believe it. (5) Yet what is
more madness than to believe in Him and say He is God's Son — he whom the Jews
condemned and the heathens hanged — and that he was born of Mary,
a maiden, without the fellowship of a man, and born of her without breach of her
body, died and was buried, and harrowed hell, and arose from death, and ascended
into Heaven, and will again on Doomsday come to judge both the quick and the
dead? (6) Who would believe this which is worth nothing, because all your lies are
unbelievable? (7) But yet it seems to you not enough to damn yourself thus in such
misbelief; but moreover you go and say shame about our immortal gods the sun and
the moon, which every man ought to worship and honor on earth."

8.   (1) This maiden thought little of what he said, and, smiling sweetly, gave him
such an answer: "I see that all your words are foolishly expressed. (2) You call those
things gods which can neither move nor steer themselves except as the high King
of Heaven commands them. (3) And they bow to Him as a creature to his Creator.
(4) There is not but one God (as I said before) who wrought all the world and every
worldly thing, and everything works His will except humankind alone. (5) Be still
then, and stop such words, for they are all witless and devoid of wisdom."

9.   (1) The emperor wondered greatly at her words and raging said, "Maiden, I see
clearly — for it is clear and evident in your remarkable words — that you were set
young to belief and to learning. (2) But from such teaching you have learned belief
which you are, in that regard, all too deeply taught when you renounce for your
Christ our immortal gods and say they are worthless and empty of good. (3) But do

(4) We schulen bringe to ende thet we bigunnen habbeth, ant tu schalt, tu motild, to curt cume seothen ant kine mede ikepen yef thu wult ti wil iwende to ure, for yef hit went agein us, ne schal the na teone ne tintreohe trukien." (5) Tha he hefde thus iseid, cleopede an of his men dearneliche to him ant sende iselede writes with his ahne kine ring yeont al his kineriche to alle the icudde clerkes, ant het ham hihin towart him hare cume swithe — ant swa muche the swithere thet, he bihet to medin ham with swithe heh mede, ant makien ham hehest in his halle yef ha theos modi motild overcume mahten ant wende the hokeres of his heathene godes upon hire heavead, thet ha were on alre erst ikennen ant icnawen thet nis bute dusilec al thet ha driveth, ant threfter thenne fordon ant fordemed yef ha nalde leaven thet ha yet lefde, ant hare lagen luvien. (6) Thes sonde wende

fol. 4v him forth as the king hehte. | (7) He heold on to herien his hethene maumez with misliche lakes long time of the dei thet he idon hefde, ant wende tha, the wari, towart his buriboldes, ant bed bringen anan this meiden bivoren him. (8) Ant seide to hire thus: "Nat ich nowther thi nome ne ich ne cnawe thi cun, ne hwucche men thu havest ihaved hiderto to meistres, ah thi schene nebscheft ant ti semliche schape schaweth wel thet tu art freomonne foster, ant ti sputi speche walde of wisdom ant of wit beore the witnesse, yef thu ne misnome onont ure maumez — thet tu se muchel misseist — ant ure godes hokerest — the thu schuldest, as we doth, heien ant herien."

---

you know what the situation is now? (4) We will bring to an end what we have begun, and you must, you argumentative babbler, come afterwards to court and receive a royal reward if you will turn your will to ours, for if it goes against us, no torment or torture will be spared you." (5) When he had said thus, he called one of his men secretly to him and sent sealed letters with his own royal ring throughout his entire kingdom to all the renowned scholars, and commanded them to greatly hasten their coming — and to hasten it even more swiftly, because he promised to honor them with a very lofty reward, and to make them highest in his hall if they could overcome this proud debater and turn the mockeries of his heathen gods upon her head, so that at first she would be willing to admit and acknowledge that all that she argues is only folly, and then afterwards be condemned and doomed if she would not abandon what she still believed and love their laws. (6) This messenger went his way forth as the king commanded. (7) He continued to worship his heathen idols with various offerings for the greater part of the day until he had finished, and he went then, the villain, toward his dwellings, and ordered this maiden brought immediately before him. (8) And he said thus to her: "I know neither your name, nor do I know your kin, nor which men you have had hitherto as teachers, but your fair face and your seemly shape show well that you are a child of noble men, and your eloquent speech would reveal wisdom and wit, if you were not mistaken about our idols — which you slander so much — and mock our gods — whom you should, as we do, honor and praise."

10.   (1) Ha onswerede ant seide: "Yef thu wult mi nome witen: ich am Katerine icleopet. (2) Yef thu wult cnawe mi cun: ich am kinges dohter. (3) Cost hehte mi feader, ant habbe ihavet hiderto swithe hehe meistres. (4) Ah forthi thet te lare thet heo me learden limpeth to idel yelp, ant falleth to biyete to wurthschipe of the worlde, ne ne helpeth nawiht eche lif to haben, ne yelpe ich nawiht therof. (5) Ah sone se ich seh the leome of the sothe lare the leadeth to thet eche lif, ich leafde al thet other ant toc me Him to Lauerd ant makede Him mi leofmon, the theos word seide thurh an of His witegen: *Perdam sapientiam sapientum et intellectum intelligentium reprobabo.* (6) 'Ich chulle fordo the wisdom of theos wise world-men,' He seith, 'ant awarpen the wit of theose world-witti.' (7) Ich herde eft theos word

fol. 5r   of another witege: *Deus autem noster in celo omnia quecumque voluit fecit. | Simulacra gentium argentum et aurum et cetera usque ad similes illis fiant.* (8) 'Ure Godd is in Heovene thet wurcheth al thet He wule. (9) Theos maumez beoth imaket of gold ant of seolver al with monnes honden: muth bute speche, hehnen bute sihthe, earen buten herunge, honden bute felunge, fet bute yonge. (10) Theo thet ham makieth mote beon ilich ham ant alle the ham trusteth.' (11) Ah nu thu seist thet ha beoth alleweldinde godes ant wult thet ich do ham wurthschipe! (12) Schaw sumhwet of ham forhwi ha beon wurthe forte beon iwurdget for ear nulle ich nowther ham heien ne herien."

11.   (1) "Nat ich hwuch thi thoht beo," quoth the king Maxence, "ah wordes thu havest inohe. (2) Ah thole nu ane hwile ant tu schald ifinden hwa the ontswerie."

---

10.   (1) She answered and said: "If you wish to know my name: I am called Katherine. (2) If you wish to know my kin, I am a king's daughter. (3) My father was called Cost, and I have had hitherto very great teachers. (4) But because the learning that they taught me pertains to idle boasting, and belongs to profit for worship of the world, and does not at all help anyone have eternal life, I do not at all boast of it. (5) But as soon as I saw the light of the true learning that leads to that eternal life, I renounced all the rest, and took Him to me as Lord and made Him my lover, who said these words through one of His prophets: *Perdam sapientiam sapientum et intellectum intellegentium reprobabo.* (6) 'I will destroy the wisdom of these wise worldly ones,' He says, 'and cast down the wit of these worldly-wise ones.' (7) I heard moreover these words from another prophet: *Deus autem noster in celo omnia quecumque voluit fecit. Simulacra gentium argentum et aurum et cetera usque ad similes illis fiant.* (8) 'Our God is in Heaven who works all that He wishes. (9) These idols are made of gold and of silver entirely by human hands: mouth without speech, eyes without sight, ears without hearing, hands without feeling, feet without movement. (10) May those who make them be like them, and all those who trust in them.' (11) But now you say that they are all-ruling gods and wish me to worship them! (12) Show something of them — for what reason are they worthy to be worshiped? — for until then I will neither honor nor praise them."

11.   (1) "I do not know what your thoughts are," said the king Maxence, "but you have more than enough words. (2) But wait now a while and you will meet one who

(3) Thes sondesmon, umbe long, tha he hefde al thet lont overgan ant thurh sohte, com ant brohte with him fifti scolmeistres: of alle the creftes the clearc ah to cunnen ant in alle wittes of worldliche wisdomes wisest o worlde. (4) The king wes swithe icwemet ant walde witen yef ha weren se wise ant se witi as me foreseide. (5) Ant ha somet seiden thet witiest ha weren of alle the meistres the weren in Estlonde ant heaved of the heste, ant mest nomecuthe icud of alle clergies.

12.   (1) "Ah thu," quethen ha, "keiser, ahest to cuthen for hwet icud thing thu hete us hider to cumene."

13.   (1) Ant he ham ontswerede: "Her is a meiden yunglich on yeres, ah se swithe witti ant wis on hire wordes thet ha with hire anes mot meistreth us alle. (2) Ah yet

fol. 5v me teoneth mare thet ha tuketh ure godes to balewe ant to | bismere ant seith hit beoth deoflen thet in ham dearieth. (3) Ich mahte inohreathe wel habben aweld hire, yef ha nalde with luve, with luther eie lanhure. (4) Ah yet me thuncheth betere thet ha beo ear overcumen with desputunge. (5) Ant yef ha theyet wule, then ha wat hire woh, withstonden agein us, ich hire wule don to the derveste death thet me mei hire demen, ant with kinewurthe yeoves yelden ow hehliche ower yong hider (yef ye agein wulleth). (6) Other, yef ow is willre forte wunie with me, ye schule beon mine readesmen in alle mine dearne runes ant mine dearne deden."

14.   (1) Tha ontswerede the an swithe prudeliche thus to the prude prince: "Hei! (2) Hwuch wis read of se cud keiser, makie se monie clerkes to cumene — ant se swithe crefti of alle clergies — of Alixandres lont the alre leaste ende to motin with a

---

shall answer you."(3) This messenger, after a long time, when he had traversed that whole land and searched it from end to end, came and brought with him fifty schoolmasters: of all the crafts which a clerk ought to know and in all the disciplines of worldly wisdom the wisest in the world. (4) The king was greatly pleased and wanted to know if they were as wise and as clever as he was told. (5) And together they said that they were the wisest of all the masters who were in the Eastern Empire and chief among the most distinguished, and the most widely known in all the branches of knowledge.

12.   (1) "But you," said they, "emperor, ought to reveal for what important matter you commanded us to come here."

13.   (1) And he answered them: "Here is a maiden young in years, but so very witty and wise in her words that she with her reasoning alone masters us all. (2) But, it angers me still more that she reviles our gods maliciously and scornfully and says it is devils that lurk inside them. (3) I could readily enough have overpowered her, if she would not have love, then at least with terrible fear. (4) But yet it seems better to me that she be first overcome with disputing. (5) And if she still will, when she knows her error, stand against us, I will put her to the most painful death that anyone could deem for her, and with royal gifts I will richly repay you for your coming here (if you want to go back). (6) Or, if it is preferable to you to stay with me, you will be my advisors in all my secret meetings and my secret matters."

14.   (1) Then one of them proudly replied to the proud prince in this way: "Hah! (2) What wise council from so famous an emperor, to make so many clerks come — and so very skilled in all the branches of knowledge — from the furthest ends

meiden! (3) Me, an mahte of ure men with his mot meistrin ant with his anes wit awarpen the alre wiseste the wuneth bi westen! (4) Ah hwuch se ha eaver beo, let bringen hire forth thet ha understonde thet ha ne stod neaver ear thene thes dei bute bivore dusie." (5) Theos meiden wes bicluset the hwile i cwarterne ant i cwalmhuse. (6) Com a sonde ant seide hire thet ha schulde cume forth to fehten i the marhen: ane agein vifti. (7) Nes this meiden nawiht hervore imenget in hire mod inwith, ah buten euch fearlac bitahte al hire feht in hire Helendes hont, ant bigon to Him to bidde theos bone:

15.

fol. 6r

(1) "Crist — Godd Godes Sune, swete softe Jesu, alre smelle swotest, Thu alwealdinde | Godd, Thi Feadres wisdom, Thu thet tahtest Thine thet ha ne sculde nowther diverin ne dreden for teone, ne for tintreohe, ne for na worldlich wontreathe, ah warnedest ham wel hu me ham walde threatin ant leaden unlaheliche, ant elnedest ham swa thet ham wes eth to drehen al thet me dude ham ant al thet ha drohen for Thi deore luve, deorewurthe Lauerd; ant seidest Theseolven: *Dum steteritis ante reges et presides, et cetera*; 'Hwene ye stondeth bivore kinges ant eorles, ne thenche ye neaver hweat ne hu ye schulen seggen, for Ich chulle yeoven ow ba tunge ant tale thet an ne schal of alle ower witherwines witen hwet he warpe a word agein ow' — Lauert, wune with me ant halt thet Tu bihete us ant sete, Jesu, swete sahen i mi muth to marhen, ant yef swuch mahte ant strengthe i mine wordes thet theo the beoth icumene ageines Thi deore nome me to under-neomene moten missen throf. (2) Awelt thurh Thi wisdom hare worldliche

of the land of Alexandria to dispute with a maiden! (3) Moreover, one of our men with his own argument can master and with his wit alone overthrow the wisest of all who lives in the west! (4) But whosoever she may be, let her be brought forth so that she may understand that before this day she never stood before anyone except fools." (5) This maiden was locked in the meantime in prison and in the death-house. (6) A messenger came and told her that she would come forth to fight in the morning: one against fifty. (7) This maiden was in no way on account of this dismayed internally in her mind, but without any fear entrusted all her fight into her Healer's hands, and began to pray this prayer to Him:

15.

(1) "Christ — God son of God, sweet soft Jesus, sweetest of all smells, You all-ruling God, Your Father's wisdom, You who taught Your own that they should neither tremble nor dread for torment, nor for torture, nor for any worldly hardship, but warned them well how people would threaten them and lead them immorally, and strengthened them so that it was easy for them to endure all that was done to them and all that they suffered for Your dear love, precious Lord; and You said Yourself: *Dum steteritis ante reges et presides, et cetera*; 'When you stand before kings and earls, do not ever think about what or how you will speak, for I will give you both tongue and tale so that not one of all your enemies will know how he may cast a word against you' — Lord, dwell with me and keep what you promised and established for us and set, Jesus, sweet words in my mouth tomorrow, and give such might and strength to my speech that those who are come against Your dear name to entrap me may miss in their aim. (2) Through Your wisdom overrule their worldly wit and through Your great strength master them so that they all may be stopped and

wit ant thurh Thi muchele mihte mestre ham swa ha beon alle istewet ant stille,
other wenden to The ant Thi nome wurdgin, the with Godd heh Feader ant with
the Hali Gast thurh-wunest in alre worlde world, áá on ecnesse." (3) Nefde ha
bute iseid swa thet an engel ne com lihtinde with swuch leome from Heovene thet
ha wes sumdel offruht ant offert, for al the cwarterne of his cume leitede o leie.
(4) Ah the engel elnede hire ant sweteliche seide:

16.

fol. 6v

(1) "Ne beo thu nawiht ofdret, Drihtines dohter! (2) Halt hardiliche o thet tu
havest bigunnen, for thi leofmon ant ti Lauert (for hwas nome thu undernome
this strif) is with the eaver ihwer i stude | ant i stalle the wel wule wite the. (3) He
bihat te thet He wule i thi muth healden flowinde weattres of wittie wordes, the schule
the flit of thine fan swifteliche avellen. (4) Ant swuch wunder ham schal thunchen of
thi wisdom thet ha wulleth alle wende to Criste, ant cume thurh martirdom to
Drihtin in Heovene. (5) Monie schule turnen to treow bileave thurh hare forbisne. (6)
Ant tu schalt sone etsterten al the strengthe of this strif thurh a stealewurhthe deth,
ant beo thenne undervon i the feire verredene ant i the murie mot of meidnes, ant
libben lives buten ende with Jesu Crist thi Lauerd, thi leofmon in Heovene. (7)
Ich hit am Michael, Godes heh-engel, ant of Heovene isent forte seggen the thus."
(8) Ant mid tet ilke, step up ant steah to the steorren. (9) Theos meiden (thet ich
munie) stot, thurh theos steavene stercliche istrenget, ant abad baldeliche athet me
com ant fatte hire to fliten with the fifti. (10) Maxence ine marhen set i kineseotle ant
bed bringen bivoren him thes modi moteres ant te meiden with ham. (11) Heo
with Cristes Cros cruchede hire overal ant com baldeliche bivoren thes feondes

---

silent, or else turn to You and worship Your name, who with God the high Father
and with the Holy Ghost lasts forever from world into world, forever in eternity."
(3) She had scarcely said this when an angel came descending with such light from
Heaven that she was somewhat frightened and afraid, for all the prison blazed
with flame from his coming. (4) But the angel encouraged her and sweetly said:

16.

(1) "Be not at all afraid, God's daughter. (2) Keep courageously to what you have
begun, for your lover and your Lord (in whose name you have undertaken this
contest), who will watch you well, is with you everywhere in all places. (3) He
promises you that He will pour into your mouth flowing waters of wise words, that
will swiftly fell the argument of your enemies. (4) And your wisdom will seem such
a wonder to them that they will all turn to Christ and come through martyrdom
to the Lord in Heaven. (5) Many will turn to true belief through their example.
(6) And you will soon escape all the violence of this strife through a stalwart death,
and then be received in the fair fellowship and in the merry meeting of maidens,
and live life without end with Jesus Christ your Lord, your lover in Heaven. (7)
I am Michael, God's archangel, and am sent from Heaven to say so to you." (8)
And with that, he rose up and ascended to the stars. (9) This maiden (whom I
have in mind) stood, stoutly strengthened from this speech, and waited boldly
until someone came and brought her to argue against the fifty. (10) Maxence in
the morning sat on the throne and ordered brought before him these proud
debaters and the maiden with them. (11) She with Christ's cross crossed herself
everywhere and came boldly before the very child of the devil and against these

an foster ant agein thes fifti, alle ferliche freken. (12) Comen alle strikinde, strengest te swithest, of eaver-euch strete forte here this strif. (13) Stoden on an half theos meistres, se monie ant unimete modi; theos meiden on other half. (14) Heo biheolden hire hokerliche alle, ant heo stot hercnende ant biheolt efter help

fol. 7r   up towart Heovene. (15) The king bigon | to wreththen thet te dei eode awei ant heo ne duden nawiht. (16) Ant the eadie Katerine bigon forte seggen:

17.   (1) "Thu," quoth ha, "keiser, navest nawt this strif rihtwisliche idealet: thu dest fifti meistres to moti with a meiden! (2) Ant havest ham bihaten — yef ha mahen on me the herre hont habben — kinewurthe meden, ant me nawiht under al, the moti, a meiden, ageines ham alle. (3) Ah ne drede ich nawiht thet mi Lauert nule wel yelde me mi hwile (for hwas nome ich underneome to fehten o this wise). (4) Ah yette me an hwet thet tu ne maht nawt wearne with rihte. (5) Yef me is ilevet thurh mi leove Lauert forte leggen ham adun, thet tu thi misbileave lete thenne lanhure ant lihte to ure."

18.   (1) "Nai!" quoth he hetterliche, as him thet hoker thuhte. (2) "Ne lith hit nawt to the to legge lahe upo me. (3) Of mine bileave — beo ha duhti other dusi — nave thu nawt to donne. (4) Do nu thet tu schalt don ant we schule lustnin hu thi Lauerd ant ti leof — thet al thi bileave is upon — wule werie to dei thine leasunges."

19.   (1) This meiden mid tet ilke lokede on other half ant lette him iwurthen, ant toc on towart thes fif sithe tene to talien o this wise: "Nu ye alles to strif beoth isturet hidere forte beon with gold ant gersum igrette — ant se feole, cuthe men

---

fifty, all formidable fighters. (12) Everyone came striding, the strongest and swiftest from every single street to hear this strife. (13) There on one side stood these masters, so many and immeasurably proud; this maiden on the other side. (14) They all stared at her scornfully, and she stood listening and looking up toward Heaven for help. (15) The king began to get angry because the day passed by and they did nothing at all. (16) And the blessed Katherine began to speak:

17.   (1) "You," said she, "emperor, have not matched this contest fairly — you make fifty masters debate with a maiden! (2) And you have promised them — if they can have the higher hand over me — kingly rewards, and me nothing at all, who argues, a maiden, against them all. (3) But I do not at all fear that my Lord will not reward me well for my time (for whose name I undertake to fight in this way). (4) But grant me one thing which you may not justly refuse. (5) If it is permitted me with the help of my beloved Lord to cast them down, that you then at least abandon your misbelief and adopt ours."

18.   (1) "No!" said he sternly, since that seemed to him an insult. (2) "It is not your business to lay the law upon me. (3) Whether it is valid or foolish, do not be concerned with my faith. (4) Now do what you will do and we will hear how your Lord and your love — in whom is all your belief — will defend your lies today."

19.   (1) This maiden at that moment looked on the other side and ignored him, and began to speak to those five times ten in this way: "Since all of you have been spurred on here to the struggle in order to be rewarded with gold and gifts — and so many, both famous men and foreigners, wait and watch to see which of us is the

fol. 7v

ba ant utcumene copnith ant kepeth hwuch ure is kempe to overcumen other—lure ow is to leosen ower swinkes lan the leoteth se lihtliche of ant spearieth ower speche, ant schome ow is to schuderin lengre under schelde ant schunien thet ye | schule to. (2) Scheoteth forth sum word ant let us ontswerien! (3) The meast kempe is icud ant kenest of ow alle of the creft, the he is nomecuthest ant meast con: cume, cuthe throf, ant thet haveth in heorte (nu we schullen talien) take ut of his tunge, ant teveli with me."

20.

(1) "Nai," quoth the cuddest an of ham alle, "ah nu we beoth of se feor for the iflut hidere, thu schalt sette sikel forth, ant seggen earst hwet tu wult, ant we schulen seothen."

21.

(1) "Ich," quoth thet meiden, "sone se ich awei weorp ower witlese lei ant leornede ant luvede the liffule leave of Hali Chirche — the ich ichosen habbe — ich aweorp with alle the glistinde wordes the beoth in ower bokes, the beoth withuten godlec ant empti withinnen, thet ye beoth with toswollen, nawt with wit ah with wint of ane wlonke wordes the thuncheth se greate, ant beoth godlese thah ant beare of euch blisse, thah ye blissen ow throf. (2) Lo, thullich is al thet ye thencheth todei forto weorri me with — Homers motes ant Aristotles turnes, Esculapies creftes ant Galienes grapes, Filistiones flites ant Platunes bokes, ant al thes writers writes thet ye wreothieth on. (3) Thah ich beo in alle of se earliche ilearet thet ich ne font nawt feole neaver min evening; thah, forthi thet ha beoth ful of idel yelp ant empti of thet hali liffule lare, al ich forsake ham her ant cwethe ham al scher up, ant

---

champion to overcome the other — it is your loss to lose the reward of your work, who take it so lightly and are sparing of your speech, and it is shame to you to shudder longer under shield and shun what you should do. (2) Shoot forth some word and let us answer! (3) Whoever is known as the greatest champion among you and keenest of the craft of all of you, he who is the most famous and knows the most: come, let him show it, and what he has in his heart, since we will speak, let him take it out with his tongue and argue with me."

20.

(1) "No," said the most famous of them all, "but since we have traveled from so far for you here, you must cut the first swath, and say first what you wish, and we will speak afterwards."

21.

(1) "I," said that maiden, "as soon as I cast away your witless law and learned and loved the life-giving belief of Holy Church — which I have chosen — I cast away with it all the glistening words that are in your books, which are without goodness and empty within, and with which you are puffed up, not with wit but only with the wind of some haughty words which seem so splendid, and yet are worthless and barren of every blessing, though you bless yourselves with them. (2) Lo, such is all that you think to fight me with today — Homer's arguments and Aristotle's subtleties, Asclepius' skills and Galen's gropings, Philistion's debates and Plato's books, and all these writers' writings which you lean on. (3) Although I was instructed in all of them so young that I never found many my equal, nevertheless, because they are full of idle yelping and empty of that holy life-giving lore, I forsake them here and give them all up completely, and say that I neither know

segge thet ich ne con ne ne cnawe na creft bute of an thet is soth wit ant wisdom ant heore eche heale thet Him riht leveth; thet is, Jesu Crist, mi Lauert ant mi leofmon the seide — as ich seide ear ant yet wule seggen —: *Perdam sapientiam sapientum et intel|lectum et cetera.* (4) 'Ich chulle fordon the wisdom of theos wise worldmen ant warpen the wit of theos world-witti.' (5) The alre schafte Schuppent schawde ure eareste aldren Adam ant Eve the wit ant te wei of lif thurh His halwunde heast, ant hefde ham bihaten (yef heo ham wel heolden) heoveneliche meden. (6) Ah the wrenchfule feont, thurh onden, with his willes weorp ham ut sone of Paraises selhthen into this liflese lif. (7) Ant al thet lihte of ham twa schulde vorleosen, yef thet Godes goddlec nere the mare, the swa muche luvede us (thah se luthere ilatet) thet He lihte nu late of heovenliche leomen; ant forthi thet He is to ure sihthe unsehelich | in His ahne cunde, com ant creap in ure forto beon isehen thrin, ant nom blod ant ban of a meidenes bodi. (8) Thus He schrudde ant hudde Him, alre thinge Schuppent, mid ure fleschliche schrud, ant schawde us His nebscheft ant weolc — hwil His wil wes — bimong worldliche men. (9) Ant tha he hefde arudd us of feondes raketehen, wende up as He walde wunien ther He wuneth, áá withuten wonunge. (10) Swa thet we witen wel, thurh wundres thet He wrahte thet na mon ne mahte, thet He is soth Godd, ant eft thurh thet He throwede ant tholede deth on Rode as dedlich mon, that He is ec soth mon: of His Feader soth Godd, ant of His moder soth mon, in anhad ba somet, soth mon ant soth Godd weldinde ant wissinde alle worldliche thing efter His wille. (11) Thes is mi Lauerd thet ich on leve. (12) Thes is al

Royal
fol. 20r

fol. 20v

---

nor acknowledge any craft but the one that is true wit and wisdom and the eternal salvation of those who believe truly in Him; that is, Jesus Christ, my Lord and my lover who said — as I said before and still will say —: *Perdam sapientiam sapientum et intellectum et cetera.* (4) 'I will destroy the wisdom of these wise worldly men and cast down the wit of these worldly-wise people.' (5) The Creator of all creatures showed our first ancestors Adam and Eve the wit and the way of life through His sanctifying commandment, and had promised them (if they guarded themselves well) heavenly reward. (6) But the crafty fiend, through jealousy, with his wiles soon cast them out of the joys of Paradise into this lifeless life. (7) And all who descended from those two would be destroyed, if God's goodness were not greater, who loved us so much (though so wickedly mannered) that He descended now recently from heavenly rays of light; and because He is to our sight invisible in His own kind, came and crept into ours in order to be seen in it, and took blood and bone from a maiden's body. (8) Thus He shrouded and hid Himself, the Creator of all things, with our fleshly shroud, and showed us His face and walked — while it was His will — among worldly men. (9) And when He had rescued us from the fiend's fetters, He went up as He wished to dwell where He dwells, forever without waning. (10) Because of this we know well, through the wonders that He worked which no man might, that He is true God, and again through the fact that He suffered and endured death on the Cross as a mortal man, that He is also true man: from His Father true God, and from His mother true man, in unity both together, true man and true God governing and guiding all worldly things after His will. (11) This is my Lord in whom I believe.

the lare thet ich nu leorni. (13) Thes is the i this strif schal strengen me agein ow. (14) In His hali nome ich schal leten lihtlich of al thet ye cunnen kasten agein me. (15) Ne beo ye so monie, for nis Him no dervre forto adweschen adun feole | then fewe, bivoren theo Him riht leveth ant luvieth."

fol. 21r

22.   (1) An for ham alle onswerede ant seide: "Yef he wes as thu seist soth Godd ant Godes sune, hu mahte he as mon derfliche deien? (2) Yef he wes soth mon, hu mahte he death overcumen? (3) Alle wise witen wel thet hit is agein riht ant agein leave of euch cundelich lahe thet Godd the is undedlich mahe deth drehen, ant deadlich mon mahe death overcumen. (4) Ant thah hit mahte nu beon thet he ba were, soth Godd ant soth mon efter thet tu munnest, an he mahte inohrathe of theos twa thing — ba somet nanesweis."

23.   (1) Heo ne sohte nawiht ah seide ananriht agein: "This is nu the derfschipe of thi dusi onsware ant te deopnesse, thet tu of thet thing thet te misthuncheth undervest the an half ant dustest adun the other: the Goddnesse of Godd for the mennesse of His monhad, as thah the Almihti ne mahte nawt theos twa misliche cundes gederin togederes. (2) Ye, ne makede He mon of lam to His ilicnesse? (3) Hwi schulde He forhohien to wurthen to thet thing thet is iwend uppon Him? (4)

fol. 21v

Ant hwen He hit mahte don buten ewt to leosen of His hehnesse, | hwi were hit Him erveth to don — the thet alle thing mei ant wule al thet god is — to neomen monnes cunde ant beon isehen soth mon Godd thah unsehlich in His ahne cunde, ant tholien as mon deth hwen duhti Him thuhte? (5) Ah yef thu wult siker beon thet

---

(12) This is all the lore that I now learn. (13) This is what will strengthen me against you in this strife. (14) In His holy name I will think little of everything that you think to cast against me. (15) Nor are you so many, for it is no harder for Him to overwhelm many than few, before those who truly believe and love Him."

22.   (1) One answered for them all and said: "If he was, as you say, true God and God's son, how might he as a man dreadfully die? (2) If he was true man, how might he overcome death? (3) All the wise know well that it is against truth and against the authority of every natural law that God who is immortal may suffer death, and that mortal man may overcome death. (4) And though it might now be that he were both, true God and true man after what you imagine, he could easily do one of these two things — but in no way both together."

23.   (1) By no means did she deliberate but said back immediately: "This is now the audacity and the wisdom of your foolish answer, that you accept half of that thing that displeases you and cast away the other: the Godness of God for the humanity of His manhood, as though the Almighty could not gather together these two separate natures. (2) On the contrary, did He not make mankind out of clay in His likeness? (3) Why should He disdain to become that thing that is modeled upon Him? (4) And when He could do it without losing anything of His dignity, why would it be hard for Him to do — He who can and will do everything that is good — to take man's nature and be seen as true human though God is invisible in His own nature, and suffer death as a human when it seemed worthy to Him? (5) But if you want to be sure that what I say is true, leave your false knowledge that you pride yourself on, and adopt

seoth beo thet ich segge, leaf thi lease wit thet tu wlenchest te in, ant liht to ure lare thet tu mahe stihen to understonden in Him Godes muchele strencthe, ant nan monnes mihte, thurh His wundri werkes ant wurthful in eorthe. (6) For nultu nawt tenne thet tu schuldest heien heanin ne hatien na mare: thet is, i soth Godd monnes unmihte thet He neodeles nom uppon Himseolven, us forto salvin ant maken us stronge thurh His unstrencthe. (7) His unstrencthe ich cleopie thet He wes as mon cundeliche ofhungret ant weri ant pinen mahte tholien. (8) In euch thing of the world beoth sutel ant ethsene the weolen of Godes wisdom, thah in this an thing He schawde ant sutelede inoh that He wes soth Godd, the leadeth euch leafful to treowe bileave ant His leove nome to herien ant to heien, tha He with His stefne the storvene astearde ant mid His word awahte the liflese liches

fol. 22r   to lif | ant to leome. (9) Thus ne dude neaver nan dedlich mon thurh his anes mihte yef He Godd nere. (10) Other, thurh wiheles ant thurh wicchecreftes, wurchith summe wundres ant bigulith unweoten, the weneth thet hit beo swa as hit on ehe bereth ham. (11) Ah thes, thurh thet He wes soth Godd, in His cunde icuplet with ure, arerde the deade, botnede blinde, the dumbe, ant te deave, healde halte and hoverede, ant euch unheale, ant draf of the wedde awariede wihtes, ant as alweldende wrahte her on worlde al thet He walde. (12) Ant yef thu nult nanesweis witen thet He wrahte thulliche wundres, lef lanhure thet tu isist: miracles thet His men makieth yette, thurh Him ant His deorewurthe nome, deies ant nihtes.

24.   (1) "Ah beo nu soth cnawes yef ich riht segge. (2) Thu seist He ne mihte nawt Godd ba beon ant mon. (3) Ah yef He nere soth Godd ant undeadlich Himseolf,

---

our lore so that you may arise to understand in Him God's great strength, and not man's might, through His wondrous and worthy works on earth. (6) For then you will not any more scoff at or hate what you should honor: that is, in true God man's weakness which He needlessly took upon Himself, to heal us and make us strong through His weakness. (7) I call it His weakness in that He was as a man naturally ahungered and weary and could endure pains. (8) In everything of the world the riches of God's wisdom are clear and evident, yet in this one thing He showed and made clear enough that He was true God, who leads every believer to true belief and to praise and exalt His beloved name, when He with His voice stirred the dead and with His word awoke the lifeless corpses to life and to light. (9) No mortal man ever did this through his own might unless He were God. (10) Others, through wiles and through witchcrafts, work certain wonders and beguile the ignorant, who think that it is just as it appears to them in the eye. (11) But this one, because he was true God, in His nature coupled with ours, raised the dead, healed the blind, the dumb, and the deaf, cured the cripples and the humpbacked, and every disease, and drove from the mad accursed demons, and as the all-powerful He worked here in the world all that He wished. (12) And if you will not in any way know that He wrought such wonders, believe at least what you see: miracles His people work still, through Him and His beloved name, by day and by night.

24.   (1) "But acknowledge truly now if I speak correctly. (2) You say He could not be both God and man. (3) But if He were not true God and Himself immortal,

hu mahte He lenen lif to the deade? (4) Ant yef He nere soth mon, hu mahte He
drehen thet He droh ant deien so derfliche? (5) Thurh this suteleth soth al thet

fol. 22v ich segge: ant tat is Godd seolf, the duste death under Him thurh | thet He is
Drihtin, meinful ant almihti. (6) Ant seolf the ilke is Godes Sune, the onont thet
He Godd wes ne mahte He drehen na deth, ant tah deide ah fleschliche for; ba
He underveng ban ant flesch on ure cunde — thet is bruchel ant dedlich — forto
deien in hire forthi thet He wes undedlich in His ahne ne in hire ne mahte He
nanesweis deien — buten in ure. (7) Thes sothe Godd ant Godes sune, the deide
onont ure cunde thet He hefde, aras ant arerde Himseolven from deathe, for thah
He were dedlich thurh thet He mon wes onont His mennesse ant deide as ich
seide, He ne losede na lif onont thet He Godd wes ne undedlichnesse onont His
Drihtnesse, ah wes eaver ant is Drihtin undedlich. (8) Thus ido dede, death ne
akaste nawt Crist, ah Crist overcom deth ant sloh hire in Himseolven."

25. (1) Alle the othere hercneden mid swithe open earen, ah herto onswerede an
for ham alle: "Yef Drihtin the darede in ure mennesse wrahte theos wundres —
as thu wult thet we leven — hwi walde He throwin as He dude ant tholien deth on

fol. 23r Rode? (2) Hwen He com to arudden of deathes raketehen | othre hwi deide He
Himseolven? (3) Ant hu mei He helpen ant beon bivoren othre, the thurh-ferde
death as heo doth? (4) Hefde He thet lanhure Himseolven aleset sum walde
hopien ant habben bileave to His alesunge."

26. (1) Yet cweth this meiden ant seide him toyeines: "Ich habbe uncnut summe
of theos cnotti cnotten (yef thu wult icnawen), ah her thu wenest yet thet tu ne

---

how could He give life to the dead? (4) And if He were not true man, how could
He suffer what He suffered and die so cruelly? (5) Through this all that I say is
shown to be the truth: and that is God Himself, who cast death down under Him
because He is the Lord, strong and almighty. (6) And the very same one is God's
Son, who insofar as He was God could suffer no death, and yet He died but in the
flesh; for He took on both bone and flesh in our nature — which is brittle and
mortal — in order to die in it because He was immortal in His own nature and in
it He could not die in any way — only in ours. (7) This true God and God's Son,
who died insofar as he had our nature, arose and raised Himself up from death,
for although He was mortal because He was man as regards His manhood and
died, as I said, He did not lose life insofar as He was God, nor immortality with
respect to His divine nature, but was ever and is the immortal Lord. (8) Thus put
to death, death did not cast down Christ, but Christ overcame death and slew it
in Himself."

25. (1) All the others listened with wide-open ears, but to this one answered for
them all: "If the Lord who hid in our humanity worked these wonders — as you
wish us to believe — why would He suffer as He did and endure death on the
Cross? (2) When He came to rescue others from death's fetters, why did He die
Himself? (3) And how can He help and be above others, who underwent death as
they do? (4) Had He at least redeemed Himself some would hope and have belief
in His redemption."

26. (1) Still this maiden spoke and said to him in reply: "I have unknotted some
of these intricate knots (if you would recognize it), but here you still think

wenen therf: thet Godd, the is unthrowlich, throwede other tholede pine other passiun o the deore Rode onont thet He Godd wes. (2) Ne mahte thet wite thu His heovenliche cunde o nanes cunnes wise felen sar ne sorhe uppon the Cruche, ah al the weane ant te wa wente uppon the unstrencthe of thet undervo flesch thet He neodeles nom with al ure nowcin bute sunne ane uppon Himseolven. (3) O Godd, the is al freo, ne mei nan uvel festnin; ne mahte me nowther Godd, onont thet He Godd wes, beatin ne binden ne neomenne halden, for He is unneomelich. (4) Ah thurh the mon thet He wes ischrudd ant ihudd with, He bicherde thene feont ant schrenchte then alde deovel ant toschrapede his hefde! (5) Nes nawt iteiet to the

fol. 23v   Treo ther He deide uppon forto drahen | buten flesch-timber, ah swa He withuten woh adweschte ant adun warp thene witherwine of Helle, mon i monnes cunde, the mid woh hefde to deth idrahen moncun thurh dedliche sunnen. (6) That wes, as ich munne, mon ant nawt Godes drihtnesse thurh-driven uppon the Rode, thah He in the ilke time soth Godd were. (7) Ah mon — for mon the misdude — tholede dom ant deide, ant Godd i mon for monnes bruche bette ant eode on bote, as His ahne goddlec lahede hit ant lokede. (8) Low, this makede Him thet He underveng mon (thet is, bicom mon) thet te bruchen thet mon hefde ibroken agein Him weren ibet thurh mon, ant thet He arise earest from deathe to live thet ne dredeth na deth. (9) Thurh Him we mahen habben sikere bileave to arisen alle efter Him. (10) Eth were ure Lauerd, liviende Godes Sune, to awarpen His unwine ant reavin him his hondiwerc — thet he with woh etheold — on euch wise in world

---

what you ought not think: that God, who is incapable of suffering, suffered or endured pain or passion on the dear Rood insofar as He was God. (2) And know that His heavenly nature might not in any kind of way feel pain or sorrow on the Cross; but all the wretchedness and woe was directed upon the weakness of that borrowed flesh that He needlessly took upon Himself with all our hardship, only without sin. (3) On God, who is completely free, no evil can fasten; nor could anyone either beat or bind or seize or hold God, inasmuch as He is God, for He is unseizable. (4) But through the man with which He was shrouded and hidden, He duped the fiend and deceived the old devil and robbed him blind! (5) Nor was anything tied in order to suffer upon the Tree where he died except for flesh-matter, so that without a doubt He, a man in human nature, overwhelmed and cast down the enemy of Hell, who had wrongfully dragged humankind down to death through deadly sins. (6) That was, as I mentioned, a man and not God's divinity pierced upon the Cross, although at that same time He was true God. (7) But humanity — for it was humanity who did wrong — suffered judgment and died, and God in humanity for humanity's mistake made it good and expiated the sin, as His own goodness ordained and determined. (8) Lo, this caused Him to take on humankind (that is, become a human) so that the breaches that humankind had committed against Him would be atoned for through humanity, and so that He who does not dread death should arise first from death to life. (9) Through Him we can all have a certain belief to rise up after Him. (10) It would have been easy for our Lord, the living God's Son, to cast down His foe and seize from him His handiwork — which he held captive with injustice — in any way in the world

thet he eaver walde: with an anlepi word; ye, with His an wil (11) Ah the witti
Weldent ant te rihtwise Godd bireadde hit swa swithe wel, thet he thet overcom

fol. 24r   mon were akast | thurh mon with meokelec ant liste, nawt with luther strencthe,
thet he ne mahte nanesweis meanen Him of wohe."

27.   (1) Hwil this eadi meiden motede this ant mealde — this ant muchele mare
— the an modgeste of ham thet mealde toyein hire warth swa awundret of hire
wittie wordes, ant swa offearet ant offruht ant alle hise feren, thet nefde heore nan
tunge to tavelin atine with. (2) Swa swithe Godes grace agaste ant agelwede ham
thet euchan biheold other as ha bidweolet weren, thet nan ne seide nawiht ah

Bodley   seten stille as stan. (3) Cwich ne cweth ther neaver an.
fol. 8r

28. |(1) Thes keiser bicapede ham, ant ase mon thet bigon to weden ant to
wurthen ut of his ahne wit, wodeliche yeide: "Hwet nu, unwreste men, ant wacre
then ei wake, of dead ant of dult wit? (2) Nu is ower stunde! (3) Hwi studgi ye nu
ant steventith se stille? (4) Nabbe ye teth ba ant tunge to sturien? (5) Is nu se
steorliche unstrenget ower strengthe ant ower wit awealt swa thet te mihte ant te
mot of a se meoke meiden schal meistren ow alle? (6) Me, yef fifti wimmen ant
thah ther ma weren hefden with wordes ower an awarpen, nere hit schendlac inoh
ant schir scheome to ow alle thet yelpeth of lare? (7) Nu is alre scheomene meast:
thet anlepi meiden with hire anes muth haveth swa bitevelet, itemet, ant iteiet alle,
italde bi tale fif sithe tene, icudde ant icorene ant of feorrene ifat, thet al ye beoth
blodles, ikimet ut of ow seolven. (8) Hwider is ower wit ant ower wisdom iwend?

---

that He ever wanted to: with a single word; yes, with His will alone. (11) But the
wise Lord and the righteous God planned it so very well that He who overcame
humankind was cast down through humankind with meekness and skill, not with
brute force, so that the Devil could in no way complain to Him of injustice."

27.   (1) While this blessed maiden disputed and declared this — this and much
more — the proudest one of them who argued against her became so astonished
by her wise words, and so afraid and affrighted, as well as all his fellows, that none
of them had a tongue to continue the argument with. (2) So thoroughly God's
grace terrified and frightened them that each one looked at the other as if they
were bewildered, so that no one said anything but sat still as stone. (3) Not one
there ever uttered a sound.

28.   (1) This emperor stared at them, and like a man who began to rage and go
out of his own wit, savagely shouted: "What now, miserable men, and weaker than
any weak ones, of dead and of dulled wit? (2) Now it is your turn! (3) Why do you
hesitate now and stand so still? (4) Do you not have both teeth and tongue to stir?
(5) Is your strength now so severely weakened and your wit so overcome that the
might and the argument of so meek a maiden will master you all? (6) Moreover,
if fifty women, and though there were more, had overthrown one of you with
words, would it not be humiliation enough and complete shame to you all who
brag of learning? (7) Now is the greatest of all shames: that a single maiden
with her own mouth has so out-argued, tamed, and tied all of you, counted by
number five times ten, known and chosen and fetched from afar, that you are
all bloodless, overcome out of yourselves. (8) Where have your wit and your

(9) Breoketh on, for bismere, ant biginneth sumhwet!"

29.   (1) Ontswerede the an the the othre heolden for hest ant heaved of ham alle and cweth to the king: "An hwet ich chulle thet tu wite: thet we habbeth witnese of alle the wise the beoth in estlonde thet neaver athet tes dei ne funde we nohwer nan swa deop ilearet the durste sputi with us, ant yef he come i place, nere he neaver se prud thet he ne talde him al tom ear he turnde from us. (2) Ah nis nawt

fol. 8v   lihtliche of this meidenes mot, for yef ich soth schal seggen, | in hire ne moteth na mon, for nawt nis hit monlich mot thet ha mealeth. (3) Ne nawt nis heo thet haveth mot, ah is an heovenlich gast in hire swa agein us thet we ne cunnen (ant tah we cuthen, ne nullen ne ne durren) warpen na word agein to weorri, ne te wreaththin Him thet ha wreotheth on. (4) For sone se ha Crist cleopede ant His nome nempnede ant te muchele mihtes of His hehnesse, ant schawde seoththen suteliche the deopnesse ant te derne run of His death o Rode, al wat awei ure worldliche wit swa we weren adrede of His drihtnesse. (5) Ant thet we kennith the wel, keiser, ant cutheth thet we leaveth thi lahe ant al thi bileave ant turneth alle to Crist. (6) Ant her we cnawlechith Him soth Godd and Godes Sune thet se muche godlec cudde us alle on eorthe thet woh haveth eni mon to weorrin Him mare. (7) This we schawith the. (8) Nu sei thet tu wult."

30.   (1) The keiser keste his heaved as wod mon of wreththe ant berninde as he wes of grome ant of teone, bed bringen o brune an ad amidde the burh, ant ba binden ham swa the fet ant te honden thet ha wrungen agein. (2) Ant i the reade lei ant

---

wisdom gone? (9) Open up, for shame, and begin something!"

29.   (1) The one whom the others held as the highest and head of them all answered and said to the king: "One thing that I want you to know: that we have the witness of all the wise who are in the east that never until this day have we found anywhere one so deeply learned who dared debate with us, and if he appeared in public, he would never be so proud that he did not consider himself entirely tame before he turned from us. (2) But there is nothing trivial about this maiden's speech, for if I will tell the truth, no human speaks in her, for it is not a human argument that she speaks. (3) Nor is it she who holds this debate, but it is a heavenly spirit in her so against us that we do not know how (and though we knew, we would not wish or dare) to cast a word against her to wage war, nor to anger Him whom she relies on. (4) For as soon as she called Christ and named His name and the great strengths of His highness, and showed afterwards clearly the deepness and the secret mystery of His death on the Cross, we were so afraid of His majesty that all our worldly wit went away. (5) And we declare this to you, emperor, and make it known that we leave your law and all your belief and all turn to Christ. (6) And here we acknowledge Him true God and God's Son who has shown so much goodness to us all on earth that anyone is wrong to fight Him further. (7) This we reveal to you. (8) Now say what you will."

30.   (1) The emperor cast his head like a madman in wrath, and burning as he was with rage and anger, commanded a funeral pyre to be set aflame in the middle of town, and commanded them bound both feet and hands so that they writhed against it. (2) And into the red flame and into that blazing fire he commanded them to be

i thet leitinde fur het warpen, euch fot. (3) As me droh ham to hare death, tha yeide thus the an ant elnede the othre: "O leove iferen, feire is us ifallen, ah yet we forgeoteth us. (4) Nu the deore Drihtin arew us ant toc read of ure alde dusischipes the we driven longe, ant haveth idiht us todei forte drehe this death thurh His milde milce, thet we forlete this lif for His treowe luve i treowe bileave

fol. 9r   ant i the cnaw|lechunge of His kinewurthe nome, hwi ne hihi we forte beon ifulhet as He het hise ear we faren heonne?"

31.   (1) As he iseid hefde, bisohten as ha stoden alle in a stevene thet tes meiden moste, i the wurthschipe of Godd, with halwende weattres bihealden ham alle. (2) Ah heo ham ontswerde ant swoteliche seide: "Ne drede ye ow nawiht, cnihtes icorene, for ye schulen beon ifulhet ant beten alle the bruchen thet ye ibroken habbeth in ower blodes rune. (3) Ant tis ferliche fur schal lihten in ow the halwende lei of the Hali Gast, the i furene tungen ontende the apostles."

32.   (1) Me weorp ham mid tis ilke word amidde the leie thear ha heven up hare honden to Heovene. (2) Ant swa somet readliche thurh seli martyrdom verden with murthe, icrunet to Criste, o the threotuthe dei of Novembres moneth. (3) Ah thet wes miracle muchel, thet nowther nes iwemmet clath thet ha hefden ne her of hare heafden, ah with se swithe lufsume leores ha leien, se rudie ant se reade ilitet eaver-euch leor, as lilie ileid to rose, thet nawt ne thuhte hit thet ha weren deade, ah thet ha slepten swoteliche a sweovete, swa thet feole turnden to treowe bileave ant tholeden anan death I the nome of Drihtin. (4) Comen Cristene a naht ant nomen hare bodies ant biburieden ham deorliche, as hit deh Drihtines cnihtes.

---

cast, every single one. (3) As they were dragged to their death, one of them cried out thus and strengthened the others: "O dear friends, things have fallen out fairly for us, but yet we forget ourselves. (4) Since the dear Lord pitied us and considered our old follies which we practiced for a long time, and has ordained for us today to suffer this death through His gentle mercy, so that we relinquish this life for His true love in true belief and in the acknowledgment of His kingly name, why do we not hasten to be baptized as He commanded His own before we depart from here?"

31.   (1) As he had said, they beseeched in one voice as they all stood, that this maiden should, in the worship of God, bathe them all with sacred waters. (2) But she answered them and sweetly said: "Do not be at all afraid, chosen knights, for you will be baptized and atone for all the breaches that you have broken by the flowing of your blood. (3) And this fearsome fire will alight in you the healing flame of the Holy Ghost, who inflamed the apostles with fiery tongues."

32.   (1) At these very words they were thrown in the middle of the fire where they raised up their hands to Heaven. (2) And so they departed together swiftly through holy martyrdom with joy, crowned to Christ, on the thirteenth day of the month of November. (3) But that was a great miracle, that neither the clothing which they had nor a hair of their heads was harmed, but with such lovely faces they lay, so flushed and glowing red every face, as a lily laid against a rose, that it did not seem that they were dead at all, but that they slept sweetly in a sleep, so that many turned to true belief and suffered death immediately in the name of the Lord. (4) Christians came by night and took their bodies and buried them tenderly, as is fitting for the Lord's knights.

33.   (1) Tha this wes ido thus, het eft the keiser thet me schulde Katerine bringe
bivoren him, ant thus to hire cleopede: "O mihti meiden! (2) O witti wummon
wurthmunt ant alle wurthschipe wurthe! (3) O schene nebschaft ant schape se |

fol. 9v   swithe semlich, thet schulde beo se prudeliche ischrud ant iprud ba with pel ant
with purpre! (4) Nim yeme of thi yuhethe; areow thi wlite ant tac read, seli, to the
seolven. (5) Ga ant gret ure godes the thu igremet havest, ant tu schalt (efter the
cwen) eaver the other beon in halle ant i bure, ant al ich chulle dihten the deden
of mi kinedom efter thet tu demest. (6) Ah yet ich segge mare: ich chulle lete
makie the of golt an ymage as cwen icrunet ant swa me schal amit te burh setten
hit on heh up. (7) Therefter me schal beoden ant bodien hit overal thet alle the
ther bigath greten hit o thi nome ant buhe thertowart, alle the wurthmunt,
burhmen ant othre. (8) On ende, thu schalt habben heheliche, as an of ure
heovenliche leafdis, of marbrestan a temple thet schal áá stonden hwil thet te
worlt stont to witnesse of thi wurthschipe."

34.   (1) Katerine ontswerede — smirkinde sumdel — ant cweth to the kinge: "Feire
uleth thi muth ant murie thu makest hit, ah ich drede thet tis dream me dreaie
towart deathe as deth meareminnes. (2) Ah al the helpeth an thin olhnunge ant tin
eie. (3) Ful wel ich chulle thet tu wite ne maht tu with nawiht wende min heorte from
Him thet ich heie ant áá wulle herien. (4) Bihat al thet tu wult; threp threfter inoh
ant threate thet tu beo weri. (5) Ne mei me wunne ne weole ne na worldes
wurthshipe,ne mei me nowther teone ne tintreohe turnen from mi

---

33.   (1) When this was so done, the emperor again commanded that Katherine
should be brought before him, and he said thus to her: "O mighty maiden! (2) O
wise woman worthy of every worship and reverence! (3) O bright face and shape
so very seemly, which should be so proudly clothed and adorned with rich and
purple clothing! (4) Take heed of your youth; have pity on your beauty and
consider, blessed one, yourself. (5) Go and greet our gods whom you have
enraged, and you will (after the queen) always be second in hall and in chamber,
and I will order the business of my kingdom entirely after what you advise. (6) But
still I say more: I will have made for you a statue of gold like a crowned queen and
it will be set high up in the middle of the town. (7) Thereafter it will be
announced and proclaimed everywhere that all who pass by there greet it in your
name and bow towards it, all in reverence to you, citizens and others. (8) Finally,
you will have honorably, as one of our heavenly ladies, a temple of marble that
will stand forever while the world stands as witness of your worship."

34.   (1) Katherine answered — smiling a little — and said to the king: "Fairly
flatters your mouth and you make it sound pleasant, but I fear that this song would
draw me toward death, as does the mermaid's. (2) But your flattery and your fear
all help you equally. (3) Full well I want you to know that you cannot with anything
turn my heart from Him whom I honor and will always praise. (4) Promise all that
you want; afterward scold enough and threaten until you are weary. (5) Neither joy
nor riches nor any world's worship, nor can torment nor torture turn me from my

leofmones luve thet ich on leve. (6) He haveth iweddet Him to mi meithhad with the ring of rihte | bileave, ant ich habbe to Him treowliche itake me. (7) Swa wit beoth ivestnet ant iteiet in an ant swa the cnotte is icnut bituhhen us tweien, thet ne mei hit liste ne luther strengthe nowther of na liviende mon lowsin ne leothien. (8) He is mi lif ant mi luve, He is thet gleadeth me, mi sothe blisse buve me, weole ant al mi wunne, ne nawt ne willni ich elles. (9) Mi swete lif, se swoteliche He smecheth me ant smealleth, thet al me thuncheth savure ant softe thet He sent me. (10) Stute nu thenne ant stew the, ant stille thine wordes, for ha beoth me unwurth, thet wite thu to wisse."

35. (1) The king ne cuthe na wit ah bigon to cwakien ant nuste hwet seggen. (2) Het o wodi wise strupen hire steort-naket ant beaten hire beare flesch ant hire freoliche bodi with cnottede schurgen. (3) Ant me swa dude sone thet hire leofliche lich litherede al a blode. (4) Ah heo hit lihtliche aber ant lahinde tholede. (5) Het hire threfter kasten i cwalmhus ant bed halden hire thrin thet ha nowther ne ete leasse ne mare tweolf dahes fulle.

36. (1) Bicom to thet te king Maxence moste fearen, ant ferde into the firreste ende of Alixandre. (2) The cwen Auguste longede forte seo this meiden. (3) Ant cleopede to hire Porphire, cnihtene prince, ant seide him a sweven thet hire wes ischawet, thet ha seh sitte theos meiden with monie hwite wurthliche men ant meidnes inohe al abute biset, ant heo wes hireseolf ther imong as hire thuhte. (4) Ant te an toc a guldene crune ant sette on hire heavet ant seide to hire | thus: "Have, cwen, a crune

---

lover's love in whom I believe. (6) He has wedded Himself to my maidenhood with the ring of right belief, and I have committed myself to Him truly. (7) We two are so fastened and tied into one and the knot is so knotted between us two, that neither the cleverness nor brute force of any living man may loosen or undo it. (8) He is my life and my love, it is He who gladdens me, my true bliss above me, my joy and all my well-being, and I desire nothing else. (9) My sweet life, so sweetly He tastes and smells to me, that everything seems delicious and pleasing which He sends me. (10) Stop now then and be silent, and still your words, for they are worthless to me, know that for certain."

35. (1) The king knew no reason but began to quake and did not know what to say. (2) In a mad fashion he ordered her stripped stark naked and her bare flesh and her beautiful body beaten with knotted scourges. (3) And it was immediately done so that her lovely body became lathered all in blood. (4) But she bore it lightly and suffered it laughing. (5) Afterward he commanded her to be cast into prison and ordered her held therein so that she ate neither less nor more for twelve full days.

36. (1) It came about that the king Maxence had to travel, and he went into the furthest end of Alexandria. (2) The queen Augusta longed to see this maiden. (3) And she called to her Porphirius, the leader of the knights, and told him a dream which had been shown to her, that she saw this maiden sit with many worthy men in white and maidens enough surrounded her, and she was there herself among them as it seemed to her. (4) And the one took a golden crown and set it on her

isent te of Heovene." (5) Ant forthi, ha seide, hire luste swithe yeorne speoke with the meiden.

37.   (1) Porphire yettede hire al thet ha yirnde ant leadde hire anan i the niht to the cwarterne. (2) Ah swuch leome ant liht leitede thrinne thet ne mahten ha nawt loki thear-ageines, ah feollen ba for fearleac dun duvelrihtes. (3) Ah an se swithe swote smeal com anan therefter thet fleide awei thet fearlac ant frovrede ham sone. (4) "Ariseth," quoth Katerine, "ne drede ye nawiht, for the deore Drihtin haveth idiht ow ba the blisfule crune of His icorene." (5) Tha ha weren iseten up sehen as the engles with smirles of aromaz smireden hire wunden, ant bieoden swa the bruchen of hire bodi, al tobroken of the beattunge, thet tet flesch ant tet fel worthen se feire thet ha awundreden ham swithe of thet sihthe. (6) Ah this meiden bigon to bealden ham bathe, ant to the cwen seide: "Cwen, icoren of Jesu Crist, beo nu stealewurthe, for thu schalt stihen bivore me to Drihtin in Heovene. (7) Ne beo thu nawiht offruht for pinen the feareth forth in an honthwile, for with swucche thu schalt buggen ant biyeote the endelease blissen. (8) Ne dred tu nawt to leaven thin eorthliche lauerd for Jesu Crist thet is King of thet eche kinedom, the yelt for the false wurthschipe of this world heoveriches wunne, for thing thet sone alith weole thet áá lesteth."

38.   (1) Feng tha Porphire to freinen this meiden hwucche weren the meden ant te endelese lif thet Godd haveth ilevet His icorene for the luren thet tis worldliche

fol. 11r   lif thet ha leoseth for the luve of rihte | bileave. (2) Heo ontswerede ant seide: "Beo nu thenne, Porphire, stille ant understont te: constu bulden a bur inwith thin

---

head and said to her thus: "Have, queen, a crown sent to you from Heaven." (5) And therefore, she said, she very eagerly desired to speak with the maiden.

37.   (1) Porphirius granted her all that she asked and led her at once in the night to the prison. (2) But such radiance and light shone inside it that they could not look at it, but both fell down headlong in fear. (3) But so very sweet a smell came immediately afterwards that that fear fled away and they were soon comforted. (4) "Arise," said Katherine, "and fear nothing, for the dear Lord has ordained for you both the blissful crown of His chosen ones." (5) When they had sat up they watched as the angels with ointments of spices smeared her wounds, and so treated the cuts in her body, all torn up from the beating, so that the flesh and the skin grew so fair that they wondered very much at that sight. (6) But this maiden began to encourage them both, and to the queen said: "Queen, chosen of Jesus Christ, be now stalwart, for you will ascend before me to the Lord in Heaven. (7) Do not be at all afraid of the pains which pass away in a moment, for with such you will buy and obtain endless bliss. (8) And fear not to leave your earthly lord for Jesus Christ who is King of that eternal kingdom, who yields the joy of the heaven-kingdom in exchange for the false worship of this world, a wealth that lasts forever in exchange for things which soon cease."

38.   (1) Then Porphirius began to ask this maiden what were the rewards and the endless life that God has granted His chosen in exchange for the losses and this worldly life which they lose for the love of true belief. (2) She answered and said: "Be still now, Porphirius, and understand: can you build a city within your heart,

heorte, al abute bitrumet with a deorewurthe wal, schininde ant schene of gimstanes steapre then is ei steorre, ant euch bolt thrinwith briht as hit bearnde ant leitede al o leie? (3) Ant al thet terin is glistinde ant gleaminde as hit were seolver other gold smeate, isteanet euch strete with deorewurthe stanes of misliche heowes imen get togederes, isliket ant ismaket as eni gles smethest, bute sloh ant slec, eaver iliche sumerlich; ant alle the burhmen seove sithe brihtre then beo sunne, gleowinde o euch gleo ant a mare iliche glead. (4) For nawiht ne derveth ham ne nawiht ne wonteth ham of al thet ha wulleth other mahe wilnin, alle singinde somet ase lifleovi, euchan with other, alle pleinde somet, alle lahinde somet, eaver iliche lusti bute longunge. (5) For ther is áá liht ant leitinde leome; ne niht nis ther neaver ne neaver na newcin. (6) Ne eileth ther na mon nowther sorhe ne sar, nowther heate ne chele, nowther hunger ne thurst, ne nan ofthunchunge. (7) For nis thear nawt bittres, ah is al beatewil, swottre ant swettre then eaver ei healewi, i thet heovenliche lond, i thet endelese lif, i the wunnen ant te weolen thurh-wuniende, ant monie ma murhthen then alle men mahten with hare muth munien ant tellen with tunge (thah ha áá talden), the neaver ne linneth nowther ne leassith ah leasteth áá mare, se lengre se mare. (8) Yef thu | yet wite wult hwucche wihtes thear beon thear as al this blisse is, yef thear is orcost other ei ahte, ich the ontswerie. (9) Al thet eaver oht is al is ther iwer, ant hwet se noht nis, thet nis ther nohwer. (10) Yef thu eskest 'Hwet oht?' nan eorthliche ehe ne mei hit seon ich segge ne nan eorthliche eare hercnin ne heren, ne heorte thenchen of mon — ant hure meale with muth — hwet te

fol. 11v

---

all surrounded with a precious wall, shining and beautiful from gemstones brighter than is any star, and every dwelling within bright as though it burned and blazed all in flame? (3) And all that is therein is glistening and gleaming as though it were silver or pure gold, each street paved with precious stones of various hues mixed together, glossed and polished as any of the smoothest glass, without mud or mire, forever like summer; and all the citizens seven times brighter than is the sun, rejoicing from every joy and forever equally glad. (4) For nothing at all either hurts them nor do they lack anything of all they want or could want, all singing together like lifelong friends, each one with the other, all playing together, all laughing together, always equally joyful without longing. (5) For there is always light and blazing radiance; nor is night ever there nor ever any distress. (6) Neither does sorrow or pain afflict any man there, neither heat nor cold, neither hunger nor thirst, nor any displeasure. (7) For nothing of bitterness is there, but everything is tasty, sweeter, and more fragrant than any healing tincture, in that heavenly land, in that endless life, in the pleasures and the blessings everlasting, and many more mirths than all people might mention with their mouths and tell with tongue (even if they talked forever), which never cease or lessen but last evermore, the longer the greater. (8) If you still wish to know what people there are at the place where all this bliss is, if there is wealth or any property, I answer you. (9) All that ever is good is there everywhere, and whatever is evil, that is nowhere. (10) If you ask, 'What good?', I say that no earthly eye can see it, and no earthly ear hearken or hear, nor human heart think — and least of all mention with mouth — what the world's

worldes Wealdent haveth iyarket alle theo the Him ariht luvieth."

39.   (1) Porphire ant Auguste worthen of theos wordes se swithe wilcweme ant se
hardi, forthi thet ha hefden isehen sihthen of Heovene, thet ha wenden from hire
abute the midniht, yarowe to al thet wa thet ei mon mahte ham yarki to drehe for
Drihtin. (2) Freineden Porphire alle his cnihtes hwer he hefde with the cwen iwunet
ant iwiket swa longe of the niht. (3) Ant Porphire ham seide: "Hwer ich habbe iwiket
ich on wel thet ye witen, for wel ow schal iwurthen yef ye me wulleth lustnin ant
leven, for nabbe ich nawt teos niht i worldliche wecchen ah habbe in heovenliche
iwaket, therin is al mi rihte bileave, thear me unwreah me the wei thet leadeth to
thet lif, ther me liveth áá i blisse buten euch bale, i wunne bute wa. (4) Forthi, yef ye
beoth mine as under me isette, ant wulleth alle with me in eche murhthe wunien,
leaveth to leven lengre o thes lease maumez — the mearreth ow ant alle theo the
ham to luteth — ant wendeth to the Wealdent the al the world wrahte: Godd
fol. 12r   heo|venlich Feader, euch godes ful. (5) Ant heieth ant herieth His an deorewurthe
Sune Jesu Crist hatte, ant te Hali Gast, Hare beire luve, the lihteth of Ham ba ant
limeth togederes swa thet nan ne mei sundri from other, alle threo an Godd almihti
overal, for He halt in His hont — thet is, wisseth ant wealt — the Heovene ant te
eorthe, the sea ant te sunne, ant alle ischepene thing sehene ant unsehene. (6) Theo
the leveth this soth ant leaveth thet lease ant buhsume ant beisume haldeth His
heastes, He haveth bihaten ham thet He ham wule leasten, thet is, blisse buten ende
i the riche of Heovene. (7) Ant hwa se is se unseli thet he this schunie, ne schal

---

Ruler has prepared for all those who love Him rightly."

39.   (1) Porphirius and Augusta became so very pleased and so hardy from these
words, because they had seen sights of Heaven, that they went from her about
midnight, prepared for all that woe that any man might ordain them to endure for
the Ruler. (2) All of his knights asked Porphirius where he had stayed with
the queen and lodged for so long into the night. (3) And Porphirius said to them:
"Where I have stayed I grant well that you know, for it will go well for you if
you will listen and believe me, for I have not this night kept awake in any worldly
watch but in a heavenly one, in which is all my true belief, where the way that leads
to that life was made clear to me where one lives forever in bliss without any
hardship, in joy without woe. (4) Therefore, if you are mine as you are placed under
me, and all want to live with me in eternal joy, leave off believing
any longer in these false idols — which mar you and all those who bow down
to them — and turn to the Ruler who made all the world: God the heavenly Father,
full of every good. (5) And honor and worship His one precious Son called Jesus
Christ, and the Holy Ghost, the love of both of Them, who proceeds from Them
both and unites Them together so that none can be sundered from the others, all
three one God almighty over all, for He holds in His hand — that is, He governs
and guides — the Heaven and the earth, the sea and the sun, and all created things
seen and unseen. (6) Those who believe this truth and leave that falsehood and
buxomly and obediently hold to His commandments, He has promised them what
He will fulfill for them, that is, bliss without end in the kingdom of Heaven. (7) And
for whomever is so foolish that he should shun this, torment and torture

him neaver teone ne tintreohe trukien in inwarde Helle. (8) To longe we habbethidriven ure dusichipes, ant He haveth itholet us, the tholemode Lauerd. (9) Ne we nusten hwet we duden athet He undutte us ant tahte us treowe ileave thurh thet eadi meiden, Katerine, thet te king pineth i cwalmhus ant thencheth to acwellen." (10) Thus he talede wel with twa hundret cnihtes ant with ma yet, thet yeven anan up hare yeomere bileave ant wurpen alle awei hare witlese lei ant wenden to Criste.

40.   (1) Crist ne foryet nawt thet he ne nom yeme to hire thet me heold yet (as the keiser het) bute mete ant mel i the cwarterne, ah with fode of Heovene thurh His ahne engel i culvrene iliche, fedde hire al the tweolf dahes as He dude Daniel thurh Abacuc the prophete i the liunes leohe ther he in lutede. (2) Ure Lauerd

fol. 12v Himseolf com with engles | ant with monie meidnes with alle, with swuch dream ant drihtfere as Drihtin deh to cumene, ant schawde Him ant sutelede Himseolf to hireseolven, ant spec with hire ant seide: "Bihalt Me, deore dohter! (3) Bihalt thin hehe Healent, for hwas nome thu havest al undernume this nowcin. (4) Beo stalewurthe ant stont wel. (5) Ne thearf thu drede na deth, for lo, with hwucche Ich habbe idiht to do the i Mi kinedom — thet is thin — with Me imeane as Mi leofmon. (6) Na thing ne dret tu, for Ich am eaver with the, do thet me do the, ant monie schulen thurh the yet turne to Me." (7) With this ilke steap up with thet heovenlich hird ant steah into the Heovene, ant heo biheolt efter hwil ha a mahte, blisful ant blithe.

41.   (1) Under this com the thurs Maxence — the wedde wulf, the heathene hunt

---

will never fail him in innermost Hell. (8) For too long have we indulged our follies, and He has suffered us, the patient Lord. (9) We did not know what we did until He revealed to us and taught us true belief through that blessed maiden, Katherine, whom the king tortures in prison and intends to kill." (10) Thus he talked well with two hundred knights and with more yet, so that they at once gave up their wretched belief and cast away all their witless law and turned to Christ.

40.   (1) Christ did not at all forget to take care of her who was still held (as the emperor commanded) without food and meal in the prison, but, with food of Heaven through His own angel in the likeness of a dove, fed her the whole twelve days as He did Daniel through Habakkuk the prophet in the lion's lair in which he lay imprisoned. (2) Our Lord Himself came with angels and with many maidens as well, with such angelic singing and a procession as it befits the Lord to come, and showed and revealed Himself to her, and spoke with her and said: "Behold Me, dear daughter! (3) Behold your high Savior, for whose name you have undertaken all this hardship. (4) Be stalwart and stand firm. (5) You need not dread any death, for lo, because of that I have ordained to put you in My kingdom — which is yours — shared with Me as My lover. (6) And dread you nothing, for I am ever with you, let be done what may be done to you, and many will yet turn to Me through you." (7) With this He rose up with that heavenly company and ascended into the Heavens, and she looked after them as long as she could, blissful and blithe.

41.   (1) At this point the demon Maxence — the mad wolf, the heathen hound —

— agein to his kineburh. (2) Theos meiden ine marhen wes ibroht bivoren him, ant he bigon to von on thisses weis towart hire: "This me were leovere, yef thu wel waldest, to habben ant to halden the cwic then to acwelle the. (3) Thu most nede, notheles, an of thes twa curen cheosen ananriht: libben, yef thu leist lac to ure liviende godes, other, yef thu nawt nult, thu schalt dreoriliche deien."

42. (1) This meiden sone anan him ontswerede ant seide: "Lef me forte libbe — swa thet ich ne leose nawt Him thet is mi lif ant mi leof, Jesu Crist mi Lauerd. (2) Ne nawiht ne drede ich na deth thet overgeath for thet endelese lif thet He

fol. 13r haveth ilevet me ananriht therefter. (3) Ah thu bithench me anan teo|nen ant tintreohen, the alre meast derve thet ei deadlich flesch mahe drehen ant drahen, for me longeth heanewart, for mi Lauerd Jesu Crist, mi deorewurthe leofmon, luttel ear me haveth ileathet. (4) Ant wel is me thet ich mot ba mi flesch ant mi blod offrin Him to lake the offrede to His Feader, for me ant for al volc, Himseolf o the Rode."

43. (1) Hwil the king weol al inwith of wreaththe, com a burh-reve (as the thet wes thes deofles budel, Belial of Helle) Cursates hehte, ant tus on heh cleopede: "O kene king! (2) O icudd keiser! (3) Yet ne seh Katerine nanes cunnes pine thet ha oht dredde. (4) Do ido dede! (5) Nu ha thus threateth ant threpeth agein the hat, hwil ha wed tus, inwith the threo dahes yarkin fowr hweoles, ant let thurh-driven threfter the spaken ant te velien with irnenne gadien swa thet te pikes ant te irnene preones se scharpe ant se sterke borien thurh, ant beore forth feor o thet other half

---

came again to his capital city. (2) This maiden in the morning was brought before him, and he began to reproach her in this way: "I would rather, if you were well willing, have and hold you alive than kill you! (3) You need, nevertheless, to choose one of these two options immediately: live, if you offer a sacrifice to our living gods, or, if you will not, you will miserably die."

42. (1) This maiden answered him at once and said: "Allow me to live — so that I do not lose Him who is my life and my love, Jesus Christ my Lord. (2) I do not fear at all any death that passes by in return for that endless life He has granted me immediately thereafter. (3) But you — come up with torments and tortures for me right away, the most cruel of all that any mortal flesh could endure and suffer, for I long to go from here, for my Lord Jesus Christ, my precious lover, summoned me a little earlier. (4) And well it is for me that I may offer both my flesh and my blood as a sacrifice to Him who offered to His Father, for me and for all folk, Himself on the Rood."

43. (1) While the king boiled all inside from wrath, there came a town-reeve (like one who was a beadle of the devil, Belial of Hell) named Cursates, and thus aloud he called out: "O mighty king! (2) O famous emperor! (3) Katherine did not yet see any of the kinds of torture that she ought to fear. (4) Make the deed done! (5) Since she thus threatens and scolds you, order while she rages like this, four wheels to be prepared within three days, and then order afterward the spokes and the rims be driven through with spikes of iron so that the points and the iron pins pierce through so sharply and so strongly, and project far on the other side

thet al the hweoles beon thurh-spitet mid kenre pikes then ei cnif, rawe bi rawe (6) Let thenne turnen hit tidliche abuten swa thet Katerine schal, with thet grisliche rune, hwen ha therbi sit ant bisith therupon, swiken hire sotschipes ant ure wil wurchen. (7) Other, yef thet ha nule no, ha schal beo tohwitheret with the hweoles swa in an honthwile thet alle the hit bihaldeth schule grure habben." (8) The king hercnede his read; ant wes sone, as he het, thes heane ant tes heatele tintreoh itimbret ant wes the thridde dei idrahen thider as the reven weren eaver iwunet. (9) fol. 13v Ant te king heold ta of | this a meiden hise kinemotes.

44.   (1) This pinfule gin wes o swuch wise iginet thet te twa turnden either withward other ant anes weis bathe; the other twa turnden anes weis alswa ah toyein the othre, swa thet hwenne the twa walden keasten uppart thing thet ha kahten, the othre walden drahen hit ant dusten dunewardes, se grisliche igreithet thet grure grap euch mon hwen he lokede thron. (2) Her amidde wes this meiden iset forte al torenden reowliche ant reowthfulliche torondin yef ha nalde hare read heren ne hercnin. (3) Ah heo keaste up hire ehnen ant cleopede towart Heovene, ful heh with hire heorte ah with stille stevene: "Almihti Godd, cuth nu Thi mihte ant menske nu Thin hehe nome, heovenliche Lauerd, ant forte festnin ham i treowe bileave the beoth to The iturnde, ant thet Maxence ant alle hise halden ham mate, smit se smeortliche herto thet al theos fower hweoles tohwitherin to stucches."

45.   (1) This wes unneathe iseit thet an engel ne com with ferlich afluht fleoninde adunewart, ant draf therto dunriht as a thunres dune ant duste hit a swuch dunt thet

---

so that all the wheels are studded with spikes sharper than any knife, row on row. (6) Then have it turned quickly about so that from that terrible movement, Katherine shall cease her follies and work our will, when she sits nearby and looks upon it. (7) Or, if she will not, she will be so whirled to pieces by the wheels that in a moment all who behold it will feel terror." (8) The king heeded his counsel; and soon, as he commanded, this heinous and hateful torture was constructed and was on the third day drawn there where the reeves were accustomed to be. (9) And then the king held his royal council concerning this one maiden.

44.   (1) This painful device was in such a way devised that two wheels turned one side by side with the other and both in one direction; the other two turned in one direction also but opposite the others, so that, when the first two would cast upward the thing which they caught, the other two would drag it and fling it downward, so fearsomely built that terror took hold of each man when he looked at it. (2) Here in the middle was this maiden set to be torn apart wretchedly and piteously ripped up if she would neither hear nor hearken to their counsel. (3) But she cast up her eyes and called toward Heaven, very loudly with her heart but with a quiet voice: "Almighty God, make known now Your might and glorify now Your high name, heavenly Lord, and in order to fasten those who are turned to You in true belief, and so that Maxence and all his people consider themselves vanquished, strike so hard here that all these four wheels shatter into fragments."

45.   (1) This had hardly been said when an angel came with a fearsome flight flying downward, and dashed straight down into it as a thunder's din and struck it such

hit bigon to cleaterin al ant tocleoven, tobursten ant tobreken as thah hit were bruchel gles, ba the treo ant tet irn, ant ruten forth with swuch rune the stucchen of bathe bimong ham as ha stoden ant seten therabuten thet ter weren isleine of thet awariede volc fowr thusent fulle. (2) Thear me mahte iheren the heathene

fol. 14r hundes yellen ant yeien ant yuren on euch half, the Cristene ken|chen ant herie then Healent, the helpeth Hise overal. (3) The keiser, al acanget, hefde iloset mon drem ant dearede, al adedet, druicninde ant dreori, ant drupest alre monne.

46. (1) The cwen stot eaver stille on heh ant biheolt al. (2) Hefde ihud hire athet ta ant hire bileave ihole theyet, ne mahte ha na mare, ah dude hire adun swithe ant forth withute fearlac o vet thidewardes, ant weorp hire bivoren then awariede wulf, ant yeide lut-stevene: "Wrecche mon thet tu hit art, hwerto wult tu wreastlin with the worldes Wealdent? (3) Hwet meadschipe maketh the, thu bittre balefule beast, to weorri The thet wrahte the ant alle worldliche thing? (4) Beo nu ken ant cnawes of thet tet tu isehen havest: hu mihti ant hu meinful, hu heh ant hu hali is thes Cristenes godd Crist thet ha herieth. (5) Hu wrakeliche wenest tu wule He, al wrathe, wreoken o the, wrecche, the haveth todriven with a dunt ant fordon, for the, todei se feole thusent?" (6) Ant monie mid alle of thet heathene folc the alle weren isihen thider forte seo this feorlich, sone se ha this sehen ant herden swa the cwen speoken, alle somet turnden ant token to yeien:

47. (1) "Witerliche, muche wurth ant wurthe alle wurthschipe is thes meidenes Godd Crist, soth Godes Sune. (2) Ant to Him we kennith ant cnaweth to Lauerd

---

a blow that it all began to clatter and split apart, burst and break up as though it were brittle glass, both the wood and the iron, and the pieces of both burst forth with such violence among them as they stood and sat around there that there were slain of that accursed folk a full four thousand. (2) There one could hear the heathen hounds yell and yelp and yowl on every side, the Christians laugh loudly and praise the Savior, who helps His own everywhere. (3) The emperor, completely demented, had lost human joy and cowered, quite mortified, swooning and sorrowful and most downcast of all men.

46. (1) The queen stood always still on high and beheld everything. (2) She had hidden herself until then and still concealed her belief, and she could not any more, but came down quickly and forth without fear on foot went forward there, and cast herself before the accursed wolf, and cried in a loud voice: "Wretched man that you are, why will you wrestle with the world's Ruler? (3) What madness, you bitter baleful beast, makes you war against Him who made you and all worldly things? (4) Be now willing to acknowledge and admit what you have seen: how mighty and how strong, how high and how holy is this Christian's God Christ whom she worships. (5) How vengefully do you think He, entirely angry, will wreak vengeance on you, wretch, He who has destroyed the wheel with one blow and put to death, because of you, so many thousands today?" (6) And many among all that heathen folk who had all come there to see this wonder, as soon as they saw this and heard the queen speak so, all together converted and began to cry out:

47. (1) "Clearly, greatly worthy and worth all worship is this maiden's God Christ, true Son of God. (2) And Him we declare and acknowledge as our Lord and high

ant to heh Healent heonne forthwardes. (3) Ant tine mix maumez alle beon amanset, for ha ne mahe nowther helpen hamseolven ne heom thet ham servith!"

fol. 14v
48. (1) The king walde weden, swa him | gromede with ham, ah with the cwen swithest. (2) Biheolt hire heterliche ant bigon to threatin hire thus, o thisse wise: "Hu nu, dame, dotest tu? (3) Cwen, acangest tu nu mid alle thes othre? (4) Hwi motest tu se meadliche? (5) Ich swerie, bi the mahtes of ure godes muchele, bute yef thu the timluker do the i the geinturn ant ure godes grete thet tu gremest nuthe, ic schal schawin hu mi sweort bite i thi swire ant leote toluki thi flesch the fuheles of the lufte. (6) Ant yet ne schalt tu nower neh se lihtliche etsterten ah strengre thu schalt tholien, for ich chulle leote luken ant teo the tittes awei of thine beare breosten ant threfter do the to deth, dervest thing to drehen."

49. (1) "Alle thine threates ne drede ich," quoth ha, "riht noht! (2) Eaver se thu mare wa ant mare weane dest me for mi neowe leofmon, the ich on with luve leve, se thu wurchest mi wil ant mi weole mare. (3) Do nu thenne hihendliche thet tu havest on heorte, for of me ne schalt tu biyeote nawiht mare."

50. (1) Sone se he understot wel thet he ne sturede hire nawt, het on hat heorte unhendeliche neomen hire, ant bute dom ananriht thurh-driven hire tittes with irnene neilles ant rende ham up hetterliche with the breost roten. (2) As thes deofles driveles drohen hire forth to fordon hire ha biseh towart Katerine ant seide: "Eadi meiden, ernde me to thi leove Lauerd for hwas luve ich tholie thet me bilimeth me thus, thet He, i the tintreohe thet ich am iturnt to, heardi min
fol. 15r heorte | thet tet wake flesch ne wursi neaver mi mod swa thet ich slakie to ofservin

---

Savior henceforth. (3) And your filthy idols are all accursed, for they can neither help themselves nor those who serve them."

48. (1) The king was about to go mad, he was so angry with them, but most angry with the queen. (2) He looked at her wrathfully and began to threaten her thus, in this way: " How now, dame, are you mad? (3) Queen, are you insane now with all these others? (4) Why do you speak so madly? (5) I swear, by the powers of our great gods, that unless you turn yourself around sooner and honor our gods whom you now anger, I will show how my sword may bite into your neck and let the birds of the sky tear into your flesh. (6) And yet you will escape nowhere near so lightly but suffer more strongly, for I will have the nipples torn and rent away from your bare breasts and after that put you to death, the cruelest thing to suffer."

49. (1) "I do not fear all your threats," said she, "not at all! (2) Ever the more woe and the more misery you do to me for my new lover, in whom I believe with love, the more you work my will and my joy. (3) Do now then quickly what you have in your heart, for from me you will get nothing more."

50. (1) As soon as he understood well that he stirred her not at all, with a hot heart he commanded her to be taken roughly, and without a trial immediately to have iron nails driven through her nipples and have them ripped up fiercely with the breast-roots. (2) As these devil's drudges dragged her forth to put her to death she looked towards Katherine and said: "Blessed maiden, intercede for me to your beloved Lord for whose love I suffer to be mutilated in this way, that He, in the torture that I am turned to, may strengthen my heart so that the weak flesh never

Heoveriche, thet ich ne forga neaver for fearlac of na pine thet beo fleschlic, the crune the Crist haveth — efter thet tu cwiddest — ilevet His icorene.”

51.   (1) “Ne dred tu nawt,” quoth Katerine, “deorewurthe cwen, ant deore with Drihtin of Heovene, for the is ilevet todei, for a lutel eorthlich lont, thet heovenliche kinedom; for a mon of lam, the the is Lauerd of lif, for this lutle pine the alith i lute hwile, endelese reste i the riche of Heovene, for this swifte pine the aswiketh se sone, blissen buten ende ant murhthen áá mare. (2) Ne nawiht ne wen thu thet tu nu forwurthe, for nu thu biginnest earst ant art ibore to libben i thet lif thet leasteth áá bute linunge.”

52.   (1) The cwen thurh thes stevene wes swithe istrenget, ant se stealewurthe thet ha veng to cleopien upo the cwelleres ant hihede ham to donne thet ham wes ihaten. (2) Ant heo duden drohen hire withute the burh geten ant tuhen hire tittes up of hire breosten bi the beare bane with eawles of irne, ant swipten of therefter with sweort hire heaved, ant heo swearf to Criste upo the threo ant twentuthe dei of Novembres moneth. (3) Ant thet wes on a Weodnesdei thet ha thus wende, martir, to the murhthes the neaver ne wonieth. (4) Porphire ananriht ferde thider i the niht, ant swucche with him of his men thet he wel truste on, ant al thes

fol. 15v leafdis licome leofliche smi|rede with smirles of aromaz swote smellinde ant biburiede hire as hit deh martyr ant cwen forte donne.

53.   (1) Me com i the marhen thet me het witen hwa hefde, agein the kinges forbod, thet licome ilead theonne. (2) Tha Porphire iseh feole the me seide hit

---

worsens my spirit so that I fear to deserve the Heaven-kingdom less, that I never forgo for fear of any pain that is fleshly, the crown which Christ — according to what you say — has granted His chosen.”

51.   (1) “Fear nothing,” said Katherine, “precious queen, and dear to the Lord of Heaven, for to you is granted today, in place of a little earthly land, that heavenly kingdom; for a man of earth, He who is Lord of life, for this little pain which passes in a little while, endless rest in the kingdom of Heaven, for this swift pain which ceases so soon, bliss without end and joy forever more. (2) Do not at all believe that you perish now, for now you begin first and are born to live in that life that lasts forever without ending.”

52.   (1) The queen was greatly strengthened through this speech, and so stalwart that she began to call upon the killers and urged them to do what was commanded them. (2) And they did drag her outside the city gates and tore her nipples up from her breasts to the bare bones with awls of iron, and swiped off her head after that with a sword, and she crossed over to Christ on the third and twentieth day of the month of November. (3) And that was on a Wednesday that she went thus, a martyr, to the joys which never end. (4) Porphirius immediately went there in the night, and with him those of his men he trusted well, and anointed all this lady’s body lovingly with sweet smelling aromatic spices and buried her as it was fitting to do for a queen and a martyr.

53.   (1) It happened in the morning that Maxence ordered it discovered who had, against the king’s prohibition, taken that body from there. (2) When Porphirius saw many guiltless people who were accused of it led off and dragged to death, he

upon gultelese leaden ant dreien to deathe, leop forth withute fearlac ant com bivoren the keiser ant keneliche cleopede: "Sei, thu Sathanesse sune, thu king forcuthest, hwet const tu to theos men thet tu thus leadest! (3) Lowr! (4) Ich am her, thu heateliche gast, with alle mine hirdmen to yelde reisun for ham. (5) Fordem nu me ant mine for we ageines thin heast thet licome awei leadden ant leiden in eorthe."

54. (1) "Nu thu art," quoth the king, "ken ant icnawes thet tu havest death ofservet ant thurh the alle the othre. (2) Ah for thu art icudd cniht ant heaved of ham alle, cheos yet of theos twa. (3) Other chear ananriht thet te othre chearren thurh the, ant tu schalt libben ant beo leof ant wurth with me. (4) Other yef thet tu nult, streche forth thi swire scharp sweord to undervonne."

55. (1) Porphire ant alle hise heolden ham togederes ant with se sothe gabbes gremeden him se sare thet he het hetterliche anan withute the burh bihefden ham euch fot, ant leaven hare bodies unburiet alle, fode to willde deor ant to luftfuheles. (2) His heaste wes ivorthet, ant alle clane bihefdet. (3) Ah for al his fol. 16r forbod, nes hit thet te bodies neren ifatte i the niht ant feire bi|buriet. (4) Nalde nawt Godd leoten His martyrs licomes liggen to forleosen, thet hefde bihaten thet an her of hare fax ne schulde forwurthen.

56. (1) Theyet nes nawt the kinges thurst, with al this blod, ikelet, ah het Katerine cumen swithe bivoren him. (2) Ha wes sone ibroht forth ant he brec on to seggen: "Thah thu beo schuldi — the ane — of ham alle clane, thah thu with thi

---

leapt forth without fear and came before the emperor and boldly called out: "Say, you son of Satan, you most infamous king, what you know to these men you lead away like this! (3) Look! (4) I am here, you hateful ghost, with all my retainers to give an answer for them. (5) Now condemn me and mine, for against your order we carried off that body and laid it in the earth."

54. (1) "Now you have," said the king, "acknowledged and made known that you have deserved death and through you all the others. (2) But since you are a famous knight and leader of them all, choose nevertheless between these two. (3) Either change your mind immediately so that the others change their minds through you, and you will live and be dear and esteemed to me. (4) Or, if you will not, stretch forth your neck to accept the sharp sword."

55. (1) Porphirius and all his men held themselves together and with such true gibes enraged him so sorely that he angrily ordered that every single one of them be beheaded at once outside the city, and all their bodies left unburied, food for wild beasts and birds of the sky. (2) His command was carried out, and all without exception were beheaded. (3) But despite his command, it happened that the bodies were fetched in the night and fittingly buried. (4) God would not let His martyrs' bodies lie destroyed, He who had promised that not a single hair of their heads would be lost.

56. (1) Even then the king's thirst, with all this blood, was not at all quenched, but he commanded that Katherine come quickly before him. (2) She was soon brought forth, and he burst out saying: "Though you are responsible — you alone —for every single one of them, though you with your witchcraft have made so many run

wicchecreft habbe imaket se monie to eornen towart hare death as ha weren wode, yet yef thu withdreiest te ant wulle greten ure godes ase forth as thu ham havest igremet ant igabbet, thu maht in alle murthe longe libbe with me ant meast schalt beo cuth ant icudd in al mi kineriche. (3) Ne lead tu us na lengre, ah loke nu bilive hwether the beo leovere don thet ich the leare ant libben yef thu swa dest, other this ilke dei se dreoriliche deien thet ham schal agrisen alle the hit bihaldeth."

57. (1) "Nai," quoth Katerine, "nis nawt grislich sihthe to seon falle thet thing, the schal arise thurh thet fal a thusentfalt te fehere, of death to lif undeathlich, ant to arise from ream to áá leastinde lahtre, from bale to eche blisse, from wa to wunne ant to weole thurh-wuniende. (2) Nawiht, king, ne kepe ich thet tu hit fir firsti, ah hat hihendliche thet tu havest in heorte, for ich am yarow to al the wa thet tu const me yarkin thet ich iseo mahe mi lufsume leofmon ant beon ibroht
fol. 16v se blithe bimong | mine feolahes the folhith Him overal i the feire ferredene of virgines in Heovene."

58. (1) The king — as the the wes fordrenct with thes deofles puissun — nuste hwet meanen ah het swithe with hire of his ehsihthe ant biheafdin utewith the barren of the burhe. (2) Heo as me ledde hire lokede ayeinwart for ludinge thet ha herde, ant seh efter hire heathene monie, wepmen ant wummen, with wringinde honden wepinde sare, ah the meidnes alre meast with sari mod ant sorhful ant te riche leafdis letten teares trondlin. (3) Ant heo biwende hire ayein, sumdel iwreathet, ant eadwat ham hare wop with thulliche wordes: "Ye leafdis ant ye meidnes, yef ye weren wise, nalde ye nawt bringe me forth towart blisse with se bale

---

towards their deaths as if they were mad, still if you restrain yourself and will honor our gods as fully as you have enraged and mocked them, you can live long with me in all joy and be the most renowned and famous in all my kingdom. (3) Now lead us astray no longer, but consider now quickly whether it is preferable to you to do what I advise you and live if you do so, or this same day to die so dreadfully that it will terrify all those who behold it."

57. (1) "No," said Katherine, "it is not a grisly sight to see that thing fall, which will rise through that fall a thousandfold more fair, from death to immortal life, and rise from wailing to everlasting laughter, from bale to every bliss, from woe to joy and to lasting happiness. (2) In no way, king, do I care for you to postpone it further, but command quickly what you have in your heart, for I am prepared for all the woe that you can contrive for me so that I can see my beautiful lover and be brought so blithely among my fellows who follow Him everywhere in the fair fellowship of virgins in Heaven."

58. (1) The king — as one who was drunk with the devil's poison — did not know what to say but commanded her to be taken quickly from his sight and beheaded outside the gates of the city. (2) As she was led she looked backwards because of a clamor that she heard, and saw behind her many heathens, men and women, weeping sorrowfully and wringing their hands, but the maidens most of all with sad and sorrowful spirits and the rich ladies letting their tears roll down. (3) And she turned around, somewhat angered, and reproached them for their weeping with these words: "You ladies and you maidens: if you were wise, you would not bring me forth

bere, nalde ye neaver remen ne makie reothe for me, the feare to eche reste into the riche of Heovene. (4) Beoth blithe, ich b. iseche ow, yef ye me blisse unneth, for ich iseo Jesu Crist, the cleopeth me ant copneth, the is mi Lauerd ant mi luve, mi lif ant mi leofmon, mi wunne ant me iweddet, mi murhthe ant mi mede ant meidene crune. (5) Ower wop wendeth al on ow seolven lest ye eft wepen echeliche in Helle for thet heathene lif thet ye in liggeth, as ye schulen alle bute yef ye forleoten, hwil ye beoth o live, ower misbileave."

59.   (1) As ha hefde iseid tus, bisohte the with the bront — as hit blikede buven hire
fol. 17r | ant sculde hire bone beon — thet he for his freolec fristede hire ant fremede the hwile thet ha buhe hire ant bede ane bone. (2) He yettede hire ant yef blitheliche leave. (3) Ant heo biheolt uppart with up aheven heorte, ant cneolinde dunewart thus to Crist cleopede: "Lauerd, leome ant lif of alle riht bileave, milde Jesu, the art Te seolf meidene mede, iheret ant iheiet beo Thu, hehe Healent! (4) Ant The ich thonki, Lauerd, thet Tu havest ileavet me ant waldest thet ich were i tale of Thine wummen. (5) Lauerd, milce me nu ant yette me thet ich yirne. (6) Ich bidde The theos bone, thet alle theo the munneth mi pine ant mi passiun — The to luve, Lauerd — ant cleopieth to me hwen ha schulen the derf of death drehen, other hwen se ha hit eaver doth, i neode ant i nowcin, hihentliche iher ham, heovenliche Healent. (7) Aflei from ham alle uvel: weorre ant wone bathe, ant untidi wederes, hunger ant euch hete the heaneth ham ant hearmith. (8) Lowr, her ich abide the bite of sweordes egge! (9) The thet deth me to death do al thet he mei don, neome

---

towards bliss with such a sorrowful clamor, and you would never lament or cause grief for me, who goes to eternal rest in the kingdom of Heaven. (4) Be happy, I beseech you, if you wish me bliss, for I see Jesus Christ, who calls and looks for me, who is my Lord and my love, my life and my lover, my joy and my spouse, my mirth and my reward and the maidens' crown. (5) Turn your weeping all on yourselves, lest afterward you weep eternally in Hell because of that heathen life in which you remain, as you all will unless you give up, while you are alive, your false belief."

59.   (1) While she had spoken thus, she asked him with the sword — as it glittered above her and was about to be her doom — that he because of his kindness would delay for her and aid her while she bowed down and prayed a prayer. (2) He assented and gave permission gladly. (3) And she looked upward with heart uplifted, and kneeling downward called to Christ thus: "Lord, light and life of all true belief, mild Jesus, who are Yourself the maidens' reward, may You be praised and glorified, high Savior! (4) And You I thank, Lord, that You have allowed me and wish that I were in the group of Your women. (5) Lord, pity me now and give me what I yearn for. (6) I pray You this prayer, that all those who remember my pain and my passion — to love You, Lord — and call to me when they must endure the pain of death, or whensoever they do it, in need and in hardship, hastily hear them, heavenly Savior. (7) Drive from them all evil: war and want both, and unseasonable weather, hunger and every hatred that injures and harms them. (8) Lo, here I await the bite of the sword's edge! (9) May he who puts me to death do all that he may do, let him take what he may

thet he neome mei: thet lif of mi licome. (10) Mi sawle ich sende to The, Healent in Heovene. (11) Hat thet ha beo iset thurh Thine hali engles i thet heovenliche hirt bimong Thine meidnes."

60.   (1) Nefde ha bute ibede swa thet ter ne com a stevene sihinde from Heovene: "Cum, Mi leove leofmon, cum nu Min iweddet, leovest an wummon! (2) Low, the

fol. 17v | yete of eche lif abit te al iopenet; the wununge of euch wunne kepeth ant copneth thi cume. (3) Lo, al the meidene mot ant tet hird of Heovene kimeth her agein the with kempene crune. (4) Cum nu, ant ne beo thu na thing o dute of al thet tu ibeden havest. (5) Alle theo the munneth the ant ti passiun, hu thu death drohe, with inwarde heorte, in eaver-euch time thet heo to the cleopien with luve ant riht bileave, Ich bihate ham hihentliche help of heoveriche."

61.   (1) Heo with theos stevene strahte vorth swiftliche the snahwite swire ant cweth to the cwellere: "Mi lif ant mi leofmon, Jesu Crist mi Lauerd, haveth nu icleopet me! (2) Do nu thenne hihentliche thet te is ihaten." (3) Ant he, as ha het him, hef thet heatele sweord up ant swipte hire of thet heaved. (4) I thet ilke stude anan iworthen twa wundres: the an of the twa wes thet ter sprong ut mid te dunt milc imenget with blod, to beoren hire wittnesse of hire hwite meithhad; the other wes thet ter engles lihten of Heovene ant heven hire on heh up, ant beren forth hire bodi ant biburieden hit i the Munt of Synai, ther Moyses fatte the lahe et ure Lauerd, from theonne as ha deide twenti dahene yong ant yette ma, as pilegrimes the wel witen seggeth. (5) Thear ure Lauerd wurcheth se feole wundres for hire as

---

take: the life of my body. (10) My soul I send to You, Savior in Heaven. (11) Command that it be set by Your holy angels in that heavenly company among Your maidens."

60.   (1) She had only just prayed like this, when there came a voice descending from Heaven: "Come, My beloved lover, come now My spouse, dearest of women! (2) Lo, the gate of eternal life awaits you all open; the dwelling of every joy waits and watches for your coming. (3) Lo, all the assembly of maidens and the company of Heaven comes here to greet you with the champions' crown. (4) Come now, and do not be in any doubt about all that you have prayed for. (5) All those who remember you and your passion, how you suffered death, in their inmost hearts, every single time they call to you with love and true belief, I promise them immediate help from the heavenly kingdom."

61.   (1) At this speech she stretched forth swiftly her snow-white neck and said to her killer: "My life and my lover, Jesus Christ my Lord, has now called me! (2) Do now then quickly what is commanded of you." (3) And he, as she ordered him, heaved up that hateful sword and swiped off her head. (4) In the same place immediately two wonders occurred: one of the two was that there sprang out with the blow milk mixed with blood, to bear witness to her white maidenhood; the other was that angels came down there from Heaven and lifted her up on high, and carried her body forth and buried it on Mount Sinai, where Moses brought the law from our Lord, from there where she died twenty days' journey and yet more, as pilgrims say who know it well. (5) There our Lord works so many wonders for her

fol. 18r na muth ne mei munnen. (6) Ah bimong ham alle this is | an of the heste· thet ter rınneth áá mare eoile iliche rive, ant striketh a stream ut of thet stanene thruh thet ha in resteth. (7) Yet, of the lutle banes the floweth ut with the eoille floweth other eoile ut, hwider se me eaver bereth ham ant hwer se ha beoth ihalden, thet healeth alle uveles ant botneth men of euch bale the rihte bileave habbeth.

62.   (1) Thus wende the eadie meiden Katerine, icrunet to Criste, from eorthliche pinen, i Novembres moneth the fif ant twentuthe dei, ant Fridei, onont te under, i the dei ant i the time thet hire deore leofmon Jesu, ure Lauerd, leafde lif o Rode for hire ant for us alle. (2) Beo He as Healent iheret ant iheiet, in alre worlde worlt, áá on ecnesse. (3) Amen.

---

that no mouth can recount them. (6) But among them all this is one of the highest: that there runs oil forever unceasingly abundant, and a stream runs out of that stone tomb that she rests in. (7) Furthermore, from the little bones which flow out with the oil another oil flows out, wherever they are carried and wherever they are kept, which heals all sicknesses and cures people of every misery who have true belief.

62.   (1) Thus went the blessed maiden Katherine, crowned to Christ, from earthly pains, in the month of November the fifth and twentieth day, and Friday, towards the third hour, on the day and at the time that her dear lover Jesus, our Lord, gave up His life on the Rood for her and for us all. (2) May He be praised and exalted as Savior, from world into all worlds, forever into eternity. (3) Amen.

EXPLANATORY NOTES TO *SANCTE KATERINE*

ABBREVIATIONS: *AS*: *Anchoritic Spirituality*, trans. Savage and Watson; **B**: Bodleian Library MS Bodley 34 [base text]; *BT*: Bosworth and Toller, *Anglo-Saxon Dictionary*; **D**: d'Ardenne and Dobson edition (1981); **E**: Einenkel, *The Life of St. Katherine*; **H**: refers to a series of sixteenth-century scribbles in various hands (see Introduction, p. 22); *HM*: *Hali Meithhad*; *MED*: *Middle English Dictionary*; *OCD*: *Oxford Classical Dictionary*; *OED*: *Oxford English Dictionary*; **R**: British Library MS Royal 17 A XXVII; **T**: British Library MS Cotton Titus D XVIII; *SJ*: *The Liflade ant te Passiun of Seinte Juliene*; *SK*: *The Martyrdom of Sancte Katerine*.

Header   *Sancte Katerine*. Katherine of Alexandria was supposedly a fourth-century saint. Little is known about her, despite the popularity of her cult throughout Europe and especially in England. According to D, in the Early Greek legend she was actually persecuted by Maximinus, not Maxentius. Maxentius won power in Italy after Constantine was proclaimed emperor after the death of his father Constantius in 306 CE, but there is no truth to the legend that he ruled in Alexandria (see pp. 204–05n1; see also explanatory note 1.1, below). Katherine's name appears here in its French form. It is likely that the audience, for whom this text was intended, read French and English as well as some Latin. For a fuller discussion of the nature of the probable audience of these texts, see Robertson, "Living Hand" and *Early English Devotional Prose*; Savage and Watson, *AS*; and Millett, "Woman in No Man's Land." On the popularity of Saint Katherine in the Middle Ages, see Christine Walsh, *Cult of St. Katherine*, especially chapters 2, "The Historical Katherine" (pp. 7–22), and 7, "The Introduction of the Cult of St. Katherine into England" (pp. 97–142).

1.1   *Costentin*. Constantine "the Great," emperor from 306–37 CE (although the traditional date given to St. Katherine's martyrdom is 305). Constantine's campaigns against Maxentius and Maximinus during the early years of his reign appear to be represented in the beginning of *SK*, though these figures are conflated with each other (*OCD*, "Constantine").

        Maxence. Though the name and position suggests Maxentius, Constantine's enemy and rival for the title Augustus in Rome from 306–12 CE, Gaius Galerius Valerius Maximinus is in fact the Roman aristocrat and governor more likely to have executed St. Katherine. The governor of Syria and Egypt in the early years of the fourth century, Maximinus was notorious for his persecution of Christians, ordering public sacrifices of all citizens in 306 and 308, and inflicting torture and death as punishment. The figure of Maxence in *SK* is likely a conflation of

Maximinus and Maxentius, possibly a result of interpretations of their similar names, or from confusion over their 311 alliance against Constantine (*OCD*, "Maximinus Gaius").

1.5   *Ylirie*. Illyria was a region of the Western Balkan peninsula.

2.1   *anes kinges Cost hehte anlepi dohter*. In John Capgrave's fifteenth-century work *The Life of Saint Katherine*, Katherine is not only Costus' learned daughter, but also the queen of Alexandria in her own right whose power is being usurped by the emperor Maxence. For an interesting discussion of the integral role of politics in Capgrave's *Katherine*, see Winstead, "Capgrave's Saint Katherine." Winstead examines the way in which Capgrave's depiction of Katherine as an active ruler complicates her status as a laudable figure. The Bodley Katherine-poet, by contrast, avoids political complications by depicting Katherine as a learned private landholder with no specific political obligations. Additionally, see Winstead, "St. Katherine's Hair" for a discussion of Katherine's princely genealogy.

        Cost. Vernacular versions of the Katherine *passio* develop Cost's bloodline so that Katherine in a sense becomes localized or nationalized, rather than remaining a distant Greek saint. Walsh, in particular, notes the "anglicization" of the tale in the fifteenth-century prose version of the legend: there, "Costas" actually becomes the elder half-brother of Constantine the Great; thus, as Walsh writes "Katherine is . . . linked both to Constantine, the man who made Christianity the official religion of the Roman Empire, and Britain [through his British mother, Helena]" (*Cult of St. Katherine*, p. 99n6). For more detail, see Walsh, *Cult of St. Katherine*, pp. 9–10 and p. 99n6.

        cleargesse. It is difficult to say precisely what the word *cleargesse* means. Katherine could not have been clerically trained, but the word suggests she had scholarly training in Latin. The audience for whom this text was intended may well have been similarly trained; although not clerical, they probably had some limited training in Latin. The word is used to describe some anchoresses in *Ancrene Wisse* (ed. Hasenfratz, "Author's Preface," p. 62, line 48). For discussion of the significance of that word in the *Ancrene Wisse*, see Robertson, "This Living Hand."

2.2   *nawt forthi that . . . telleth wel to*. Although the precise audience of this text is unknown, it is likely that many of its readers were women who had been "ladies" in secular life; thus, this comment here would have particular resonance for the audience.

3.3   *Modi meistres ant . . . menske al up*. This passage both establishes Katherine's position as a dominant intellectual figure and highlights the steadfastness and power granted to her by the Holy Spirit (3.2). The careful declaration that many learned men have been overcome by her knowledge foreshadows her competition with and victory over the fifty masters that begins at 11.3.

        crefti crokes. D glosses "crokes" as "sophistries" (p. 302), referring to the art of formal philosophical dispute. There is a connection here to the Devil's "crafty tricks" as though philosophical argument were itself a weapon of the devil; for example, see 6.1, where "crokinde creftes" refers specifically to the devil's tricks. Note the patristic suspicion of formal classical rhetoric and logic, which can be used to obscure truth. Compare also *SK*,11.3, and see the explanatory note to those sentences, below.

4.1   *burdeboldes*. D notes that this word translates the Latin *palatio patris* (p. 301). Literally, the term means "birth-castle" or where Katherine was born, the place of her heritage.

4.3   *seide hire thet sothe*. The literal translation is "told her that truthfully," with *thet* (as well as *this* and *hwet* of 4.2) referring to the antecedent *swuch nurth* of 4.1. For the sake of clarity, however, we have freely translated *thet sothe* as "the truth," following Savage and Watson's translation (*AS*, p. 263).

4.7   *hwet hit mahte . . . al his kineriche*. B appears to be missing a verb, and this problem is duplicated in R and T. The Latin text offers no help here. D notes the similarity between the Middle English "yeinen" (see *MED yeinen* (v.), sense a, "to be useful or profitable; avail; help," which we have translated as "gain") and the cognate "geinen" (see *MED geinen* (v.), sense 2, "to oppose"). This second cognate, according to D, would have been "ȝeinin" in the AB dialect; the scribe of the exemplar may have conflated the two terms, hence our translation. See D, pp. 209–10n63, for a more extended explanation.

4.10   *Rode-taken*. I.e., the sign of the cross.

5.2   *scheop*. We have translated this verb as "shape" to illustrate both the very physical sense of creation (God shaping Adam from clay with His hands) and also to demonstrate the modern cognate. See *MED shapen* (v.), sense 1.

5.5   *sculde*. D notes that the "sc" spelling is common in the B manuscript, although T and R invariably spell "sch," (see D, p. xlv). This spelling is a holdover from Anglo-Saxon.

6.5   *thurh thet*. D glosses as "by reason of the fact that" (p. 340).

7.3   *lahe sprung*. AB's *lahe* corresponds to the later Middle English *laue*, both descendants of Old English *lagu*, "law" (*BT, lagu* (n.)). There are two ways to translate the phrase *lahe sprung*, as we see it: first, to consider AB *lahe* as an adjectival form of *laue*, following Savage and Watson's translation "legitimate source" (*AS*, p. 265); or, (the more questionable option) to translate *hefde lahe sprung* as "had originated from law." Given the lack of preposition, though, we have translated based on Savage and Watson.

7.5   *Me hwet is . . . ant te deade?* Contrast Maxence's elaborate and detailed description of Christian doctrine with his very general reference to his own pagan religion. See Bernau, "Christian *Corpus*," for a discussion of this "lack of specificity" (pp. 124–26). Maxence gives a clear summary of the Nicene Creed. The Nicene Creed, affirmed at the Council of Nicea in 325 CE, is the set of words of faith all Catholics are expected to proclaim. According to the *Catholic Encyclopedia*, those words are:

We believe (I believe) in one God, the Father Almighty, maker of heaven and earth, and of all things visible and invisible. And in one Lord Jesus Christ, the only begotten Son of God, and born of the Father before all ages. (God of God) light of light, true God of true God. Begotten not made, consubstantial to the Father, by whom all things were made. Who for us men and for our salvation came down from heaven. And was incarnate of the Holy Ghost and of the Virgin Mary and was made man; was crucified also for us under Pontius Pilate, suffered and was buried; and the third day rose again according to the Scriptures. And ascended into heaven, sits at the right hand of the Father, and shall come again with glory to judge the living and the dead, of whose Kingdom there shall be no end. And (I believe) in the Holy Ghost, the Lord and Giver of life, who proceeds from the Father (and the Son), who together with the Father and the Son is to be adored and glorified, who spoke by the Prophets. And one holy, catholic, and apostolic Church. We confess (I confess) one baptism for the remission of sins. And we look for (I look for) the resurrection of the dead and the life of the world to come. Amen.

akennet. See *MED akennen*, (v.2), sense 2a, which cites this occurrence.

9.3   *Ah wastu nu hwet is?* Literally, "But do you know what is now?" Our translation follows D's suggestion on p. 216n143. Savage and Watson's translation is also helpful: "Do you know what happens now?" (*AS*, p. 265).

9.4   *motild*. This descriptor is unique to the AB texts. D glosses as "female debater, wrangling woman" (p. 323); *MED motild* (n.) defines as "A female disputant, debater; female advocate." Compare Maxence's use here with the term in *On Lofsong of Ure Lefdi*, line 305: "Ich . . . bidde þin ore, þet tu beo mi motild aʒeines mine soule fan," where *motild* has the connotation of advocate or intercessor as well (ed. Morris, *Old English Homilies*, p. 205). See also 9.5 of *SK*, where "theos modi motild" is used more neutrally, to mean "this proud debater." We have translated the term "motild" in this instance as "argumentative babbler," to get at the pejorative sense of the term as it is used here. Compare Savage and Watson's translation: "you spitfire" (*AS*, p. 265). The word itself only survives in the three examples cited and is most likely derived from Old English *mót* + *-ild*. Of note is that this now obscure noun (*mot*) only survives in occasional legal use as "moot," where it refers to legislative or judicial meetings (see *BT mót* (n.)), or to a formal argument about law conducted by legal students discussing hypothetical cases.

9.5   *ikennen ant icnawen*. On why this is "willing to admit and acknowledge," see D, pp. 217–18n154–5.

10.4–5   *Ah forthi thet . . . Him to Lauerd*. Katherine's dual movement from a worldly position to spiritual one, first in her declaration of her abandonment of worldly knowledge for spiritual knowledge, and later in her renunciation of worldly spouses for the heavenly Spouse, differentiates her from the other two virgin martyrs of the Katherine Group, who have no such worldly position. A number of critics have explored the implications that this dual emphasis has for Katherine's construction as a gendered figure and as a role model for different audiences. See Jenkins and Lewis "Introduction" to *St. Katherine of Alexandria*;

Francomano, "'Lady, you are quite a chatterbox'"; Winstead, "St. Katherine's Hair"; and Reames, "St. Katherine."

10.5   *Perdam sapientiam sapientum et intellectum intelligentium reprobabo.* Isaias 29:4; as quoted in 1 Corinthians 1:19. This reference is repeated at 21.3.

10.7   *Deus autem noster . . . similes illis fiant.* Vulgate Psalm 113:3–8. This quotation indirectly implies that if the pagans are like *their* gods, then Katherine herself must in turn be like *her* god, an implication that is borne out in her eventual martyrdom.

11.3   *creftes.* In order to maintain the alliteration, our translation maintains the modern cognate. However, the sense of this passage supports *OED*'s reading of *craft* here ((n.), sense 5b) as a specific branch of knowledge, possibly referring to the seven Liberal Arts, traditionally grammar, rhetoric, and logic (the Trivium) and arithmetic, geometry, astronomy, and music (the Quadrivium).

13.2   *to balewe ant to bismere.* This phrase functions as a dative of purpose and reference, following Latinate functions of the dative. We have translated *balewe* and *bismere* as adverbs. D also glosses as adverbs "maliciously and contumaciously" (p. 28). This construction is not in the Latin text but seems to follow a Latin dative of purpose and reference. Savage and Watson also translate as adverbs "abusively and insultingly" (*AS*, p. 267).

14.4   *thet ha understonde . . . bute bivore dusie.* A difficult line to translate. The Latin text reads *ut cognoscat se nondum uidisse aut audisse preter hodie sapientem* (D, p. 159, lines 290–91) [in order that she understand that not yet has she before today seen or heard wisdom except]. After dealing with the indirect statement within an *ut* clause of result, the Middle English translator has modified the text to make the clerks' arrogance all the more clear. We have translated as "so that she may understand that before this day she never stood except before fools" to keep as much literal meaning as possible; an "anyone" is implied by "thene" (than) with the sense that Katherine has never stood before anyone besides, or other than, fools.

15.1   *Dum steteritis ante reges et presides, et cetera.* Compare Matthew 10:18–20, Mark 13:9–11, and Luke 21:12–15.

16.1–29.8 *Ne beo thu . . . thet tu wult.* The contest with the fifty masters is the episode of Katherine's *vita* that has caused the most controversy in terms of its potential to be read as a religious precedent allowing women to teach and preach. See Bernau, "Christian *Corpus*," p. 122, on Katherine's status as a dangerous preacher; Francomano, "'Lady, you are quite a chatterbox,'" on Katherine's talkativeness and persuasive abilities; Frazier, "Katherine's Place," p. 236; and Blamires, "Women and Preaching," for medieval theological debates regarding women preachers and heresy.

16.2   *i stude ant i stalle.* An alliterative turn of phrase, meaning literally "in place and in place;" we have used D's gloss for the phrase in our translation (see D, p. 332).

18.1   *thet hoker thuhte.* We have consulted D's gloss (p. 315) in our translation of this phrase.

19.3   *cume, cuthe . . . take.* These verbs are subjunctives with hortatory force. D (p. 226n302) notes that *cume* and *cuthe*, while subjunctive forms, function as imperatives.

20.1   *sette sikel forth.* Literally, "set the sickle forth." D glosses the phrase as "begin reaping, start the harvest, cut the first swathe (?)" (p. 330). We have followed D's and Savage and Watson's "cut the first swathe." This invitation is a serious mistake on the philosophers' part, although, as Savage and Watson point out "in theory it would be to the philosophers' advantage to speak second." They continue that despite this, "letting [Katherine] speak first is evidently a major, and telltale, tactical blunder" (*AS*, p. 424n18).

21.2   *Homers motes ant . . . ant Platunes bokes.* Christian audiences frequently had mixed feelings regarding the wisdom of classical writers. Here, Katherine whole-heartedly condemns Homer, Aristotle, Asclepius, Galen, Philistion, and Plato. In contrast, the fifteenth-century *Dicts and Sayings of the Philosophers* regards the sayings of many of these philosophers as highly valuable, and the text is considered as part of the medieval genre of "wisdom literature" (see Sutton's introduction). More often, though, Christian writers regarded classical texts with cautious pragmatism, as in St. Augustine's equation of the plundering of the Egyptians' gold with the Christians' use of classical material. See *On Christian Doctrine*, book 2, chapter 60, where he writes: "If those who are called philosophers, especially the Platonists, have said things which are indeed true and are well accommodated to our faith, they should not be feared; rather, what they have said should be taken from them as from unjust possessors and converted to our use" (trans. Robertson, p. 75).

21.3   *Perdam sapientiam sapientum et intellectum et cetera.* 1 Corinthians 1:19.

21.4   *wit.* D'Ardenne and Dobson point out that although *wit* is not the most accurate translation of *disciplinam*, it does serve the purpose of alliteration. See D, p. 229n328.

21.7   *ilatet.* D'Ardenne and Dobson emend both R and T following the use of this phrase in *SJ* (see D's long discussion, p. 230n333).

22.1–4   *An for ham . . . ba somet nanesweis.* Maxence here echoes the Nicene Creed. See above, note 7.5.

23.1–11 *Heo ne sohte . . . . thet He walde.* Here Katherine explains the simultaneous humanity and divinity of Christ, arguments related to such influential treatises as Anselm's *Cur Deus Homo*.

23.1   *derfschipe.* A difficult word to translate. D glosses as "secret, hidden meaning"; *MED derfshipe* citing this occurrence only, glosses as "Irreverence, sacrilege (compare *derfnesse*)"; E glosses as "baseness, vileness" but includes the translation "strength" (p. 158, 46) ; the Latin source presented in E (p. 46) has: *hec est subtilitas* [this is the subtlety]. Savage and Watson translate derfschipe as "subtlety" (*AS*, p. 270). However, compare *MED derfnesse* (n.), sense a, meaning "audacity, irreverence, sacrilege." This meaning seems to be a later development of the noun "derf" (used frequently in the Katherine Group to refer to suffering, pain, torment, or the act of martyrdom) not attested until the fifteenth century. We have decided to translate the term as "wicked" to connect with this earlier meaning, as well as reveal the immoral connotations of the philosophers' overly clever but ultimately false arguments.

D explains that here the English author changes the sense of the Latin source: "The whole run of the English sentence leads up to the proposition that he could do one of these two things, suffer death or overcome death, but not both at once; it is not designed to pose the alternatives that he could be either God or man, but not both" (p. 231n359).

23.3   *iwend uppon*. Compare Savage and Watson, *AS* (p. 278). The actual meaning of *wenden* is "to turn," so supposedly Katherine builds on the image of humanity as clay, and God as the great Shaper (or potter).

23.8   *In euch thing . . . of Godes wisdom*. The *cleargesse* Katherine has already demonstrated her accomplished book-learning by the sophisticated Christological discussion with the fifty teachers. Here, however, she also shows an aptitude for discerning God's presence in the natural, living world, a kind of divinely inspired wisdom that exists outside of her books. The signs of God's presence in the living world, briefly described here, are of course later expanded in greater detail in St. Bonaventure's *Itinerarium Mentis in Deum* (*Mind's Road to God*), especially in section 2: "Of the Reflection of God in His Traces in the Sensible World" (see Boas trans., pp. 14–21). The Welsh life of Katherine places more emphasis on this natural divine wisdom, rather than on her bookish learning. See Cartwright, "*Buchedd Catrin*," p. 73.

24.6   *seolf the ilke*. I.e., the self-same.

26.2   *bute sunne ane*. "Except sin alone." Christ took upon Himself all the hardships of humanity except for their sinful state (since He was perfect).

26.4   *toschrapede his hefde!* See *MED scrapen* (v.) and *shrapen* (v.). D glosses as "Scratch to shreds, lacerated" from Old English *scrapian* (*BT*, *scrapian* (v.)). See also the textual note to 26.4, since the manuscript reading in R and T is most likely corrupt. Savage and Watson translate as "lacerated his head" (*AS*, p. 272), as a reference to Genesis 3:15, God's curse upon the devil: "I will put enmity between you and the woman, and between your offspring and hers; he [i.e., humankind] will crush your head, and you will strike his heel." The sense is that when Christ took human form, He deceived the devil, and figuratively "crushed his head" by conquering death and redeeming humankind. Compare *MED shaven* (v.), sense 2a, "to deceive someone"; in later Middle English to give someone a "close shave" essentially means to rob, deceive, or otherwise trick them, thus our translation of *robbed him blind*.

26.8   *te bruchen thet mon hefde ibroken agein Him*. I.e., the transgressions that mankind had committed against Him (based on D's gloss, p. 301).

28.3   *studgi.* See D's note, pp. 241–42n464.

30.1–2   *bringen . . . warpen.* These verbs are infinitives as a result of the indirect command initiated by *bed* and *het*, respectively. A passive construction introduced in the following sentence *As me droh ham* (30.3) (literally "as one dragged them," but in AB meant "as they were dragged"), we have translated these two verbs as passives.

31.3   *furene tungen.* The image of a fiery tongue recalls Pentecost (Whitsunday), a Christian feast that commemorates the descent of the Holy Ghost upon the Apostles, fifty days after the resurrection of Christ; see Acts 2:1–4.

33.3   *pel ant with purpre.* "Pall," according to the *OED* (citing this line), is a fine cloth "used for the robes of persons of high rank." However, *MED pel* (n.2) notes "a furred skin used as lining or trim on a garment." It seems most likely that Maxence is suggesting a purple robe trimmed with fur, an appropriate gift for a lady high in status at his court.

33.4   *seli.* D suggests a possible translation here of "innocent" (p. 330), an interesting alternative that pairs well with Maxence's eventual blaming of Katherine for the deaths of the fifty masters, Augusta, and Porphirius and his knights. The Middle English terms traverse a spectrum of possible meanings, from "holy, blessed" (sense 1a), to "innocent" (sense 2a), to "foolish" (sense 2b) as it is applied to John the "sely" carpenter of Chaucer's Miller's Tale (*CT* I[A] 3423, 3601, 3614). The term's modern descendent is the contemporary word "silly."

34.1–10   *Katerine ontswerede — smirkinde . . . thu to wisse.* In this passage Katherine shifts tracks from dense theological discussion to a discourse more grounded in matters concerning gender, marriage, and sex. The shift is appropriate here, as Maxence has, in true fiendish form, posed temptations for her similar to those of the world ("ich chulle dihten . . . efter thet tu demest," 33.5), the flesh ("tu schalt . . . eaver the other beon . . . i bure," 33.5), and the devil, in offering to make her an object of idolatrous worship (33.5–8). Katherine grounds her rebuttal upon her relationship with her true Husband, and in turn engages questions of gender that emerged both in the fictional landscapes of romance as well as in actual women's lives. For the idea of marriage in these saints' lives see Bugge, *Virginitas*, and Robertson, *Early English Devotional Prose*. See Wogan-Browne, "Virgin's Tale," p. 169, and *Saints' Lives*, specifically chapters 1.2, 3, and 4.1, on the romance structure of virgin martyr tales. See also Jenkins and Lewis, "Introduction" to *St. Katherine of Alexandria*, pp. 13–15, and Lewis, "Pilgrimage," pp. 47–51, for discussions of Katherine as *sponsa Christi*; and see also Walsh, "Role of the Normans," p. 33, for more on Katherine's divinely wedded virginity as a model for real women, particularly Christina of Markyate.

34.1   *meareminnes.* See *MED mere-maiden* (n.), sense b: "one who misleads or deceives."

34.7   *wit.* First person dual pronoun.

35.2–4   *Het o wodi . . . . et lahinde tholede.* The Bodley author specifies that Katherine, is beaten *with cnottede schurgen, . . . hit lihtliche aber and lahinde tholede* ("with knotted scourges . . . bore it lightly and suffered it laughing"); he later emphasizes the angels' healing ministrations. Concerning these details, Jacobus de Voragine writes that Katherine was "stripped and beaten with scorpions, and then thrown into a dark cell" (trans. Ryan and Ripperger, p. 712). Jacobus says nothing of her reaction to these tortures. This could be proof that the Bodley Katherine is like the Bodley Juliana in being what Margherita calls a "self-consciously Germanic English narrative" ("Desiring Narrative," p. 358), sharing in the Anglo-Saxon sensibilities present in Old English saints' lives. In "Pain and Saint Making," Dendle notes that most "Old English saints' lives . . . reflect the anesthetic tradition" in which "the saint is invulnerable to the tortures" (p. 46). This apparent invulnerability was important in Anglo-Saxon culture, where "[t]rial by ordeal" was believed to make "manifest what was hidden, by inscribing on the bodies of the guilty the marks of sin that already stained the soul" (p. 51). An accused person whose wounds healed quickly and cleanly would be judged innocent, a circumstance that places greater importance on Katherine's ability to ignore her tormentors and to recover quickly from Maxence's abuse, as well as shedding a different light on the unburned appearance of the martyred masters at 32.3, and on the prayer of the queen at 50.2.

37.3　　*Ah an se swithe swote smeal com anan.* A sweet smell, in contrast with the stench of death, is associated with Christ and faith in 2 Corinthians 2:14–16. Sweet smells thus imply holiness. Memorable examples can be found not only in religious narratives (such as the miraculous smell of the invisible rose and lily crowns in Chaucer's Second Nun's Tale [*CT* VIII[G] 229, 247]), but also in romances with religious components, e.g., the sweet odor associated with Sir Guy's corpse in *The Stanzaic Guy of Warwick* (ed. Wiggins, lines 3524–27) or the odor associated with the appearance of the Grail in Arthurian romances.

37.5　　*bieoden.* See *OED bego* (v.), sense 6, which cites this occurrence. D glosses as "to tend (a wound)" (p. 299).

　　　　bruchen of hire bodi. Compare the earlier use of the phrase to refer to a loss of virginity at 7.5; the phrase also occurs in *HM* 8.12, and in *On Lofsong of ure Louerde* (ed. Morris, *Old English Homilies*, p. 205). This is the only occurrence of the phrase that does *not* specifically refer to the loss of virginity.

38.2　　*bur inwith thin heorte.* See Apocalypse 21:10–27, where the New Jerusalem (Heaven) is described as a city. See also Augustine's *De Civitate Dei*, where the New Jerusalem is a condition of being, not just a place. While Jacobus entirely omits mention of the city, the English version expands the Latin version's account, and anticipates the elaborate description of the New Jerusalem found in *Pearl*.

38.7　　*beatewil.* See D, p. 257–58n618 on this difficult term; d'Ardenne and Dobson note that *MED* has "of good will, benevolent; ?humble," which makes little sense given the context.

　　　　the neaver ne linneth nowther ne leassith ah leasteth áá mare, se lengre se mare. The author's use of the instrumental here (the longer, the greater) to describe the proportions of heavenly pleasures looks ahead to the *Pearl*-poet's similar use, as the maiden explains the difficult rationale of the Parable of the Vineyard: "Now

he that stod the long day stable / And thou to payment come hym byfore —
Thenne the lasse in werke to take more able, / And *ever the lenger the lasse, the
more*" (ed. Stanbury, lines 597–600, emphasis ours). While the maiden's words
reveal an indirect proportion, as opposed to Katherine's direct proportion, the
similar, if reversed, expressions both emphasize the difficulty, if not the
impossibility, of describing Heavenly reward in measurable terms which the
mortal mind can conceptualize.

38.8   *thear as*. Our translation is based on D's gloss of *as* in this instance as "at the
         place in which" (p. 298).

38.10   *nan eorthliche ehe . . . Him ariht luvieth*. 1 Corinthians 2:9.

39.1   *wilcweme. MED* glosses as "pleased, satisfied," but see also the Middle English
         meanings of *queme* (adj., sense 1), which describe the word as a quality that is
         "pleasing, acceptable (to God, Christ)." Also compare the Old English *wel-
         gecwéme*, "well-pleasing" (*BT, wel-gecwéme* (adj.)).

39.2–3   *Freineden Porphire alle . . . i worldliche wecchen*. Clearly Porphirius' knights wonder
         if he has been committing adultery with the queen, hence the pun between
         "wordlich wecchen" and "heovenliche iwaket." Their almost schoolgirl interest
         in their commander's whereabouts demonstrates their interest not only in the
         fabliaux potential of such a holy story (compare the conception of Christ and the
         portrayal of Joseph as the *senex amans*) but moreover, a faithful loyalty to their
         commander, as evidenced by their immediate conversion to Christianity. In such
         a way, they are ideal thanes, following their commander to death with absolute
         loyalty.

39.3   *therin is al mi rihte bileave*. See corresponding textual note. Both D (pp.
         259–60n638–39) and E (p. 143n1751) agree that the exemplar for all three
         manuscripts was corrupt and that the scribes of the manuscripts did their best
         to emend the line. Our modern editors emend as "þear as me [learde me mi]
         rihte bileaue" (D) and "þer as me rihte mi bileaue" (E). The corresponding Latin
         text reads *quibus michi uia uite reuelata est et uere deitatis cognitio reserata* (D, pp.
         185–86, lines 808–09): [in which [heavenly watches] the road of life was revealed
         to me and, truly, the knowledge of the deity was made accessible] (translation
         ours). This text forms the basis for D's emendation of "þear as me [learde me
         mi] rihte bileaue" [there as I was taught my true belief]. We have gone with a less
         extreme emendation of T's text.

40.1   *as He dude Daniel*. See the apocryphal Bel and the Dragon (Daniel 14:30–38) for
         the story of Daniel being fed by Habakkuk.

40.5   *with hwucche*. Bodley lacks an explicit noun for "hwucche" [which] to modify. D
         inserted "duheðe" [company] (see *MED douthe* (n.), sense 1c) to give a noun for
         "hwuchhe" to modify, and they translate as "with company." We are translating
         "with" according to *MED with* (prep.), sense 14c, as "because of," which is
         attested also in *Ancrene Wisse*. We are translating "which" according to *MED
         which* (pron.), sense 2b as "that." With this adjusted translation the antecedent
         for "hwucche" is "death" earlier in the same sentence.

43.1   *deofles budel.* A "beadle," in this context, refers to a person "who delivers the message or executes the mandate of an authority" (*OED, beadle* (n.), sense 2). Although the term can describe anyone from a simple messenger to a town-crier, the word "beadle" is sometimes pejorative; compare *SJ* 19.1, as well as *Piers Plowman*, where beadles make up part of the retinue "that regneth with the false" and attends the marriage of Mede and Falsehood: "Bedelles and bailliues and brokoures of chaffare" (B.II.53, 59). We have translated the term as "beadle" throughout to preserve the alliteration, though the word is somewhat obsolete.

    Belial. Belial is a standard name for a demon or devil; the name is also assigned to the demon adversary in *SJ.*

43.4   *Do ido dede.* I.e., "make an end of the matter" (D, p. 305).

43.5   *wed.* "Rage, rave, become mad," a word that would more appropriately describe Maxence than Katherine.

    fowr hweoles. A wheel of torture also occurs in *SJ* (see 60.1–61.1). *SK* and *SJ* clearly are related; d'Ardenne and Dobson explore the question of which text preceded the other, but come to no conclusion about the chronology (see D, pp. 263–65n700). See also Bernau, "Christian *Corpus*," p. 119, for the wheel's associations with knowledge and learning.

44.3   *mate.* See *MED mat* (adj., sense 1b); the figurative meaning of the adjective to mean "helpless, powerless; overcome, defeated" comes from the literal origin of the word in the term "check-mate" (see sense 1a). D (p. 268n725) provides a thorough etymological discussion of this word, whose earliest occurrence (preceding even those referring to chess) is in this line.

    tohwitherin. Compare 43.7, where the same verb describes the supposed fate for Katherine. Unbeknownst to them, the emperor and his henchman are powerless to dole out this fate, which will instead be meted out upon their invention.

46.5   *todriven with a dunt.* "Broken to pieces with a blow." While none of the manuscripts specify that the wheel is meant here, we have included it in our translation for clarity.

48.6   *Ant yet ne . . . thing to drehen.* Sarah Salih, in "Performing Virginity," comments on the fact that only the queen, and not Katherine herself, has her breasts ripped off. Salih posits the virgin as belonging to a gender category distinct from the usual male/female divisions, noting that the virgin martyrs are never tormented through the specifically female parts of their bodies. The queen, who falls into the firmly female-gendered category of "wife," has one of the most visible signs of her femininity, her breasts, mangled during her martyrdom, "a torture enacted on the specifically female body of a rebellious wife . . . The tortures of the virgin heroines are never sexualized in this manner; the texts refuse to mark their naked bodies as female" (p. 104). For a detailed discussion of virgin martyrs whose breasts *are* mutilated, see Kristen Wolf, "Severed Breast." While the text does differentiate the sexualized violence meted on the queen from the torture inflicted on the virgin, in our view both are sexualized, albeit in different ways; see Margherita, *Romance of Origins*, who asserts that we readers, "like Eleusius himself," are repeatedly "made to gaze with prurient interest at the spectacle of [Juliana's] broken female body" (p. 49).

53.2   *the me seide hit upon*. Literally, "upon whom it was said."

53.3   *Lowr!* Another possible translation is "Listen!" or simply "Lo!" but we have chosen "Look!" based both on the context (Porphirius is looking for the perpetrator of the crime) but also on D's evidence that the AB interjection *lowr* may be related to Old English *lo we*, or "let us look" (p. 277n809). See *BT lá* (interj.) meaning "Lo! Oh! Ah!" and *BT lócian* (v.2) meaning "to apply one's sight to ascertain."

54.4   *to undervonne*. The inflected infinitive indicates the text's Anglo-Saxon roots. It also suggests a sense of necessity that Porphirius must, both according to Maxence's law and God's law, accept the martyrdom that is being offered to him. Our translation has followed the glossing of the line in the *MED* definition of *underfon* ((v.), sense 8b) which means "to accept (martyrdom, death, evils, etc.)," rather than E's and D's glossing of "receive" to emphasize the role Porphirius' free choices take in determining his fate. In addition, the term *undervonne* is notable in that the verb, in the sense of accepting death (in the same definition in *MED*) is universally used in religious contexts: see *Early English Homilies* in Cotton Vespasian D XIV: "Gyf we god underfengen of Godes hande, hwy ne scule we eac yfel underfon?" (ed. Warner, p. 126, line 6) [If we accept goodness from God's hand, why will we not also accept evil?]; *HM* 33.11: "He underveth blitheliche ant bicluppeth swoteliche the alre ladlukeste" [He (Christ) receives happily and embraces sweetly the loathsomest of all]; *Ancrene Wisse*: "Ant tah ne gruchede he nawt, ah underueng hit eadmodliche forte learen hise" (ed. Millett, p. 46, lines 1003–04) [And then he did not complain, but accepted it humbly to teach his own]; "Lofsong of our Louerde": "Ich bidde the thet ich mote under uon in obedience bothe wone and weole" (in *Þe Wohunge* ed. Meredith, p. 13, lines 126–27) [I pray you that I might receive in obedience both poverty and wealth]. The point is that even though the evil Maxence demands that Porphirius stretch out his neck to accept his martyrdom, he still speaks using holy language; God himself uses Maxence and speaks through him.

55.1   *hise*. We have provided "men" in the translation, as the "hise" acts as a substantive adjective, and could be translated simply as "his own." E provides "knights" (p. 112).

         heolden ham togederes. Literally, "held themselves together"; i.e., "stayed together."

55.2   *alle clane bihefdet*. The verb form (*bihefdet*) is the third person singular, which in the context of the sentence would imply that either Maxence beheaded them or, presumably, one of his henchmen. Since the subject of this verbal phrase is missing, we have translated as a passive.

55.3   *nes hit thet te bodies neren ifatte*. Literally, "it was not that the bodies were not fetched . . ." This use of the mutually canceling double negative represents a significant departure from the Old English use of double (or triple, or quadruple) negatives for emphasis, as D points out (p. 278n823). The use of the double negative here implies a kind of secretiveness, or slyness, to the action of the anonymous Christians who bury Porphirius and his knights.

57.2   *mine feolahes the . . . virgines in Heovene.* Katherine refers here to the 144,000 virgins who reside with Christ in Heaven, described in Apocalypse 14:1–5.

58.1   *swithe with hire.* This idiom, literally "quickly with her," is glossed by D as "take her quickly" (p. 344). According to Dobson, this idiom means "take her quickly" but the "with" here suggests an ellipsis of the verb (p. 344).

59.1   *bone.* Here the word is a form of *MED bane* (n.) meaning, possibly "slayer, murderer" (sense 1a, which is paralleled by the Morton translation), "destroyer" (sense 2a), or "destruction . . . death, doom" (sense 3); based in Old English *bana* (*BT, bana* (n.)), meaning killer or manslayer, the word remains in the modern if slightly archaic sounding "bane." However, also possible is a pun with the term *bon* (*MED* (n.2), sense 1a) meaning a prayer, or "a favor asked for" in prayer, which appears later in this sentence, where Katherine "buhe hire ant bede ane bone." This reading of 59.1 makes sense since the sword, for Katherine, signifies both her bodily destruction as well as the answer to her "bone," her prayer.

   ha₂. The feminine singular pronoun, literally "she," but in this context "it," referring to the soul. The term is feminine as it translates Latin *anima*.

60.1–61.1   *Mi lif ant . . . . nu icleopet me.* The echoing here of language from the Canticle of Canticles remarks clearly on the association in the Middle Ages of heavenly love with romantic love. Numerous religious, male and female, refer to themselves as the "brides" of Christ and to Christ as the "bridegroom" or "lover." See in particular the *Shewings of Julian of Norwich*, the *Book of Margery Kempe*, and, much later, the writings of Teresa of Avila and John of the Cross. For discussions of the bride of Christ or *sponsa Christi* motif see references in note 34.1.

61.3   *Ant he, as . . . of thet heaved.* See Cartwright, "*Buchedd Catrin*," p. 58, for information on the association of Katherine with John the Baptist.

61.4   *milc imenget with . . . hire hwite meithhad.* For a discussion of this passage and Katherine's connections with fertility, see Walsh, "Role of the Normans," p. 27.

   as pilegrims the wel witen. On Katherine and pilgrims, see Lewis, "Pilgrimage."

61.4–7   *beren forth hire bodi . . . . rihte bileave habbeth.* See Walsh, "Role of the Normans," for a discussion of the movement of some of Katherine's relics from Sinai to Rouen (pp. 21–23) and on the need for faith in the occurrence of miracles (pp. 26–27). Lewis, "Pilgrimage," also discusses the finger bones at Rouen (pp. 44–45). In "*Buchedd Catrin*," Cartwright examines this section of the Middle Welsh versions, in which the healing oil flows from Katherine's breast instead of from her bones (pp. 78–81).

62.1   *i Novembres moneth the fif ant twentuthe dei.* 25 November is Katherine's feast day. According to the Gospels (see Matthew 27:46–50, Mark 15:34–37, and Luke 23:44–46), Christ died in the ninth hour, not the third (for a discussion see D, pp. 285–86n914–15).

under. Refers to the undern, the third canonical hour, the prayer said daily according to the ecclesiastical timetable, at approximately 9am.

TEXTUAL NOTES TO *SANCTE KATERINE*

ABBREVIATIONS: *BT*: Bosworth and Toller, *Anglo-Saxon Dictionary*; **D**: d'Ardenne and Dobson edition (1981); **H**: a series of sixteenth-century scribbles in various hands (see Introduction, p. 22); **MS**: Oxford, Bodleian Library MS Bodley 34 [base text]; **R**: British Library MS Royal A XXVIII; **T**: British Library MS Cotton Titus D XVIII.

Our edition is based on Bodley 34's text; on those occasions when the MS reading has not sufficed, we have supplemented based on the Royal manuscript (R), or emended following d'Ardenne's and Dobson's edition from 1981 (D). However, in general we have worked to conserve B's reading whenever possible. We refer readers who wish to compare all three manuscripts of *SK* to D's edition, which presents an excellent triple text manuscript reading as well as an emended text of the Bodley 34 reading.

Title	Fol. 1r is heavily damaged and stained almost entirely brown. The title is virtually illegible; we follow Ker's reconstruction.
1.1	*Costentin*. The rubricated capital *C* is very faintly visible, 1.2 cm. The indicator letter has been cropped.
1.5	*ter he etstutte*. So R. MS is unreadable.
1.6	*siker*. So D, R, T. MS: the second letter is unreadable.
	cume. So D, R, T. MS: *cunne*. MS's scribe mistakenly writes an extra minim.
	warth. So D, R, T. MS: *war*.
1.8	*I*. MS: the capital is badly faded.
	of₂. So D, R, T. MS: unreadable. To the right of the line, the symbol ∞ is written in another hand.
2.1	*I*. MS: small rubricated capital, 6 mm.
2.2	*offearet*. MS: *a* inserted above the line.
3.1	*Theos*. MS: large rubricated capital *Þ*, 1.3 cm.
3.2	*evening*. So D, R, T. MS: *euenig*.
3.3	*se*. MS: inserted above the line.
	ant cwethen. MS: this phrase is marked for insertion in the right margin.
	menske. So D, R, T. MS: *meske*.
4.1	*Thus*. MS: small rubricated capital *Þ*, 7 mm.
	wiste. MS: corrected from *wil*.
	áá. MS: *a*. This word is usually spelled *áá* in MS. Because of this, and to avoid confusion with the definite article, we have silently emended those occurrences of *a* to *áá* throughout this volume.
	bur. So D, R, T. MS: *burh*.
	towart. MS: *o* inserted above the line.

aweariede. So D, following R's *awariede.* MS: *aweari,* with the last three letters almost illegible.

of$_2$. MS: corrected from *ef.*

4.2   *hwet$_1$.* So D, R. MS: *wet.* T: *hwat.*

4.3   *wreaththe.* MS: *wreadthe.* The MS-scribe often does not cross the top of ð, making it resemble *d* throughout the manuscript.

iwurthen. MS: *iwurden;* the ð has not been crossed. D, R, T: *wurðen.*

4.5   *heathene.* So D, T. MS: *headene;* another uncrossed ð. R: *heðene.*

4.7   *geinin.* So MS, altered from *geinen.*

4.11   *steavene.* MS: decorative line filler in red follows this word to the end of the line.

5.1   *Gretunge.* MS: large rubricated capital *G,* 1 cm, with indicator letter cropped.

5.2   *fordeth.* So D, R, T. MS: *forthdeth.*

6.1   *The.* MS: large rubricated capital Þ, 2.6 cm, with indicator letter cropped.

ahten. So D, R, T. MS: *ahte.*

thurh. MS: Þ$_2$ inserted above the line.

gold. MS: *d* inserted above the line.

6.2   *sehen.* So D, T. MS, R: *schulen.* See D, p. 213n101.

6.3   *nawiht.* So D. MS: *nawhit.* The scribe often inverts *h* and *i* in this and similar words. We have silently emended obvious examples of metathesis such as this.

6.6   *gremieth.* So D, R. MS: *gremied,* with uncrossed ð.

7.1   *The.* MS: small rubricated capital Þ, 7 mm.

swithe. So D, R, T. MS: *swide,* with uncrossed ð.

7.2   *Thi.* MS: small rubricated capital Þ, 6 mm, with indicator letter cropped.

7.3   *lahe sprung.* So MS, R, and T. D (p. 214–15n116) emends to *lahet.*

7.5   *Me.* MS: small rubricated capital *M,* 4 mm, with indicator letter cropped.

8.1   *Theos.* MS: large rubricated capital Þ, 2.1 cm, with indicator letter cropped.

9.1   *The.* MS: small rubricated capital Þ, 6 mm.

yung. So D, R, T. MS: *gung.*

9.2   *forcwethest.* So D, R, T. MS: *forcwedest,* with uncrossed ð.

undedliche. So R. MS: *undeðliche.* D, T: *undeadliche.* It seems likely here that the MS-scribe interchanged *d* and ð.

9.3   *nu hwet.* So D, following T's *nu hwat.* MS: *wet.* R: *hwet.*

9.4   *kine mede.* So D, R, T. MS: *þine mede.*

9.5   *dearneliche.* So T. MS: *dearliche.* R: *dernliche.* D emends to *dearnliche.*

het ham. So D, R, T. MS: *thet ha.*

medin. So D, R. MS: *meaðin.* T: *meden.*

thet$_2$. So D. MS: *þe.* It appears that the MS-scribe has forgotten to cross the þ, his usual abbreviation for *þet.*

9.7   *hethene.* So R. MS: *heaðne.* D, T: *heaðene.*

9.8   *Nat.* MS: small rubricated capital *N,* 6 mm.

misseist. So D, R, T. MS: *mis seist seist.*

thu$_3$. So D. MS, R, T omit. See D, p. 219n166.

10.1   *Ha.* MS: small rubricated capital *H,* 6 mm.

10.4   *wurthschipe.* So D, R, T. MS: *wu?rdschipe* with the unclear letter probably otiose.

10.7	Beginning on fol. 5r is the first series of sixteenth-century scribblings (hereafter noted as hand "H"). The majority of these notations are most likely "pen-trials made in a lawyer's office," most likely somewhere in Herefordshire (Ker, p. xiii). Halfway down the page in the right margin is *Th*, which is repeated further below, along with a few other scribbles and *This in* written at the bottom of the page.
	argentum. So D, R, T. MS: *ar.*
10.8	*Godd.* So D, R, T. MS: *goþ.*
10.9	*sihthe.* So D, R, T. MS: *siðhðe.*
10.11	*wurthschipe.* So D, R, T. MS: *wurdschipe*; ð is uncrossed.
11.3	*Thes.* MS: small rubricated capital Þ, 6 mm.
	long. So D, R, T. MS: *log.* The scribe likely forgot a macron indicating *n*.
13.2	*tuketh.* So D, R, T. MS: *tuket.*
	seith. So D, R, T. MS: *seid.*
13.3	*yef.* So D, R, T. MS: *gef.*
13.6	*runes.* So D, R, T. MS: *run*, with a stroke through the following ampersand that could signify *-es*; D reads it as an otiose mark.
14.4	*stod.* So D. MS: *stoð*, with a very faded stroke on the *d*-ascender signifying ð.
14.5	*Theos.* MS: small rubricated capital Þ, 8 mm.
14.7	*nawiht.* So D, R, T. MS: *nawhit.* Metathesis corrected for sense.
15.1	*Crist.* MS: small rubricated capital C, 5 mm.
	Godd. In the top margin of fol. 6r, H: *This indenture made the xii daye of July in the fowerth yere of the Rey* (see Ker, p. xiii).
	sculde. MS: *sclude.* We have emended the metathesis. D, R, T: *schulde.*
	swete₂. MS: *swete swete.* D, R, T: *swucche.*
	yef. So D, R. MS: *gef.* T: *ʒif.*
15.2	*worlde world.* So D, R, T. MS: *world.*
15.3	*Nefde.* MS: small rubricated capital N, 5 mm.
16.6	*strengthe.* MS: *strengðeðeð.*
	mot. MS, R, T omit. Emended for sense following D (see p. 223n262).
	meidnes. So D, T. MS: *meiðdnes.* R: *meidenes.*
	lives. So MS, corrected from *liven.*
	buten. So D. R, T omit. MS: *livesi.* D's emendation allows the phrase to translate as "life without end" (see pp. 223–24n262).
16.9	*Theos.* MS: small rubricated capital Þ, 1.2 cm.
	abad. So D, R, T. MS: *abaɫd.*
16.13	*unimete.* So D, R. MS: *unimeð.* T: *unimet.* See D, p. 225n275.
16.14	*heo.* So D, R, T. MS omits. See D, p. 225n275.
	hercnende. So T. MS, R: *hercnede.* D emends to *hercneð.*
16.16	*seggen.* MS: decorative line filler in red follows this word to the end of the line.
17.1	*Thu.* MS: large rubricated capital Þ, 2.1 cm.
18.1	*thuhte.* So D, R, T. MS: *þuþte.*
18.4	*dei.* So R. T: *dai.* MS, D: *de.*
19.1	*Nu.* MS: large rubricated capital N, 8 mm.
	lihtliche. MS: *lihteliche.* D, R, T: *lutel.*

19.3	*the₃*. So D, based on T's *þeo*. MS, R: *þet*.
	nomecuthest. So D, R, T. MS: *nomecudest*; the *ð* is uncrossed.
	talien. So D, R, T. MS: *talien*, corrected to *tallien*, with *i* inserted above the line in red.
	of₂. So D, R, T. MS: *on*.
20.1	*nu*. So D, R, T. MS omits.
21.1	*Ich*. MS: large rubricated capital *I*, 1.1 cm.
	glistinde. So D, R, T. MS: *gllistinde*.
	nawt. So D, R, T. MS: *nawit*.
21.2	*Aristotles*. So D, R. MS: *aristocles*. T: *aristoles*.
	wreothieth. So D, R, T. MS: *wreoðien on*. See D, p. 228n318.
21.3	*ich beo*. So D, R, T. MS omits. We emend to provide a subject.
	ilearet. So MS, altered from *ileared*.
	ham₂. So D, R, T. MS omits.
21.3–28.1	After fol. 7v, three leaves have clearly been torn out of the manuscript. We have supplied the missing text from R.
21.5	*hefde ham bihaten*. So D, T. R omits.
21.7	*se luthere ilatet*. So D. See p. 230n333. R: *he luðere ahte*. T: *þe luðere lihte*.
21.10	*soth mon and soth Godd*. So D, T. R: *soth godd and soth mon*. See D, p. 230n345.
21.15	*adun*. So D, T. R omits. See D, p. 230n350.
	theo. So D, T. R: *þet*.
	riht leveth and luvieth. So D, T. R: *luvieð riht and leveð*. See D, p. 230n351.
23.1	*dustest*. So D, T. R: *dudest*. See D, p. 231n362.
	the₃. So D. R, T omit.
	His. So D, T. R omits.
23.2	*His*. So D, T. R: *is*.
23.4	*hit Him*. So D, T. R omits.
	erveth. R: ~~h~~*erveth*.
	to₂. So D, T. R omits.
	duhti. So D. R, T omit. See D, p. 232n370–71.
23.8	*leome*. So D, T. R: *leomen*. See D, pp. 233–34n385.
23.10	*weneth*. R: ~~ne~~ *weneth*.
23.11	*thes*. So D, T. R: *wes*.
	euch. So D, T. R: *eveh*.
23.12	*makieth*. Emended from R's *maket* to agree with *men*. The phrase *miracles thet his men maket yette* reads in T as follows: *miracles thet beth maked yet*. In either reading the phrase is problematic; D emends to *miracles þet [bi] his men beoð [i]maket ʒette*, which more closely paraphrases the Latin "que si ab eo gesta non credis, fieri ab hominibus in nomine eius, uel certe multotiens facta, cognosce" (see p. 234n394–95).
24.6	*onont*. So D, T. R: *on nont*.
25.1	*leven*. So D, T. R: *ileven*.
25.3	*helpen ant beon*. So D, T. R: *helpen oðre ant beon*.
26.1	*wult*. R: *t* inserted above the line.
26.2	*ne sorhe uppon . . . te wa wente*. So D, T (though D emends *wente* to *wende*). R omits. See D, p. 236n427.
26.3	*He₁*. So D, T. R: *Godd*. See D, p. 237n432.

26.4	*his*. So D, T. R omits. See D, p. 237n434–35.
26.5	*forto*. So D, T. R: *to*.
	moncun. So D, T. R: *mon to*.
26.7	*misdude — tholede*. So D, T. R: *misdude bette ant eode on bote ant þolede*, most likely looking ahead to the *bette ant eode on bote* of the next line.
26.8	*ibet*. So D, T. R: *ibroken*. See D, p. 238n445.
	deathe to live thet ne dredeth na deth. So D, T. R: *deaðe þet ne dredeð na deð to live*. See D, p. 238n446.
26.9	*Him we mahen*. R: *we mahten him*; the scribe has indicated that *him* should precede *we*. We have emended *mahten* to *mahen* following D and T.
26.10	*he eaver*. So D, T. R: *heaver*.
26.11	*Godd*. R: ~~we~~ *Godd*.
	swithe. So D, T. R: *swide*, with uncrossed ð.
27.1	*ant alle his feren*. So D, T. R omits. See D, p. 238n456–57.
	atine. R: *atint*. T: *a dint*. D writes that this word is "one of the trickiest problems in the text" (p. 239n457). d'Ardenne and Dobson choose this form because it accords with *tavelin* and because it is closest to the recorded form. See their lengthy discussion on pp. 238–40n457.
27.2	*agelwede*. R: *ageide*. As it appears in the manuscripts, *ageide* in R and *agide* in T, this word is unidentifiable; thus D follows the Old English word *agelwan* (*BT*, *a-gelwan* (v.)). See D's detailed discussion on p. 240n458.
28.1	*Thes*. MS: large rubricated capital *Þ*, 2 cm.
	thet. So D, R, T. MS omits.
	dead. So D. MS, T: *deað*. R: *ded*.
28.5	*unstrenget*. So D, R. MS: *unstreged*. T: *unstrengðet*.
28.7	*ikimet*. So T. MS, D, R: *bikimet*. We have emended following T's close spelling to *akimed* (see *OED akimed* (adj.)).
	ut. So D. MS, R, T omit. D argues that this must have been omitted by eyeskip (p. 243n473).
29.1	*Ontswerede*. MS: large rubricated capital *O*, 7 mm.
	nohwer. MS: *h* inserted above the line.
	al tom. So R, T. MS: *acomen*. D emends to *atomet*.
	turnde. So D, R, T. MS: *turde*.
29.2	*mot₂*. So T. MS: *us acomen*. R omits. D eme nds to *us atomet*. We have adopted T's reading following the Old English phrase *habban gemot* ("hold a council"); compare to D, pp. 245–46n483–84, who compares the Old English but ultimately emends; see also note 29.1 to *al tom*, above. See also *BT*, *ge-mót* (n.).
29.5	*cutheth*. So D, R, T. MS: *cudeth*.
29.8	*wult*. So D, T. MS, R: *wult nu*, repeating the *nu* at the beginning of the line.
30.1	*The*. MS: large rubricated capital *Þ*, 3.5 cm. The indicator letter has been cropped.
31.3	*fur*. So D, R, T. MS omits.
32.1	*Me*. MS: small rubricated capital *M*, 6 mm.
32.3	*iwemmet*. So D, T. MS: *iweumet*. The MS-scribe probably missed a minim. See D, p. 249n519. R: *iweommet*.
	her. MS: *her* ~~thet ha~~.

	lufsume. So D, T. MS: *leufsume*. See D, p. 249n520. R: *lufsum*.
	turnden. So D, R, T. MS: *turden*.
33.1	*Tha*. MS: small rubricated capital Þ, 1.2 cm.
33.2	*wurthschipe*. MS: decorative line filler in red follows this word to the end of the line.
34.1	*Katerine*. MS: large rubricated capital *K*, 1.4 cm.
34.2	*thin*. So D, R, T. MS: *thing*.
34.3	*áá*. MS omits. D, R: *a*. T: *ai*.
34.5	*wurthshipe*. So MS, with h_2 altered from *c*.
34.8	*buve*. So D, T. MS: *bune*. R: *bunen*.
35.1	*The*. MS: small rubricated capital Þ, 1.2 cm. The indicator letter is cropped.
35.4	*hit lihtliche*. So D, R, T. MS: *hihtliche*, with h_2 altered from *t*.
35.5	*kasten*. So R, T. MS: *kestten*. D: *kesten*.
35.5	*nowther*. So D, R, T. MS: *nowder*, with uncrossed *ð*.
	tweolf. MS: *o* inserted above the line.
36.1	*Bicom*. MS: large rubricated capital *B*, 9 mm.
36.3	*wurthliche*. So D, R, T. MS: *wurliche*.
	hire$_3$. So D, R, T. MS omits.
36.4	*Ant*. So D, R, T. MS: *And þet*.
	thus. MS: originally omitted, but inserted in the left margin.
	On fol. 10v, bottom margin, H: *A medycyn for*, in heavily smeared ink and upside down.
37.1	*Porphire*. MS: space has been left for a large capital *P* which was never inserted, but the indicator letter in the left margin is clear.
37.3	*smeal*. MS: *a* inserted above the line.
37.5	*of hire*. So D, R, T. MS: *of hire of hire*.
37.6	*the*. So D, T. MS: *þe þe*. R omits.
37.8	*wurthschipe*. So D, T. MS: *wurdschipe*, with uncrossed *ð*. R: *wurschipe*.
38.1	*Feng*. So D, R, T. MS: *Wende*. D argues that MS's *wende* is the result of misreading (p. 254n598).
	worldliche. So D, T. MS: *worlðliche*, with l_1 inserted above the line. R: *worldlich*.
38.2	*constu*. MS: space has been left for a large capital *C* that was never inserted. Most likely the paragraph break here would have indicated a pause and new emphasis on the main body of Katherine's sermon, since the text would probably have been read aloud. We have continued the paragraph and indicated emphasis with a colon.
	deorewurthe. So D, R. MS: *deorepurðe*. T: *derewurðe*.
	schene. So D. MS, R, T: *schenre*. All three manuscripts have the comparative *schenre*, but according to D, it makes better sense to avoid the comparative here. D also points out the R scribe's attempt to correct the error, by writing *schenre þen eni ʒimstanes*. See p. 255n604.
38.3	*slec*. So D, R, T. MS: *slech*, with the *c* inserted above the line. Possibly the MS-scribe forgot to cancel the *h*. D emends this to follow the other manuscripts and provide a discussion of the etymology of this unusual word (p. 256n609).
	o. MS: *os*. D, R, T: *of*.
38.4	*other*$_2$. So D, T. MS: *oder*, with uncrossed *ð*. R: *oðere*.

longunge. MS: *lungunge*. We have emended based on the sense of the line in MS, where the blessed are described as not lacking anything *thet ha wulleth other mahe wilnin*. R: *linunge*. T: *blinnunge*. D emends to *linnunge*; see D's discussion on emending, p. 257n614.

38.7   *linneth*. So D, R. MS: *limieð*, perhaps an error in strokes, but also the scribe's difficulty with this suggests that he may not have been familiar with this word (D, p. 258n622). T: *blimneð*.

       ne₂. So D, R, T. MS: *ne ne*.

       leasteth. MS: *a* inserted above the line.

38.10   *Wealdent*. MS: *a* inserted above the line.

39.1   *Porphire*. MS: space has been left for a large capital *P* that was never inserted.

39.2   *Porphire*. MS: *Porhphire*, with *h₁* canceled.

39.3   *therin is al mi rihte bileave*. Our emendation is based on T's *þer is al mi rihte bileaue*. MS: *þear as me þear as me rihte bileaue*. D emends to *thear as me [learde me mi]*. R: *þer as mi rihte bileaue schawde me*.

39.4   *isette*. So D, following T. MS: *isete*. R: *iset*.

39.6   *haldeth*. So D, R, T. MS: *halðeð*.

       blisse. MS: *blissen*.

39.7   *schal*. So D, R, T. MS omits.

40.1   *Crist*. MS: space has been left for a large capital *C* that was never inserted.

40.2   *Bihalt*. So D. MS: *Bihaldt*, with the *dt* ligatured. R, T: *bihald*.

40.3   *Healent*. MS: *e₂* inserted above the line.

       nowcin. So D, R, T. MS: *newcin*.

40.5   *hwucche*. So MS. D: *hwucche duheðe*. See also the corresponding explanatory note.

41.1   *Under*. MS: space has been left for a large capital *U* that was never inserted.

42.1   *This*. MS: space has been left for a large capital *Þ* that was never inserted.

       mi₃. So D, R, T. MS: *ni*.

42.2   Top margin of fol. 13r. H: *This byll mad fo*.

43.1   *Hwil*. MS: space has been left for a large capital *H* that was never inserted.

       weol. So D, R, T. MS. *wweol*.

43.5   *pikes₂*. So R. MS and T omit. D makes a compelling argument to emend to *spikes kenre* (p. 265n704). However, we have decided to emend our text from R based on the lack of evidence for the existence of *spikes* before the fourteenth century (with the exception of two occurrences in the late-thirteenth century *Middle English Sea Terms* [see *MED spike* (n.1), sense a]). "Pikes," however, is well-attested in early Middle English; in particular, see the Worcester fragment of *Body and Soul* where it is specifically designated as an instrument of torture: "Nu me wulleþ prikien þeo pikes inne helle" (see *MED pike* (n.1), sense a).

44.1   *This*. MS: space has been left for a large capital *Þ* that was never inserted.

       swuch. So D, R, T. MS: *swuhc*.

       turnden either. So D, R, T. MS: *turden eider*. Both *ð*s are uncrossed.

       turnden₂. So D, R, T. MS: *turden*, with the *ð* uncrossed.

       kahten. So R. MS: *chachten*. D has emended to *cahten*, following T.

       othre₂. So D, T. MS: *odre* with the *ð* uncrossed. R: *oðer*.

44.3   *stille*. So D, R, T. MS omits.

Almihti. So D, R, T. MS: *al mihte.*

menske. So D, R, T. MS: *meske.*

thet₁. So D; see p. 268n724. MS, R, T omit.

smeortliche. So D. MS: *smeordtliche.* R, T: *smertliche.*

45.2   *then.* MS: *þene* with final *e* canceled out.

Healent. MS: *e₂* inserted above the line.

45.3   *hefde.* So D, R, T. MS: *hef.*

46.1   *The.* MS: space has been left for a large capital *Þ* that was never inserted.

46.2   *ha.* So D, T. MS, R omit.

wreastlin. MS: *a* inserted above the line.

Wealdent. So D, T. MS: *welalden.* R: *weldent.*

46.3   *worldliche.* So D, R, T. MS: *worldlich.*

46.6   *isihen.* So D, T. MS: *isehene.* R: *isehen.* Emended for sense to mean "have journeyed." As D points out, it would have been easy for the scribe to be distracted by the *isehen* that appears in the line above or *sehen* in the line below to produce a form meaning "were seen" (p. 272n750).

47.1   *Godd.* So D, R, T. MS: *goðd.*

47.3   *heom.* So D, R. MS: *ha?m,* most likely either a garbled *a* or a midword correction from *ham.* The third letter is unreadable. See D's discussion on pp. 272–73n756, where they argue that *heom* is what the scribe intended to write. T: *ham.*

48.2   *Hu.* MS: space has been left for a large capital *H* that was never inserted.

dotest tu. So D, after R's and T's *dotestu.* MS: *dutest tu.*

49.2   *weane.* So D, R, T. MS: *wene.*

50.1   *Sone.* MS: space has been left for a large capital *S* that was never inserted.

50.2   *deofles.* So D. MS: *deoflel,* though the *l* looks like it could have been altered to or from an *s.* R: *deoules.* T: *deoueles.*

hire forth. So D. MS, R, T omit.

bilimeth. So D, R, T. MS: *bilimieð.*

flesch. So R. MS, T: *vles* (*vles=fles*). We have emended to *flesch* for ease of comprehension.

slakie. So T. MS, R: *earni.* D emends to *earhi,* citing a misreading of the exemplar (see p. 274n781).

na. MS: inserted above the line.

51.1   *Ne.* MS: space has been left for a large capital *N* that was never inserted.

deorewurthe. So D, R. MS: *deorewrðe.* T: *derewurðe.*

51.2   *linunge.* So R. MS: *longunge.* T: *ende.* D emends to *linnunge.*

52.1   *istrenget.* So D, R, T. MS: *istreget.*

52.4   In left margin of fol. 15v, H: very faint, illegible writing, most likely Latin.

53.1   *Me.* MS: space has been left for a large capital *M* that was never inserted.

thet me. MS, R, T omit. D adds this for sense (see p. 276n804).

53.2   *Sathanesse.* So MS. D: *Sathanase,* following T (see p. 277n808). Rather than implying a female Satan (as the *-esse* at first glance indicates), *satanasse* and *sathanasse* are common variants of the word *satanas* (see *MED* (n.)). See the *Sayings of St. Bede,* line 235: "If ȝe miȝtten at-blenche from þe sori satanasse"; and the *Quatrefoil of Love,* line 96: "Sary sathanasse soughte þam belyue, for to wakken oure waa." According to the *MED*, *SK* is the only text with the variant of *sathanesse*.

53.5	*eorthe*. So D, R, T. MS: *eorde*.
54.1	*Nu*. MS: space has been left for a large capital *N* that was never inserted.
55.2	*bihefdet*. So MS, corrected from *bihefden*, with *t* inserted above canceled *n*.
55.4	*forwurthen*. So D, following R. MS: *forwurdthen*. T: *forlosen*.
56.1	*Theyet*. MS: space has been left for a large capital Þ that was never inserted.
	thurst. So D, R, T. MS omits.
56.2	*ant₂*. So D, T. MS, R omit.
57.1	*Nai*. MS: space has been left for a large capital *N* that was never inserted.
58.1	*The*. MS: space has been left for a large capital Þ that was never inserted.
	nuste. So D, R, T. MS: *and nuste*.
	ehsihthe. So D, R. MS: *hehsihðe*. T: *sihðe*.
58.2	*heathene*. So D, T. MS: *headene*, with an uncrossed ð. R: *heðene*.
58.4	*Lauerd*. MS: space has been left for a large capital *L* that was never inserted. The indicator letter appears twice (*ll*) in the left margin.
59.4	*ileavet*. So T. MS: *ileveð*. R: *ilenet*. D emends to *ileuet*.
59.7	*wone*. So D, T. MS: *weone*. R: *weane*.
60.1	*Nefde*. MS: space has been left for a large capital *N* that was never inserted.
61.1	*Heo*. MS: large rubricated capital *H*, 2.1 cm. The indicator letter has been cropped. This capital and the next are the work of the second rubricator, using a much better quality ink.
61.7	*botneth*. MS: a letter has been erased after this word.
62.1	*Thus*. MS: large rubricated capital Þ, 2.5 cm.

THE LIFLADE ANT TE PASSIUN OF SEINTE MARGARETE

I the Feaderes ant i thes Sunes ant i thes Hali Gastes nome, her biginneth the Liflade ant te Passiun of Seinte Margarete.

1.   (1) Efter ure Lauerdes pine ant His passiun, ant His death o Rode ant His ariste of death, ant eft er His upastihunge, as He steah to Heovene, weren monie martyrs, wepme ba ant wummen, to deathes misliche idon for the nome of Drihtin; ant, as icudde kempen, overcomen ant akeasten hare threo cunne van, the veont, ant teos wake worlt, ant hare licomes lustes, ant wenden of theos weanen to weole ant to eche wunne icrunet to Criste.

fol. 18v
2.   (1) Theyet weren monie ma thene nu beon misbilevede | men, the heheden ant hereden hethene maumez, of stanes ant of stockes wrecches iwrahte. (2) Ah Ich, an Godes theowe, Teochimus inemed, ilered i Godes lei, habbe iredd ant araht moni mislich leaf, ant neaver i nan stude ne mahte Ich understonden of nan the were wurthe forto beon iwurget as hit deh Drihtin, bute the hehe Healent an thet is in Heovene, the wunede hwil His wille wes amonc worldliche men, ant bottnede blinde, the dumbe, ant te deave, ant te deade arerde to leome ant to live; ant cruneth His icorene, the deth dreheth for Him other eni neowcin. (3) Ant alle Cristene men, thet beoth of Crist icleopet, swa yef ha nutteth

---

In the name of the Father and of the Son and of the Holy Ghost, here begins the Life and the Passion of St Margaret.

1.   (1) After our Lord's pain and His passion, and His death on the Cross and his resurrection from death, and after His ascension, as He rose to Heaven, there were many martyrs, both men and women, wrongly put to death in the name of the Ruler; and, as well-known warriors, they overcame and cast down their three kinds of foes, the fiend, and this weak world, and the lusts of their bodies, and they went from these woes to prosperity and everlasting joy, crowned to Christ.

2.   (1) Even then, there were many more false believers than there are now, who extolled and praised heathen idols, wretched things wrought from stones and sticks. (2) But I, God's own servant, named Teochimus, learned in God's law, have read and interpreted many kinds of books, and never in any place might I comprehend any who were worthy to be worshiped as it befits the Ruler, except the lofty Savior who is in Heaven, who dwelled while it was His will among worldly men, and cured the blind, the dumb, and the deaf, and raised the dead to light and to life, and crowns His chosen, who endure death or any hardship for Him. (3) And

hare nome, hafeth ilened thet lif thet echeliche lesteth. (4) Ich, fulhet i font o the almihti Fedres nome ant o the witti Sunes nome ant o thes Hali Gastes, wes i the ilke time liviende i londe tha thet eadie meiden, Margarete bi nome, feht with the feond ant with his eorthliche limen, ant overcom ant acaste ham, ant biyet hit iwriten of the writers tha, al hire passiun ant hire pinfule deth thet ha dreh for Drihtin.

3.   (1) Hercneth! (2) Alle the earen ant herunge habbeth, widewen with tha iweddede, ant te meidnes nomeliche, lusten swithe yeorliche hu ha schulen luvien the liviende Lauerd ant libben i meithhad, thet Him his mihte leovest, swa thet ha moten, thurh thet eadie meiden the we munneth todei with meithhades menske, thet seli meidnes song singen with this meiden ant with thet heovenliche hird echeliche in Heovene. |

fol. 19r   (1) This meiden thet we munieth wes Margarete ihaten, ant hire flesliche
4.   feder Theodosie hehte, of thet hethene folc patriarche ant prince. (2) Ah heo, as the deorwurthe Drihtin hit dihte, into a burh wes ibroht to veden ant to vostrin, from the muchele Antioche fiftene milen. (3) Tha ha hefde of helde yeres fiftene, ant hire moder wes iwend the wei thet worldliche men alle schulen wenden, ha warth theo the hefde iwist ant iwenet hire swa lengre swa levere, ant alle hire luveden thet hire on lokeden, as theo thet Godd luvede, the heovenliche Lauerd, ant yef hire the grace of the Hali Gast, swa thet ha ches Him to luve ant to lefmon, ant bitahte in His hond the menske of hire meithhad, hire wil ant hire werc, ant al

---

he has granted to all Christian people who are called so after Christ, if they profit by their name, that life which lasts forever. (4) I, baptized in the font in the almighty Father's name and in the wise Son's name and in the Holy Ghost's, was at that same time living in a land where that blessed maiden, Margaret by name, fought with the fiend and with his earthly followers, and overcame and cast them down, and I gained hold of that which was written by the writers then concerning all her suffering and her painful death that she endured for the Ruler.

3.   (1) Listen! (2) All who have ears and hearing, widows with the wedded and the maidens especially, let them listen very eagerly to how they should love the living Lord and live in virginity, which to him is the best-loved virtue, so that they may, through that blessed maiden whom we commemorate today, with the strength of virginity, sing that holy maiden's song both with this maiden along with that heavenly host forever in Heaven.

4.   (1) This maiden that we commemorate was called Margaret, and her fleshly father called Theodosius, of that heathen folk patriarch and prince. (2) But she, as the dear Lord ordained it, was brought into a city to be nurtured and fostered, fifteen miles from Antioch the Great. (3) When she was fifteen years of age, and her mother was gone the way that all worldly ones must go, she became, to her who had raised her and weaned her, increasingly dear over time, and all loved her who looked on her as she whom God loved, the heavenly Lord, and who had given her the grace of the Holy Ghost, so that she chose Him as love and beloved, and delivered into His hand the honor of her virginity, her will and her work, and

thet heo eaver i the world i wald hahte, to witen ant to welden with al hireseolven. (4) Thus ha wes ant wiste, meokest áá meiden, with othre meidnes o the feld hire fostermodres hahte, ant herde on euich half hire hu me droh to deathe Cristes icorene for rihte bileave, ant yirnde ant walde yeorne, yef Godes wil were, thet ha moste beon an of the moni moder-bern thet swa muchel drohen ant drehheden for Drihtin.

5.   (1) Bitimde umbe stunde thet ter com ut of Asye towart Antioche the veondes an foster, to herien i the hehe burh hise hethene godes. (2) Olibrius hehte, schireve of the lond, thet alle the lefden o the liviende Godd fordude ant

fol. 19v   fordemde. (3) As he wende a dei his wei, seh this seli | meiden Margarete as ha wes ant wiste upo the feld hire fostermodres schep, the schimede ant schan al of wlite ant of westume.

6.   (1) He het his hird hetterliche: "Nemeth hire swithe! (2) Yef heo is freo wummon, Ich hire wule habben ant halden to wive. (3) Ant yef heo theowe is, Ich cheose hire to chevese, ant hire wule freohin with gersum ant with golde; ant wel schal hire iwurthen for hire lufsume leor with al thet Ich welde." (4) As the knihtes wolden warpen honden on hire, ha bigon to clepien ant callen to Criste thus:

7.   (1) "Have, Lauerd, milce ant merci of Thi wummon. (2) Ne ne let Tu neavre mi sawle forleosen with the forlorene, ne with the luthere mi lif, the beoth al blodi biblodeget of sunne. (3) Jesu Crist, Godes Sune, beo Thu eaver mi gleo ant mi gledunge; the mot Ich áá mare hehen ant herien. (4) Hald, hehe Lauerd, min heorte, Ich biseche The, in treowe bileve, ant biwite Thu mi bodi — thet is al bitaht to The — from flesliche fulthen, thet neaver mi sawle ne isuled beo in

---

all that she ever owned in the world in her keeping, to keep and to rule over entirely for her. (4) Thus she tended and looked after, ever the meekest maiden, with other maidens in the field, her foster-mother's sheep, and heard on every side of her how Christ's chosen ones were being put to death for true belief, and she yearned and wished earnestly, if it were God's will, that she might be one of the many mother's children who suffered and endured so much for the Ruler.

5.   (1) It befell after a time that there came out of Asia towards Antioch the fiend's own foster-child, to honor his heathen gods in the capital city. (2) Olibrius he was called, the governor of that land, who condemned and killed all who believed in the living God. (3) As he went his way one day, he saw this holy maiden Margaret in the field, who shimmered and shone all of face and form, as she pastured and guarded her foster-mother's sheep.

6.   (1) He ordered his men fiercely: "Seize her at once! (2) If she is a free woman, I will have her and marry her. (3) And if she is a slave, I choose her as a concubine, and will free her with treasure and with gold, and it shall go well for her because of her lovely countenance, with all that I rule over." (4) As the knights would lay hands on her, she began to cry and call to Christ thus:

7.   (1) "Have, Lord, compassion and mercy on your woman. (2) Never let my soul perish with the lost, nor my life with the wicked men, who are all stained bloody with sin. (3) Jesus Christ, God's Son, may You be ever my joy and my gladness, who I may evermore honor and praise. (4) Hold, lofty Lord, my heart, I beseech You, in true belief, and protect my body — which is completely given over to You

sunne thurh thet licomes lust thet lutle hwile liketh. (5) Lauerd, lustu to me. (6) Ich habbe a deore gimstan, ant Ich hit habbe iyeve The — mi meithhad I mene, blostme brihtest i bodi the hit bereth ant biwit wel. (7) Ne let Tu neaver the unwiht warpen hit i wurthinc, for hit is the leof, hit is him thinge lothest, ant weorreth ant warpeth ever thertoward | with alles cunnes wrenches. (8) Lauerd, Thu were me ant wite hit ever to The. (9) Ne thole Thu never the unwiht thet he wori mi wit ne wonie mi wisdom, ah send me Thi sonde, Helent, of Heovene, thet cuthe me ant kenne hu Ich onswerie schule thes schuckes schireve. (10) For Ich iseo me, Lauerd, bistepped ant bistonden ase lomb with wedde wulves, ant ase the fuhel the is ivon in thes fuheleres grune, ase fisc ahon on hoke, ase ra inumen i nette. (11) Heh Helent, help me, ne leaf Thu me never nu i luthere mennes honde."

8. (1) The knihtes, for ha spec thus, charden euchan ayein ant cwethen to hare lauerd: "Ne mei thi mihte habben na man with this meiden, for ha ne heheth nan of ure hethene godes, ah leveth o the Lauerd the the Gius fordemden ant drohen to deathe, ant hethene hongeden ant heven on Rode."

9. (1) Olibrius the luthere, tha he this iherde, changede his chere, ant het bilive bringin hire biforen him. (2) Sone se ha icume wes, he cleopede to hire thus: "Cuth me," quoth he, "yif thu art foster of freomon other theowe-wummon."

10. (1) The eadi meiden Margarete sone him ontswerede, ant softeliche seide: "Freo wummon Ich am thah ant Godes thewe."

— from fleshly filth, so that my soul may never be sullied in sin through that fleshly desire that pleases for a little while. (5) Lord, listen to me. (6) I have a precious gemstone, and I have given it to you — my virginity I mean, the brightest blossom in the body that holds and protects it well. (7) May you never let the Fiend cast it into the mire, for (just as) it is dear to you, it is the most loathsome thing to him, and he makes war and always attacks it with all kinds of wiles. (8) Lord, defend me and hold it ever for Yourself. (9) May You never suffer the devil to make war against my wit or lessen my wisdom, but send me Your messenger, Healer, from Heaven, who may show me and make known to me how I should answer this sheriff of the demon. (10) For I see myself, Lord, beset and surrounded as a lamb among mad wolves, and like the bird that is caught in the fowler's trap, like a fish hung on a hook, like a roe taken in a net. (11) Lofty Healer, help me, and may You never leave me in wicked men's hands."

8. (1) The knights, as she spoke thus, all returned and said to their lord: "No man can have power against this maiden, for she worships none of our heathen gods, but believes in the Lord whom the Jews condemned and put to death, and whom the heathens hung and raised on the Cross."

9. (1) The wicked Olibrius, when he heard this, changed his countenance, and ordered her immediately to be brought before him. (2) As soon as she had come, he spoke to her thus: "Tell me," said he, "if you are the foster-child of a freeman or a slave-woman."

10. (1) The blessed maiden Margaret answered him right away, and softly said: "I am a free woman though I am also God's servant."

11.   (1) "Ye," quoth he, "ah hwet godd hehest ant herestu?"

12.   (1) "Ich hehe," quoth ha, "Heh-Feader, Healent in Heovene, ant His deorwurthe Sune, Jesu Crist hatte; ant Him Ich habbe, meiden, mi meithhad

fol. 20v   iyettet, ant lu|vie to leofmon ant leve on ase on Lauerd."

13.   (1) "Ye," quoth he lude. (2) "Levestu ant luvest te the reufulliche deide ant reuliche on Rode?"

14.   (1) "Nai," quoth ha, "ah theo the wenden to fordon Him, thine forthfedres, beoth forfaren reuliche ant forloren lutherliche; ant He liveth, Kine-bern icrunet in His kinedom, Keiser of kinges, echeliche in Heovene."

15.   (1) The wari of theos wordes wearth utnume wrath, ant het hire kasten in cwarterne ant i cwalhus athet he hefde betere bithoht him o hwucche wise he walde merren hire meithhad, ant ferde him thenne swa forth into Antioche ant hehede hise hethene godes as hit lomp ant lei to his luthere bileve. (2) Het hire i the other dei bringen bivoren him.

16.   (1) Ha wes sone ibroht forth, ant he bigon to seggen: "Meiden, have merci ant milce of the seolven. (2) Nim yeme of thi yuhethe ant of thi semliche schape, of thi schene nebschaft. (3) Wurch efter mi wil ant wurge mine maumez, ant the schal wel iwurthen bivoren the heste of min hirt, with al thet Ich i world hah ant i wald habbe."

17.   (1) Margarete, mildest ant meidene meokest, ontswerede him ant seide: "Wite hit tu nu yif thu wult — for He hit wat ful wel the haveth iseilet to Himseolf me ant mi meithhad — thet tu ne maht nanes weis, with weole ne

---

11.   (1) "Yes," said he, "but what god do you praise and worship?"

12.   (1) "I worship," said she, "the High-Father, the Savior in Heaven, and his precious Son, named Jesus Christ; and I, a maiden, have given my maidenhood to Him, and love him as a beloved and believe in him as a Lord."

13.   (1) "Indeed," said he loudly. (2) "You believe in and you love Him who pitiably and miserably died on the Cross?"

14.   (1) "No," said she, "but those who thought to condemn him, your fore-fathers, are miserably dead and wickedly damned; and He lives, a Prince crowned in His kingdom, Ruler of kings, forever in Heaven."

15.   (1) At these words, the villain became exceedingly angry, and ordered her cast into a prison and torture-chamber until he had better considered in what way he might mar her maidenhead, and he went his way forth then into Antioch and worshiped his heathen gods as it was fitting and proper for his wicked belief. (2) He ordered her on the next day brought before him.

16.   (1) She was soon brought forth, and he began to say: "Maiden, have mercy and compassion for yourself. (2) Take care for your youth and for your seemly shape, for your bright face. (3) Do according to my will and worship my idols, and it shall go well for you, more than the best of my household with all that I own in the world and have in possession."

17.   (1) Margaret, the mildest and meekest maiden, answered him and said: "Know it now if you will — because He knows it full well who has sealed me to himself and my virginity — that in no way may you, with wealth or with joy, with woe

fol. 21r   with wune, with wa ne with wont|rethe, ne with nan worldlich thing, wenden me
ne wrenchen ut of the wei thet Ich am in bigunne to ganne. (2) Ant unwurth thet
wite thu me beoth thine wordes, for Him ane Ich luvie ant habbe to bileve the
weld ant wisseth with His wit windes ant wederes, ant al thet biset is with se ant
with sunne. (3) Buven ba ant bineothen, al buheth to Him ant beieth. (4) Ant to-
eke this: thet He is se mihti ant se meinful, He is leoflukest lif forto lokin upon
ant swotest to smellen; ne ne His swote savour ne His almihti mihte ne His
makelese lufsumlec never mare ne mei lutli ne aliggen, for He ne alith never, ah
liveth áá in are, ant His muchele mihte lesteth áá mare.”

18.   (1) “Let!” quoth Olibrius, “Ne beoth thes wordes noht wurth. (2) Ah an-hwet
wite thu: bute yif thu swike ham, mi swerd schal forswelten ant forswolhen thi
flesc, ant therefter thine ban schulen beon forbernde o berninde gleden. (3) Ah
yif thu wult leve me, thu schalt beon mi leofmon ant min iweddede wif, ant welden
ase lefdi al thet Ich i wald hah ant am of lauerd.” |

fol. 20b   (1) “Ich ileve the,” quoth ha, “wel of thine biheaste. (2) Ah have thu hit, ant ti luve,
19.   for Ich habe a leovere thet Ich nulle for nan leosen ne leaven. (3) Thu swenchest the
to swithe, ant warpest me is wa fore awei thine hwile, for al me is an,” quoth ha, “thin
fol. 21r   olhnung ant thin eie. (4) | Ich wulle bitechen mi bodi to eaver- euich bitternesse thet
tu const on bithenchen, ne bite hit ne se sare with thon thet Ich mote meidene mede
habben in Heovene. (5) Drihtin deide for us, the deorwurthe Lauerd, ant ne drede Ich
na deth forto drehen for Him. (6) He haveth His merke on me iseiled with His in-seil;
ne mei unc lif ne deth nother twemen otwa.”

---

or with wretchedness, nor with any worldly thing, turn or wrench me out of the
way that I have begun to follow. (2) And know that your words are worthless to me
for I love and hold my faith in Him alone, who rules and guides with his wit the
winds and weathers, and all that is surrounded with the sea and with the sun. (3)
Both above and below, all obey Him and pay homage. (4) And also this: because
He is so mighty and so powerful, He is the most lovely being to look upon, and
the sweetest to smell; nor can His sweet savor or His almighty power or His
matchless beauty ever lessen or cease, for He never ceases, but lives forever in
honor, and his great might lasts forevermore.”

18.   (1) “Stop!” said Olibrius, “These words are worth nothing. (2) But know one
thing: unless you cease them, my sword will destroy and devour your flesh, and
thereafter your bones shall be burned up on burning coals. (3) But if you will
believe me, you will be my beloved and my wedded wife, and as a lady rule over
all that I keep in possession and am lord over.”

19.   (1) “I believe,” said she, “that you are good for your promise. (2) But keep it
and your love, for I have a dearer one that I will not lose or leave for any other.
(3) You trouble yourself too much, and unfortunately waste your time, for it is all
one to me,” said she, “your flattery and your anger. (4) I will commit my body to
every cruelty that you can contrive, and may it bite never so sorely provided that
I may as a maiden have my reward in Heaven. (5) The Ruler died for us, the dear
Lord, and I am not afraid to endure death for Him. (6) He has sealed His mark
upon me with His seal, and neither life nor death can divide us in two.”

fol. 21v
20.
(1) "Na?" quoth he, "Is hit swa? | (2) Neometh hire swithe," quoth he to his cwel-leres. (3) "Strupeth hire steort-naket ant hongeth hire on heh up, ant beteth hire bere bodi with bittere besmen." (4) Tha awariede werlahen leiden se lutherliche on hire leofliche lich thet hit brec overal ant litherede o blode. (5) Thet eadie meiden ahef hire heorte heh up towart heovene ant cleopede to Criste:

21.
(1) "Lauerd, in The is al min hope. (2) Hald me mi wit wel swa, ant mi wil, to The, thet hit ne forwurthe naut for wa thet me do me ne for wele nowther. (3) Ne lef Thu never mine fan — the feondes, I mene — habben ne holden hare hoker of me, as ha walden yef ha me mahten awarpen; ah swa ne schulen ha never me ne nan other thet ariht luvieth The. (4) Heovenliche Lauerd, Thin nome beo iblescet. (5) Lauerd, loke to me ant have merci of me; softe me mi sar swa ant salve mine wunden thet hit ne seme nohwer ne suteli o mi samblant thet Ich derf drehe." (6) The cwelleres leiden se lutherliche on hire lich thet tet blod bearst ut ant strac adun of hire bodi as streem deth of welle.

22.
(1) Olibrius the luthere, reve bute rewthe, hwil me yerdede hire thus yeomerliche, yeide: "Stute nu ant stew thine unwitti wordes, ant hercne, meiden, mi read, ant wel the schal iwurthen."

fol. 22r
23.
(1) Alle the thear weren, wepmen ant wum|men, remden of reowthe ant meanden thes meiden, ant summe of ham seiden: "Margarete, Margarete, meide swa muche wurth yef thu wel waldest, wa is us thet we seoth thi softe leofliche lich toluken se ladliche! (2) Weila, wummon, hwuch wlite thu leosest ant forletest for thi misbileave! (3) The reve is reowliche wrath, ant wule iwis fordo the. (4) Ah luve

---

20.
(1) "No?" said he. "Is it so? (2) Seize her at once!" said he to his executioners. (3) "Strip her stark-naked and hang her high up, and beat her bare body with cruel rods." (4) Then the accursed scoundrels laid so miserably on her lovely body that it burst forth overall and was lathered in blood. (5) That blessed maiden heaved her heart up high toward Heaven and cried out to Christ:

21.
(1) "Lord, in You is all my hope. (2) Protect well my wit, and my will also, to You, so that it may not become enfeebled in any way for woe that anyone does to me, nor for weal either. (3) Never allow my foes — the fiends, I mean — to have or hold me in contempt, as they would if they could cast me down; but this they will never do to me or to anyone else who loves You rightly. (4) Heavenly Lord, may Your name be blessed. (5) Lord, look to me and have mercy on me, soften for me my wound and also salve my wounds so that it may neither seem anywhere upon my face that I endure pain." (6) The executioners laid so miserably upon her lovely body that the blood burst out and flowed down her body as a stream does from a spring.

22.
(1) Olibrius the wretched, the ruler without mercy, while she was beaten cruelly, called out: "Stop now and stay your unwise words and listen, maiden, to my advice, and it shall go well for you."

23.
(1) All who were there, men and women, cried out for pity and lamented this maiden, and some of them said: "Margaret, Margaret, maid worth so much if you wished for it well, it is woeful for us that we see your soft lovely body torn so horribly! (2) Alas, woman, what a loveliness you lose and give up for your misbelief! (3) The governor is cruelly angry, and will certainly destroy you. (4) But love him

nu ant lef him ant tu schalt, wummone meast, wunne ant weole wealden."

24.   (1) "O," quoth ha, "wrecches, unweoten bute wit! (2) Weila, hwet wene ye? (3) Yef mi lich is toloken, mi sawle schal resten with the rihtwise. (4) Sorhe ant licomes sar is sawulene heale. (5) Ah leve ye, Ich reade ow, o the liviende Godd, mihti ant meinful ant euch godes ful, the hereth theo the Him cleopieth to, ant heovene-getes openeth! (6) For ow nulle Ich iheren, ne heien nan of ower godes, the dumbe beoth ant deave, ant blinde ant bute mihte, with monnes hond imakede."

25.   (1) "Ah thu wurchest," quoth ha tha to Olibrium the luthere, "thine feader werkes, the feondes of Helle. (2) Me, thu heathene hund, the hehe Healent is min help. (3) Yef He haveth iyettet te mi licome to teluken, He wule, thu heatele reve, arudde mi sawle ut of thine honden ant heoven hire into Heovene, thah thu hongi me her. (4) Ant tu, grisliche gra, thu luthere liun lath Godd, thi mihte schal

fol. 22v   unmuclin ant melten to riht noht, ant tu schalt eaver i sar | ant i sorhe swelten, hwen Ich gomeni with Godd ant gleadie buten ende."

26.   (1) He o wraththe warth forneh ut of his witte, ant het swithe bitterliche hongin hire ant heoven up herre then ha ear wes, ant with sweord scharpe ant ewles of irne hire freoliche flesch toronden ant torenden. (2) Ant heo biseh on heh up, ant bigon to seggen:

27.   (1) "Helle-hundes, Lauerd, habbet bitrummet me, ant hare read thet heaneth me haveth al biset me. (2) Ah Thu, hehe Healent, beo umbe me to helpen.

---

and believe him now, greatest woman, and you will rule over joy and wealth."

24.   (1) "Oh," said she, "wretches, fools without wit! (2) Alas, what are you thinking? (3) If my body is torn apart, my soul shall rest with the righteous. (4) Pain and suffering of the body is the soul's salvation. (5) But believe, I advise you, in the living God, mighty and powerful and full of everything that is good, who hears those that call to Him, and the Heaven-gates will open! (6) For I will not listen to you, nor worship any of your gods who are deaf and dumb, and blind and without power, made by the hand of a human.

25.   (1) "But you," said she then to Olibrius the wicked, "work the deeds of your father, the fiends of Hell. (2) But, you heathen hound, the high Savior is my help. (3) If He has granted that my body be torn apart, He will, you hateful governor, deliver my soul out of your hands and lift it into heaven, though you hang me here. (4) And you, disgusting devil, wicked lion hateful to God, your power will diminish and melt to nothing, and you will forever swelter in pain and in sorrow, while I rejoice with God and be glad forever."

26.   (1) He went almost out of his mind from anger and immediately ordered her cruelly hung up and raised higher than she was before, and her comely flesh cut up and torn in pieces with sharp swords and awls of iron. (2) And she looked up on high, and began to say:

27.   (1) "Hell-hounds, Lord, have surrounded me, and the gathering of those who afflict me has completely beset me. (2) But You, high Savior, be close to help me.

(3) Arude, reowfule Godd, mi sawle of sweordes egge ant of hundes hond, for nabbe Ich bute hire ane. (4) Lowse me, Lauerd, ut of the liunes muth, ant mi meoke mildschipe of the an-ihurnde hornes. (5) Glede me, Godd, with Thi gleo ant yef me hope of heale, thet mi bone mote thurh-thurli the Heovene. (6) Send me Thi sonde i culvrenene heowe, the cume me to helpe, thet Ich mi meithhad mote wite to The unwemmet. (7) Ant lef me yet iseon, Lauerd, yef Thi wil is, the awariede wiht the weorreth ayein me — ant cuth Thi mahte on me, almihti Godd, thet Ich him overcume mahe, swa thet alle meidnes eaver mare thurh me the mare trusten on The. (8) Beo Thi nome iblesced, alre bleo brihtest, in alre worldene worlt, áá on ecnesse. (9) Amen."

fol. 23r

28. (1) Hwil thet ha spec thus, me tolec hire swa thet te luthere | reve, for the strong rune of the blodi stream, ne nan other thet ter wes ne mahte for muche grure lokin thiderwardes; ah hudden hare heafden, the heardeste-iheortet, under hare mantles for thet seorfule sar thet heo on hire isehen. (2) Yet spec ant seide Olibrius the luthere: "Hwet bihalt, meiden, thet tu ne buest to me, ne nult habbe milce ne merci of the seolven? (3) Ye, ne felest tu thi flesch al tolimet ant toluken thurh thet Ich hit hate? (4) Ah buh nu ant bei to me ear then thu deie o dreori deth ant derf, for yef thu ne dest no, thu schalt swelten thurh sweord ant al beo limmel toloken. (5) Ant Ich wulle tellen, hwen thu al totoren art, in euchanes sihthe the sit nu ant sith the, alle thine seonewwen."

---

(3) Deliver, merciful God, my soul from the sword's edge and from the hound's grasp, for I have only it. (4) Loose me, Lord, from the lion's mouth, and my meek mildness from the unicorn's horn. (5) Gladden me God, with your bliss, and give me hope of salvation, so that my prayer might pierce through to Heaven. (6) Send me your messenger in the shape of a dove, which comes to help me, so that I may preserve my virginity unblemished for You. (7) And allow me still to see, Lord, if it is Your will, the accursed being which makes war against me — and show your power in me, almighty God, so that I may overcome him so that all maidens forever more may, through me, trust in You the more. (8) May Your name be blessed, brightest face of all, world in all worlds, forever into eternity. (9) Amen."

28. (1) While she spoke thus, she was torn apart to the extent that, because of the strong running of the bloody stream, neither the wicked governor nor anyone else who was there could look at her, because of the great horror; but hid their heads, the hardest-hearted, under their mantles because of that terrible pain that they saw her in. (2) Yet Olibrius the wicked spoke and said: "What do you see, maiden, that you will not bow to me, nor will have pity or mercy on yourself? (3) Yea, do you not feel your flesh completely dismembered and torn apart since I ordered it? (4) But bow now and submit to me before you die in dreary and painful death, for if you do nothing, you will suffer by the sword and be completely dismembered limb from limb. (5) And I will count, when you are all torn apart, in the sight of everyone who sits now and sees you, all your sinews."

29.   (1) "Me, heateliche hund," quoth ha tha, "thah thu al swa do, me schendest tu nawt. (2) Hwen mi sawle bith bivoren Godes sihthe in Heovene, lutel me is hwat me do mid mi bodi on eorthe. (3) Ah the schulde scheomien, thu scheomelese schucke (yef thu scheome cuthest) the thulli mot haldest with a yung meiden, ant spillest al thi hwile ant ne spedest nawiht. (4) For yef Ich wrahte the wil of the flesch thet tu fearest as thu wult with, mi sawle schulde sinken, alswa as thu schalt,

fol. 23v   to sorhen in helle. (5) Ah for|thi Ich wulle wel thet mi flesch forfeare her, thet softe Jesu cruni mi sawle i the selhthen of Heovene, ant efter Domesdei do ham ba togederes, to weolen ant to eche wunnen thurh-wuniende." (6) He warth se wrath thet forneh wod he walde iwurthen. (7) Bed, bi lives coste, keasten hire i cwalmhus, ant swa me dude sone. (8) Ant wes as thah hit were the seovethe time of the dei thet me droh hire thus into dorkest wan, ant wurst in to cumene. (9) Ant heo hef up hire hond ant blecede al hire bodi with the taken of the Hali Rode. (10) As me reat hire inwart, ha bigon to bidden theos bone to ure Lauerd:

30.   (1) "Deorewurthe Drihtin, thah Thine domes dearne beon, alle ha beoth duhtie thah. (2) Alle heovenliche thing, ant heorthliche bathe, buheth The ant beieth. (3) Thu art hope ant help to alle thet Te herieth. (4) Thu art foster ant feader to helplese children. (5) Thu art weddede weole, ant widewene warant, ant meidenes mede. (6) Thu art wunne of the world, Jesu Crist, Kine-bern, Godd iknnet of Godd, as liht is of leome. (7) Loke, Lauerd, to me, mi lif, mi luve, mi leofmon, ant milce me, Thi meiden. (8) Min ahne flesliche feader dude ant draf

---

29.   (1) "But, hateful hound," said she then, "when you do all this, you shame me not at all. (2) When my soul is before God's sight in Heaven, it matters little to me what anyone does with my body on earth. (3) But you should be ashamed, you shameless devil (if you could understand shame) that you hold such a debate with a young maiden, and waste all your time, and succeed at nothing. (4) For if I worked the will of the body, which you will do what you want with, my soul would sink, as yours will, to pains in hell. (5) But because of this I desire well that my flesh perish here, so that sweet Jesus may crown my soul in the joys of Heaven, and after Doomsday will reunite them together, to prosperity and to every joy everlasting." (6) He became so angry that he nearly went mad. (7) He ordered his executioners, on the pain of death, to cast her in prison, and so it was done immediately. (8) It was then at about the seventh hour of the day that she was dragged like this into the darkest dwelling, and the worst one could enter. (9) And she lifted up her hand and blessed her whole body with the sign of the Holy Cross. (10) As she was drawn inward, she began to make this prayer to our Lord:

30.   (1) "Dear Lord, although Your judgments are hidden, nevertheless they are all worthy. (2) All heavenly things and all earthly things bow to and obey You. (3) You are the hope and help to all who glorify You. (4) You are the foster-parent and father to helpless children. (5) You are joy to the wedded, and protector of widows, and maidens' reward. (6) You are the joy of the world, Jesus Christ, royal Prince, God born of God, as light from a flame. (7) Watch over me, Lord, to me, my life, my love, my beloved, and pity me, Your maiden. (8) My own fleshly father sent and drove

me awei, his anlepi dohter, ant mine freond aren me for Thi luve, Lauerd, famen ant feondes. (9) Ah The Ich halde, Healent, ba for feader ant for freond. (10) Ne forlet

fol. 24r Tu me nawt, | liviende Lauerd. (11) Bihald me ant help me, ant lef me thet Ich mote legge mine ehnen o the luthre unwiht the weorreth ayein me, ant lef me deme with him, Drihtin of dome. (12) He heaneth me ant heateth, ant Ich neaver nuste thet he ewt of min hearm eaveryete hefde. (13) Ah swuch is his cunde, ant swa is ful of atter his ontfule heorte, thet he heateth euch god, ant euch hali thing ant halewinde is him lath. (14) Thu art, Drihtin, Domesmon of cwike ant of deade. (15) Dem bituhen unc twa, ne wraththe Thu The, mi wunne, for sahe thet Ich segge. (16) For an thing I bische The eaver ant overal: thet Tu wite to The mi meithhad unmerret, mi sawle from sunne, mi wit ant mi wisdom from unwitlese wiht. (17) In The is, min Healent, al thet Ich wilni. (18) Beo Thu áá iblescet, Ordfrume ant Ende, bute ende ant ord, áá on ecnesse."

31.   (1) Hire vostermoder wes an thet frovredee hire, ant com to the cwalmhus ant brohte hire to fode bred ant burnes drunch thet ha bi livede. (2) Heo tha ant monie ma biheolden thurh an eilthurl as ha bed hire beoden. (3) Ant com ut of an hurne hihendliche towart hire an unwiht of helle on ane drakes liche, se grislich thet ham gras with thet sehen thet unselhthe glistinde as thah he al overguld were. (4) His lockes ant his longe berd blikeden al of golde, ant his grisliche teth semden of swart

fol. 24v irn. (5) His twa ehnen | steareden steappre then the steoren ant ten gimstanes, brade ase bascins in his ihurnde heaved on either half on his heh hokede nease. (6) Of his

---

me away, his only daughter, and my friends, because of Your love, Lord, are foes and fiends. (9) But I hold You, Savior, both as father and friend. (10) Do not forsake me, living Lord. (11) Watch over me and help me, and give me leave that I might lay my eyes on the loathsome fiend who wages war against me, and give me leave to argue with him, God of judgment. (12) He afflicts me and hates me, and I never knew that he had any harm from me at any time before this. (13) But such is his nature, and his envious heart is so full of poison, that he hates every good thing, and every holy and sacred thing is loathsome to him. (14) You are, Ruler, Judge of the living and the dead. (15) Judge between us two, but do not become angry, my joy, for the words that I speak. (16) For one thing I beseech you forever and over all else: that You keep to Yourself my virginity unmarred, my soul from sin, my wit and my wisdom from the witless creature. (17) In You, my Savior, is all that I wish for. (18) May You be forever blessed, beginning and end, without end and beginning, forever in eternity."

31.   (1) Her foster-mother was one of those who comforted her, and came to the prison and brought her bread for food and drink from the spring by which she lived. (2) She and many more beheld her through a window as she made her prayers. (3) And there came quickly out of a corner toward her a demon of hell like a dragon, so frightening that they were horrified when they saw that evil thing glistening as though he were all gilded over. (4) His locks and his long beard gleamed all with gold, and his grisly teeth seemed made of blackened iron. (5) His two eyes, broad as basins in his horned head on either side of his hooked nose, stared brighter than the stars and gemstones. (6) From his disgusting mouth

speatewile muth sperclede fur ut, ant of his nease-thurles threste smorthrinde smoke, smecche forcuthest. (7) Ant lahte ut his tunge, se long thet he swong hire abuten his swire, ant semde as thah a scharp sweord of his muth scheate, the glistnede ase gleam deth ant leitede al o leie. (8) Ant al warth thet stude ful of strong ant of stearc stench, ant of thes schucke schadewe schimmede ant schan al. (9) He strahte him ant sturede toward tis meoke meiden, ant geapede with his ge-now upon hire ungeinliche, ant bigon to crahien ant crenge with swire, as the the hire walde forswolhe mid alle. (10) Yef ha agrisen wes of thet grisliche gra, nes na muche wunder. (11) Hire bleo bigon to blakien for the grure thet grap hire, ant for the fearlac offruht, foryet hire bone thet ha ibeden hefde, thet ha iseon moste then unsehene unwiht, ne nawt ne thohte thron thet hire nu were ituthet hire bone, ah smat smeortliche adun hire cneon to ther eorthe, ant hef hire honden up hehe toward Heovene, ant with theos bone to Crist thus cleopede:

32. (1) "Unseheliche Godd, euch godes ful, hwas wreaththe is se gromful thet helle

fol. 25r ware ant heovenes, | ant alle cwike thinges cwakieth therayeines — ayein this eisfule wiht thet hit ne eili me nawt, help me, mi Lauerd. (2) Thu wrahtest ant wealdest alle worldliche thing. (3) Theo thet Te heieth ant herieth in Heovene ant alle the thinges the eardith on eorthe — the fisches the i the flodes fleoteth with finnes, the flihinde fuheles the fleoth bi the lufte, ant al thet iwraht is, — wurcheth thet Ti wil is ant halt Thine heastes, bute mon ane. (4) The sunne reccheth hire rune withuten euch reste; the mone ant te steorren the walketh bi the lufte ne stutteth ne ne studegith,

---

fire sparkled out, and from his nostrils smoldering smoke pressed out, most hateful of stinks. (7) And he darted out his tongue, so long that he flung it about his neck, and it seemed as though a sharp sword, which glistened like a beam of light does and burned all in flame, shot out of his mouth. (8) And everything in that place was full of a strong and a foul stench, and everything shimmered and shone from the reflection of this demon. (9) He moved and made his way toward this meek maiden, and gaped with his mouth over her threateningly, and began to stretch and arch his neck, as though he would swallow her completely. (10) If she was frightened of that fearsome fiend, it was not a great wonder. (11) Her face began to grow pale because of the horror that gripped her, and frightened because of the terror, she forgot her prayer that she had made that she might see that unseen devil, nor did she think about the fact that her prayer was now granted to her, but she fell hard on her knees down to the earth, and lifted her hands up high toward Heaven, and with this prayer to Christ cried out thus:

32. (1) "Invisible God, full of every goodness, whose wrath is so fierce that the inhabitants of hell and heaven, and all living things tremble before it — help me, my Lord, against this terrible creature, so that it does not harm me. (2) You created and rule over every worldly thing. (3) Those that honor and glorify You in Heaven, and all things which dwell on earth — the fish that swim with fins in the flood, the flying fowls that fly in the air, and all that is created — do that which is Your will and uphold your orders, except for humankind. (4) The sun proceeds on course without any rest; the moon and the stars which move through the firmament neither stay nor stop, but stir evermore, nor do they ever

ah sturieth áá mare, ne nohwider of the wei thet Tu havest iwraht ham ne wrencheth ha neavre. (5) Thu steorest the sea-strem, thet hit flede ne mot fir then Thu merkest. (6) The windes, the wederes, the wudes ant te weattres buheth The ant beith. (7) Feondes habbeth fearlac, ant engles, of Thin eie. (8) The wurmes ant te wilde deor thet o this wald wunieth libbet efter the lahe thet Tu ham havest iloket, luvewende Lauerd. (9) Ant Tu loke to me ant help me, Thin hondiwerc, for al min hope is o The. (10) Thu herhedest Helle ant overcome ase kempe the acursede gast the fundeth to fordo me. (11) Ah her me nu ant help me, for nabbe Ich i min nowcin nanes cunnes elne bute Thin ane. (12) With this uvel wite me, for Ich truste al o The, ant Ti wil iwurthe hit, deorwurthe Lauerd, thet Ich thurh Thi strengthe mahe stonden with him, ant his muchele overgart thet Ich hit mote

fol. 25v afeallen. (13) Low, he fundeth swithe | me to forswolhen, ant weneth to beore me into his balefule hole ther he wuneth inne. (14) Ah o Thin blisfule nome Ich blesci me nuthe." (15) Ant droh tha endelong hire, ant thwertover threfter, the deorewurthe taken of the deore Rode thet He on reste. (16) Ant te drake reasde to hire mid tet ilke, ant sette his sariliche muth, ant unmeathlich muchel, on heh on hire heaved, ant rahte ut his tunge to the ile of hire helen ant swengde hire in ant forswelh into his wide wombe — ah Criste to wurthmund ant him to wrather heale. (17) For the Rode-taken redliche arudde hire thet ha wes with iwepnet, ant warth his bone sone, swa thet his bodi tobearst omidhepes otwa. (18) Ant thet eadi meiden allunge unmerret, withuten eaver-euch wem, wende ut of his wombe, heriende on heh hire Healent in Heovene.

---

turn aside anywhere from the way that You have made for them. (5) You stir the sea-stream, so that it may not flow further than You have designed. (6) The winds, the weathers, the woods, and the waters bow to You and obey. (7) Fiends and angels are in fear of your anger. (8) The serpents and the wild beasts that dwell in the forest live after the laws that You have ordained for them, beloved Lord. (9) And may You watch over me and help me, Your handiwork, for all my hope is in You. (10) You harrowed Hell and overcame as a champion the accursed spirit that is trying to destroy me. (11) But hear me now and help me, for in my distress I have no strength of any kind except for You alone. (12) Guard me against this evil, for I trust all in You, and may it be Your will, dear Lord, that I through Your strength may stand against him, and that I may cast down his great arrogance. (13) Lo, he tries greatly to swallow me up, and thinks to bear me into his baleful pit in which he dwells. (14) But in Your blissful name I bless myself now." (15) And then she drew on herself downwards, and cross-wise thereafter, the beloved token of the dear Cross that He rested upon. (16) And the dragon rushed to her at that moment, and set his horrible mouth, immoderately great, on high above her head, and stretched out his tongue to the hard skin of her heels, and swung her in and swallowed her up in his big belly — but to Christ's honor and destruction to him. (17) For the Rood-token that she was armed with speedily defended her and soon became his slayer, so that his body burst in two at the middle. (18) And that blessed maiden entirely unharmed, without any spot, came out of his belly, praising aloud her Savior in Heaven.

33. (1) As ha biheold, ant lokinde upon hire riht half, tha seh ha hwer set an unsehen unwiht, muche deale blackre then eaver eani blamon, se grislich, se ladlich, thet ne mahte hit na mon redliche areachen, ant his twa honden to his cnurnede cneon heteveste ibunden. (2) Ant heo, tha ha seh this, feng to thonkin thus ant herien hire Healent:

fol. 26r (1) |"Brihtest bleo of alle thet eaver weren iborene, blostme iblowen ant **34.** iboren of meidenes bosum, Jesu Godd, Godes bearn, iblescet ibeo Thu. (2) Ich am gomeful ant glead, Lauerd, for Thi godlec, Keiser of kinges, Drihtin undeadlich. (3) Thu haldest ant hevest up treowe bileave. (4) Thu art welle of wisdom, ant euch wunne waxeth ant awakeneth of The. (5) Thu art englene weole, thet wealdest ant witest ham withuten wonunge. (6) Me gomeneth ant gleadeth al of gasteliche murhthen. Me, mihti Godd makeles, is thet eani wunder? (7) Ye, iseo Ich, Lauerd, blowinde mine bileave. (8) Ich habbe isehen hu the feond the wende to fordo me tofeol efne atwa, ant felde hu his fule stench strac ant sturede aweiwart. (9) Ich habbe isehen the wurse of Helle her awarpen ant te monslahe islein, the stronge thurs astorven. (10) Ich habbe isehen his overgart ant his egede orhel ferliche avellet. (11) Ich habbe isehe the Rode the arudde me se redliche of his reowliche rake, hu ha thet balefule wurm ant thet bittre beast makede to bersten. (12) Ich habbe isehen hali ant halwende eoli as hit lihte to me, ant Ich me seolf smelle of The, swote Jesu, swottre then eaver eani thing thet is on eorthe. (13) Ich habbe isehen blisse ant Ich blissi me throf. (14) I weole ant i wunne is nu thet Ich wunie, ne nes me neaver se wa as me is wel nu. (15) The Ich hit thoncki,

---

33. (1) As she watched, and looking upon her right side, then she saw that there sat a strange fiend, a good deal blacker than ever any black person, so grisly, so loathsome, that no one could readily recount it, and his two hands firmly bound to his gnarled knees. (2) And she, when she saw this, began to thank and praise her Savior thus:

34. (1) "Brightest face of all that ever was born, blossom bloomed and borne from the maiden's breast, Jesus God, God's child, blessed be You. (2) I am joyful and glad, Lord, for your goodness, Emperor of kings, immortal Ruler. (3) You guard and lift up true belief. (4) You are the well of wisdom, and every joy wakes and awakens from You. (5) You are the joy of angels, who rules over and protects them without ceasing. (6) I rejoice and am glad all because of ghostly mirth. But, mighty matchless God, is that any wonder? (7) Yea, I see, Lord, my belief blossoming. (8) I have seen how the fiend, who came to destroy me, fell apart exactly in two, and I felt how his foul stench flowed and moved away. (9) I have seen here the devil of Hell cast down and the man-slayer slain, the strong demon destroyed. (10) I have seen his arrogance and his foolish pride terribly laid low. (11) I have seen the Cross which defended me so readily from his cruel jaws, and how it made that baleful worm and that bitter beast burst. (12) I have seen holy and healing oil as it descended to me, and I myself smell of You, sweet Jesus, sweeter than ever any thing that is on earth. (13) I have seen bliss and therefore I make myself blissful. (14) In wealth and in joy is now that place where I dwell, and it was never so woeful for me as it is now well for me. (15) I thank You for it,

fol. 26v tholemode Lauerd. (16) Ich habbe adun | the drake idust ant his kenschipe akest, ant he swelteth thet me wende to forswolhen. (17) Ich am kempe ant he is cravant ant overcumen. (18) Ah The Ich thonki throf, the kingene King art, echeliche icrunet, sorhfule ant sari ant sunfule toturn, wondrinde ant wrecches ant wonlese wisent, castel of strengthe ayein the stronge unwiht, meidenes murhthe ant martyrs crune, mel-seotel softest ant guldene yerde, alre gold smeatest ant glistinde gimstan, of alle seheliche thing ant unseheliche ba swotest ant swetest, alre schefte Schuppent, thrumnesse threovald ant anvald the-hwethere, thrile i threo hades ant an in an hehschipe, heh hali Godd, euch godes ful, beo Thu eaver ant áá iheret ant iheiet bute linnunge."

35. (1) As ha hefde iheret thus longe ure Lauerd, com thet grisliche gra creopinde hire towart, ant heold hire bi the vet, ant ase sorhfulest thing sariliche seide: "Marherete, meiden, inoh thu havest ido me. (2) Ne pine thu me na mare with the eadie beoden thet tu biddest se ofte, for ha bindeth me swithe sare mid alle, ant makieth me se unstrong thet Ich ne fele with me nanes cunnes strengthe. (3) Thu havest grimliche ibroht mi brother to grunde ant islein then sleheste deovel of

fol. 27r Helle, the Ich o drake liche sende to forswolhe the ant merren | with his muchele mein the mihte of thi meithhad, ant makien thet tu nere na mare imong moncun imuneget on eorthe. (4) Thu cwenctest ant acwaldest him with the hali Rode, ant me thu makest to steorven with the strengthe of thine beoden, the beoth the se munde. (5) Ah leaf me ant let me gan, leafdi, Ich the bidde." (6) Thet milde meiden

---

long-suffering Lord. (16) I have dashed down the dragon and cast down his fierceness, and he who thought to swallow me suffers. (17) I am the champion and he is defeated and overcome. (18) But I thank You for that, who are King of kings, crowned eternally, a refuge for the sorrowful and the sorry and the sinful, a guide for the wandering and the wretched and the hopeless, a castle of strength against the powerful demon, maidens' mirth and martyrs' crown, softest seat at the feast and golden scepter, purest of all gold and glistening gemstone, of all things both seen and unseen the sweetest and most fragrant, the Creator of all creatures, threefold Trinity and nevertheless one, threefold in three persons and one on high, high holy God, full of every goodness, may You forever and ever be praised and worshiped without end."

35. (1) While she had long praised our Lord in this way, that fearsome fiend came creeping toward her, and held her by the foot, and like the most sorrowful thing sadly said: "Margaret, maiden, you have done enough to me. (2) Do not trouble yourself anymore with the blessed prayers that you make so often, for they bind me all up very painfully, and make me so weak that I do not feel any kind of strength in me. (3) You have grimly brought my brother to ground and have slain then the slyest devil of Hell, whom I sent in a dragon's shape to swallow you and mar with his great might the strength of your maidenhood, and make it so that you would never more be remembered among humankind on earth. (4) You killed and destroyed him with the holy Cross, and you are destroying me with the strength of your prayers, which are so present in your mind. (5) But leave me and let me go, lady, I pray you." (6) That mild maiden Margaret gripped that grisly

Margarete grap thet grisliche thing, thet hire ne agras nawiht, ant heteveste toc him bi thet eateliche top ant hef him up ant duste him dunriht to ther eorthe, ant sette hire riht fot on his ruhe swire ant feng on thus to speokene:

36. (1) "Stute nu, earme steorve, ant swic nuthe lanhure, swikele swarte deovel, thet tu ne derve me nawt mare for mi meithhad. (2) Ne helpeth the nawiht, for Ich habbe to help min Healent in Heovene, ant te worldes Wealdent is ihwer mi warant. (3) Thah thu strong were tha thu weorredest me, He wes muchele strengre the hefde to biwite me." (4) With this, tha thudde ha o the thurs feste with hire fot with euchan of theose word: "Stute nu, uvele gast, to gremie me mare. (5) Stute nu, alde monslahe, thet tu ne slea heonnevorth Cristes icorene. (6) Stute nu, wleatewile wiht, to astenche me with the stench the of thi muth stiheth. (7) Ich am mi Lauerdes lomb, ant He is min Hirde. (8) Ich am Godes theowe ant His threl to don al thet His deore wil | is. (9) Beo He áá iblescet thet blithe haveth imaked me in endelese blissen."

fol. 27v

37. (1) Hwil thet ha spec thus o thet speatewile wiht, se ther lihtinde com into the cwalmhus a leome from Heovene, ant semde as thah ha sehe i the glistende glem the deorewurthe Rode reache to the heovene. (2) Ant set a culvre thron ant thus to hire cleopede: "Meiden eadi an, Margarete, art tu, for Paraise yeten aren yarowe iopenet te nu." (3) Ant heo leat lahe to hire leove Lauerd, ant thonkede Him yeorne with inwarde heorte.

38. (1) Thet liht alei lutlen, ant heo biturde hire tha ant cweth to thet unwiht: "Cuth me," quoth ha, "swithe, forcuthest alre thinge, of hweat cunde thu beo."

---

thing, which did not terrify her in any way, and grabbed him cruelly, took him by that hideous hair on his head, and heaved him up and flung him straight down to the earth, and set her right foot on his shaggy neck and began to speak to him thus:

36. (1) "Stop now, wretched pestilence, and cease now at least, deceitful black devil, so that you do not bother me any more because of my maidenhead. (2) It does not help you in any way, since I have as my help the Savior in Heaven, and the world's Ruler is everywhere my protector. (3) Although you were strong when you warred against me, He who protected me was much stronger." (4) With this, then she stamped hard on the demon with her foot with each of these words: "Cease now, evil spirit, to anger me more. (5) Cease now, old manslayer, that you slay not henceforth Christ's chosen. (6) Cease now, disgusting creature, assailing me with the stench that arises from your mouth. (7) I am my Lord's lamb, and He is my Shepherd. (8) I am God's servant and his thrall to do all that is His dear will. (9) May He be forever blessed who has made me happy in endless bliss."

37. (1) While she spoke thus to that disgusting creature, so there came into the prison a light descending from Heaven, and it seemed as though she saw in the glistening gleam the beloved Cross reach to the heavens. (2) And a dove sat thereon and called out to her thus: "You are a blessed maiden, Margaret, for the gates of Heaven are now opened ready for you." (3) And she bowed low to her beloved Lord, and thanked him earnestly in her innermost heart.

38. (1) That light faded gradually, and she turned around then and said to that demon: "Show me," said she, "quickly, most loathsome of all things, what your nature is."

39. (1) "Leafdi," quoth he, "leowse thi fot thenne of mi necke ant swa lanhure leothe me, meiden an eadiest, thet Ich ethie mahe; ant Ich mot nede (notheles min unwilles hit is) don thet ti wil is."

40. (1) The milde meiden dude swa — lowsede ant leothede a lutel hire hele — ant he bigon to breoken on speatewilliche thus to speokene: "Wult tu witen, lufsume leafdi, hu Ich hatte? (2) Ah hwet se of mi nome beo, Ich habbe efter Belzebub meast monnes bone ibeon, ant forswolhen hare swinc, ant to aswinden

fol. 28r imaket the meden thet ha moni yer hefden ham iyarket with sum of mi|ne wiheles, thet Ich wrencte ham adun hwen ha lest wenden. (3) Ne neaver yet ne mahte me overcume na mon bute thu nuthe. (4) Thu haldest me i bondes, ant havest her iblend me, ant art mi brotheres bone, Rufines the rehest ant te readwisest of alle theo in Helle. (5) Crist wuneth in the, forthi thu wurchest with us al thet ti wil is. (6) Ne nawt nart tu, wummon, othre wummen ilich. (7) Me thuncheth thet tu schinest schenre then the sunne, ah over alle thine limen the leitith of leome, the fingres se freoliche (me thuncheth), ant se freoliche feire, ant se briht blikinde, thet tu the with blescedest ant makedest te merke of the mihti Rode the reavede me mi brother, ant me with bale bondes bitterliche bindest, thet Ich lokin ne mei, swa thet liht leometh ant leiteth, me thuncheth."

41. (1) "Thu fikest," quoth ha, "ful wiht! Ah cuth me thet Ich easki."

42. (1) "Wumme, leafdi!" quoth he tha. (2) "Wa me mine lives, bute Ich hit am thet weorri áá with rihtwise. (3) Of the unseli sunfule me thuncheth Ich am al

---

39. (1) "Lady," said he, "loosen your foot then from my neck and so at least release me, maiden most blessed, that I might breathe; and though it is against my wishes, I must needs do what your will is."

40. (1) The mild maiden did so — loosed and released her heel a little — and he began to burst forth horribly to speak in this way: "Do you wish to know, lovely lady, what I am called? (2) But whatever my name may be, I have after Beelzebub been the slayer of the most men, and devoured their labor, and I made perish with some of my wiles the rewards which they had for many years prepared for themselves, from which I wrenched them aside when they least expected. (3) And never yet could anyone overcome me except for you now. (4) You hold me in bonds, and have here blinded me, and are the slayer of my brother, Ruffin, the boldest and wisest of counsel of all those in Hell. (5) Christ dwells in you, so that you work against us everything that is your will. (6) You are not anything, woman, like other women. (7) It seems to me that you shine brighter than the sun, but over all your limbs that the light blazes upon, the fingers are so fine, it seems, and so beautifully fair, and shining so bright, with which you crossed yourself and which made the mark of the mighty Cross which tore my brother from me, and you have bound me bitterly with cruel bonds, that I may not look, since the light gleams so and shines, I think."

41. (1) "You flatter," said she, "demon! But tell me what I ask."

42. (1) "Woe is me, lady!" said he then. (2) "Woe betide my life for I am he who wars always against the righteous. (3) Of the miserably sinful I think that I am

siker; ah the gode Ich ga áá bisiliche abuten, ant ham Ich folhi neodelukest, the cunnith to beon cleane withuten monnes man ant fleoth flesches fulthen, yef Ich mahte eanies weis makien ham to fallen ant fulen hamseolven.

fol. 28v

43.

(1) "Monie Ich habbe awarpen the wenden mine wi|heles ful witerliche etwrenchen, ant o thisse wise: Ich leote otherhwiles a cleane mon wunien neh a cleane wummon, thet Ich nawhit towart ham ne warpe ne ne weorri, ah leote ham al iwurthen. (2) Ich leote ham talkin of Godd ant tevelin of godlec, ant trewliche luvien ham withuten uvel wilnunge ant alle unwreste willes, thet either of his ahne, ant of the othres ba, treowliche beo trusti, ant te sikerure beon to sitten bi hamseolven ant gominen togederes. (3) Thenne thurh this sikerlec seche Ich earst upon ham, ant scheote swithe dearnliche ant wundi, ear ha witen hit, with swithe attri healewi hare unwarre heorte. (4) Lihtliche on alre earest, with luveliche lates, with steape bihaldunge either on other, ant with plohe-speche sputte to mare, se longe thet ha toggith ant tollith togederes. (5) Thenne thudde Ich in ham luvefule thohtes, on earest hare unthonkes, ah swa waxeth thet wa, thurh thet ha hit theavieth, thet ham thuncheth god throf. (6) Ant Ich thus, hwen ha leoteth me, (ne ne letteth me nawt ne ne steorith hamseolf ne ne stondeth strongliche ayein) leade ham i the leiven ant i the ladliche lake of thet suti sunne. (7) Yef ha edstonden wulleth mine unwreste wrenches ant mine swikele swenges, wreastlin ha moten ant witherin with hamseolven, ne me akeasten ha ne mahen ear ha |

fol. 29r

hamseolven overcumen. (8) Lath me is ant notheles nedlunge Ich do hit — cuthe the hu ha mahen best overcume me. (9) Lowse me the hwile, leafdi, ant leothe me.

---

certain, but I go always busily about the good, and I follow most diligently those who try to be chaste without sexual intercourse with anyone and flee the filths of the flesh, if I might in any way make them fall and befoul themselves.

43.

(1) "Many have I cast down who thought to entirely escape my wiles, and in this way: I allow sometimes a chaste man to dwell near a chaste woman, whom I in no way either attack or war against, but leave them be entirely. (2) I let them talk of God and debate about goodness, and truly love each other without evil desire or any wicked wills, so each may be truly confident of his own feelings, and more secure to sit by themselves and rejoice together. (3) Then through this security I first make an attack upon them, and shoot so secretly and, before they know it, wound their unwary hearts with a very venomous drug. (4) Gently first of all, with loving looks, with amorous gazing from one to the other, I incite them on to more with playful speech, so long that they flirt and wrestle playfully together. (5) Then I thrust upon them lustful thoughts, at first against their will, but that evil grows so much, because they allow it, that to them it seems good. (6) And thus I, when they let me (and they neither hinder me in any way nor restrain themselves nor stand strongly against me) lead them into the bog and into the loathly lake of that foul sin. (7) If they will withstand my evil tricks and my deceitful strokes, they must wrestle and struggle with themselves, and they cannot overthrow me before they overcome themselves. (8) It is loathsome to me and nonetheless necessary that I do it — I make known to you how they may best overcome me. (9) Release me meanwhile, lady, and loose me.

44.　　　(1) "This beoth the wepnen thet me wurst wundith, ant witeth ham unwemmet ant strengeth ham sterclukest ayein me ant ayein hare wake lustes. (2) Thet beoth: eoten meokeliche ant meatheluker drinken, do thet flesh i sum derf, ne neaver ne beon idel, hali monne bone for ham, with hare ahne beodefule thohtes thet ha schulen thenchen bimong hare benen, ayein hare unwerste thohtes thet Ich in ham thudde, thenchen hit is thurh me thet hare lust leadeth ham to wurche to wundre, thenchen yef ha beieth me, to hu bitter beast ha buheth, ant hwas luve ha forleteth. (3) Hu lufsum thing ha leoseth, thet is, with meithhad meidenes menske, ant te luve of the luveliche Lauerd of Heovene ant of the lufsume cwen, englene leafdi. (4) Ant henlunges makieth ham with al thet heovenliche hird, ant unmenskith hamseolf bimong worldliche men, ant forleoseth the luve nawt ane of heh in Heovene ah of lah ec on eorthe, ant makieth the engles murne ant us of muche murhthe to lahhe se lude, the seoth ham lihte se lah of se swithe hehe, from the heste in Heovene to the laheste in Helle. (5) This ha moten ofte munien bi hamseolfen, |

fol. 29v　　　thenchen hu swart thing ant suti is thet sunne,

　　　thenchen of helle-wa ant of heoveriche wunne,

　　　hare ahne death ant Drihtenes munegin ful ilome,

　　　ant te grisle ant te grure thet bith et te dome.

(6) Thenchen thet te licunge of thet fleschliche lust alith se swithe sone, ant te pine thervore leasteth áá mare. (7) Ant sone se ha gulteth eawiht, gan anan vorthriht,

---

44.　　　(1) "These are the weapons that wound me the worst, and guard them unblemished and strengthen them most strongly against me and against their weak lusts. (2) They are: to eat meekly and drink more meekly, to put the flesh in some pain, and never be idle, for holy men to pray for them, with their own spiritual thoughts that they should think during their prayers against their evil thoughts which I thrust upon them, to think it is through me that their lust leads them shamefully, to think that if they obey me, to how bitter a beast they bow, and whose love they give up. (3) How lovely a thing they lose, that is, with maidenhood the strength of maidens, and the love of the lovely Lord of Heaven and of the beloved queen, the lady of angels. (4) And they make themselves vile before that whole heavenly host, and dishonor themselves among worldly men, and lose altogether not only the love of the high in Heaven, but also of the low on earth, and they make the angels mourn and us laugh so loudly from much mirth, we who see them descend so low from so very high, from the highest in Heaven to the lowest in Hell. (5) This they should often call to mind by themselves,

　　　To think of how black and filthy a thing is that sin,

　　　To think of hell-woe and of heavenly joys,

　　　To call to mind very often their own death and the Ruler's very often,

　　　And the horror and the terror that will be at Judgment Day.

(6) To think that the pleasure of that fleshly lust dies so very soon, and the pain that results lasts forevermore. (7) And as soon as they sin in any way, they ought to

thet ha ne firstin hit nawt, to schawen hit i schrifte, ne beo hit ne se lutel ne se liht sunne. (8) For thet is under sunne thinge me lathest, thet me ofte eorne to schrift of his sunne. (9) For thet lutle Ich mei makien to muchelin unmeathliche yef me hut ant heleth hit; ah sone se hit ischawet bith birewsinde i schrifte, thenne scheometh me therwith, ant fleo ham from schuderinde as Ich ischend were. (10) Thah se feor ant se forth ha mahen beon istopen in sotliche to luvien thet nanes weis ne schulen ha stewen hare heorten, ne etstutten ne etstonden the strengthe of mine swenges hwil thet ha somet beoth. (11) Ne nis thear na bote bute fleo thenne, thet nowther ne beo nohwer ane with other, ne seon ham ne sompnin ne sitten togederes withuten wittnesse thet mahe iseon hweat ha don ant heren hwet ha seggen. (12) Yef

fol. 30r   ha thus ne letteth me | ah theavieth me ant tholieth, ant weneth thah to edwrenchen, Ich leade ham with leas luve lutlen ant lutlen into se deop dunge thet ha druncnith therin; ant sperki in ham sperken of lustes se luthere thet ha forberneth inwith ant thurh thet brune ablindeth, thet ha nabbeth sihthe hamseolve to biseonne. (13) Thet mein of hare heorte mealteth thurh the heate, ant forwur-theth hare wit ant woreth hare wisdom, swa thet nulleth ha nawt wite thet ha ahten to witen wel. (14) Loke nu hwuch wunder: ha beoth se cleane overcumen, ant swa Ich habbe iblent ham, thet ha blindlunge gath forth ant forseoth Godd ant ham-seolven foryeoteth, swa thet ha lutherliche, hwen ha lest weneth, ferliche falleth fule ant fenniliche i flescliche fulthen, ant for a lust thet alith in an hondhwile, leoseth ba the luve of Godd ant te worldes wurthschipe. (15) Ah theo the stealewurthe beoth

---

go straightaway at once to reveal it in confession so that they do not delay it at all, be it never so little nor so light a sin. (8) For that is the most hateful thing to me under the sun: when someone yearns to confess his sin frequently. (9) For that little sin I may cause to increase immoderately if one hides and conceals it; but as soon as it is shown in repentance in confession, then they shame me with that, and I flee from them shuddering as if I were destroyed. (10) However they may be so far and so fully advanced to love foolishly that in no way shall they restrain their hearts, nor withstand or resist the strength of my tricks while they are together. (11) Nor is there any remedy but flight then, so that neither should be anywhere with the other, nor should they see each other nor meet together nor sit together without a third party who may see what they do and hear what they say. (12) If thus they do not hinder me but tolerate and allow me and think then to withstand me, I lead them with false love little by little into the deep dung so that they drown therein; and kindle in them sparks of lust so wicked that they burn up inside and through that burning go blind, so that they do not have the sight to see themselves. (13) That power of their hearts melts in the heat, and their wit grows weak and wars against their wisdom, so that they do not wish to know in any way that they ought to guard themselves well. (14) Look now what a wonder it is: they are so completely overcome, and I have blinded them so, that they blindly go forth and forsake God and forget themselves, so that they wretchedly, when they least expect, fall terribly and foully in fleshly filth, and for a desire that dies in an instant, lose both the love of God and the world's worship. (15) But those that are

ant sterke toyein me, swa thet ha ham with me wecchinde werien, se uvel me thuncheth throf thet al Ich am dreori athet ha beon thurh me sumdel idervet, ant am in hare beddes se bisi ham abuten thet summes weis ha schulen ham sclepinde sulen. (16) Ah the Rode-merke merreth me overal, ant meast ed te nuthe." (17) Ant with this ilke bigon to yeien ant to yuren:

fol. 30v

45. (1) "Margarete, meiden, to hwon schal Ich iwurthen? | (2) Mine wepnen, wumme, allunge aren awarpen. (3) Yet were hit thurh a mon, ah is thurh a meiden! (4) This yet me thuncheth wurst, thet al thct cun thet tu art icumen ant ikennet of beoth alle in ure bondes, ant tu art edbroken ham — alre wundre meast, thet tu the ane havest overgan thi feader ant ti moder, meies ant mehes ba, ant al the ende thet tu ant heo habbeth in ieardet, ant Crist ane havest icoren to leofmon ant to lauerd. (5) Beatest us ant bindest ant to death fordemest. (6) Wei! (7) Wake beo we nu ant noht wurth mid alle, hwen a meiden ure muchele overgart thus avealleth."

46. (1) "Stew the!" quoth ha, "sari wiht, ant sei me hwer thu wunest meast, of hwet cun thu art ikumen of, ant ti cunde cuth me, ant thurh hwas heaste heane ye hali men ant hearmith, ant weorrith hare werkes."

47. (1) "Ah sei me, seli meithen, hweonne is the ilenet i thine leothebeie limen se stealewurthe strengthe? (2) Of hwet cunde kimeth the thi luve ant ti bileave, thet leith me se lahe? (3) Cuth me nu ant ken me hwi the worldes Wealdent wuneth, wummon, in the, ant hu He com into the, ant Ich chulle makie the war of alle mine wiheles."

---

stalwart and strong against me, so that they defend themselves vigilantly against me, that seems so evil to me that I am completely cruel until they are through me somewhat injured, and I am in their beds so busy about them that in some way they will soil themselves sleeping. (16) But the sign of the Cross mars me all over, and most of all now from you." (17) And with this same speech he began to whine and howl:

45. (1) "Margaret, maiden, what will become of me? (2) My weapons, alas, are completely destroyed. (3) Yet it could be through a man, but is through a maiden! (4) This I think is the worst, that all that family that you have come from are entirely in our bonds, and you have escaped from them, and the greatest of all wonders, that you have surpassed your father and mother, both kinsmen and kinswomen, and all the region that you and they have dwelled in, and have chosen Christ alone as your beloved and your lord. (5) You beat us and bind us and condemn us to death! (6) Alas! (7) We are weak now and worth nothing at all, when a maiden lays low our great arrogance like this."

46. (1) "Shut up!" said she, "sorry creature, and tell me where you most often live, of what kin you are born from, and show me your nature, and by whose command you afflict and harm holy men, and make war against their works."

47. (1) "But tell me, holy maiden, from whence is granted to you such stalwart strength in your supple limbs? (2) From what nature comes to you your love and your faith, which lays me so low? (3) Show me now and make known to me why the world's Ruler dwells, woman, in you, and how He came into you, and I shall make you aware of all my wiles."

48.   (1) "Steu the ant stille beo," quoth ha, "of thin easkunge. (2) Ye nart tu nawt
wurthe, awariede ful wiht, to here mi steavene ant hure to understonden se

fol. 31r   dearne ant se derf thing of Godes dihel|nesse. (3) Ah hwet se Ich am ant hwuch
se Ich am, thurh Godes grace Ich hit am — wilyeove unofservet, thet He haveth
me iyettet, for yelde hit Himseolven. (4) Ah swithe cuth me ant ken thet Ich easki
efter."

49.   (1) "Ye," quoth he, "Ich mot nede. (2) Sathanas the unseli, the for his prude
of parais lihte se lahe; he is keiser ant king, icrunet of us alle. (3) Ant hwerto
schulde Ich telle the ant with talen tealen, lufsume leafdi, of ure cunde ant ure
cun, thet tu cost the seolf iseon i Jamemes ant i Manbres bokes ibrevet? (4) Swuch
fearlac Ich fele for sihthen thet Ich iseo Crist seche to the thet speoken I ne dear
nawt, ah diveri ant dearie, drupest alre thinge. (5) Thah, hwen thu wult witen, we
livieth bi the lufte al thet measte deal, eadi meiden, ant ure weies beoth abufen
with the windes. (6) Ant beoth áá wakere to wurchen al thet wa thet we eaver mahe
moncun, ant mest rihtwise men ant meidnes, as thu art. (7) For Jesu Crist, Godes
bern, wes of meiden iboren, ant thurh the mihte of meithhad wes moncun
iborhen, binumen ant bireavet us al thet we ahten. (8) Nu thu wast, leafdi, thet tu
wite waldest: hwer we meast wunieth ant hwi we meast heaneth ant heatieth the
meidnes. (9) Yet yef thu wite wult hwi we weorith meast rihtwise theines, Ich the

fol. 31v   onswerie: for onde thet et áá ant eaver ure heorte. (10) We witen | ha beoth
iwrahte to stihen to thet stude thet we of feollen; ant us thuncheth hokerlich ant
swithe hofles throf, swa thet teone ontent us, ant we iwurtheth wode thurh the

---

48.   (1) "Shut up and be still," said she, "of your demand. (2) You are not worthy,
accursed foul creature, to hear my voice and especially to understand the secret
and hidden matter of God's mystery.(3) But whoever and whatever I am, I am it
through God's grace — an undeserved gift that He has given me to pay it back to
Him. (4) But show me immediately and tell me what I ask for."

49.   (1) "Yes," said he, "I must necessarily. (2) Satan the unholy, for his pride of
Paradise fell so low; he is emperor and king, crowned by us all. (3) And for what
purpose should I speak with you and tell tales, lovely lady, of our kind and our kin
which you can see for yourself set down in the books of James and Mambres? (4)
In visions in which I see Christ coming to you I feel such terror that I dare not
speak, but shiver and quake with fear, most downcast of all things. (5) However,
since you wish to know, we live in the air for the most part, holy maiden, and our
ways are above with the winds. (6) And we are forever watchful to work all that woe
that we ever may against humankind, and for the most against righteous men and
maidens, as you are. (7) For Jesus Christ, God's child, was born of a maiden, and
through the might of maidenhood was humankind born, and all that we owned
was taken away and robbed from us. (8) Now you know, lady, what you wanted to
know: where we dwell most often and why we most often afflict and hate the
maidens. (9) Yet if you want to know why we war against the righteous most, I will
answer you: because of envy that eats at our hearts forever and ever. (10) We know
that they are made to ascend to that place that we fell from; and we think it
disgraceful and very senseless, so that injury inflames us and we have become mad

grome thet us grometh áá with the gode. (11) For thet is ure cunde thet I the schulde kennen. (12) Beon sorhful ant sari for euch monnes selhthe, gomenin hwen he gulteth, ne neaver mare ne beo gleade bute of uvel ane. (13) This is ure cunde, makelese meiden. (14) Ah, deore Drihtines lomb, leothe me a lutel ant leowse, leafdi, thi fot the sit me se sare. (15) Ich halsi the o Godes half, heh heovenlich Feader, ant o Jesues nome, His an sulliche Sune, thet mon ne wummon ne mahe neaver mare heonnevorth warpe me heonne. (16) Ah thu, brihte burde, bind me on eorthe, ant ne warp thu me nawt neother into Helle. (17) For Salomon the wise, hwile he her wunede bitunde us in a tunne. (18) Ant comen Babilones men ant wenden forte habben golthord ifunden, ant tobreken thet feat, ant we forth ant fulden tha the widnesse of the worlde."

50.   (1) "Stille beo thu stille," quoth ha, "earmest alre thinge! (2) Ne schalt tu, alde schucke, motin with me mare. (3) Ah flih, sorhfule feond, of min ehsihthe, ant def thider as thu mon ne derve na mare." (4) With thet ilke the eorthe totweamde ant

fol. 32r   bitunde him, ant | he rarinde rad ruglunge into Helle.

51.   (1) Ine marhen sende hise men Olibrius the luthere to bringen hire bivoren him, ant heo blescede hire ant com baldeliche forth. (2) Striken men thiderward of eaver-euch strete forto seo thet sorhe thet me walde leggen on hire leofliche bodi yef ha to the reves read ne buhe ne ne beide.

52.   (1) "Meiden," quoth he, "Margarete, yet Ich bidde ant bodie thet tu wurche mi wil ant wurthgi mine maumez, ant te tide ant te time schal beon iblescet thet tu ibore were."

---

through the rage that enrages us forever against the good. (11) For that is our nature that I must make known to you. (12) We are sorrowful and sorry for each man's joy, we rejoice when he sins, and we are never more glad except for evil alone. (13) This is our nature, matchless maiden. (14) Ah, dear lamb of God, release me a little and loose, lady, your foot which sits upon me so sorely. (15) I entreat you on God's behalf, the high heavenly Father, and in Jesus' name, His one wondrous Son, that neither man nor woman may evermore henceforth cast me out of here. (16) But you, bright lady, bind me on the earth, and do not cast me lower into Hell. (17) For Solomon the wise, while he dwelled here confined us in a jar. (18) And the men of Babylon came and thought to have found a gold-hoard and broke that vessel in pieces, and we came forth then and filled the wideness of the world."

50.   (1) "Be silent forever," said she, "most wretched of all things! (2) You shall not, old devil, dispute with me more. (3) But fly, sorrowful fiend, out of my eyesight, and dive down there so you can never injure man more." (4) At that moment the earth yawned open and swallowed him up, and roaring he rode backwards into Hell.

51.   (1) In the morning Olibrius the wicked sent his men to bring her before him, and she blessed herself and came boldly forth. (2) People made their way there from every street to see what pain that would be inflicted on her lovely body if she neither obeyed nor bowed to the governor's advice.

52.   (1) "Maiden," said he, "Margaret, I still order and command that you work my will and worship my idols, and the tide and the time that you were born shall be blessed."

53.   (1) "Nai," quoth ha, "ne kepe Ich nawt thet me blesci me swa. (2) Ah hit were thi gein ant ti god bathe thet tu, the geast unblescet, efter blesceunge ga ant heie Godd almihti, heh heovenliche Feader, ant His selcuthe Sune, Jesu Crist, thet is soth mon ant Godd notheletere. (3) Ah thu witlese wiht wurchest as thu art wurthe, blodles ant banles, dumbe ant deave bathe. (4) Ant yet tu wurchest wurse, for the unsehene unwihtes wunieth ham inwith, ant tu ase thine lauerdes luvest ham ant heiest."

54.   (1) Him bigon to gremien, ant o grome gredde: "Strupeth hire steort-naket ant heoveth hire on heh up, swa thet ha hongi to mede of hire hokeres, ant ontendeth hire bodi with bearninde teaperes." (2) The driveles unduhtie swa

fol. 32v   duden sone, thet te hude snawhwit swartede as hit sner|cte, ant bearst on to bleinin as hit aras overal. (3) Ant hire leofliche lich reschte of the leie swa thet alle remden thet on hire softe siden sehen thet rewthe.

55.   (1) Ant heo bigon to bidden Davithes bone: "Heh Healent Godd, with the halewende fur of the Hali Gast, moncune frovre, fure min heorte, ant let te lei of Thi luve leiti i mine lenden."

56.   (1) Yet him cweth Olibrius, revene lutherest: "Lef, meiden, mi read: wurch thet Ich wilni ear then thu thet lif lutherliche lete."

57.   (1) "Lutherliche Ich livede," quoth ha, "yef Ich the ilefde. (2) Ah yef Ich thus deie, mi death is deorewurthe, ant dure into eche live. (3) Thu swenchest te swithe ant ne spedest nawiht; forte wurchen on me, meiden an thet Ich am, ah wergest the seolven. (4) Mi Lauerd haveth mine limen sunderliche iseilet, ant haveth,

---

53.   (1) "No," said she, "I do not care at all to be blessed like that. (2) But it would be both to your gain and your good that you, who goes unblessed, should go looking for a blessing and honor God almighty, the high heavenly Father, and His wondrous Son, Jesus Christ, who is true man and God nevertheless. (3) But you create a witless creature, as worthy as you are, bloodless and boneless, deaf and dumb both. (4) And yet you do worse, for the invisible demons dwell within them and you love them and worship them as your lords."

54.   (1) He began to grow angry, and in rage cried out: "Strip her stark-naked and lift her up on high, so that she hangs as a reward for her mockeries, and burn her body with burning tapers." (2) The worthless drudges did so at once so that her snow-white skin blackened as it scorched, and burst into blisters as it rose up everywhere. (3) And her lovely body crackled from the flame so that all cried out who saw that pitiful sight on her soft sides.

55.   (1) And she began to make the prayer of David: "High Savior God, with the healing fire of the Holy Ghost, humankind's comfort, inflame my heart and let the flame of Your love burn in my loins."

56.   (1) Again Olibrius spoke, the wickedest of governors: "Believe, maiden, my advice: do what I wish before you lose your life cruelly."

57.   (1) "Wickedly would I live," said she, "if I believed you. (2) But if I die thus, my death is dear, and a door into everlasting life. (3) You work so hard and achieve nothing for what you do to me, a maiden that I am, but you weary yourself. (4) My Lord has specially sealed my limbs and has, for my gemstone

to mi gimstan thet Ich yettede Him, iyarket ant iyeve me kempene crune."

58. (1) I ha warth he swithe wod, ant bed o wreththe bringen forth a vetles ful of weattre, ant binden hire bathe the fet ant te honden, ant dusten to the grunde, thet ha death drohe ant druncnede therinne. (2) Me dude as he don het; ant heo biheold on heh up ant cleopede towart Heovene:

59. (1) "Alre Kingene king, brec mine bondes, thet Ich ant alle thet soth hit heien The ant herien. (2) This weater mote iwurthe me wunsum ant softe, ant lef me

fol. 33r thet hit to me beo beath of blisse ant fulluht of font|stan, halhunge ant leome of echelich heale. (3) Cume the Hali Gast o culres iliche, the o Thi blisfule nome blesci theos weattres. (4) Festne with fulluht mi sawle to Theseolven, ant with thes ilke weattres wesch me withinnen ant warp from me awei eaver-euch sunne, ant bring me to Thi brihte bur, Brudgume of wunne. (5) Ich undervo her fulluht o deore Drihtines nome, ant on His deorewurthe Sunes, ant o thes Hali Gastes; on Godd i godlec ituinet ant untodealet." (6) Nefde bute iseid swa thet al the eorthe ne bigon to cwakien ant to cwavien. (7) Ant com a culvre beornind se briht as thah ha bearnde, ant brohte a guldene crune, ant sette hire o thet seli meidenes heaved. (8) With thet ilke breken ant bursten hire bendes, ant heo, ase schene ase schininde sunne, wende up of the weater, singinde a loft-song thet Davith the witege wrahte feor therbivoren Criste to wurthmunt. (9) "Mi lufsume Lauerd," quoth ha, "He cutheth ase King thet He rixleth ariht. (10) Feierlec ant strengthe beoth Hise schrudes, ant igurd He is ham on, thet a cumeliche fearen ant semliche sitten."

---

that I granted to him, prepared and given me the champion's crown."

58. (1) Then he became intensely maddened, and in wrath ordered a vessel full of water brought forth, and bound her both by the feet and hands, and flung her to the bottom so that she would be put to death and drowned therein. (2) It was done as he had ordered; and she looked up on high and cried out toward Heaven:

59. (1) "King of all kings, break my bonds, so that I and all who see it may honor and worship You. (2) May this water become pleasant and mild, and agreeable to me and allow it to be a bath of bliss and baptism in the font, a hallowing and light of eternal salvation. (3) May the Holy Ghost come in the likeness of a dove, which in Your blessed name may bless these waters. (4) Fasten with baptism my soul to Yourself, and with these same waters wash me within and cast away from me every sin, and bring me to Your bright bower, Bridegroom of joy. (5) I accept here baptism in the dear Lord's name and in His dear Son's and in the Holy Ghost's: one God in goodness enclosed and undivided." (6) She had just said so when all the earth began to quake and to quiver. (7) And there came a dove glowing as bright as though it burned, and brought a golden crown, and set it on that blessed maiden's head. (8) At that moment her bonds broke and burst, and she, as bright as the shining sun, came up out of the water, singing a praise-song that David the prophet wrote long before that time to the glory of Christ. (9) "My beloved Lord," said she, "He makes known as King that He rules rightly. (10) Beauty and strength are his garments, and He is girded in them so that they appear comely and sit seemingly."

60. (1) "Cum," quoth the culvre with schilinde stevene, "ant stih to the wunne ant to the weole of Heovene. (2) Eadi were thu, meiden, tha thu chure meithhad, the of alle mihtes is cwen. (3) Forthi thu schalt áá bruken in blisse buten ende crunene brihtest." |

fol. 33v

61. (1) O thet ilke time turnden to ure Lauerd fif thusent men yet withuten itald children ant wummen, ant alle weren ananriht, as the reve het hit, o Cristes kinewurthe nome hefdes bicorven, in a burh of Armenie Caplimet inempnet, alle heriende Godd with up-aheve stevene, ant stihen — alle martyrs — with murhthe to Heovene.

62. (1) The reve rudnede al of grome se him gromede, ant warth swa wrath ant swa awed thet he al o wodschipe demde hire to deathe. (2) Ant het on hot heorte thet me hire heved with schiminde ant scharp sweord, with blikinde ant bitel brond totweamde from the bodie. (3) Leiden honden on hire theo the ihaten weren, ant bunden hire thet tet blod bearst ut et te neiles, ant withute the burh ledden to biheafdin.

63. (1) "Meiden," quoth Malcus, "streche forth thet swire scharp sweord to undervon, for Ich mot thi bone beon (ant thet me is wa vore) yef Ich mahte therwith, for Ich iseo Godd Seolf with His eadie engles bitrumme the abuten."

64. (1) "Abid me thenne, brother," quoth ha, "hwil thet Ich ibidde me, ant biteache Him mi gast ant mi bodi bathe, to ro ant to reste."

65. (1) "Ibide the," quoth he, "baldeliche hwil the god liketh." (2) Ant heo bigon on hire cneon forte cneolin adun, ant blithe with theos bone ber on heh iheven up honden towart Heovene:

---

60. (1) "Come," said the dove with a ringing voice, "and ascend to the joy and to the bliss of Heaven. (2) Blessed were you, maiden, when you chose virginity, which is queen of all virtues. (3) Therefore you will enjoy the brightest of crowns forever in bliss without end."

61. (1) At that same time five thousand men turned to our Lord still without counting children and women, and all were immediately, as the governor ordered it, beheaded in Christ's royal name, in a city of Armenie called Caplimet, all praising God with uplifted voices, and ascended — all martyrs — with mirth to Heaven.

62. (1) The governor reddened completely from rage which enraged him, and became so angry and so maddened that, entirely in madness, he condemned her to death. (2) And in hot heart he ordered that her head be severed from her body with a shining and sharp sword, with a bright and biting blade. (3) Those who were commanded laid hands on her, and bound her so that the blood burst out at the nails, and they led her outside of the city to be beheaded.

63. (1) "Maiden," said Malchus, "stretch forth your neck to submit to the sharp sword, for I must be your slayer (and that is grievous to me), if I might do it with this sword, because I see God Himself with his blessed angels surround you."

64. (1) "Wait for me then, brother," said she, "while I make my prayers and give to Him both my soul and my body both, to repose and to rest."

65. (1) "Pray," said he, "boldly while it pleases you." (2) And she began to kneel down on her knees, and with this prayer happily lifted her hands up on high towards Heaven:

fol. 34r

66. |(1) "Drihtin, leodes Lauerd, duhtie thah ha dearne beon ant derve Thine domes. (2) Me is nu death idemet her, ant with The lif ilenet — Thi milde milce Ich thonki hit. (3) Thu, folkes Feader of frumscheft, schuptest al thet ischepen is. (4) Thu, wisest wurhte of alle, merkedest the heovene ant mete with Thi strahte hond, ant with The icluhte the eorthe. (5) Thu, steoresmon of sea-stream, Thu, wissent ant wealdent of alle wiht the iwrahte beoth, seheliche ant unsehene, buh Thine earen, Healent Godd, ant bei to mine benen. (6) Ich bidde ant biseche The, thet art mi weole ant wunne, thet hwa se eaver boc writ of mi liflade, other biyet hit iwriten, other halt hit ant haveth oftest on honde, other hwa se hit eaver redeth other thene redere blitheliche lusteth, Wealdent of Heovene, wurthe ham alle sone hare sunnen foryevene. (7) Hwa se on mi nome maketh chapele other chirche, other findeth in ham liht other lampe, the leome yef ham, Lauerd, ant yette ham of Heovene. (8) I thet hus ther wummon pineth o childe, sone se ha munneth mi nome ant mi pine, Lauerd — Lauerd, hihendliche help hire ant her hire bene. (9) Ne i the hus ne beo iboren na mislimet bearn, nowther halt ne hoveret, nowther dumbe ne deaf ne

fol. 34v idemet of deofle. (10) Ant hwa se eaver mi nome munegeth with | muthe, luveliche Lauerd, et te Laste Dom ales him from deathe."

67. (1) With this tha thuhte hit as thah a thunre dunede. (2) Ant com a culvre, se briht as thah ha bearnde, of Heovene with a rode leitinde of liht ant of leome. (3) Ant te meiden duvelunge feol dun to ther eorthe. (4) Ant com the culvre ant ran hire ant rihte up with the Rode ant seide hire sweteliche to, with swotest a steavene:

---

66. (1) "Ruler, Lord of men, though they are mysterious and difficult, your judgments are excellent. (2) Now I am condemned to death here, and life with You granted — for that I thank Your mild mercy. (3) You, the people's father of creation, created everything that is made. (4) You, the wisest creator of everything, marked and measured out the heavens with your outstretched hand and with Your clenched hand the earth. (5) You, steersman of the sea-stream, You, guardian and ruler of all creatures that are created, seen and unseen, incline Your ears, Savior God, and assent to my prayers. (6) I bid and beseech You, who are my joy and my bliss, that whoever writes a book about my life, or obtains it written, or holds it and has it often in hand, or whoever reads it or listens eagerly to a reader, Savior of Heaven, may all their sins be forgiven of them immediately. (7) Who so in my name makes a chapel or church, or provides in them light or lamp, give them, Lord, and grant them the light of Heaven. (8) In that house where a woman suffers in childbed, as soon as they call to mind my name and my suffering, Lord — Lord, quickly help her and hear her prayer. (9) Nor may there be born in the house any misshapen child, neither lame nor hunch-backed, neither deaf nor dumb nor ordained for the devil. (10) And who so ever mentions my name with mouth, lovely Lord, at the Last Judgment deliver him from death."

67. (1) At this then it seemed as though a thunder-clap resounded. (2) And there came a dove, as bright as if it burned, from Heaven with a cross gleaming with light and with radiance. (3) And the maiden fell headlong down to the earth. (4) And the dove came and touched her and raised her up with the Rood and said to her sweetly,

"Eadi art tu, meiden, bimong alle wummen, thet eoli halwende havest ant halsum isoht efter, ant alle sunfule men imuneget i thine benen ant i thine eadie beoden. (5) Bi Meseolf Ich swerie, ant bi Min heovenlich hird, thet tine beoden beoth the treoweliche ituthet, ant for alle theo iherd the thu vore ibeden havest. (6) Ant muche mare is iyeven to theo the munieth thi nome, ant iyettet moni thing thet nu nis nawt imuneget. (7) Hwer se eaver thi bodi other ei of thine ban beon, other boc of thi pine, cume the sunfule mon ant legge his muth therupon, Ich salvi him his sunnen. (8) Ne ne schal nan unwiht wunien in the wanes ther thi martyrdom is iwriten inne, ant alle of the hus schulen gleadien i Godes grith ant i gasteliche luve. (9) Ant alle the the biddeth, to yarkin Ich yetti ham of hare bruchen bote. (10) Ant tu art eadi, ant te stude thet tu on restest, ant alle theo the thurh the

fol. 35r   schulen turne to Me. | (11) Cum nu, for Ich kepe the, brud to thi Brudgume. (12) Cum, leof, to thi lif, for Ich copni thi cume. (13) Brihtest bur abit te — leof, hihe the to me! (14) Cum nu to Mi kinedom, leaf thet leode se lah, ant tu schalt wealde with Me al thet Ich i wald ah."

68.   (1) The stevene stutte ant heo stod up, alre burde blithest, ant bigon to bidden theo the hire abuten weren ant hire death biwopen thet ha schulde tholien. (2) "Leoteth nu ant leaveth," quoth ha, "ower ladliche nurth, ant gleadieth alle with me the me god unnen — for ye habbeth iherd (yef ye hercneden riht) hwet te hehe Healent haveth me bihaten. (3) Ant as ye luvieth ow seolf, leofliche Ich ow leare thet ye habben mi nome muchel ine munde, for Ich chulle bidden for theo blitheliche in Heovene the ofte munneth mi nome ant

---

with the sweetest voice: "Blessed are you, maiden, among all women, who have sought after that healing and hallowing oil, and who remembers all sinful men in your prayers and in your blessed petitions. (5) By Myself I swear, and by My heavenly host, that your prayers are securely granted to you, and heard for all those for whom you have prayed. (6) And much more is given to those who remember your name, and many things granted which are not mentioned now. (7) Where so ever your body or any of your bones are, or a book of your passion should the sinful man come and lay his mouth upon it I shall heal him of his sins. (8) Nor will any demon dwell in the places in which your martyrdom is written, and all the house will rejoice in God's peace and in ghostly love. (9) And all who pray to you to prepare them I will grant them remedy for their sins. (10) And you are blessed and the place upon which you rest, and all those who through you will turn to Me. (11) Come now, for I await you, Bride to the Bridegroom. (12) Come, beloved, to your life, for I long for your coming. (13) The brightest bower awaits you — beloved, hasten to me! (14) Come now to my kingdom, leave that lowly people, and you shall rule with me all that I own in possession."

68.   (1) The voice ceased and she stood up, happiest of all women, and began to pray for them who were about her and bewailed her death that they should endure it. (2) "Cease now and leave off," said she, "your loathly noise, and rejoice all with me who wish me well — for you have heard (if you listened rightly) what the high Savior has promised me. (3) And as you love yourself, lovingly I exhort you to have my name much in mind, for I will happily pray for those in Heaven who often

munegeth on eorthe. (4) With blithe heorte beoreth me genge forte herien the King thet haveth icore me, worldes Wurhte ant Wealdent of alle iwrahte thinges. (5) The Ich thonki throf; The Ich heie ant herie, heovenliche Healent. (6) For Thi deorewurthe nome Ich habbe idrohe nowcin, ant neome death nuthe, ant Tu nim me to The, Godd, of al thet god is ordfrume ant ende. (7) Beo Thu áá iblescet, ant Ti blisfule Sune, Jesu Crist bi His nome, with the Hali Gast, thet glit of Inc bathe.

fol. 35v (8) Ye, threo ant tah an, in hades totweamet, in | heheschipe untodealet, iteit ant itunet, an Godd unagin. (9) Wurthschipe ant wurthmunt wurthe to The ane from worlde into worlde áá on ecnesse."

69.   (1) Efter theos bone tha beah ha the swire, ant cweth to the cwellere, "Do nu, brother, hihendliche thet te is ihaten."

70.   (1) "Nai!" quoth he. (2) "Nulle Ich no, for Ich habbe iherd hu Drihtines deore muth haveth with the imotet."

71.   (1) "Thu most!" quoth the meiden. (2) "Nedunge don hit, for yef thu ne dest no, ne schalt tu habbe with me dale in Heoveriche." (3) Ant he with thet hef up hetelest alre wepne ant smat smertliche adun, thet te dunt defde in. (4) Ant thet bodi beide ant thet scherpe sweord scher hire with the schuldren, ant te bodi beah to ther eorthe. (5) Ant te gast steah up to thet istirrede bur, blithe to Heovene. (6) He the thene dunt yef yeide mit tet ilke: "Drihtin, do me merci ant milce of this dede! (7) Of this sunne, Lauerd, loke me salve!" (8) Ant feol of fearlac adun on hire riht halve.

---

remember my name and speak it on earth.(4) With a happy heart accompany me to praise the King that has crowned me, the world's Creator and the Ruler of all created things. (5) I thank you for it; You I praise and worship, heavenly Savior. (6) For Your dear name I have undergone hardship, and now suffer death, and may You take me to You, God of all that is good, beginning and end. (7) May You be blessed forever, and Your blissful Son, Jesus Christ by His name, with the Holy Ghost which proceeds from you both. (8) You, three and nevertheless one, divided into persons, undivided in glory, bound together and enclosed, one God without beginning. (9) May honor and glory go to You alone from world into world forever into eternity."

69.   (1) After this prayer then she bowed her neck, and said to the executioner: "Do now, brother, quickly what you are ordered."

70.   (1) "No," said he. (2) "I will not, for I have heard how the Lord's dear mouth has spoken with you."

71.   (1) "You must!" said she. (2) "Do it against your will, for if you do not you will not have your share in the Heaven-kingdom." (3) And with that he heaved up the cruelest of all weapons and smote smartly down, so that the blow sank in. (4) And that body gave way and the sharp sword sheared her at the shoulders, and the body bowed to the earth. (5) And the spirit rose up to that starry bower, joyful to Heaven. (6) Then he who gave the blow cried out at that moment: "Lord, grant me mercy and compassion for this deed! (7) Behold, Lord, and heal me of this sin!" (8) And from fear he fell down on her right side.

72.   (1) Comen lihtinde tha the engles of leome, ant seten ant sungen on hire bodi bilehwit ant iblesceden hit. (2) The feondes the ther weren, deadliche idorven, fengen to yeien: "Margarete, meiden, leothe nuthe lanhure ant lowse ure bondes. (3) We beoth wel icnawen thet nis na lauerd bute Godd, the thu on levest." (4)

fol. 36r   Turnden tha thurh this to Crist swithe monie | ant comen dumbe ant deave to hire bodi as hit lei, and botneden alle. (5) The engles, as ha beren the sawle in hare bearmes, sihen towart heovene, ant sungen ase ha stuhen up with sweteste stevene: "*Sanctus, sanctus, sanctus Dominus Deus Sabaot, (et cetera).* (6) Hali is, hali is the Lauerd of heovenliche weordes! (7) Heovene is ful, ant eorthe, of Thine wurthfule weolen! (8) Alre wihte Wealdent in hehnesse, heal us! (9) lblescet beo the bearnes cume the com i Drihtines nome — heale in hehnesse!" (10) With thet, tha bigunnen the gastes of Helle to theoten ant to yellen. (11) Ant tuhen alle to hire bodi the untrume weren ant hefden hare heale.

73.   (1) Com Ich, Teochimus, ant toc hire leofliche lich, ant ber ant brohte hit ayein into Antioches burh with murthe unimete, ant dude hit i grave-stan in hire grandame hus, the wes icleopet Clete. (2) Ich ah wel to wite this, for Ich, i pine of prisun ther ha wes iput in, font hire flutunge ant fedde flesches fode. (3) And Ich iseh hwer ha feaht with the ferliche feond ant hire bonen that ha bed wrat o boc-felle, ant hire liflade al lette don o leave. (4) Ant sende hit sothliche iwriten wide yont te worlde.

---

72.   (1) There came descending then the angels of light, and they sat and sang over her innocent body and blessed it. (2) The fiends who were there, severely injured, began to cry out: "Margaret, maiden, release us now at least and loosen our bonds. (3) We well know that there is no lord but God, in whom you believe." (4) Then through this a great many there turned to Christ, and the deaf and the dumb came to her body as it lay, and all were cured. (5) The angels, as they carried the soul in their bosoms, made their way toward Heaven and sang as they rose up with the sweetest voices: "*Holy, Holy, Holy Lord God of Hosts (and so on).* (6) Holy is, Holy is the Lord of heavenly hosts! (7) Heaven is full, and earth, of your glorious joys! (8) Ruler of all creatures in glory, save us! (9) Blessed be the coming of the child who comes in the Lord's name — salvation in glory!" (10) With that the spirits of Hell began then to howl and yell. (11) And all who were infirm proceeded to her body and received healing.

73.   (1) I, Teochimus, came and took her lovely body and bore it and brought it again into the city of Antioch with immeasurable mirth, and placed it in a stone coffin in her grandmother's house, who was called Clete. (2) Truly I ought to know this well, for I, during her suffering in the prison where she was put, found her sustenance and fed her food for the body. (3) And I saw where she fought with the fearsome fiend and her prayers that she made I wrote down on parchment, and her entire life I had put down on the page. (4) And I sent it truly written everywhere throughout the world.

74.   (1) Thus the eadi meiden, Margarete bi nome, i the moneth thet ure ledene

fol. 36v   — thet is, ald Englis — *Efterlithe* inempnet, ant *Julium* o Latin, o the twen|tuthe dei, deide with tintrohe ant wende from thes weanen to lif thet áá lesteth, to blisse bute balesith, to wunne buten euch wa.

75.   (1) Alle theo the this iherd heorteliche habbeth: in ower beoden blitheluker munneth this meiden, thet ha with the bonen thet ha bed on eorthe bidde yet for ow i the blisse of Heovene,

thear ha schineth seovevalt schenre then the sunne,

i sy ant i selhthe mare then eani muth cuthen hit cunne.

(2) Ant i thet englene hird singeth áá unsulet,

thet mon ne wummon ne mei thet his flesch-fulet.

(3) Ant we bituhe the engles, thurh hire erndunge,

moten yet iseo hire ant heren hire singen.

(4) Igret iwurthe Godd Feader, ant His Sune iseinet,

the Hali Gast iheiet, theos threo in an itheinet

of engles ant of eorthmen withuten ende. (5) AMEN.

---

74.   (1) Thus the blessed maiden, Margaret by name, in the month that our language — that is, Old English — calls Efterlithe, and *Julium* in Latin, on the twentieth day died with torment and went from these woes to the life that lasts forever, to bliss without suffering, to joy without any woe.

75.   (1) All those who have devotedly listened to this: remember in your prayers this maiden more happily, so that she with the prayers that she made on earth may still intercede for you in the bliss of Heaven,

where she shines seven times brighter than the sun,

in victory and in more happiness than any mouth could tell it.

(2) And in that host of angels she sings forever unsoiled,

which no man or woman may who is flesh-fouled.

(3) And we among the angels, because of her intercession,

may yet see her and hear her sing.

(4) May God the Father be magnified, and His Son blessed,

the Holy Ghost glorified, these three in one,

served by angels and men on earth without end. (5) AMEN.

EXPLANATORY NOTES TO *SEINTE MARGARETE*

ABBREVIATIONS: *AW*: *Ancrene Wisse*, ed. Hasenfratz; **B**: Bodleian Library MS Bodley 34 [base text]; *BT*: Bosworth and Toller, *Anglo-Saxon Dictionary*; **H**: refers to a series of sixteenth-century scribbles in various hands (see Introduction, p. 22); *HM*: *Hali Meithhad*; **M**: Mack edition (1934); **MED**: *Middle English Dictionary*; **MWB**: Millett and Wogan-Browne edition (1990); *OED*: *Oxford English Dictionary*; **R**: British Library MS Royal 17 A XXVII; *SJ*: *The Liflade ant te Passiun of Seinte Juliene*; *SK*: *The Martyrdom of Sancte Katerine*; *SM*: *The Liflade and te Passiun of Seinte Margarete*.

Header   *Seinte Margarete.* St. Margaret probably was never an historical person. According to M, if she had existed, her martyrdom would have taken place in Antioch in Pisidia (what is today central Turkey) in the first decade of the fourth century under the joint rule of Diocletian and Maximian (p. ix). Her legend was extremely popular, especially in England and even before the Norman Conquest, as is attested by two surviving accounts of her passion in Old English (see Clayton and Magennis, *Old English Lives*). She was a patron saint of childbirth and many in labor either invoked her name or wore amulets that referred to her. See Farmer, *Oxford Dictionary of Saints*, for a summary of her legend, which exists in both prose and verse versions in the vernacular (for a list of the versions and languages see Spencer, "Legend," p. 198). Margaret's legend is also present in the eastern church, where she is known as St. Marina, a circumstance that was noted as early as the tenth century, when Surius quotes Symeon Metaphrastes' note on *Marina, quam latinae ecclesiae Margaritam vocant* [Marina, who the Latin churches call Margaret] (Spencer, "Legend," p. 197). For more on the Marina-Margaret connection, and on the curious differences in their iconography and roles as saints, see Larson, "Cults of Sts Margaret and Marina."

1.1   *Efter ure Lauerdes . . . icrunet to Criste.* This opening, as is common in the legends of virgin martyrs, places the saint's life clearly within the context of Christ's passion and resurrection. For further discussion of this life as an *imitatio Christi*, see Cadwallader, "The Virgin, the Dragon and the Theorist," pp. 72–117.

2.2   *Ich, an Godes theowe, Teochimus.* Teochimus, the narrator, claims both to have gathered the sources for Margaret's legend and to have been an eye-witness to her encounter with the dragon. This presence of an eye-witness serves the purpose both of authorizing the text as historically "real" as well as providing a lens through which the reader can view the text; i.e., Teochimus, a spectator of the dragon-fight and the martyrdom, not only negotiates the story through his pen but through his eye, and thus personalizes as well as authenticates the text.

119

See the opening Prologue to Capgrave's *Life of St. Katherine* for an elaborate use of this authorizing device — there, the narrator receives his source texts for Katherine's biography not only through Athanasius, the supposed original author of the Katherine legend, but through the anonymous English priest who wrote the first part of Katherine's life in the "straungeness of his derk langage" (ed. Winstead, Prologue, line 62). See also explanatory note 73.1. McFadden reports that, in the Old English lives of St. Margaret, Teochimus is not only the author of her story, but her foster-father as well, thus bringing his participation in the narrative to an even more personal level ("'Books of Life'," p. 479).

moni mislich leaf. See *MED lef* (n.1), sense 2a: "a leaf of a book, page, sheet." Teochimus' assertion that he has both read and written many pages guarantees his literacy — a quality not necessarily shared by his audience. The comment also calls to mind the opening of Laȝamon's *Brut*: "Laweman þes bokes bieolde an þe leues tornde / he ham loueliche bi-helde" (ed. Brook and Leslie, lines 24–25), in which the "leaves" represent the book in its particulars, rather than simply an abstract idea of literacy or knowledge.

2.4   *eorthliche limen.* See *MED lim* (n.1), sense 4a, where "limen" is explained as an extension of the literal body of Christ, whose "limbs" constitute those followers of the true faith. In return, the followers of the devil, or those wicked agents who work his will on earth, are his "limbs," as in 28.1 of *SJ*, where Juliana refers to Eleusius and his torturers as "deofles limen."

3.1   *Hercneth!* While this text may have originally been composed with a listening audience in mind, it is not clear whether this version was read or listened to; see Millett's discussion of the audience of the Katherine Group in "Audience of the Saints' Lives."

3.2   *widewen with tha . . . te meidnes nomeliche.* Winstead considers this address clear evidence that the text was written for a female audience. She also notes that at specific places (see 27.7 and 30.5) the translator has adjusted his adaptation from the gender-neutral Latin text to involve women directly, which does not happen in *SK* or *SJ* (*Virgin Martyrs*, p. 35).

the we munneth todei. See 74.1: "*Julium* o Latin, o the twentuthe dei" (20 July). Douglas Gray suggests that the text "was written after the establishment of St. Margaret's Day as a major feast day in the English church by the Council of Oxford in 1222" (*Middle English Literature*, p. 281).

thet seli meidnes . . . echeliche in Heovene. Compare Apocalypse 14:3–4.

4.1   *ant hire flesliche feder Theodosie hehte.* Winstead points out that in the Latin version, it is clear that Margaret's pagan father despises her: "Odiosa erat suo patri, et dilecta erat Domino Iesu Christo" (M, p. 128) [She was hated by her father, and beloved by Lord Jesus Christ] (*Virgin Martyrs*, p. 62n107). The translator here has omitted any mention of animosity between father and daughter (*Virgin Martyrs*, p. 62).

4.3   *to welden with al hireseolven.* See MWB's translation: "on her own account" (p. 47). We have tried to follow a more literal sense here; but the idea still is that

Margaret has bestowed not only her virginity, but also the keeping of her worldly goods on God. While this would seem a nonsensical idea, Robertson suggests that throughout the legend, Margaret relies on not just a "spiritual commitment . . . to Christ" but a bodily one as well ("Corporeality," p. 274).

4.4   *hire fostermodres hahte. hahte* is a translation of the Latin *oves* and according to M is the "earliest recorded use of O[ld] E[nglish] *eoht* with the meaning of 'livestock'," (M, p. 60n4/30). As Margaret has commended herself so thoroughly into God's keeping, she is the ideal shepherd for not just the literal flock of sheep but the spiritual flock, the rest of Christianity.

       moder-bern. M describes this word as "a genitive compound not elsewhere recorded in M[iddle] E[nglish]" but which survives in our phrases "every mother's child," or "every mother's son" (M, p. 60n6/3).

5.2   *schireve* leads to our modern word "sheriff." See *MED shir-reve*. The Latin text reads *prefectus*.

5.3   *seh this seli meiden Margarete.* Wogan-Browne discusses Olibrius' destructive gaze in "Virgin's Tale." Compared to the dragon and his brother demon, it is easy to overlook the centrality of Olibrius' villainy in this tale. However, as in note 2.4 above, Olibrius represents one of those "limbs" of the devil who become the actual agents through which evil is worked on earth. Wogan-Browne states that "his gaze [upon Margaret is] as prehensile as the dragon's tongue" ("Virgin's Tale," p. 180). It is because of this gaze that she is seized and thrown into prison, the initial swallowing that precedes the swallowing by the dragon. An interesting comparison on looking is Part II of *AW*, which advises against anchoresses allowing their faces to be visible in the window of the cell. It elaborates on the plight of Dinah (Genesis 34:1 ff.): "al thet uvel of Dina thet ich spec of herre, al com nawt for-thi thet te wummen lokeden cangliche o wepmen, ah for heo unwriyen heom in monnes ech-siththe ant duden hwar-thurch ha machten fallen in sunne" (ed. Hasenfratz, p. 102, lines 96–98) [all the evil of Dinah which I spoke of above, all came not because the women looked foolishly on men, but because they uncovered themselves in man's sight and did that through which they might fall into sin].

6.2–3 *Yef heo his . . . thet Ich welde.* While Olibrius' prurient intentions here do not explicitly constitute a sexual threat, his rage at her refusal suggests a kind of rape-wish. However, Wogan-Browne downplays this sexual threat: despite Olibrius' sexual interest, Margaret remains inviolable ("Virgin's Tale," p. 176). Indeed, she becomes the violator in her assaults on the dragon, Ruffin, and his unnamed demon brother late in the text. Some critics have argued that the rape threat here is displaced into the dragon episode, as Margaret is involuntarily subjected to the powerful force of male appetite (see explanatory note 31.3 below).

6.3   *ant wel schal . . . thet Ich welde.* The Latin text reads: *et bene ei faciam in domo mea* (M, p. 129/16) [and I will do well for her in my house/holdings]. Mi translates "iwurthen" as "reward" while the sense of the word is much more similar to "faciam." The writers, both of the Latin and the English text, speak by implication here — if she is a slave, and ends up being Olibrius' concubine, she will have a much better life because of his great power and possessions than she would as a slave working in the fields tending sheep.

7.2   *the beoth al blodi biblodeget of sunne.* Margaret's description of the sinners evokes the image of her own body, which will be completely covered in blood later on in the tale. However, Margaret's "biblodeget" body is a sanctifying one, which affects the spectators (and the audience) with pity, and thus moves them toward devotion. Robertson also brings up another possibility, whereby the image of the sinners, covered in a bloody mess from their sin, evokes images of "birth, whose blood and pain are the result of femininity" ("Corporeality," p. 275). Margaret's choice of words, Robertson argues, demonstrates the corporeal type of spirituality accorded to female saints.

7.5   *gimstan.* Jewels are conventionally associated with virginity in saints' lives. The specific associations of Margaret with a pearl (Latin *margarita*), according to MWB, dates from Jacobus de Voragine's thirteenth-century version of Margaret's life in his *Golden Legend*: "Margaret comes from *margarita*, which is the Latin name for a pearl; and this precious gem is shining, white, small, and endowed with virtue. So Saint Margaret was shining white by her virginity, small by her humility, and endowed with the power to work miracles" (*Golden Legend*, p. 351; see also MWB, p. 154). For further discussion of the earliest appearances of the words *pearl* and *margarite* in English see M, p. 60n6/28. Earl argues that the associations of St. Margaret with pearls is the inspiration behind the Middle English *Pearl*-maiden ("Pearl Maiden").

7.7   *unwiht.* This word, literally translated as "un-being," refers to the devil, who has undone himself (we have initially translated as "Un-Being" and thereafter translated the word as "fiend"). The *MED* reports the vast majority of uses of the term in the thirteenth century (almost all of them are from the B manuscript), with one reported in the fifteenth-century *Pater Noster of Richard Ermyte* (*unwight* (n.)).

9.1   *changede his chere.* MWB translates as "his countenance darkened" (p. 49). The Latin reads: *immutavit vultum faciei sue* [changed the expression of his face] (M, p. 130/5).

12.1   *Ich hehe, quoth . . . ase on Lauerd.* Wogan-Browne ("Powers of Record," p. 80) describes the Katherine Group saints' lives as a "feminized nuptial romance," in which the heroine, who represents the "ideal solitary self," focuses entirely on her Bridegroom in an "eroticization of waiting." These observations are particularly apt here, where in Margaret's first public proclamation of her spiritual and sexual allegiances, she contextualizes herself in not just a hagiographical but a romance narrative as well.

16.3   *the schal wel iwurthen.* See explanatory note 6.3 above. MWB has again translated as "I shall reward you," smoothing over the literal sense of "iwurthen."

17.1   *the haveth iseilet . . . ant mi meithhad.* The seal is an image fraught with scriptural references, as those who were claimed by God are stamped with His seal; in the

New Testament, see in particular John 3:33 and 6:27, 1 Corinthians 9:2, 2 Corinthians 1:22, Ephesians 4:30, and 2 Timothy 2:19. Most significant for our text, however, is the Canticle of Canticles 4:12: "My sister, my spouse, is a garden enclosed, a garden enclosed, a fountain sealed up"; and, especially, 8:6: "Put me as a seal upon thy heart, as a seal upon thy arm, for love is strong as death, jealousy as hard as hell, the lamps thereof are fire and flames." Compare 55.1 and the corresponding explanatory note.

to. See M's gloss of "to" that refers to this line: "as the object of" (p. 116).

17.4   *swotest to smellen*. Holiness is conventionally associated with sweet smells; this tradition extends to Chaucer's Second Nun's Tale and Malory's *Morte D'Arthure*, where the appearance of the Holy Grail is always accompanied by a pleasant smell. See also *SK* explanatory note 37.3. For a discussion of the odor of sanctity, see Susan Ashbrook Harvey, *Ancient Christianity and the Olfactory Imagination*.

19.6   *iseiled with His in-seil*. See explanatory note 17.1 above.

unc. A clear marker of the AB dialect's strong Anglo-Saxon roots, this is a first person pronoun in the dual form, meaning "we two" (*BT*, *unc* (dat.), sense 1). The dative case makes for difficult translation, but we have treated the verb "twemen" as taking the dative as object. See also 68.7, which features the second person form of the dual: "thet glit of Inc bathe" [which proceeds from you both].

21.5   *softe me mi . . . Ich derf drehe*. Dendle explains some basic premises of hagiographical writing in terms of the extent to which the martyrs feel or complain about the presence of physical pain. In some of the earliest saints' lives, the martyrs explicitly suffer but are "able to ignore the pain because of inner fortitude" ("Pain and Saint-Making," pp. 41–42). Clearly, Margaret is aware that she will suffer pain, but prays for invincibility.

22.1   *reve bute rewthe*. As opposed to the infinitely merciful *Drihtin* to whom Margaret has been praying. A consistent contrast has been set up here between the lordly governor, who rules without proper judgment and is thus an extension, a "limb" of the devil, and the heavenly governor, the ruler who assists his subjects when they are in need. In a sense this contrast perfectly encapsulates not only the problem of personal spiritual governorship versus earthly living but also the key problem of early Christianity, where Roman rulers saw the Christians' allegiance to another "lord" as a threat. The Roman Emperor is not only the supreme political power but also the supreme spiritual power, whereas for Christians the two are to be separated; earthly power and riches must be disdained in favor of spiritual riches.

24.1–6   *"O," quoth ha . . . . monnes hond imakede*. In response to the spectators' attempt to read her body, Margaret directs or almost preaches that they should interpret her suffering differently. For discussions of this issue, see Lewis, "'Lete me suffre'," and Sarah Salih, "Performing Virginity." Compare also 54.1–3, and the corresponding explanatory note.

24.6   *nan of ower . . . monnes hond imakede*. Katherine describes idols in similar terms. See *SK* 10.9.

25.1–4   *Ah thu wurchest . . . gleadie buten ende*. Margaret's words here are spirited, aggressive, and disruptive. Illustrations of these increasingly hostile dialogues between the saint and Olibrius survive in the *Queen Mary Psalter*, where a fourteenth-century English illustrator has accompanied a saints' calendar with drawings depicting various moments in the legend. See plates 307–14 and plate 259 (b and c) of the *Queen Mary's Psalter* facsimile for these illustrations (ed. Warner). See also pp. 92–98 of *Virgin Martyrs* for Winstead's excellent discussion of the iconography of feminine disruption that is present in the drawings depicting Margaret's interrogations.

25.4   *swelten*. See *MED swelten* (v.1), sense 1a: "to cease living, perish, die." While this is the more common meaning of the word, we have translated as "swelter" according to *swelteren* (v.), sense a: "to become weak or faint from heat, swelter; faint." The words are etymologically related, and "swelter" more accurately conveys both the sense that Olibrius, forever suffering in hell, is not in fact *dying*, but rather enduring eternal torment. "Swelter" also implies the kind of environment Olibrius will have to endure.

27.4   *Lowse me, Lauerd . . . an-ihurnde hornes*. Compare Vulgate Psalm 21:22: "Save me from the lion's mouth; and my lowness from the horns of the unicorns."

          an-ihurnde. Literally, "one-horned." Unicorns, traditionally trapped by virgins, in whose lap the beast calmly lays its head while the hunters wait in ambush, are an important part of religious symbolism; e.g. Luke 1:69: "[He] hath raised up an horn of salvation to us, in the house of David his servant." For a comprehensive discussion of the iconography of the Virgin and the Unicorn in medieval and Renaissance art, see Lyall, *The Lady and the Unicorn*. Christ is frequently associated with the unicorn because of the beast's legendary power to resurrect itself after it has been slaughtered, and because of the purifying power of its horn. See T. H. White, *Bestiary*, pp. 20–21. The dangerous unicorn of Daniel is most likely the inspiration for the unicorn of *AW*, which is associated with anger (ed. Hasenfratz, p. 225, lines 283–93), although this may reflect the frequent conflation of the gentle but powerful unicorn and the more fierce, dangerous monoceros (or rhinoceros) in the bestiary material. See also MWB's note on p. 154.

27.5   *thet mi bone mote thurh-thurli the Heovene*. According to the *MED thirlen* (v.), this is the only occurrence of the verb "thurh-thurlen" to mean "pierce [the heavens]," in prayer. However, other texts refer to the capability of prayer to pierce Heaven. See chapter 38 to the Middle English *Cloud of Unknowing*: "And whi peersith it heven, this lityl schort preier of o litil silable?" (line 1386). Margaret's prayers are anything but "o litil silable"; indeed, she proves much more loquacious than Olibrius and the devil put together. The fervent devotion of Margaret's prayers, though, serve the same purpose of the later *Cloud*'s single syllable-prayers: that is, the quality of the prayers "preyed with a fulle spirite" (*Cloud*, line 1387) and serve to drown out other dialogues with God "unmydfuly mumlyd in the teeth" (*Cloud*, line 1383). The fierceness of Margaret's prayers serve to drown out the droning and potentially distracting background noise of Olibrius, the misdirected commentary of the spectators (see 23.1–4), and the soft-spoken manipulations of the devil.

27.6   *culvrenene*. The dove signals the end of the flood of Genesis 8. See also Matthew 3:16, Mark 1:10, Luke 3:22, and John 1:32 for the appearance of the dove (the Holy Spirit) at the baptism of Jesus. However, the dove's frequent appearance in the Canticle of Canticles makes it the perfect messenger for Margaret, as the Bride and the Bridegroom (Christ) frequently describe each other in terms of doves or turtledoves: see Canticle of Canticles 1:9, 1:14, 2:10, 2:14, 4:1, 5:2, 5:12 and 6:8.

29.7   *Bed*. We have translated as "He ordered [the executioners]," as the object is explicitly missing here, but are understood to be the same servants who have been torturing Margaret.

        bi lives coste. Literally, "by the cost of [their] life." MWB has translated as "on pain of death" (p. 57). There is a growing sense that, as the knights who originally seize Margaret expressed reservations on account of her fervent devotion to her faith (see 8.1), these "cwelleres" may not have the eagerness to destroy her that Olibrius does.

29.8   *Ant wes as . . . in to cumene*. According to MWB, in the synoptic gospels, darkness descends during Christ's crucifixion from the sixth hour through the ninth hour; see, for example, Matthew 27:45 (p. 154).

30.1–7 *Deorwurthe Drihtin . . . Thi meiden*. See MWB p. 154n56/19–26 and 56/23 for Vulgate Psalms containing these same motifs.

31.2   *eilthurl*. This window represents both the diegetic boundary between Margaret and her audience (both the literal audience and the readerly audience) but also the real physical world of the anchoress, who is provided for by her community through a window. Meanwhile, "she, in turn, supports and inspires [that] community through her prayers, her faith, and her heroic resistance to temptation. The anchoress's contact with the outside world, like Margaret's, is through a window" (Winstead, *Virgin Martyrs*, pp. 38–39).

31.3–32.18 *Ant com ut . . . Healent in Heovene*. See K. Smith, "Snake-Maiden," for a discussion of Margaret's battle with the dragon as a folk motif. See also Spencer, "Legend," p. 198, on medieval and late classical hagiographers' skepticism regarding this section.

31.3   *ane drakes liche*. "Like a dragon" rather than simply a dragon. Medieval dragons are frequently synonymous with enormous snakes; in addition to the biblical association between dragons and satanic forces (see Apocalypse 12, 20), McFadden notes that "Serpents are traditional enemies of virgins, so the serpentine dragon . . . hints more strongly at the sexual nature of Olibrius's offer" ("'The Books of Life'," p. 483). We would also add that there is a kind of resolution to the threats of rape in this scene. Earlier, Margaret prays for her virginity to remain intact. Here she is literally *raptus* in the dragon's jaws — that is, her very body seized against her will, and she is helpless in the grasp of an aggressive, masculine, and, building on McFadden's point, sexualized force. However, the higher power of the sign of the Cross prevents this *raptus* from being completed (i.e., her being wholly consumed by the dragon). In the process of this interruption, the dragon is feminized in a sense, in that his body becomes the locus of the classic vaginal wound, which is violently penetrated by the emerging Margaret in a conflation of rape- and birth-images.

ham gras. An impersonal construction that takes the dative, literally meaning "It was horror to them" or, translated more smoothly, "they were horrified."

with thet sehen thet unselhthe glistinde. See M, p. 66n20/21: "*wið þet* would form a conjunctive phrase, 'by reason of the fact that,' or perhaps better 'when that, when' (they saw that wicked creature glistening)."

31.5   *brade ase bascins.* Robertson discusses the implications of the imagery of washbasins in the eyes of the dragon, who is not only "a figure of wonder" but evocative of "the everyday world of the female contemplatives for whom this work was written" ("Corporeality," p. 278).

31.6   *sperclede.* MWB translates as "flickered," which perhaps captures the image better. We have translated more literally, since the sense is that fire is "belching out" of the dragon's mouth; however this sense of the verb "sparkle" was still in use as late as 1864 in Tennyson's *Aylmer's Field*: "Or when some heat of difference sparkled out" (*Works*, p. 150, line 705).

        threste. "Pressed out" or "issued forth." MWB translates as "streamed out."

31.11   *ne nawt ne . . . ituthet hire bone.* The frequent occurrence in Middle English of multiple negatives makes a literal translation of this line nearly impossible. Multiple negatives often imply emphasis; here, the triple negative emphasizes the fact that Margaret, in her initial terror at the sight of the dragon, *completely* forgot that God, in sending the dragon to her, grants her prayer that she might see her enemy face to face.

32.1–14 *Unseheliche Godd, euch . . . blesci me nuthe.* This prayer is infused with motifs taken from Vulgate Psalms 68:35; 103:19–32; 145:6; and 148:3–10.

32.5   *merkest.* This word is clearly in the present tense, but we have translated it as imperfect to maintain consistency with "havest iwraht" of 32.4.

32.14   *Ich blesci me.* The sense is "I cross myself" but we have translated it as "bless" in order to preserve the alliteration; the sense is that Margaret draws the symbol of the cross.

32.16   *mid tet ilke.* MWB usefully glosses this phrase as "at that moment." Literally the phrase translates as "with that same."

        forswelh into his wide wombe. Although Margaret has prayed to Christ to deliver her from the dragon, she has instead been delivered "*to* him . . . experienc[ing] complete submersion in her prison within a prison," exemplifying "the descent-return archetype" (Dendle, "Pain and Saint-Making, p. 49) typical of romance narratives. In addition, this entrance into the dragon's mouth evokes images of Christ's entry into the Hell-mouth in the account of the Harrowing; another literal swallowing that results in a glorious rebirth as the Hebrew patriarchs are rescued and brought to Heaven. K. Smith makes an argument for the connection between the St. Margaret material and the folk-motif of the Snake-Maiden, which encompasses both the Melusine legend and the serpent-kissing episode in the *Book of John Mandeville* (ed. Kohanski and Benson, lines 304–41). See "Snake-Maiden," pp. 259–63, for a discussion of the two stories as cognates.

33.1   *blackre then eaver eani blamon*. See *MED blo-man* (n.) which refers to a "black-skinned African, an Ethiopian, blackamoor." The majority of the lines cited refer to the "blo-man" coming from Africa, or, more specifically, Ethiopia. See the *Early South-English Legendary*, which describes a "deuel . . . / . . . swarttore þane euere ani blouȝman" (p. 372, line 174–76). While it seems more likely that the author is here thinking of a comparison with a black African (rather than a Muslim), what is important to note is the idea of racial alterity here, which frequently conflated black Africans and Muslims together. This idea of racial difference, coupled with the religious difference of the ever-threatening Muslim expansion, merged with satanic imagery later in the Middle Ages, to produce numerous examples of traditionally evil or satanic characters (such as King Herod and the demon Belyall in the N-Town plays) in literature praying to "Mahoun" (Mohammed) — another name for Satan.

34.9   *monslahe*. The term itself is rare, and this is the only recorded instance, to our knowledge, of it used as an epithet for the devil. See *OED manslaghe* (n.), "man-slayer" [murderer]; *MED mon-slaȝe* (n.), sense b, "one who destroys the soul"; and *BT*'s Old English *mann-slaga* (n.), "homicide, man-slayer." The Old High German cognate *manslago* has the same meaning as the Old English term (see *OED*).

34.18 *toturn*. M refers to the occurrence of this word in the text as the "only occurrence in English" (p. 117). The *MED* provides this line as the only place where the word is used.

       mel-seotel. MWB translates as "seat at the feast" or "banqueting seat." M glosses as "meal-seat," which I have followed here.

35.3   *merren with his . . . of thi meithhad*. The fiend's words here further confirm Wogan-Browne's claim that the saint's body is essentially inviolable ("Virgin's Tale"). But also see Savage, "Translation of the Feminine," pp. 184–85, for a discussion of the virgin martyr's "female body as a literal element which it is impossible to interpret further."

35.4   *munde*. See *MED minde* (adj.), sense a, "present in consciousness or concern," which cites this line.

35.6   *Thet milde meiden . . . his ruhe swire*. Margaret's treatment of the demon here is mild compared to other versions of her legend. In particular, see the Old English life (in *Old English Lives of St Margaret*, ed. Clayton and Magennis, pp. 124–25), where she "gegrap þane deofol þa be þæm locce and hine on eorþan awearp and his swyþran ege utastang and ealle his ban heo tobrysde" [grabbed the devil by the hair and threw him to the ground and she put out his right eye and shattered all his bones] (ed. Clayton and Magennis, pp. 124–25). Dendle points out the increased violence of the Old English versions over other vernacular versions of the Margaret legend: "Margaret is not as interested in learning about demons as she is in pummeling them" ("Pain and Saint-Making," p. 49).

40.4   *Rufines*. A conventional name for the devil. St. Jerome wrote a treatise called *Contra rufinum* (see D, p. xxv), and the demonic dragon of the Old English legend of St. Margaret is called "Ruffus" (Price, "Virgin and the Dragon," p. 339). Most important for this text, though, is the reference in *AW* to the character: "Nabbe ye alswa of Ruffin the deovel, Beliales brother, in ower Englische boc of Seinte Margarete?" ["Do not you also have [the story] of Ruffin the devil, Belial's brother, in your English book of St. Margaret?"] (ed. Hasenfratz, p. 261, lines 4:795–96). The reference to the story reveals two important details: first, that the AB version of Margaret's story was most likely in circulation *before* the composition of *AW*; and second, that while there are some indications that *Margaret* was written to be read aloud, the private ownership of the book may indicate private reading by an anchoress. See Hasenfratz's explanatory note to these lines in the *AW*. For a useful discussion of the dragon in various incarnations of the Margaret legend, as well as insight into medieval understandings of demonology, see Price, "Virgin and the Dragon."

43.1–7 *Monie Ich habbe . . . ha hamseolven overcumen*. Hassel notes that "This depiction of a sexual temptation that is always at issue in social relations between men and women cautions women to avoid such contact altogether" (*Choosing Not to Marry*, p. 66). See also *SJ* 48.2–5. Elliott ("Women and Confession," p. 42) points out "the potential dangers that might arise from the privileged rapport between confessor and penitent." While the text here does not explicitly refer to a male clergyman and his female confessee, it is likely that a "cleane mon [and] . . . a cleane wummon" (43.1), both virgins, are both professional religious. These relationships between religious men and women are necessary because only male religious can hear confession. Elliott further illustrates medieval anxieties about these relationships by describing Thomas of Cantimpré's *Concerning Bees*, which addresses the problem that "many clerics are more tempted by women who appear to have embraced a religious way of life. Likewise women, who would automatically spurn the attractions of secular men . . . frequently cannot resist the allure of holy men, monks, or other ecclesiastics" ("Women and Confession," p. 42).

43.5   *thudde*. While the sense of the term, according to *MED thudden* (v.), sense c, is to force or impose thoughts upon the object, the sexual nature of the language (we have translated it as "to thrust" according to sense b) is unmistakable, and perfectly fitting given the temptations that the devil is setting before chaste men and women.

44.4   *the seoth ham . . . laheste in helle*. Further discussion of this idea of the maiden falling from her high tower to the lowest pit of Hell can be found in *HM*, 2.5, 14.3–5, 17.4.

44.5   *thenchen hu swart . . . et te dome*. A brief rhymed verse which is echoed, with some variation, in *AW* (ed. Hasenfratz, p. 258, lines 749–57). The author of *AW* recommends that the female contemplative use this verse as an aid to meditation. These lines represent the second explicit connection between the two texts (see also explanatory note 40.4 above).

44.7   *gulteth*. "Gulteth" is the present third singular, but because of the plural "ha" and because of the previous context, we have translated in the plural sense.

44.15   *ha schulen ham sclepinde sulen*. The reference is to nocturnal orgasm, a subject of some interest to theologians given the uncertain level of willing involvement of the subject. Writers of the penitentials and of confessional treatises often discussed the question of whether a man who had experienced nocturnal emission could receive the Eucharist, or whether he had to undergo penance beforehand. For an extended discussion of this question, see Pierre J. Payer, *Sex and the Penitentials*, pp. 49–52. The penitentials are silent on the subject of women's nocturnal orgasm, however.

49.3   *i Jamemes ant i Manbres bokes*. According to legend, the two sorcerers who opposed Moses and Aaron of Exodus 7:11–12; see Price, "Virgin and the Dragon," p. 345 and p. 356n27. The two characters are mentioned briefly in several Old English texts, including that of Ælfric, who refers to their practicing of "deofles cræft" (Price, p. 356n27). See also M, p. xxix, and MWB, p. 155n72/6–7.

49.5   *ant ure weies . . . with the windes*. MWB translates as "our ways that we travel are up among the winds." We should understand "weie" here as "street" or, more specifically, "the route along which someone or something is moving" (*MED wei* (n.), sense 2a, which cites this line). See MWB, p. 155n72/9, for references to the origin of the demons' dwelling place.

49.7   *For Jesu Crist . . . thet we ahten*. The devil explains here that he especially hates female virgins because Christ was born of a virgin. Thus, this text emphasizes the distinctive power virginity affords women.

49.17   *For Salomon the . . . in a tunne*. Solomon was believed to have power over the Jinn who he confined to a jar. In the pseudo-epigraphical Old Testament book *The Testament of Solomon*, king Solomon summons forth countless demons, interrogates them about divine matters, forces them to construct the Temple of God, and finally imprisons them in leather flasks sealed magically with Solomon's signet-ring (*Testament of Solomon*, trans. Conybeare, p. 42). See also note 49.3 above. For discussion of the *SM*-author's knowledge of demonology, see M, pp. xxviii–xxix.

54.1–3   *Him bigon to . . . . sehen thet rewthe*. Wogan-Browne ("Virgin's Tale," p. 177) discusses the particular tortures that Margaret undergoes as a "formulaic . . . beating [which] outlines the virgin's body as the locus of argument in a manner different from the represented torture of male saints, in which tortures are addressed to a more fully articulated body (heads, hands, feet etc.) as part of juridical argument and contest." See also p. 191n44 for specific examples of male martyrs whose hands and feet are pierced in comparison to Margaret, whose body suffers *as a whole*. However, in the lines that follow, Margaret forcibly re-creates this torturing fire as a holy fire through her prayers, "a personal female Pentecost, more eloquent and more searing than ever in her love for God" ("Virgin's Tale," p. 179). Some scholars read the torment episodes in the saints' lives as voyeuristic sexualized violence which perhaps constitutes a sadistic rape narrative. See, for example, Innes-Parker, "Sexual Violence"; Gravdal, *Ravishing Maidens*; and Gaunt, *Gender and Genre*. However, see Salih, *Versions of Virginity*, pp. 80–98, for her discussion of ways that contemporary criticism (especially that of Laura Mulvey) potentially obscures medieval evaluations of pain. While we cannot deny the sexual nature of the violence done to Queen Augusta of *SK* (52.2), whose nipples are pierced before her breasts are torn off her body, Katherine's, Margaret's, and Juliana's bodies are not tormented in such female-specific locations on the body. While the spectacle of the naked, bleeding female body certainly evokes notions of sexual violence, the ways in which the saints use their torment, and command their torment to be read by spectators, suggests that torture in these narratives functions as well to reflect on the bestial nature of their tormentors and as pedagogical tool for educating the audience, in that the image evokes the theater of the naked, bleeding body of Christ.

54.3   *Ant hire leofliche . . . sehen thet rewthe*. See explanatory note 21.5. Dendle does not discuss the actual pain that Margaret herself goes through in his essay; however, this scene of brutal torture deflects the physical pain from Margaret to the spectators who watch her. Whereas in earlier saints' lives, such as those of St. Andreas, Conon of Nazareth, and Blandina of Lyons, physical suffering enables the saints themselves to become spiritually stronger (see Dendle, "Pain and Saint-Making," pp. 39–42), here, the physical torment enables the onlookers to develop "rewthe" — that sorrow that is the first step of spiritual growth.

55.1   *Ant heo bigon to bidden Davithes bone*. This particular prayer is never explicitly articulated by David in the Bible, though repeated references to God as purgative or purifying fire (Malachi 3:1–3, Hebrews 12:29, and 1 Corinthians 13–16) abound, as well as descriptions of God's judgment by fire (e.g., Isaias 66:16). However, Margaret's description of love as fire, and of love of God as erotic (in her loins) echoes the words of the Beloved in the Canticle of Canticles: "love is strong as death . . . the lamps thereof are fire and flames (8:6) This reference makes sense in that the Canticle was often considered a lovesong between David and Bathsheba (despite the fact that the Bride speaks here). In addition, because the Bride sings these verses, the prayer further emphasizes Margaret's role as *sponsa Christi* (bride of Christ).

59.1   *Alre Kingene king . . . The ant herien*. Compare Vulgate Psalm 115:16–17.

59.3–4 *o Thi blisfule . . . . awei eaver-euch sunne*. Hassel examines the connection between baptism imagery and Margaret's status as the patron saint of childbirth in *Choosing Not to Marry*. See particularly p. 68.

59.4   *Brudgume*. Here and at 67.11 the Latin Mombritius version, as well as Jacobus de Voragine's version, have no corresponding mention of the spousal devotion shared between Margaret and God. Postlewate, in her study on the Old French versions of Margaret's legend, describes the same choice of vocabulary in the French, also based on the Mombritius version: "she is Christ's *espouse* and *amie*" ("Vernacular Hagiography," p. 118). This change in both vernacular adaptations from the Latin text may reflect either a later common Latin version that served as a basis for both translations, or the independent incorporation, on the part of both translators, of contemporary trends in theology. Astell refers to the renewed interest in the Song of Songs during the twelfth century; the metaphor of the Bride came to reference not simply the church, but "the new Eve, the woman within each one, the Bride of God" (*Song of Songs*, p. 7), and as a result, individual devotion began to reflect the importance of a more personal, intimate relationship with God.

59.10   *Feierlec ant strengthe . . . ant semliche sitten.* Compare Vulgate Psalm 92:1.

63.1   *Malcus.* Malchus, Margaret's executioner, appears abruptly here; he consistently appears in the same role in Latin and vernacular versions of the saint's life. Their revealing conversation continues at 69.1; despite his reluctance to execute Margaret, Malchus functions as an instrument of God, one that Margaret herself arguably wields. In John 18:10–11, Malchus is named as the servant of the Jewish high priest Caiaphas who participated in the arrest of Jesus. One of the disciples, Simon Peter, in order to interfere with the arrest, cuts off the servant's ear which, in Luke (22:50–51) only, is said to have been healed by Jesus. See also note 71.8 below.

66.4   *merkedest the heovene . . . icluhte the eorthe.* Compare Vulgate Wisdom 11:21–22 on God's ordering of the world.

66.6   *hwa se hit . . . hare sunnen foryevene.* Postlewate identifies this as "the crucial moment in the use of the saint's life as exemplum. The members of the audience, by the very act of reading and listening to the saint's story, discover that they are engaged in an act of devotion that will protect them" ("Vernacular Hagiography," p. 128). Margaret does not directly address the reading (or listening) audience of her life, but her prayer here enfolds them into the ongoing devotional momentum of her story. In some ways, Margaret dictates here how her own sainthood should be read. Compare 24.1–6; see also the explanatory note to those lines.

66.8   *I thet hus . . . her hire bene.* Margaret is first associated with women and childbirth by Wace in his French version of the legend. See M, p. 79n46/34 ff. for the history of St. Margaret as the patron saint of childbirth. Most likely the association grew out of the safe "rebirth" of Margaret from the dragon's "wide wombe" (32.16), though the subsequent explosion of the dragon would not necessarily give hope to laboring mothers. Larson explores the history of Margaret's role as intercessor in childbirth ("Who is the Master"). Accounts of the legend which call into question the veracity of the dragon-story (such as the version by Jacobo de Voragine) also omit Margaret's benediction of children and laboring mothers.

67.3   *Ant te meiden . . . to ther eorthe.* This action is a conventional sign of abjection before God as well as a part of clerical ordination.

67.4   *Eadi art tu, meiden, bimong alle wummen.* Compare Luke 1:28. The echoing here of Gabriel's words to Mary at the Annunciation further confirms Margaret's role as spouse of God.

        benen ant i thine eadie beoden. In translating as "petitions" we have followed MWB, as "benen" and "beoden" are essentially the same thing — prayers.

67.11–14   *Cum nu . . . . i wald ah.* This passage in which Christ beckons Margaret to join him as his bridegroom echoes Song of Songs 4:8: "Come with me from Lebanon, my bride, come with me from Lebanon. Descend from the crest of Amana . . . from the lions' dens and the mountain haunts of the leopards."

67.14   *tu schalt wealde . . . i wald ah.* Here, Christ clearly echoes Olibrius' numerous temptations of not just material wealth but temporal power: "ant wel schal hire i-wurthen . . . with al thet Ich welde" (6.3). Now (as opposed to earlier in the text),

Margaret will rule over her Heavenly domain and reap the reward for bestowing her virginity on Christ.

68.7　　*Inc.* See explanatory note 19.6 (*unc*).

68.8　　*Ye, threo ant . . . an Godd unagin.* Margaret's prayer here echoes the Athanasian Creed, as she reaffirms the trinitarian doctrine of the Church in her final blessing and prayer. The Athanasian Creed is similar to the Nicene Creed. See *SK* explanatory note 7.5.

71.8　　*Ant feol of fearlac adun on hire riht halve.* The collapse of Malchus on Margaret's right side here clearly parallels that of Dismas, whose story is based on Luke 23:39–43. The apocryphal Gospel of Nicodemus identifies the Good Thief as Dysmas, who is crucified on the right side of the Lord (see James, *Apocryphal New Testament*, p. 104). After his execution, Dysmas became the patron saint of prisoners, thieves, and especially condemned prisoners. While this is the last we read of Malchus in our text, Nicholas Bozon, in his Anglo-Norman life of Saint Margaret offers some kind words as to the penitent executioner's fate: "Meix par cele pleyne de vertuwe / Jeo crey k'il prist bon fin" [Because of her full of virtue, / I think he came to a good end] ("La Vie Sein(te) Margaret(e)," trans. Klenke, lines 306–07, p. 41).

72.5　　*Sanctus, sanctus, sanctus Dominus Deus Sabaot.* The author quotes the *Sanctus* of the Mass, which draws on the song of praise heard by Isaiah in Isaiah 6:3.

73.1　　*Com Ich, Teochimus.* The re-entry of Teochimus into the text is abrupt, and serves as a kind of structural end-bracket for the narrative and passion of the saint. However, unlike Teochimus' initial self-introduction (2.2–4), here he explains not only his role in writing the life of Margaret, but his actual participation in her story. McFadden suggests that "Theotimus [*sic*] fulfills the literal and mimetic levels of the narrative by participating in the martyrdom, recording the events for future use, and leaving physical artifacts to point to her narrative." This fulfills the purpose of personalizing the narrative as well as "giv[ing] the text a sense of immediacy" ("'Books of Life'," p. 479).

74.1　　*ald Englis.* This is the first recorded use of the term "Old English" to describe the pre-Conquest vernacular (see *MED English* (n. (orig. adj.)), sense 2c). It signals the author's self-consciousness as both an English author and one trained in Latin.

75.1–4　　*thear ha schineth . . . eorthmen withuten ende.* The text again lapses into verse in this prayer. For the first instance of verse, see 44.8.

TEXTUAL NOTES TO *SEINTE MARGARETE*

ABBREVIATIONS: **B₂**: later scribal hand in MS; **H**: a series of sixteenth-century scribbles in various hands (see Introduction, p. 22); **M**: Mack edition (1934); **MS**: Bodleian Library MS Bodley 34 [base text]; **MWB**: Millett and Wogan-Browne edition (1990); **R**: British Library MS Royal 17 A XXVII; **SM**: *The Liflade ant te Passiun of Seinte Margarete*.

SM presents some complications as a later scribe (B₂) reviewed the beginning of the text and made corrections. When possible we have adapted these corrections. We have closely consulted M (1934) for a faithful transcription of Bodley 34 as well as R, and we refer readers who wish to examine the Royal manuscript version of this text to this edition, which provides a parallel text transcription from both manuscripts. In addition, we have examined MWB's helpful edition and translation, which bases its more liberal emendations on R.

Header	Written in red by a different hand. *Biginneth*. So M, MWB. MS: *biginned*.
1.1	*Efter*. MS: large rubricated capital *E*, 1.5 cm.
	steah. So MS, with *a* inserted above the line.
2.1	*Theyet*. MS: large rubricated capital *Þ*, 2.3 cm.
	Beginning on fol. 18v, a second scribe (designated here as B₂) has inserted numerous corrections to the text, possibly based on a copy similar to R.
	of stanes and of stockes. So MS, M, MWB. B₂ has corrected to: *of stockes ant of stanes ant of stockes*. R: *of stockes ant of stanes*.
2.2	*theowe*. So MS, with *o* inserted above the line.
	habbe iredd ant araht. So B₂, MWB. MS, M: *redde ant arahte*. R: *habbe ired ant araht*.
	as hit deh Drihtin, bute. So B₂, R. MS, M, MWB: *as drihtin deh to donne*.
	blinde. So B₂, MWB, R. MS, M omit.
	dreheth for Him. So B₂, MWB, R. MS, M: *drehen*.
2.3	*thet beoth of Crist icleopet*. So B₂, MWB, R. MS, M omit.
2.4	*fulhet*. So MS, corrected from *folhet*.
	almihti. So M, MWB, R. MS: *al mihtei*.
	ant o the witti Sunes nome. So MWB, R. B₂: *and o þe witti suns nome*. MS, M omit.
	ilke. So B₂, MWB, R. MS, M omit.
3.1	*Hercneth*. MS: space has been left for a large capital *H* that was never inserted.
4.1	*This*. MS: space has been left for a large capital *Þ* that was never inserted.
4.3	*the hefde*. Corrected from *the ha hefde* by B₂. So MWB. M, R omit.
	hire₂. So B₂, MWB, R. MS, M omit.
	hire wil ant . . . i wald hahte. So M, MWB. MS: the entire line has been canceled. R omits.

4.4   *áá meiden*. B₂ has deleted MS's *alre mild* and inserted *a meiden* in the right
           margin. R: *an meiden*. M, MWB retain *alre milde*.

           for rihte bileave. So B₂, MWB, R. MS, M omit.

           drohen ant drehheden. So B₂, MWB. MS: *drohen*, which M reads as *drehen*. R:
           drohen.

5.1   *Bitimde*. MS: space has been left for a large capital *B* that was never inserted.

5.3   *a dei*. So B₂, MWB, R. MS, M omit.

           fostermodres. So M, MWB. MS: *fostmodres*.

6.2   *is*. MS: *his*. Emended to avoid confusion with pronoun *his*.

7.1   *Have*. MS: space has been left for a large capital *H* that was never inserted.
           We have generally followed MS's paragraph markings, adding additional
           breaks to clearly define dialogue. In addition, we have consulted MWB's
           paragraph divisions when in need of clarification.

7.4   *Thu*. So B₂, MWB, R. MS, M omit.

           flesliche. So B₂, MWB, R. MS, M: *ulche*.

           hwile. So MWB, R. MS, M: *while*.

7.6   *bereth*. So M, MWB, R. MS: the word is smudged and very difficult to read;
           only *b*, *r*, and the top of the *ð* are clear.

7.7   *hit is₂*. So B₂, MWB, replacing MS's *&* (*ant*), retained by M. R: *hit is*.

           thertoward with alles. So B₂, R. M, MWB. MS: *thertoward* ~~with willes with werkes~~
           with alles, with cancellation most likely by B₂.

7.8   *wite hit ever*. So M, MWB, R. MS: *wit ~~me~~ ever*; with *hit* inserted above.

7.11   *i luthere mennes*. So M, MWB. MS: *iluthers menne*. Emended for sense,
           following R's *i luthere monne*.

8.1   *The*. MS: space has been left for a large capital *Þ* that was never inserted.

10.1   *thah*. B₂: *ant thah*. MS, M omit. MWB: *am, ant þah Godes*. R: *ant tah*.

11.1   *ah*. MS: *ah* is inserted above the line.

12.1   *leve on ase on Lauerd*. So B₂, MWB. MS, M: *leve ase lauerd*. R: *leue as on lauerd*.

13.1   *Ye*. So B₂, R, corrected from MS's *hu dele*. M, MWB retain *hu dele*.

           lude. So B₂, MWB, R. MS, M omit.

15.1   *ant i cwalhus*. So MS, with *ant i* inserted in the margin.

16.1   *seggen*. So MWB, R. MS, M: *segen*.

           Meiden. MS: space has been left for a large capital *M* that was never inserted.
           In this case the indicator letter has been partially trimmed off.

16.3   *ant₂*. So B₂, MWB, R. MS, M omit.

17.1   *him*. So B₂, MWB, R. MS, M omit.

           In the top margin of fol. 21r, H: *In the Name of god ?u on I georg*.

           Margarete. MS: *a₂* inserted above the line.

           wel the. MS: *wel ~~he~~ þe*.

           iseilet. So M, MWB, R. MS: *iseiset*.

           to Himseolf me ant. So MWB, MS. B, M: *me to himseolf ant*. R: *to him me seolf*.

           meithhad. MS: *meidhad*.

           nanes. So MWB, R. MS, M: *nans*.

           Between fols. 20a and 21 there is a small strip of parchment, known as fol.
           20b, which contains corrected text on one side, written by B₂. See the
           textual note to 19.1–3 below.

           wrenchen ut of. MS: *ut* inserted above the line.

17.3   *buheth*. So M, MWB, R. MS: *buhed*.

        ant beieth. So B₂, MWB, R. MS, M omit.

17.4   *He is leoflukest lif forto*. So B₂, MWB, R. MS: *he leoflukest to*. M: *he is leoflukest to*.

        ne His swote . . . ne His makelese. So B₂, MWB, R. MS, M omit.

        lufsumlec. MS: *his lufsumlec*. This *his* becomes redundant with B₂'s insertion.

        never mare ne mei. So MS. Corrected by B₂ to *never mare ne mei neaver mare*.

18.1   *Let*. MS: space has been left for a large capital *L* that was never inserted.

        wurth. So MWB, R. MS, M: *wurhth*.

18.3   *Ich i wald*. So B, with *i* inserted above the line.

19.1–3 *Ich ileve the . . . ant thin eie*. MS: ~~e leove qð ha hwar to luste þe warpen al awei þi ne hwile~~. Space has been left for a capital *M* (for the deleted phrase *Me leove*) that was never inserted. The indicator letter has been cropped. Following MS, the narrative jumps straight from Olibrius' offer to marry Margaret to her declaration that she will undergo any sort of bodily torment so long as she is able to keep her place in heaven. From R, it is apparent that fol. 20br, pasted between leaves 20 and 21, belongs between these two speeches, and we have inserted the text in place of the canceled line, following MWB. M transcribes the text insert on p. 12n4.

19.1   *beheaste*. So B₂, with *aste* inserted above the line.

19.2   *leovere*. So MWB, R. B₂: *leovevere*.

19.3   *thine hwile*. So MWB, R. B₂: *thine thine hwile*. Redundant *thine* removed.

        quoth ha. B₂: inserted above the line.

        olhnung. So MWB, R. B₂: *olhnigi*.

21.1   *Lauerd*. MS: space has been left for a large capital *L* that was never inserted.

        hope. MS: *mine hope* ~~ant min hu~~.

21.3   *luvieth*. MS: *luvied*.

        The. So M, MWB, R. MS: *þe he*.

22.1   *Olibrius*. MS: space has been left for a large capital *O* that was never inserted. The indicator letter has been cropped.

23.1   In the top margin of fol. 22r, H: *I Rychard Vnet of ledbury In the com*. In the right margin the name *Anne* is faintly distinguishable and slightly below it *Ry*, both written by H.

        meanden. MS: *a* inserted above the line.

25.4   In the top margin of fol. 22v, H: *Iohn Altermonger the worste that ever*. In the left margin; H: *This*, followed by unclear scribble filling up the rest of the margin.

        liun. So M, MWB, R. MS: *lim*.

        tu₂. MS: *?u*. A smudge on the page makes the first letter impossible to read.

        unmuclin. So M. Emended based on R's *unmuchelin*. MS: *unmutlin*, retained by MWB.

26.1   *wraththe*. MS: *wradðe*.

        hire₂. MS: *hire* ~~leo~~.

26.2   *seggen*. MS: there is a long decorative mark between *segge* and *n*.

27.1   *Helle-hundes*. MS: space has been left for a large capital *H* that was never inserted.

27.3   *reowfule*. MS: *o* inserted above the line.

        hundes. So M, MWB, R. MS: *hondes*.

	bute. So M, MWB, R. MS: *but?*. The last letter is garbled and may have been modified from an *a*. M states that the original letter was a *u*.
27.6	*Send*. So MS, corrected from *sende*.
27.8	*iblesced*. So M, MS, with *s* inserted above the word and *d* appearing to have been corrected from *t*. MWB, R: *iblescet*.
	áá. MS: *áá* ~~itts~~.
27.9	*Amen*. So R. MS omits.
28.1	*Hwil*. MS: space has been left for a large capital H that was never inserted. The indicator letter has been cropped.
	In the right margin of fol. 23r, H: very faint scribbling.
	hudden. MS: *huden*; d_2 is inserted above the line.
	iheortet. MS: *i heorttet*.
28.5	*hwen*. MS: *h* is inserted above the line.
29.1	*Me*. MS: space has been left for a large capital *M* that was never inserted.
29.2	*eorthe*. MS: ~~t~~*eorthe*.
29.6	*warth*. So MWB, R. MS, M omit.
30.1	*Deorewurthe*. MS: space has been left for a large capital D that was never inserted.
30.10	In the top margin of fol. 24r, H: *To hi[?] lord got that made bothe see and*.
31.1	*Hire*. MS: space has been left for a large capital *H* that was never inserted.
	cwalmhus. MS: *h* is inserted above the line.
	bi livede. So M, MWB, R. MS: *bilevide*.
31.3	*ane*. So M, MWB, R. MS: *ana*.
31.4	*swart*. So M, MWB, R. MS: the word might be *sward*. The last letter has been altered from *d* to *t* or vice versa.
31.7	*scharp sweord*. MS: *sweord scharp*, but corrected via markers *a* and *b*; *a* appears over *scharp* and *b* over *sweord* to indicate the word order should be reversed.
31.11	*then*. MS: inserted above the line.
	ant₃. So MWB, R. MS omits.
	with. MS: inserted above the line.
32.1	*Unseheliche*. MS: space has been left for a large capital *U* that was never inserted.
	wreaththe. So M, MWB. MS: *wreaðe*.
	mi Lauerd. So M, MWB. MS: *mi la lauerd*. At the turn of the line, MS has an extra *la* which has been omitted here.
32.3	*heastes*. So M, MWB. MS: *heastest*.
32.4	*iwraht*. So MS, with *r* inserted above the line.
	neavre. So MS, with *a* inserted above the line.
32.13	In the bottom margin of fol. 25v, upside down, H: *This bill th*.
32.18	*Heovene*. MS: decorative lines are inserted between e^2 and *n*, and between *n* and e^3.
	eaver-euch. MS: *eavereuch* ~~sor~~.
33.1	*As*. MS: space has been left for a large capital *A* that was never inserted. The indicator letter in the margin appears to be written by a later hand.
	ant₁. MS: inserted above the line. M, MWB, R omit.
33.2	*Healent*. MS: decorative lines are inserted between e^2 and *n*, and *n* and *t*.

34.1 In the top margin of fol. 26r, H: *?ee a Rychard Sebourne of.*

Brihtest. MS: space has been left for a large capital *B* that was never inserted.

34.6 *murhthen.* So MWB, R. MS, M: *murhden.*

34.10 *ferliche.* So R, M. MS, MWB: *earheliche.*

34.12 *eoli.* MS: *e* is inserted above the line.

34.13 *isehen.* So MWB, R. MS, M: *sehen.*

34.15 *thoncki.* MS: *þonki*; *c* is inserted above the line.

34.18 *sorhfule.* MS: *sorfule*; *h* is inserted above the line.

thing. So M, R. MS, MWB omit.

Godd. MS: *godð.*

35.1 *As.* MS: space has been left for a large capital *A* that was never inserted.

35.2 *biddest.* So MWB, R. MS, M: *bidest.*

35.3 In the bottom margin of fol. 27r, upside down, H: *This bill made the,* followed by two incomplete letters.

meithhad. So M. So MWB, R. MS: *meidhad,* though the ink is blurred and the *d* is unclear.

35.6 *Margarete.* So MWB, R. MS, M: *margarte.*

36.1 *Stute.* MS: space has been left for a large capital *S* that was never inserted. The indicator letter in the left margin appears to be written by a later hand.

36.2 *worldes.* So M, MWB, R. MS: *worldess,* though M reads as an unfinished *worldest.*

is ihwer. MS: *iwer*; *is* and *h* are inserted above the line.

36.3 *biwite.* MS: *wite,* with *bi* inserted above the line.

36.5 *monslahe.* So M, MWB, R. MS: *monslae.*

heonnevorth. So M, MWB, from R's *heonneforð.* MS: *heonnevord.*

36.7 *He.* So MS, corrected from *ha.*

36.9 *blissen.* MS: rubricated decorative line filler follows this word to the end of the line.

37.1 *Hwil.* MS: rubricated large capital *H,* 1.5 cm. With this capital, the work of the first rubricator resumes off and on throughout the rest of the manuscript. The second rubricator does not return.

speatewile. So MS, with *a* inserted above the line.

Rode. MS: *rode t.*

38.1 *unwiht.* MS: rubricated decorative line filler follows this word to the end of the line.

Cuth. MS: rubricated large capital *C,* 1 cm.

forcuthest. So MWB, R. MS, M: *forcudest.*

40.1 *speokene.* MS: rubricated decorative line filler follows this word to the end of the line.

Wult. MS: rubricated capital wynn with decorative flourish at the bottom, total 3 cm.

40.2 *beo.* MS: *beo ~~ihe~~,* with *ihe* partially erased.

40.4 *rehest.* So M, MWB, R. MS: *rehe.*

40.5 *wuneth.* So M, MWB, R. MS: *wuned.*

40.7 *leometh.* So M, MWB, R. MS: *leomed.*

42.1 *leafdi.* So M, MWB. MS: *leasdi.* R: *lefdi.*

42.3 *fulthen.* So M, MWB, R. MS: *fulden.*

43.1	*Monie*. MS: space has been left for a large capital *M* that was never inserted.
	nawhit. So M, MWB. MS: *nawt*; *hi* is inserted above the line.
43.6	*leade*. MS: a redundant *ich*, in a later hand, has been inserted prior to this word above the line; R duplicates this syntax but does not include the earlier *ich* at the beginning of the sentence. Both M and MWB omit.
43.8	*notheles*. So MS, with *n* inserted above the line.
44.1	*This*. MS: space has been left for a large capital Þ that was never inserted.
	sterclukest. So MS, with *c* inserted above the line.
44.4	*ec*. So MWB, R. MS: *hec* is inserted above the line in a later hand (not B₂); M retains MS's reading.
44.9	*muchelin*. So R. MWB, MS: *mutlin*. M: *muclin*.
	hit ischawet. So M, MWB, R. MS: *hit is ischawet*, with *is* inserted above the line. There remains the possibility that *bith* is a mistake for *with*, which would accompany the following *birewsinde* far more smoothly.
44.11	*thear*. MS: *þer*; *a* is inserted above the line.
	seggen. MS: *segen*; *g* is inserted above the line.
44.13	*forwurtheth*. So MWB, R. MS, M: *forwurdeth*.
	ahten to. So M, MWB, R. MS omits.
44.14	*ha₁*. So M, MWB, R. MS: *ah*.
	hwen. So MS, with *h* inserted above the line.
	wurthschipe. So MWB, R. MS, M: *wurdschipe*.
44.16	*ed te nuthe*. So M, MWB, R. MS: *edten ende*.
45.1	In the bottom right corner of fol. 30v, upside down, H: *I The I*.
	Margarete. MS: space has been left for a large capital *M* that was never inserted.
	iwurthen. So MWB, R. MS, M: *iwurden*.
45.7	*ant*. So M, MWB, R. MS: *ah*, with *h* inserted above the line.
46.1	*Stew*. MS: space has been left for a large capital *S* that was never inserted. The indicator letter in the left margin is in a later hand.
48.2	In the top margin of fol. 31r, H: *Tomy h on? My own ffrind I pray yow*[?] followed by faint scribbles. The right margin contains very faint marks that are impossible to decipher. In the bottom right corner of the page, H has written *I The*, upside down.
48.3	*unofservet*. So MWB, R. MS, M: *unoservet*.
49.2	*Sathanas*. MS: space has been left for a large capital *S* that was never inserted. MS contains two indicator letters in the left margin, one contemporary and one in a later hand.
49.7	*meithhad*. So M, MWB, R. MS: *meidhad*.
49.8	*we₁*. So MS, inserted above the line.
49.9	*weorith*. So MS, M. MWB: *weorrið*. R omits.
49.10	*hofles*. So M, MWB, R. MS: *holes*.
	iwurtheth. So MWB, R. MS, M: *iwurdeth*.
49.15	*sulliche*. So M, MWB, R. MS: *susliche*, with *s* possibly modified to *l*.
50.1	*Stille*. MS: space has been left for a large capital *S* that was never inserted. The indicator letter in the left margin is in a later hand.
50.3	*feond*. So M. MS: the last letter appears to have been altered from *t*. MWB: *feont*. R: *þing*.

50.4	*ilke*. So MWB, R. MS, M: *illke*.
51.1	*Ine*. MS: space has been left for a large capital *I* that was never inserted.
52.1	*Meiden*. MS: space has been left for a large capital *M* that was never inserted.
53.2	*selcuthe*. So MWB. MS, M: *selcude*.
	Godd₂. So M, MWB, R. MS: *goð*.
54.1	*Him*. MS: space has been left for a large capital *H* that was never inserted.
55.1	*frovre, fure*. So M, MWB, R. MS: *frovre, frovre*.
	let. So M, MWB, R. MS omits.
56.1	*Lef*. MS: space has been left for a large capital *L* that was never inserted. The indicator letter in the left margin is in a later hand.
57.4	*haveth₁*. So M, MWB, R. MS: *haved*.
58.1	*death*. So M, MWB. R: *deð*. MS: *deah*.
59.1	*Alre*. MS: space has been left for a large capital *A* that was never inserted. The indicator letter in the left margin is in a later hand.
59.2	*echelich*. So M, MWB, R. MS: *eche lif*.
59.6	*eorthe*. So MWB, R. MS: *eorde*. M reads MS as *eorthe*.
	cwakien. MS: corrected from *chakien*.
59.7	*ant brohte*. So M, R. MS, MWB omit.
59.8	*wurthmunt*. So MWB, R. MS, M: *wurdmunt*.
59.9	*cutheth*. So MWB. MS, M, R: *cudeð*.
60.1	*Cum*. MS: space has been left for a large capital *C* that was never inserted.
	stevene. MS: *stettvene*.
61.1	*O*. MS: space has been left for a large capital *O* that was never inserted. The edge of the indicator letter in the left margin is visible; the rest has been cropped.
	turnden. So R. MS, M, MWB: *turden*.
	murhthe. So MWB. MS, M: *murhde*. R: *murhðen*.
62.1	*The*. MS: space has been left for a large capital *Þ* that was never inserted.
	warth. So M, MWB. MS: *ward*. R omits.
62.2	*schimminde*. So M, MWB, R. MS: *schimninde*.
	with₂. So M, MWB. MS: *wid*. R omits.
63.1	*Meiden*. MS: space has been left for a large capital *M* that was never inserted.
64.1	*thet*. MS: inserted above the line.
65.1	*quoth he*. So M, MWB, R. MS omits.
66.1	*Drihtin*. MS: space has been left for a large capital *D* that was never inserted. The indicator letter in the left margin is written in a later hand.
	thah. So M, MWB. MS: *thetah*. This word mistakenly begins with a crossed *þ*.
	dearne. MS: *derne*; with *a* is inserted above the line.
66.3	*al*. So M, MWB, R. MS: *a*.
66.6	*iwriten*. MS: *iwritent*.
66.7	*ham₃*. So R. MS, M, MWB: *him*.
66.8	*mi nome*. So MWB, R. MS, M: *þi nome*.
66.10	In the bottom margin of fol. 34v, upside down, H: *This indenture made the xv / he sc he that in ? ? ?*. (The cursive, here, is partially illegible.)
	Ant hwa. MS: the descender on the *wynn* goes nearly to the bottom of the page.
	Laste. So M, R. MS: *lelaste*. MWB: *leaste*.
	him. So MWB. MS: *ham*.

67.1   *With.* MS: space has been left for a large capital *wynn* that was never inserted.

67.4   *thine eadie.* MS: *þene* corrected to *þine*; *eadie* inserted above the line.

67.7   *other₂.* So MWB, R. MS, M: *oder.*

67.8   *hus.* So M, MWB, R. MS: *thus.*

67.13   *abit.* So MWB, R. MS, M: *abitd.*

68.1   *The.* MS: space has been left for a large capital *Þ* that was never inserted. In the space remaining in the left margin, *þ* has been written in a later hand.

        blithest. So MWB. MS, M: *blidest.* R omits.

68.2   *quoth ha.* MS: inserted above the line.

        ye₂. So MWB, R. MS: *ge.* M reads as ʒ.

68.3   *mi₂.* So M, MWB, R. MS: *ni.*

68.6   *Ich.* So MS, with *c* inserted above the line.

68.8   In the bottom margin of fol. 35v, upside down, H: *A medycyn for.*

        threo. MS: *þeo*; *r* is inserted above the line.

        heheschipe. So M, MWB, R. MS: *he hehschipe.*

68.9   *Wurthschipe.* So MWB, R. MS, M: *wurdschipe.*

69.1   *Efter.* MS: space has been left for a large capital *E* that was never inserted.

71.2   *dale in.* MS: *dale* ~~wið~~ *in.*

71.3   *smertliche.* So M, R. MS: *smeetliche.* MWB: *smeortliche.*

71.4   *schuldren.* So MWB, R. MS: *scluldren.* M reads as *schildren.*

        ant te bodi beah. So MS, with *te bodi* inserted in the right margin.

71.5   *Heovene.* MS: *heovne*; *e₂* is inserted above the line.

72.1   *Comen.* MS: space has been left for a large capital *C* that was never inserted.

        lihtinde. So M, MWB, R. MS: *lihtinte.*

72.9   *bearnes.* MS: *bearn̄es.*

73.1   *Com.* MS: large rubricated capital *C*, 1.1 cm. At the end of this line *re heale* (from *hare heale* 72.11) has been bumped from the previous line, as indicated by a red colophon mark.

73.3   *hwer.* MS: *wer*, with *h* added above the line.

73.4   *yont te worlde.* MS: *worlde* is placed on the next line directly below *yont te.*

74.1   *Thus.* MS: large rubricated capital *Þ*, 2.1 cm.

        balesith. So MWB, R. MS, M: *balesið* (p. 52, line 35).

        euch wa. MS: following this phrase, decorative rubricated line filler continues to the end of the line.

75.1   *Alle.* MS: large rubricated capital *A*, 2.1 cm. The indicator letter has been cropped.

        muth. So M, MWB, R. MS: *mud.*

75.2   *Ant.* So MWB. M, MS: *an.* R omits.

75.3   *bituhe.* So MS, with *i* inserted above the line.

        singen. MS: following this word, decorated rubricated line filler continues to the end of the line.

75.4   *Igret.* MS: large rubricated capital *I*, 1.4 cm. The indicator letter has been cropped.

75.5   *AMEN.* MS: this word is all in capitals.

THE LIFLADE ANT TE PASSIUN OF SEINTE JULIENE

I the Feaderes ant i the Sunes ant i the Hali Gastes nome, Her Biginneth the liflade ant te passiun of Seinte Juliene.

1.   (1) In ure Lauerdes luve, the Feader is of frumscheft, ant i the deore wurthmunt of His deorewurthe Sune, ant i the heiunge of the Hali Gast, the of ham ba glideth, an Godd unaginninde, euch godes ful: alle leawede men the understonden ne mahen Latines ledene, litheth ant lusteth the liflade of a

fol. 37r   meiden, | thet is of Latin iturnd to Englische leode, with thon thet teos hali leafdi in Heovene luvie us the mare, ant thurh this lihinde lif leade us to thet eche, thurh hire eadi erndunge, thet Crist is swithe icweme.

2.   (1) Theos meiden ant teos martyr thet Ich of munne wes Juliene inempnet, i Nichomedese burh al of heathene cun icumen ant akennet, ant hire fleshliche feader Affrican hehte, the heande ant heascede mest men the weren Cristene ant droh ham thurh derve pinen to deathe. (2) Ah heo, as theo thet te hehe heovenliche Lauerd hefde His luve ilenet, leafde hire ealdrene lahen ant bigon

---

In the name of the Father and of the Son and of the Holy Ghost, here begins the life and the passion of Saint Juliana.

1.   (1) In the love of our Lord, who is the Father of creation, and in the dear worship of His precious Son, and in the praise of the Holy Ghost, who proceeds from them both, one God without beginning, full of every good thing: all unlearned people who cannot understand the language of Latin, hear and listen to the life of a maiden, which is translated from Latin into the English language, so that this holy lady in Heaven may love us the more, and through this deceitful life may lead us to that eternal one, through her blessed intercession, which is very pleasing to Christ.

2.   (1) This maiden and this martyr that I commemorate was named Juliana, came from and was born to an entirely heathen family in the city of Nichomedia, and her fleshly father was called Africanus, who oppressed and persecuted most men who were Christian and put them to death through terrible tortures. (2) But she, as one to whom the high heavenly Lord had given His love, left her elders' laws and began

to luvien then áá liviende God, the lufsume Lauerd thet schupte alle scheaftes ant wealdeth ant wisseth, efter thet His wil is, al thet ischeapen is.

3. (1) Wes i thon time, as the redunge telleth, the modi Maximien keiser i Rome heriende ant heiende heathene maumez with unimeath muchel hird ant with heh duhethe, ant fordemde alle theo the o Drihtin bilefden. (2) Thes mihti Maximien luvede an Eleusium bivoren monie of his men: akennet of heh cun, ant swithe riche of rente, ant yung mon of yeres. (3) Thes yunge mon Eleusius, thet thus wes wel with the king, hefde iunne feolahschipe to Affrican ant wes iwunet ofte to

fol. 37v cumen with him | to his in ant iseon his dohter.

4. (1) As he hefde enchere bihalden swithe yeorne hire utnume feire ant freoliche yuhethe, felde him iwundet inwith in his heorte with the flan the of luve fleoth, swa thet him thuhte thet ne mahte he nanes weis withute the lechnunge of hire luve libben. (2) Ant efter lutle stunde withute long stevene, wes himseolf sonde to Affrican hire feader, ant bisohte him yeorne thet he hire yeve him, ant he hire walde menskin with al thet he mahte as the thing i the world thet he meast luvede. (3) Affrican wiste thet he wes swithe freo-iboren ant walde wel bicumen him a freoi-boren burde, ant yetede him his bone. (4) Ha wes him sone ihondsald, thah hit hire unwil were, ah ha truste upon Him thet ne truked na mon thet trewliche Him truste, on ant eode to chirche euche dahethes dei to leornin Godes lare, biddinde yeorne with reowfule reames thet He wissede hire o hwuche wise ha mahte witen hire meithhath from mones man unwemmet.

---

to love then the ever living God, the lovely Lord who created all creatures, and rules and directs, according to His will, all that is created.

3. (1) In that time, as the legend tells, the proud emperor Maximian was in Rome worshiping and praising heathen idols with an immeasurably large court and with a noble company, and he condemned all those who believed in the Ruler. (2) This mighty Maximian loved, above many of his men, one Eleusius: descended from noble kin, and very rich from rent, and a young man of years. (3) This young man Eleusius, who was so well off with the king, had given friendship to Africanus and was accustomed often to come with him to his house and to see his daughter.

4. (1) When he had at one time beheld very earnestly her exceedingly fair and beautiful youth, he felt himself wounded inside in his heart with the arrows which fly from love, so that it seemed to him that he could not in any way live without the medicine of her love. (2) And after a little while without a long delay, he was himself the messenger to Africanus her father, and he eagerly besought Africanus to give her to him, and he would honor her with everything that he might as the thing that he loved most in the world. (3) Africanus knew that he was of very noble birth and that a nobly born lady would suit him well, and granted him his boon. (4) She was soon betrothed to him, although she was unwilling, but she trusted in Him who does not fail anyone who truly trusts in Him, and went to church at dawn every day to learn God's lore, praying earnestly with pitiful cries that He guide her as to what way she might keep her maidenhood unblemished from sex with a man.

5.

fol. 38r

(1) Elewsius, thet luvede hire, thuhte swithe longe thet ha neren to brudlac ant to bed ibrohte. (2) Ah heo, forte werien hire with him summe hwile, | sende him to seggen thet nalde ha nawt lihten se lahe to luvien, ne nalde ha neolechin him for na liviende mon ear then he were under Maximien, hehest i Rome, thet is heh reve. (3) He, ase timliche as he hefde iherd this, biyeted te keiser thet he yette him al thet he walde, ant lette, as me luvede tha, leaden him i cure up o fowr hweoles ant teon him yeonte tun thron from strete to strete. (4) Al the cure wes overtild thet he wes itohen on, with purpres ant pelles, with ciclatuns ant cendals ant deorewurthe clathes, as the thet se heh thing hefde to heden ant se riche refschipe to rihten ant to readen. (5) Tha he hefde thus idon, sende hire thus to seggen: hire wil he hefde iwraht; nu his ha schulde wurchen.

6.

fol. 38v

(1) Juliene the eadie, Jhesu Cristes leofmon, of his blisfule luve balde hire seolven, ant sende him al openliche bi sonde to seggen: "This word ha send te: 'For nawt thu havest iswech te. (2) Wreathe se thu wreathe, do thet tu do wult. (3) Nule ich, ne ne mei ich lengre heolen hit te: yef thu wult leaven the lahen thet tu livest in ant leven i Godd Feader ant in His deorwurthe Sune, ant i the Hali Gast folkene frovre an Godd | thet is igret with euches cunnes gode, ich chule wel neome the. (4) Ant yef thet tu nult no, thu art windi of me ant other luve sech the.'" (5) Tha the hehe reve iherde this ondswere bigon to wrethen swithe, ant cleopede hire feder forth ant feng on to tellen hwuch word ha sende him. (6) Efter thet, he wende forte habben al thet heo wilnede.

5.

(1) To Eleusius, who loved her, it seemed too long that they were not brought to marriage and bed. (2) But she, in order to defend herself against him for some time, sent for him to say that she did not at all wish to descend so low to love, nor did she wish to approach him for any living man until he was directly beneath Maximian, the highest in Rome, that is, the high reeve. (3) He, as soon as he had heard this, obtained from the emperor the promise that he would grant him all that he wished; and, as was the custom, he had him set in a four-wheeled chariot and drawn through the town in it from street to street. (4) The entire chariot that he was drawn in was canopied with purple cloths and satin, with cloth of gold and fine linen and precious cloths, like one who had to attend to so high a thing and had to direct and arrange so powerful a governorship. (5) When he had done this he sent to her to say thus: he had fulfilled her wish, now she should fulfill his.

6.

(1) Juliana the blessed, Jesus Christ's beloved, emboldened herself with His blissful love, and sent to him by messenger to say entirely in public: "This word she sends to you: 'You have troubled yourself for nothing. (2) Angry as you may be, do what you will. (3) I will not, nor can I, conceal it from you any longer: if you will leave the law that you live in and believe in God the Father, and in His precious Son, and in the Holy Ghost, comfort of men, one God who is glorified with every kind of good, I will well accept you. (4) And if you will not, you are done with me and should seek another love.'" (5) When the high reeve heard this answer he began to grow very angry, and he called her father forth and began to tell what message she sent him. (6) After that, he expected to have everything that he wished.

7. (1) Affrican, hire feader, wundrede him swithe ant bigon to swerien: "Bi the ilke godes thet me is lath to gremien, beo hit soth thet tu seist, to wrather heale ha seith hit! (2) Ant ich wulle o great grome al biteachen hire the, ant tu do hire al thet tu wult."

8. (1) He thonkede him, ant heo wes icleopet forth. (2) Ant Affrican, hire feader, feng on earst feire on to lokin yef he mahte with eani luve speden. (3) "Juliene," quoth he, "mi deorewurthe dohter! (4) Sei me hwi thu forsakest thi sy ant ti selhthe, the weolen ant te wunnen the walden awakenen ant waxen of the wedlac thet ich reade the to. (5) Hit nis nan ethelich thing the refschipe of Rome, and tu maht, yef thu wult, beon burhene leafdi ant of alle the londes the therto liggeth."

9. (1) Juliene the eadie ontswerede him ant seide, "Yef he wule luvien ant leven Godd almihti thenne mei he speoken throf ant speden inohreathe. (2) For yef he thet nule no, ich segge the thet soth is ne schal he wiven on me. (3) Sei nu hwet ti wil is."

fol. 39r

10. (1) Affrican wreathede ant | swor swithe deopliche: "For the drihtfule godd Apollo, mi lauerd, ant mi deore leafdi, the deorewurthe Diane, thet ich muche luvie, yef thu haldest her-on, ich schal leote wilde deor toluken ant toteore the ant yeove thi flesch fode to fuheles of the lufte."

11. (1) Juliene him ondswerede ant softeliche seide, "Ne lef thu nawt, leove feader, thet tu offeare me swa. (2) Ich swerie ayein the, for Jhesu Crist, Godes Sune, thet ich on leve ant luvie as leoflukest ant lufsumest Lauerd, thah ich cwic beo forbearnd

---

7. (1) Africanus, her father, was very surprised and began to swear: "By the same gods that I hate to anger, if what you say is true, she says it to disastrous fortune! (2) And in great anger I will hand her over entirely to you, and you may do to her all that you wish."

8. (1) He thanked him, and she was called forth. (2) And Africanus, her father, began at first to see whether he might succeed with any love. (3) "Juliana," he said, "my precious daughter! (4) Say to me why you forsake your triumph and your happiness, the good fortune and delight which would awaken and wax from the wedlock that I recommend to you. (5) It, the reeveship of Rome, is no inconsiderable thing and you might, if you wish, be the lady of the city and of all the lands which lie nearby."

9. (1) Juliana the blessed answered him and said: "If he will love and believe in God Almighty then he may speak about it and succeed soon enough. (2) But if he does not wish that, I say to you that it is true he shall not marry me. (3) Say now what your will is."

10. (1) Africanus grew angry and swore very deeply: "By the noble god Apollo, my lord, and by my dear lady, the precious Diana, whom I love very much, if you hold to this, I will have wild beasts pull and tear you to pieces and give your flesh as food to the birds of the sky!"

11. (1) Juliana answered him and softly said: "Do not at all believe, dear father, that you frighten me with this. (2) I swear again to you, for Jesus Christ, God's Son, in whom I believe and love as the most lovely and most gracious Lord, that were

bathe lim ant lith i leitinde leie, nulle, ich the her-onont — threate se thu threate — buhe ne beien."

12.   (1) Affrican feng eft on, ant to fondin | ongon yef he mahte eanisweis with olhnunge wenden hire heorte, ant leoftede luveliche ant seide hire sikerliche, thet ne schulde ha lihtliche wilni na wunne thet ha ne schulde wealden, with then an thet ha walde hire wil wenden.

13.   (1) "Nai," quoth ha "thet nis nawt. (2) Schulde ich do me to him, thet alle deoflen is bitaht ant to eche death fordemet, to forwurthe with him, worlt buten ende, i the putte of Helle for his wedlackes weole other for ei wunne? (3) To sothe ich hit segge the: unwurth hit is me. (4) Ich chulle thet he wite hit ful wel, ant tu eke mid al, ich am to an iweddet thet ich chulle treowliche withute leas luvien thet is unlich him ant alle worltliche men. (5) Ne nulle ich neaver mare Him lihen ne

fol. 39v lea|ven, for weole ne for wunne, for wa ne for wontreathe, thet ye me mahen wurchen."

14.   (1) Hire feader feng on to wreaththin swithe ferliche ant easkede hire hokerliche, "Ant hwet is he, thes were thet tu art to iweddet, thet tu havest withute me se forth thi luve ilenet, thet tu letest lutel of al thet tu schuldest luvien? (2) Ne ich nes neaver — thet ich wite — yet with him icnawen."

15.   (1) "For Gode," quoth the meiden, "thin hearm is the mare. (2) Nawt forthi thet tu navest iherd of him yare: thet is, Jhesu, Godes Sune, thet forte alesen moncun thet schulde beon forloren al, lette lif o Rode. (3) Ich ne seh Him neaver,

---

I burned alive both limb and joint in flaming fire, I would not, in regard to this — threaten however you threaten — bow to or obey you."

12.   (1) Africanus started again, and tried to test if he might in any way turn her heart with flattery, and cajoled kindly and said to her that certainly, she would not lightly desire any delight that she would not possess on the condition that she would change her will.

13.   (1) "No," said she, "that is nothing. (2) Should I join myself to him who is entirely committed to devils and doomed to eternal death, to perish with him, world without end, in the pit of Hell for the benefit of his wedlock or for any reward? (3) To you I truly say: it is worthless to me. (4) I wish that he knew full well and you also with everyone: I am wedded to one whom I will truly love without lies who is unlike him and all worldly men. (5) I will never more lie to or leave Him for fortune or joy, for woe or for misery, which you may do to me."

14.   (1) Her father began to grow very horribly angry and asked her mockingly, "And who is he, this husband to whom you are wedded, to whom you have given your love, without me, so far that you make light of all that you should love? (2) As of now, I was never — that I know — introduced to him!"

15.   (1) "By God," said the maiden, "your harm is the greater! (2) It is not because you have not heard of him before: that is, Jesus, God's Son, who in order to redeem mankind that would be completely lost, relinquished his life on the Rood.

ant thet me ofthuncheth, ah ich Him luvie ant wulle don ant leve on as o Lauerd. (4) Ne schal me firsen Him from nowther deovel ne mon."

16.   (1) "For mi lif," quoth hire feader, "the schal lathin his luve for thu schalt habbe throf hearm ant scheome bathe. (2) Ant nu thu schalt on alre earst, as on ernesse swa beon ibeaten with bittere besmen thet tu wani thet tu were, wummon of wummone bosum, to wrather heale eauer iboren i the worlde."

17.   (1) "Swa much," quoth thet meiden, "ich beo Him the leovere se ich derfre thing for His luve drehe. (2) Wurch thu thet ti wil is."

18.   (1) "Ye," quoth he, "blitheliche!"

19.   (1) Ant het swithe heatterliche strupen hire steort-naket ant leggen se luther
fol. 40r | liche on hire leofliche lich thet hit litheri o blode. (2) Me nom hire ant dude swa thet hit yeat adun of the yerden ant heo bigon to yeien: "Beaten se ye beaten, ye Beliales budeles, ne mahe ye nowther mi luve ne mi bileave lutlin towart te liviende Godd, mi leofsume leofmon, the luvewurthe Lauerd; ne nulle ich leven ower read, the forreadeth ow seolf; ne the mix maumez — the beoth thes feondes fetles — heien ne herien for teone ne for tintreohe thet ye me mahe timbrin."

20.   (1) "Na, nult tu?" quoth Affrican. (2) "Hit schal sone sutelin, for ich chulle sende the nu ant biteache thi bodi to Eleusium the riche thet reve is over Rome ant he schal the forreaden ant makie to forswelten, as his ahne wil is, thurh al thet eauer sar is."

---

(3) I never saw Him and that displeases me, but I love Him and will do so and believe in Him as Lord. (4) Nor shall either devil or man take me away from Him."

16.   (1) "Upon my life," said her father, "His love will become hateful to you, for you will have both harm and shame for it. (2) And now you will, first of all, as a foretaste be beaten so with sharp rods that you will lament that you were ever born to evil fortune in the world, a woman from a woman's womb."

17.   (1) "I will be," said that maiden, "so much the more beloved to Him as I suffer the more grievous thing for His love. (2) Work what is your will!"

18.   (1) "Yes," said he, "happily!"

19.   (1) And he very fiercely ordered her to be stripped stark-naked and beaten so wickedly on her lovely body that it lathered in blood. (2) She was seized and it was done so that blood poured down off the rods and she began to cry out: "However badly you beat me, you beadles of Belial, you can lessen neither my love nor my belief toward the living God, my beloved lover, the loveworthy Lord; nor will I believe your advice, which leads you to destruction; nor will I praise or glorify your filthy idols — which are vessels of the Fiend — for any pain or torture that you may contrive."

20.   (1) "No, will you not?" said Africanus. (2) "It shall soon be clear, for I will send you now and surrender your body to Eleusius the noble who is reeve of Rome, and he will lead you to destruction and make you die in agony as is his own will, through all that is ever painful."

21. (1) "Ye," quoth this meiden, "thet mei Godd welden. (2) Ne mahe ye nawt do me bute thet He wule theavien ant tholien ow to donne to mucli mi mede ant te murhthe thet lith to meithhades menske. (3) For eaver se ye nu her mearreth me mare, se mi crune schal beon brihttre ba ant fehere. (4) Forthi, ich chulle blitheliche ant with blithe heorte drehen eaver-euch derf for mi leofmones luve the lufsume Lauerd, ant softe me bith euch sar in His servise. (5) Thu wult, thu

fol. 40v seist, ayeove me to Eleusium the luthere: Ayef | me, for nawiht ne yeove ich for inc nowther. (6) Thet ye mahen ane pine me here, ah hit ne hearmeth me nawt; ah helpeth ant heveth up ant maketh mine murhthes monifalde in Heovene. (7) Ant yef ye doth me to death, hit bith deore to Godd, ant ich schal blithe bicumen to endelese blissen, ant ye schulen, wrecches — wei ower wurthes, thet ye weren i the worlt iboren ant ibroht forth to wrather heale — ye schule sinken adun to sar ant to eche sorhe, to bitternesse ant to bale deope into Helle."

22. (1) Affrican hire feader bitterliche iteonet bitaht te hire Eleusium, the luthere reve of Rome, ant lette bringen hire bivoren his ehsihthe as he set ant demde the hehe burh-domes. (2) As he biseh ant biheold hire lufsume leor lilies ilicnesse, ant rudi ase rose, ant under hire nebscheft al se freoliche ischapet, weorp a sic as a wiht thet sare were iwundet. (3) His heorte feng to heaten ant his meari mealten; the rawen rahten of luve thurh euch lith of his limes. (4) Ant inwith bearnde of brune swa ant cwakede, as of calde, thet him thuhte in his thonc thet ne bede he

---

21. (1) "Yes," said this maiden, "God may control that. (2) You may do nothing to me except what He will permit and allow you to do to multiply my reward and the mirth that pertains to maidenhood's honor. (3) For however much you hurt me here, the more my crown will be both brighter and fairer. (4) Therefore, I will joyfully and with a joyful heart endure every single suffering for the love of my beloved, the lovely Lord, and every torment will be soft to me in His service. (5) You wish, you say, to give me up to Eleusius the wicked: give me to him, for I care nothing at all for either of you two! (6) You who can only torture me here but it harms me not at all, but helps me and lifts me up and makes my mirths manifold in Heaven. (7) And if you put me to death, it will be dear to God, and I will become happy because of endless blisses, and you will, you wretches — alas for your fates, that you were born into the world and brought forth to evil fortune — you will sink down to suffering and to eternal sorrow, to bitterness and to bale, deep into Hell!"

22. (1) Africanus her father, bitterly enraged gave her to Eleusius, the wicked reeve of Rome, and had her brought before his eyes as he sat and decided the high city court judgments. (2) As he saw and beheld her lovely face in the likeness of a lily and red as rose, and everything below her face so beautifully shaped, he heaved a sigh like a creature that was sorely wounded. (3) His heart began to heat up and his marrow to melt; the rays of love reached through every joint of his limbs. (4) And inside he burned from fire so and quaked, as if from cold, that it seemed to him in his mind that he wanted no kind of bliss in the world but her

Royal
59v

23.

i the worlt nanes cunnes blisse bute hire bodi ane, to wealden hire with wil efter thet he walde. (5) Ant bigon with swotnesse soffte to seggen:

(1) "Mi lif ant mi leofmon ant leafdi yef thu wel wult, | bithench thet ich in Rome richest am ant iboren hehest. (2) Hwi dest tu us ba so wa thurh thi muchele unwit ant wurchest so wrathe? (3) Nulli ich the na mare uvel then thi seolf waldest. (4) Ah leof me were thet tu thi luthere thonc lefdest, ant te wel schal with alle wunne iwurthen, ant neaver of thi wil ne schulde the nawt wontin. (5) Ant loke alswa the lahen as al thet cun, thet tu art of icumen ant akennet, on leveth ant luvieth. (6) Hwi leavest tu ham the ane, ant wurtheth ha the so lathe? (7) Ne wen thu nawt the ane with thi wisdom to overstihen ham alle."

24.

Royal
fol. 60r

(1) "Let," quoth ha, "Elewsi, ant stew swucche wordes, for ne beoth ha riht nohtes. (2) For, yef thu cneowe ant were cuth with the King thet is over alle kinges icrunet in Heovene, lutel waldest tu leoten of ower lahelese lahen thet leareth ow to luten dedliche schaften, as ye schulden to | Godd, ant gremieth ower Schuppent. (3) For the cwike deovlen doth ham-thrin, on hwet ye bileveth, ant hwen so ye herieth ham, ye herieth thet unhwiht ant buheth as to healent. (4) Ant he wule ower hwile bitterliche yelden, for ne wergeth he neaver to wurchen ow al thet wandrethe, world àà buten ende. (5) Do thet tu don wult, for nulle ich the nan other don, bute yef thu lithe and leve min lare, ant luvie Godd almihti, ant leave alle the lahen thet tu list inne."

---

body alone, to possess her with his will according to what he wished. (5) And he began with sweetness to say softly:

23.

(1) "My life and my beloved and lady, if you wish well, consider that I am the richest in Rome and the highest born. (2) Why do you do such woe to us both through your great lack of reason and act so angrily? (3) I wish you no more evil than you yourself wish. (4) But I would prefer that you leave your wicked purpose, and it will go well for you with every joy, and you will never lack anything you desire. (5) And consider, in comparison, the customs which all your kin, whom you are come from and are descended from, believe in and love. (6) Why do you alone abandon them, and why have they become so loathsome to you? (7) Do not at all expect yourself alone, with all your wisdom, to overpass them all!"

24.

(1) "Cease," said she, "Eleusius, and stop such words because they are not at all right! (2) For if you knew and were familar with the King who is crowned over all kings in Heaven, little would you esteem your lawless customs which teach you to bow down to lifeless idols as you should to God, and which anger your Creator. (3) For the living devils set themselves inside of them, in whom you believe, and whenever you praise them, you praise that demon and bow to it as if to a savior. (4) And He will bitterly repay your time, for He will never grow weary working for you all that woe, world forever without end. (5) Do what you wish to do, for I will do nothing else for you, unless you listen to and believe my teaching, and love God Almighty, and abandon all the customs to which you are in subjection."

25.   (1) "Me, leof," quoth Elewsius, "yef me swa | biluvede, hit were sone iseid the keiser ant ikudd to the kinge, ant he me walde warpen ut of mine wike ant demen me to deathe."

26.   (1) Ant heo him onswerede: "Yef thu dredest so muchel an dedlich mon the liveth al ayein lay, and leneth al his luve in liflese schaften, on his Schuppent scheome, ant art offruht swa to leosen his freontschipe, schuld ich thenne forsaken Jhesu Crist, Godes sune, the is ort ant ende of al thet eaver god is, the wule efter this lif — thet ich lete lutel of — for His lufsum luve, thet ich livie with Himseolf i the sy ant the selhthe of heovenriches wunnen? (2) Speche thu maht spillen ant ne speden nawiht! (3) Thah thu me buste and beate, as thet is bitaht te, ant to derve pine don me ant to dreori deth, thah thu, famon, flea me, ne schal | tu for na slaht, the sonre seo me slakien to luvien ant to leven o then liviende Godd, alre gume Lauerd."

resume
Bodley
fol. 41r

27.   (1) The reve feng to rudnin i grome of great heorte, ant het his heathene men strupin hire steort-naket ant strecchen o ther eorthe, ant hwil thet eaver six men mahten idrehen, beaten hire beare bodi, thet ha al were bigoten of the blode. (2) Ha duden al as he bed, ant hwil thet ha beoten hire bigunnen to yeien: "This is a biginnunge of the sar ant of the scheome thet tu schalt drehen yef thu nult to ure wil buhen ant beien. (3) Ah yet thu maht, yef thu wult, burhe the seolfen. (4) Ant yef thu mare withseist, alre monne, wurthe him wurst of wa ant of wontreathe the ne wurche the meast."

---

25.   (1) "But beloved," said Eleusius, "if I were so inclined, it would soon be told to the emperor and reported to the king, and he would cast me out of my office and condemn me to death!"

26.   (1) And she answered him: "If you dread so much one mortal man, who lives entirely against the law, and who bestows all his love on lifeless things, a shame upon his Shaper, and if you are so afraid to lose his friendship, should I then forsake Jesus Christ, God's Son, who is the beginning and the end of all that is ever good, who wishes after this life — which I care little for — for his lovely love that I live with Him in the triumph and the happiness of the joys of the heavenly kingdom? (2) You can waste speech and succeed not at all! (3) Though you buffet me and beat me, since it is your right, and put me to cruel torture and to a dreary death, although you, enemy, flay me, you will not, for any slaughter, see me slacken in loving and believing in the living God, Lord of all men."

27.   (1) The reeve began to grow red from rage in his swollen heart, and commanded his heathen men to strip her stark-naked and to stretch her upon the earth, and for six men to beat her bare body for as long as they could, so that she was entirely drenched from the blood. (2) They did entirely as he ordered and while they beat her they began to shout: "This is a beginning of the pain and of the shame that you will endure if you will not bow to and obey our will! (3) But yet, you may save yourself if you wish. (4) And if you still refuse, may there be misfortune and misery of all men to he who does not do his best to work on you."

28.   (1) "Doth," quoth ha, "deofles limen al thet te deoflen — hwas driveles ye beoth — driveth ow te donne. (2) Lutel me is of ower luve, leasse of ower laththe, ant of thes threates riht noht. (3) Wite ye hit to wisse!"

29.   (1) "Nu," cweden ha, "Wa him the ne fondi todei for te wurche the wurst!"

30.   (1) Ther wes sorhe to seon on hire freoliche flesch hu ha ferden therwith. (2) Ah heo hit al thuldeliche tholede for Drihtin, ant hwen ha felde meast sar,

fol. 41v   sikerlukest seide, "Haldeth longe | ne leave ye neaver for nulle ich leaven His luve thet ich on leve ne for luve nowther ne for luther eie."

31.   (1) Eleusius iherde this ant feng his neb to rudnin ant tendrin ut of teone. (2) Ant hehte swithe neomen hire ant teon bi the top up. (3) Ant swa me dude sone, swa thet ha hongede feor from ther eorthe, bi the vax ane ant leiden tha se lutherliche on hire on euch halve thet euch dunt defde in hire leofliche lich, the biyet of the yerden al o gure-blode. (4) "Lauerd Godd almihti," quoth ha, "loke to Thi meiden. (5) Thu fondedest Abraham, ant fundest him treowe; lef me thet ich mote The treowliche luvien. (6) Halt me, Healent min, Jhesu Crist, Godes Sune, as Thu havest bigunnen, for nam ich strong of na thing buten of Thi strengthe. (7) Ant o The i truste al, ant nawt o me seolven, ant her ich bihate The swuch hope ich habbe to Thin help. (8) Milde Godd almihti, ne schal neaver mi luve ne mi bileave towart Te lutlin ne lihen for na derf ne for na death thet ich schule drehen."

32.   (1) Tha Eleusius seh thet ha thus feng on to festnin hire seolven i sothe bileave, thohte he walde don hire anan ut of dahene, ant bed bilive bringen forth

---

28.   (1) "Do," said she, "you devil's limbs, all that the devils — whose drudges you are — drive you to do. (2) Your love matters little to me, your loathing less, and these threats matter nothing at all! (3) Know it for certain!"

29.   (1) "Now," said they, "Woe to him who does not try today to do the worst to you!"

30.   (1) There was sorrow then to see how they fared with her beautiful flesh. (2) But she patiently endured it all for the Lord, and when she felt the worst, she said most certainly, "Keep it up for a while and do not ever stop, for I will not leave His love which I believe in, neither for love nor for any wickedness."

31.   (1) Eleusius heard this and his face began to grow red and inflamed from rage. (2) And he commanded quickly that she be seized and pulled up by the hair. (3) And it was soon done, so that she hung far from the earth by the hair alone, and they laid then on her so horribly on every side that every blow sank into her lovely body, which became completely drenched in gore-blood from the rods. (4) "Lord God Almighty," said she, "Watch over Your maiden! (5) You tested Abraham and found him true; grant that I may truly love you. (6) Hold fast to me, my Savior, Jesus Christ, God's Son, as you have begun to, for I am not strong from anything but from Your strength. (7) And I trust entirely in You and not in myself, and here I vow to You that I have this hope in your help. (8) Mild God Almighty, neither my love nor my belief in you shall ever lighten or prove false because of any pain or any death that I will suffer."

32.   (1) When Eleusius saw that she began to fortify herself in true belief, he thought he would immediately put her days to an end, and he ordered quickly for

fol. 42r brune-wallinde bres, ant healden hit se, wal-|-hat hehe up on hire heaved thet hit urne endelong hire leofliche lich adun to hire helen. (2) Me dude al as he het. (3) Ah the worldes Wealdent — thet wiste Sein Juhan His ewangliste unhurt i the veat of wallinde eoli ther he wes idon in, thet ase hal com up throf as he wes hal meiden — the ilke lives Lauerd wiste Him unwemmet, His brud, of the bres thet wes wallinde, swa thet ne thuhte hit hire buten ase wlech weater al thet ha felde. (4) Eleusius warth wod tha nuste hwet segen, ah hehte swithe don hire ut of his eh sihthe, ant dreaien in to dorc hus, to prisunes pine. (5) Ant swa ha wes idon sone.

33. (1) Heo, as ha thrinne wes, i theosternesse hire ane, feng to cleopien to Crist ant bidde theos bone: "Lauerd Godd almihti, mi murhthe ant mi mede, mi sy ant al the selhthe thet ich efter seche, Thu sist al hu ich am bisteathet ant bistonden, festne mi bileave! (2) Riht me ant read me, for al mi trust is on The. (3) Steor me ant streng me, for al mi strengthe is of The. (4) Mi feader ant mi moder, forthi thet ich nule The forsaken, habbeth forsake me; ant al mi nestfalde cun, thet schulde beo me best freond, beoth me meast feondes, ant mine inhinen, alre

fol. 42v meast heamen. (5) Herewurthe Healent, habbe | ich Thin anes help: Ich am wilcweme. (6) Ne forleaf Thu me nawt, luviende Lauerd. (7) As Thu biwistest Daniel bimong the wode liuns ilatet se luthere, ant te threo children the chearre nalden from the lahen thet ha schulden luvien, Ananie ant Azarie ant Misahel inempnet, as Thu, al Wealdent, biwistest ham unwemmet with thet ferliche fur i the furneise, swa Thu, wunne of the worlt, wite me ant were, ant witere ant wisse

---

boiling molten brass to be brought forth, and commanded it to be poured boiling hot, so high up on her head that it flowed along her lovely body down to her heels. (2) Everything was done as he commanded. (3) But the world's Ruler — who kept Saint John His Evangelist unhurt in the vat of boiling oil in which he was placed, so that he arose from it as whole as if he were a whole virgin — the same Lord of life kept His bride for Himself, untouched by the brass that was boiling, so that all that she felt seemed to her nothing but lukewarm water. (4) Eleusius became mad then and did not know what to say, but ordered her quickly taken out of his eyesight and dragged into a dark house, to the pain of prison. (5) And so she was soon put there.

33. (1) She, since she was inside in the darkness alone, began to call out to Christ and prayed this prayer: "Lord God Almighty, my joy and my reward, my triumph and all the happiness I seek, you see how I am all beset and surrounded: make fast my belief! (2) Guide me and advise me, for all my trust is in you. (3) Steer me and strengthen me, for all my strength is from you. (4) Because I will not forsake you, my father and my mother have forsaken me; and all my closest kin, those who should be my best friends, are my greatest foes, and my household, the greatest of all churls. (5) Praiseworthy Savior, I have your help alone: I am well pleased. (6) Do not forsake me, loving Lord. (7) As you guarded Daniel among the wild lions looking so wicked, and the three children named Ananie and Azarie and Misahel who would not turn aside from the laws that they would love, as you, Ruler of all, protected them unblemished from that fearsome fire in the furnace, so you, joy of the world, guard and defend me, and protect and guide through

thurh Thi wisdom to wite me with sunne. (8) Lauerd, lives lattow, lead me thurh this lease, this lutle leastinde lif, to the havene of heale, as Thu leaddest Israeles leode of Egipte bute schip, dru-fot, thurh the Reade Sea ant asenchtest hare van the ferden ham efter. (9) Ant Tu, folkes Feader, aval mine vamen, ant Tu, Drihtin, todrif the deovel thet me derveth for ne mei na monnes strengthe withuten Thin stonden him toyeines. (10) Lef me thet ich mote, mihti meinfule Godd, iseon him ischeomet yet, the weneth me to schrenchen ant schunchen of the nearowe wei thet leadeth to eche lif. (11) Loke me from his lath, liviende Lauerth. (12) Make me war ant wite me with his crefti crokes thet ha me ne crechen. (13) Were me swa with then unwine, helpleses Heale, thet Tu beo iheiet

fol. 43r   ant iheret eavre in eorthe as in Heovene. | (14) Beo thu áá iblescet, Lauerd, as Thu were ant art ant schalt beon in eche."

34.   (1) As ha theos bone hefde ibeden, com a kempe of Helle on englene heowe, ant feng on to motin thus with this meiden: "Juliene, mi leofmon, thu havest for mi luve muchel idrohen ant idrahen. (2) Thu havest feorliche fan thet te fehteth ayein. (3) Ha greithith theo grome nu alles cunnes pinen. (4) Ne mei ich tholien thet ha thus mearren the na mare! (5) Thu art inoh ifondet ant tu havest mi freondschipe inoh swithe ofservet. (6) Me areoweth thi sar! (7) Ah hercne nuthe mi read: wurch Eleusius wil, for ich the yeove leave."

35.   (1) Thes meiden wes awundret swithe of thes wordes ant as ha wes offearet, feng on to freinin: "Hwet wiht," quoth ha, "art tu thet thulli word me bringest?"

---

your wisdom to keep me from sin. (8) Lord, leader of life, lead me through this false life, this little lasting life, to the harbor of salvation, just as you led Israel's people from Egypt without a ship, dry footed, through the Red Sea and drowned their foes who followed after them. (9) And you, Father of the people, fell my foes, and you, Ruler, drive off the devil who torments me, for no man's strength may stand against him without your strength! (10) Give me leave that I might, mighty powerful God, see him shamed yet, he who thinks to deceive me and frighten me away from the narrow path that leads to eternal life. (11) Protect me from his malice, living Lord. (12) Make me wary and guard me against his crafty tricks so that they do not catch me. (13) Defend me so against the fiend, Savior of the helpless, that you may be praised and glorified forever on earth as in Heaven. (14) May you be forever blessed, Lord, as you were and are and shall be into eternity."

34.   (1) Just as she had prayed this prayer, a champion of Hell came in the shape of an angel, and began to speak thus with this maiden: "Juliana, my beloved, you have received and suffered much for my love. (2) You have frightening foes who fight against you. (3) Enraged, they are preparing all kinds of tortures for you. (4) I cannot abide them to harm you any more! (5) You are tested enough and you have earned my friendship plenty enough. (6) Your pain grieves me! (7) Now listen to my advice: do Eleusius' will, for I give you leave."

35.   (1) This maiden was quite astonished by these words and since she was frightened she began to ask: "What creature," said she, "are you who brings such words to me?"

36.　　　(1) "Ich hit am," quoth the unwiht, "Godes heh engel, forte segge the this ısent te from Heovene." (2) Ha wundrede hire swithe, ant as theo the nes nawt of lihte bileave, stille, bute steavene on heh in hire heorte cleopede to Criste.

37.　　　(1) "Jhesu," quoth ha, "Godes Sune thet art Thi Feader wisdom, wisse me, Thi wummon, hwet me beo to donne. (2) Ant yef Thi deore wil is, do me to understonden thet the this seith me yef he beo Thi sonde."

38.
fol. 43v　　(1) Ant com sihinde adun softe from Heovene, a stevene thet seide, "Juliene the eadie, | iblescet beo the time thet tu ibore were. (2) Nule nawt thi leofmon tholie na leas thing to lihe the longe. (3) Hit is the stronge unwiht the stont ter of Helle! (4) Ga nu neor ant nim him, ant with the bondes thet ter beoth bind him heteveste. (5) Godd almihti yeveth the mahte forte don hit, ant tu schalt leaden him al efter thet te liketh, ant he schal al telle the — unthonc in his teth — thet tu wilnest to witen, ant kenne the ant cuthen al thet tu easkest."

39.　　　(1) This eadi meiden, as ha wes iwisset thurh then engel, leop to ant ilahte him ant seide: "Sei me swithe hwet tu beo ant hweonene ant hwa the hider sende."

40.　　　(1) Ant he with thet ilke feng to wenden heowes ant warth swuch as he wes: unhwiht of Helle. (2) "Leafdi," quoth he, "leaf me ant ich chulle seggen."

41.　　　(1) "Do swithe sei me, for ich chulle lowse the ant leten hwen me thuncheth!"

42.　　　(1) "Deore leafdi," quoth he tha, "ich hit am, the deovel Belial, of alle unwreste unwihtes the wurste ant meast awariet, for nis me neaver wel ne nes, bute hwen ich makede moncun to wurche to wundre. (2) Ich hit am thet weorp ut

---

36.　　　(1) "I am he," said the fiend, "God's high angel sent to you from Heaven to say this to you." (2) She was very surprised, and, since she was not of an unquestioning nature, silently, but in a loud voice in her heart, called out to Christ:

37.　　　(1) "Jesus," said she, "God's Son who is your Father's wisdom, guide me, your woman, as to what I should do. (2) And if it is Your dear will, make me understand whether he who says this to me is Your messenger."

38.　　　(1) And a voice came, descending down softly from Heaven, which said: "Juliana the holy, blessed be the time that you were born. (2) Your beloved will not suffer any false thing to deceive you for long. (3) It is the fierce demon from Hell who stands there! (4) Go near him now and grab him, and with the bonds which are there bind him cruelly tight. (5) God almighty gives you the strength to do it, and you shall control him completely just as you please; and he will tell you — damn his teeth! — everything that you wish to know, and declare and make known to you all that you ask."

39.　　　(1) This blessed maiden, since she was guided by the angel, leapt forward and caught hold of him and said: "Say to me quickly what you are, and where you came from, and who sent you here!"

40.　　　(1) And at that moment he began to change shape and became such as he was: a fiend of hell. (2) "Lady," said he, "release me and I shall tell you."

41.　　　(1) "Do tell me quickly, for I will release you and let you go when I like!"

42.　　　(1) "Dear lady," said he then, "I am he, the devil Belial, of all the wretched devils the worst and the most wicked, for I am not and was not ever happy except when I made mankind commit shameful actions. (2) I am the one who cast out Adam

Adam ant Eve of Paraise selhthe; ant ich hit am thet makede Caym the acursede acwalde his brother Abel. (3) Ant ich hit am thet makede Nabugodonosor, the kene king of Caldey, makien the maumez igoten al of golde, ant ich | hit am thet makede thet te threo children icoren over the othre weren idust to fordon i thet ferliche fur of the muchele oven. (4) Ant ich hit am thet makede then muchele witti witege, Ysaie, beon isahet thurh ant thurh to deathe. (5) Ant ich hit am thet makede to ontenden Jerusalem ant Godes deore temple todriven al to duste. (6) Ant ich hit am thet makede ant readde Israeles folc to leaven i the wildernesse the Lauerd thet alesde ham of Pharaones theowdom ant makede ham godes igotene to heien ant to herien! (7) Ant ich hit am the reafde the riche Iob his ahte, swa thet he weolewede of wontrethe i the mixne. (8) Ant ich hit am thet sumchearre wes thurh the wise Salomon ethalden. (9) Ant ich hit am thet makede Sein Iuhan the Baptiste beon heafdes bicorven, ant Seinte Stephene isteanet, ant ich hit am thet spec thurh Simunes muth, the wicche the weorrede eaver ayein Peter ant Pawel. (10) Ant ich hit am the readde Nerun, the riche keiser of Rome, to don o rode Peter ant to biheafdin Pawel. (11) Ant ich makede the cniht to thurlin Godes side with scharpe speres ord! (12) Thah ich talde aldei yet ich mahte tellen, for ma wundres ich habbe iwraht thene ich mahte munien, ant ma monne bone ibeon then ei of mine brethren."

fol. 44r

fol. 44v   (1) "Do sei me," quoth the meithen, "hwa sende the to me, ant hwa | is

43.   meister over the."

44.   (1) "Leafdi," quoth he, "Belzeebub, the balde thurs of Helle."

---

and Eve from the happiness of Paradise; and I am the one who made Cain the accursed kill his brother Abel. (3) I am the one who made Nebuchadnezzar, the cruel king of Caldee, make the idols cast entirely of gold, and I am the one who made it so that the three children chosen over the others were flung into that fearsome fire of the huge oven. (4) And I am the one who caused the great wise prophet, Isaiah, to be sawed through and through to death at that time. (5) And I am the one who caused Jerusalem to be burned and God's dear temple reduced entirely to ash. (6) And I am the one who made and advised Israel's folk to abandon the Lord who freed them from Pharaoh's thralldom, in the wilderness; and they made for themselves gods cast of metal to praise and to worship! (7) And I am the one who stole the rich Job's goods, so that he wallowed from misery in the midden-heap. (8) And I am the one who once was held captive by Solomon the wise. (9) And I am the one who caused Saint John the Baptist to be beheaded, and Saint Steven be stoned, and I am the one who spoke through the mouth of Simon, the witch, who always made war against Peter and Paul. (10) And I am the one who advised Nero, the rich emperor of Rome, to crucify Peter and to behead Paul. (11) And I made the knight pierce God's side with a sharp spear's point! (12) If I spoke all day I might tell more, for more crimes have I wrought than I can recall, and I have been the bane of more people than any of my brothers."

43.   (1) "Do tell me," said the maiden, "who sent you to me and who is master over you."

44.   (1) "Lady," said he, "Beelzebub, the bold demon of Hell."

45. (1) "Hwet is," quoth ha, "his werc? (2) Ant hwet wurcheth he mest?"

46. (1) "Leafdi, yef thi wil is, he ifint euch uvel ant bithencheth hit al, ant sendeth us thenne thider as him thuncheth. (2) Ant hwen we nawt ne spedeth, ne ne mahen wrenchen sum rihtwis of the weie, we dearieth ant ne durren nohwer cume bivoren him, ant he heterliche hat theo thet habbeth iwraht efter his wille, hwer se ha us ifinden, beaten us ant binden, ant don us mare wa on then ei mon mahte tholien. (3) Forthi we moten, leafdi, buhen swithe ant beien to ure luvewurthe feader ant wurchen alle his willes."

47. (1) "Sei," quoth ha, "witerluker yet, hu ye wurcheth ant o hwuche wise ye bichearreth Godes children."

48. (1) "Leafdi," quoth he, "Juliene, the ich font ant habbe ifolhet me to wrather heale, ich wende iwis to leade the into thine ealdrene lahen ant makie to leaven the luve of thi Lauerd, ant feng on to fondin the, ah ich am aveallet. (2) Ich chulle kenne the nu al thet tu easkest: hwer se we eaver iseoth mon other wummon eani god biginnen, we wepnith us ayein ham ant makieth iswiken al thet best mahte wenden hare heorte, ant makien ham to thenchen thohtes ther-toyelnes, ant wendeth to other willes thet ham wulleth hearmin. (3) Ant makieth ham forte

fol. 45r leose lust for te bidde yeorne thet Godd bineo|me ham the wil thet we in ham warpeth. (4) Ant ha unstrengith therwith, ant we strengeth therwith on ham, and overstiheth al, ear ha lest wcncn. (5) Ant yef we seoth ham yeornliche sechen to chirche, ant ter swithe bi hamseolf bireowsin hare sunnen, ant leofliche lustnin Hali Chirche lare, ther we beoth yetten bisiliche ham abuten (ant mare ther then

---

45. (1) "What," said she, "is his work? (2) And what does he do the most?"

46. (1) "Lady, if it is your will, he discovers every evil and devises it all, and he sends us then to where it seems best. (2) And when we do not succeed and cannot wrench someone righteous from the right path, we cower and do not dare come before him, and he fiercely orders those who have done his will, wherever they find us, to bind us and beat us and to work us more woe than any man might endure. (3) Therefore we must, lady, bow down to and obey our lovable father, and carry out all his desires."

47. (1) "Say," said she, "more plainly still, how you operate and in what ways you deceive God's children."

48. (1) "Lady," said he, "Juliana, whom I have found and have followed to evil fortune, I truly thought to lead you into your elders' laws and make you leave the love of your Lord, and I began to test you, but I am defeated. (2) I will now declare to you all that you ask: wheresoever we see man or woman begin any good, we arm ourselves against them and make them desert all that might turn their hearts to the best, and make them think thoughts to the contrary, and turn to other desires that will harm them. (3) And we make them lose the desire to pray eagerly that God deprive them of the desire that we put in them. (4) And they grow weak with it, and we grow strong in them from that desire, and engulf them completely, before they least expect it. (5) And if we see them eagerly visit church, and there, all by themselves, repent of their sins and lovingly listen to Holy Church's teaching, there we are still busily about them (and more there than

elleshwer) to letten ham, yef we mahen, wrenchen hare thonkes towart unnette thinges. (6) Ah hwucche se beoth se stealewurthe thet ha understonden ham, ant warpeth ut with strengthe ut of hare heorte unwreaste willes thet ich ham in warpe, ant yeornliche yeiyeth efter Godes grace to help ant to heale, ant thenne meast hwen the preost in with the Messe noteth Godes licome, thet He nom of thet lathlese meiden. (7) Ther is riht bileave ant inwardliche bonen swa icweme to Godd thet i thet ilke time we biginneth to fleon ant turneth to fluhte. (8) This is al thet we doth Cristemen, ant eggith eaver to uvele."

49.   (1) "Me, ye eateliche wihtes," quoth thet eadi wummon, "hu durre ye eaver neomen ow to Cristes icorene?"

50.   (1) "Me sei me, seli meiden," quoth he, "hu derst tu halde me ant hondlin se heterliche bute thuh thet tu art trusti o thi Lauerd. (2) Ant ich do as thu dest,

fol. 45v   truste o mi lauerd thet is meister | of alle mixschipes, ant wurche his wil over al ase forth as i mei. (3) Ant yef ich mahte forthre ich walde beo the feinre. (4) Ah nat i hwet unseli sith makede me her to sechen, bute mi muchele unselhthe sohte the to seonne. (5) Wumme áá — thet sihthe se sariliche hit sit me. (6) Ne set me neaver na thing se luthere ne se sare. (7) Wei hwi nefde ich iwist hwuch weane me wes towart? (8) Ne mi kinewurthe feader ne cuthe nawt warnin of thulli wa his foster? (9) Forlet me nu, leafdi, ant ich chulle al bileave the ant folhin an other, other ich chulle forwreie the to mi meinfule feader. (10) Ah wel ich warni the vore, hit nis nawt thin biheve."

---

elsewhere) to hinder them if we may, and to wrench their thoughts toward vain things. (6) But whoever is so stalwart that they understand, with strength from their hearts they cast out from the wicked desires that I cast into them, and eagerly cry after God's grace for help and for salvation, and especially when the priest during the Mass partakes of God's body, which He took from that flawless maiden. (7) There true belief and heartfelt prayers are so pleasing to God that at that same time we begin to flee and turn to flight. (8) This is all that we do to Christians and we egg them on always to evil."

49.   (1) "But, you hateful fiends," said that blessed woman, "how dare you ever visit Christ's chosen ones?"

50.   (1) "But tell me, blessed maiden," said he, "how dare you hold me and handle me so violently, unless you are confident in your lord. (2) And I do as you do: trust in my lord who is master of all villainies, and do his will over everything as far as I may. (3) And if I could do further, I would be the gladder. (4) But I do not know what unhappy fate made me search here unless my great ill luck sought to see you. (5) Woe is me forever — so sorely does that sight grieve me! (6) Nothing ever grieved me so wickedly or so painfully. (7) Alas, why did I not know what wretchedness was upon me? (8) And did my royal father not think to warn his child of such woe? (9) Let me go now, lady, and I will leave you completely alone and follow another, or I will denounce you to my mighty father. (10) But I warn you well beforehand, it is not to your benefit."

51.   (1) "O," quoth ha, Juliene, Jhesu Cristes leofmon, "threatest tu me, wrecche?(2) The schal iwurthen, Godd hit wat, godes the wurse."

52.   (1) Ant grap a great raketehe, thet ha wes with ibunden, ant bond bihinden his rug ba twa his honden thet him wrong euch neil ant blakede of the blode, ant duste him ruglunge adun riht to ther eorthe. (2) Ant stondinde o the steorve, nom hire ahne bondes ant bigon to beaten then Belial of Helle, ant he to rarin reowliche, to yuren ant to yein, ant heo leide on se lutherliche thet wa wes him o live.

53.
fol. 46r   (1) "O mi leafdi Juliene," quoth he, "evening with apostel, patriarchen ilich, ant leof with alle martyrs, englene feolahe, ant archanlene freond! (2) Frithe | me ane hwile, ich halsi the o Godes half, ant on His Sune Rode thet we se muchel dredeth, ant o the pine ant o the death thet He droh for moncun milce have ant merci, wummon, of mi wrecchedom."

54.   (1) "Stew the, steorve of Helle!" quoth thet eadie meiden. (2) "Merci nan nis with the, forthi ne ahest tu nan milce to ifinden! (3) Ah sei me swithe, mare of the wa thet tu havest mid woh iwraht mon."

55.   (1) "Leafdi, leaf the hwile ant hald thine eadi honden. (2) Ich habbe iblend men ant ibroken ham the schuldren ant te schonken, i fur iwarpen ham ant i water, ant hare ahne blod ich habbe ofte imaket ham to spitten ant to speowen, ant te an to sclein then other, ant a hon him seolven. (3) Me, witti wummon, hu wult tu thet ich endi the the tale the waxeth áá as ich telle? (4) Se feole ich habbe ifulet of theo the neren iblescet nawt se wel as ham bihofde, thet ne mahte hit na mon rikenin ne

---

51.   (1) "Oh," said she, Juliana, Christ's beloved, "do you threaten me, wretch? (2) It will turn out, God knows it, so much the worse for you."

52.   (1) And she grabbed a great chain that she was bound with, and bound both his two hands behind his back so that each of his nails twisted painfully and became black from the blood, and flung him backwards straight down to the earth. (2) And, standing on top of that pestilent creature, she seized her own bonds and began then to beat Belial of Hell, and he began to howl pitifully, to yowl and yell, and she laid on so fiercely that he was sorry to be alive.

53.   (1) "Oh my lady Juliana," said he, "equal to the apostle, like the patriarchs, and beloved among all the martyrs, angels' fellow and archangels' friend! (2) Spare me for a minute, I beg you in God's name and on his Son's Cross which we dread so much, and on the pain and the death that he suffered for humankind: have pity and mercy, woman, upon my wretchedness."

54.   (1) "Shut up, you pestilence from Hell!" said that blessed maiden. (2) "There is no mercy for you because you should not enjoy any mercy! (3) But tell me quickly more of the woe that you have wrongfully wrought upon humans."

55.   (1) "Lady, leave off a moment and hold back your blessed hands. (2) I have blinded men and broken them, both shoulders and shanks, flung them into fire and water, I have often made them spit and spew their own blood, and the one to slay the other, and then hang himself. (3) But, wise woman, how do you wish me to end for you the tale which always grows as I tell it? (4) I have befouled so many of those who were not so well blessed as they should have been, that no man might

reden. (5) Of al thet uvel i the world, hwet wult tu wurse? (6) Ich am, of the sprunges, the an thet hit meast of springeth, ne neaver athet tis dei nes ich thus ihondlet. (7) O, the mihte of meithhad, hu thu art iwepnet to weorrin ayein us! (8) Yet tu wurchest us wurst, of al thet us wa deth, as thu dudest eavre. (9) Ah we schule sechen efter wrake on alle theo thet te biwiteth, ne ne schulen ha neaver beo sker of ure weorre. (10) We wulleth meidenes áá mare heanen ant heatien, |

ant thah monie etsterten us, summe schulen stutten. (11) O Jhesu, Godes Sune, The havest Thin hehe seotel o meithhades mihte — hire to muche menske — wa wurchest Tu us therwith! (12) To wel Thu witest ham the treowliche habbeth hire in heorte ihalden, yef ha milde ant meoke beon as meiden deh to beonne." (13) With thet he this hefde iseid, bigon swa te yuren thet monie weren awundret hwet tet yur were.

56.   (1) Eleusius, the reve, het lokin yef ha livede ant bringen hire bivoren him yef ha were o live. (2) Heo the weren ihaten forth ant funden hire thus, ant of thet grisliche gra weren agrisen swithe, leadden hire thah forth. (3) Ant heo leac eaver efter hire then laddliche of Helle thet olhnede swithe ant bed tus ant bisohte, "Mi leove leafdi Juliene, ne make thu me nawt men to hutung ne to hokere; thu havest ido me wa inoh, thah thu ne do me wurse! (4) Ich habbe, wumme, forloren mi leove feaderes freontschipe. (5) Ne neaver mare her onuven ne der ich cumen bivoren him. (6) Mihti meiden, leaf me o Godes half, ich halsi the! (7) Ne beoth Cristene men — yef hit is soth thet me seith — merciable ant milzfule? (8) Ant tu art bute reowthe! (9) Have merci of me for the Lauerdes luve, thi luvewurthe

---

reckon nor estimate it. (5) Of all that evil in the world, what worse do you want? (6) I am, of the wells of all that evil in the world, the one from which it wells up the most, and never until this day was I treated so. (7) Oh, the might of maidenhood, how you are armed to wage war against us! (8) Even now, out of everyone who hurts us, you do us the worst, as you always did. (9) But we will strive for vengeance on all those who protect you, and they will never be free from our war. (10) We will ever more humiliate and hate maidens, and although many escape us, some shall not escape. (11) Oh Jesus, God's Son, you who have your high seat in maidenhood's might — a great honor to her — you work us woe through that! (12) You protect them too well who truly have her held in the heart, if they be mild and meek as a maiden should be." (13) As soon as he had said this, he began to howl so that many were wondering what that howl could be.

56.   (1) Eleusius the reeve demanded to see if she lived, and ordered her brought before him if she were alive. (2) Those who were ordered went forth and found her so, and were very terrified of that grisly evil spirit, though they yet led her forth. (3) And she dragged always behind her the loathly thing from Hell who cajoled very much and begged thus and besought her: "My dear lady Juliana, do not let everyone hoot and holler at me; you have done me enough woe, even if you do me no worse! (4) Woman, I have lost my dear father's friendship. (5) And never again from here on do I dare come before him. (6) Mighty maiden, release me for God's sake, I beg you! (7) Are not Christian people — if it is true what you tell me — merciful and mild? (8) And you are without pity! (9) Have mercy on me, for the Lord's love, your love-worthy

fol. 47r

leafdi, i the bidde." (10) Ant heo leac him eaver endelong the cheping chepmenne to hutıng. (11) Ant heo leiden to him, sum with | stan, sum with ban, ant sleatten on him hundes, ant leiden to with honden. (12) As he wes imaket tus earmest alre thinge, ant berde as the ful wiht, thet ter flue monie, se thet eadi wummon wergede sumhwet, ant reat him with the raketehe unrudeliche swithe ant weorp him forth from hire awei into a put of fulthe.

57.   (1) Com baldeliche forth bivore the reve as he set on his dom seotle, schiminde hire nebscheaft schene as the sunne. (2) The reve, tha he seh hire, thuhte muche sullich ant bigon to seggen: "Juliene, sei me ant beo soth cnawes: hwer were the itaht theose wicchecreftes, thet tu ne telest na tale of nanes cunnes tintreohe, ne ne dredest nowther death ne cwike deoflen?"

58.   (1) "Her me, heathene hund," quoth thet eadi meiden. (2) "Ich heie ant herie Godd feader, ant His sulliche Sune, Jhesu Crist hatte, ant te Hali Gast, Godd as the othre, threo ant nawt threo godes, ah is eaver an ant ihwer untweamet. (3) He, kempene King, haveth todei overcumen Helles bule, Belial, baldest of alle, ant ti sire Sathanas thet tu levest upon. (4) Ant ti feader hatest, ant his heaste forthest ant wel bisemeth the to beon ant bikimeth to beo streon of a swuch strunde. (5) Ah eaver beo acurset, colt of swuch cunde! (6) The mihti mildfule Godd, thet

fol. 47v

ich áá munne, yef me mihte of Heo|vene, him forte hearmin ant te forte schenden, ant makien to scheomien thct schalt swucche shuken heien ant herien. (7) Weila, as thu were iboren, wrecche, o wrathe time, thet ti sari sawle ant ti sorhfule gast schal with swucche ploiveren pleien in Helle! (8) Reve, areow the

---

lady, I pray you." (10) And she dragged him always along, to the hooting of the marketing merchants. (11) And they laid on him, some with stones, some with bones, and set hounds on him, and laid on him with hands. (12) So while he became the most miserable of all things, and cried aloud as a foul creature so that many flew there, that blessed woman became wearied somewhat and she flung him with the chain very roughly and cast him forth away from her into a pit of filth.

57.   (1) She came boldly forth before the reeve as he sat on his judgment seat, her face bright, blazing like the sun. (2) The reeve, when he saw her, thought it a great marvel and began to say: "Juliana, tell me and be truthful: where were you taught those witchcrafts, by which you hold no account of any kind of torment, nor fear neither death nor living devils?"

58.   (1) "Hear me, heathen hound," said that blessed maiden. (2) "I praise and glorify God the Father and his marvelous son called Jesus Christ and the Holy Ghost, God as the other gods, three and not three but always one and everywhere undivided. (3) He, king of champions, has today overcome Hell's bull Belial, boldest of all, and your sire Satan, whom you believe in. (4) And your father ordered you, and you carry out his order; and it suits you well and becomes you to be the progeny of such a race. (5) But may you always be cursed, colt of such a stock! (6) May the mighty merciful God, whom I always keep in mind, give me might from Heaven to hurt him and put him to shame, and to make ashamed whoever will praise and glorify such fiends. (7) Alas, wretch, that you were born at an evil hour, because your sorry soul and your sorrowful ghost will play with such playfellows in Hell! (8) Reeve,

seolven. (9) Unseli mon, bisih the, hei Godd, ant her me! (10) Jhesu is se milzful thet He walde blitheliche Heovenes heale to alle. (11) Ah hwa se o bote ne geath ne schal he beon i borhen.”

59.   (1) “Ye!” quoth Eleusius. (2) “Haldest tu yetten up o thi yuhelunge? (3) Wenest tu thet we beon se eth to biwihelin? (4) Ah we schulen iseo nu, for hit schal sone sutelin hu thi wichecreft schal wite the ant werien.”

60.   (1) Ant lette o wodi wise a swithe wunderlich hweol meten ant makien, ant thurh-spitien hit al with spaken ant felien, thicke ant threofalt with irnene gadien, kene to keorven al thet ha rinen to ase neil-cnives. (2) Ant stod the axtreo istraht o twa half into stanene postles, thet hit, as hit turnde, ne overtoke nohwer bineothen to ther eorthe. (3) Grisen him mahte thet sehe hu hit gront into hwet se hit ofrahte. (4) Me brohte hire vorth, as Beliales budel bet, ant bunden hire therto hearde ant heteveste. (5) He dude on either half hire fowre of hise cnihtes

fol. 48r forte turnen thet hweol with hondlen imaket thron o thet eadi | meiden, se swithe as ha mahten; ant het, o lif ant o leomen, swingen hit swiftliche ant turnen hit abuten. (6) Ant heo, as the deovel spurede ham to donne, duden hit unsperliche thet ha bigon to broken al as thet istelede irn strac hire in over al, ant from the top to the tan, áá as hit turnde, tolimede hire ant toleac lith ba ant lire. (7) Bursten hire banes ant thet meari bearst ut, imenget with the blode. (8) Ther me mahte iseon alre sorhene meast, the i thet stude stode.

61.   (1) As ha yeide to Godd ant walde ayeoven hire gast into His honden, se ther

---

pity yourself. (9) Unhappy man, behold, yourself praise God and hear me! (10) Jesus is so merciful that he happily desires Heaven’s salvation for everyone. (11) But whoever does not do penance will not be saved.”

59.   (1) “Indeed!” said Eleusius. (2) “Do you still keep to your squawking? (3) Do you think that we are so easy to beguile? (4) But we will see now, for it will soon become clear how your witchcraft guards and keeps you.”

60.   (1) And frantically he had fashioned and made a most terrifying wheel, and had it filled throughout with spokes and with rims, thick and threefold with spikes of sharp iron, to carve everything that they came upon like razors. (2) And the axle stood, extended on both sides into stone pillars, so that as it turned, the wheel did not reach anywhere underneath on the earth. (3) It could terrify anyone who saw how it ground into whatever it came upon. (4) She was brought forth, as Belial’s beadle bid, and they bound her to it hard and cruelly tight. (5) He placed four of his knights on either side of her to turn that wheel, with handles made for it, as hard as they could on that blessed maiden, and he ordered them, upon life and limb, to swing it swiftly and to turn it about. (6) And they, as the devil spurred them to do, did so unsparingly so that she began to break apart as that steel-hard iron struck her all over, and from the top to the toes always as it turned, it dismembered her and pulled apart both limb and flesh. (7) Her bones burst and that marrow burst out mingled with the blood. (8) Whoever stood in that place could see there the greatest of all sorrows.

61.   (1) As she cried out to God and wished to give up her ghost into His hands,

lihtinde com an engel of Heovene, ant reat to thet hweol swa thet hit al toreafde. (2) Bursten hire bondes, ant breken alle clane, ant heo, ase fischhal as thah ha nefde nohwer hurtes ifelet, feng to thonki thus Godd with honden up ahevene: "Drihtin undeathlich, an Godd almihti alle othre unlich, Heovene wruhte ant eorthes ant alle iwrahte thinges, The ich thonki todei alle Thine deden. (3) Thu makedest mon of lame ant yeve him liviende gast ilich to Theseolven, ant settest for his sake al thet i the worlt is. (4) Ah he forgulte him anan thurh the eggunge of Eve, ant wes iput sone ut of paraise selhthen. (5) Weox swa his team her thet ne mahte hit na mon tellen, ah swa swithe hit sunegede thet tu hit forsenctest al in Noees flod bute eahte thet Tu frithedest. (6) Thu chure | seoththen i the alde lahe, Abraham ant Isaac, Jacob ant his children, ant yeve to Joseph (thet wes the yungeste) hap i Pharaones halle. (7) Longe ther efter Thu leddest Moyses, thet Tu se muchel luvedest, bute brugge ant bat thurh the Reade Sea ant al his cunredden, thear as al Pharaones ferde fordrencte. (8) Ant feddest ham fowrti yer i the wildernesse with heovenliche fode, ant wurpe under hare vet hare fan alle ant brohtest ham, thurh Iosue, into Ierusalemes lond thet Tu ham bihete. (9) Ther wes i Samueles dei Saul the forme king, kempene icorenest. (10) In a weorre as he wes, Thu dudest i the lutle Davith the selhthe thet he slong ant ofsloh with a stan to deathe the stronge Golie, ant readdest him to rixlen i Saules riche. (11) Thus Thu makest, milde Godd, alle theo muchele the makieth ham meoke, ant theo the heith ham her leist swithe lahe. (12) Threfter, tha the thuhte — ithonket hit beo the! — lihtest hider to us of heovenliche leomen ant nome blod ant ban

fol. 48v

---

an angel of Heaven came descending, and it crashed into that wheel so that it shattered completely. (2) Her bonds burst and broke up completely, and she, as fish-whole as though she had nowhere felt hurt, began to thank God thus with her hands uplifted: "Immortal Lord, one almighty God unlike all others, maker of Heaven and of earth and of all created things, I thank you today for all of your deeds. (3) You made man from earth and gave him a living spirit similar to yourself and made for his sake all that is in the world. (4) But he fell into sin right away because Eve egged him on and he was soon put out of the joys of paradise. (5) His progeny grew so much here that no one could tell it, but they sinned so much that you drowned them all in Noah's flood, except for eight whom you protected. (6) Afterwards, in the old law, you chose Abraham and Isaac, Jacob and his children, and gave to Joseph (who was the youngest) happiness in Pharaoh's hall. (7) Long after that you led Moses, whom you loved so much, and all of his kindred through the Red Sea without a bridge or boat, whereas all the Pharaoh's host drowned. (8) And you fed them for forty years in the wilderness with heavenly food and cast under their feet all of their foes and, by means of Joshua, you brought them into the land of Jerusalem which you had promised to them. (9) In Samuel's day Saul was the first king, the choicest of champions. (10) When he was at war, You bestowed on the little David such grace that he slung and slew to death with one stone the strong Goliath, and advised him to rule in Saul's kingdom. (11) Thus you make great, mild God, all those who make themselves meek, and those who glorify themselves here you lay very low. (12) After that, when it pleased you — may you be thanked for it! — you came down to us here

i thet meare meiden, ant were I Bethleem iboren moncun to heale. (13) Ant to the hirden schawdest te, thet te engles to The tahten, ant of the threo kinges were kinewurdliche iwurdget, weoxe ant wrahtest wundres. (14) Ah ear, Thu were ioffret ant with lac aleset ant i Iordanes flum of Sein Iuhan ifulhet. (15) Thu healdest alle unhale ant te deade of deathe. (16) Aleast, as the biluvede, lettest an

of | the tweolve thet Tu hefdest icoren chapi the ant sullen, ant tholedest pine ant passiun thurh Giwes read o Rode, deidest, ant were idon dead i thruh of stane. (17) Stepe adun ant struptest ant herhedest Helle arise, ant Thin ariste cuddest Thine icorene, ant stuhe abuve the steorren into the heste heovene. (18) Ant kimest, King, o Domesdei to deme cwike ant deade. (19) Thu art hope of heale. (20) Thu art rihtwises weole ant sunfules salve. (21) Thu art an thet al maht ant nult nawt bute riht. (22) Iblescet beo Thu eavre the ah eaver-euch thing heien ant herien; ant ich do, deore Drihtin, Thi meiden, an thet ich am, ant luvie The to leofmon luvewende Lauerd thet havest se muche for me iwraht withute mine wurthes. (23) Beo, mi blisfule Godd, with me, ant wite me with the deoveles driveles ant with hare creftes. (24) Wurch yet swucche wundres, forthi deorewurthe nome, thet te reve rudni ant scheomie with his schucke ant Tu beo áá iwurdget, as Thu art wurthe wurthmunt, from worlde into worlde. (25) Amen withuten ende."

62.　　(1) With this as ha stute, stoden the cwelleres, ant yeiden lud-stevene: "Mihti Lauerd is The thet Juliene on leveth. (2) Ne nis na godd buten He, we beoth wel

---

from heavenly light and took blood and bone in that noble maiden, and were born in Bethlehem for the salvation of humankind. (13) And to the shepherds you showed yourself, whom the angels led to you, and you were royally worshiped by the three kings, and grew and worked wonders. (14) But before that, you were offered and redeemed with a gift, and baptized in the river Jordan by Saint John. (15) You healed all the sick and raised the dead from death. (16) Finally, as it pleased you, you let one of the twelve that you had chosen trade and sell you, and, through the Jews' plot, you suffered pain and passion on the Cross, died, and were put dead in a coffin of stone. (17) You stepped down and stripped and harrowed Hell, arose, and made known your Resurrection to your chosen ones, and ascended above the stars into the highest heaven. (18) And you will come, king, on Doomsday to judge the quick and dead. (19) You are hope for salvation. (20) You are the wealth of the righteous and the salve of the sinful. (21) You are the one who can do all and wishes for nothing but justice. (22) Blessed be you forever, whom every creature ought to praise and glorify; and I do, dear Lord, your maiden, alone that I am, and I love you as a lover, lovely Lord, you who have done so much for me without any merits of mine. (23) Be with me, my blissful God, and guard me against the devil's drudges and against their tricks. (24) Work yet such wonders, for your precious name, that the reeve with his devils may redden and be shamed and you may always be glorified, since you are worthy of worship, from world into world. (25) Amen without end."

62.　　(1) With this, as she stopped, the executioners stood and yelled loud-voiced: "A mighty Lord is the one whom Juliana believes in. (2) There is no God but he, we

icnawen. (3) Reve, us reoweth ure sith thet we se longe habbeth ilevet thine reades." (4) Ant wenden alle anesweis abute fif hundret, the stoden ant yeiden alle in a stevene: "Luvewurthe wummon, we wendeth alle to thet Godd thet tu on trustest. | (5) Forlore beo thu, reve, with false bileave, ant iblescet beo Crist ant alle His icorene. (6) Do nu deadliche on us al thet tu do maht. (7) Make us, reve, ananriht misliche pinen. (8) Ontend fur ant feche hweol! (9) Greithe al thet tu const grimliche bithenchen. (10) Forthe al thi feaders wil, thes feondes of Helle. (11) To longe he heold us as he halt te nuthe, ah we schulen heonne forth halden to Jhesu, Godes kinewurthe Sune, moncun Alesent." (12) Swa the reve gromede thet he gristbetede. (13) Wod he walde iwurthen! (14) Ant sende o wodi wise forth to Maximien, the mihti caisere of Rome, her of hwet he readde. (15) Ant he ham het euch fot, heafdes bikeorven. (16) Fif hundret itald of wepmen, ant of wimmen an hundret ant thritti, thrungen euch an bivoren other forte beo bihefdet. (17) Ant ferden alle martyrs, with murhthe, to Heovene.

63.

(1) Eleusius the hwile lette his men makien a muche fur mid alle, ant bed binden hire swa the fet ant te honden, ant keasten hire into the brune cwic to forbearnen. (2) As ha lokede up ant seh this lei leiten, biheolt towart Heovene with honden a hevene, ant thus to Crist cleopede:

64.

(1) "Ne forleaf Thu me nawt nu i this nede, Lauerd of live! (2) Mildheortfule Godd, milce me, Thi meiden, ant mid Ti softe grace salve mine sunnen. (3) Jhesu, mi selhthe, ne warp Thu me nawt ut of Thin ehsihthe! (4) Bihald me ant help me, ant of this reade lei reaf ant arude me, swa thet | tes unseli ne thurve nawt

---

acknowledge. (3) Reeve, our conduct grieves us that we have so long believed in your counsels." (4) And they all converted, about five hundred, who stood and cried all in one voice: "Loveworthy woman, we all turn to that God whom you trust. (5) Lost are you, reeve, with false belief and blessed be Christ and all his chosen. (6) Now do to us cruelly everything that you can do. (7) Make for us, reeve, all kinds of tortures right now. (8) Kindle the fire and fetch the wheel! (9) Prepare all that you can cruelly contrive! (10) Carry out completely your father's will, the fiend from Hell. (11) Too long he held us as he holds you now, but we will henceforth hold to Jesus, God's royal Son, humankind's redeemer." (12) The reeve was so angry that he ground his teeth. (13) He was about to go mad! (14) And he sent frantically forth to Maximian, the mighty emperor of Rome, to find out what he advised about it. (15) And Maximian ordered that the heads be chopped off of every one of them. (16) Five hundred men in total, and of women one hundred and thirty, thronged each one before the other to be beheaded. (17) And they made their way with mirth, all martyrs, to Heaven.

63.

(1) Eleusius meanwhile also had his men make a huge fire, and ordered them to bind her, both the feet and the hands, and cast her into the fire alive to burn up. (2) As she looked up and saw this flame lit, she looked toward Heaven with hands upraised and cried out thus to Christ:

64.

(1) "Do not forsake me now in this need, Lord of life! (2) Mild-hearted God, pity me, your maiden, and with your gentle grace salve my sins. (3) Jesus, my happiness, do not cast me out of your eyesight! (4) Behold me and help me, and take and rescue me from this red flame so that these wicked men may not have

seggen: 'Thi Lauerd thet tu levest on ant schulde thi scheld beon, hwer is he nuthe?' (5) Ne bidde ich nawt, Drihtin, this for deathes drednesse; ah false swa hare lahe ant festne i Thine icorene treowe bileave. (6) Schaw, mi mihti Godd, Thi meinfule mahte ant hihendliche iher me, iheiyet ant iheret áá on ecnesse."

65.		(1) Nefde ha bute iseid swa thet an engel ne com se briht as thah he bearnde to thet ferliche fur, ant i thet lei lihte, ant acwente hit anan, eaver-euch sperke. (2) Ant heo stod unhurt ther amidheppes, heriende ure Healent with heheste stevene. (3) The reve seh hit acwenct ant bigon to cwakien, se grundliche him gromede, ant set te balefule beast, as eaver ei iburst bar thet grunde his tuskes, ant feng on to feamin ant gristbeatien grisliche upo this meoke meiden, ant thohte with hwuch mest wa he mahte hire awealden. (4) Ant het fecchen a veat, ant with pich fullen, ant wallen hit walm-hat ant het warpen hire thrin, hwen hit meast were iheat ant wodelukest weolle.

66.		(1) As me dude hire thrin ha cleopede to Drihtin, ant hit colede anan ant warth hire ase wunsum as thah hit were a wlech beath, iwlaht for then anes in for te beathien. (2) Ant smat up ayein theo the iyarket hit hefden, ant forschaldede
fol. 50v	of ham, as hit up scheat | alle italde bi tale, seove sithe tene, ant forthre yet five. (3) Tha the reve this iseh, rende hise clathes ant toc himseolf bi the top ant feng to fiten his feonden ant lastin his lauerd.

67.		(1) "Swithe," quoth he, "with hire ut of min ehsihthe thet ich ne seo hire nawt heonne forth mare, ear the buc of hire bodi ant tet heaved liflese liggen isundret."

---

cause to say: 'Your Lord, in whom you believe and who should be your shield — where is he now?' (5) I do not beg this, Lord, for fear of death; but falsify their law and fasten true belief in your chosen ones. (6) Show, my mighty God, your strong power and quickly hear me; be praised and glorified forever into eternity."

65.		(1) She had scarcely said so when an angel came, as bright as though he burned, to that fearsome fire and he alighted into that flame and quenched it at once, every single spark. (2) And she stood there unhurt in the midst of it, praising our Savior with the loudest voice. (3) The reeve saw it quenched and began to shake, so deeply did it anger him: and the baleful beast sat, like any bristled boar that ever ground his tusks, and began to foam and horribly grind his teeth at this meek maiden, and considered by what greatest pain he might master her. (4) And he ordered a vessel fetched and filled with pitch, and boiled it boiling-hot and commanded her to be cast inside, when it was the hottest and boiled most bitterly.

66.		(1) As she was placed inside it she cried out to the Lord and it cooled immediately and became as pleasant for her as though it were a luke-warm bath, made warm just for the purpose of bathing. (2) And it surged up against those who had prepared it and scalded them to death as it shot up, all told in number seven times ten, and five still more. (3) When the reeve saw this, he tore his clothes and grabbed himself by the hair and began to quarrel with his fiends and curse his lord.

67.		(1) "Quickly!" said he, "get her out of my eyesight so that I do not see her any more before the trunk of her body and the lifeless head lie sundered!" (2) As soon

(2) Sone se ha this iherde, ha herede Godd of Heovene ant warth utnume glead, forthis ha helde iwilnet. (3) Me leadde hire ant leac forth, ant heo wes ethluke.

68. (1) As ha stutte i thet stude ther the fordemde schulden death drehen, tha com the ilke Belial thet ha hefde ibeaten feorren to bihinden ant bigon to yeien: "A, stalewurthe men, ne spearie ye hire nawiht. (2) Ha haveth us alle scheome idon. (3) Schendeth hire nuthe! (4) Yeldeth hire yarow borh efter thet ha wurthe is. (5) A, stalewurthe men, doth hire bilive to death buten abade."

69. (1) Juliene the eadie openede hire ehnen ant biheold towart him, as he thus seide; ant tet bali blencte, ant breid him ayeinwart bihinden hare schuldren as for a schoten arewe. (2) "Wumme thet ich libbe," quoth he, "ich beo nunan ilaht. (3) Ah ilecche ha me eft, ne finde ich na leche. (4) Igripe ha me eanes ne ga i neaver mare threfter o grene." (5) Ant leac him ayeinwart, as the beare unhwiht, in alre diche deofle wei — ne mahte nawt letten. (6) As ha schulde stupin ant strecche

fol. 51r forth | thet swire, ha bed first, ant feng on thus for te learen theo the ther weren:

70. (1) "Lusteth me, leove men, ant litheth ane hwile. (2) Bireowsith ower sunnen, ant salvith with soth schrift ant with deathbote! (3) Leaveth ower unlahan ant buldeth upo treowe eorthe thet ne dredeth na val for wind ne for wedere. (4) Lokith thet te heovenliche Lauerd beo grund-wal of al thet ye wurcheth, for thet stont studevest, falle thet falle. (5) Yeieth to Godd in Hali Chirche thet He yeove ow wit wel forte donne, ant strenge ow with His strengthe ayein the strongc unwiht thet secheth eaver ant áá ow to forswolhen. (6) Lustnith lustiliche hali writes lare ant livieth threfter.

---

as she heard this, she praised God of Heaven and became exceedingly glad, since she had desired this. (3) She was led and dragged forth, and she was easy to drag.

68. (1) As she paused in that place where the condemned were accustomed to suffer death, then that same Belial whom she had beaten came from far behind and began to cry out: "Ah, stalwart men, do not spare her at all! (2) She has put us all to shame. (3) Kill her now! (4) Give her ready repayment for what she deserves. (5) Ah, stalwart men, put her to death now without delay!"

69. (1) Juliana the blessed opened her eyes and looked toward him as he said thus, and that evil one flinched and sprang backwards behind their shoulders as if in fear of a fired arrow. (2) "Woe is me that I live!" said he, "I am soon caught. (3) But should she catch me again I will not find rescue. (4) Once she grasps me, I will nevermore afterwards live on the earth." (5) And he jerked himself backwards, like the Devil himself, into the ditch of all demons – he could not stop himself. (6) As she was about to stoop and stretch forth the neck, she prayed first and began thus to instruct those who were there:

70. (1) "Listen to me, dear people, and hear me for a while. (2) Repent your sins and heal them with true shrift and with penance! (3) Leave your evil customs and build upon trustworthy ground so that you fear no fall from wind or from weather. (4) See to it that the heavenly Lord is the foundation of all that you do, for He stands steadfast, fall what may befall. (5) Cry out to God in Holy Church so that he gives you the knowledge to do well and strengthens you with His strength against the strong fiend, who seeks always and forever to swallow you. (6) Listen eagerly to Holy Scripture's teaching and live according to it. (7) It is well for him who is

(7) Wel him the waketh wel ant i this lutle hwile wit her himseolven, ant heorteliche siketh ofte for his sunnen. (8) This worlt went awei as the weater the eorneth, ant ase sweven imet aswint hire murhthe, ant al nis bute a leas wind thet we i this worlt livieth. (9) Leaveth thet leas is ant leoteth lutel throf, ant secheth thet sothe lif thet áá leasteth, for this lif ye schulen leoten — ant nuten ye neaver hwenne — ant reopen ripe of thet sed thet ye her seowen; thet is, undervo yeld of wa other of wunne efter ower werkes. (10) Swithe ich biseche ow thet ye bidden for me, brethren ant sustren." (11) Ant custe | ham coss of peis alle as ha stoden. (12) Ant biheold uppart, ant hehede hire stevene:

fol. 51v

71.   (1) "Lauerd Godd almihti, ich thonki The of Thine yeoven. (2) Nim yeme to me nuthe. (3) Thu luvest over alle thing treowe bileave, ne lef Thu neaver to Thi va Thin ilicnesse thet Tu ruddest of death thurh Thi death o Rode! (4) Ne let Tu me neaver deien i the eche death of Helle! (5) Underveng me to The ant do me with thine i thet englene hird with meidenes imeane. (6) Ich ayeove The mi gast, deorrewurthe Drihtin, ant do hit, blisfule Godd for Thin iblescede nome to ro ant to reste." (7) With thet ilke ha beide hire ant beah duvelunge adun, bihefdet, to ther eorthe. (8) Ant te eadie engles with the sawle singinde sihen into Heovene.

72.   (1) Anan threfter, sone com a seli wummon bi Nichomedesse burh o rade towart Rome. (2) Sophie wes inempnet, of heh cun akennet, ant nom this meidenes bodi ant ber hit into hire schip biwunden swithe deorliche i deorrewurthe clathes. (3) As ha weren i watere com a storm thet te schip ne mahte

---

very vigilant and who in this little time here guards himself, and heartily sighs often for his sins. (8) This world wends away like the water which flows, and, like a dream dreamt, its joy fades away, and all that we experience in this world is nothing but a false wind. (9) Leave what is false and reckon it little, and seek that true life that lasts forever, for you will leave this life — and you never know when — and reap the harvest from that seed which you sow here; that is, accept the yield of woe or of joy according to your works. (10) Earnestly, I beseech you that you pray for me, brothers and sisters." (11) And she kissed them all with the kiss of peace as they stood. (12) And she looked upward, and raised up her voice:

71.   (1) "Lord God Almighty, I thank You for Your gifts. (2) Take care of me now! (3) You love above all things true belief; do not ever leave to your foe your likeness, which you rescued from death through your death on the Rood! (4) Do not ever abandon me to die in the unending death of Hell! (5) Take me to you and place me with your own in that angels' company among the fellowship of maidens. (6) I give you my spirit, precious Lord, and commit it, blissful God, for your blessed name, to peace and to rest." (7) With that she bent herself and bowed headlong down, beheaded, to the earth. (8) And the blessed angels singing departed with the soul into Heaven.

72.   (1) Soon afterwards, there came a holy woman riding toward Rome by the city of Nicomedia. (2) She was called Sophie, descended from high kin, and she took this maiden's body, wrapped very preciously in rich clothes, and carried it into her ship. (3) When they were on the water, there came a storm through which no

na mon steorin, ant drof ham to drue lond in to Champaine. (4) Ther lette Sophie, from the sea a mile setten a chirche ant duden hire bodi thrin in a stanene thruh, hehliche, as hit deh halhe to donne.

fol. 52r
73. (1) The reve sone se he wiste thet ha wes awei ilead, leop | for hihthe with lut men into a bat ant bigon to rowen swiftliche efter, for te reavin hit ham ant i the sea senchen. (2) Ant arisen stormes se sterke ant se stronge, thet te bordes of this bat bursten ant tobreken, ant te sea sencte him on his thrituthe sum, ant therto yet fowre, ant draf ham adrenchet dead to the londe, ther ase wilde deor limmel toluken ham ant tolimeden eaver-euch lith from the lire. (3) Ant te unseli sawlen sunken to Helle, to forswelten i sar ant i sorhe eaver.

74. (1) Thus the eadi Juliene wende thurh pinen, from worldliche weanen to Heoveriches wunnen, i the nomecuthe burh Nicomede inempnet, i the sixtenthe dei of Feoverreres moneth, the fowrtuthe kalende of Mearch thet is seoththen.

75. (1) Heo us erndi to Godd the grace of Himseolven the rixleth in threohad ant tah is untweamet. (2) Iheret ant iheiet beo He Him ane as He wes ant is eaver in eche.

76. (1) Hwen Drihtin o domesdei windweth his hweate
Ant warpeth thet dusti chef to Hellene heate,
He mote beon a corn i Godes guldene edene,
The turnde this of Latin to Englischc lcdene,
Ant he thet her least on wrat swa as he cuthe. (2) AMEN.

---

man could steer the ship, and it drove them onto dry land into Campagna. (4) There Sophie, a mile from the sea, founded a church and placed her body inside in a coffin of stone, solemnly, as one ought to do for a saint.

73. (1) The reeve, as soon as he learned that she had been carried off, hastily leaped into a boat with a few men and began to row swiftly after, in order to seize the body from them and sink it into the sea. (2) And there arose storms so stark and so strong that the boards of this boat burst and broke apart, and the sea sank him and thirty of his men, and still four more in addition, and drove them drowned dead to land, where wild beasts tore them apart limb from limb and ripped every single joint from the flesh. (3) And the unholy souls sank to Hell, to perish miserably in pain and in sorrow forever.

74. (1) Thus the blessed Juliana passed through torments, from worldly woes to the joys of the heavenly kingdom, in the renowned city named Nicomedia on the sixteenth day of the month of February, which is after the fourteenth Calends of March.

75. (1) May she, through her pleading to God, secure for us the grace of Him who rules in the Trinity and yet is undivided. (2) May he be praised and glorified, Him alone, as He was and is, forever into eternity.

76. (1) When the Lord on Doomsday winnows his wheat
And drives that dusty chaff to hellish heat,
May he be a grain on God's golden threshing floor,
Who translated this from Latin into the English language,
As well as he who last wrote in this book as best he could. (2) AMEN.

EXPLANATORY NOTES TO *SEINTE JULIENE*

ABBREVIATIONS: *AS*: *Anchoritic Spirituality*, trans. Savage and Watson; *AW*: *Ancrene Wisse*, ed. Hasenfratz; **B**: Bodleian Library MS 34 [base text]; **B₂**: Bodleian Library MS 285; *CT*: *Canterbury Tales*; **D**: d'Ardenne edition (1961); *HM*: *Hali Meithhad*; *MED*: *Middle English Dictionary*; *OCD*: *Oxford Classical Dictionary*; *OCE*: *Original Catholic Encyclopedia*; *OED*: *Oxford English Dictionary*; **R**: British Library MS Royal 17 A XXVII; *SJ*: *The Liflade ant te Passiun of Seinte Juliene*; *SK*: *The Martyrdom of Sancte Katerine*; *SM*: *The Liflade and te Passiun of Seinte Margarete*.

Header *Seinte Juliene.* Juliana was an early fourth-century virgin and martyr who probably was martyred at Cumae or Naples, and whose cult in England goes back at least as far as Bede's late ninth-century *Martyrology*. See Farmer, *Oxford Dictionary of Saints*, p. 280. Bodley 34 gives Juliana a French name, which reinforces the argument that the milieu in which these works were produced was at least trilingual. It is likely that the readers of these texts knew how to read English and French and a certain degree of Latin. See the note to the header of *SK*. For a discussion of multilingual literacy in this period see Robertson, "This Living Hand."

1.1 *alle leawede men . . . to Englische leode.* This passage shares with *SM* a self-consciousness about its status as a translation into English. Compare *SM* 74.1. This life is clearly addressed to those who did not understand Latin — that is, untrained lay audiences. Women in the religious life in this period were unlikely to have been trained in Latin as were their male counterparts. Notice also that this life stresses that it should be listened to rather than read, suggesting that at one point the narrative was read aloud, as opposed to read privately. *SJ*'s rhetorical flourishes contribute, according to Ursula Schaefer, to a skillful combination of highly literate, Latinate translation with powerful oral/aural formulaic language. See Schaefer, "Twin Collocations," pp. 188–91, for her specific discussion of how the dense pairing of semantically or phonologically similar nouns and verbs affects the orality and aurality of this text.

2.1 *Nichomedese.* During the reign of Diocletian, Nicomedia was the largest metropolis in the Roman province of Bithynia in what is now northwest Turkey Diocletian established the City as capital of the Eastern Roman Empire in 286 CE and it remained so until 330, when Constantine the Great moved the capital to Byzantium (thereafter Constantinople). See *OCE*, "Diocletian."

3.1 *i thon, time.* I.e., the early fourth century, when Maximian (d. 310) and Diocletian (d. 312) ruled and persecuted Christians together. See Eusebius' account of the

169

Diocletian persecutions in Book VIII of his *Church History*; chapters 5 and 6 cover the oppression of Christians in Nicomedia, which were especially brutal. The suppression of Christian practices began in Nicomedia in February 303 CE. See *OCD*, "Nicomedia."

3.3   *wes wel with the king.* I.e., "got along well with the king," or "was well off with the king"; D glosses as "was on good terms with" (p. 137); Savage and Watson translate as "was thus so favored by the king" (*AS*, p. 306).

4.1   *As he hefde . . . hire luve libben.* This version of the persecution of the female saint draws on traditional courtly love imagery to describe Eleusius' attraction to Juliana. Compare, for instance, *Roman de la Rose*, the Lover's torment at the hands of the God of Love when he first beholds the Rose: "I was in great pain and anguish because of my doubled danger: I didn't know what to do, what to say, or where to find a physician for my wound . . . but my heart drew me toward the rosebud, for it longed for no other place" (trans. Dahlberg, p. 54). Gayle Margherita discusses the *Juliana*-author's use of French courtly love discourse in this text, in an English culture that had not yet seen the instantiation of courtly love in its vernacular literature: "Eleusius's courtly discourse conceals an aggressive and sadistic subtext that is, in the legend, allied with both pagan and Norman political hegemony. The text sets up an analogy between early Christians and Anglo-Saxon aristocrats, marginalized under pagan and Norman domination respectively" (*Romance of Origins*, p. 47). This suggestion sets up a productive context from which to read the legend's agenda of English myth-making and the attempt at establishing vernacular authority.

4.3   *Affrican wiste thet . . . him his bone.* Here some of the concerns of secular marriage practices are made evident as Eleusius considers the class similarity between himself and Juliana. Concerns over marriage are at the forefront of *SJ*, when Juliana must negotiate between her pledge to marry Christ and the cultural expectation of her secular marriage. A useful historical comparison is Christina of Markyate, whose insistence that she is already married (to Christ) helps her annul her marriage to Beohtred; see the *Life of Christina of Markyate*, ed. and trans., Talbot.

4.4   *hire unwil.* Literally, "to her displeasure." However, we have attempted to include the concept of willing consent in our translation, an essential element in medieval marriage practice. For more on marriage law and practice in the Middle Ages, see McCarthy, *Marriage in Medieval England*; Sheehan, *Marriage, Family, and Law*; Noonan, "Power to Choose"; and most recently McSheffrey, *Marriage, Sex, and Civic Culture*.

5.4   *with purpres ant pelles.* See also the explanatory note to *SK* 33.3, where this same phrase is used to describe an upper class woman's clothing.

6.1–4   *Juliene the eadie . . . . luve sech the.* Hassel, in *Choosing Not to Marry*, discusses in detail the unique position Juliana occupies (as opposed to Katherine or Margaret) in that the marriage proposal Eleusius offers is "most appealing for a young woman" (p. 70). Eleusius' social rank equals that of Juliana's own family, and he approaches her initially in a romantic and socially appropriate way. The potential legitimacy of this earthly marriage, however, emphasizes Juliana's role as a Bride of Christ, which she reaffirms at 13.4. For more discussion of the contrast between this earthly marriage and her marriage to Christ, see Hassel, *Choosing Not to Marry*, pp. 70–71.

14.1–2   *Hire feader feng . . . . with him icnawen.* Christina of Markyate's conflict with her parents is similar to that of Juliana and Africanus: both daughters have rejected the parents' traditional right to select a spouse for their child, a selection in which the family has a lot at stake, since a good marriage could be of significant economic and social benefit to the family. Christina's parents plead, threaten, and abuse her in their attempts to persuade her to abandon her commitment to Christ. Like Christina, Juliana claims a prior "marriage" to Christ as an impediment to a secular marriage. See *Life of Christina of Markyate*, ed. and trans. Talbot. For a discussion of the legitimacy of her marriage vows to Christ in the secular sphere see Head, "Marriages of Christina of Markyate." See Hassel, *Choosing Not to Marry*, p. 75, on Juliana's complete alienation from her family and society.

19.2   *Beliales budeles.* The name Belial comes from 2 Corinthians 6:15, and is a common name for the devil or one of his henchmen. In this context (as in 60.4 below), *budeles* are senior lieutenants who execute the orders of a superior authority (*OED beadle* (n.), sense 2a). See also *SK* 43.1 and the corresponding explanatory note.

21.3–4   *For eaver se . . . . in His servise.* Especially emphasized in this life is Christ's ability to provide all that a secular husband can and more. Eleusius tempts Juliana with material wealth and status, which mean nothing to her compared to the spiritual wealth and status afforded to her by Christ. This contrast evokes Matthew 6:19–21 as well as Matthew 22:21. Compare also *SM* 6.3 and 67.14, as well as the corresponding explanatory notes.

22.2   *lilies ilicnesse, ant rudi ase rose.* The white lily is traditionally associated in saints' lives with purity and the red rose with blood. Compare, for example, the faces of the converted pagan scholars after their execution (*SK* 32.3), or Chaucer's Second Nun's interpretation of Saint Cecilia's name (*CT* VIII[G] 85–91) and especially Saint Cecilia's association with roses and lilies (*CT* VIII[G] 218–24 and 246–52). Romance heroines are also conventionally described as white-skinned and red-cheeked.

22.3–4   *His heorte feng . . . . thet he walde.* On Eleusius' reaction to Juliana's beauty, compare Gower's Tale of Apollonius, where the daughter of the King of Pentapolis thinks about Apollonius:

> Hire herte is hot as eny fyr,
> And otherwhile it is acale;
> Now is sche red, nou is sche pale
> Riht after the condicion
> Of hire ymaginacion. (*Confessio Amantis*, ed. Peck, 8.846–50)

While Genius might certainly accuse Eleusius of "mislok" (*CA* 1.334), his love-symptoms, however, prefigure the sadistic and violent character he will become. This description, in addition to participating in the subtext of courtly love, also evokes images and sensations disturbingly evocative of hellfire and fury, particularly in the melting bone marrow and alternation of hot and cold. Compare, for example, the melting of sinners' bodies in Purgatory in Passus II of *The Vision of Tundale*, ed. Foster, lines 339–44, or the torment of fire and ice in Passus III, lines 365–80 (though much of this imagery originates in Bede's Vision of Drythelm from the *Ecclesiastical History* [see Foster's Introduction to *Tundale*, pp. 179–90]). In addition, Margherita points out the parallel between the psychological torment Eleusius experiences at Juliana's hands, and the physical torture he inflicts on her later, which includes bursting her bone marrow and snapping all of her limbs (*Romance of Origins*, pp. 46–47).

23.5–6   *Ant loke alswa . . . . the so lathe*? Eleusius' tactic here is to make a direct comparison between these ancient pagan customs and Juliana's kin group (the *alswa . . . as* construction). In this way he appeals (or attempts to appeal) to her sense of duty to her *gens* or to her domestic impulses toward her family. The strong link in Roman culture between the patriarchal family and the family's own personal pagan gods is evident in the iconographic image of Aeneas, departing the wreckage of Troy while carrying his father Anchises on his shoulders and the bust of the family gods, while leading his young son by the hand (his wife, Creusa, forgotten, disappears behind him). This attempt at manipulation fails utterly, as Juliana has wholeheartedly renounced this system of simultaneous religious worship and family honor in favor of a heavenly family.

24.3   *cwike deovlen*. In response, Juliana equates Eleusius' gods (the same gods whose loyalty he has thrust upon her) with living demons, predicting the infernal family the governor will adopt when he ends up in Hell.

24.4   *world àà buten ende*. An adverbial phrase, basically "forever and forever and forever," although it is tempting to read this as a prepositional "in the world that is forever without end" (i.e., Hell). We suspect that both senses are implied.

25.1   *Me, leof . . . me to deathe*. Eleusius' pragmatic but ultimately cowardly response to Juliana's challenge signifies the end of his courtly sweet-talk. His refusal to enter into what would be a holy marriage bond with Juliana is worth contrasting with Valerian's response to Saint Cecilia on their wedding night in Chaucer's Second Nun's Tale; when she warns him gently of a holy angel who loves her and who will slay Valerian if he touches her, the bridegroom responds:

> "If I shal trusten thee,
> Lat me that aungel se and hym biholde;
> And if that it a verray angel bee,
> Thanne wol I doon as thou has prayed me;
> And if thou love another man, for sothe
> Right with this swerd thanne wol I sle yow bothe"
> (*CT* VIII[G] 163–68)

Evidently Valerian has been reading up on Gower's Tale of Nectanabus, but he also demonstrates a remarkable ability to listen to his holy wife and to see what for Eleusius would be an impossibility. In contrast, Eleusius fears the loss of his secular office and ultimately death (which fear Valerian conquers in his visit to the catacombs).

27.1   *bigoten of the blode*. "Covered over" or "drenched" in blood. The image of Juliana naked, covered in her own blood, and the particular phrasing here not only draws attention to the sadistic and potentially violent erotic subtext of the tale but more importantly to the analogy drawn between the image of the naked, feminized, tortured body of Christ and the virgin martyrs who love him. D points out a useful Anglo-Saxon parallel in the *Dream of the Rood*, where the Cross describes how it became entirely "mid blode . . . begoten" after Christ's side was pierced (line 48, quoted in D, p. 79).

27.4   *wurthe him wurst*. Literally, "it becomes him the worst."

30.2   *ne for luve nowther ne for luther*. Juliana refers to the gentleness with which both Africanus and Eleusius began their attempts at persuasion, and to the wicked anger with which they ended it.

31.4–7   *Lauerd Godd almighti . . . . to Thin help*. Compare Vulgate Psalm 17.

32.3   *Ah the worldes . . . wes hal meiden*. In *De Praescriptione Haereteticorum* [Of the Prescription against Heretics], Chapter 36, Tertullian states that John was thrown into a cauldron of boiling oil from which he emerged unscathed before the Porta Latina in Rome.

33.7–8   *As Thu biwistest . . . . ferden ham efter*. For the story of Daniel in the lions' den, see Daniel 6. The tale of the Hebrew children cast into the furnace is found in Daniel 3, where they are called Sidrach, Misach, and Abdenago (Daniel 1:6–7 tells of the children's renaming). The Parting of the Red Sea is found in Exodus 14 (the full story of the escape from Egypt, including Passover and a celebratory hymn of praise to God, is recounted in Exodus 13–15).

34.1   *com a kempe of Helle on englene heowe*. The scenario of a demon disguised as an angel most likely originates from 2 Corinthians 11:14, where Paul states, "And no wonder, for Satan himself masquerades as an angel of light." This episode in *SJ* is remarkable for its violence, in that many of the tortures Juliana inflicts on Belial in some ways approach those torments she receives at the hands of her father and Eleusius. However, the episode also points to, as Hassel notes, "the difficulties of faith facing holy women" (*Choosing Not to Marry*, p. 74). In particular, the words of Belial-as-angel represent what suffering but flawed Christians want to hear, but what the martyr must resist: that Juliana need not suffer more pain and that her spiritual striving is finished. In many ways, Belial's words are so convincing because, in his assertion that "Ne mei ich tholien thet ha thus mearren the na mare" (34.4) and "Me areoweth thi sar" (34.6), he echoes, in some ways, the grief of the Father for the torments of the Son (typologically re-enacted by God's testing of Abraham in Genesis 22:1–19). The false angel scenario can be compared to the apocryphal story of the postlapsarian life of Adam and Eve in the *Vita Adae et Evae*; in this text, as recounted by Rosemary Woolf, Adam and Eve do penance by immersing themselves in the Jordan and Euphrates (respectively) for one month. After two weeks, the devil comes to Eve disguised as an angel and asks her to leave off her penance and exit the river (Woolf, "Fall of Man," pp. 19–20). In both the cases of Eve and Juliana, the false messenger expresses the unstated desire of these two women, the ultimate temptation voluntarily to give up suffering. Unfortunately for Eve, she gives in yet again, whereas Juliana does not. For more on this episode, see Hassel, *Choosing Not to Marry*, pp. 74–77, and Woolf, "Fall of Man," pp. 19–20.

37.1   *hwet me beo to donne*. Literally, "what there is for me to do." The impersonal construction ("me beo") is a common form in highly inflected languages. The inflected infinitive usually indicates obligation, hence our translation "what I should do."

38.5   *unthonc in his teth*. "Ingratitude in his teeth" – i.e., "against his will" or "despite himself." Winstead translates as "willy-nilly" (*Chaste Passions*, p. 18), and Watson and Savage as "even against his will" (*AS*, p. 313). This idiom is used only in AB texts; compare *HM* 41.7 and the *AW* 4:699–700, which Hasenfratz glosses as "damn his teeth (i.e., despite himself)" (p. 254, lines 698–703). Curiously, all three instances involve the phrase in reference to the virgin/anchoress's power to further frustrate and enrage the devil by resisting his temptations. D suggests that this phrase became modified from contact with Old French *malgré suen* ("despite his"), resulting in the extremely common Middle English phrase *maugre his heed* (*face*, *teeth*, &c.) (p. 135), meaning "in spite of his wishes."

42.1   *Deore leafdi . . . scharpe speres ord*. The devil recites and takes credit for the major catastrophes of the Bible from Genesis through the Gospels. See note to 61.3–18 below.

42.2   *Adam ant Eve . . . Caym the acursede acwalde his brother Abel*. For the Biblical account of Adam and Eve being cast out of Paradise, see Genesis 3:1–19. On the murder of Abel and God's cursing of Cain, see Genesis 4:3–15.

42.3   *te threo children*. On Nebuchadnezzar and the idol of gold and the attempted burning of Sidrach, Misach, and Abdenago, see Daniel 3. See also the note to 33.7–8 above.

42.4   *Ant ich hit . . . thurh to deathe*. This story of Isaiah's death is told in the apocryphal book, the Ascension of Isaiah, in which Manasseh, his heart taken over by Bel'ar (Belial), has the prophet cut in two with a wooden saw.

42.5   *Godes deore temple todriven al to duste*. On the destruction of the temple of Jerusalem by the armies of Nebuchadnezzar, see 2 Kings 25:8–17 and 2 Chronicles 36:17–21.

42.6   *ant makede ham . . . . ant to herien*. Exodus 32:1–6 describes the creation of the golden calf, which seems to be the *godes* to which the demon refers.

42.7   *the riche Iob*. For Job's lamentation on the dung-hill, see Job 2:7–8.

42.9   *Sein Iuhan the . . . Seinte Stephene isteanet.* For the death of John the Baptist, see Matthew 14:1–12. For the death of Stephen, see Acts 7:54–59.

        Simunes muth, the . . . Peter ant Pawel. Simon Magus, whose encounter with Peter and Philip is narrated in Acts 8:9–25, gave rise to a long string of apocryphal works. His struggles in Rome against Peter and Paul are variously told, though perhaps most influentially in the "Philosophumena" of Hippolytus of Rome and in the Acts of St. Peter.

42.10   *Ant ich hit . . . to biheafdin Pawel.* Paul's martyrdom, though not told in the Bible, is narrated by Eusebius in his *Ecclesiastical History* 2.25, and also appears in Patristic sources such as Tertullian's *De Praescriptione*, Chapter 36.

42.11   *the cniht to thurlin Godes side with scharpe speres ord.* On the piercing of Christ's side at the Crucifixion, see John 19:34. This unnamed knight was later associated with Longinus, who according to tradition was miraculously cured of blindness when the blood and water from Christ's wound ran into his eyes.

44.1   *Belzeebub.* The name Beelzebub comes from Ba'al-zebub, the god of the Philistine city of Ekron (see 2 Kings 1:2), and is a synonym for Satan. See *MED Belzebub* (n.), sense c. Also compare Luke 11:15 of the Wycliffite Bible where Satan is identified as "Belsebub, prince of deuelis."

46.3   *ure luvewurthe feader.* This is the first of several times that Belial mentions his father, Satan. The terms Belial uses to describe him ("luvewurthe feader" [46.3], "mi kinewurthe feader" [50.8], "mi meinfule feader" [50.9], and "mi leove feader" [56.4]) unwittingly — and perhaps unflatteringly — juxtapose Satan with God, the true paternal authority. One key distinction between the promises that serve as the foundation of these relationships (Belial's with Satan; Juliana's with God) is that the demonic one is easily broken. Unlike Juliana, Belial betrays his father, while Juliana stands firm, even under torture.

48.2–8 *hwer se we . . . . eaver to uvele.* Belial describes here his assaults on religious men and women who attempt to pray together, revealing yet more anxiety about the necessary relationship between female religious and their confessors and priests. See the explanatory note to *SM* 43.1–43.9.

48.4   *overstiheth.* We have taken some liberty with the translation of this word, which *MED* defines as "prevail over" (*overstihen* (v.), sense c.). The verb also describes rising water, as in Jacob and Joseph:" Þer nas in Þis worldhul non so heiŏ, Þat tis vnirude flod muchel no ouersteiŏ" (*MED overstihen* (v.), sense a.) These rapidly rising flood waters appropriately describe the growing desire the devils plant in well-meaning religious, who can become engulfed in their weakened state.

48.6   *hwen the preost . . . noteth Godes licome.* I.e., when the priest receives the Eucharist, thereby partaking of God's body.

52.1   *euch neil ant blakede of the blode.* This vivid and violent image of bleeding fingernails, although not unique to these texts, appears elsewhere in the cluster of texts that collectively make up what is known as the AB group. In the

"Lofsong of Ure Louerde" (*Þe Wohunge of Ure Laured*, ed. Thompson), the visionary describes, in a kind of emotional climax, "ha þe bunden swa heteli faste þ[et] te blod wrang ut at / tine finger neiles" (lines 467-70) [how they bound you so cruelly tight that blood was twisted out from your finger-nails].

52.2   *wa wes him o live*. Literally, "it was woe for him [to be] alive," the phrase is glossed in the *MED* as "grief weighed upon him" (*wo* (n.), sense 7a, citing this line). However, see also *MED alive* (adj./adv.), sense 3a, which glosses as "he was ever so wretched" (not citing this line). Either way, the sense is clear though the idiom becomes awkward when translated literally. Both Savage and Watson (*AS*, p. 315) and Winstead (*Chaste Passions*, p. 20) translate as "he was sorry to be alive," which we have followed.

55.5–6   *Of al thet . . . . meast of springeth*. Our translation departs from the original here in syntax, though the Middle English text can be translated more literally: "Of all that evil in the world, what more do you want? I am, of the wills . . ." We have translated so that the antecedent of "hit" (55.6) is clear: "al thet uvel."

55.7   *O, the mihte . . . weorrin ayein us*. The physical power of virgins receives repeated emphasis in the saints' lives, especially in terms of how the virgins wield this power over devils. Juliana and Margaret display this power frequently, as they torture their demons in between their own episodes of being tortured. Compare *SM* 35.3; see also the corresponding explanatory note.

56.3   *ne make thu . . . ne to hokere*. *hutung* is likely a substitute gerund, though D notes that the ending is unusual (p. 103). A literal translation of this passage would read: "do not turn me into [an object of] scorn and mocking for people." Savage and Watson maintain this sense with "don't make me the derision and scorn of humanity!" (*AS*, p. 316). We have translated the whole phrase liberally here, both to maintain alliteration as well as to include the vocal component of both *hutung* (shouting at, hooting at; *OED hoot* (v.)) and *hokere* (mockery, derision, scornful speech, *MED hoker* (n.), sense b).

56.12   *thet ter flue monie*. "so that many flew there," i.e., hurried there in order to see what was going on. We have translated "flue" literally in order to preserve the alliteration.

57.2   *beo soth cnawes*. This phrase, literally "to be truly acknowledging," is used only in AB texts, *SK*, *SJ*, *HM*, and *AW*. *MED knoues* (adj./adv.) defines it as "acknowledging" but glosses this whole phrase as "confess or acknowledge truly." See D's extensive note on the possible origin of "soth-cnawes" (pp. 164–65).

58.2   *Ich heie ant . . . ant ihwer untweamet*. Here Juliana echoes the Apostles' Creed.

60.1–8   *Ant lette o . . . . thet stude stode*. Compare the wheel of torture in *SK* 43.5–44.2.

60.1   *felien*. "Fellies" literally, but we have followed the less literal translation of "rims," the part of the wheel to which the tire is attached. See *MED felwes*.

60.4   *budel*. See the explanatory note to 19.2 above, as well as the explanatory note to *SK* 43.1.

ant bunden hire. "and they bound her"; "they" refers to the henchmen who are the object of the "bet" (ordered) in the previous clause.

61.2   *fischhal*. Literally "fish-whole"; Compare *Alliterative Morte Arthure*, line 2709: "The freke shall be fish-hole within four houres" (ed. Benson); and *The Wars of Alexander*, line 2700: "As fast was he fysch-hale & Philip he callis" (ed. Duggan and Turville-Petre). D compares the term to the German idiom *gesund wie ein Fisch* (p. 91) or *gesund wie ein fisch im wasser* [fit as a fish in water]. *OED* glosses "fish-whole . . . as sound as a fish; thoroughly sound or healthy." The term is not recorded in use after 1599. This idiom is perhaps echoed in such modern if old-fashioned phrases as "healthy as a horse."

61.3–18   *Thu makedest mon . . . . cwike ant deode*. Here Juliana summarizes the major events of the Old and New Testaments. On the narrative level, by doing so she instantiates herself in this ancient and venerated Christian history. On a didactic level, though, this summary and catalogue of the major events in the Bible remind the female religious audience of scriptural events that they themselves most likely could not read. Compare also 42.1–11, where Belial takes credit for the great catastrophes in Scripture; this catalogue also marks an opportunity for Scriptural education.

61.4   *thurh the eggunge of Eve*. Literally "through Eve's egging." We have translated liberally here to maintain clearly and preserve the essence of this flavorful Norse-derived term. See also Savage and Watson, who translate as "through the urging of Eve" (*AS*, p. 317).

61.5   *hit sunegede*. Literally, "it sinned", "it" referring to the "team" (progeny) of the previous clause, a quantitative singular noun. We have translated this singular as a plural (they), to remind the reader of the numerous individuals within the collective "team" whose degraded morality was responsible for the Flood.

61.14   *Thu were ioffret*. I.e., in the temple for circumcision. See Luke 2:21–40. The gift through which Juliana is redeemed is the pair of young doves or pigeons (2:24) offered in sacrifice to the Lord at the time of his circumcision. The feast of the circumcision, January 1ˢᵗ, was celebrated in the Western Catholic Church until Vatican II, when it was changed to the Feast of the Virgin, although it is celebrated still in the Eastern Orthodox tradition. Considered the first day that Christ shed his blood for mankind, the Feast marks the opening of New Year's festivities in *Sir Gawain and the Green Knight*.

62.1–3   *Mihti Lauerd is . . . . ilevet thine reades*. These sentences contain strong echoes of the Creed, fulfilling the purpose not only of an articulation and affirmation of faith but of declaring a Christian community or congregation, albeit a short-lived one.

62.14   *sende o wodi . . . hwet he readde*. *Sende* should be understood as "sent [a message to find out]" (See D, p. 123) or "inquired." See also *MED senden* (v.2) senses 5e and 6b.

       o wodi wise. Literally, "in an insane manner." We have followed D's suggestion and translated the adverbial phrase as "frantically" (p. 140).

63.1   *swa . . . ant*. We have translated as "both . . . and" following *MED so* (adv.), sense
            12c, which cites this occurrence, and D, p. 58n3. Both sources admit that this
            instance of *swa* is confusing, and there are no other recordings of the adverb
            being used this way; D speculates that *swa the* could be a corruption of *bathe*,
            although she does not emend.

65.3   *The reve seh . . . mahte hire awealden*. This simile indicates Eleusius' increasingly
            bestial behavior, comparing him to a boar, the most dangerous quarry in the
            hunt. The former courtly lover has been transformed into a beast without reason
            — the conventional enemy of the serene and rational virgin martyr. Several texts
            use comparison to a boar to imply bravery or fierceness in combat (often in a
            positive light): compare, for example, *Cursor Mundi*, "Þe sargantz þat ware brem
            als bare" (ed. Morris, line 4899). Instead, *SJ*'s author clearly compares Eleusius
            in his rage to the violence of an unpredictable and dangerous animal. The famous
            boar-hunt from *Sir Gawain and the Green Knight* demonstrates the clear peril of
            hunting the animal: "The frothe femed at his mouth unfayr by the wykes, /
            Whettes his whyte tusches . . . / He had hurt so mony beforne / That all thoght
            then ful lothe / Be more with his tusches torne, / That breme was and braynwod
            both" (ed. Burrow, lines 1572–73, and 1577–80). This boar, literally backed into
            a corner, exhibits some of the same behavior and madness as Eleusius.

66.2   *smat up*. See *MED smiten* (v.) sense 7c . Savage and Watson translate as "dashed"
            (*AS*, p. 319) and D glosses as "shot, dashed" (p. 24). We have taken some liberty
            with the translation to more clearly indicate a violent movement of water.

69.5   *in alre diche deofle wei*. This phrase presents some difficulty in translation. The
            case of *diche* is unclear; D (p. 147) suggests the form is corrupt or possibly a
            genitive adjective, hence Winstead's translation: "a devil of a ditch" (*Chaste
            Passions*, p. 25). We have taken *diche* as the object of the preposition, and *alre
            deofle* as a genitive plural, following Watson's translation instead of Winstead. The
            sense is that the "ditch of all demons" is an epithet for Hell. (However, compare
            Jacobus de Voragine's version of the legend, where after Juliana drags Belial
            through the crowd, she throws him into quite the devil of a ditch — the latrine!)

70.1–71.6   *Lusteth me, leove . . . . ant to reste*. Hassel discusses Juliana's role as preacher:
            "Juliana translates otherwise inaccessible biblical truth into a form that is both
            accessible to its audience and persuasive . . . Her act of biblical translation
            resonates with the middle English version of her own life, in that, like the
            unknown translator of the Latin story, she renders the clerical language of
            sacred texts into the vernacular, enabling the understanding of a wider
            audience, one that included women" (*Choosing Not to Marry*, p. 78). Juliana's
            translation of the holy word to her audience reflects back on the act of
            translation that takes place in the rendering of her *Vita* into the vernacular, an
            act which could potentially mangle the body of the authoritative Latin text. This
            use of translation and transformation in her sermon additionally expresses the
            aesthetic dream of the perfect organic text in the English vernacular, a method
            of response to the anxieties about translating the Latin into English.

70.3   *buldeth upo treowe . . . ne for wedere.* Compare Matthew 7:24–25: "Therefore everyone who hears these words of mine and puts them into practice is like a wise man who built his house on the rock. The rain came down, the streams rose, and the winds blew and beat against that house; yet it did not fall, because it had its foundation on the rock."

70.11   *coss of peis.* The kiss of peace is symbolic of the charitable Christian community Juliana has forged here, and functions as a token of spiritual love and friendship as well as a kind of benediction. See *OED kiss* (n.), sense 6c, which cites this line, as well as *OED pax* (n.), sense 2.

71.3   *Thin ilicnesse.* I.e., humanity. Winstead's translation here, "one made in your image" (*Chaste Passions*, p. 25) clarifies the sense of the passage.

72.2   *Sophie.* Sophia (or Sephonia) transported the saint's body to Italy and had it buried in Campania. The motif of the rudderless boat usually signifies abandonment to the will of God. See, for example, *The Voyage of Saint Brendan* or Chaucer's Man of Law's Tale.

74.1   *the sixtenthe dei . . . kalende of Mearch.* The feast day of Saint Juliana is February 16th in the Western Catholic Church and December 21st in the Eastern Orthodox Church. *Kalende* is the first day of each month in the Roman calendar. The "fourteenth Calends of March" is the fourteenth day counted back from the first of March, or 16 February.

76.1   *Hwen Drihtin o . . . to Englische ledene.* The author falls into rhymed verse here: aabbc. Compare the ending of *SM* 75.1–4. In B, just after this verse on fol. 52r, a poem has been inserted in a sixteenth-century secretary hand. Ker (*Facsimile of MS Bodley 34*, p. xiv) transcribes this addition as:

> Whan Iudge at domesday dothe winnow his wheat
> And drives dustye chaffe into hellishe heat
> god make him a corne, in Eden to duell
> that owt of latinethis treatise did freat
> and him that last wrote Amen *Quoth* Maidwell.

ABBREVIATIONS: *BT*: Bosworth and Toller, *Anglo-Saxon Dictionary*; **D**: d'Ardenne (1961); **H**: a series of sixteenth-century scribbles in various hands (see Introduction, p. 22); *HM*: *Hali Meithhad*; **MS**: Bodleian Library MS Bodley 34 [base text]; **R**: British Library MS Royal 17 A XXVII; *SJ*: *The Liflade ant te Passiun Seinte Juliene*; *SK*: *The Martyrdom of Sancte Katerine*; *SM*: *The Liflade and te Passiun of Seinte Margarete*.

Before 1.1	Header is in faded red ink of poor quality, in a different hand than the header to *SM*, which appears on fol. 18r.
1.1	*In*. MS: large rubricated capital *I*, 3.3 cm.
	ba. MS: *baðe*.
	unaginninde. MS: *unagin*. We have adopted D's emendation following her suggestion that *unagin* is a corrupted form; see p. 169 for her discussion of this word. *MED* (*unagunnen* (pp1.)) also suggests that this word in *SJ* is an error for *unagunnen*, a well-attested Old English past participle meaning "uncreated." See also *BT*, *un-águnnen* (adj.).
	icweme. MS: rubricated decorative line filler follows this word to the end of line.
2.1	*Theos*. MS: large rubricated capital *Þ*, 2.5 cm with flourish; indicator letter is visible in the left margin.
	al. MS: *alt* (i.e. a second *l* is canceled).
2.2	*God*. MS: *goð*.
	scheaftes. So MS, with *a* inserted above the line.
	is₂. MS: *s* enlarged with flourish, followed by rubricated decorative line filler to the end of the line.
3.1	*Wes*: MS: large rubricated capital wynn, 1.9 cm; indicator letter is visible in the left margin.
3.3	*dohter*. MS: rubricated decorative line filler follows this word to the end of the line.
4.1	*As*. MS: large rubricated capital *A*, 3.2 cm counting flourish.
	utnume. So D, following R. MS: *utnunme*.
4.2	*stunde*. MS: *stonde*, corrected to *stunde*.
4.4	*wes*. So D, following R. MS: *þes*.
	thet₂. So D, following R. MS: *ha*.
	unwemmet. MS: rubricated decorative line filler follows this word to the end of the line.
5.1	*Elewsius*. MS: large rubricated capital *E*, 1.1 cm.
	swithe. So D. MS: *swðe*. R omits.

5.2   *hwile*. So MS, with *h* inserted above the line.

         In the top margin of 38r, H: *Willelmus Sebourne This indent*.

6.1   *him al*. MS: *him ~~to~~ al*.

6.5   *habben*. MS: *habben idon*. R condenses; the full phrase in R reads: *efter thet hewende to habben his iwil*. We have emended to match the sense of R. D also suggests that *idon* was incorporated later (p. 8n2).

7.1   *seith*. So D. MS: *sehð*. R: *seide*.

8.4   *reade*. MS: *~~t~~reade* (*t* canceled).

9.1   *Godd*. MS: *gdd*, with *o* inserted above the line.

         speoken. So D, following R. MS omits.

9.2   *For*. So MS, D. R omits.

10.1   In the top margin of fol. 39r, H: *In the Name of god Amen I george Wyssham of tedestorn In the Com*.

11.2   *for*. So D, R. MS omits.

12.1   *Affrican*. MS: the *a* of *affrican* has been added in a different hand. Space is left for a capital here which was never added. No indicator letter is visible in the margin; this letter was most likely trimmed off before binding.

13.4   *ich₂*. So MS, corrected from *ih*.

13.5   In the bottom margin of fol. 39v, H has scribbled a short phrase upside down and heavily smeared: *mas N(?) . . . bus(?)*. Versions of the same phrase are repeated in the same hand on fols. 40v, 41v, 42v, and 57r. H has also written, in the bottom margin and perpendicular to the text: *he shal* or possibly *he that*. And in the left margin, H: *felix quem sue (?) Aliena . . .*

14.1   *Hire*. MS: large rubricated capital *H*, 1.9 cm.

16.2   *wani thet tu*. MS, R: omit. D argues that an earlier manuscript must have dropped a term for "lament," which, to fill out the clause, would have been followed by *thet tu*. Because of the nearby *thet tu* (*besmen thet tu*), these words were left out by eyeskip. We have followed D's suggested emendation (p. 14n1).

17.2   *Wurch*. So, D, following R. MS: a word, ending with *d* or possibly *ð*, has been erased and is unreadable.

19.1   *het*. So D, following R. MS: omits.

         leggen. So D, to agree with *strupen*. MS: *leggeth*. R: *beten*.

         thet. So D, following R's *swa luðere þet hire leofliche liche liðeri al oblode*. MS: *ant*. *Thet* is needed to finish out the result clause started in *se* earlier in the same sentence.

21.1   *Ye*. MS: large rubricated capital *ʒ*; indicator letter is visible in the margin.

21.7   *to₄*. So R. MS: *se*. We have emended to *to* following the fairly common phrase *to wrather heale* at 7.1, 16.2, and 48.1. D emends to *te*.

22.1   *Affrican*. MS: *ffrican*. MS: space has been left for a capital *A* that was never inserted. The indicator letter in the left margin has been inserted by a later hand.

22.2   *rudi*. MS: *~~te~~ rudi*.

22.4   *bearnde*. So MS, with *a* inserted above the line.

23.1   *Mi*. MS: space has been left for a large capital *M* that was never inserted. The indicator letter in the left margin has been added by a later hand.

23.5	*on.* So D. R: *of.* It is possible that *of* is not a mistake, since the word often follows or precedes *akennet*; however more likely it is a mistake for *on*, which should accompany *leven.*
23.6	*ha.* So D. R: omits.
24.2	*schulden to.* R: *schulden to schulden to.*
26.1	*efter.* So D. R: *hefter.*
	thet ich livie. So D. R: *leve.* D substitutes this phrase since the R reading "is clumsy, and certainly corrupt." She argues that this phrase was probably omitted because of the repetition of *luve* and *leve* here (p. 20n6).
	i. So D. R: omits.
26.2	*maht.* MS: *mahen*, which is a 2nd person plural. We have emended to *maht* (2nd person singular) to agree with singular *ye.* However, see D, p. 16n1, where she emends to *thet yit . . . mahen*, so that *yit* (2nd person dual pronoun) agrees with *mahen.* Both R and MS read *thet ye [. . .] mahen*, so some emendation is needed.
26.3	*thah.* So D. R: *thah ne schaltu.* The scribe has anticipated the *ne schaltu* at the end of the line.
	for na. Our text follows the MS manuscript again starting here. We have omitted the first word of MS, fol. 41r (*tu*) in order to avoid repetition with *schaltu*, the previous word in R.
	slaht. MS: *schalt*, corrected sloppily to *slaht*, or possibly to *sclaht*. This mistake was evidently because of *schalt* written at the very end of the preceding folio (now lost). See D, p. 22n3.
27.1	*The.* MS: space has been left for a capital Þ that was never inserted. The indicator letter has been cropped, but a later hand has inserted þ into the empty space.
27.2	*ant of the scheome thet tu schalt.* So D, following R's: *ant te scheome thet tu schalt.* MS: *schalt ant of the scheome.* We have adopted D's emendation in order to clarify the syntax.
27.3	*wult.* MS: *wult ase.* R: *wult bithench.* D makes the point that *ase*, the final word on fol. 40v, preceded another short phrase that is now lost, and as such emends to *ase wise wis wummon*, as an example of what might have followed on the next page (p. 18n6). We have stayed with R's reading. Following *wult*, we have adopted our text from the R manuscript, since the next folio is missing from MS.
28.1	*Doth.* MS: *deð*, with *d* added in a later hand. Space has been left for a capital *D* that was never inserted. The original indicator latter has been cropped. D reads as *[D]oð*.
	al thet te deoflen. MS: this phrase is inserted above the line.
29.1	*Nu.* So MS, R. D reads MS as *Na.* Both Savage and Watson, and Winstead translate as "No."
31.1	*Eleusius.* MS: space has been left for a capital *E* that was never inserted; indicator letter is visible in the margin.
31.3	*ant leiden.* So MS, R. The subject is dropped, largely because of the previous line *me dude sone*, although this phrase is passive. D emends to *ant ha leiden*

to clarify the implied subject "they." We have retained the manuscript reading here, since the plural subject is implied by the plural *leiden*.

biyet. So D, R. MS: *yet*.

31.7 *swuch*. So D, R. MS: *swuc*.

31.8 *schule*. So MS, but with *h* and *u* ligatured. See also D, p. 24n4.

32.1 *Tha*. MS: space has been left for a capital *Þ* that was never inserted. The indicator letter has been cropped, but a later hand has inserted *þ* in the margin.

anan. MS: ~~of~~ *anan*.

endelong. So D, R. MS: *enddelong*.

helen. MS: *heælen*.

32.4 *warth*. So D, R. MS omits.

33.1 *Heo*. MS: space has been left for a capital *H* that was never inserted. The indicator letter has been cropped, but a later hand has inserted *h* in the left margin.

murhthe. So D, R. MS: *murhde*.

33.2 *mi*. MS: a word has been erased following *mi*; the space has been left empty. See D, p. 26n6.

33.4 *habbeth*. So D, R. MS: *habbe*.

33.7 *with*. MS: *wid*.

33.10 *schunchen*. MS: ~~thun~~ *shunchen*.

33.14 *eche*. MS: rubricated decorative line filler follows this word to the end of line.

34.1 *As*. MS: large rubricated capital *A*, 1.7 cm. The indicator letter is visible in the left margin.

this. So D, R. MS: *his*.

34.7 *hercne*. So D, R. MS omits.

leave. MS: rubricated decorative line filler follows this word to the end of line.

35.1 *Thes*. MS: large rubricated capital *Þ*, 2.2 cm; indicator letter is visible in the left margin.

36.2 *cleopede*. So MS, but written over an erasure; the earlier word is not discernible.

Criste. MS: rubricated decorative line filler follows this word to the end of line; it has been copied over an entire erased line which is not discernible.

37.1 *Jhesu*. MS: large rubricated capital *I*, 2.3 cm.

37.2 *thet the*. So D, R. MS: *thet the thet*.

38.1 *softe*. So D, R. MS: *fofte*.

seide. MS: *seide* ~~hire~~.

In the bottom margin of fol. 43v, H has written two words, through smeared ink has made them illegible.

38.2 *to*. So D. MS: *ta*.

leofmon. So MS, with o_1 inserted above the line.

40.1 *wenden*. So D, R. MS: *hwenden*.

41.1 *thuncheth*. MS: rubricated decorative line follows this word to the end of the line.

42.1 *Deore*. MS: large rubricated capital *D*, 9 mm.

unwihtes. So D. MS: *unwhihtes*.

42.8 *sumchearre*. So MS, with *a* inserted above the line.

42.12	*brethren*. MS: rubricated decorative line filler follows this word to the end of line.
43.1	*Du*. MS: large rubricated capital *D*, 6 mm; indicator letter is visible in the left margin.
	In the bottom margin of fol. 44v the page, upside down, H: *I george Wyshame de Tedestorne in the Com' of herff' yeo man doethe*. See also the textual note to *HM* 2.5, which mentions George's father Thomas as well as Ker, *Facsimile to MS Bodley 34*, p. xiv, on the Wysham family of Herefordshire.
46.3	*luvewurthe*. So D. MS: *luvewrthe*. R: *leowunde lauerd*.
	willes. MS: rubricated decorative line filler follows this word to the end of line.
47.1	*Sei*. MS: large rubricated capital *S*, 8 mm.
	wurcheth. So D, R. MS: *wurchen*.
	bichearreth. So MS, with *a* inserted above the line.
48.2	*easkest*. So MS, with *a* inserted above the line.
48.3	A number of small lacunae are in the bottom half of fol. 45r; the scribe has worked around them.
48.4	*ha*. So D. MS omits. R: *heo*.
	strengeth. So D, R. MS: *strenged*.
	and overstiheth al. So D, R. MS omits.
	ear. So D. MS: *car*. R: *er*.
48.6	*warpeth*. MS, R: *ant warpeth*. We have followed D's emendation (see p. 38n4).
48.8	*uvele*. MS: rubricated decorative line filler follows this word to the end of line.
49.1	*Me*. MS: large rubricated capital *M*, 7 mm. The indicator letter has been cropped, but a later hand has inserted *m* in the left margin.
50.9	*mi*. So D, R. MS omits.
51.1	*O*. So MS. D, R: *A*.
	threatest tu. So D, following R's *threatestu*. MS: *threates tu*.
	ha. MS: *þa* added above the line in a different hand.
53.1	*O*. MS: large rubricated capital *O*, 7 mm. The indicator letter has been cropped, but a later hand has inserted *o* in the left margin.
	freond. So D, R. MS: *freonð*.
53.2	In the top margin of fol. 46r, a later hand (late 15th–early 16th c.) has written *E E ♣ a a b c d e f g*.
	me. So D, R. MS omits.
	dredeth. So D, R. MS: *ðredeð*.
54.1	*Stew*. MS: space has been left for a capital *S* that was never inserted. The indicator letter is visible in the left margin; a later hand has also inserted *s* in the left margin.
54.2	*ahest*. MS: *a* inserted above the line.
54.3	*mid*. So D, R. MS: *ant of*.
55.7	*hu*. So R. D, MS: *as*.
55.12	*ihalden*. So D. Both MS and R have an infinitive form; MS: *forte halden* and R: *to halden*, which presents difficulty in translation. D argues that the mistake must have occurred in an earlier manuscript (p. 44n1).
56.1	*Eleusius*. MS: space has been left for a capital *E* that was never inserted. The indicator letter is cropped, but a later hand has inserted *e* in the left margin.
	bringen. So D, R. MS: *brugen*.

56.3	*hutung ne to hokere*. See the explanatory note to this line.
56.7	*Ne*. So D, R. MS: *ȝe*.
56.10	*chepmenne*. So R. MS: *champmen*, which D emends to *chapmen*.
56.12	*As*. MS: space has been left for a capital *A* that was never inserted. The indicator letter is visible in the left margin; a later hand has also inserted *a* in the left margin.
	him₁. So D, R. MS: *hit*.
58.1	*Her*. MS: space has been left for a capital *H* that was never inserted. The indicator letter is visible in the left margin; a later hand has also inserted *h* in the left margin.
58.3	*alle*. MS: ~~healle~~.
58.6	*shuken*. MS: ~~swuken~~, with *shuken* inserted in the margin. D reads the insert as *schuken*.
59.1	*Ye*. MS: space has been left for a large capital *ȝ* that was never inserted.
60.4	*Me*. MS: space has been left for a large capital *M* that was never inserted.
60.6	*ant from*. MS: *ant ~~heo~~ from*.
61.1	*As*. MS: *s*; space has been left for a large capital *A* that was never inserted. An indicator letter in a later hand has been inserted in the left margin, but is cropped.
61.2	*Drihtin*. MS: *rihtin*; space has been left for a large capital *D* that was never inserted. An indicator letter in a later hand has been inserted in the left margin, but is cropped.
61.5	*thet₁*. So D, R. MS omits.
61.7	*leddest Moyses*. So D. MS: *leddest þurh Moyses*. R: *leddest moysen þurh*. The mistaken *þurh* was likely inserted here through eyeskip to *þurh þe Reade Sea* in an earlier copy. See D, p. 54n1.
	ant₁. So D, R. MS omits.
	cunredden. MS: *cunredden ~~ant fedest~~*. The mistake anticipates *ant feddest* in the line directly below.
61.10	*weorre*. So MS, with *r* inserted above the line.
61.13	*hirden*. MS: ~~children~~, with *hirden* inserted in the left margin.
61.16	*idon*. So MS, with *i* inserted above the line.
61.24	*art*. So D, following R. MS: *arrt*.
61.24–25	*worlde into worlde. Amen*. So D. We have followed D's emendation, and regularized the syntax of this common idiom; compare *HM* 21.8 and *SW* 14.9. MS: *worlde into worlde. Amen wið uten ende*. R: *amen*.
62.1	*With*. MS: space has been left for a large capital wynn that was never inserted.
62.5	In the top margin of fol. 49v, H has written *T*(?) repeatedly, then written: (?)*hes Thomas Willelmus Ricus henricus willhelmus . . . ??* . In the left margin, H has written: *This bill made the xᵗʰ daye of Maye*.
62.8	*Ontend*. So D. MS: *on tentd*. R: *tend*.
62.9	*tu*. So D. MS omits. R: *þu*.
62.17	*to Heovene*. MS: *to ~~crist~~ heovene*.
63.1	*Eleusius*. MS: space has been left for a large capital *E* that was never inserted.
64.1	*Ne*. MS: space has been left for a large capital *N* that was never inserted.
64.4	In the top margin of fol. 50r, H: *Thomas*.

64.6	*Schaw*. So D. MS: *schwau*, with *h* added above the line. R omits.
	iheiyet. So MS, with *ʒ* inserted above the line.
	iheret. So D. MS: *ihere*. R omits.
65.1	*Nefde*. MS: space has been left for a large capital *N* that was never inserted.
	to . . . ant i. MS: The scribe misplaces *ant₁*, putting it before *to thet ferliche* and omitting it before *i thet lei*. D suggests that the scribe made this mistake while in the process of expanding the line (p. 60n2). He also may have anticipated *ant* while looking at the line below.
65.3	*feng*. So D, R. MS: *fen*.
65.4	*were iheat*. MS: *were ~~hat~~ iheat*.
66.1	*As*. MS: space has been left for a large capital *A* that was never inserted.
	hire₁. So D, R. MS omits.
66.3	*feonden*. MS: *feont*. We have emended for plural sense following R's *mawmez*. The sense here is that Eleusius curses the demon or demons he has been blasphemously worshiping. D emends to "weon" for a sense similar to R's.
67.1	*Swithe*. MS: large rubricated capital *S*, 1 cm; indicator letter is visible in left margin.
	heaved. MS: *heavet*, with *t* corrected to *d*.
67.2	*Godd*. So D, R. MS: *goð*.
68.1	*ilke*. So D, R. MS: *illeke*.
	spearie. So MS, with *a* inserted above the line.
68.5	*abade*. MS: rubricated decorative line filler follows this word to the end of the line.
69.1	*Juliene*. MS: large rubricated capital *I*, 2.7 cm.
	openede. So D, R. MS: *openenede*.
	bali. So R. MS: *beali*. D emends to *Belial* (see D's glossary entry under *beali*, p. 78). We have emended more conservatively, taking R's *bali* as an adjectival form of *bale*, following the *MED* (*bali* (adj.)).
69.5	*the*. MS: inserted in the margin.
69.6	*weren*. MS: rubricated decorative line filler follows this word to the end of the line.
70.1	*Lusteth*. MS: large rubricated capital *L*, 1.3 cm.
70.3	*buldeth*. So D, R. MS: *buldes*.
70.4	*grund*. So MS, corrected from *grunt*.
70.5	*secheth*. So D. MS, R: *seleð*. D asserts that *seleð* here represents an error, since the word does not exist in a similar context in other Middle English texts (see p. 123, under D's glossary entry for *seleð*). Middle English *sellen* with the sense of "to betray" might work; however this verb takes the form of *sullen* in AB (e.g. *SJ* 61.16).
71.1	*Lauerd*. MS: large rubricated capital *L*, 1.3 cm.
72.1	*Anan*. MS: large rubricated capital *A*, 2.5 cm.
	Nichomedesse. So MS, with *h* inserted above the line.
72.4	*halhe*. MS: *ahalhe*.
73.1	*The*. MS: large rubricated capital *Þ*, 2.5 cm.
	leop. So D. MS: *leup*. R omits.

On the sixteenth-century additions to this page, see the explanatory note to
76.1. See also the Introduction, pp. 20 and 22, especially p. 22n83.

the. So D. MS: *thea*. R: omits.

73.2   *ham₁*. So D, R. MS: *him*.

adrenchet. MS: *adrenetchet*.

74.1   *Thus*. MS: large rubricated capital Þ, 2.5cm.

75.1   *Heo*. MS: large rubricated capital *H*, 1.4 cm; the indicator letter is visible in
the left margin.

76.1   *Hwen*. MS: large rubricated capital *H*, 1.4 cm; indicator letter is visible in
the left margin.

warpeth. MS: the original word has been erased and replaced with *weopð*,
which is barely legible and written in a different hand. *MED* suggests that
weorpð was intended (*werpen* (v.), sense 8b). We have emended to *warpeth*,
the common conjugation of this form of the verb in the Katherine Group
(see *SM* 7.7, *SJ* 48.3, and *HM* 22.13 and 27.11). D speculates that the
erased word may have been *deð* (p. 70n4).

Epistel of meidenhad meidene frovre.

fol. 52v
1.
(1) *Avdi, filia, et vide, et inclina aurem tuam, et obliviscere populum tuum et domum patris tui.* (2) Davith the psalmwruhte speketh i the Sawter towart Godes spuse, thet is, euch meiden thet haveth meidene theawes, ant seith: "Iher me, dohter, bihald ant bei thin eare, ant foryet ti folc ant tines feader hus." (3) Nim yeme hwet euch word beo sunderliche to seggen: "Iher me, dohter," he seith. (4) "Dohter" he cleopeth hire, forthi thet ha understonde thet he hire luveliche lives luve leareth, as feader ah his dohter, ant heo him as hire feader the blitheluker lustni. (5) "Iher me, deore dohter," thet is, "yeornne lustne me with earen of thin heavet." (6) "Ant bihald," thet is, "opene to understonde me the ehnen of thin heorte." (7) "Ant bei thin eare," thet is, "beo buhsum to mi lare." (8) Heo mei ondswerien ant seggen: "Ant hwet is nu this lare thet tu nimest se deopliche ant learst me se yeorne?" (9) Low, this: "Forget ti folc ant tines feader hus." (10) "Thi folc" he cleopeth, Davith, the gederunge inwith the of fleschliche thonkes, the leathieth the ant dreaieth with har procunges to flesliche fulthen, to licomliche lustes, ant eggith the to brudlac ant to weres cluppunge, ant makieth the to thenchen hwuch delit were

---

A letter on virginity for the encouragement of virgins.

1.
(1) *Listen, daughter, and look, and incline your ears, and forget your people and the home of your father.* (2) David the psalm-writer speaks in the Psalter to God's spouse, that is, every maiden that has maidens' virtues, and says: "Hear me, daughter, behold and bend your ear, and forget your folk and your father's house." (3) Take heed of what each word separately says: "Hear me, daughter," he says. (4) "Daughter," he calls her, so that she understand that he teaches her lovingly love of life, as a father ought to do for his daughter, and so that she listen to him as her father the more gladly. (5) "Hear me, dear daughter," that is, "carefully listen to me with the ears of your head." (6) "And behold," that is, "open the eyes of your heart to understand me." (7) "And bend your ear," that is, "be obedient to my teaching." (8) She may answer and say: "And what now is this teaching that you take so seriously, and teach me so carefully?" (9) Lo, this: "Forget your folk and your father's house." (10) "Your folk," he, David, calls, the gathering inside you of fleshly thoughts, which incite and draw you with their prickings to fleshly filths, to bodily desires, and egg you on to wedlock and to a husband's embrace, and make you

189

fol. 53r

thrin, hwuch eise i the richedom thet theos leafdis habbeth, hu muche mahte of inker streon | awakenin. (11) A, fals folc of swikel read, as thi muth uleth as thu schawest forth al thet god thuncheth, ant helest al thet bittre bale thet is therunder, ant al thet muchele lure thet terof ariseth! (12) "Forget al this folc, mi deorewurthe dohter," seith Davith the witege. (13) Thet is, thes thonkes warp ut of thin heorte. (14) This is Babilones folc, the deofles here of Helle, thet is umbe forte leaden into the worldes theowdom Syones dohter.

2.   (1) "Syon" wes sumhwile icleopet the hehe tur of Jerusalem, ant seith "Syon" ase muchel on Englische ledene ase "heh sihthe." (2) Ant bitacneth this tur the hehnesse of meithhad, the bihald, as of heh, alle widewen under hire ant weddede bathe. (3) For theos, ase flesches threalles, beoth i worldes theowdom ant wunieth lahe on eorthe, ant meiden stont, thurh heh lif, i the tur of Jerusalem. (4) Nawt of lah on eorthe, ah of the hehe in Heovene, the is bitacnet thurh this, of thet Syon ha bihalt al the worlt under hire, ant thurh englene liflade ant heovenlich thet ha lead, thah ha licomliche wunie upon eorthe, ha is as i Syon — the hehe tur of Heovene — freo over alle from worldliche weanen. (5) Ah Babilones folc (thet ich ear nempnede), the deofles here of Helle, thet beoth flesches lustes ant feondes eggunge, weorrith ant warpeth eaver | towart tis tur forte keasten hit adun ant drahen hire into theowdom thet stont se hehe therin ant is icleopet, forthi, Syones dohter.

fol. 53v

---

imagine what delight would be in it, what ease in the riches that these ladies have, how much might arise from your children. (11) Ah, false folk of deceitful counsel, how your mouth flatters as you put forth all that seems good, and conceal all that bitter bale that is underneath, and all that great loss that arises from it! (12) "Forget all this folk, my beloved daughter," says David the prophet. (13) That is, cast these thoughts out of your heart. (14) This is Babylon's folk, the devil's army of Hell, which aims to lead Syon's daughter into the world's bondage.

2.   (1) "Syon" in the past was called the high tower of Jerusalem, and "Syon" says the same as " high sight" in the English language. (2) And this tower betokens the high rank of maidenhood, which beholds, as from on high, both all widows and the wedded underneath her. (3) For these, as thralls of the flesh, are in the world's bondage and dwell low on the earth, and a maiden stands, through the lofty life, in the tower of Jerusalem. (4) Not from low of earth, but from the height of Heaven, which is signified through this, from that Sion she beholds all the world under her, and through the angelic and heavenly life that she leads, although she dwells bodily upon the earth, she is as if in Syon — the high tower of Heaven — completely free from the world's miseries. (5) But Babylon's folk (which I mentioned earlier), the devil's army of Hell, which are the lusts of the flesh and the egging on of the fiends, make war and always assail this tower to cast it down and drag her into slavery who stands so high inside and who is called, because of this, Syon's daughter.

3.   (1) Ant nis ha witerliche akeast ant into theowdom idrahen, the of se swithe heh
stal of se muche digneté ant swuch wurthschipe as hit is to beo Godes spuse —
Jesu Cristes brude, the Lauerdes leofmon thet alle thinges buheth, of al worlt
leafdi as He is of al Lauerd, ilich Him in halschipe, unwemmet as He is, ant thet eadi
meiden His deorrewurthe moder, ilich His hali engles ant His heste halhen — se
freo of hireseolven thet ha nawiht ne thearf of other thing thenchen bute ane of
hire Leofmon with treowe luve cwemen, for He wule carie for hire, thet ha haveth
itake to, of al thet hire bihoveth hwil ha riht luveth Him with sothe bileave — nis
ha thenne sariliche, as ich seide ear, akeast ant into theowdom idrahen, the, of se
muchel hehschipe ant se seli freodom schal lihte se lahe into a monnes
theowdom, swa thet ha naveth nawt freo of hireseolven, ant trukien, for a mon of
lam, the heovenliche Lauerd, ant lutlin hire leafdischipe ase muchel as hire
leatere were is leasse wurth ant leasse haveth then hefde ear hire earre, ant of Godes
fol. 54r   brude ant His freo dohter — for ba togederes ha is — biki | meth theow under mon
ant his threl, to don al ant drehen thet him liketh, ne sitte hit hire se uvele, ant
of se seli sikernesse as ha wes in ant mahte beon under Godes warde, deth hire into
drechunge, to dihten hus ant hinen ant to se monie earmthen, to carien for se
feole thing, teonen tholien ant gromen ant scheomen umbe stunde, drehen se
moni wa for se wac hure as the worlt foryelt eaver ed ten ende; nis theos witerliche akeast? (2) Nis this theowdom inoh, ayein thet ilke freolec thet ha hefde hwil
ha wes Syones dohter?

---

3.   (1) And is she not truly cast down and dragged into slavery, who from so very
high a place, from so much dignity and such worship as it is to be God's spouse
— Jesus Christ's bride, the Lord's lover whom all things obey, lady of all the world
as he is Lord of all, like Him in wholeness, unblemished as He is, and that blessed
maiden His dear mother, like His holy angels and His highest saints — so free
from herself that she need not at all think of any other thing except only of how
to please her Lover with true love, for He will provide for her, He whom she has
taken, everything that she needs while she loves Him rightly with true belief —
is not she then grievously, as I said before, cast down and dragged into slavery,
who from so much eminence and such blessed freedom shall descend so low into a
man's slavery, so that she has nothing free of her own, and shall leave, for a man
of clay, the heavenly Lord, and lessen her ladyship by as much as her latter
husband is worth less and has less than her former one had, and from God's bride
and his free daughter — for she is both together — she becomes a slave under a
man and his thrall, to do everything and to endure what pleases him, however
badly it sits with her, and from such holy security as she was in and could have
been under God's protection, puts herself into drudgery, to manage household
and servants, so many miseries, to see to so many things, to endure adversities
and annoyances and sometimes shames, to suffer so many woes for so poor a wage
as the world ever pays in the end; is not this maiden truly cast down? (2) Is this
not slavery aplenty, in exchange for that same freedom that she had while she was
Syon's daughter?

(3) Ant thah nis inempnet her nawt of heovenliche luren, the passith alle withuten evenunge. (4) Sikerlicke, swa hit feareth.

4.   (1) Serve Godd ane, ant alle thing schule the turne to gode, ant tac the to Him treowliche ant tu schalt beo freo from alle worldliche weanen. (2) Ne mei nan uvel hearmi the, for as Seinte Pawel seith, alle thing turneth then gode to gode. (3) Ne mei na thing wonti the, the berest Him thet al wealt inwith thi breoste. (4) Ant swuch swettnesse thu schalt ifinden in His luve ant in His servise, ant habbe se muche murhthe throf ant licunge i thin heorte thet tu naldest changin thet stat thet tu livest in forte beo cwen icrunet. (5) Se hende is ure Lauerd thet nule He

fol. 54v   nawt thet His icorene beon her withute mede, | for se muchel confort is in His grace thet al ham sit thet ha seoth, ant thah hit thunche othre men thet ha drehen hearde, hit ne derveth ham nawt, ah thuncheth ham softe ant habbeth mare delit thrin then ei other habbe i licunge of the worlt. (6) This ure Lauerd yeveth ham her as on earnnesse of eche mede thet schal cume threfter. (7) Thus, habbeth Godes freond al the frut of this worlt thet ha forsaken habbeth o wunderliche wise ant Heovene ed ten ende.

5.   (1) Nu thenne, on other half, nim the to the worlde, ant eaver se thu mare havest, se the schal mare trukien, ant servin — hwen thu naldest Godd — thes fikele worlt ant frakele, ant schalt beo sare idervet under hire as hire threal on a thusent wisen, ayeines an licunge habben twa ofthunchunges, ant se ofte beon imaket earm of an ethlich mon thet tu list under, for nawt other for nohtunge, thet te schal lathi thi lif ant bireowe thi sith thet tu eaver dudest te into swuch theowdom for worldliche

---

(3) And yet there is nothing mentioned here of heavenly losses, which surpass everything else without comparison. (4) Truly so it goes.

4.   (1) Serve God alone, and all things will turn out well for you, and commit yourself truly to Him and you will be free from all worldly sorrows. (2) Nor may any evil harm you, for as Saint Paul says, all things turn out well for the good. (3) Nor can anything be lacking for you who carry Him who rules everything inwardly in your heart. (4) And you will find so much sweetness in His love and in His service, and have so much mirth from it and pleasure in your heart that you would not exchange that state that you live in to be a crowned queen. (5) So gracious is our Lord that He does not wish that His chosen be here without reward, for there is so much comfort in His grace that all that they see suits them, and though it may seem to others that they suffer bitterly, it does not hurt them at all, but seems soft to them and they have more delight in it than any other has in pleasure of the world. (6) Our Lord gives them this here as a pledge of the eternal reward that will come afterward. (7) Thus God's friends have all the fruit of this world that they have forsaken and, in a wondrous way, Heaven at the end.

5.   (1) Now then, on the other hand, turn yourself to the world, and always the more you have, the more it will fail you, and you will serve — when you would not serve God — this fickle and foul world, and you will be terribly troubled under her as her thrall in a thousand ways, in place of one pleasure you have two displeasures, and so often be made wretched for the worthless man that you lie under, for nothing or a trifle, you will loathe your life and regret   your   actions   that   you   ever   put   yourself   into   such

wunne thet tu wendest to biyeotene, ant havest ifunden weane thrin ant wontrethe
rive. (2) Al is thet tu wendest golt iwurthe to meastling. (3) Al is nawt thet ti folc
fol. 55r (of hwam I spec thruppe) biheten the to ifinden. (4) Nu thu wast thet ha hab|beth
bichearret te as treitres; for under weole, i wunnes stude, thu havest her ofte
Helle, ant bute yef thu withbreide the thu bredest te thet other, as doth thes
cwenes, thes riche cuntasses, theos modie leafdis of hare liflade. (5) Sothliche, yef ha
bithencheth ham riht ant icnawlecheth soth, ich habbe ham to witnesse: ha lickith
honi of thornes. (6) Ha buggeth al thet swete with twa dale of bittre (ant thet schal
forthre i this writ beon openliche ischawet). (7) Nis hit nower neh gold al thet ter
schineth, nat thah, na mon bute hamseolfen hwet ham sticheth ofte.

6.   (1) Hwen thus is of the riche, hwet wenest tu of the povre the beoth wacliche
iyeven ant biset on uvele, as gentile wummen meast alle nu on worlde the nabbeth
hwerwith buggen ham brudgume onont ham, ant yeoveth ham to theowdom of
an etheluker mon with al thet ha habbeth? (2) Weilawe, Jesu Godd, hwuch un-
wurthe chaffere! (3) Wel were ham weren ha on hare brudlakes dei iboren to
biburien.

7.   (1) Forthi, seli meiden, forget ti folc as Davith bit; thet is, do awei the thonckes
the prokieth thin heorte thurh licomliche lustes ant leathieth the ant eggith towart
thullich theowdom for fleschliche fulthen. (2) Foryet ec thi feader hus, as Davith
fol. 55v read threfter. (3) "Thi fea|der" he cleopeth thet untheaw thet streonede the of thi
moder: thet ilke unhende flesches brune, thet bearnninde yeohthe of thet

---

slavery for worldly joy that you expected to gain, and have misery and hardship
aplenty there. (2) All that you thought gold becomes brass. (3) All is nothing that
your folk (of whom I spoke earlier) promised you would find. (4) Now you know
that they have tricked you like traitors, for under joy, in place of happiness, you
often have Hell here, and unless you withdraw yourself you breed for yourself that
other [Hell], as do these queens, these rich countesses, these proud ladies from
their lives. (5) Truly, if they consider rightly and confess the truth, I take them to
witness: they lick honey from thorns. (6) They buy all that sweetness with two
parts of bitterness (and that will be shown clearly further on in this writing). (7)
All that shines there is not by any means gold, though no one except themselves
knows what often pricks them.

6.   (1) When it is this way for the rich, what do you expect of the poor who are unworthily given in marriage and evilly provided for, like almost all gentle women in the
world now who do not have the wherewithal to buy themselves a bridegroom of
the same rank as themselves, and who give themselves to slavery for a more
worthless man with everything that they have? (2) Weilaway, Jesus God, what a
worthless trade! (3) It would be better for them were they taken to be buried on
their wedding day.

7.   (1) Therefore, blessed maiden, forget your folk as David bids; that is, do away
with the thoughts that prick your heart through bodily desires and which invite you
and egg you on towards such slavery for fleshly filth. (2) Forget also your father's
house, as David advises next. (3) "Your father," he calls that wantonness which begot
you on your mother: that same filthy flesh's flame, that burning itch of that

licomliche lust bivore thet wleatewile werc, thet bestelich gederunge, thet scheomelese sompnunge, thet ful of fulthe stinkinde ant untohe dede. (4) Hit is thah i wedlac summes weies to tholien, as me schal efter iheren. (5) Yef thu easkest hwi Godd scheop swuch thing to beonne, ich the ondswerie. (6) Godd ne scheop hit neaver swuch, ah Adam ant Eve turnden hit to beo swuch thurh hare sunne ant merden ure cunde, thet is, this untheawes hus, ant haveth, mare hearm is, al to muche lauerdom ant meistrie thrinne. (7) This cunde merreth us thet Davith cleopeth "thi feadres hus" — thet is, the lust of lecherie thet rixleth therwithinnen. (8) Foryet ant ga ut throf with wil of thin heorte, ant Godd wule, efter the wil, yeove the strengthe sikerliche of His deore grace. (9) Ne thearf thu bute wilnin ant leote Godd wurchen. (10) Have trust on His help: ne schalt tu na thing godes bisechen ne biginnen thet He hit nule endin. (11) Eaver bidde His grace, ant overkim with hire help the ilke wake cunde the draheth into theowdom, ant into fulthe fenniliche akeasteth se monie.

8.   (1) *Et concupiscet rex decorem tuum.* (2) "Ant thenne wule," seith Davith, "the king wilni thi wlite." (3) The King of alle kinges desireth the to leofmon. (4) Ant

fol. 56r   tu | thenne, eadi meiden, thet art iloten to Him with meithhades merke, ne brec thu nawt thet seil thet seileth inc togederes. (5) Halt thi nome thurh hwam thu art to Him iweddet, ne leos thu neaver for a lust ant for ethelich delit of an hondhwile thet ilke thing the ne mei neaver beon acoveret. (6) Meithhad is thet tresor thet, beo hit eanes forloren, ne bith hit neaver ifunden; meithhad is the blostme thet, beo ha fulliche eanes forcorven, ne spruteth ha eft neaver. (7) Ah

---

bodily desire before that disgusting act, that beastly gathering, that shameless union, that stinking and wanton deed full of filth. (4) It still is to be suffered in wedlock in some ways, as you will hear later. (5) If you ask why God made such a thing to be, I will answer you. (6) God never shaped it so, but Adam and Eve changed it to be like this through their sin and marred our nature, that is, the house of this wantonness, in which it has, even worse, all too much lordship and mastery. (7) This nature mars us that David calls "your father's house" — that is, the lust for lechery that rules inside it. (8) Forget and go out of it with the will of your heart, and God will, according to that will, certainly give you strength from His dear grace. (9) You need only will it, and let God do the work. (10) Have trust in His help: you will neither ask for nor undertake anything good that He will not carry out. (11) Always pray for His grace, and overcome with its help the same weak nature that drags you into slavery, and miserably casts so many into the muck.

8.   (1) *And the king will desire your beauty.* (2) "And then," says David, "the king will desire your beauty." (3) The King of all kings desires you as a lover. (4) And you then, blessed maiden, who are assigned to him with the mark of maidenhood, do not ever break that seal which seals you both together. (5) Keep your name through which you are wedded to Him, and never lose for a desire and for the worthless delight of a moment that same thing which may never be recovered. (6) Maidenhood is that treasure that once it be lost, may never be found; maidenhood is that blossom that, once it be fully cut, never sprouts afterward. (7) Although

thah falewi sumchere mid misliche thonkes, ha mei eft grenin neaver the leatere. (8) Meithhad is thet steorre thet, beo ha eanes of the est igan adun i the west, neaver eft ne ariseth ha; meithhad is thet an yeove iyettet te of Heovene. (9) Do thu hit eanes awei ne schalt tu neaver nan other swuch acovrin, for meithhad is Heovene cwen ant worldes alesendnesse, thurh hwam we beoth iborhen, mihte over alle mihtes ant cwemest Crist of alle. (10) Forthi thu ahest, meiden, se deorliche to witen hit, for hit is se heh thing ant se swithe leof Godd ant se licwurthe, ant thet an lure thet is withuten coverunge. (11) Yef hit is Godd leof thet is Himseolf swa ilich hit nis na wunder, for He is leoflukest thing ant buten eavereuch bruche, ant wes eaver ant is cleane over alle thing, ant over alle thinge luveth cleannesse. (12) Ant hwet is lufsumre thing ant mare to herien bimong eorthliche thing then the mihte of

fol. 56v meithhad, | bute bruche ant cleane, ibrowden on Himseolven the maketh of eorthlich mon ant wummon Heovene engel, of heame hine, of fa freont, help of thet te hearmith? (13) Ure flesch is ure fa ant heaneth us ant hearmith se ofte as ha us fuleth, ah yef ha wit hire withute bruche cleane, ha is us swithe godd freond ant help of treowe hine. (14) For in hire ant thurh hire thu ofearnest, meiden, to beon englene evening i the eche blisse of Heovene, ant with god rihte, hwen thu hare liflade i thi bruchele flesch bute bruche leadest. (15) Engel ant meiden beoth evening i vertu i meithhades mihte, thah eadinesse ham twinni yetten ant totweame. (16) Ant thah hare meithhad beo eadiure nuthe, thin is the mare strengthe to halden, ant schal with mare mede beo the foryolden. (17) This mihte is thet an thet

---

it withers sometimes with wandering thoughts, it can still grow green afterward. (8) Maidenhood is that star that, once it goes down from the east into the west, will never after will rise again; maidenhood is that one gift given to you from Heaven. (9) Throw it away once, and you will never recover any other like it, for maidenhood is the queen of Heaven and the world's redemption, through which we are saved, strength over all strengths and of all things most pleasing to Christ. (10) Therefore you ought, maiden, to guard it so dearly, for it is so great a thing and so very beloved to God and so praiseworthy, and that one loss that is without recovery. (11) It is no wonder if it is beloved to God who is Himself so similar, for he is the loveliest thing and without any breach, and ever was and is clean above all things, and over all things loves cleanness. (12) And what is a lovelier thing and more praiseworthy among earthly things than the might of maidenhood, without breach and clean, resembling Himself, who makes from an earthly man and woman an angel of Heaven, from the churl a servant, from the foe a friend, help from that which harms you? (13) Our flesh is our foe and hurts us and harms us as often as it befouls us, but if it keeps itself clean without breach, then it is a very good friend for us and the help of a true servant. (14) For in it and through it you deserve, maiden, to be the equal of angels in the eternal bliss of Heaven, and with good reason, when you lead their life in your frail flesh without breach. (15) Angel and maiden are equal in virtue through the might of maidenhood, though holiness may still part and separate them. (16) And though their maidenhood may be more blessed now, yours takes more strength to guard, and will be rewarded with a greater gift to you. (17) This power is that one that

fol. 57r

i this deadliche lif schaweth in hire an estat of the blisse undeadlich i thet eadi lond, as brude ne nimeth gume ne brudgume brude, ant teacheth her on eorthe, in hire liflade, the liflade of Heovene, ant i this worlt thet is icleopet "lond of unlicnesse," edhalt hire burde in licnesse of heovenlich cunde, thah ha beo utlahe throf ant i licome of lam, ant i bestes bodi neh liveth Heovene engel. (18) Nis | this mihte of alle swithe to herien? (19) This is yet the vertu the halt ure bruchele veat, thet is, ure feble flesch as Seinte Pawel leareth, in hal halinesse. (20) Ant as thet swote smirles ant deorest of othre, thet is icleopet basme, wit thet deade licome thet is therwith ismiret from rotunge, alswa deth meidenhad meidenes cwike flesch withute wemmunge. (21) Halt alse hire limen ant hire fif wittes (sihthe ant herunge, smechunge ant smellunge, ant euch limes felunge) thet ha ne merren ne ne mealten, thurh licomliche lustes, i fleschliche fulthen the Godd haveth thurh His grace se muche luve iunnen, thet ha ne beoth of theo iliche bi hwam hit is iwriten thus thurh the prophete thet ha in hare wurthinge as eaveres forroteden — thet is, eavereuch wif thet is hire were threal ant liveth i wurthinge, he ant heo bathe. (22) Ah nis nawt bi theos iseid thet ha forrotieth thrin yef ha hare wedlac laheliche haldeth, ah the ilke sari wrecches the i the fule wurthinge unwedde waleweth beoth the Deofles eaveres, thet rit ham ant spureth ham to don al thet he wule. (23) Theos walewith i wurthinge ant forrotieth thrin athet ha arisen thurh bireowsunge ant healen ham with soth schrift ant with deadbote.

---

in this mortal life shows in it one state of the immortal bliss in that blessed land, where bride does not take bridegroom nor bridegroom bride, and teaches here on earth, in its own way of life, the life of Heaven, and in this world that is called the "land of unlikeness," keeps to its original nature in likeness of heavenly nature, although it is an exile from there and in a body of clay, and in a beast's body lives almost like an angel of Heaven. (18) Is not this power, over everything else, very worthy of praise? (19) This is yet the virtue that holds our frail vessel, that is, our feeble flesh as Saint Paul teaches, in complete holiness. (20) And as that sweet and most precious ointment above all others, which is called balm, protects that dead body that is anointed with it from rotting, so does maidenhood keep the maiden's flesh alive without corruption. (21) It also guards her limbs and her five senses (sight and hearing, tasting and smelling, and each limbs' sensation) so that those upon whom God has bestowed so much love through His grace do not come to harm nor dissolve, through bodily desires, into fleshly filth, and so that they are not like those about whom it is written by the prophet in this way, that they rotted in their dung as do boars — that is, every wife who is thrall to her husband and lives in dung, he and she both. (22) But by this it does not mean that they rot in there if they lawfully keep their marriage, but the same sorry wretches who wallow unwedded in the foul dung are the beasts of the Devil, who rides them and spurs them to do all that he wishes. (23) These wallow in dung and rot in there until they arise through repentance and heal themselves with true confession and with penance.

9.   (1) Eadi meiden, understont te in hu heh digneté the mihte of meithhad halt
fol. 57v   te. (2) Ah se thu herre stondest, beo sarre offe | aret to fallen, for se herre degré,
se the fal is wurse. (3) The ontfule Deovel bihalt te se hehe istihe towart Heovene
thurh meithhades mihte. (4) Thet him is mihte lathest, for thurh ure Leafdi
meithhad — the hit bigon earst, the meiden Marie — he forleas the lauerdom on
moncun on eorthe, ant wes Helle irobbet ant Heovene bith ifullet. (5) Sith the
folhin hire troden, meiden, gan as heo dude the offrede hire meithhad earst to
ure Lauerd, for hwon thet He cheas hire bimong alle wummen forte beon His
moder ant thurh hire meithhad moncun alesen. (6) Nu bihalt te alde feond ant
sith the i this mihte stonde se hehe — ilich hire ant hire Sune, as engel in
Heovene, i meithhades menske! — ant toswelleth of grome ant scheoteth niht ant
dei his earewen, idrencte of an attri healewi, towart tin heorte, to wundi the with
wac wil ant makien to fallen — as Crist te forbeode! (7) Ant eaver se thu
strengeluker stondest agein him, se he o teone ant o grome wodeluker weorreth,
for swa muche the hokerluker him thuncheth to beon overcumen, thet thing se
feble as flesch is (ant nomeliche of wummon) schal him overstihen. (8) Euch
fleschlich wil ant lust of leccherie the ariseth i the heorte is thes feondes fla, ah
hit ne wundeth the nawt bute hit festni in the ant leave se longe thet tu waldest
fol. 58r   thet ti wil were ibroht to werke. (9) Hwil | thi wit edstont ant chastieth thi wil,
thah thi lust beore to thet te leof were, ne hearmeth hit te nawiht ne suleth thi
sawle, for wit is hire scheld under Godes grace. (10) Hwil the scheld is ihal, thet

---

9.   (1) Blessed maiden, understand in what high dignity the might of maidenhood holds you. (2) But the higher you stand, the more sorely you should be
afraid to fall, for the higher the degree, the worse the fall. (3) The envious Devil
sees you risen so high towards Heaven through maidenhood's might. (4) That
might is most loathsome to him, for through our Lady's maidenhood — who first
began it, the maiden Mary — he lost the lordship over humankind on earth, and
Hell was robbed and Heaven will be filled. (5) He sees you follow in her footsteps,
maiden, and go as did she who offered her maidenhood first to our Lord, at the
time when He chose her among all women to be His mother and through her
maidenhood to redeem humankind. (6) Now the old fiend beholds you and sees
you stand so high in this might — like her and her Son, as an angel in Heaven,
in maidenhood's honor! — and he swells from rage and shoots his arrows night
and day, dipped in a poisonous ointment, towards your heart to wound you with a
weak will and make you fall — may Christ forbid it! (7) And ever the more strongly
you stand against him, the more madly he attacks in wrath and in rage, for it seems
to him so much more shameful to be overcome, that a thing as feeble as the flesh is
(and namely of a woman) should surpass him. (8) Each fleshly wish and desire for
lechery that arises in the heart is this fiend's arrow, but it wounds you not at all unless
it fastens inside you and remains so long that you wish that your desire were out in
action. (9) While your wit stands firm and controls your will, though your desire is
inclined to that which would be pleasing to you, it neither harms you at all nor soils
your soul, for wit is its shield under God's grace. (10) While the shield is

is the wisdom of thi wit, thet hit ne breoke ne beie, thah thi fleschliche wil fals beo therunder ant walde as hire luste, thes feondes flan fleoth ayein alle on him-seolven.

10.   (1) Ant loke wel hwervore: Ure licomes lust is thes feondes foster, ure wit is Godes dohter, ant ba beoth us inwith. (2) Forthi her is áá feht, ant mot beon áá nede, for ne truketh neaver mare hwil we her wunieth weorre ham bitweonen. (3) Ah wel is him thet folheth Wit, Godes dohter, for ha halt with Meithhad thet is ure suster. (4) Ah thi Wil, on other half, of thet licomliche lust halt with Leccherie, thet is the deofles streon as heo is, ant Sunne hire moder. (5) Leccherie o meithhad with help of fleschlich wil weorreth o this wise: hire forme fulst is sihthe. (6) Yef thu bihaldest ofte ant stikelunge on ei mon, leccherie ananriht greitheth hire with thet to weorrin o thi meithhad ant secheth erst upon hire nebbe to nebbe. (7) Speche is hire other help. (8) Yef ye threfter thenne speoketh togedere folliche ant talkith of unnet, Leccherie seith

fol. 58v   scheome the menske of thi meithhad ant tuketh hire al to wundre ant | threat to don hire scheome ant hearmin threfter, ant halt hire forewart. (9) For sone se cos kimeth forth (thet is hire thridde fulst) thenne spit Leccherie to scheome ant to schendlac Meithhad o the nebbe. (10) The feorthe fulst to bismere ant to merren Meithhad thet is unhende felunge. (11) Wite hire thenne, for yef ye thenne hondlith ow in ei stude untuliche, thenne smit Leccherie o the mihte of Meithhad ant wundeth hire sare. (12) Thet dreori dede on ende geveth thet deathes-dunt — weila, thet reowthe!

---

whole — that is, the judgment of your reason — so that it neither breaks nor bends, though your fleshly will is false under it and would do as it desired, this fiend's arrows all fly back on himself.

10.   (1) And look well why: our body's lust is this fiend's foster-child, our wit is God's daughter, and both are within us. (2) Therefore here there is always battle and must always be out of necessity, for the war between them never ceases while we dwell here. (3) But well it is for him who follows Wit, God's daughter, for she stands with Maidenhood who is our sister. (4) But your Will, on the other hand, out of that bodily lust, stands with Lechery who, as she is, is the devil's child, and Sin her mother. (5) Lechery wages war upon Maidenhood in this way with the help of fleshly will: her first help is sight. (6) If you look often and intently upon any man, right away Lechery readies herself with that to wage war on your maidenhood, and she first advances on her face to face. (7) Speech is her other help. (8) If after that you then speak together foolishly and talk about silly things, Lechery speaks shame about the power of your maidenhood and reviles her scandalously and threatens to put her to shame and to harm her thereafter, and she keeps her vow. (9) For as soon as the kiss comes forth (which is her third help), then Lechery spits at Maidenhood in the face to her shame and to her disgrace. (10) The fourth help to besmear and mar Maidenhood is indecent touching. (11) Guard her then, for if you then handle each other improperly in any place, then Lechery smites upon the might of Maidenhood and wounds her terribly. (12) That dreary deed in the end gives the death-blow — alas, what a pity!

(13) Ne acwiketh neaver Meithhad efter thet wunde. (14) Wei! The sehe thenne hu the engles beoth isweamet the seoth hare suster se seorhfuliche aveallet, ant te deoflen hoppin ant, kenchinde, beaten honden togederes — stani were his heorte yef ha ne mealte i teares!

11. (1) Wite the, seli meiden. (2) Me seith thet eise maketh theof. (3) Flih alle the thing ant forbuh yeorne thet tus unbotelich lure mahe of arisen. (4) Thet is, on alre earst the stude ant te time the mahten bringe the on mis forte donne. (5) With othre untheawes me mei stondinde fehten, ah ayein lecherie thu most turne the rug yef thu wult overcumen ant with fluht fehten. (6) Ant sothes yef thu thenchest ant bihaldest on heh towart te muchele mede thet meithhad abideth, thu wult leote lihtliche ant abeoren blitheliche the derf thet tu drehest onont ti

fol. 59r fleschliche wil ant ti licomes lust, thet tu forberest her | ant ane hwile leavest for blisse thet kimeth throf withuten eani ende. (7) Ant hwuch is the blisse? (8) Low, Godd Himseolf seith thurh the prophete: "Theo the habbeth from ham forcorven flesches lustes ant haldeth Mine Sabaz" (thet is, "haldeth ham i reste from thet fleschliche werc ant haldeth Me forewart"), "Ich bihate ham," He seith, "i Mi kineriche to yeoven ham stude ant betere nome then sunen ant dehtren."

12. (1) Hwa mahte wilni mare? (2) *Eunuchus qui servaverit sabata mea, et cetera.* (3) Hwa mei thenche the weole, the wunne, ant te blisse, the hehschipe of this mede thet tes ilke lut word bicluppeth abuten? (4) "Ich chulle," He seith, "yeoven ham stude ant nome betere then sunen ant dehtren." (5) Sulli biheste! (6) Ah hit is ilich thet thet ham is bihaten, to singen with engles (hwas feolahes ha beoth thurh

---

(13) Maidenhood never revives after that wound. (14) Alas! Whoever then sees how upset the angels are who see their sister so sorrowfully overthrown, and the devils hop and, leering, clap their hands together — stony would be his heart if he did not dissolve into tears!

11. (1) Guard yourself, blessed maiden. (2) It is said that opportunity makes a thief. (3) Flee all those things and shun earnestly that from which irremediable loss can arise in this way. (4) That is, first of all the place and the time that might lead you to do amiss. (5) Against other vices you may fight standing, but against lechery you must turn your back if you wish to overcome it and fight it with flight. (6) And truly if you think and behold on high toward the great reward that awaits maidenhood, you will take it lightly and blithely bear the difficulty that you endure concerning your fleshly will and your body's lust, which you shun here and give up for a time, in exchange for the bliss that comes from it without any end. (7) And what is this bliss? (8) Lo, God Himself says through the prophet: "Those who have cut out the flesh's lusts from themselves and hold My Sabbath," (that is: "keep themselves in rest from that fleshly deed and keep their promise to Me"), "I promise," he says, "to give them a place in My kingdom and a better name than sons and daughters."

12. (1) Who could wish for more? (2) *The eunuch who keeps my Sabbaths, etc.* (3) Who can imagine the happiness, the joy, and the bliss, the eminence of this reward that this same short word contains? (4) "I will," He says, "give them a place and a name better than sons and daughters." (5) Wondrous promise! (6) But it is like the one that is promised to them, to sing with the angels (whose fellows they are through

liflade of Heovene theyet ther ha wunieth, fleschliche, on eorthe): to singe thet swete song ant thet englene drem, utnume murie — thet nan halhe ne mei bute meiden ane — singen in Heovene, ant folhin Godd almihti, euch godes ful, hwider se He eaver wendeth as the othre ne mahe nawt, thah ha alle beon His sunen ant alle Hise dehtren. (7) Ne nan of thes othres crunen, ne hare wlite, ne hare weden ne mahen evenin to hare, se unimete brihte ha beoth ant schene to biseon on.

13.

fol. 59v

(1) Ant hwet bith hare anes song, ant efter Godd hare anes yong hwider se He eaver | turneth, ant hare fare, se feier bivoren alle the othre? (2) Understond ant nim yeme: al hare song in Heovene is forte herien Godd of His grace ant of His goddede. (3) The iweddede thonkith Him thet ha, lanhure, hwen ha alles walden fallen dune-wart, ne feollen nawt with alle adun for wedlac ham ikepte — the ilke lahe the Godd haveth istald for the unstronge. (4) For wel wiste ure Lauerd thet alle ne mahten nawt halden ham i the hehe of meithhades mihte, ah seide tha He spec throf: *Non omnes capiunt verbum istud.* (5) "Ne undervoth nawt," quoth He, "this ilke word alle." (6) *Quis potest capere capiat.* (7) "Hwa se hit mei underneomen, underneome, Ich reade," quoth He. (8) Other is thet Godd hat ant other is thet He reat. (9) The ilke thinges Godd hat thet mon mot nede halden the wule beon iborhen, ant theo beoth to alle men o live iliche imeane. (10) His reades beoth of heh thing ant to His leoveste freond (the lut i thisse worlde) ant derve beoth to fullen, ant lihte thah hwa se haveth riht luve to Him ant treowe bileave. (11) Ah hwa se halt ham earneth him overfullet ful, ant overeorninde met of heovenliche mede. (12) Swuch is meithhades read,

---

the lifestyle of Heaven though still they dwell there, bodily, on earth): to sing that sweet song and that angels' music, especially joyful — which no saint can do but a maiden only — to sing in Heaven, and to follow God almighty, full of every good, wherever He goes as those others cannot, though they are all His sons and all His daughters. (7) And none of these others' crowns, nor their beauty, nor their clothes can compare to theirs, so immeasurably bright they are and shining to look upon.

13.

(1) And what will be their only song, and after God their only course, where so ever He turns, and their fortune, so fair before all the others? (2) Understand and take heed: their entire song in Heaven is to praise God for His grace and for His goodness. (3) The wedded thank Him that they, at least, when they all would fall downward, did not fall down with everyone because wedlock protected them — the same law that God established for the weak. (4) For well did our Lord know that not everyone could hold themselves high in the might of maidenhood, but said when he spoke of it: *Not all take that word.* (5) "Not everyone may receive," said he, "this same word." (6) *He who is able to take it may take it.* (7) "Who so may receive it, receive it, I advise," said He. (8) One is what God orders and another is what he advises. (9) The one who wants to be saved must keep to the same things that God commands, and those are shared by all living people alike. (10) His counsels are about lofty matters and for his dearest friends (the few in this world) and are difficult to fulfill, though easy for whoever has the proper love for Him and true belief. (11) But whoever keeps to them earns an overflowing cup for himself, and an overrunning measure of heavenly reward. (12) Such is the counsel of

thet Godd ne hat nawt ah reat hwuch se His wule beon of the lut of His leoveste freond, ant, as His deorling deore, don His read ant earnin him crune upo crune. (13) Alswa, Seinte Pawel yeveth read to meidnes, thet meidnes beoth as he wes, ant

fol. 60r   seith thet wel is ham | thet swa ham mahen halden; ne hat he hit nan other weis, for eaver se deorre thing se is dervre to biwitene, ant yef hit were ihaten ant nawt tenne ihalden the bruche were deadlich sunne. (14) Forthi, wes wedlac ilahet in Hali Chirche as bed te seke, to ihente the unstronge the ne mahen stonden i the hehe hul ant se neh Heovene as meithhades mihte.

14.   (1) This is, thenne, hare song, the beoth i lahe of wedlac: thonki Godd ant herien thet He greithede ham lanhure, tha ha walden of meidnes hehschipe, a swuch stude into lihten thet ha neren nawt ihurt, thah ha weren ilahet; ant hwet se ha thrin hurten ham with ealmesdeden healden. (2) This singeth, thenne, iweddede, thet ha, thurh Godes milce ant merci of His grace, tha ha driven dunewart, i wedlac etstutten ant i the bed of His lahe softeliche lihten. (3) For hwa se swa falleth of meithhades menske thet wedlakes hevel bedd nawt ham ne ihente, se ferliche ha driveth dun to ther eorthe thet al ham is tolimet, lith ba ant lire. (4) Theos ne schulen neaver song singen in Heovene ah schulen weimeres leod áámare in Helle, bute yef bireowsunge areare ham to live ant heale ham with soth schrift ant with deadbote; for yef ha thus beoth acwiket ant imaket hale, ha beoth i widewene reng ant schulen i widewene ring bivore the iweddede singen in Heovene. (5)

fol. 60v   Thet is, thenne, hare song: to herien hare Drihtin | ant thonkin Him yeorne thet

---

maidenhood, which God does not order but advises for whoever wishes to be among the few of his dearest friends, and, as his dear darling, to follow his counsel and earn for himself a crown above crowns. (13) Also, Saint Paul gives advice to maidens that maidens should be as he was, and says that it is well for them who can keep themselves so; and he does not order it in any other way, for always the more dear a thing is, the harder it is to guard it, and if it were ordered and then not kept the breach would be a deadly sin. (14) Therefore, wedlock was made lawful in Holy Church as a bed for the sick, to catch the weak who can not stand on the high hill and so near Heaven as can the might of maidenhood.

14.   (1) This, then, is their song, who are in the law of wedlock: to thank and to praise God and that he at least prepared for them, when they would have gone from the high place of maidenhood, such a place to descend to, so that, though they were brought low, they would not be hurt; and however they hurt themselves in there they healed with almsdeeds. (2) This, then, the wedded sing, that they, through God's pity and the mercy of His grace, though they fell downward, in wedlock they stopped and in the bed of His law softly landed. (3) For whoever falls so from maidenhood's strength that wedlock's woven bed may not catch them, so terrifyingly they fall down to the earth that they are entirely dismembered, both joint and flesh. (4) These will never sing the song in Heaven but will sing songs of lamentation evermore in Hell, unless repentance raises them to life and heals them with true confession and with penance; for if they are thus quickened and made whole, they are in the widows' circle and will sing in the widows' circle before the wedded in Heaven. (5) That, then, is their song: to praise their Lord and thank him earnestly

His mihte heolt ham i cleanschipe chaste efter thet ha hefden ifondet flesches fulthe ant yettede ham i this worlt to beten hare sunnen.

15.   (1) Swote beoth theos songes, ah al is meidenes song unilich theose, with engles imeane, dream over alle the dreames in Heovene. (2) In heore ring, ther Godd Seolf ant His deore moder — the deorewurthe Meiden, the heovenliche cwen — leadeth i thet eadi trume of schimminde meidnes. (3) Ne moten nane buten heo hoppin ne singen, for thet is áá hare song, thonki Godd ant herien thet He on ham se muche grace yef of Himseolven thet ha forsoken for Him euch eorthlich mon ant heolden ham cleane áá from fleschliche fulthen i bodi ant i breoste, ant i stude of mon of lam token lives Lauerd, the King of hehe blisse, forhwi He mensketh ham se muchel bivoren alle the othre as the brudgume deth his weddede spuse.

16.   (1) This song ne muhen nane buten heo singen. (2) Al (as ich seide ear) folhith ure Lauerd, ant tah nawt overal, for i the menske of meithhad ant in hire mihte ne muhe nane folhin Him, ne thet eadi Meiden, englene leafdi ant meidenes menske, bute meidnes ane. (3) Ant forthi is hare aturn se briht ant se schene bivoren alle othre

fol. 61r   thet ha gath eaver nest Godd hwider se | He turneth. (4) Ant alle ha beoth icrunet the blissith in Heovene with kempene crune, ah the meidnes habbeth, upo theo the is to alle iliche imeane, a gerlondesche schinende schenre then the sunne, "auriole" ihaten o Latines ledene. (5) The flurs the beoth idrahe thron, ne the gimmes thrin, te tellen of hare evene nis na monnes speche. (6) Thus, feole privileges schawith ful sutelliche hwucche beoth ther meidnes, ant sundrith ham from the othre with thus feole mensken, world buten ende.

---

that His power holds them chaste in purity after they have tested the flesh's filth and allowed them to atone for their sins in this world.

15.   (1) Sweet are these songs, but the maiden's song is entirely unlike those, shared with angels, the song over all the songs in Heaven. (2) In their circle, there God Himself and His dear mother — the dear Maiden, the heavenly queen — lead in that blessed company of shining maidens. (3) No one but they may dance or sing, for that is always their song, to thank and to praise God that He gave to them so much grace of Himself that they forsook for him every earthly man and kept themselves clean forever from fleshly filth in the body and in the heart, and in place of a man of earth they took the Lord of life, the King of high bliss, because he honors them so much above all the others as the bridegroom does his wedded spouse.

16.   (1) This song no one but they may sing. (2) All (as I said before) follow our Lord, and yet not entirely, for in the honor of maidenhood and in its power none may follow Him, nor that blessed Maiden, the angels' lady and maidens' glory, except for maidens alone. (3) And therefore their appearance is so bright and so shining above all others that they go next to God where ever he turns. (4) And all those who rejoice in Heaven are crowned with the champions' crown, but the maidens, in addition to that which is shared by all equally, have a diadem shining brighter than the sun called, "aureola" in the language of Latin. (5) To tell of the nature of the flowers that are drawn on it, or the gems in it, there is no man's speech. (6) Thus, many privileges show very clearly which ones there are the maidens and with many honors distinguish them from the others, world without end.

17. (1) Of thes threo hat (meithhad ant widewehad, ant wedlac is the thridde) thu maht, bı the degrez oł hare blisse, icnawen hwuch ant bi hu muchel the an passeth the othre. (2) For wedlac haveth frut thrittifald in Heovene, widewehad sixtifald. (3) Meithhad, with hundretfald, overgeath bathe. (4) Loke thenne herbi, hwa se of hire meithhad lihteth into wedlac, bi hu monie degréz ha falleth dunewardes; ha is an hundret degréz ihehet towart Heovene hwil ha meithhad halt, as the frut preoveth, ant leapeth into wedlac — thet is, dun neother to the thrittuthe — over thrie twenti ant yet ma bi tene. (5) Nis this, ed en cherre, a muche lupe dunewart? (6) Ant tah, hit is to tholien ant Godd haveth ilahet hit (as ich ear seide) leste, hwa se leope ant ther ne edstode lanhure, nawt nere thet kepte him ant drive adun fol. 61v swirevorth withuten ike│punge deope into Helle. (7) Of theos nis nawt to speokene, for ha beoth iscrippet ut of lives writ in Heovene.

18. (1) Ah schawi we yet witerluker (as we ear biheten) hwet drehen the iweddede, thet tu icnawe therbi hu murie thu maht libben, meiden, i thi meithhad over thet heo libbeth — to-eche the murhthe ant te menske in Heovene thet muth ne mei munnen. (2) Nu thu art iweddet, ant of se heh se lahe iliht: of englene ilicnesse, of Jesu Cristes leofmon, of leafdi in Heovene, into flesches fulthe, into beastes liflade, into monnes theowdom, ant into worldes weane. (3) Sei nu — hwet frut, ant for hwuch thing meast is it al forthi, other ane dale, thervore? (4) Beo nu soth cnawes! (5) Forte keli thi lust with fulthe of thi licome? (6) For Gode, hit is speatewile forte thenche thron, ant forte speoken throf yet speatewilre. (7) Loke thenne hwuch beo

---

17. (1) Of these three states (maidenhood and widowhood, and wedlock is the third) you may, by the degrees of their bliss, know what and by how much the one surpasses the others. (2) For wedlock has a thirty-fold fruit in Heaven, widowhood sixty-fold. (3) Maidenhood, with a hundred-fold, surpasses both. (4) See then by this: whoever descends into wedlock from her maidenhood, by how many degrees she falls downwards; she is lifted toward Heaven one hundred degrees while she keeps her maidenhood, as the fruit proves, and she leaps into wedlock — that is, down lower to the thirtieth — over three twenties and yet more by ten. (5) Is this not, at one time, a great leap downward? (6) And yet, it is to be endured and God has decreed it (as I said before) since if anyone who leapt and did not stop there at least, there would be nothing nearby that would catch him, and he would fall downward headlong without protection deep into Hell. (7) Of these ones there is nothing to say for they are scraped out of the book of life in Heaven.

18. (1) But let us show yet more clearly (as we promised before) what the wedded suffer, from that you may know by that how joyfully you can live, maiden, in your maidenhood over what they live — in addition to the mirth and the glory of Heaven that no mouth can tell. (2) Now you are wedded, and descended from so high to so low: from the angels' equal, from Jesus Christ's lover, from a lady in Heaven, into flesh's filth, into a beast's life, into a man's slavery, and into the world's misery. (3) Say now — for what fruit, and mostly for what reason — is it completely for this reason, or partly, for this? (4) Reveal the truth now! (5) To cool your lust with the filth of your body? (6) By God, it is disgusting to think about that, and to speak about it yet more disgusting. (7) See then what that same thing is and what it

thet seolve thing ant thet dede to donne. (8) Al thet fule delit is with fulthe aleid as thu turnest thin hond, ah thet ladliche least leafeth ant lest forth, ant te ofthunchunge throf longe threfter; ant te unseli horlinges the unlaheliche hit hantith habbeth in inwarde Helle: for thet hwilinde lust, endelese pine bute yef heo hit leaven, ant hit on eorthe under schrift bitterliche beten. (9) Forhohe forte don hit, thet te thuncheth uvel of ant eil forte heren; for hwen hit is thullich —

fol. 62r

ant muchele ladluker then ei welitohe muth for scheome | mahe seggen — hwet maketh hit iluvet bituhhe beasteliche men bute hare muchele untheaw? (10) Thet bereth ham, ase beastes, to al thet ham lusteth, as thah ha nefden wit in ham ne tweire schad — as mon haveth — ba of god ant of uvel, of kumelich ant unkumelich, na mare then beastes thet dumbe neb habbeth!

19. (1) Ah leasse then beastes yet, for theos doth hare cunde (bute wit thah ha beon) in a time of the yer. (2) Moni halt him to a make ne nule, efter thet lure, neaver neomen other. (3) Ant mon, thet schulde habbe wit ant don al thet he dude efter hire wilnunge, folheth thet fulthe in eaver-euch time ant nimeth an efter an, ant moni (thet is wurse) monie togederes. (4) Lo nu hu this untheaw ne eveneth the nawt ane to wittlese beastes, dumbe ant broke-rugget, ibuhe towart eorthe — thu thet art i wit wraht to Godes ilicnesse, ant iriht bodi up ant heaved towart Heovene, forthi thet tu schuldest thin heorte Heoven thiderwart as thin eritage is ant eorthe forhohien — nim yeme hu this untheaw ne maketh the nawt ane evening ne ilich ham, ah deth muchel eateluker ant mare to witen the forschuptest te seolf, willes

---

is to do the deed. (8) All that foul delight is sated with filth as you turn your hand, but that loathsome sin lingers and lasts on, and the grief from it long afterward; and the unholy whores who unlawfully practice it have within an inward Hell: for that transitory lust endless pain unless they leave it and bitterly atone for it on earth in penance. (9) Scorn to do that, which seems evil to you and disgusting to hear about; for when it is such — and much more loathsome than any respectable mouth may speak of for shame — what makes it loved among beastly men except for their great viciousness? (10) That incites them, like beasts, to everything that they desire, as though they had no wit in them nor the ability — as a person has — to tell the difference between both good and evil, seemly and unseemly, no more than do the beasts, which have dumb snouts!

19. (1) But less than beasts yet, for those follow their instinct (although they are without wit) at one time of the year. (2) Many a one keeps itself to one mate and will not, after its loss, ever take another. (3) And man, who should have wit and should do everything that he does after its wish, follows that filth every time and takes one after another, and many (which is worse) take many together. (4) See now how this vice does not only just compare you to witless beasts, dumb and hunch-backed, bowed towards the earth — you who are wrought in God's likeness in the mind, and with an upright body and head uplifted towards Heaven, because you should hold your heart towards Heaven where your heritage is, and scorn the earth — take heed how this vice does not only make you equal and similar to them, but makes you much more horrible and more blameworthy, you who pervert yourself, willingly and

ant waldes, into hare cunde. (5) The leoseth thenne se heh thing — the mihte ant te biheve of meithhades menske — for se ful fulthe as is ischawet thruppe, hwa se

fol. 62v   of engel lihteth to iwurthen lahre | then a beast for se ladli cheaffere, loki hu ha spede!

20.   (1) "Nai," thu wult seggen, "for thet fulthe nis hit nawt. (2) Ah monnes elne is muche wurth, ant me bihoveth his help to fluttunge ant te fode. (3) Of wif ant weres gederunge worldes weole awakeneth, ant streon of feire children the gleadieth muchel the ealdren." (4) Nu thu havest iseid tus ant thuncheth thet tu havest iseid soth, ah ich chulle schawin hit al with falsschipe ismethet. (5) Ah on alre earst, hwet weole other wunne se ther eaver of cume, to deore hit bith aboht thet tu the seolf sulest fore ant yevest thin beare bodi to tukin swa to wundre ant feare with se scheomeliche, with swuch uncoverlich lure as meithhades menske is ant te mede, for worldlich biyete. (6) Wa wurthe thet cheaffeare, for ei hwilinde weole sullen meithhad awei, the cwen is of Heovene! (7) For alswa as of this lure nis nan acoverunge, alswa is euch wurth unwurth hertowart.

21.   (1) Thu seist thet muche confort haveth wif of hire were the beoth wel igederet, ant either is alles weis ipaiet of other. (2) Ye, ah hit is seltscene on eorthe. (3) Beo nu thah swuch hare confort ant hare delit, hwerin is hit al meast buten i flesches fulthe other in worldes vanité, the wurtheth al to sorhe ant to sar

fol. 63r   on ende? (4) Ant nawt ane on | ende ah eaver umbe hwile, for moni thing schal ham wreathen ant gremien ant makie to carien, ant for hare othres uvel

---

readily into their kind. (5) Whoever then loses so lofty a thing — the might and the advantage of maidenhood's honor — for so foul a filth as is shown above, whoever falls from an angel to become lower than a beast for such a bad bargain, look at how she prospers!

20.   (1) "No," you will say, "it is not at all for that filth. (2) But a man's strength is worth a great deal, and I need his help for sustenance and for food. (3) From the union of wife and husband the world's happiness awakens, and a line of fair children who give much joy to the parents." (4) Now you have said so and think that you have said the truth, but I will show that it is all glossed over with falsehood. (5) But first of all, whatever happiness or joy so comes from there, it is too dearly bought that you soil yourself for it and give your bare body to be ill-treated so terribly and be dealt with so shamefully, with such an irrecoverable loss as is the honor and the reward of maidenhood, for worldly profit. (6) Cursed be that bargain, to sell off maidenhood, the queen of Heaven, in exchange for any passing pleasure! (7) For just as there is no recovering from this loss, so every thing of worth is worthless in comparison.

21.   (1) You say that the wife has much comfort of her husband if they are well-matched, and either is in all ways satisfied with the other. (2) Yes, but it is seldom seen on earth. (3) Though their comfort and their delight be like this now, what is in it mostly but the flesh's filth or the world's vanity, which all come to sorrow and to pain in the end? (4) And not only in the end but always, for many things will anger and annoy them and cause them to worry, and to grieve and to sigh for each other's

sorhin ant siken. (5) Moni thing ham schal twinnin, ant tweamen, thet lath is leovie men, ant deathes dunt on ende either from other, swa thet ne bith hit nanes weis thet tet elne ne schal endin in earmthe. (6) Ant eaver se hare murhthe wes mare togederes, se the sorhe is sarre ed te twinnunge. (7) Wa is him, forthi, as Seint Austin seith, thet is with to muche luve to ei eorthlich thing iteiet, for eaver bith thet swete aboht with twa dale of bittre, ant a fals wunne with moni soth teone. (8) Ah wel is hire thet luveth Godd, for Him ne mei ha nanes weis (bute yef ha lihe Him ant His luve leave) neaver mare leosen, ah schal ifinden Him áá swetture ant savurure from worlde into worlde, áá on ecnesse.

22. (1) Thu speke thruppe of monnes help to flutunge ant to fode. (2) Wala; lutel therf thu carien for thin anes liveneth, a meoke meiden as thu art ant His deor leofmon the is alre thinge Lauerd, thet He ne mahe lihtliche thet He nule gleadliche ifinde the largeliche al thet te bihoveth. (3) Ant tah thu wone hefdest other drehdest

fol. 63v eani derf for His deorew|urthe luve, as the othre doth for monnes, to goder heale thin He hit tholeth to fondi the hwether thu beo treowe, ant greitheth thi mede monifald in Heovene. (4) Under monnes help thu schalt sare beon idervet for his ant for the worldes luve, the beoth ba swikele, ant wakien i moni care nawt ane for the seolf (ase thearf Godes spuse) ah schalt for monie othre, ase wel for the lathe ofte as for the leove, ant mare beon idrechet then ei drivel i the hus other ei ihuret hine, ant tin anes dale bruken ofte with bale ant bitterliche abuggen. (5) Lutel witen herof the selie Godes spuses the, i se swote eise withute swuch trubuil, i

---

misfortunes. (5) Many things will separate them, and death's blow, which is hateful to loving people, in the end will part one from the other, so that there is no way that comfort will not end in grief. (6) And always the more their joy was together, the more painful is the sorrow at their parting. (7) Woe to him, therefore, as Saint Augustine says, who is tied to any earthly thing with too much love, for always will sweetness be paid for with two parts of bitterness, and a false joy with many true sorrows. (8) But it is well for her who loves God, for she may not in any way (unless she lies to Him and leaves His love) ever lose Him, but will find Him ever sweeter and more savory from world into world, forever into eternity.

22. (1) You speak above of a man's help for sustenance and for food. (2) Look here: A meek maiden as you are and the dear lover of Him who is Lord of all things, you need worry little about your own sustenance that he cannot easily, that he will not gladly, generously provide you all that you need. (3) And if you had want or suffered any hardship for His dear love, as the other does for a man's, He allows it for your benefit to test whether you are true, and he prepares your reward manifold in Heaven. (4) Subject to a man's help you will be sorely troubled for his and for the world's love, which are both treacherous, and you will lie awake in many worries not only for yourself (as God's spouse should) but for many others, as often for the loathsome as often for the beloved, and you will be more oppressed than any drudge in the house or any hired hand, and will get your own share with misery and will pay for it bitterly. (5) Little of this do the blessed spouses of God know who, in such pleasant ease without such trouble,

gastelich este ant i breoste reste, luvieth the sothe Luve ant in His anes servise hare lif leadeth. (6) Inoh wel ham is her ah unlich elleshwer. (7) Alle worldes weole ham is inoh rive. (8) Al ha habbeth therof thet ha wel wilnith; al thet eaver Godd isith thet ham wule freamien. (9) Ne mei na worldlich unhap bireavin ham hare weole for ha beoth riche ant weolefule inwith i the heorte. (10) Al the este ant al the eise is ther as the othre beoth godlese ant ignahene, nabben ha neaver se muchel withuten i the worlde, for thet ha beoth offearet eaver forte leosen, ant yiscith thah efter muchel muche deale mare. (11) With earmthe biwinneth hit; with fearlac biwiteth hit; forleoseth hit with sorhe. (12) Swinketh | to biyeotene; biyeoteth forte leosen; leoseth forte sorhin. (13) Thus this worldes hweol warpeth ham abuten. (14) Theoves hit steoleth ham; reavers hit robbith. (15) Hare overherren witith ham ant wreatheth. (16) Mohthe fret te clathes ant cwalm sleath thet ahte, ant tah nane of theos ne makie to forwurthen weole ther ase muchel is; eaver se ther mare is, se ma beoth thet hit wastith. (17) Ant nat ich neaver hwi me seith thet heo hit al weldeth, thet, wullen ha nullen ha, biwinneth ant biwiteth hit to se monie othre, nawt ane to hare freond ah to hare fan fulle. (18) Ne habben ne mahen throf — thah ha hit hefden isworen — bute hare anes dale. (19) This is nu forthi iseid thet tu seidest thruppe thet ter walde wakenin of wif ant weres somnunge richesce ant worldes weole, thet tu understonde hu lutel hit freameth ham yet her i this worlt, teke thet hit reaveth ham the hehe riche of Heovene bute ha povre beon therin with halinesse of heorte.

fol. 64r

---

in spiritual bliss and in peace of mind, love the true Love and lead their lives in His service alone. (6) It is well enough for them here but different elsewhere. (7) All the world's joy is abundant enough for them. (8) They have all from there that they well wish for: God sees to everything that will ever benefit them. (9) Nor may any worldly misfortune deprive them of their joy for they are rich and well-off within the heart. (10) All the joy and comfort is there, whereas the others are impoverished and gnawed at by worry, however much they have, because they are always afraid to lose it, and still they itch for a great deal more. (11) With misery they obtain it; with fear they guard it; with sorrow they lose it. (12) They work to gain it; they gain it to lose it; they lose it to grieve for it. (13) Thus this world's wheel whirls them about. (14) Thieves steal it from them; raiders rob it. (15) Their overlords punish them and make them angry. (16) The moth eats up the clothes and pestilence slays the livestock, and though none of these things may make wealth perish where there is much of it; always the more there is, the more there are who waste it. (17) And I never know why it is said that they have everything, who, will they or nill they, win it and guard it for so many others, not only for their friends but for their absolute enemies. (18) They can not have anything from that — though they had sworn to have it — except for their own portion. (19) This is now said because you said above that there would arise from the union of husband and wife riches and the world's happiness, so that you may understand how little it helps them yet here in this world, apart from the fact that it robs from them the high kingdom of Heaven unless they are inwardly poor with holiness of heart.

23.

(1) Thus, wummon — yef thu havest were efter thi wil, ant wunne ba of worldes weole — the schal nede itiden. (2) Ant hwet yef ha beoth the wone, thet tu nabbe thi wil with him ne weole nowther, ant schalt grevin godles inwith westi wahes, ant te breades wone brede thi bearn-team, ant teke this, liggen under

fol. 64v   la|thest mon, thet, thah thu hefdest alle weole, he went hit te to weane? (3) For beo hit nu thet te beo richedom rive, ant tine wide wahes wlonke ant weolefule, ant habbe monie under the hirdmen in halle, ant ti were beo the wrath, other iwurthe the lath swa thet inker either heasci with other — hwet worltlich weole mei beo the wunne? (4) Hwen he bith ute havest ayein his cume sar care ant eie. (5) Hwil he bith et hame alle thine wide wanes thuncheth the to nearewe. (6) His lokunge on ageasteth the. (7) His ladliche nurth ant his untohe bere maketh the to agrisen. (8) Chit te ant cheoweth the ant scheomeliche schent te; tuketh the to bismere as huler his hore; beateth the ant busteth the as his ibohte threl ant his ethele theowe. (9) Thine banes aketh the ant ti flesch smeorteth the, thin heorte withinne the swelleth of sar grome ant ti neb utewith tendreth ut of teone. (10) Hwuch shal beo the sompnunge bituhen ow i bedde? (11) Me theo the best luvieth ham tobeoreth ofte thrin, thah ha na semblant ne makien ine marhen, ant ofte of moni nohtunge, ne luvien ha ham neaver swa, bitterliche bi hamseolf teonith either. (12) Heo schal his wil muchel hire unwil drehen — ne luvie ha him neaver swa wel — with muche weane ofte. (13) Alle his fulitohchipes ant his unhende gomenes, ne beon ha neaver swa with fulthe bifunden (nomeliche, i bedde), ha schal, wulle ha

fol. 65r   nulle ha, tho|lien ham alle.

23.

(1) This, woman — if you have a husband for your desire, and happiness also in world's joy — shall certainly happen to you. (2) And what if they are missing for you, so that you have neither your desire with him nor wealth, and will grieve impoverished within empty walls, and to lack of bread breed your offspring, and besides this, will lie under the most loathsome man, who, though you had every kind of wealth, he turns it into suffering? (3) For suppose now that for you riches are plentiful, and your wide walls proud and prosperous, and you have many servants under you in hall, and yet your husband is angry with you, or becomes loathsome to you so that either of you both are angry with the other — what worldly wealth may be a joy to you? (4) When he is out you have terrible anxiety and dread about his return. (5) While he is at home all your wide walls seem to you too narrow. (6) His gazing on you frightens you. (7) His loathly noise and his wanton uproar make you frightened. (8) He chides you and nags you and shamefully disgraces you, ill-treats you insultingly as a lecher does his whore, beats you and buffers you as his purchased thrall and his born slave. (9) Your bones ache and your flesh smarts, your heart within you swells from bitter anger and on the outside your face burns with rage. (10) What will the joining between you in bed be like? (11) Even those who love each other best often quarrel in there, though they do not show it in the morning, and often, however well they love each other, they bitterly irritate each other over many nothings when they are by themselves. (12) She must endure his will greatly against her will — however much she loves him — often with great misery. (13) All his foulnesses and his indecent love play however filled with filth they may be (in bed, that is!), she must, will she nill she, endure them all.

24. (1) Crist schilde euch meiden to freinin other to wilnin forte witen hwucche ha beon, for theo the fondith ham meast ifindeth ham forcuthest, ant cleopieth ham selie iwiss the nuten neaver hwet hit is, ant heatieth thet ha hantith. (2) Ah hwa se lith i leifen deope bisuncken, thah him thunche uvel throf, he ne schal nawt up acoverin hwen he walde. (3) Bisih the, seli wummon: beo the cnotte icnut eanes of wedlac, beo he cangun other crupel, beo he hwuch se he eaver beo, thu most to him halden. (4) Yef thu art feier ant with gleade chere bicleopest alle feire, ne schalt tu o nane wise wite the with unword ne with uvel blame. (5) Yef thu art unwurthlich and wratheliche ilatet thu maht — ba to othre ant to thi were — iwurthen the unwurthre. (6) Yef thu iwurthest him unwurth ant he as unwurth the, other yef thu him muche luvest ant he let lutel to the, hit greveth the se swithe thet tu wult inohreathe (ase monie doth) makien him poisun ant yeoven bale i bote stude; other, hwa se swa nule don medi with wicchen ant forsaken forte drahen his luve towart hire Crist ant hire Cristendom ant rihte bileave. (7) Nu hwet blisse mei theos bruken the luveth hire were wel ant ha habbe his laththe other cunqueari his luve o thulliche wise?

fol. 65v

25. (1) Hwenne schulde ich al habben | irikenet thet springeth bituhe theo the thus beoth igederet? (2) Yef ha ne mei nawt temen ha is icleopet gealde. (3) Hire lauerd luveth hire ant wurthgeth the leasse, ant heo, as theo thet wurst is throf, biwepeth hire wurthes ant cleopeth ham wunne ant weolefule the temeth hare teames.

26. (1) Ah nu iwurthe hit al thet ha habbe hire wil of streon thet ha wilneth; ant loki we hwuch wunne throf hire iwurthe: i the streonunge throf, is anan hire flesch

---

24. (1) May Christ shield every maiden against asking or wanting to know what they are, for those who experience them the most find them the most hateful, and they call those blessed indeed who never know what they are, and hate those who practice it. (2) But whoever lies deeply sunk in the swamp will not rise out of it when he wants to, though it seems wretched. (3) Look, blessed woman: once the knot of wedlock is knotted, be he idiot or cripple, be he what so ever he may be, you must stay with him. (4) If you are fair and speak to everyone pleasantly with glad cheer, you will not be able to protect yourself in any way against slander or nasty gossip. (5) If you are base and bad-tempered you may — both to others and to your husband — become more worthless. (6) If you become worthless to him and he just as worthless to you, or if you love him very much and he thinks little of you, it grieves you so much that you will quickly enough (as many do) make poison for him and give misery in remedy's place; or, she who does not want to do so will traffic with witches and forsake Christ and her Christianity and true belief in order to draw his love to her. (7) Now what bliss may she enjoy who loves her husband well and has his hatred or wins his love in such a way?

25. (1) When should I have accounted for everything that arises between those who are joined in this way? (2) If she cannot conceive she is called barren. (3) Her lord her loves and respects her the less, and she, as she that has the worst thereof, bewails her fate and calls those women happy and joyful who bear their children.

26. (1) But now, say it happens that she has all her desire for a child that she wishes for; and let us look at what happiness she gets from that: in the conceiving

with thet fulthe ituket (as hit is ear ishawet); i the burtherne throf is hevinesse ant heard sar eaver umbe stunde; in his iborenesse alre stiche strengest ant death otherhwiles; in his fostrunge forth moni earm-hwile. (2) Sone se hit lihteth i this lif mare hit bringeth with him care then blisse, nomeliche to the moder. (3) For yef hit is misboren — as hit ilome ilimpeth — ant wonti ei of his limen other sum misfeare, hit is sorhe to hire ant to al his cun scheome, upbrud in uvel muth, tale bimong alle. (4) Yef hit wel iboren is ant thuncheth wel forthlich, fearlac of his lure is anan with him iboren; for nis ha neaver bute care leste hit misfeare, athet owther of ham twa ear leose other. (5) Ant ofte hit itimeth thet tet leoveste bearn ant iboht bitterlukest sorheth ant sweameth meast his ealdren on ende. (6) Nu

fol. 66r hwet wunne haveth the moder, the | haveth of thet forschuppet bearn sar ant scheome bathe, ant fearlac of thet forthlich athet ha hit leose?

27.   (1) For Gode, thah hit nere neaver for Godes luve, ne for hope of Heovene, ne for dred of Helle — thu ahtest, wummon, this werc for thi flesches halschipe, for thi licomes luve, ant ti bodies heale over alle thing to schunien. (2) For ase Seinte Pawel seith, euch sunne thet me deth is withute the bodi bute this ane. (3) Alle the othre sunnen ne beoth bute sunnen, ah this is sunne, ant ec uncumelecheth the ant unwurdthgeth thi bodi, suleth thi sawle ant maketh schuldi towart Godd ant fuleth thi flesch ec. (4) Gultest o twa half. (5) Wreathest then Alwealdent with thet suti sunne ant dest woh to the seolf, thet tu al willes se scheomeliche tukest. (6) Ga we nu forthre ant loki we hwuch wunne ariseth threfter i burtherne of bearne, hwen thet streon in the awakeneth ant waxeth, ant hu monie earmthen anan

---

of that, her flesh is at once soiled with that filth (as it has been shown before); in the carrying of it, there is always heaviness and hard pain; in its birth the strongest of all stabbing pains and sometimes death; in its upbringing many a weary hour. (2) As soon as it comes into this life it brings with it more worry than joy, especially to the mother. (3) For if it is born deformed — as it often happens — and lacks any of its limbs or some other misfortune, it is sorrowful for her and shame to all its kin, scorn for evil mouths, a tale among all. (4) If it is well born and seems fully vigorous, fear of its loss is at the same time born with it; for she is never without worry lest it come to harm, until either of those two first loses the other. (5) And often it happens that that dearest and most bitterly paid for child upsets and grieves his parents the most in the end. (6) Now what joy does the mother have, who from that deformed child has both sorrow and shame, and fear for that healthy one until she loses it?

27.   (1) By God, even if it were not ever for love of God, nor for hope of Heaven, nor for fear of Hell, you ought, woman, for your flesh's wholeness, for your body's love, and your body's health, shun that deed over everything. (2) For as Saint Paul says, each sin that one does is outside the body except for this alone. (3) All the other sins are nothing but sins, but this is sin, and also mars you and degrades your body, soils your soul and makes you guilty before God and also fouls your flesh. (4) You are guilty on two sides. (5) You anger the All-Ruler with that filthy sin and you do harm to yourself, in that you entirely willingly mistreated yourself so shamefully. (6) Let us now go further and look at what joy arises thereafter in the carrying of the child, when that offspring in you awakens and grows, and how many miseries awaken at

awakenith therwith, the wurcheth the wa inoh, fehteth o thi seolve flesch ant weorrith with feole weanen o thin ahne cunde. (7) Thi rudie neb schal leanin ant ase gres grenin. (8) Thine ehnen schule doskin ant underneothe wonnin, ant of thi breines turnunge thin heaved aken sare. (9) Inwith, i thi wombe, swel in thi butte the bereth the forth as a weater-bulge, thine thearmes thralunge ant stiches i thi fol. 66v   lonke, ant i thi lendene sar eche rive, | hevinesse in euch lim, thine breostes burtherne o thine twa pappes, ant te milcstrunden the the of striketh. (10) Al is with a weolewunge thi wlite overwarpen, thi muth is bitter, ant walh al thet tu cheowest. (11) Ant hwet mete se thi mahe hokerliche underveth (thet is, with unlust) warpeth hit eft ut. (12) Inwith al thi weole ant ti weres wunne forwurthest a wrecche. (13) The cares ayein thi pinunge thraen bineometh the nahtes slepes. (14) Hwen hit thenne therto kimeth, thet sore sorhfule angoise, thet stronge ant stikinde stiche, thet unroles uvel, thet pine over pine, thet wondrinde yeomerunge, hwil thu swenchest terwith ant thine deathes dute; scheome teke thet sar with the alde wifes scheome creft, the cunnen of thet wa-sith, hwas help the bihoveth, ne beo hit neaver se uncumelich; ant nede most hit tholien, thet te therin itimeth.

28.   (1) Ne thunche the nan uvel of, for we ne edwiteth nawt wifes hare weanen, thet ure alre modres drehden on us seolven, ah we schawith ham forth forte warni meidnes thet ha beon the leasse efterwart swuch thing ant witen herthurh the betere hwet ham beo to donne.

---

once with that, which work woe enough for you, fight against your own flesh and make war upon your own nature with many miseries. (7) Your rosy face will grow lean and become green as grass. (8) Your eyes will grow dim and will darken underneath, and from your brain's turning your head aches sorely. (9) Inside, in your womb, a swelling in your belly that puffs you up like a water-skin, your bowels' pain and stitches in your side, and pain in your aching loins, heaviness in every limb, your breast's burden of your two paps, and the streams of milk that flow from them. (10) Your beauty is completely ruined with wilting, your mouth is bitter, and all that you chew nauseating. (11) And what food your stomach scornfully accepts (that is, with distaste) it casts out again. (12) In the middle of all your happiness and your husband's joy you degenerate into a wretch. (13) The worries about your labor pains deprive you of sleep at night. (14) Then when it comes to it, that sore sorrowful anguish, that strong and stabbing stitch, that nonstop suffering, that pain above pain, that restless wailing, while you labor with it and with fear of your death, shame along with the pain, with the shameful craft of the old women who know about that painful experience, and whose help you need, however indecent it may be; and you must suffer it all, whatever happens to you then.

28.   (1) Do not consider any of this evil, for we do not at all blame wives for their miseries, which all our mothers suffered for ourselves, but we put them forward to warn maidens so that they seek such a thing less eagerly and may know better, through this, what they should do.

29.   (1) Efter al this kimeth, of thet bearn ibore thus, wanunge ant wepunge the schal abute midniht makie the to wakien, other theo thet ti stude halts (the thu

fol. 67r   most for carien). (2) Ant, hwet! — the cader fulthen ant bearmes | umbe stunde, to feskin ant to fostrin hit se moni earm-hwile, ant his waxunge se let, ant se slaw his thriftre! (3) Ant eaver habbe sar care ant lokin efter al this hwenne hit forwurthe, ant bringe on his moder sorhe upo sorhe. (4) Thah thu riche beo ant nurrice habbe thu most, as moder, carien for al thet hire limpeth to donne.

30.   (1) Theose ant othre earmthen the of wedlac awakenith Seinte Pawel biluketh in ane lut wordes: *Tribulaciones carnis et cetera.* (2) Thet is on Englisch: "theo thet thulliche beoth schulen derf drehen." (3) Hwa se thencheth on al this, ant o mare thet ter is, ant nule withbuhe thet thing thet hit al of awakeneth, ha is heardre-iheortet then adamantines stan ant mare amead (yef ha mei) then is meadschipe seolf. (4) Hire ahne fa ant hire feont, heateth hireseolfen.

31.   (1) Lutel wat meiden of al this ilke weane: of wifes wa with hire were, ne of hare werc se wleateful the ha wurcheth imeane, ne of thet sar ne of thet sut i the burtherne of bearn ant his iborenesse, of nurrices wecches, ne of hire wa-sithes of thet fode fostrunge, hu muchel ha schule ed eanes in his muth famplin nowther to bigan hit ne his cader-clutes. (2) Thah this beon of to speokene unwurthliche thinges, thes the mare ha schawith i hwuch theodom wifes beoth, the thullich

fol. 67v   mote drehen, | ant meidnes i hwuch freodom, the freo beoth from ham alle. (3) Ant hwet yef ich easki yet — thah hit thunche egede — hu thet wif stonde the

---

29.   (1) After all this there comes, from that child born in this way, wailing and weeping which will wake you up around midnight, or the one who takes your place (for whom you have to care). (2) And, look! — the filth in the cradle and sometimes in your lap, to swaddle it and feed it for so many weary hours, and its growth so sluggish, and so slow its thriving! (3) And ever to have intense worry and to anticipate when, after all this, it could die, and bring upon its mother sorrow upon sorrow. (4) Though you may be rich and have a nurse you must, as a mother, worry about everything that falls to her to do.

30.   (1) These and other miseries which arise from wedlock Saint Paul expresses in few words: *The tribulations of the flesh, et cetera.* (2) That is in English: "those that are like this will endure hardship." (3) Whoever thinks on all this, and on more that there is, and will not avoid that deed from which it all arises, she is more hardhearted than a stone of adamant and madder (if she may be) than madness itself. (4) Her own foe and her fiend, she hates herself.

31.   (1) Little does the maiden know of all this same misery: of the wife's woe with her husband, nor of their deed — so disgusting! — that they do together, nor of that pain nor of that grief in the carrying of a child and birth, of the nurse's vigils, nor of her woeful times in the raising of that child, how much food she should stuff into his mouth at one time, neither to bespatter it nor its baby clothes. (2) Although these are unworthy things to speak of, they show all the more what slavery wives are in, who must endure them, and in what freedom maidens are in, who are free from them all. (3) And what if I ask yet — although it may seem silly — how it goes for that wife who, when she comes in, hears her

ihereth hwen ha kimeth in hire bearn schreamen, sith the cat et te fliche ant ed te hude the hund, hire cake bearnen o the stan ant hire kelf suken, the crohe eornen i the fur, ant te cheorl chideth? (4) Thah hit beo egede i sahe, hit ah, meiden, to eggi the swithre therfrommart, for nawt ne thuncheth hit hire egede thet hit fondeth! (5) Ne therf thet seli meiden, thet haveth al idon hire ut of thullich theowdom as Godes freo dohter ant His Sunes spuse, drehe nawiht swucches.

32.   (1) Forthi, seli meiden, forsac al thulli sorhe for utnume mede thet tu ahtest to don withuten euch hure, for nu ich habbe ihalden min biheaste thruppe: thet ich walde schawin with falschipe ismethet thet te moni an seith (ant thuncheth thet hit soth beo) of the selhthe ant te sy thet te iweddede habbeth, thet hit ne feareth nawt swa as weneth thet sith utewith ah feareth al otherweis, of poure ba ant riche, of lathe ba ant leovie, thet te weane ihwer passeth the wunne, ant te lure overal al the biyete.

33.   (1) Nu thenne, seli meiden, thet Davith cleopeth "dohter": iher thi feader ant hercne his read, thet he the i the frumthe of this writ readde. (2) "Foryet ti folc," thet liheth the of weres ant worldes wunne, thet beoth thine thohtes the swikelliche lea | thieth the towart alle weane. (3) Ant "forsac thi feader hus," as hit is thruppe iopenet, ant tac the to Him treowliche. (4) With him thu schalt wealden — as with thi were iweddet — worlt buten ende, heovenliche wunnen. (5) Eadi is His spuse, hwas meithhad is unwemmet hwen He on hire streoneth; ant hwen ha

fol. 68r

---

child scream, sees the cat at the flitch and the hound at the hide, her cake burning on the stone and her calf sucking, the crock running into the fire, and the churl chides her? (4) Though it may be silly to say, it ought, maiden, to urge you more strongly away from it, for it does not seem silly at all to her who experiences it! (5) Nor does that blessed maiden, who has entirely escaped such slavery as God's free daughter and his Son's spouse, need to endure anything of such things.

32.   (1) Therefore, blessed maiden, forsake all such sorrow for surpassing reward which you ought to do without any compensation, for now I have kept my promise above: that I would show that what many a one says to you (and it seems that it is true) about the happiness and the success which the wedded have, is glossed over with falsehood, and that it does not at all fare so as she who sees from outside thinks, but it fares entirely otherwise, both for the poor and the rich, for both those who hate and those who love, so that everywhere the woe surpasses the joy, and the loss entirely surpasses all the gain.

33.   (1) Now then, blessed maiden, whom David calls "daughter": hear your father and listen to his counsel, which he advised you in the beginning of this treatise. (2) "Forget your folk," who lie to you about the joy of husbands and the world, which are your thoughts which deceitfully incite you towards every woe. (3) And "forsake your father's house," as it is explained above, and commit yourself to Him truly. (4) With Him you shall possess — as with your wedded husband — the world without end, heavenly joy. (5) Blessed is his spouse, whose maidenhood is unmarred when He procreates with her; and when she gives birth by Him she neither temeth of Him ne swinketh ne ne pineth. (6) Eadi is the Were hwen nan ne mei beo meiden bute yef heo Him luvie, ne freo bute yef heo Him servi, hwas streon is undeathlich ant hwas marhe-yeve is the kinedom of Heovene. (7) Nu thenne, seli meiden, yef the is weole leof, nim the Him to Lauerd thet wealdeth al thet is ant wes ant eaver schal iwurthen. (8) For thah He beo richest Him ane over alle, the alre measte povre the Him to were cheoseth is Him wel icweme. (9) Yef thet tu wilnest were the muche wlite habbe, nim Him of hwas wlite beoth awundret of the sunne ant te mone, upo hwas nebscheft the engles ne beoth neaver fulle to bihalden. (10) For hwen He yeveth feirlec to al thet is feier in Heovene ant in eorthe, muchele mare He haveth withuten ei etlunge ethalden to Himseolven. (11) Ant thah hwen He thus is alre thinge feherest, He underveth blitheliche ant bicluppeth swoteliche the alre ladlukeste ant maketh ham seove sithe schenre then the sunne.

34.
fol. 68v

(1) Yef the were leof streon, nim the to Him under hwam thu schalt, i thi meithhad, te|men dehtren ant sunen of gasteliche teames, the neaver deie ne mahen ah schulen áá bivore the pleien in Heovene, thet beoth the vertuz thet He streoneth in the thurh His swete grace, as rihtwissnesse ant warschipe ayeines untheawes, mesure ant mete ant gastelich strengthe to withstonde the feond ant ayein sunne, simplete of semblant, buhsumnesse ant stilthe, tholemodnesse ant reowfulnesse of euch monnes sorhe, gleadschipe i the Hali Gast ant pes i thi breoste of onde ant of wreaththe, of yisceunge ant of euch untheawes weorre, mekelec ant miltschipe ant swotnesse of heorte, the limpeth — alre thinge best — to meithhades

---

toils nor suffers. (6) Blessed is the Husband when no one may be a maiden unless she loves Him, or free unless she serves Him, whose offspring is immortal and whose morning-gift is the kingdom of Heaven. (7) Now then, blessed maiden, if wealth is dear to you, take to yourself Him as Lord who possesses all that is and was and ever will be. (8) For though He may be richest of all by Himself over all, the poorest of all who chooses Him as a husband is well pleasing to Him. (9) If what you desire is a husband who has great beauty, take Him at whose beauty both the sun and the moon marvel, upon whose face the angels are never weary of looking. (10) For when he gives fairness to all that is fair in Heaven and in earth, He has kept back, beyond calculation, much more for Himself. (11) And even though He is the fairest of all things, he happily receives and sweetly embraces the loathsomest of all and makes them seven times brighter than the sun.

34.

(1) If children are dear to you, commit yourself to Him with whom you will, in your maidenhood, bear daughters and sons of a spiritual progeny, who never die, and never can, but will always play before you in Heaven, which are the virtues that He begets upon you through His sweet grace, such as righteousness and vigilance against vices, measure and moderation and spiritual strength to withstand the fiend and against sin, modesty of manner, obedience and silence, patience and pity for every person's sorrow, gladness in the Holy Ghost and peace in your heart from envy and from wrath, from covetousness and from the attack of every vice, meekness and mildness and sweetness of heart, which belongs — best of all things — to maidenhood's

mihte. (2) This is meidenes team, Godes Sune spuse, thet schal áá libben ant pleien buten ende bivoren hire in Heovene.

35.   (1) Ah thah thu, meiden, beo with unbruche of thi bodi, ant tu habbe prude, onde, other wreaththe, yisceunge, other wac wil inwith i thin heorte — thu forhorest te with the unwiht of Helle, ant he streoneth on the the team thet tu temest. (2) Hwen thi Were alwealdent, thet tu the to weddest, sith ant understont tis, thet His fa forlith the ant thet tu temest of him thet Him is teame lathest, He forheccheth the anan (as hit nis na wunder!) ant cwetheth the al cwite him thet tu of temest. (3) Ne kepeth He with na mon, ant hure with His famon, nan half dale. (4) The luvieth eawiht | buten Him — ant hwet se ha for Him luvieth — ha wreatheth Him swithe.

fol. 69r

36.   (1) Over alle thing, wite the thet tu ne temi prude bi thes deofles streonunge, for heo of alle untheawes is his ealdeste dohter. (2) Earst ha wakenede of him theyet he wes in Heovene, forneh with him evenald, ant swa ha keaste hire feader sone se ha ibore wes, from the heste Heovene into Helle grunde, bute coverunge, ant makede of heh-engel eatelukest deofel. (3) The thus adun duste hire heovenliche feader, hwet wule ha don bi hire eorthliche modres the temeth hire in horedom of then lathe Unwiht, the hellene schucke? (4) Hwen Godd se wracfulliche fordemde His heh-engel the streonede hire in Heovene, hwet wule He don bi thet lam ant wurmene mete the of the Deofel temeth hire in eawbruche on eorthe? (5) Yef thu havest, with meithhad, meokelec ant mildschipe, Godd is i thin heorte, ah yef ther is overhohe other ei prude in, He is utlahe throf; for ne muhen ha nanes weis

---

might. (2) This is the maiden's family, God's Son's spouse, which will live forever and play without end before her in Heaven.

35.   (1) But although you, maiden, may be without breach of your body, if you have pride, envy, or wrath, avarice, or weak will inside in your heart, — you whore yourself with the fiend of Hell, and he begets on you the offspring which you bear. (2) When your all powerful Husband, to whom you wed yourself, sees and understands this, that his foe lies with you, and that by him you are breeding what is to Him the most loathsome of broods, He shuts you out at once (as it is no wonder!) and declares you completely free to go to him with whom you are breeding. (3) He does not go halves with anyone, and least of all with his foe. (4) Whoever loves aught but Him — and whatever they love instead of Him — enrages him greatly.

36.   (1) Above all things, guard yourself so you do not beget pride by copulation with this devil, for she of all vices is his eldest daughter. (2) She first sprang from him while he was still in Heaven, almost the same age as him, and, as soon as she was born, she cast her father, irrecoverably, from the highest Heaven into the deep of Hell, and made from the high angel the most hateful devil. (3) If she cast down her heavenly father like this, what will she do to her earthly mothers who breed her in whoredom with that loathly Fiend, the hellish devil? (4) When God so vengefully condemned His archangel who spawned her in Heaven, what will He do to that earth and worms' food that breeds her in adultery by the Devil on earth? (5) If you have, along with maidenhood, meekness and mildness, God is in your heart, but if there is arrogance or any pride inside, He is an outlaw from there, for in no way can they live together in a single heart, when they could not dwell together at all in Heaven.

beddin in a breoste, ne ne muhen nawt somet eardin in Heovene. (6) Theonne Godd weorp hire sone se ha iboren wes, ant as thah ha nuste hwuch wei ha come theonewart, ne con ha neaver mare ifinden nan wei ayeinwart, ah eardinde her on eorthe bihat eche wununge alle hire modres, al beon ha meidnes, with hire

fol. 69v   awea | riede feader in inwarde Helle.

37.   (1) Wite the, meiden, with hire. (2) Ha cwikede of cleane cunde, as is in engles evene, ant cleaneste breosten bredeth hire yetten. (3) The beste ha asaileth, ant wel ha der hopien to beo kempe over mon, the overcom engel. (4) Nis ha nawt i clathes ne i feahunge utewith (thah hit beo merke throf ant makunge otherhwiles), ah under hwit other blac, ant ase wel under grei ase under grene, ant áá ha luteth i the heorte. (5) Sone se thu telest te betere then another, beo hit hwervore se hit eaver beo, ant havest of ei overhohe, ant thuncheth hofles ant hoker of eawt thet me seith the other deth yetten, thu merrest thin meithhad ant brekest ti wedlac towart Godd ant of His fa temest.

38.   (1) Ne tele thu nawt ethelich, al beo thu meiden, to widewen ne to iweddede. (2) For alswa as a charbucle is betere then a jacinct i the evene of hare cunde, ant thah is betere a briht jacinct then a charbucle won, alswa passeth meiden, onont te mihte of meithhad, widewen ant iweddede; ant tah is betere a milde wif other a meoke widewe then a prud meiden. (3) For theos, for hare sunnen thet ha i flesches fulthe folhith other fulieth, leoteth ham lahe ant ethliche, ant beoth sare ofdret of Godes luthere eie; ant as the eadi sunegilt Marie Magdaleine, with bittre

fol. 70r   wopes bireowsith hare gultes ant inwardluker luvieth Godd, alswa as heo | dude,

---

(6) God cast her out of there as soon as she was born, and as though she did not know which way she came from there, she could never afterwards find a way back, but living here on earth she promises an eternal dwelling place for all her mothers, although they are maidens, with her accursed father in innermost Hell.

37.   (1) Guard yourself, maiden, against her. (2) She quickened from a pure nature, as it is in the nature of an angel, and the cleanest hearts breed her still. (3) She assails the best, and she, who overcame an angel, may dare well hope to be a champion over a person. (4) She is not found in clothes or adornment on the outside (though it may be the mark of her and sometimes the marking), but under white or black, and as much under gray as under green cloth, and she always lies hidden in the heart. (5) As soon as you consider yourself better than another, for whatever reason it may be, and have disdain for anyone, and consider unreasonable and contemptible anything that someone says or does to you, you mar your maidenhood and break your marriage to God and give birth by his enemy.

38.   (1) Although you are a maiden, do not consider widows and the wedded worthless. (2) For just as a carbuncle is better than a jacinth in the quality of their nature, and though a bright jacinth is better than a dull carbuncle, so the maiden, with respect to the might of maidenhood, surpasses widows and the wedded, and nevertheless a mild wife or a meek widow is better than a proud maiden. (3) For these, because of their sins which they follow or practice in filth of the flesh, consider themselves lowly and worthless, and are sorely afraid of God's terrible

for hare forgevenesse. (4) Ant te othre, the haldeth ham unforgult ant cleane, beoth ase sikere unlusti ant wlecche. (5) Unneathe liveth i Godes luve, withuten euch heate of the Hali Gast the bearneth se lihte withute wastinde, brune in alle His icorene. (6) Ant te othre, in an heate of an honthwile, beoth imelt mare ant iyotten i Godd then the othre in a wlecheunge al hare lifsithen.

39. (1) Forthi, eadi meiden, Godes Sunes spuse, ne beo thu nawt to trusti ane to thi meithhad withuten other god ant theawfule mihtes ant over al, miltschipe ant meokeschipe of heorte, efter the forbisne of thet eadi meiden over alle othre, Marie, Godes moder. (2) For tha the hehengel Gabriel grette hire ant brohte hire to tidinge of Godes akennesse, loke hu lah ha lette hire, tha ha ontswerede thus bi hireseolven. (3) "Efter thi word," quoth ha, "mote me iwurthen. (4) Low, her mi Lauerdes threl." (5) Ant tah ha ful were of alle gode theawes, ane of hire meokelec ha seide ant song to Elizabeth. (6) "For mi Lauerd biseh His thuftenes meokelec, me schulen cleopien," quoth ha, "eadi alle leoden." (7) Nim yeme, meiden, ant understont herbi thet mare for hire meokelec then for hire meithhad ha lette thet ha ifont swuch grace ed ure Lauerd. (8) For al meithhad, meokelec is muche wurth, ant meithhad withuten hit is ethelich ant unwurth; for alswa is fol. 70v meiden i meithhad bu|te meokeschipe as is withute liht eolie in a lampe.

40. (1) Eadi Godes spuse, have theos ilke mihte thet tu ne thunche theostri ah schine ase sunne i thi Weres sihthe. (2) Feahi thi meithhad with alle gode theawes the thuncheth Him feire. (3) Have eaver i thin heorte the eadieste of

---

wrath; and, like the blessed sinner Mary Magdalene, they repent their sins with bitter weeping and more ardently love God, just as she did, because of their forgiveness. (4) And the others, who consider themselves free from guilt and pure, are certainly lazy and lukewarm. (5) Scarcely do they live in God's love, without any heat of the Holy Ghost which burns so bright without consuming, a fire in all His chosen. (6) And the others, in the heat of one moment, are melted and refined more in God than the others in a state of indifference all their lifetimes.

39. (1) Therefore, blessed maiden, spouse of God's Son, do not be too trusting in your maidenhood alone without other good and virtuous strengths and above all, mildness and meekness of heart, after the example of that blessed maiden above all others, Mary, mother of God. (2) For when the archangel Gabriel greeted her and brought to her tidings of God's incarnation, look how lowly she considered herself, when she answered thus of herself. (3) "According to your word," said she, "may it happen to me. (4) Lo, here is my Lord's servant." (5) And though she was full of all good virtues she spoke only of her meekness and sang to Elizabeth. (6) "Because my Lord saw the meekness of His handmaid, all peoples," said she "will call me blessed." (7) Take heed, maiden, and understand by this that she thought that she obtained such grace from our Lord more for her meekness than for her maidenhood. (8) For all maidenhood, meekness is worth much, and maidenhood without it is cheap and worthless; for a maiden in maidenhood without meekness is like oil in an unlit lamp.

40. (1) Blessed spouse of God, hold this same power so that you do not seem dark but shine like the sun in the sight of your Husband. (2) Adorn your maidenhood with all good virtues that seem lovely to Him. (3) Hold ever in your heart the most

meidnes ant meithhades moder, ant bisech hire áá thet ha the lihte ant yeove luve ant strengthe for te folhin i meithhad hire theawes. (4) Thench o Seinte Katerrine, o Seinte Margarete, Seinte Enneis, Seinte Juliene, ant Seinte Cecille, ant o the othre hali meidnes in Heovene: hu ha nawt ane ne forsoken kinges sunes ant eorles, with alle worldliche weolen ant eorthliche wunnen, ah tholeden stronge pinen ear ha walden neomen ham ant derf death on ende. (5) Thench hu wel ham is nu ant hu ha blissith thervore bituhe Godes earmes, cwenes of Heovene. (6) Ant yef hit eaver timeth thet ti licomes lust — thurh the false feont — leathie the towart flesliche fulthen, ontswere i thi thoht thus: "Ne geineth the nawt, sweoke! (7) Thullich ich chulle beon in meidenes liflade, ilich Heovene engel. (8) Ich chulle halde me hal thurh the grace of Godd, as cunde me makede, thet Paraise selhthe undervo me al, swuch as weren ear ha agulten his eareste hinen. (9) Allunge swuch ich chulle beon fol. 71r as is mi deore Leofmon, mi deorewurthe La|uerd, ant as thet eadi meiden the He Him cheas to moder. (10) Al swuch ich chulle wite me treowliche unwemmet, as ich am Him iweddet, ne nulle ich nawt, for a lust of ane lutle hwile (thah hit thunche delit) awei warpe thet thing hwas lure ich schal biremen withuten coverunge ant with eche brune abuggen in Helle. (11) Thu wrenchful ful wiht! (12) Al for nawt thu prokest me to forgulten ant forgan the blisse upo blisse, the crune upo crune of meidenes mede, ant willes ant waldes warpe me as wrecche i thi leirwite, ant for thet englene song of meithhades menske, with the ant with thine greden áá ant granin i the eche grure of Helle."

---

blessed of maidens and maidenhood's mother, and beseech her always to enlighten you and to give you love and strength to follow her virtues in maidenhood. (4) Think of Saint Katherine, of Saint Margaret, Saint Agnes, Saint Juliana, and Saint Cecilia, and of the other holy maidens in Heaven: how they not only forsook the sons of kings and earls, with all worldly wealth and earthly pleasures, but suffered strong torments and a cruel death in the end before they would accept them. (5) Think how well it is now for them and how they rejoice for that in between God's arms, queens of Heaven. (6) And if it ever happens that your body's lust — through the false fiend — should incite you towards fleshly filth, answer in your thought thus: "It helps you not at all, traitor! (7) I will be, in a maiden's life, just like an angel in Heaven. (8) I will keep myself whole through the grace of God, as nature made me, so that the bliss of Paradise may receive me fully, just like its first shepherds were before they sinned. (9) I will be completely like my dear Lover is, my precious Lord, and like that blessed maiden whom He chose as His mother. (10) Justly so I will keep myself truly unblemished, as I am wedded to Him, and I will not, for the lust of a little while (though it may seem a delight) cast away that thing whose loss I will bewail as irrecoverable and pay for with eternal fire in Hell. (11) You crafty foul creature! (12) All for nothing you prick me to commit sin and to forgo the bliss upon bliss, the crown upon crown of a maiden's reward, and willingly and voluntarily cast myself as a wretch into your punishment in hell for fornication, and instead of that song of the angels about maidenhood's honor, to cry out and groan with you and yours forever in the eternal terror of Hell."

41.   (1) Yef thu thus ontswerest to thi licomes lust ant to the Feondes fondunge he schal fleo the with scheome. (2) Ant yef he alles efter this inohreathe etstonde ant halt on to eili thi flesch ant prokie thin heorte, thi Lauerd Godd hit theaveth him, to muchli thi mede. (3) For as Seinte Pawel seith: "ne bith nan icrunet bute hwa se treoweliche i thulli feht fehte ant with strong cokkunge overcume hire seolf." (4) For thenne is the Deofel with his ahne turn scheomeliche awarpen hwen thu, as the Apostle seith ne schalt tu beon icrunet bute thu beo asailet. (5) Yef Godd

fol. 71v   wule cruni the, He wule leote ful wel the | Unwiht asaili the thet tu earni, therthurh, kempene crune. (6) Forthi, hit is the meast god thet hwen he greveth the meast ant towart te with fondunge wodeluker weorreth yef thu wel wrist te under Godes wengen. (7) For thurh his weorre he yarketh the (unthonc in his teth) the blisse ant te crune of Cristes icorene.

42.   (1) Ant Jesu Crist, leve hire thurh Thi blescede nome, ant alle theo the leaveth luve of lami mon forte beon His leofmon, ant leve ham swa hare heorte halden to Him thet hare flesches eggunge, ne the feondes fondunge, ne nan of his eorthliche limen ne wori hare heorte-wit ne wrenche ham ut of the wei thet ha beoth in iyongen, ant helpe ham swa in Him to hehin towart Heovene, athet ha beon istihe thider as hare brudlac schal, in al thet eaver sel is, with thene seli Brudgume thet siheth alle selhthe of sitten buten ende. (2) AMEN.

---

41.   (1) If you answer thus to your body's lust and to the Fiend's temptation he will flee from you with shame. (2) And if after all this he perhaps resists and continues to afflict your flesh and prick your heart, then your Lord God allows him to do so, to increase your reward. (3) For as Saint Paul says: "no one is crowned except for whoever truly fights in such a fight and with a great struggle overcomes herself." (4) For then the Devil is shamefully overthrown with his own trick when, as the Apostle says, you will not be crowned unless you are assailed. (5) If God desires to crown you, He will allow the Fiend to assail you thoroughly so that, through that, you may earn the champion's crown. (6) Therefore, it is the best for you when he grieves you the most and more madly makes war against you with temptation if you take cover well under God's wings. (7) For through his attack he prepares you (damn his teeth!) for the bliss and the crown of Christ's chosen ones.

42.   (1) And, Jesus Christ, grant to her through Your blessed name, and to all those who leave the love of an earthly man to be His lover, and grant to them that their hearts keep to Him so that neither the urging of their flesh, nor the fiend's temptation, nor any of his earthly followers neither trouble their mind nor wrench them out of the path they have walked on, and so help them to ascend toward Heaven in Him, until they have arisen to where their marriage will be, in all that ever is good, to sit forever with that blessed Bridegroom from whom everything good is derived. (2) AMEN.

EXPLANATORY NOTES TO *HALI MEITHHAD*

ABBREVIATIONS: **AS**: *Anchoritic Spirituality*, trans. Savage and Watson; **AW**: *Ancrene Wisse*, ed. Hasenfratz; **B**: Bodleian Library MS Bodley 34 [base text]; **BT**: Bosworth and Toller, *Anglo-Saxon Dictionary*; **CT**: *Canterbury Tales*; **F**: Furnivall edition (1922); **HM**: *Hali Meithhad*; **M**: Millett edition (1982); **MED**: *Middle English Dictionary;* **MWB**: Millett and Wogan-Browne edition (1990); **OED**: *Oxford English Dictionary*; **PL**: *Patrologiae Cursus Completus*; **SJ**: *The Liflade and te Passiun of Seinte Juliene*; **SK**: *The Martyrdom of Sancte Katerine*; **SM**: *The Liflade and te Passiun of Seinte Margarete*; **SW**: *Sawles Warde*; **T**: British Library MS Cotton Titus D XVIII; **Whiting**: Whiting, *Proverbs, Sentences, and Proverbial Phrases*.

Header   *Epistel of meindenhad meidene frovre.* HM participates in and responds to a body of medieval writing known simply as virginity literature, which has its roots in a large body of patristic writing concerning virginity (for an overview of this material, see Lapidge and Herren's introduction to Aldhelm's *De Virginitate*, pp. 51–58 and 191–92n8). While no direct source for the Middle English text can be accounted for, the author most likely had at his disposal a number of Latin compositions about virginity as well as other pastoral material. Bella Millett has exhaustively traced many of these attributions in the 1982 edition, and, where pertinent, we have listed them below. Most likely though, as M writes, *HM*'s author based at least part of his text on the following main sources: (1) Hildebert of Lavardin's letter to Athalisa; (2) Gregory the Great's *Regula Pastoralis*; and (3) Bernard of Clairvaux's *De Moribus et Officio Episcoporum*. The most important and influential of these works on *HM* is that of Hildebert: this letter, of which at least ten manuscript copies survive, demonstrates both the kind of advisory relationship between virgin recluse and clergyman modeled in texts from the *Life of Christina of Markyate* to *AW*, as well as points to the far-reaching influence of conventional models of virginity literature. Those readers who wish to consult the direct passages of Hildebert, Gregory, or Bernard should consult M's thorough explanatory notes, as well as her introduction, "Sources," pp. xlv–lii; we have included some short pertinent passages with translations below, which unless otherwise cited, are our own. The source study of *HM* reveals that the oft-cited sensitive and surprisingly realistic description of pregnancy and childbirth (see 27.6–14) in fact springs from a conventional body of texts written by clergymen for the purpose of deterring women from marriage.

1.1   *Audi, filia, et . . . domum patris tui.* Compare Vulgate Psalm 44:11. This text is often cited in works on virginity, including Jerome's letter on virginity to Eustochium, as well as Part III of the twelfth-century *Speculum Virginum*, a popular dialogue on virginity, of which twenty-seven manuscripts survive (see the appendix of *Listen Daughter* for a partial translation by Barbara Newman, as well as the critical edition by Jutta Seyfarth). Millett notes that the interpretation of Psalm 44:11 is borrowed from Alan of Lille's *Summa de Arte Praedicatoria*, Chapter 47, PL 210.195 (see M, p. 25n1/1–2). In addition, the emphasis on listening, "Audi," might indicate a listening rather than a reading audience. We do not know for certain for whom the AB texts were written and therefore what kind of literacy that audience possessed. For a discussion of female literacy in this period and concerning these texts see Robertson, "This Living Hand."

1.2   *Davith*. According to Millett, the spelling of David's name here represents an Anglo-French pronunciation (see M, p. 25n1/2). However, alternatively this orthography might reflect Welsh pronunciation and, if so, would further strengthen Dobson's proposition that the text emanated from the Herefordshire border. See Dobson, *Origins of Ancrene Wisse*, p. 115–73. See also the explanatory note 31.1.

          Godes spuse. While contemplatives were conventionally described as married to Christ, the Bodley 34 texts develop this metaphor to the extreme; as is clear from the previous tales of Saints Katherine, Margaret, and Juliana, the virgins' spiritual marriage to Christ conflicts with their fathers' or other superiors' secular plans for the dispensing of their sexuality; the consistent misunderstanding of the spiritual implications of the women's divine marriage is one of the marks of pagan mulishness — see, for example, *SJ* 14.1–2, where Africanus demands to know the identity of this husband to whom he has not yet been introduced. For the particular relevance of the *Sponsa Christi* motif for women, see Bugge, *Virginitas*, and Robertson, *Early English Devotional Prose*, especially Chapter 5 on *HM*, pp. 77–93. See also Valerian's response to Cecilia's claim in Chaucer's Second Nun's Tale [*CT* VIII[G] 162–68].

1.3   *Nim yeme hwet . . . sunderliche to seggen*. *HM*'s author directly addresses the reader throughout the text, engaging her in an imaginative dialogue with his material. Margaret Hostetler notes that this pattern reflects a larger agenda, in which the male author creates a number of "reader-characters," one of which is the *seli meiden* addressed so frequently in the first half of the text. This figure, Hostetler claims, is invited to participate in an exegesis of Psalm 44 and thus to engage actively and imaginatively with the discourse rather than passively accepting it (see "Characterized Reader," especially pp. 95–96 on the virgin exegete). See also explanatory note 27.6–14.

1.4   *lives luve*. Love of eternal life. The concept appears as an allegorical figure in *SW* 24.1 and following.

1.10   *inker*. The genitive plural of the dual pronoun: literally, "of your two."

2.1   *Syon . . . the hehe tur of Jerusalem*. Millett notes that the description of Sion as "a tower" (*tur*) follows "the traditional (though inadmissable) etymology of *Sion* as *specula* 'watch tower'" (M, p. 26n2/5). Scripture also points to the possibility of Sion as the literal tower of Jerusalem; see 1 Chronicles 11:5: "David took the castle of Sion, which is the city of David," i.e., Jerusalem. However, more important for our text is the association between the image of the tower and virginity, both in terms of how the tower image protects virginity but also elevates it in status above more normative sexual roles. In particular, see the legend of Saint Barbara, another early Christian martyr: the tower becomes not only a way for Barbara's father to encase and enclose her sexuality, but for Barbara herself to use and manipulate for further worship of the Christian God (see Winstead's translation from the *South English Legendary*, in *Chaste Passions*, pp. 39–43). Roberta Gilchrist discusses the uses of architectural space in the constructions of medieval genders and sexualities, explaining that the "gendering of the body was achieved with reference to physical boundaries and architectural spaces, especially the tendencies to link female and religious spaces, and to locate them in the most segregated settings, achieved through boundaries or height; in particular the siting of women's chambers in the upper reaches of towers. Space was used to construct and reinforce a gendering of women's bodies which emphasized chastity and purity" ("Medieval Bodies," p. 57). For Gilchrist's extended treatment of how space and gender are mutually constitutive, see *Gender and Material Culture*. Finally, Christopher Cannon suggests that defensive structures such as the tower feature prominently in the AB texts because the environment in which they were presumably produced (on the Herefordshire/Wales border) was sprinkled with similar defensive structures. See his "The Place of the Self: *Ancrene Wisse* and the *Katherine Group*" in *Grounds of English Literature*.

2.4   *englene liflade*. Consecrated virgins aimed to imitate the life of angels (*vita angelica*) through contemplation of God (see M, pp. xxviii–xxx). We have followed both M and MWB as well as Savage and Watson in liberally translating this phrase as "angelic life"; literally the phrase translates to "life of angels."

        thah ha licomliche . . . from worldiche weanen. Speaking of the grace of God, Paul writes that those who receive it come not to Sinai, with its physical revelations and restrictions, but "to mount Sion, and to the city of the living God, the heavenly Jerusalem, and to the company of many thousands of angels" (Hebrews 12:22). That this special state is especially accessible to virgins can be seen in the fact that Paul proceeds and follows this passage with admonitions against fornication (12:16 and 13:4). On Sion as a tower, see the explanatory note to 2.1, above.

3.1   *mon of lam*. The author focuses on the literally earthen nature of men due to the fact that they are made of clay (see Genesis 2:7). The phrase also occurs in *SK* 23.2 and 51.1, *SJ* 61.3, and *HM* 15.3.

4.2   *alle thing turneth then gode to gode*. The reference is to Romans 8:28, where the *gode* people for whom things will turn out *gode* are those who truly love God.

4.4   *forte beo cwen icrunet*. This particular *cwen icrunet* is an earthly queen. The virgin, already a crowned queen of Heaven, has no desire to exchange her state to be a temporal queen with an inferior lord. See also the explanatory note 5.5.

4.7   *Thus, habbeth Godes . . . ed ten ende*. HM varies remarkably from other tracts on virginity, such as Saint Jerome's *Letter to Eustochium* and Aldhelm's *De virginitate*. Both Aldhelm and Jerome emphasize the rewards a virgin can attain in the afterlife, whereas *HM* focuses on the rewards in this life as well as in heaven. See *Woman Defamed*, ed. Blamires, pp. 74–76 for excerpts of the *Letter*, and Aldhelm's *De Virginitate*, as well as Robertson, *Early English Devotional Prose*, pp. 77–93.

5.4   *thes cwenes . . . theos modie leafdis*. These references to queens, rich countesses, and proud ladies might be an indication that the text was written for an audience of upper-class women, though perhaps those unfortunate younger daughters for whom the families could not afford an expensive marriage. See also the explanatory note 6.1, below.

5.5   *ha lickith honi of thornes*. Proverbial; see Whiting H439. This is a conventional description of the difficulties of earthly life. It is interesting to note that the virgin saint Gertrude the Great (d. 1302) was said to have had a vision in which Christ told her that "with my enemies you have licked the dust (compare Psalm 71:9) and sucked honey among thorns. Come back to me now, and I will inebriate you with the torrent of my divine pleasure (Psalm 35:9)" (Gertrude, *Herald of Divine Love*, p. 95).

5.7   *Nat thah . . . ham sticheth ofte*. M notes the echo of Jerome, *Adversus Jovinianum* 1.48 (p. 28n4/13–14). This is the very text against which the Wife of Bath protests so vociferously in her Prologue (*CT* III[D] 673–75); we might only imagine how Chaucer's Wife would respond to a text such as *HM*. Ironically, despite its misogyny, Jerome makes similar arguments against marriage and in praise of virginity in *Adversus Jovinianum*, though he seems to be addressing an audience of men. For a translated excerpt of this text, see Beidler's introduction to *The Wife of Bath, Geoffrey Chaucer*, pp. 21–23.

6.1   *hwet wenest tu of the povre*. Despite the reference to the poor, this text is clearly addressed to women of upper social status — although perhaps gentlewomen of little inheritance. At times, women entered nunneries or were placed there by their parents especially because they (or their family) could afford dowry for a convent but not for a husband. Aristocratic marriage practices in the Middle Ages often involved the alliance of a member of one class with a member of another. The social desire to marry someone of equal or higher rank (though sometimes aristocrats who were losing money had to marry below their rank) occasionally conflicted with religious expectations of marriage, which argued that marriage should be based on consent alone (for praise of marriage based on consent see, for example, Langland's *Piers Plowman*, B.IX.108–18). For a discussion of marriage practices in the Middle Ages, see Sheehan, *Marriage, Family and Law*. For a critique of marriage practices more concerned with property transfer than affirmations of consent, see the marriage arrangements of Lady Mede in Passus 2 of *Piers Plowman* (B).

6.3   *on hare brudlakes dei iboren to biburien*. This imagery most likely alludes to ritual practices concerning anchoresses, who, Clay notes, were "carried to burial on their wedding-day"; that is, they were ritually buried within an anchor-hold as a tomb. See Clay (*Hermits and Anchorites*, pp. 193–98) for a description of the burial ceremony often practiced at anchoritic enclosure.

8.1   *Et concupiscet rex decorem tuum.* Compare Vulgate Psalm 44:12. M cites Alan of Lille's *Summa de Arte Praedicatoria*, Chapter 47, PL 210.195, as the source for this passage (p. 29n5/10–11): '*Et' sic 'concupiscet rex decorem tuum', ille scilicet rex, qui est rex regum, et dominus dominantium* ['And' thus 'the king will desire your beauty', that king of course, who is the king of kings, and the lord of lords].

8.4   *thet seil thet seileth inc togederes.* The seal of virginity is based on the Canticle of Canticles 4:12: "My sister, my spouse, is a garden enclosed, a garden enclosed, a fountain sealed up." See Innes-Parker ("Fragmentation and Reconstruction," pp. 29–30) for a discussion of the intact body as a necessary aspect of holy life. See also the explanatory note to *SM* 17.1.

8.6   *ne bith hit neaver ifunden.* The rigid irrecoverability of virginity proves flexible to later examples of female contemplatives, particularly Margery Kempe. Margery's non-virginal status becomes a point of contention and ridicule when Christ commands her to wear white clothing as a symbol of her status as (renewed) virgin. For a discussion of how the ideological framework of a text like *HM* could have influenced Margery Kempe, see Bosse, "Female Sexual Behavior."

8.12   *of heame hine.* This is a confusing phrase, as the clear sense from the rest of the passage indicates that the two terms should be antonyms. Compare also *SJ* 33.4: "al mi nestfalde cun, thet schulde beo me best freond, beoth me meast feondes, ant mine inhinen, alre meast heamen" [all my closest kin, those who should be my best friends, are my greatest foes, and my household, the greatest of all churls]. However, see *The Owl and the Nightingale*, lines 1115–16: "Vor children gromes, heme & hine. / Hi þencheþ alle of þire pine," where the terms, if not synonymous, at least represent similar ideas: household servants. Millett emends to *heane* following T's reading, but suggests that this rare Middle English noun is related to the verb *heanen*, "to injure, oppress, persecute" (*MED henen* (v.), sense a), thus a translation of "oppressors," not otherwise attested in Middle English (see M, pp. 30–31n6/2). It should be noted, however, that the adjective *heane* survives to mean "contemptible, hateful, injurious" (*MED hen* (adj.), sense b) as in *SK* 43.8: "thes heane ant tes heatele tintreoh" [this heinous and this hateful torture]. We have retained B's reading of *heame* with the assumption that "churls" or "yokel" is antonomous with the concept of an obedient and faithful servant; however we admit that the reading, like other readings, is tenuous.

8.12–21   *Ant hwet is . . . . as eaveres forroteden.* M cites an extended passage in Bernard of Clairvaux's *De Moribus et Officio Episcoporum* as the source for this section (p. 30n5/31–6/29). However, she also notes Bernard's ultimate source: the *Speculum Virginum*, from which a brief quotation is warranted: "What is the beauty of this virgin, so esteemed by the royal gaze? What beauty does this king, who is the creator of heaven and earth, desire in the virgin? What is this beauty that God seeks in you? Would you like to know? It is the beauty of righteousness, the form of a praiseworthy life, the light of understanding, the grace of heavenly discipline, the love of God, the hatred of the world or anything else of that kind that the rational soul acquires through longing for virtues or hatred of vices" (trans. Newman, *Listen Daughter*, p. 282).

8.15   *Engel ant meiden*. On the virginal qualities of the afterlife, see Matthew 22:30, Mark 12:25, and Luke 20:34–36, where proof is found in the presumed lack of marriage among angels.

8.17   *ant i this . . . liveth Heovene engel*. As a source for this passage, Millett cites Bernard's *Sermo 27 in Cantica*, which, in turn, draws its phrase *regio dissimilitudinis* (land of unlikeness) from Augustine's *Confessions*, 7.10 (M, p. 32n6/15–18 and 6/15–16). For the image of life on earth as exile, see Hebrews 11:13–16. See also her discussion, pp. xxvi–xxviii.

       burde. The Titus manuscript reads *burðe*; most likely the scribe simply forgot to cross the *ð*. The term here presents a theological conundrum, in that *burde/burðe* is not simply the "birth" or "birthright" of the individual, nor its *cunde* or nature, but its origin as well. As the virtue of virginity here lives out its *liflade* in *licnesse* to the Heavenly life, there is a sense that this virtue preserves the original nature of the creation of God; that is, the nature uncorrupted and stained by the deeds of Adam and Eve. Since all human beings are descended from the marred state of humanity, the theological impossibility of a person living according to this original nature is solved by the author's attention to the abstracted virtue of virginity: this quality preserves the original chaste nature of humanity, but in the body of the virgin struggles against impure thoughts. The virgin's success in the process of this struggle is what makes her so unique.

8.18–19   *Nis this mihte . . . in hal halinesse*. See 1 Thessalonians 4:3–5.

8.21–22   *as eaveres forroteden . . . the Deofles eaveres*. The Middle English term *eaveres* is troublesome, and is still defined, according to *MED* and *OED* as "boar" (compare *MED ever* (n.), sense 1 and *OED* "ever" (n.)), derived from the Old English *eofor* (*BT, eofor* (n.), sense 1a). Compare Celtic lore wherein evil men are turned into boars that ravage the countryside as Twrch Trwyth in the Irish story of *Culhwch and Olwen*. We have similarly translated as "boars." However, identifying an echo here of Joel 1:17 ("the beasts have rotted in their dung"), Tolkien ("Devil's Coach-Horses," pp. 333–34) advises translating the word as "horses" based on its relationship to the Middle English term *aver* meaning "draft horse" or "beast of burden" (*MED, aver* (n.1), sense 1). MWB translate as "Devil's cart-horses" (p. 13); Savage and Watson as "beasts of burden" (*AS*, p. 229). While at first the image of a draft-horse wallowing in dung or muck might still seem to make little sense, compare Chaucer's Friar's Tale (*CT* III[D] 1539–65), which features a similar image — though luckily these "caples thre" do not end up going to the devil.

8.23   *with soth schrift ant with deadbote*. Compare *SW* 7.3.

9.1–7   *Eadi meiden . . . . schal him overstihen*. M cites Gregory's *Regula Pastoralis*, Book III, Chapter 28 (p. 33n7/6–24): *Admonendi sunt peccata carnis ignorantes, ut tanto sollicitius praecipitem ruinam metuant, quanto altius stant. Admonendi sunt, ut noverint, quia quo magis loco prominenti consistunt, eo crebrioribus sagittis insidiatoris impetuntur. Qui tanto ardentius solet erigi, quanto robustius se conspicit vinci; tantoque intolerabilius dedignatur vinci, quanto contra se videt per integra infirmae carnis castra pugnari* [those who are innocent of the sins of the flesh are to be admonished to dread all the more anxiously headlong ruin, the loftier the eminence on which they stand. We should admonish them to realise that the more conspicuous their position, the more numerous are the arrows hurled against them by him who lies in wait for us. The more stoutly he sees himself worsted, the more energetically does he bestir himself. The more intolerable to him is his shame of being conquered, the more clearly he perceives that he is opposed by an unbroken barrier of weak flesh] (trans. Davis, p. 195).

9.2   *se herre degré, se the fal is wurse*. Proverbial; see Whiting D156.

9.5   *the offrede hire meithhad earst to ure Lauerd*. According to Millett, in Augustine's *De Sancta Virginitate* 4: "Mary was thought to have made a vow of virginity before the Annunciation" (M, p. 33n7/11–15). This tradition is later expanded in medieval writings. When ordered by the priests to take a husband in the N-Town plays, for example, Mary exclaims: "mannys felaschep shal nevyr flowe me! / I wyl levyn evyr in chastyté / Be the grace of Goddys wylle!" (ed. Sugano, 10.37–39). For a discussion of the practice of chaste marriage in the Middle Ages see Dyan Elliott, *Spiritual Marriage*.

10.3–4   *Wit, Godes dohter . . . that is ure suster. . . Leccherie, thet is the deofles streon. . . ant Sunne hire moder*. The personification of virtues and vices has a long tradition in Christian literature, perhaps most influentially represented in Prudentius' *Psychomachia* (ca. 405), where they battle for souls in Virgilian epic form. A much later example from an English writer is John Gower's *Mirour de l'Omme* (ca. 1377), where Wit (Reason) is male and weds God's seven daughters, the virtues, so that together they might stand against the Devil and the seven vices that have been engendered incestuously upon his daughter, Sin. In Gower's genealogies, Virginity is specifically the second daughter of the virtue of Chastity, which is set, as here, against the vice of Lechery (*Mirour de l'Omme*, trans. Wilson, lines 16573 ff.). This passage recalls the ongoing battle between Wit, the husband ("Godes cunestable," 4.1) and Will, the unruly wife in *SW*.

10.5–13   *weorreth o this wise . . . . efter thet wunde*. M cites Alan of Lille's *Summa de Arte Praedicatoria*, chapter 5, *PL* 210.122, as a source for this passage describing the five strategies of lust (p. 34n8/7–31). See also p. 34n8/8–20 for an extended discussion of the development of this topos, which originates in Ovid's *Metamorphoses*. Part II of *AW* describes a similar battle between virginity and lechery: "Earest scheot the arewen of the licht echnen, the fleoth lichtliche forth ase flaa thet is i-vithered ant stiketh i there heorte, ther-efter schaketh hire spere ant neolachet upon hire, ant mid schakinde word yeveth speres wunde. | Sweordes dunt [is] dun-riht — thet is, the hondlunge — for sweord smit of nech ant yeveth deathes dunt, ant hit is wei-la-wei nech i-do with ham the cumeth swa nech togederes, thet outher hondli other other i-fele other" [First lechery shoots the arrows from the wanton eyes, which fly lightly forth as a shaft which is feathered and sticks in the heart; afterwards, she shakes her spear and closes in upon her, and with an agitating word, gives the wound of the spear. A sword's blow — that is, human touching — comes straight down, for a sword smites from near-by and gives death's blow; and it is, alas, nearly finished for those who come so close together, who either handle each other or touch each other] (ed. Hasenfratz, p. 105, lines 132–37).

10.8   *seith scheome.* "Speaks shame of"; i.e., slanders.

11.6–13.13   *Ant sothes yef . . . were deadlich sunne.* M cites an extended section of Book III, Chapter 28 of Gregory's *Regula Pastoralis* as the source for this section (p. 35n8/31–10/13). On traditions of personification, see the explanatory note to 10.3–4, above.

12.2   *Eunuchus qui servaverit sabata mea, et cetera.* Isaias 56:4–5, discussed by Augustine in *De Sancta Virginitate*, pp. 234–35.

12.6–13.2   *singen with engles . . . . of His goddede.* M cites Hildebert of Lavardin's Letter to Athalisa as a source for this passage: *Virginitas angelicam redolens conversationem, cantat canticum novum, canticum felix, canticum quod nemo potest dicere praeter eos 'qui cum mulieribus non sunt coinquinati'* (p. 36n9/13–15) [Virginity smelling of angelic association, sings a new song, a happy song, a song which no one can speak of except those 'who are not polluted with women]; and *Porro canticum omnium laudem Creatoris et actiones intellige gratiarum. Laudant ergo Christum virgines, Christum laudant viduae, laudant etiam conjugatae. Laudant conjugatae, quia . . .* (pp. 36–37n9/24–25) [Further understand that the song of all (of them is) praise of the Creator and gestures of thanks. Therefore the virgins praise Christ, the widows praise Christ, and the wedded also praise. The wedded praise, because . . .].

12.6   *His sunen ant alle Hise dehtren.* On the virgins singing before God's throne, see Apocalypse 14:3–4. Though the Bible cites these virgins as male (they are specifically undefiled by women), exegetes have long taken the passage to be gender-neutral.

13.4   *Non omnes capiunt verbum istud.* See Matthew 19:10–12.

13.8–13   *Other is thet . . . . were deadlich sunne.* This description of the difference between God's commandments versus his advice corresponds in some ways to the "Author's Preface" in *AW*: "Nan ancre, bi mi read, ne schal makien professiun — thet is, bihaten ase heast — bute threo thinges: thet beoth obedience, chastete, ant stude steathel-vestenesse . . . For hwa-se nimeth thing on hond ant bihat hit Godd as heast for-te don hit, ha bint hire ther-to, ant sunegeth deadliche i the bruche, yef ha hit breketh willes. Yef ha hit ne bihat nawt, ha hit mei do thah ant leaven hwen ha wel wule, as of mete, of drunch, flesch forgan other fisch, alle other swucche thinges . . . Theos ant thulliche othre beoth alle i freo wil to don other to leten hwil me wule ant hwen me wule, bute ha beon bihaten. Ah chearite — thet is, luve — ant eadmodnesse ant tholemodenesse . . . theos ant thulliche othre . . . ne beoth nawt monnes fundles, ne riwle thet mon stalde, ah beoth Godes heastes" [No anchoress, by my advice, shall make profession — that is, promise as a vow — except for three things: those are obedience, chastity, and steadfastness of place . . . For whosoever takes a thing in hand and promises it to God as a vow to do it, she binds herself to it and sins mortally in the breach if she breaks it willingly. If she does not promise it, she can do it nevertheless and stop when she well wants, with food, with drink, to forgo meat or fish, all other such things . . . These and such others are all in free will to do or to stop while one wants and when one wants, unless they are promised. But charity — that is, love — and humility and patience . . . these and such others . . . are not man's invention, or a rule which man established, but are God's commandments] (ed. Hasenfratz, pp. 62–63, lines 54–67).

13.11   *ful.* F translates as a past participle of *fullen*: "filled overfull." We have followed M and translated as "cup" based on *MED ful* (n.), sense 1: "A cup; a drinking cup or bowl." All examples of the use of this word are from the twelfth and thirteenth centuries; thus it would make sense for this author to use the word.

13.12   *crune upo crune.* While the literal sense of *upo* is "upon," we have translated as "above" to get at the idea of a crown that surpasses the worth of other crowns.

13.13   *Alswa, Seinte Pawel . . . ham mahen halden.* Paul's famous advice, found in 1 Corinthians 7:8 and 25–26, is a favorite among those recommending celibacy as the surest means of avoiding sin.

Seinte Pawel yeveth read. M cites Gregory's *Regula Pastoralis*, Book 3, Chapter 27, as the likely source for this passage (p. 37n10/14–15): *Hinc est enim quod peritus medicinae coelestis Apostolus non tam sanos instituit, quam infirmis medicamenta monstravit, dicens: 'De quibus scripsistis mihi: Bonum est homini mulierem non tangere; propter fornicationem autem unusquisque suam habeat uxorem, et unaquaeque suum virum habeat'* [I Cor. 7:1–2]. *Qui enim fornicationis metum praemisit, profecto non stantibus praeceptum contulit; sed ne fortasse in terram ruerent, lectum cadentibus ostendit* [Hence it is that the Apostle, versed in celestial medicine, did not so much prescribe for the hale, as point out the remedies for the weak, when he said: *'Concerning the things whereof you wrote to me, it is good for a man not to touch a woman, but for fear of fornication, let every man have his own wife, and let every woman have her own husband.'* (See 1 Corinthians 7:1–2) For in setting out beforehand the fear of fornication, he surely did not give a precept to those who stood on their feet, but pointed out the bed to such as were falling] (trans. Davis, p. 189).

14.1   *tha ha walden of meidnes hehschipe.* An odd use of the auxiliary *walden*. F translates as "when they fell short of maidenhoods [sic] elevation"; MWB as "when they were about to fall from the virgin's high estate." *MED* cites this line as a "modal auxiliary expressing wish or desire . . . past form with past meaning with implied inf[initive]" (*willen* (v.1), sense 9g). Usually in this construction the implied verb is one that has appeared in a previous line, possibly as part of the same sentence, and *most* often is some expression of "to go," "to be," "to do," or "to get," as in the other lines cited in 9g. Our translation of "would have gone" follows more closely the usual pattern of this construction, though F and MWB adhere to the image of the maiden falling from the high tower only to be caught by the bed of marriage.

14.3–5   *For hwa se . . . . beten hare sunnen.* See Evans for a discussion of what she calls the "'willed' virginity" characterized by this passage ("Jew, the Host and the Virgin Martyr," p. 174).

14.3   *ham is tolimet.* An impersonal construction, literally: "it is dismembered to them."

15.3   *for thet is . . . of hehe blisse.* M cites Hildebert's Letter to Athalisa as a source for
            this passage (p. 38n11/4–9): *Laudant innuptae, quia ex eo habent ut quibus licuit
            hominibus nubere virginibus, spiritu Deo nubere malint, et carne virgines et spiritu* [see
            I Cor. 7:34]. *Ecce sacrarum virginum canticum sacrum, canticum non vetus sed novum,
            non illius scilicet Adae, in quo et per quem mentis et carnis corrupta est integritas, sed ejus
            in quo et per quem non solum sanata, sed etiam super angelos glorificata est humanitas.
            Hujus laus et exaltatio virtutis canticum est quod ignorant viduae, quod nesciunt
            conjugatae.* [The unwedded give praise, because from that they consider that it
            was allowed for such virgins to marry men, although they preferred to marry
            God in spirit, virgins both in flesh and spirit. Behold the holy song of holy
            virgins, not an old song but a new one, certainly not the song of that Adam, in
            which and through which the soundness of mind and flesh is spoiled, but of this
            human nature is not only healed in it and through it, but also is glorified above
            the angels.]

15.3   *mon of lam.* See the explanatory note to 3.1, above.

16.4   *Ant alle ha . . . o Latines ledene.* For discussion of the source of this description of
            the rewards in Heaven for those who keep Christ's commandments of Matthew
            19:18–19, see M (p. 39n11/17–20), who observes that ultimately the text here
            seems to derive from Bede's glossing of Exodus 25:25 in *De Tabernaculo et Vasis
            ejus* 6. However, see also Wogan-Browne, who points out the secular courtliness
            of the "ring-dance," noting that "[this scene] invoke[s] a specifically high
            medieval ideal of the aristocratic heroine, one shared to a large extent with
            courtly literature and secular romance" (*Saints' Lives*, p. 23). This observation
            emphasizes the author's use of secular devices to imply heavenly station;
            compare also explanatory notes 4.4 and 5.5.

17.1–7   *Of thes threo . . . . writ in Heovene.* According to MWB, this discussion of the
            relative rewards of virginity, widowhood, and marriage is a patristic
            interpretation of Matthew 13:23 ("But he that received the seed upon good
            ground, is he that heareth the word, and understandeth, and beareth fruit, and
            yieldeth the one an hundred-fold, and another sixty, and another thirty")
            common in literature on virginity (p. 151n20/17–21). Hassel (*Choosing Not to
            Marry*, p. 39) sees *HM*'s emphasis on precise numerical values for virginity,
            widowhood, and wifehood as "appeals to earthly rank" that overwhelm the
            spiritual meaning of the parable. Aquinas' *Catena Aurea* cites Jerome, where the
            hundred-fold fruits are ascribed to virgins, the sixty-fold to widows and con-
            tinent persons, and the thirty-fold to chaste wedlock (1.494). Augustine, in his
            Quæstiones Evangeliorum, ranks the rewards differently, and notes that the
            hundred-fold fruit signifies martyrs, the sixty-fold fruit virgins, and the thirty-
            fold fruit the wedded (1.493).

17.7   *lives writ.* That is, the Book of Life, made famous for its appearance in
            Apocalypse 3:5 and 20:12–15.

18.1   *Ah schawi we . . . drehen the iweddede.* See Savage, "Translation of the Feminine,"
            for analysis of *HM* not only as a virginity text but also as a text on martyrdom,

particularly "marriage as an unsuccessful martyrdom" (p. 194). Likewise, Hassel (*Choosing Not to Marry*, p. 33) calls *HM* "a sermon on virginity that says more about marriage than staying single." Although M points out the source of many of the details of the difficulties of married life in Hildebert of Lavardin, the author also includes an unusually extensive engagement with the quotidian lives its readers choose to leave behind. For a discussion of this emphasis on "quotidian psychological realism" in the AB texts in general see Robertson, *Early English Devotional Prose*.

18.9–19.3 *hwet maketh hit . . . . monie togederes.* M cites Alan of Lille's *Summa de Arte Praedicatoria*, Chapter 5, PL 210.123 as source for this passage (p. 40n12/27–13/3): *lechery* [sic] *hominem in pecudem mutat; imo, homo per eam infra pecudem degenerat, cum pecus servat concupiscendi tempora, tu concupiscis omni hora; pecus servat naturam, tu debaccharis in eam; pecus servat unitatem paris, tu ad plures discurris* [lechery changes a man into an animal; no indeed, a man through that sinks lower than an animal, since an animal keeps to the seasons of carnal longing while you desire sex at every hour; an animal serves nature, you revel furiously in it; an animal keeps one mate, you run about to many].

18.10 *dumbe neb.* A dumb snout or face, that is, lacking the ability to speak or clearly communicate, and thus also lacking intellectual ability and discrimination (see *MED domb*, (adj.), sense 5a, which cites this line).

19.4 *Lo nu hu . . . ant eorthe forhohien.* The upright posture of mankind is attributed to a desire for Heaven (see M, p. 41n13/3–8).

forthi thet tu . . . thin eritage is. Compare Matthew 6:19–21.

20.5–6 *Ah on alre . . . is of Heovene!* M cites Hildebert's Letter to Athalisa as a source for this passage (p. 41n13/19–25): *Praeterea ex nuptiis nulla speratur impune felicitas, quam primo necesse est quadam carnis commistione comparari. Infeliciter ei succedit, quae successum virginitatis mercatur impendio . . . Impar mercimonium est, brevem quaestum jactura perenni comparare; minus sibi providet quisquis gratiae virginitatis aliquid anteponit* [In addition, no happiness is safely hoped for from marriage, which foremost needs to be secured by means of a certain mingling of the flesh. It turns out unluckily for her, who is trafficked, with the cost (being) the continuance of (her) virginity . . . It is an uneven merchandise, a short-lived profit to compare with eternal loss; whoever places anything before the pleasantness of virginity provides too little for herself.]

21.7–8 *Wa is him . . . . áá on ecnesse.* M cites Augustine's *Confessions* here as a probable source for 21.7–8 (p. 42n14/4–10), respectively: *Miser eram, et miser est omnis animus vinctus amicitia rerum mortalium* [I was in misery, and misery is the state of every soul overcome by friendship with mortal things] (trans. Chadwick, Book 4, Chapter 6, p. 58) and *Beatus qui amat te* [God], *et amicum in te, et inimicum propter te. Solus enim nullum charum amittit, cui omnes in illo chari sunt, qui non amittitur . . . Te nemo amittit, nisi qui dimittit* [Happy is the person who loves you] (Tobit 13:18) and his friend in you, and his enemy because of you (Matthew 5:44). Though left alone, he loses none dear to him; for all are dear in the one who cannot be lost. . . . None loses you unless he abandons you] (trans. Chadwick, Book 4, Chapter 9, p. 61).

22.4   *tin anes dale*. "Your own share" refers to the bride's dowry.

22.11   *With earmthe biwinneth . . . hit with sorhe*. This description is a conventional formula used by patristic and scholastic writers to describe avarice; for other examples of this description, see M, p. 43n14/34–5. This passage reveals the author's dependence on these types of sources as well as a more flexible understanding of greed than is traditionally assumed. The ambiguous "muchel" of 22.10, and the series of "hit" (articulated three times in 22.11) refer to a desired object much more tenuous and ambiguous than a simple lust for money. Richard Newhauser, in his study on greed in the early Middle Ages, writes that avarice often manifests as a "desire for intangible objects" such as "honor, knowledge, [or] life itself" as much as it refers to a desire for money (*Early History of Greed*, p. xiv).

22.13   *this worldes hweol*. I.e., the wheel of Fortune, a common medieval image often denoting the impermanence of material goods and/or worldly status. Fortune and her wheel appear as both a rich component of philosophical discourse as well as a well-known trope of medieval narrative. For the former, see Boethius, *The Consolation of Philosophy*, Book 2, in which Lady Philosophy urges the ailing philosopher to relinquish his attachment to Fortune; in Poem 7 (trans. Green, pp. 39–40), she offers the example of death, the great equalizer, as one of the many demonstrations of the fruitlessness of relying on Fortune. As regards the narrative trope, see, for a vivid and famous example, the *Alliterative Morte Arthure*, lines 3218–3393, in which Arthur dreams of his terrifying downfall on Fortune's wheel. Finally, it is worth noting, in addition to this conventional imagery, the preoccupation with images of the wheel in the Bodley 34 texts (compare the would-be tortures devised for Katherine and for Juliana), where the ultimate goal, for professed nuns, anchoresses, or virgin martyrs, is to eventually transcend the significance and effectiveness of worldly pain as well as worldly joy.

22.14–15 *Theoves hit steoleth . . . ham ant wreatheth*. M cites Hildebert of Lavardin's *Letter to Athalisa* as a source for this passage (p. 43n15/2–3): *Virginitati tamen divitiae praeferuntur, sed eis aerugo suspecta est, sed tinea demolitur, sed insidiantur latrunculi, sed timetur majoris violentia potestatis* [Yet riches are preferred to virginity, but rust is suspected by them, and the moth destroys it, and thieves lie in wait for it, and the violence of great power is feared].

22.16   *ahte*. A general term referring most likely to cattle (compare Savage and Watson's translation, *AS*, p. 236, as well as *SK* 4.1), but often livestock in general, including sheep. See Millett's note in *Ancrene Wisse*, which explains that the term "can [also] mean possessions [or] money" (ed. Millett, 2.285). Compare also *hahte*, a similar term referring to sheep, in *SM* 4.4.

22.17   *wullen ha nullen ha*. "They wish to they do not wish to"; a proverb leading to "will they, nill they" and eventually to "willy nilly." According to the *OED*, this is the earliest known occurrence of the phrase. See Whiting, W277.

23.2   *grevin*. M and MWB emend to *granin*. See M, p. 43n15/18. F reads B as *grenin* as a variant of *granen* "to groan," related to Anglo-Saxon *gránian* (see F, p. 42n444 and p. 87, entry under *granen*) See also *BT*, *gránian* (v.).

23.8   *ethele theowe*. See M, p. 44n15/30, who argues that the term refers to "a serf born on the estate."

24.4–7   *Yef thu art . . . o thulliche wise?* M cites Hildebert's *Letter to Athalisa* as a source for this pessimistic passage on marriage (p. 45n16/13–24 and 16/31–17/13): *Si formosa est, difficile caret infamia; deformem maritus aspernatur. Nunquam lectus est sine rixa, cujus vel pudet vel taedet conjugalem. Porro consequens est ut ei vir displiceat quae viro placere non quaerit. Quae non quaerit, sagaciores sollicitat aniculas, maleficiis assidet et, ut acquiret gratiam, projicit innocentiam. Quae igitur quies est animae, cui vel maritus est pro supplicio, vel conscientia pro flagello?* [If she is beautiful, it is difficult for her to be without disgrace; the husband despises the ugly wife. The bed is never without quarrel, of which she is either ashamed or weary. Furthermore, it is logical that her husband displeases her who does not seek to please her husband. She who doesn't seek (to do this), she solicits very clever little old women, sits with witches and, to get a favor, throws away innocence. Therefore who is quiet of heart, for whom there is either a husband for punishment, or conscience for a scourge?] and *Magni soboles emitur, cujus conceptus infestatio est pudicitiae, partus vitae. Ea in lucem progrediens, auspicium sollicitudinis est, non materia gaudiorum. Vitiosa quippe progenies odium suscitat. Cum vero bona est, timor nascitur amittendi. Quis autem animo locus est gaudii, qui vel inflammatur odio, vel timore cruciatur?* [Offspring is purchased dearly, of which the conception is a disturbance of chastity, and its birth a disturbance of life. Advancing into the light, it is an omen of anxiety, not the stuff of rejoicing. Certainly a deformed child arouses hatred. When the child is in fact sound, fear arises of its being lost. Now, what place is there in the spirit for joy, which is either inflamed with hatred, or tortured with fear?]. See also 27.6–14 for the anxieties surrounding childbirth.

27.2–3   *For ase Seinte Pawel . . . unwurdthgeth thi bodi*. See 1 Corinthians 6:18.

27.6–14   *Ga we nu . . . . te therin itimeth*. Hostetler describes this famous passage as "a mass of affective detail" signaling the imaginative movement of the "reader-character" into the role of wife and mother. Hostetler points out two other rhetorical details worth noting: first, that the author ceases to address the reader as *meiden* and switches to *wummon* (compare 18.1, 22.2 to 27.1); second, that the "narrator uses a debate format, laying out the reader-character's imagined points and refuting them one by one" ("Characterized Reader," p. 98). These details illustrate both the author's strategic use of rhetoric in engaging his reader, as well as the invitation to the female reader to engage with multiple roles — i.e., exegete, virgin, wife, mother, and debater (though perhaps a more appropriate term would be *motild*; see the explanatory note to *SK* 9.4). In terms of source material, though, the author has based this sensitive account of childbirth and child-rearing, according to M, on an expansion of a description of pregnancy in Hildebert of Lavardin. The discomforts of pregnancy appear also in other religious letters, such as those of Osbert of Clare (see M, p. 46n17/23–18/4).

27.8   *thi breines turnunge.* "Your brain's turning," i.e., dizziness (see *MED brain* (n.1),
         sense a, meaning "vertigo, dizziness" as well as MWB's translation). We have
         translated literally, following Savage and Watson. This phrase, a striking
         description of the source of dizziness, is one of the few examples in the
         Katherine Group of a kenning, a holdover from Anglo-Saxon poetic tradition,
         a metaphor or periphrastic expression referring to a thing by description, rather
         than simply naming it, for example: "whale-road" (sea); "sword storm" (battle);
         "horse of the sea" (ship).

27.9   *swel in.* M's emendation (see p. 46n17/30); see also our corresponding textual
         note. The presence of *swel* here presents crucial interpretive issues, as the term
         is never used (as verb or noun) to describe natural pregnancy, but consistently
         to describe either pathological, physical swelling or the swelling of the
         heart/mind to pride or anger, implying (at least in this case) a connection
         between the sickness of inflammation and moral disobedience. *MED* defines
         swelle (n.) as "A morbid swelling in the body or a bodily part." Compare *AW*
         4.1182–87, where the author compares lascivious temptations to a bodily wound,
         which the anchoress should not concern herself with "bute hit to swithe swelle
         thurh skiles yettunge with to muchel delit up toward te heorte, ah drinc thenne
         atter-lathe ant drif thet swealm ayein-ward frommard te heorte – thet is to
         seggen, thench o the attri pine thet Godd dronc o the rode, ant te swealm schal
         setten" [unless it swell too terribly up toward the heart throught he consent of
         reason with too much delight, but drink then the antidote and drive the
         inflammation away from the heart – that is to say, think on the poisonous pain
         that God drank on the Cross, and the inflammation will subside] (ed.
         Hasenfratz, p. 288, lines 1184–87).

28.1   *we ne edwiteth . . . forte warni meidnes.* The moral distinction between marriage
         and virginity is based in the first letter of Paul to the Corinthians, chapter 7;
         Paul is careful to point out that marriage should not be condemned, though
         virginity is preferable. Patristic commentators on both Paul as well as the subject
         of virginity generally clarify that they do not wish to detract from marriage;
         Jerome has a particularly interesting take on praising marriage in his letter to
         Eustochium: *Laudo nuptias, laudo coniugium, sed quia mihi virgines generant* [I
         praise wedlock, I praise marriage; but it is because they produce virgins for me]
         (letter 22, trans. Wright, pp. 94–95).

30.1   *Theose ant othre . . . ane lut wordes.* M cites Hildebert's Letter to Athalisa as a
         source for this passage (p. 47n18/26–27): *Haec et alia nuptiarum sunt incommoda,
         quae numerare longum ducens Apostolus, 'tribulationem', inquit, 'sustinebunt huiusmodi*
         [These and other things of marriage are disagreeable, which the Apostle,
         considering them tedious to number, says 'they tolerate the tribulation of this
         manner of life'].

         Tribulaciones carnis et cetera. See 1 Corinthians 7:28.

31.1   *Lutel wat meiden . . . ne his caderclutes.* M cites Hildebert of Lavardin's Letter to
         Athalisa as a source for this passage (p. 48n18/32–19/5): *Virginitas maritalis ignara
         negotii, non labores puerperae, non novi partus spurcitias experitur . . . virginitas*

vigilias nutricis ignorans, quam multa supellectile, quibusve sorbitiunculis alumnus indigeat, non requirit [Virginity ignorant of the business of marriage, does not know about childbirth labors, nor about the filthinesses of a new baby . . . virginity being ignorant of the vigils of the wet-nurse, does not enquire after just how much stuff, or what portions of food the child may need].

bigan. See *MED, bigon* (v.1), sense a: "to cover." All of the examples, including the Royal manuscript of Juliana (compare d'Ardenne's edition, p. 22/187) use this verb to mean "cover (something) with blood." Compare the Bodley reading of this line in *SJ*, which reads "bigoten" (27.1 of our text). As M notes (p. 48n19/4), this is the only example of this verb referring to a substance besides blood (in this case, food). We have chosen to translate *bigon* as "bespatter."

cader-clutes. Cader is a Welsh word for cradle. The presence of this term provides additional evidence for the theory that the text was produced in Herefordshire near the Welsh border. See Dobson, *Origins of Ancrene Wisse*, pp. 115–16 and 323–24. Dobson also discusses the Welsh origin of this word on pp. 115–16.

31.3   *fliche.* "A side of an animal" sometimes referring to beef but more often to pork, as in a side of bacon (*OED flitch* (n.1)).

33.5–6   *Eadi is . . . kinedom of Heovene.* M cites Hildebert's Letter to Athalisa as a source for this passage (p. 49n19/32–20/3 and 20/3–4): *Beata nimirum sponsa, cujus pudor dum concipit non deperit; dum generat, non laborat. Beatissimus autem sponsus cui, nisi cohaereat, nulla virgo est; nulla casta, nisi eum diligat; nulla libera, nisi ei serviat* [Certainly (God's) spouse (is) blessed, whose purity does not perish while she conceives; who does not suffer while she produces life. And most blessed (is) the husband, whom, unless she clings to Him, she is no virgin; not clean, unless she loves Him; not free, unless she serves Him] and *Ejus prole nihil vivacius, cum qua nulla propagatur mortalitas. Ejus dote nihil utilius, in quo sufficientam comitatur aeternitas* [(There is) nothing more long-lived than His offspring, to whom no mortality is spread. Nothing is more profitable than His dowry, in which eternity accompanies sufficiency].

33.6   *marhe-yeve.* I.e., a dowry. See *MED yeve* (n.), sense 2b.

33.8   *thah He beo . . . Him wel icweme.* M cites Hildebert's Letter to Athalisa as a source for this passage (p. 49n20/7–8): *pauperi libens copulatur, dives in omnes qui invocant illum* [with pleasure He marries the poor, rich among all those who call upon Him].

33.9   *upo hwas nebscheft . . . fulle to bihalden.* Compare 1 Peter 1:12.

34.1–2   *Yef the were . . . hire in Heovene.* The image of virtues as spiritual children can be traced back to Origen, *Homilies on Numbers* (see M, p. xli).

35.1–36.1   *Ah thah thu . . . his ealdeste dohter.* M cites Hildebert's Letter to Athalisa as the source for this discussion of adultery with the devil (p. 50n20/29–21/5): *Unum tamen est quo ille sponsam ablaterat, et propriam diffitetur: hujus etenim ratio dissidii, sola mentis est corruptela. Mentis deformitas offendit virum, sponsalia diripit, abjudicat dotem, eliminat introductam. Mentem tuus amans explorat, et ex ejus qualitate vel dictat repudium, vel maritum pollicetur. Huic autem suspecta est superbia, nec fieri potest ut cum eo in gratia revertatur* [There is one (reason) however for which he sets aside his spouse, and denies his own: indeed the reason for this separation is corruption of the mind alone. Deformity of the mind displeases the Husband, lays waste the betrothal feast, rightfully takes away the dowry, carries the new bride (lit., "the one who has been introduced") out the door. Your lover tests your mind, and based on its quality he either declares divorce, or promises marriage. Yet still for this, pride is suspected, and it cannot happen that she comes back in favor with Him].

36.1–38.6   *Over alle thing . . . al hare lifsithen.* Pride particularly threatens the virgin's salvation because she has something that wives and widows do not: physical purity. Thus this sin has the capacity to upset the traditional order of the female estates (e.g., virgins, widows, wives). Aldhelm, in his tract on virginity, demonstrates particular interest in this matter, since some evidence points to his addressing a mixed audience: virgins and women who have cast off their husbands to pursue a chaste life — hence the terms "chastity" and "virginity" have different meanings (see the introduction to *De Virginitate*, trans. Lapidge and Herren, pp. 51–58). Aldhelm's strong words on proud virgins (as opposed to humble chaste women) are worth noting: "because they judge themselves to be chastely celibate and to be thoroughly free from all the dregs of filth, inflated with (over-) confidence in their virginity they arrogantly swell up and in no way do they turn away the most cruel monster Pride, devourer of the other virtues, with the nose-ring of humility . . . Virgins of Christ and raw recruits of the Church must therefore fight with muscular energy against the horrendous monster of Pride and at the same time against those seven wild beasts of virulent vices [i.e., the Seven Deadly Sins], who with rabid molars and venomous bicuspids strive to mangle violently whoever is unarmed and despoiled of the breastplate of virginity and stripped of the shield of modesty" (trans. Lapidge and Herren, pp. 67–68).

36.5–37.3   *for ne muhen . . . . the overcom engel.* M cites Hildebert's Letter to Athalisa as the source for this passage (p. 51n21/16–25): *Diversum est utrique hospitium, nec in eodem cohabitant animo, quibus cohabitare non licuit in coelo. In coelo nimirum nata est superbia, sed velut immemor qua inde via ceciderit, illuc ultra redire non novit. Ea de supernis corruens, et parentans in terris, omnibus suis apud inferos aeternam pepigit mansionem. Ipsa ex purissimis et simplicibus orta substantiis, puros adhuc animos inquietat, ausa victoriam sperare de homine, quae de angelo triumphavit* [It is a hostile lodging for both of them, and they do not live together in the same heart, those who are not allowed to live together in heaven. Pride was undoubtedly born in heaven, but as if (she was) forgetful of which way she fell from there, in addition she did not know how to return to that place. She, falling down from on high, and appearing on the ground, has made an eternal dwelling place for all her own in hell. Risen from the most clean and pure substances herself, even now she disturbs clean souls, having dared to hope for victory over man, she who triumphed over an angel].

37.4   *hwit other blac. . . grei . . . grene*. The colors probably refer to the different habits of the religious orders. If the grey refers to the Franciscan grey-friars, then this text of *HM* would have to be dated after 1224, the year that the Franciscans first came to England. Millett has argued that the work most closely associated with *HM*, *AW*, should be linked with the Dominicans; see "New Answers, New Questions." For an earlier argument for the Augustinian origins of the *AW* and the *Katherine Group*, see Dobson, *Origins of Ancrene Wisse*, p. 16ff. The *AW* itself argues that a contemplative should not be concerned with the different orders but rather should ally herself with the Order of St. James, which is unconcerned with the color of habits. See ed. Hasenfratz, pp. 64–67, lines 79–129.

38.1–2   *Ne tele thu . . . a prud meiden*. M cites a longer passage from Book III, Chapter 28 of Gregory's *Regula Pastoralis*; *HM*'s author evidently condensed this material for this section (M, p. 52n21/32–22/4). Davis' translation of this section reads as follows: "Those who are innocent of sins of the flesh are to be admonished not to prefer themselves in the eminence of their loftier estate, seeing that they do not know how many better things are done by those of inferior estate in these matters. For on the assessment of the righteous Judge, the character of our conduct reverses the merit due to our rank. Indeed, who, taking the more outward appearances of objects, does not know that in the realm of gems the garnet is preferred to the jacinth, yet the blue jacinth is preferred to the pale garnet, because what the order of nature has denied to the former, is added to it by the phase of its beauty, and though the latter is superior in the order of nature, it is depreciated by the quality of its colour? So, then, in the case of man there are some who, though of higher rank, are inferior, and others who are in a lower estate, are better, because the latter by their good way of life transcend the character of the lower estate, while the former fall short of the merit of their higher estate by not living up to it" (p. 198).

38.2   *charbucle₁ . . . jacinct*. Precious gems appear in the Bible such as in the description of the ornaments of Aaron and his sons in Exodus 39:10–12: "And he set four rows of precious stones in it. In the first row was a sardius, a topaz, an emerald. In the second, a carbuncle, a sapphire and a jasper. In the third a ligurius, an agate, and an amethyst." Compare also the description in Apocalypse of the New Jerusalem and its gem-rich edification (Apocolapyse 21:18–21). Jewels such as these were of special interest in the Middle Ages and often accrued moral meaning or powers of healing and protection, as discussed in medieval lapidaries. The Peterborough Lapidary, for example, reports that the carbuncle, or "Carbuncculus is a precios stone, & he schineþ as feyre whose schynyng is not ouercom by nyȝt" (Evans and Serjeantson, *English Mediaeval Lapidaries*, p. 82)

     is betere a milde wif other a meoke widewe then a prud meiden. This phrase, Newman notes, is "ubiquitous in . . . virginity literature" (*From Virile Woman*, pp. 256–57n47). For example, Newman cites Augustine, *Enarrationes in Psalmos*, 99.13; Caesarius of Arles, *Homilies* 12; the *Speculum virginum*; and Thomas of Froidmont, *Liber de modo bene vivendi ad sororem* 22.64 (*From Virile Woman*, pp. 256–57n47).

38.3   *eadi sunegilt Marie Magdaleine*. Mary Magdalene's identification as a repentant sinner originates in the conflation of the anonymous repentant woman of Luke 7:37–50 and of the "Mary who is called Magdalen" of Luke 8:2 (though Mary Magdalene is mentioned numerous other times in the New Testament). Gregory the Great first identified the two figures as the same, and this identification was later confirmed by Augustine (see Aquinas' *Catena Aurea*, 3.258).

38.4   *Ant te othre . . . unlusti ant wlecche*. See Apocalypse 3:15–16.

39.3   *Efter thi word . . . mi Lauerdes threl*. See Luke 1:38.

39.5   *Elizabeth*. Mother of John the Baptist and wife of Zacharias. Elizabeth's visitation with the Virgin is narrated in Luke 1:39–55.

39.6   *For mi Lauerd . . . eadi alle leoden*. See Luke 1:48.

39.8   *eolie in a lampe*. This image of the virgin like an oil lamp is common in virginity literature and is derived from Matthew 25:1–13, the parable of the wise and foolish virgins. See Chrysostom, who says they "denote the gifts of virginity." Jerome agrees though he is insistent that the parable applies not exclusively to virgins but to the whole human race. Origen glosses "lamps" to mean "natural faculties." For Hilary they are "the lights of bright souls shining forth in the sacrament of baptism" or human bodies. For Augustine the lamps are their good works that shine before them. For Hilary the oil is "the fruit of good works" and for Jerome, "the ornament of good works"; for Augustine, the oil designates the joy that springs forth in accord with God's anointment. For Origen oil is "the word of teaching with which the lamps are filled" (*Catena Aurea* 1.3, pp. 844–45).

40.4   *Thench o Seinte Katerrine . . . ant Seinte Cecille*. This short list of martyrdoms includes the names of the virgins in the Katherine Group texts, and perhaps provides some hints as to other martyrdoms that the audience of *HM* was reading or to which they might have had access. Saint Agnes (*Seinte Enneis*) was a virgin martyr whose legend places her death during the Diocletian persecutions; Saint Cecilia was most likely a legendary figure, though one later made famous in Chaucer's Second Nun's Tale. B omits Saint Lucy from this short list, although T does include her here.

40.8   *as weren ear ha agulten his eareste hinen*. See Jerome, *Epistles* 22:19. It was generally accepted by the Church Fathers that Adam and Eve remained virgins until after the Fall, although Augustine later argued that sexual intercourse would have taken place in Paradise (see M, pp. xxix–xxx).

40.12   *leir-wite*. From Old English *leger-wite*, the term was used in legal treatises to specify a fine levied for fornication, in particular with a female slave; see *MED leir-wite* (n.), sense b. *HM* has the only recorded instance of this term being used in a figurative sense.

41.3   *as Seinte Pawel . . . overcume hire seolf*. See 2 Timothy 2:5 and 1 Corinthians 9:24–27.

41.4   *as the Apostle seith*. This probably is a reference to James 1:12 (see M, p. 55n23/33–24/1 and MWB, p. 153n42/12–13).

41.6   *wrist te under Godes wengen*. This image of sheltering under God's wings appears frequently in the Psalms. In particular, see Vulgate Psalms 16:8, 35:8, 56:2, and 60:5. This image also appears in *SW* 15.1 and 43.2.

41.7   *damn his teeth*. For a similar phrase see *SJ* explanatory note 38.5.

Textual Notes to *Hali Meithhad*

ABBREVIATIONS: *CT*: *Canterbury Tales*; **F**: Furnivall edition (1922); *HM*: *Hali Meithhad*; **M**: Millett edition (1982); *MED*: *Middle English Dictionary;* **MS**: Bodleian Library MS Bodley 34 [base text]; **MWB**: Millett and Wogan-Browne edition (1990); *OED*: *Oxford English Dictionary*; **T**: British Library MS Cotton Titus D XVIII; **Whiting**: Whiting, *Proverbs, Sentences, and Proverbial Phrases*.

1.2	*meidene.* So T. MS: *meiið.* M emends to *meið.*
1.3	*word.* So M, T. MS: *worð.*
1.4	*lustni.* So M, T. MS: *lustin.*
1.8	*Heo mei ondswerien ant seggen.* So M. T: *Ho mei onsweren & seien.* MS omits.
	yeorne. So M, T. MS:*ȝeone.*
1.10	*makieth.* So M, following *dreaieth* of 1.10. MS: *makied.* T: *maken.*
1.11	*bittre.* So M, following standard AB spelling of the word. MS: *bittri.* T: *bitter.*
1.12	*deorewurthe.* So M, T. MS: *deorewrthe.*
2.1	*seith.* So T. MS omits. M emends to *Syon seith.*
2.3	*worldes.* So M. MS: *worlddes.*
	lahe. So F, M, T. MS: the word has been inserted in the right margin with the final two letters cropped (the first upstroke of *h* is visible).
	eorthe. So M, T. MS: *eordthe.*
2.4	*ha₄.* MS: *ant.* T: *and.* As is, the sentence makes little sense without an independent clause governing *thurh . . . eorthe.* M retains the MS reading and adds just before it *ha stiheð gasteliche,* following Dobson's suggestion (see p. 26n2/11–14). We have emended more conservatively, since neither MS nor T contain this phrase.
2.5	*hire.* So M, T. MS omits.
	icleopet. So MS, corrected from *icleoped.*
	In the bottom margin of fol. 53v, upside down; H: *Thomas Wysham de Tedestorne in com' hereff gent in ducentis sterlingorum soluend'.* See also the textual note to *SJ* 43.1, which mentions Thomas's son George as well as Ker, *Facsimile of MS Bodley 34,* p. xiv, on the Wysham family of Herefordshire.
3.1	*wurthschipe.* MS: There is an otiose descender between *s* and *c.*
	al₂. So M, T. MS omits.
	thet₃. So M, following T's *þat.* MS omits.
	hire leafdischipe. MS: *hire ~~leafdhi~~ leafdischipe.*
	in₂. So M, T. MS omits.
	earmthen. So M, T. MS: *earmden.*

4.5   *beon.* M, T: *beo.* MS omits.

4.6   *earnnesse.* So MS, with *a* inserted above the line.

5.1   *servin.* So MS, T. M: *serve.* M argues that an imperative is necessary here
             rather than the infinitive *servin* which appears in both manuscripts. She
             suggests the scribe made an error following the previous word *trukien* (M,
             p. 27n3/31). However, our sense is that the modal *schal* governs both
             infinitives, *trukien* and *servin.*

             ofthunchunges. So M, T. MS: *ofthunchunge.*

6.1   *the₁.* So M, T. MS omits.

             wummen. So M, following T's *wimmen.* MS: *wummon.*

7.1   *the₃.* So M, T. MS omits.

             fleschliche. So M, T. MS: *flecsliche.*

7.6   *this.* So M, following T's *tis.* MS omits.

             hearm. So M. MS: *hearrm.* T: *harm.*

7.8   *the₂.* So M, T. MS omits.

7.10   *biginnen.* Our emendation, from T's *bigunnen.* MS: *luvien.* M emends to
             iunnen, citing MS's *luvien* as "bad sense" and T's *bigunnen* as "bad
             grammar" (see p. 29n5/6). We agree that the passage is problematic and
             reflects corruption in both manuscripts, and have opted for a more
             conservative emendation. *Biginnen* replicates the nice alliteration of T
             and presents the idea that whatever the virgin strives to undertake (see
             MED, biginnen (v.5), sense a) or "to begin," God will see through to its
             completion (*endin*).

8.3   *desireth.* Our emendation. MS, M: *desiri.* T: *desire.* Although the *MED* cites
             the MS reading as an early form of the verb, we think it highly likely,
             especially given T's reading, that *desiri/desire* is a scribal error. A *þ*
             immediately follows the word in both manuscripts, and it makes sense
             that the scribe would have mistakenly elided the final *þ* of *desiriþ/desireþ*
             with the following *þe.*

8.4   *meithhades.* So M. MS: *meidhades.*

8.5   *Halt.* So M. MS: *hwalt.* According to M, the scribe anticipated the following
             hwam (p. 30n5/13).

             the. MS: *þee.*

8.8   *yeove.* So M, T. MS omits.

8.10   *to.* So T. MS omits. M emends to *te,* explaining that in most cases forms of
             ah (here, *ahest*) followed by an infinitive (in this case, *witen*) are usually
             followed by the *to* particle (p. 30n5/26).

             withuten. So M. MS: *wituten.* T: *wiðute.*

8.11   *leof.* So F, M, T. MS omits.

             nis. So M, T. MS omits.

             bruche. So F, M, T. MS: *bruge,* corrected to *bruche* in a different hand. We
             have adapted the correction following other editions.

8.12   *eorthliche.* So M, T. MS: *eordlich.*

             maketh. So M, T. MS: *maked.*

             eorthlich. So M, T. MS: *eordlich.*

             heame. So MS. M, T: *heane.* See M's long discussion of the possibility that the
             MS-scribe is right. She argues that *heane* as "oppressor" fits the sense of

the passage better than the more neutral *heame*, "inhabitant," despite the fact that *heane* is not a known word (M, pp. 30–31n6/2).

8.14   *ofearnest*. So M, T. MS: *earanest*, with a_1 inserted above the line.

        meiden. So M, T. MS: *meden*.

        god. So M, T. MS: *goð*.

8.15   *meithhades*. So M. MS: *meidhades*. T: *meidenhades*.

8.16   *eadiure*. So M, T. MS: *ed ure*. F emends to *ediure*, noting that "the *i* has been erased" (p. 16).

        halden. MS: ~~halden~~ *halden*. It appears that the scribe first wrote *haeden*, tried to correct to *halden*, then crossed the word out and wrote on a fresh section of the line.

8.17   *i this$_1$*. So M, T. MS: *is the*.

        gume. MS: *gumi~~n~~e*, with *e* inserted above the *i*.

        licnesse. So M, T. MS: *cleannesse*. The scribe most likely made this mistake by repetition from the earlier *unlicnesse*.

        throf. So M, T. MS: *threof*.

8.21   *licomliche lustes*. So T. MS: *licome lustest*. M emends to *licomes lustes*. We have adopted T's reading based on the presence of the phrase in *HM* lines 1.10, 7.1, 7.3, 10.4.

        theo iliche. So M. MS: *the ilich*. T: *þa iliche*. M suggests that T's *iliche* should be read as a plural noun, and has adjusted the pronoun to reflect this (p. 32n6/27).

        wurthinge$_2$. So M, T. MS: *wurdinge*.

8.23   *walewith*. So M. MS: *waleweth*.

        with$_1$. So M, T. MS: *wid*.

9.1   *meithhad*. So M. MS: *meidhad*.

9.2   *offearet*. So M, T. MS: *offeaaret*. The scribe repeated the *a* when he began the next page (fol. 57v).

9.4   *thurh*. So MS, with *r* inserted above the line.

        ure. So M, T. MS: *hire*.

        earst. MS: *earest*.

9.5   *wummen*. So M. MS: *wummem*. T: *wimmen*.

9.6   *the$_1$*. So M, T. MS omits.

        scheoteth. So M. MS: *scheoted*. T: *schoteð*.

        healewi. So MS, with *a* inserted above the line.

9.9   *nawiht*. So MS, with *ih* inserted above the line.

9.10   *thes*. So M. MS: it appears that the scribe wrote *ses*, then attempted to correct by adding a descender to the initial long *s*. T: *þe*.

        fleoth. So M, T. MS: *beod*.

10.4   *other*. So M, T. MS: *oder*.

10.6   *greitheth*. So M, T. MS: *greideð*.

10.8   *speoketh*. So M. MS: *sweoked*. F reads as *speoked* but notes the mistake in spelling (p. 22). T: *speken*.

10.9   *fulst*. So M, T. MS: *fulht*.

        Meithhad. So M. MS: *meiðhað*. T: *meidenhad*.

11.6   *throf*. So M, T. MS: *threof*.

12.2   *servaverit*. So M, T. MS: *seminaverunt*.

12.6   *halhe*. So M, following T's *halhes*. MS: *habbe*.

13.1   *bith*. So M. MS: *bið*. T: *beð*.

13.4   *istud*. So M. MS: *istuð*. T: *hoc*.

13.12   *as*. So M, T. MS: *al*.

13.13   *thet meidnes beoth*. MS: *þe meidnes beoð*. M, T: *to beon*.

14.2   *softeliche*. So M, T. MS: *fofteliche*.

14.4   *leod*. So T. MS: *leo*. M emends to *leoth*.

15.1   *is*. So M, T. MS omits.

15.2   *leadeth*. So M. M argues that a plural verb is needed here to follow the plural subject (p. 38n11/3). MS, T: *leat*.

16.2   *muhe*. So M, T. MS: *muhten*.

16.3   *gath*. So M, T. MS: *gad*.

16.4   *schinende*. So T. MS omits. M emends to *schininde*.

        auriole. So T. MS: *an urle*, which M argues is a corruption of *auriole* (p. 39n11/19). We have emended to T's reading in the Middle English and transposed to the Latin term in the translation.

16.5   *gimmes*. So M. MS: *ʒimmies*.

        te. So M, T. MS: *ne*.

16.6   *meidnes*. So M, T. MS: *meiðnes*.

17.1   *Of*. So T. MS: *ʒef of*. M retains MS's reading. MWB emend to *ʒet of*. M makes sense of the incomplete if-clause by emending *widewehad, ant wedlac is þe þridde* to *widewehad ant [wedlachad], wedlac is þe þridde*. See M, pp. 39–40n25–26 for a helpful discussion of the corruption of this line in MS; also see Dobson, *Origins*, pp. 161–62n3. Most likely T's scribe simplified what was originally an "if . . . then" correlative by dropping the *ʒef*, and we have adopted this reading.

17.4   *preoveth*. So M, T. MS: *preoved*.

        leapeth. So M, T. MS: *leaped*.

17.6   *haveth*. So M, T. MS: *haved*.

17.7   *beoth*. So M, T. MS: *beod*.

18.1   *to-eche*. So MS. M, T: *teke*.

18.4   *soth cnawes*. So M, T. MS: *soþ cwawes*.

18.8   *habbeth*. So M. MS: omits.

        leaven. MS: *le leaven*. The scribe began the word at the very end of a line, then canceled and wrote on the next line.

18.9   *thet₁*. So M, following T's *þat*. MS: *ant*.

19.3   *folheth*. So M, T. MS: *foheth*.

19.5   *meithhades*. So M. MS: *meidhades*. T: *meidenhades*.

        cheaffere. So MS, with *a* inserted above the line.

21.1   *ipaiet*. So MS, with i_2 inserted above the line.

21.2   *ah*. So M, T. MS: *ahi*.

21.5   *earmthe*. So M, T. MS: *earmde*.

21.6   *twinnunge*. So M, following T's *twinninge*. MS: *twinnnunge*.

22.2   *He₁*. So M, T. MS: *ʒe*.

22.3   *thin He*. So M, T. MS: *him þe*.

22.5   *se*. So M, T. MS: *þe i þe*.

        leadeth. So M, T. MS: *leaðeð*.

22.10	*Al*. So M, T. MS: *as*.
22.13	*worldes*. So MS, with *l* inserted above the line.
22.14	*steoleth*. So M. MS: *steoled*.
	hit₂. So M, T. MS: *hit hit*.
22.16	*forwurthen*. So M, T. MS: *forwurden*.
23.1	*schal nede*. So M, T. MS: *ne schal*.
23.2	*grevin*. MS: *grenin*. T: *greni*. M: *granin*. M suggests that the word *granin* might have been intended to mean "groan (in childbirth)" (though this use is not attested before 1300; see *MED gronen* (v.1) sense b). See her discussion of the various alternatives offered by editors from Tolkien onward (pp. 43–44n15/18). The first *n* of *grenin* in MS could be a slightly smudged *v*, hence our emendation. *Greven* is a verb that appears in *HM*, though indirectly; i.e. *HM* 24.6: *hit greveth the se swithe*.
23.3	*were*. MS: *weres*.
23.9	*tendreth*. So MS, corrected from *tendren*, with *ð* written over *n₂*.
23.12	*drehen — ne luvie ha him neaver swa wel*. So M, T. MS omits; the line as it stands is missing a verb. M believes that the MS-scribe has accidentally missed the line (p. 44n16/2–3).
23.13	*gomenes*. So M, T. MS: *gonienes*.
	wulle. MS: *wulla*, with *e* inserted above the canceled *a*.
24.1	*ifindeth*. So M, T. MS: *ifinðeð*.
24.3	*he₃*. So M, T. MS omits.
24.4	*tu*. So M, T. MS omits.
24.5	*unwurthlich and wratheliche*. So M, T. MS: *unwurðliche*.
24.7	*cunqueari*. So MS, with *a* inserted above the line.
25.1	*irikenet*. MS: *al irikinet*, with *al* significantly faded. The scribe appears to have repeated the word from the previous page and then erased.
26.1	*habbe*. MS: *nab habbe*.
	ant₁. So M, T. MS omits.
	fostrunge. So M. MS: *fosttrunge*. T: *fostringe*.
26.3	*upbrud*. So M, T. MS: *upbrrud*, with *r₂* inserted above the line.
	bimong. So M, T. MS: *bimon*.
26.4	*forthlich*. So M, T. MS: *forlich*.
	misfeare. MS: *ne misfeare*.
27.1	*hit*. MS: inserted above the line.
27.3	*sunnen₁*. So M, T. MS: *sunen*.
27.4	*Gultest*. So M. MS, T: *gulteð*, the plural form of the verb, whereas the singular is needed. M argues the scribe of the common ancestor was misled by the series of third person singular verbs into substituting *gulteth* for this word (p. 46n17/21).
27.5	*thet₂*. So M, following T's *þat*. MS: *ant*.
27.6	*awakenith*. So M. MS, T: *awakeneð*, the singular form of the verb (though it looks like a plural), whereas the plural is needed. M explains that the scribe probably accidentally repeated the *awakeneð* in the preceding line (p. 46n17/25).

27.9   *swel in*. So M. MS, T: *swelin*. Reading this word as two words makes the best sense of the phrase, according to M (p. 46n17/30). See also the corresponding explanatory note.

lonke. MS: ~~wombe~~ *lonke*.

27.11   *mete*. So M, T. MS omits.

27.13   *cares*. So M. MS: *carest*. T: *care*. An emendation to T's reading would not make sense as the main verb, *bineometh*, is in the plural form.

27.14   *stikinde*. So M, T. MS: *stinkinde*.

28.1   *meidnes*. So M, T. MS: *meiðnes*.

29.1   *thet ti*. So M, following T's *þat ti*. MS: *þe hire*.

29.3   *upo sorhe*. So M, T. MS omits (see M, p. 47n18/23).

31.1   *werc*. So M, T. MS: *were*.

wleateful. So MS, with e_1 inserted above the line.

sut. So M. MS, T: *suti*. The normal use of *suti* to mean "filthy, disgusting" does not quite fit here, hence Tolkien's original suggestion of *sut* (see M, p. 48n19/1).

ha schule. So M, T. MS: *hit is*.

31.4   *swithre*. So M, T. MS: *swithe*.

33.5   *His*. MS: *þis*, corrected above the line to *ihis*.

33.7   *Lauerd*. So M, T. MS: *lauerð*.

34.1   *tholemodnesse*. So M, T. MS: *tholomodnesse*.

mekelec. So T. MS: *metelec*. M: *meokelec*.

meithhades. So M. MS: *meihades*. T: *meidenhades*.

35.1   *i thin*. So M, T. MS omits.

36.1   *his*. So M, T. MS: *hiss*.

36.2 ha_2 . . . *hire*. So M, T. MS: *hire keaste ure*. M argues that MS's reading "obscures the contrast between Pride's heavenly father (21/9) and her earthly mothers" (p. 51n21/6).

36.3   *ha*. So M, T. MS: *he*.

36.5 $muhen_2$. So T. MS: *maken*. M: *mahten*.

36.6   *eardinde*. So M, T. MS: *earmðe*.

bihat. So M, T. MS: *bihalt*.

$hire_2$. So M, F. MS, T: *hare*. M follows F in emending; here, Pride's mothers (i.e., prideful maidens are not the fiend's daughters, but rather his whores (p. 51n21/21).

37.5   *Sone*. So M, T. MS: *son*.

38.2 $charbucle_1$. So M, T. MS: *charbuche*.

onont. So M, T. MS: *onon*.

38.3 as_1. So M, T. MS: *al*.

bireowsith. So M. MS, T: *bireowseth*. Compare the textual note to 23.13; the subjects are the mild wives and meek widows of the previous lines, though the MSS readings are in the singular. M makes the point that the scribe of the common exemplar may have read *Marie Magdaleine* as the subject (p. 53n22/7), hence the singular form.

inwardluker. So M. MS: *inwarðluker*. T: *inwardlukest*.

38.5   *liveth*. So T. MS omits.

39.1	*to trusti.* So M, T. MS: *trust.*
	meithhad. So M. MS: *meidhad.* T: *meidenhad.*
	theawfule. MS: *þeawfufele.*
39.2	*lah.* So M, T. MS: *þah.*
39.6	*His.* So M, T. MS: *þis.*
39.8	*hit.* MS: *þis hit.*
	withute. So M, T. MS: *wid ute.*
40.1	*i thi.* So M, T. MS: *ant ti.*
40.4	*meidnes.* So M, T. MS: *meiðnes.*
40.6	*ti.* So M, T. MS: *tu.*
	the₂. M, T. MS omits.
40.7	*engel.* So M, T. MS: *e engtel.* The first *e* is repeated most likely because of a lacuna in the fols. 70r–v which extends diagonally through seven lines; the scribe has heretofore neatly written around the slit.
40.9	*deorewurthe.* So M, from T's *derewurðe.* MS: *deorewurde.*
40.10	*me.* So M, T. MS omits.
40.12	*blisse upo blisse.* So M, T. MS: *blisse o up o blisse.*
	meithhades. So M. MS: *meidhades.* T: *meidenhades.*
41.2	*thi₂* So M, T. MS: *ant ti.*
41.6	*greveth.* So M, T. MS: *greved.*
	Godes. So M, T. MS: *goder.*
42.1	*leve hire.* MS: *leve me hire.*
	ant₂. So M, T. MS omits.
	beon₂. MS: this word is inserted above the line.
	eorthliche limen. MS: between these words the scribe has written several words which have been erased.

SAWLES WARDE

I the Feaderes ant i the Sunes and i the Hali Gastes nome, her bigineth Sawles Warde.

fol. 72r
1. (1) *Si sciret paterfamilias qua hora fur venturus esset, vigilaret utique et non sineret perfodi domum suam.*

2. (1) Ure Lauerd i the Godspel teacheth us thurh a bisne hu we ahen wearliche to biwiten us seolven with the unwiht of Helle ant with his wrenches. (2) "Yef thes lauerd wiste," he seith, "hwenne ant hwuch time the theof walde cume to his hus, he walde wakien; ne nalde he nawt tholien the theof forte breoken hire."

3. (1) This hus the ure Lauerd speketh of is seolf the mon. (2) Inwith, the monnes wit i this hus is the huse lauerd, ant te fulitohe wif mei beon wil ihaten, thet, ga the hus efter hire, ha diht hit al to wundre bute Wit ase lauerd chasti hire the betere ant bineome hire muchel of thet ha walde. (3) Ant tah walde al hire hird folhin hire overal yef Wit ne forbude ham, for alle hit beoth untohene ant rechelese hinen bute yef he ham rihte. (4) Ant hwucche beoth theos hinen? (5) Summe beoth withuten ant summe withinnen. (6) Theo withuten beoth the monnes fif wittes, sihthe ant herunge, smechunge ant smeallunge, ant euch limes felunge.

In the name of the Father and of the Son and of the Holy Ghost, here begins "The Soul's Guardianship."

1. (1) *If the head of the household knew at what hour the thief was about to come, he would certainly remain awake and would not leave his house alone to be broken into.*

2. (1) Our Lord in the Gospel teaches us through a parable how we ought warily guard ourselves against the fiend of Hell and against his wiles. (2) "If the lord knew these things," he says, "when and at what time the thief would come to his house, he would stay awake; and he would not suffer the thief to break into it."

3. (1) This house which our Lord speaks of is humanity itself. (2) Inside, the person's wit in this house is the lord of the household, and the unruly wife can be called Will, who, should that household follow her will, she brings it all to ruin unless Wit as lord restrains her better and takes away from her much of what she desires. (3) And yet still all her household would follow her in everything if Wit did not forbid them, because are all unruly and reckless servants unless he corrects them. (4) And who are these servants? (5) Some are outside and some inside. (6) Those outside are the person's five senses, sight and hearing, tasting and smelling, and feeling in every member.

249

(7) Theos beoth hinen under Wit as under huse lauerd, ant hwer se he is yemeles nis hare nan the ne feareth ofte untoheliche ant gulteth ilome, other i fol semblant other in uvel dede. (8) Inwith, beoth his hinen in se moni mislich thonc to cwemen wel the husewif ayein Godes wille, ant swerieth somet readliche thet

fol. 72v efter hire hit schal | gan. (9) Thah we hit ne here nawt, we mahen iwiten hare nurhth ant hare untohe bere, athet Wit cume forth ant ba with eie ant with luve tuhte ham the betere. (10) Ne bith neaver his hus, for theos hinen, wel iwist for hwon thet he slepe other ohwider fare from hame, thet is, hwen mon foryet his wit ant let ham iwurthen. (11) Ah ne bihoveth hit nawt thet tis hus beo irobbet, for ther is inne the tresor thet Godd yef Himseolf fore — thet is, monnes sawle. (12) Forte breoke this hus efter this tresor, thet Godd bohte mid His death ant lette lif o Rode, is moni theof abuten ba bi dei ant bi niht, unseheliche gasttes with alle unwreaste theawes. (13) Ant ayein euch god theaw the biwiteth i this hus, Godes deore castel, under Wittes wissunge thet is huse lauerd, is eaver hire untheaw forte sechen inyong abute the wahes to amurthrin hire thrinne. (14) Thet heaved throf is the Feont the meistreth ham alle. (15) Ayeines him ant his keis, the husebonde (thet is, Wit) warneth his hus thus: ure Lauerd haveth ileanet him frovre of His dehtren, thet beoth to understonden the fowr heaved theawes. (16) The earste is Warschipe icleopet, ant te other is ihaten Gasteliche Strengthe, ant te thridde is Meath, Rihtwisnesse the feorthe.

---

(7) These are servants under Wit as under the household lord, and wherever he is negligent there is not anyone who does not often act rudely and sin frequently, either in wicked behavior or in evil deed. (8) Inside, his servants are in so many various thoughts busy to please well the housewife against God's will, and they swear unanimously that it will go after her desire. (9) Although we hear it not, we can perceive their noise and their unruly uproar, until Wit comes forth and both with fear and with love teaches them the better. (10) Because of those servants his house is never well guarded if he should sleep or fare anywhere from home; that is, when man forgets his wit and lets them be. (11) But this house must not be robbed, for inside there is the treasure for which God gave Himself — that is, man's soul. (12) There is many a thief nearby both by day and by night to break into this house after this treasure, which God bought with his death and gave up life on the Cross — unseen spirits with wicked vices. (13) And against every good virtue who guards in this house — God's dear castle — under the guidance of Wit who is the household lord, there is always its vice seeking entrance around the walls in order to murder her inside. (14) The head of them is the Fiend who rules them all. (15) Against him and his henchmen, the husband (that is, Wit) protects his house thus: our Lord has lent him the comfort of His daughters, who are to be understood as the four cardinal virtues. (16) The first is called Vigilance, and the other is called Spiritual Strength, and the third is Moderation, Righteousness the fourth.

fol. 73r
4.

(1) Wit the husbonde, Godes cunestable, cleopeth War|schipe forth ant makıth hıre durewart, the warliche loki hwam ha leote in ant ut, ant of feor bihalde alle the cuminde: hwuch beo wurthe inyong to habben other beon bisteken thrute. (2) Strengthe stont nest hire thet, yef ei wule in Warschipes unthonkes warni Strengthe fore, thet is hire suster, ant heo hit ut warpe. (3) The thridde suster, thet is Meath, hire he maketh meistre over his willesfule hird (thet we ear of speken), thet ha leare ham mete, thet me "meosure" hat, the middel of twa uveles, for thet is theaw in euch stude ant tuht forte halden, ant hateth ham alle thet nan of ham ayein hire nohwer with unmeath ne ga over mete. (4) The feorthe suster, Rihtwisnesse, sit on hest as deme ant beateth theo the agulteth ant cruneth theo the wel doth, ant demeth euchan his dom efter his rihte. (5) For dret of hire, nimeth this hird — euch efter thet he is — his warde to witene: the ehnen hare, the muth his, the earen hare, the honden hare, ant euch alswa of the othre wit thet onont him ne schal nan untheaw cumen in.

5.

fol. 73v

(1) As this is ido thus ant is al stille thrinne, Warschipe, thet áá is waker, is offearet lest sum fortruste him ant feole o slepe ant foryeme his warde. (2) Ant sent ham in a sonde thet ha wel cnaweth, of feorren icumen, forte offearen theo the beoth | overhardi, ant theo the yemelese beoth halden ham wakere. (3) He is undervon in ant swithe bihalden of ham alle, for lonc he is ant leane, ant his leor deathlich ant blac ant elheowet, ant euch her thuncheth thet stont in his heaved up.

4.

(1) Wit the husband, God's constable, calls Vigilance forth and makes her door-keeper, who carefully watches whom she lets in and out, and from afar beholds all who are coming: which are worthy to have entrance or to be shut outside. (2) Strength stands next to her so that if anything will go against Vigilance's will she first warns Strength, who is her sister, and she casts it out. (3) The third sister, which is Moderation, he makes her master over his willful household (which we spoke of before), so that she teaches them moderation, which some call "measure," the middle between two evils, for that is a virtue in each place and the right course to hold, and she bids them all that none of them should in no way go against her with excess nor with too much moderation. (4) The fourth sister, Righteousness, sits in the highest place as a judge and beats those who sin and crowns those who do well, and gives each one his sentence after his right. (5) For dread of her this household undertakes — each according to what he is — to keep his guard: the eyes theirs, the mouth his, the ears theirs, the hands theirs, and also each of the other wits so that through him no vice shall come in.

5.

(1) When this has been done thus and all is still therein, Vigilance, who is always watchful, is fearful lest someone trust too much and fall asleep and neglect his watch. (2) And she sends into them a messenger whom they know well, come from afar, in order to frighten those who are overbold, and to keep more watchful those who are careless. (3) He is received inside and greatly beheld by them all, for he is lank and lean, and his face death-like and pale and of an unearthly hue, and every hair on his head seems to stand up.

(4) Warschipe hat him tellen bivoren ham hwet he beo ant hweonene he comme ant hwet he ther seche.

6.   (1) "Ne mei Ich," he seith, "nohwer speoken bute Ich habbe god lust. (2) Lustnith me thenne: Fearlac Ich hatte, ant am Deathes sonde ant Deathes munegunge, ant am icumen bivore hire to warnin ow of hire cume." (3) Warschipe, thet best con bisetten hire wordes ant ec hire werkes, speketh for ham alle ant freineth hweonene ha cume ant hwuch hird ha leade.

7.   (1) Fearlac hire ontswereth, "Ich nat nawt the time, for ha ne seide hit me nawt. (2) Ah eaver lokith hwenne, for hire wune is to cumen bi stale, ferliche ant unmundlunge hwen me least weneth. (3) Of hire hird thet tu easkest, Ich the ondswerie: ha lihteth hwer se ha eaver kimeth with a thusent deoflen; ant euchan bereth a gret boc al of sunnen iwriten with swarte smeale leattres, ant an unrude raketehe gledread of fure forte binden ant to drahen into inwarde Helle hwuch se he mei preovin fol. 74r thurh his boc, thet is on euch sunne enbre|vet thet he with wil other with word other with werc wrahtte in al his lifsithe — bute thet he haveth ibet earthon with soth schrift ant with deadbote."

8.   (1) Ant Warschipe hire easketh, "Hweonene cumest tu, Fearlac, Deathes munegunge?"

9.   (1) "Ich cume," he seith, "of Helle."

10.   (1) "Of Helle?" ha seith, Warschipe. "Ant havest tu isehen Helle?"

11.   (1) "Ye," seith Fearlac, "witerliche, ofte ant ilome."

---

(4) Vigilance orders him to tell in their presence what he is and where he comes from and what he seeks there.

6.   (1) "I may not," he says, "speak anywhere unless I have full attention. (2) Listen to me then: Fear I am called, and I am Death's messenger and remembrance of Death, and I have come before her to warn you of her coming." (3) Vigilance, who can best fashion her words and also her deeds, speaks for them all and asks where she comes from and what host she leads.

7.   (1) Fear answers her, "I do not know the time, for she has not told it to me. (2) But always look thence, for her custom is to come by stealth, suddenly and unexpectedly when one least expects. (3) Of her host which you ask about, I will answer you: she alights wheresoever she comes with a thousand devils; and each one bears a great book all of sins written with small dark letters, and a cruel chain red-hot from fire in order to bind and drag into innermost Hell whoever he may prove through his book, in which every sin is inscribed, which he wrought in all his lifetime with will or with word or with deed — except what he has atoned for before then with true shrift and with repentance."

8.   (1) And Vigilance asks, "From where do you come, Fear, remembrance of Death?"

9.   (1) "I come," he says, "from Hell."

10.   (1) "From Hell?" she, Vigilance, says, "And have you seen Hell?"

11.   (1) "Yes," says Fear, "certainly, and very often."

12. (1) "Nu," seith thenne Warschipe, "for thi trowthe, treoweliche tele us hwuch is Helle ant hwet tu havest isehen thrin."

13. (1) "Ant Ich," he seith, Fearlac, "o mi trowthe, blitheliche nawt tah efter thet hit is — for thet ne mei na tunge tellen — ah efter thet Ich mei ant con, thertowart Ich chulle reodien.

14. (1) "Helle is wid withute met ant deop withute grunde, ful of brune unevenlich, for ne mei nan eorthlich fur evenin thertowart; ful of stench untholelich, for ne mahte in eorthe na cwic thing hit tholien; ful of sorhe untalelich, for ne mei na muth, for wrecchedom ne for wa, rikenin hit ne tellen. (2) So thicke is thrinne the theosternesse thet me hire mei grapin, for thet fur ne yeveth na liht ah blent ham the ehnen the ther beoth with a smorthrinde smoke, smeche forcuthest. (3) Ant tah i thet ilke swarte theosternesse swarte thinges ha iseoth, as deoflen thet ham meallith ant derveth áá ant dreccheth with alles cunnes pinen, ant iteilede draken,

fol. 74v grisliche ase deoflen, the forswolheth ham ihal ant speoweth ham | eft ut bivoren ant bihinden, otherhwile torendeth ham ant tocheoweth ham euch greot, ant heo eft iwurtheth hal to a swuch bale bute bote as ha ear weren. (4) Ant ful wel ha iseoth (ham to grisle ant to grure, ant to echen hare pine) the lathe Helle-wurmes, tadden ant froggen the freoteth ham ut te ehnen ant te nease-gristles. (5) Ant sniketh in ant ut neddren ant eauroskes — nawt ilich theose her ah hundret sithe grisluker — et muth ant et earen, ed ehnen ant ed neavele ant ed te breoste-holke as meathen i forrotet flesch, eaveryete thickest. (6) Ther is remunge i the brune ant tothes

---

12. (1) "Now," says Vigilance then, "by your faith, truly tell us what Hell is and what you have seen therein."

13. (1) "And I," he says, Fear, "upon my faith gladly, though not according to what it is — for that no tongue may tell — but I will strive to do what I am able.

14. (1) "Hell is wide without measure and deep without bottom, full of an incomparable fire — for no earthly fire may compare with it — full of unbearable stench — for no living thing on earth can tolerate it — full of indescribable sorrow — for no mouth may, for wretchedness or for woe, describe it or tell it. (2) So thick is the darkness therein that one could grasp it, for that fire gives no light but blinds the eyes of them who are there with a smothering smoke, a smell most loathsome. (3) And even so in that same black darkness they perceive black things, such as devils that beat them and afflict them always and harass them with all kinds of tortures, and dragons with tails, grisly as devils, which swallow them whole and spew them out after before and behind, or tear them up and chew them up every piece, and they afterward become whole as they were before for such a suffering without remedy. (4) And full well they see (a horror and a terror for them, and to increase their pain) the loathsome Hell-worms, toads and frogs which gnaw out the eyes and the nose-gristles. (5) And in and out creep snakes and water-frogs — not like those here but a hundred times more hideous — through the mouth and through the ears, through the eyes and through the navel and through the breast-hollow, like maggots in rotten flesh, thickest as ever. (6) There is wailing in the fire and

hechelunge i the snawi weattres. (7) Ferliche ha flutteth from the heate into the chele, ne neaver nuten ha of theos twa hwether ham thuncheth wurse, for either is untholelich. (8) Ant i this ferliche mong the leatere thurh the earre derveth the mare. (9) Thet fur ham forbearneth al to colen calde; thet pich ham forwalleth athet ha beon formealte ant eft acwikieth anan to drehen al thet ilke (ant muche deale wurse) áá withuten ende. (10) Ant tis ilke unhope is ham meast pine, thet nan naveth neaver mare hope of nan acoverunge, ah aren sikere of euch uvel to thurhleasten i wa, from world into worlde, áá on echnesse. (11) Euch athrusmeth other, ant euch is othres pine, ant euchan heateth other — ant himseolven — as |
fol. 75r   the blake deovel. (12) Ant eaver se ha i this world luveden ham mare, se ha ther heatieth ham swithere. (13) Ant either curseth other, ant fret of the othres earen ant te nease alswa. (14) Ich habbe bigunne to tellen of thing thet Ich ne mahte nawt bringe to eni ende, thah Ich hefde a thusent tungen of stele ant talde athet ha weren alle forwerede. (15) Ah thencheth nu herthurh hwuch the measte pine beo. (16) For the leaste pine is se heard thet, hefde a mon islein ba mi feader ant mi moder ant al the ende of mi cun, ant ido me seolven al the scheome ant te hearm thet cwic mon mahte tholien, ant Ich isehe thes mon i the ilke leaste pine thet Ich iseh in Helle, Ich walde (yef hit mahte beon) tholien a thusent deathes to arudden him ut throf, swa is the sihthe grislich ant reowthful to bihalden. (17) For thah neaver nere nan other pine bute to iseon eaver the unseli gastes ant hare grisliche schape — biseon on hare grimfule ant grurefule nebbes, ant heren hare rarunge ant hu

---

the chattering of teeth in the icy waters. (7) Quickly they flit from the heat into the cold, and they never know of those two which seems worse to them, for either is intolerable. (8) And in this terrible mix the latter afflicts them more because of the former. (9) That fire burns them up all to cold coals; that pitch boils them up until they are completely melted and again resurrects them at once to suffer all the same (and a great deal worse) forever without end. (10) And this same despair is the greatest pain to them, that they will not ever more have hope of any recovery but are certain of every evil to last in woe, from world into world, forever into eternity. (11) Each suffocates the other, and each is the other's suffering, and each one hates the other — and himself — like the black devil. (12) And always the more they loved someone in this world, the more they hate them there. (13) And each one curses the other, and gnaws at the other's ears and the nose also. (14) I have begun to tell of the things that I could not bring to any end, although I had a thousand tongues of steel and spoke until they were all worn out. (15) But consider now through this what the greatest pain may be. (16) For the least pain is so hard that, had a man slain both my father and my mother and all the remainder of my kin, and done to myself all the shame and the harm that a living man might suffer, and I saw this man in the same least pain that I saw in Hell, I would (if it might be) suffer a thousand deaths to deliver him out of there, the sight is so terrible and pitiful to behold. (17) For though there were never any other pain except to see the unholy spirits and their grisly shapes, to look upon their fierce and terrible faces, and to hear their roaring, and how with insults they blame and

ha with hokeres edwiteth ant upbreideth euchan his sunnen — this schenthlac ant te grure of ham were unimete pine, ant hure tholien ant abeoren hare unirude duntes with mealles istelet, ant with hare eawles gledreade hare dustlunges as thah hit were a pilche-clut euchan towart other i misliche pinen! (18) O Helle, Deathes hus

fol. 75v — wununge of wanunge, of grure ant of granunge, heatel | ham ant heard, wan of alle wontreathes, buri of bale ant bold of eavereuch bitternesse, thu lathest lont of alle, thu dorc stude ifullet of alle dreorinesses — Ich cwakie of grisle ant of grure, ant euch ban scheketh me ant euch her me rueth up of thi munegunge, for nis ther na stevene bituhhe the fordemde bute 'Wumme!' ant 'Wa is me!' ant 'Wa beo the!' ant 'Wa beo the!' 'Wa!' ha yeieth ant wa ha habbeth, ne of al thet eaver wa is ne schal ham neaver wontin. (19) The swuch wununge ofearneth for ei hwilinde blisse her o thisse worlde, wel were him yef thet he neaver ibore nere. (20) Bi this ye mahen sumdel witen hwuch is Helle, for iwis, Ich habbe thrin isehen a thusent sithe wurse, ant from theonne kimeth Death with a thusent deoflen hiderwart, as Ich seide, ant Ich com thus," quoth Fearlac, "for te warnin ow fore ant tellen ow theos tidinges."

15.   (1) "Nu Lauerd Godd," quoth Warschipe, "wardi us ant werie, ant rihte us ant reade hwet us beo to donne, ant we beon the warre ant wakere to witen us on euch half under Godes wengen. (2) Yef we wel werieth ant witeth ure hus ant Godes deore tresor thet He haveth bitaht us, cume Death hwen ha wule! (3) Ne thurve we nowther beon ofdred for hire ne for Helle, for ure death bith deore

---

upbraid everyone for his sins, this shame and terror for them would be an incomparable pain, and especially to suffer and endure their cruel blows with clubs of steel, and with their red-hot awls flinging each one toward the other — as though they were a leather-scrap! — into various pains. (18) Oh Hell, Death's house — dwelling-place of wailing, of great fright, and of groaning; cruel and hateful home, abode of afflictions, city of sorrow and hall of every bitterness, you most loathsome land of all, you dark place full of all drearinesses — I quake from horror and from terror, and every bone shakes me and each single hair stands up at your remembrance, for there is there no voice among the damned but "Alas!" and "Woe is me!" and "Woe be to you!" and "Woe be to you!" and "Woe!" they cry and woe they have, nor will they ever lack anything that is woe. (19) He who earns such a dwelling for any transitory bliss here in this world, it would have been better for him had he never been born. (20) By this you may know something about what Hell is like, for certainly I have seen in there a thousand times worse, and from thence comes Death with a thousand devils towards here, as I said, and thus I have come," said Fear, "in order to warn you beforehand and tell you these tidings."

15.   (1) "Now may Lord God," says Vigilance, "guard us and defend us, and direct us and advise what there is for us to do, and may we be the more wary and watchful to guard ourselves on every side under God's wings. (2) If we well defend and guard our house well and God's dear treasure which he has entrusted to us, come Death when she will! (3) We do not need to be afraid either of her or of Hell,

fol. 76r

Godd ant ingong into Heovene. (4) Of theos fikelinde world ne of hire false blisse ne neome we neaver yeme, for al thet is on eorthe nis bute as a schadewe, for al wurtheth | to noht bute thet deore tresor, Godes deorewurthe feh thet is us bitaht to witene. (5) Ich habbe thervore sar care, for Ich iseo," seith Warschipe, "hu the Unwhiht with his ferd ase liun iburst geath abuten ure hus, sechinde yeornliche hu he hit forswolhe. (6) Ant tis Ich mei," seith Warschipe, "warnin ow of his lath ant for his wrenches, ah Ich ne mei nawt ageines his strengthe."

16.

(1) "Do nu," quoth Strengthe, "Warschipe, suster, thet te limpet to the ant warne us of his wiheles, for of al his strengthe ne drede we nawiht, for nis his strengthe noht wurth bute hwer se he ifindeth etheliche ant wake, unwarnede of treowe bileave. (2) The apostle seith, 'Etstont then feont ant he flith ananriht.' (3) Schulde we thenne fleon him? (4) Ye, nis Godd ure scheld? (5) Ant alle beoth ure wepnen of His deore grace, ant Godd is on ure half ant stont bi us i fehte. (6) Yef he schute towart me with weole ant wunne of the world, with este of flesches lustes, of thulliche nesche wepnen Ich mahte carien summes weis, ah ne mei me na thing heardes offearen, ne nowcin ne na wone falsi min heorte ne wursi mi bileave towart Him thet yeveth me alle mine strengthen."

17.

fol. 76v

(1) "For ba me ah," quoth Meath, "ant for heart of nowcin ant for wone of wunne, dreden ant carien. (2) For moni for to muchel heard of wa thet he dreheth forget ure Lauerd, ant ma thah for nesche ant for flesches licunge for|yemeth ham ofte. (3) Bituhhen heard ant nesche, bituhhe wa of this world ant to muche wunne,

---

for our death will be dear to God and our entry into Heaven. (4) May we never take heed of this false world and of her false bliss, for all that is on earth is nothing but a shadow, for all turns to nothing except for that dear treasure, God's precious property which is given to us to guard. (5) Therefore I have great worry, for I see," says Vigilance, "how the Fiend with his army like an enraged lion goes about our house, seeking eagerly how he may swallow it up. (6) And I can do this," says Vigilance, "warn you of his hatred because of his tricks, but I can do nothing against his strength."

16.

(1) "Do now," says Strength, "Vigilance, sister, that which belongs to you and warns us of his wiles, for all of his strength we do not fear in any way, for his strength is not worthy except where he finds one easy and weak, unprotected by true belief. (2) The apostle says, 'Withstand the fiend and he flees immediately.' (3) Should we then flee him? (4) Yea, is not God our shield? (5) And all of our weapons are from His dear grace, and God is on our side and stands by us in the fight. (6) If he shoots towards me with wealth and the pleasure of the world, with the luxury of the flesh's lust, I might be somehow afraid of such soft weapons, but nothing hard may frighten me, and neither suffering nor want may falsify my heart nor weaken my belief towards Him who gives me all my strength."

17.

(1) "For both," says Moderation, "the hardness of suffering and for the lack of joy, one ought to dread and to be anxious. (2) For many forget our Lord because they suffer too much bitter adversity, and even more because of softness and for flesh's pleasure neglect themselves often. (3) Between hardness and softness, between the woe of this world and too much pleasure,

bituhhe muchel ant lutel, is in euch worldlich thing the middel wei guldene. (4) Yef we hire haldeth, thenne ga we sikerliche, ne therf us nowther for Death ne for deovel dreden. (5) Hwet se beo of heardes, ne drede Ich nawiht nesches, for ne mei na wunne ne na flesches licunge ne licomlich este bringe me over the middel of mesure ant of mete."

18.   (1) Rihtwissnesse speketh nu: "Mi suster," ha seith, "Warschipe, the haveth wit ant schad bituhhe god ant uvel, ant wat hwet is in euch thing to cheosen ant to schunien, readeth us ant leareth for te yeme lutel alle fallinde thing ant witen warliche theo the schulen áá lesten. (2) Ant seith as ha soth, seith thet thurh unweotenesse ne mei ha nawt sunegin, ant tah nis nawt siker of the unwihtes strengthe, as theo the halt hire wac — thah ha beo muche wurth to ure alre ehnen — ant demeth hire unmihti onont hireseolven to etstonden with his turnes, ant deth ase the wise. (3) Mi suster Strengthe is swithe bald ant seith thet nawiht heardes ne mei hire offearen; ah thah ha ne trust nawt on hire ahne wepnen ah deth o Godes grace, ant thet Ich demi riht ant wisdom to donne. (4) Mi thridde suster, Meath,

fol. 77r   speketh of the middel sti bituhhe riht ant luft thet lut cunnen halden, | ant seith i nesche ha is bald, ant heard mei hire offearen; ant forthi ne yelpeth ha of na sikernesse, ant deth as the wise. (5) Mi meoster is to do riht forte demen, ant Ich deme meseolf thet Ich thurh me ne do hit nawt, for al thet god is of Godd thet we her habbeth. (6) Nu is riht thenne thet we demen us seolf eaver unmihtie to werien ant to witen us other ei god to halden withute Godes helpe. (7) The rihtwise

---

between much and little, there is in every thing the golden middle way. (4) If we keep to it then we go securely, and we need not fear either Death or the Devil. (5) What there may be of suffering, I do not dread any softness, for no joy nor flesh's pleasure nor fleshly luxury may bring me away from the middle of measure and of moderation."

18.   (1) Righteousness speaks now: "My sister," she says, "Vigilance, who has wit and discrimination between good and evil, and knows what is to be chosen and to be shunned in each instance, advises us and teaches us to heed little every transitory thing and to guard warily those which will last always. (2) And as one who speaks the truth she says that although she may not sin through ignorance, she is not confident concerning the Fiend's strength, as she considers herself weak — although she is worth much in the eyes of all us — and she judges herself powerless on her part to stand firm against his tricks, and she does as the wise do. (3) My sister Strength is very brave and says that no hardship may frighten her; but nevertheless she does not trust at all in her own weapons but does trust in God's grace, and that I consider right and wise to do. (4) My third sister, Moderation, speaks of the middle path between right and left which few can hold, and she says in softness she is brave, and hardship may frighten her; and therefore she does not boast of any certainty, and she does as the wise do. (5) My role is to do right in order to judge, and I judge that I do not do it at all through myself, because all the good which we have here is from God. (6) Now it is right then that we judge ourselves always powerless to defend and to guard ourselves or to hold to any goodness without God's help. (7) The righteous God

Godd wule thet we demen us seolf etheliche ant lahe (ne beo we neaver swucche), for thenne demeth He us muche wurth ant gode ant halt for His dehtren. (8) For thah mi forme suster war beo of euch uvel, ant min other strong beo toyeines euch nowcin, ant mi thridde meathful in alles cunnes estes, ant Ich do riht ant deme, bute we, with al this, milde beon ant meoke ant halden us wake, Godd mei mid rihte fordemen us of al this thurh ure prude. (9) Ant forthi is riht dom thet we, al ure god, thonkin Him ane."

19. (1) Wit, the husebonde, Godes cunestable, hereth alle hare sahen ant thonketh God yeorne with swithe glead heorte of se riche lane as beoth theos sustren, His fowr dehtren thet He haveth ileanet him on helpe forte wite wel ant werien his castel ant Godes deorewurthe feh thet is biloke thrinne.

20. (1) The willesfule husewif halt hire al stille, ant al thet hird thet ha wes iwunet
fol. 77v to dreaien efter hire turneth | ham treowliche to Wit hare lauerd, ant to theos fowr sustren.

21. (1) Umben ane stunde speketh eft Warschipe ant seith, "Ich iseo a sonde cumen, swithe gledd icheret, feier ant freolich ant leofliche aturnet."

22. (1) "Let him in," seith Wit. "Yef Godd wule, he bringeth us gleade tidinges, ant thet us were muche neod, for Fearlac, Deathes sonde, haveth with his offearet us swithe mid alle." (2) Warschipe let him in ant he gret Wit, then lauerd, ant al thet hird seothen with lahhinde chere. (3) Ant ha yeldeth him his gretunge ant beoth alle ilihtet ant igleadet, ham thuncheth, of his onsihthe, for al thet hus schineth ant schimmeth of his leome. (4) He easketh ham yef ham biluveth to heren him ane hwile.

---

wishes that we judge ourselves worthless and low (may we never be so), for then He judges us greatly worthy and good and considers us his daughters. (8) For although my first sister is aware of every evil, and my other is strong against every adversity, and my third moderate in all kinds of pleasures, and I do rightly and judge, unless we with all of this are mild and meek and consider ourselves weak, God may rightly condemn us for all this because of our pride. (9) And therefore, it is a correct judgment that we, for all our good, should thank Him alone."

19. (1) Wit, the husband, God's constable, hears all their words and thanks God earnestly with a very glad heart for so rich a loan as these sisters are, His four daughters that He has loaned him as help to guard and defend his castle well and God's precious property that is enclosed inside.

20. (1) The willful housewife keeps entirely silent, and all that household that she was accustomed to draw after her turn truly to Wit their lord, and to those four sisters.

21. (1) After a while Vigilance speaks again and says, "I see a messenger come, very glad in appearance, fair and handsome and beautifully dressed."

22. (1) "Let him in," says Wit. "If God wishes, he brings us glad tidings, and that we need very much, for Fear, Death's messenger, has with his tidings frightened us greatly indeed." (2) Vigilance lets him in and he greets Wit, the lord, and all that household afterwards with a laughing expression. (3) And they return his greeting and are all lightened and gladdened, it seems to them, because of his appearance, for all that house shines and shimmers from his gleam. (4) He asks them if it pleases them to listen to him for a while.

23.   (1) "Ye," quoth ha (Rihtwisnesse), "wel us biluveth hit, ant wel is riht thet we the litheliche lustnin."

24.   (1) "Hercnith nu thenne," he seith, "ant yeornliche understondeth. (2) Ich am Murthes sonde ant munegunge of eche lif, ant Lives Luve ihaten, ant cume riht from Heovene thet Ich habbe isehen nu ant ofte ear, the blisse thet na monnes tunge ne mei of tellen. (3) The iblescede Godd iseh ow offruhte ant sumdel drupnin of thet Fearlac talde of Death ant of Helle, ant sende me to gleadien ow, nawt forthi thet hit ne beo al soth, thet he seide (ant thet schulen alle uvele fondin ant ifinden)

fol. 78r   ah ye with the fulst of Godd ne thurve na thing dreden, for He sit on | heh thet is ow on helpe, ant is alwealdent thet haveth ow to witene."

25.   (1) "A!" seith Warschipe, "welcume, Lives Luve! (2) Ant for the luve of Godd seolf, yef thu eaver sehe Him, tele us sumhwet of Him ant of His eche blisse."

26.   (1) "Ye, i seoth," quoth Lives Luve, Murhthes sonde, "Ich habbe isehen Him ofte; nawt tah alswa as He is, for ayein the brihtnesse ant te liht of His leor, the sunne-gleam is dosc ant thuncheth a schadewe, ant forthi ne mahte Ich nawt ayein the leome of His wlite lokin ne bihalden, bute thurh a schene schawere bituhhe me ant Him thet schilde mine ehnen. (2) Swa Ich habbe ofte isehen the Hali Thrumnesse — Feader ant Sune ant Hali Gast, threo an untodealet — ah lutle hwile Ich mahte tholie the leome. (3) Ah summes weis Ich mahte bihalden ure Lauerd Jesu Crist, Godes Sune, thet bohte us o Rode, hu He sit blisful on His Feader riht half thet is alwealdent. (4) Rixleth i thet eche lif bute linnunge, se unimete feier thet te engles ne beoth neaver ful on Him to bihalden. (5) Ant yet

---

23.   (1) "Yes," said she (Righteousness), "it pleases us well, and it is right well that we listen meekly to you."

24.   (1) "Listen now then," he says, "and earnestly understand. (2) I am Mirth's messenger and the remembrance of eternal life and am called Love of Life, and come straight from Heaven which I have seen now and often before, the bliss of which no man's tongue may tell of. (3) The blessed God sees you frightened and somewhat downcast from what Fear told of Death and of Hell, and sent me to gladden you, not because it is not all true, what he said (and, all the evil ones will discover that and find out); but you need fear nothing with the help of God, for He sits on high who is a help to you and is the Almighty who has you to guard."

25.   (1) "Ah!" says Vigilance, "welcome, Love of Life! (2) And for the love of God Himself, if you ever saw Him, tell us something of Him and of His eternal bliss."

26.   (1) "Yes, in truth," says Love of Life, Mirth's messenger, "I have often seen Him; though not just as He is, for against the brightness and the light of His face, the sun-gleam is dark and seems a shadow, and therefore I cannot look toward or behold the light of His face, except through a shining mirror between me and Him that shields my eyes. (2) Also I have often seen the Holy Trinity — Father and Son and Holy Ghost, three in one undivided — but I could endure the light only a little while. (3) But in some way I could behold our Lord Jesus Christ, the Son of God, who redeemed us on the Cross, how He sits blissfully on the right side of His Father who is almighty. (4) He rules in that eternal life without end, so immeasurably fair that the angels are never tired of looking upon Him. (5) And

ich iseh etscene the studen of His wunden, ant hu He schaweth ham His Feader to cuthen hu He luvede us ant hu He wes buhsum to Him the sende Him swa to alesen us; ant bisecheth Him áá for moncunnes heale.

27.
fol. 78v

(1) "Efter Him, Ich iseh on heh over alle heovenliche wordes the eadi meiden His moder, Marie inempnet, sitten in | a trone se swithe briht with gimmes istirret, ant hire wlite se weoleful thet euch eorthlich liht is theoster therayeines. (2) Thear Ich iseh as ha bit hire deorewurthe Sune se yeornliche ant se inwardliche for theo thet hire servith, ant He hire getteth blitheliche al thet ha bisecheth.

28.

(1) "Thet liht tha Ich ne mahte lengre tholien, Ich biseh to the engles ant to the archangles ant to the othre the beoth buven ham, iblescede gastes the beoth áá bivore Godd ant servith Him eaver ant singeth áá unwerget. (2) Nihe wordes ther beoth, ah hu ha beoth iordret ant sunderliche isette, the an buve the othre, ant euchanes meoster, were long to tellen. (3) Se muche murhthe Ich hefde on hare onsihthe thet ne mahte Ich longe hwile elleshwider lokin.

29.

(1) "Efter ham Ich iseh towart te patriarches ant te prophetes, the makieth swuch murhthe thet ha aren nuthe i thet ilke lont of blisse thet ha hefden of feor igret ear on eorthe. (2) Ant seoth nu al thet isothet thet ha hefden longe ear icwiddet of ure Lauerd, as He hefde ischawed ham i gastelich sihthe. (3) Ich iseh the apostles, poure ant lah on eorthe, ifullet ant bigoten al of unimete blisse sitten i trones, ant al under hare vet thet heh is i the worlde, yarowe forte demen i the dei of dome kinges ant keiseres ant alle cunreadnes of alles cunnes ledenes.

---

yet I saw clearly the places of His wounds, and how He shows them to His Father to make known how He loved us and how He was obedient to Him who sent Him thus to save us; and He beseeches Him always for mankind's salvation.

27.

(1) "After Him, I saw on high over all the heavenly hosts the blessed maiden His mother, named Mary, sitting on a throne so very bright starred with gems, and her face so joyful that every earthly light is dark in comparison. (2) There I watched as she prays to her precious Son so eagerly and so earnestly for those who serve her, and He grants her blissfully all that she requests.

28.

(1) "When I could no longer endure that light, I looked to the angels and to the archangels and to the others that are above them, the blessed spirits who are always before God and serve Him always and sing forever unwearied. (2) Nine hosts there are, but how they are ordered and separately set out, the one above the other, and each one's occupation, would be long to tell. (3) I had so much joy in their sight that I might not, for a long while, look elsewhere.

29.

(1) "After them I looked towards the patriarchs and the prophets, who make such mirth that they are now in that same land of bliss that they had from far away prayed for before on earth. (2) And they see now verified that which they had long before prophesied about our Lord, as he had showed them in spiritual sight. (3) I saw the apostles, poor and lowly on earth, entirely filled and drenched with immeasurable bliss sitting in thrones, and everything that is great in this world under their feet, ready to judge on the day of doom kings and emperors and all tribes of all kinds of languages.

fol. 79r
30. (1) | "Ich biheolt te martyrs ant hare unimete murhthe, the tholeden her pinen ant death for ure Lauerd, ant lihtliche talden to alles cunnes neowcins ant eorthliche tintreohen ageines the blisse thet Godd in hare heorte schawede ham to cumene.

31. (1) "Efter ham Ich biheolt the cunfessurs hird the liveden i god lif ant haliliche deiden, the schineth as doth steorren i the eche blissen, ant seoth Godd in His wlite thet haveth alle teares iwipet of hare ehnen.

32. (1) "Ich iseh thet schene ant thet brihte ferreden of the eadi meidnes ilikest towart engles, ant feolahlukest with ham blissin ant gleadien, the libbinde i flesche overgath flesches lahe ant overcumeth cunde, the leadeth heovenlich lif in eorthe as ha wunieth. (2) Hare murhthe ant hare blisse, the feierleac of hare wlite, the swetnesse of hare song — ne mei na tunge tellen. (3) Alle ha singeth the ther beoth, ah hare song ne mahe nane buten heo singen. (4) Se swote smeal ham folheth hwider se ha wendeth thet me mahte libben áá bi the swotnesse. (5) Hwam se heo bisecheth fore is sikerliche iborhen, for agein hare bisocnen Godd Himseolf ariseth, thet alle the othre halhen sittende ihereth."

33. (1) "Swithe wel," quoth Warschipe, "liketh us thet tu seist. (2) Ah nu thu havest se wel iseid of euch a setnesse of the seli sunderlepes, sumhwet sei us nu hwuch blisse is to alle iliche meane." (3) Ant Lives Luve hire ondswereth:

fol. 79v
34. (1) | "The imeane blisse is seovenfald: lengthe of lif, wit, ant luve; ant of the luve a gleadunge withute met murie; loftsong ant lihtschipe; ant sikernesse is the seovethe."

---

30. (1) "I beheld the martyrs and their immeasurable mirth, who suffered here pains and death for our Lord, and considered all kinds of sufferings and earthly torments light compared with the bliss to come which God showed them in their hearts.

31. (1) "After them I beheld the host of confessors who lived a good life and died blessedly, who shine as do the stars in eternal bliss, and see God in His beauty who has wiped all tears from their eyes.

32. (1) "I saw that shining and that bright company of blessed maidens most like angels, and most suited to be blissful and rejoice with them, who living in the flesh, surpass the flesh's law and overcome nature, who lead a heavenly life on earth while they live there. (2) Their mirth and their bliss, the beauty of their faces, the sweetness of their song — no tongue may tell. (3) All of them sing who are there, but their song none but they may sing. (4) So sweet a smell follows them wherever they go that one might live forever from the sweetness. (5) Whomever they pray for is definitely saved, for because of their requests God himself rises, who, seated, hears all the other saints."

33. (1) "Very much," said Vigilance, "do we like what you say. (2) But now you have said so well of every order of the holy ones separately, tell us now what bliss is for all alike in common." (3) And Love of Life answers her:

34. (1) "The communal bliss is seven-fold: length of life, wit, and love; and from that love a gladness joyful without moderation; a song of praise and lightness; and security is the seventh."

35.   (1) "Thah Ich this," seith Warschipe, "sumdel understonde, thu most unwreo this witerluker ant openin to theos othre."

36.   (1) "Ant hit schal beon," seith Lives Luve, "Warschipe, as thu wilnest."

37.   (1) "Ha livieth ááá in a wlite thet is brihtre seovevald ant schenre then the sunne, ant eaver in a strengthe to don (buten euch swinc) al thet ha wulleth, ant eaver mare in a steal in al thet eaver god is withute wonunge, withuten euch thing thet mahe hearmin other eilin, in al thet eaver is softe other swote. (2) Ant hare lif is Godes sihthe ant Godes cnawlechunge, as ure Lauerd seide: 'Thet is,' quoth He, 'eche lif, to seon ant cnawen soth Godd ant Him thet He sende — Jesu Crist ure Lauerd — to ure alesnesse.' (3) Ant beoth forthi ilich Him i the ilke wlite thet He is, for ha seoth him as He is nebbe to nebbe. (4) Ha beoth se wise thet ha witen alle Godes reades, His runes ant His domes, the derne beoth ant deopre then eni sea dingle. (5) Ha seoth i Godd alle thing, ant witen of al thet is ant wes ant eaver schal iwurthen: hwet hit beo, hwi, ant hwerto, ant hwerof hit bigunne.

38.   (1) "Ha luvieth God withute met for thet ha understondeth hu He haveth bi ham idon thurh His muchele godlec, ant hwet ha ahen His deorewurthe milce to yelden. (2) Ant euchan luveth other ase muchel as himseolven.

fol. 80r   (1) "Se gleade ha beoth of Godd thet al is hare blisse se muchel | thet ne mei
39.   hit munne, na muth ne spealie na speche. (2) Forthi thet euchan luveth other as himseolven, euchan haveth of othres god ase muche murhthe as of his ahne. (3) Bi this ye mahen seon ant witen thet euchan haveth sunderlepes ase feole gleadschipes as ha beoth monie alle, ant euch of the ilke gleadschipes is to eavereuch

---

35.   (1) "Though I," says Vigilance, "somewhat understand this, you must reveal this more plainly and explain it to these others."

36.   (1) "And it will be," says Love of Life, "Vigilance, as you wish."

37.   (1) "They live forever in a splendor that is brighter sevenfold and more beautiful than the sun, and always in strength (without any effort) to do all that they wish, and forevermore in a state of all that is ever good without ceasing, without anything that might harm or annoy, in all that is ever soft and sweet. (2) And their life is the sight of God and the knowledge of God, as our Lord said: 'That is,' said He, 'eternal life, to see and to know true God and Him whom He sent — Jesus Christ our Lord — for our deliverance.' (3) And therefore they are like Him in the same splendor that He is in, for they see Him as He is face to face. (4) They are so wise that they understand all God's plans, His secret counsels and His judgments, which are secret and deeper than any sea trench. (5) They see in God all things and know of all that is and was and ever will be: what it is, why, and wherefore, and from where it began.

38.   (1) "They love God without measure since they understand what He has done for them through His great goodness, and what they ought to give back for His precious mercy. (2) And each one loves the other as much as himself.

39.   (1) "They are so glad in God that all their bliss is so great that it may not be remembered, nor may any mouth or speech describe it. (2) Since each one loves the other as himself, each one has of the other's good fortune as much mirth as of his own. (3) By this you may see and know that each one has separately as many gladnesses as they all are many, and each of the same gladnesses is to every one

an ase muche gleadunge as his ahne sunderliche. (4) Yet over al this, hwen euchan luveth Godd mare then himseolven ant then alle the othre, mare he gleadeth of Godd withuten ei etlunge then of his ahne gleadunge ant of alle the othres. (5) Neometh nu thenne yeme! (6) Yef neaver anes heorte ne mei in hire undervon hire ahne gleadunge sunderliche — se unimete muchel is the anlepi blisse — hu is hit thet ha nimeth in hire thus monie ant thus muchele? (7) Forthi seide ure Lauerd to theo the Him hefden icwemet: *Intra in gaudium, et cetera.* (8) 'Ga,' quoth He, 'into thi Lauerdes blisse.' (9) Thu most al gan thrin, ant al beon bigotten thrin, for in the ne mei hit nanes weis neomen in. (10) Herof ha herieth Godd ant singeth áá, unwerget, eaver iliche lusti in His loft-songes as hit iwriten is: *Beati qui habitant, et cetera.* (11) 'Eadi beoth theo, Lauerd, the i Thin hus wunieth. (12) Ha schulen herien The from worlde into worlde.'

40.
fol. 80v

(1)"Ha beoth alle as lihte ant as swifte as the sunne-gleam the scheot from est into west ase thin | ehe-lid tuneth ant openeth, for hwer se eaver the gast wule the bodi is ananriht withute lettunge. (2) For ne mei ham na thing ageines etstonden, for euch an is almihti to don al thet he wule; ye, makie to cwakien Heovene ba ant eorthe with His an finger.

41.

(1) "Sikere ha beoth of al this: of thulli lif, of thulli wit, of thulli luve ant gleadunge throf, ant of thulli blisse, thet hit ne mei neaver mare lutlin ne wursin ne neome nan ende. (2) This lutle Ich habbe iseid of thet Ich iseh in Heovene, ah nower neh ne seh Ich al, ne thet yet thet Ich seh ne con Ich half tellen."

42.

(1) "Witerliche," quoth Warschipe. (2) "Wel we understondeth thet tu havest ibeo

---

as much gladness as his own separately. (4) Yet over all this, when each one loves God more than himself and than all the others, the more he rejoices in God without any estimation more than from his own gladness and that of all the others. (5) Now then, take heed! (6) If never once may a heart receive in itself its own gladness separately — so immeasurably great is the single bliss — how is it that they take in itself so many and so much? (7) Because our Lord said to those who had pleased Him: *Enter into rejoicing, etc.* (8) 'Go,' said He, 'into your Lord's bliss.' (9) You must all go into it, and be completely suffused by it, for it cannot in any way enter into you. (10) Because of this they praise God and sing forever unwearied, ever alike happy in His praise-songs as it is written: *Blessed are those who live, etc.* (11) 'Blessed are those, Lord, who dwell in Your house. (12) They will praise You from world into world.'

40.

(1) "They are all as light and as swift as the sun-beam which shoots from east into west in the blink of an eye as your eyelid closes and opens, for wheresoever the spirit wishes to go the body is at once without delay. (2) For nothing may stand against them, for each one is almighty to do what he wishes; yea, he makes both heaven and earth quake with His one finger.

41.

(1) "They are certain of all this: of such life, of such wit, of such love and gladness thereof, and of such bliss, that it may never more diminish nor worsen nor come to any end. (2) This little I have said of what I saw in Heaven, but I saw nowhere near all, nor can I tell half of that which I saw."

42.

(1) "Certainly," says Vigilance. (2) "Well do we understand that you have been

thear ant soth havest iseid trof efter thi sihthe. (3) Ant wel is him thet is war ant bisith him hu he mahe beast halden his hus — thet Godes tresor is in — ayeines Godes unwine, the weorreth thertowart áá with untheawes; for thet schal bringen him thider as he schal al this thet tu havest ispeken of an hundret sithe mare, of blisse buten euch bale folhin ant ifinden."

43.

Royal fol. 10a

(1) Quoth Strengthe: "Hwen hit swa is, hwet mei tweamen us from Godd ant halden us theonne? (2) Ich am siker ine Godd thet ne schal lif ne deth — ne wa ne wunne nowther — | todealen us ant His luve thet al this haveth us iyarcket, yef we as treowe tresurers witeth wel His tresor thet is bitaht us to halden, as we schulen ful wel under His wengen."

44.   (1) "Warpeth ut," quoth Warschipe, "Farlac, ure fa! Nis nawt riht thet an hus halde theos tweien; for ther as Murthes sonde is, ant soth Luve of eche Lif, Farlac is fleme."

45.   (1) "Nu, ut!" quoth Strenthe. "Farlac, ne schaltu na lengere leven in ure ende."

46.   (1) "Nu," quoth he, "Ich seide for god al thet Ich seide, ant thah hit muri nere, nes na lessere mi tale then wes Murhthes sondes, ne unbihefre to ow, thah hit ne beo so licwurthe ne icweme."

47.   (1) "Either of ow," quoth Meath, "haveth his stunde to speokene, ne nis incker nothres tale to schunien in his time. (2) Thu warnest of wa; he telleth of wunne; muche neod is thet me ow ba yeornliche hercni. (3) Flute nu, Farlac, thah hwil Lives Luve is herinne, ant thole with efne heorte the dom of Rihtwisnesse, for thu schal ful blitheliche beon underfon in as ofte as Lives Luve stutteth for to spekene."

---

there and have told the truth of that according to your sight. (3) And it is well for him who is wary and looks to how he may best protect his house — which God's treasure is in — against God's enemy, who makes war upon it always with vices; for that will bring him to where he will seek and find all this of which you spoke and a hundred times more, of bliss without any hardship."

43.   (1) Says Strength: "When it is so, what may separate us from God and keep us from there? (2) I am certain in God that neither will life nor death — nor woe or joy either — will divide us from His love which has prepared all this for us, if we as true treasurers guard well His treasure that is given to us to keep, as we will full well under His wings."

44.   (1) "Cast out," says Vigilance, "Fear, our foe! It is not right that a house should hold these two; for where Mirth's messenger is, and true Love of eternal Life, Fear is an outlaw."

45.   (1) "Now, out!" says Strength. "Fear, you will no longer remain in our quarter."

46.   (1) "Now," says he, "I said for good all that I said, and though it was not cheerful, my tale was no less important than was that of Mirth's messenger, nor less profitable to you, though it is not so agreeable or pleasant."

47.   (1) "Each of you," says Moderation, "has his turn to speak and neither of your tales should be shunned during its turn. (2) You warn of woe; he tells of joy; there is much need for one to listen to you both earnestly. (3) Depart now, Fear, while Love of Life is here, and endure with an even heart the judgment of Righteousness, for you will very happily be received in as often as Love of Life ceases to speak."

48. (1) Nu is Wil thet husewif al stille — thet er wes so willesful — al ituht efter Wittes wissunge, thet is husebonde. (2) Ant al thet hird halt him stille, thet wes iwunet to beon fulitohen ant don efter Wil, hare lefdi, ant nawt efter Wit.(3) Lustneth nu his lare ant fondeth, eavereuch an, efter thet him limpeth to thurh theos twa sonden thet ha iherd habbeth, ant thet fowr sustren lerden thruppe: for euch untheawes inyong his warde te witene ant te warden treowliche.

fol. 10b
49. (1) | Thus ah mon te thenchen ofte ant ilome ant with thulliche thohtes awecchen his heorte, the i slep of yemeles forget hire sawle heale, efter theos twa sonden: from Helle sihthe biseon to the blisse of Heovene; to habben farlac of thet an, luve toward thet other, ant leaden him ant his hinen (thet beoth his limen alle) nawt efter that his Wil, the untohe lefdi, ant his lust leareth ah efter thet Wit wul, thet is husebonde; tuhten ant teachen thet Wit ga ever biuore ant drahe Wil efter him to al thet he dihteth ant demeth to donne, ant with the fowr sustren, the fowr heved theawes, Warschipe ant Strencthe in Godd, ant Meth ant Rihtwisnesse, witen Godes treosor — thet is, his ahne sawle — i the hus of the bodi from the theof of Helle. (2) Thulli thoht maketh mon te fleon alle untheawes ant ontent his heorte toward the blisse of Heovene, thet ure Lauerd yeve us thurh His hali milce, thet with the Feder ant te Sune ant te Hali Gast rixleth in threohad áá buten ende. (3) AMEN.

50. (1) Par seinte charité, biddeth a Pater Noster for Johan thet theos boc wrat.

51. (1) Hwa se this writ haveth ired

---

48. (1) Now Will that housewife is entirely silent — who before was so willful — fully guided according to the instruction of Wit, who is husband. (2) And all that company holds itself still, that was accustomed to be foolish and follow Will, their lady, and not after Wit. (3) They listen now to his lore and concern themselves, every one, about what pertains to them because of these two messengers whom they have heard, and what the four sisters taught previously: to keep his watch and defend truly against every vice's entrance.

49. (1) Thus one ought to think often and frequently of these two messengers, and with such thoughts awaken one's heart, which in the sleep of negligence forgets its soul's salvation: from the sight of Hell to look up to the bliss of Heaven, to have fear of that one, love toward that other, and to lead himself and his servants (which are all his limbs) not according to what his Will, the unruly lady, and his desire teaches, but according to what Wit who is husband wishes, to discipline and teach that Wit goes always before and draws Will after him in all that he orders and judges necessary to be done, and with the four sisters, the four chief virtues, Vigilance and Strength in God, and Moderation and Righteousness, to guard from the thief of Hell God's treasure — that is, his own soul — in the house of the body. (2) Such a thought makes one flee all vices and inflames one's heart toward the bliss of Heaven, which our Lord gave us through His holy mercy, who with the Father and the Son and the Holy Ghost rules in the Trinity forever without end. (3) AMEN.

50. (1) For holy charity, pray an *Our Father* for John who copied this book.

51. (1) Whoever has read this writing

52.	(1) Ant Crist him haveth swa isped,
53.	(1) Ich bidde par seinte charité
54.	(1) Thet ye bidden ofte for me:
55.	(1) Áá *Pater Noster* ant *Ave Marie*,
56.	(1) Thet Ich mote thet lif her drehen,
57.	(1) Ant ure Lauerd wel icwemen
58.	(1) I mi yuhethe ant in min elde,
59.	(1) Thet Ich mote Jhesu Crist mi sawle yelden. AMEN.

52.	(1) And Christ has so him profited,
53.	(1) I pray for holy charity
54.	(1) That you pray often for me:
55.	(1) *Our Father* and *Hail Mary* always,
56.	(1) That I might lead my life here,
57.	(1) And please our Lord well
58.	(1) In my youth and in my old age,
59.	(1) That I may yield my soul to Christ. AMEN.

EXPLANATORY NOTES TO *SAWLES WARDE*

ABBREVIATIONS: *AW*: *Ancrene Wisse*, ed. Hasenfratz; **B**: Bodleian Library MS Bodley 34 [base text]; **BS**: Bennett and Smithers edition (1968); ***BT***: Bosworth and Toller, *Anglo-Saxon Dictionary*; ***CT***: *Canterbury Tales*; ***HM***: *Hali Meithhad*; ***MED***: Middle English Dictionary; **MWB**: Millett and Wogan-Browne edition (1990); ***OED***: *Oxford English Dictionary*; **R**: British Library MS Royal 17 A XXVII; ***SJ***: *The Liflade ant te Passiun of Seinte Juliene*; ***SM***: *The Liflade and te Passiun of Seinte Margarete*; ***SW***: *Sawles Warde*; **T**: British Library MS Cotton Titus D XVIII; **W**: Wilson edition (1938).

Header   *Sawles Warde. SW* is a translation of a sermon, "De Custodia Interioris Hominis," attributed to St. Anselm by R. W. Southern and F. S. Schmitt (*Memorials of St. Anselm*). Generations of critics falsely identified the source as Hugh of St. Victor's *De Anima* 4.13–15, though Becker points out that this false identification was used "before *De Custodia* was edited critically" ("Source Text," pp. 44–45). Robertson notes that scholars have insufficiently acknowledged "De Custodia" (*Early English Devotional Prose*, p. 208).

1.1   *Si sciret paterfamilias . . . perfodi domum suam.* Compare Matthew 24:43 and Luke 12:39. Perkins identifies this verse as the "pericope" from which the rest of the text develops: "The figural nature of the verse is already apparent in the Gospel, and . . . initiates a process of narrative and figurative development" ("Reading the Bible," p. 211). Perkins discusses the rich interplay of metaphor and biblical allusion, where reference to the "theof" (sin, the Devil) entering the "hus" (body) to steal the "tresure" (soul) consistently relies and builds upon images from Gospel verses, particularly Luke (12:36, 34, and 39) and Matthew (6:20). Perkins' exhaustive identification of scriptural verses tied to the text of *SW* has been extremely helpful in compiling these notes, and many of our references have been borrowed from his discussion.

3.2   *te fulitohe wif mei beon wil ihaten.* Hassel sees the introduction of Will as wife as "disrupt[ing] neat dualism, preventing a simple dichotomy of gender . . . although she is contrasted most obviously with Reason, Will is also envisioned as an alternative or opposite to the other women in the narrative, the four virginal Virtues. The role or image of women in *Sawles Warde* is not consistent and stable. Rather, the meaning of women in the text depends on position, their relationship to masculine authority" (*Choosing Not to Marry*, p. 87). For an earlier discussion of gender in *SW* see Robertson, *Early English Devotional Prose*, pp. 126–43; for a more recent discussion see Masha Raskolnikov, *Body against Soul*.

Wit is the translator's word for the Latin *animus*, which refers specifically to the intellectual powers of the soul rather than the spirit of the soul (*anima*). Wit regularly appears in Middle English allegorical texts, often representing the intellectual powers of reasoning and standing in for the Latin term *ratio*. However, compare the use of the term in Langland and Chaucer, where *wit* describes natural human intelligence as opposed to knowledge based on education or *auctoritas*. In *Piers Plowman*, Will often must rely on his "kynde wit" (natural wit) instead of the corrupt words of clerics. See for example Conscience's declaration in regards to the practices of clerical orders: "'by Criste, kynde wit me telleth / It is wikked to wage yow" (B.XX.268–69). Chaucer's Friar Thomas, in contrast, relies solely on his natural intelligence when he should be using this natural intelligence together with the Scriptures in his preaching: "I have to day been at youre chirche at messe, / And seyd a sermon after my symple wit — / Nat al after the text of hooly writ" (*CT* III[D] 1788–90).

3.7   *fol semblant*. This line is the first occurrence of "semblant" in Middle English, borrowed from the French word for "face." Skaffari notes that this example shows "great adherence to the orthography of the *source language*" ("Lexical Borrowings, p. 89, italics in original) which could demonstrate a very recent borrowing from the French. This phrase is one of two entirely "French-derived elements" in the text (Skaffari, "Lexical Borrowings," p. 92), and the first instance of a phrase which was to become common in later Middle English. However, the *MED* distinguishes *falssemblaunt* (*fals* (adj.), sense 1b) as in Gower's quasi-allegorical use in the *Confessio Amantis* ("treacherous, untrustworthy"), and *fol semblaunt* (*fol* (adj.), sense 2) which cites this line of *SW* to mean "evil appearance or demeanor." The difference lies in the prefix *fals* rooted in Latin *falsum* and *fol* rooted in Old French *fol* ("foolish, mad, crazy" [Hindley et al., p. 323] which carries over to Middle English to mean not just "foolish, stupid" [*MED fol* (adj.), sense 1a] but "sinful, wicked" [sense 1b] as well). Hence we should be cautious about making any connection here between *fol semblant* and the later *falssemblaunt*.

3.8   *efter hire*. I.e., according to her will.

3.9   *ham*. Refers to the "hinen" the five senses, while "wit" remains in the singular since it refers to the singular sense.

3.11–13   *Ah ne bihoveth . . . amurthrin hire thrinne*. The author's description of the thief and murderer here allegorically describes the process of sin and temptation; the numerous thieves represent the vices (classified under the Seven Deadly Sins) and the guards their opposing virtues. In keeping with the pervasive emphasis on vigilance in *SW*, the idea is that should the guards fail to maintain watch, the vices may approach the house, break in, and steal the most sacred treasure: the human soul. This metaphor for sin and temptation builds on Matthew 24:43 and Luke 12:39. See Hassel's discussion of this metaphor as it compares to *AW* (*Choosing Not to Marry*, pp. 91–95).

3.13   *Godes deore castel*. For a history of the metaphor of self as castle, see Christina Whitehead, *Castles of the Mind*, as well as Christopher Cannon's discussion of the role defensive structures play in the imagination of the authors of the Katherine Group in his *Grounds of English Literature*.

3.15   *keis*. A word of Welsh origins, from *cais* (plural *caisiaid*), referring to a historical class of sergeants, policemen of a kind who helped enforce the law and carry out executions (Breeze, "Welsh Cais," p. 298). Breeze argues that the term carried extremely "penetrating implications for the forms of evil" due to the historical role of the *caisiaid* in Wales and the marches, hence the use of the term for the devil's henchmen (p. 303). See Breeze for a thorough discussion of the origins and contexts of the term and its implications in English and Welsh. The presence of Welsh terms in the Katherine Group indicates to some extent the geographical origin of the language: see Dobson, *Origins of Ancrene Wisse*, pp. 115–16; as well as Russell-Smith, "*Keis in Sawles Warde*." Other Welsh terms in the Katherine Group include *cader* (*HM* 29.2), *cokkunge* (*HM* 41.3), *genow* (*SM* 31.9). See also Cannon, *Grounds of English Literature*, pp. 139–71, for a discussion of the significance of the Welsh marches to the imagination of the Katherine Group.

    ure Lauerd haveth . . . of his dehtren. Originally described as the Four Virtues in "De Custodia," *SW*'s four daughters are an early English incarnation of the Four Daughters of God: Vigilance, Strength, Moderation, and Righteousness (Robertson, *Early English Devotional Prose*, p. 130). A more traditional version of the Four Daughters, such as that in *Piers Plowman*, consists of Truth, Mercy, Justice, and Peace. The daughters play a different role in *SW*, as they are frequently depicted in other English literatures as debating the righteousness of the possible salvation of humanity through Christ's sacrifice (compare the *Castle of Perseverance* [lines 3129–3649], *Piers Plowman* B.XVIII, and the Salutation in the Mary Play of the N-Town cycle). For an early and yet-to-be superseded discussion of the history of the Four Daughters of God see Traver, "The Four Daughters of God: A Mirror," as well as her monograph *The Four Daughters of God*.

3.16   *The earste is . . . Rihtwisnesse the feorthe*. To the Latin source's list of the cardinal virtues Prudentia, Fortitudo and Iustitia, the author adds Temperentia, in Middle English, *meath*.

    Warschipe. Literally, "ware-ship," i.e., the quality of being watchful and aware. See *MED warshipe* (n.), sense a. Savage and Watson translate as "Caution." It should be noted that Warschipe in *SW* does not solely concern awareness of one's physical space, but a moral watchfulness as well, hence the alternative translation, "prudence" (see *MED warshipe* (n.), sense b).

4.1   *Wit, the husbonde, Godes cunestable*. Though the texts in the Katherine Group have been read frequently as intentionally nativist works, as part of the first movement to compose in the vernacular again after the Norman conquest, the language itself demonstrates the international nature of early Middle English. Skaffari points out that this phrase uses words of French (*conestable*), Germanic (*God*), and Scandinavian (*hus-bonda*) origins ("Lexical Borrowings," p. 82). The line also records the first instance of *cunestable* in Middle English and means "the chief officer of the household, court, administration, or military forces of a ruler" (*OED constable* (n.), sense 1). See also W, p. 47n42. See also BS who note that constable used as "'governor of a (royal) fortress' is perhaps more appropriate than 'chief officer of a household' (*OED* s.v. 1) and perhaps more likely to be in the mind of a [West Midlands] writer at a time when royal castles were being built to hold the Welsh border" (p. 421n43).

4.3   *Meath . . . tuht forte halden.* Price ("Moderation in *Sawles Warde*") illustrates the implications of the different manuscript readings of these lines. Our text follows B and T, whereas R reads, instead of "the middel of twa uveles," "þe middel of twa þing" (W, p. 6). Price considers this difference "a good example of the *lectio difficilior* principle" and chooses the B/T text over R since it illustrates more closely the Ciceronian and Aristotelian concepts of moderation, such as those discussed in Aquinas' *De medio virtutum*. However, Price does not consider this single instance to be enough evidence to consider *SW* as a part of the "early thirteenth century's assimilation of Aristotelian material," although it does reflect the "author's command of contemporary intellectual interests" while placing them in the context of "psycho-moral thinking" (pp. 116–17).

mete, thet me "meosure" hat. Of note is that the writer here defines "meosure" according to another synonym; thus Dor suggests that *meosure* may be a recent loan word from French ("Post-Dating Romance"). The *MED* lists the earliest occurrences of "mesure" in *SW* (this line) and the roughly contemporary Trinity College, Cambridge Homilies.

5.3   *lonc.* Related to "lank" according to *MED lank* (adj.), sense a, which cites this line to mean "skinny, lean." T reads "long" which refers to height or stature (*MED long* (adj.1), sense 1b). "Lank" or "lanky" implies, in modern idiom at least, height in addition to skinniness, hence our translation.

leor. Derived from Old English *hleor*, this native term for "face" is used twice in the text, here and at 26.1 (*BT, hleor* (n.)). Skaffari notes that both instances are used in alliterative passages ("Lexical Borrowings," p. 86), and the author's choice of this term (over the two other words — *nebbe* and *wlite* — used throughout the text for "face") indicates an attempt to link native vocabulary with native poetic devices.

elheowet. Literally, "ill-hued."

6.3   *thet best con bisetten hire wordes.* I.e., express herself.

7.1–2   *Ich nat nawt . . . . me least weneth.* These lines conflate several biblical verses, and also echo the earlier pericope for the entire text (see the explanatory note 1.1). Compare in particular Matthew 24:36 (where Christ predicts the end of days: "But of that day and hour no one knoweth: no, not the angels of heaven, but the Father alone"); Matthew 25:13 (on the parable of the foolish and wise virgins: "Watch ye therefore, because you know not the day nor the hour"); and 1 Thessalonians 5:2 ("For yourselves know perfectly that the day of the Lord shall come as a thief in the night") and 5:6 ("Therefore, let us not sleep, as others do: but let us watch, and be sober"). Two separate topics of interest to the author of

SW seem to be raised between these lines and 1.1–2.2: first, the author further emphasizes the need for constant vigilance against sin, given Death's penchant for arriving suddenly and unexpectedly. Secondly, through biblical allusion, the author may be referring to the double use of the thief metaphor: while it often stands in (as in 1.1) for sinfulness, and sometimes even for the Devil himself, the reversal of the metaphor to indicate Christ's coming in 1 Thessalonians indicates the power of choice, as indicated by the two thieves on either side of Christ during the Crucifixion.

7.3   *euchan bereth a gret boc al of sunnen.* See Apocalypse 20:12–15.

with soth schrift ant with deadbote. Compare *HM* 8.23.

8.1–13.1   *Ant Warschipe hire . . . Ich chulle reodien.* Eggebroten, who asserts that *SW* is a translation of Hugh of St. Victor's *De anima*, sees this playful dramatic dialogue as evidence that our text was intended for "gently bred young women . . . of landed families, familiar with courteous life centered on the great hall of a manor or castlel [sic]." Thus, the arrival of a visitor from the outside world who came bearing exciting news would be familiar to the female audience of the tale ("*Sawles Warde*: A Retelling of De Anima," p. 32). However, compare Perkins' overview of *SW*'s changes from the source; he notes that the drastic reduction of active dialogue like this from "De Custodia" suits *SW* better to its central task of sermonizing ("Reading the Bible," p. 211).

9.1–14.20   *Ich cume . . . ow theos tidinges.* According to W, the details of the descriptions of Hell are additions by the Middle English adapter, as it is far more detailed than its Latin source. There are two major sources for medieval descriptions of Hell: *The Vision of St. Paul* (an early Christian apocryphal account of St. Paul's visions of heaven and hell) and the sixth-century *Sunday Letter* (see W, p. 53n90). Robertson argues that such detailed description is characteristic of texts written for women and the uneducated (*Early English Devotional Prose*, pp. 126–94).

14.4   *ham to grisle ant to grure.* MWB glosses as "to their horror."

14.6   *Ther is remunge . . . the snawi weattres.* Compare Matthew 24:51, 25:30, and 22:13.

hechelunge. W notes this as the only occurrence of the word in Middle English (p. 57n109). *MED* defines *hechelynges* as the combing or heckling of flax. Following *tothes*, it is defined as "gnashing or chattering of teeth." Alone, a *hechele* is "an instrument for carding flax" (*MED hechel(e* (n.)) which would not seem to relate clearly to the chattering of teeth! We have based our translation on the typical English translation of Matthew 24:51, upon which the text is based: *stridor dentium* — "gnashing of teeth."

14.10   *unhope.* W notes the rarity of the term *unhope.* Compare *AW*: "hit walde to swithe hurten ower heorte ant makien ow swa offeraret, thet ye mahten sone — thet Godd forbeode ow! — fallen i desesperance — thet is, in an unhope ant an unbileave for-te beon i-borhen" [it would too severely wound your heart and make you so afraid that you could soon — may God forbid that for you — fall into despair — that is, into a hopelessness and a disbelief that you will be saved] (ed. Hasenfratz, p. 64, lines 72–74). According to *MED*, *unhope* (n.) is only otherwise used in the fifteenth-century *Complaint Against Hope*. The more common term is *wanhope* (n.), though *MED* does not record any uses of it before 1325.

14.13   *fret of.* Compare a similar use of the same verb just a few lines earlier at 14.4: "tadden ant froggen the freoteth ham ut te ehnen ant te nease-gristles." *MED* suggests that the verb *freten*, when followed by *of*, would mean "to partake of, to eat of" (*freten* (v.1), senses 1a(b)). We have translated somewhat more liberally as "gnaws at" in order to evoke the earlier image of toads and frogs gnawing. The echo is possibly intentional on the part of the author since the sinners are not only gnawed on by the worms of Hell but become worms of Hell through their continual and corrosive hatred of each other.

14.17   *pilche-clut.* *MED* cites this line (*pilche* (n.), sense g) as meaning "a ragged pilch." MWB translates as "a scrap of hide" (p. 93), and W as "rags, old cloth" (p. 111). The *OED* cites two instances of the phrase, one in this line of *SW*, and the other in *Richard Coer de Lyon*, line 6806 (A version).

14.18   *O Helle, Deathes hus . . . ham neaver wontin.* Fearlac's rhetorically terrifying apostrophe to Hell features concrete details of suffering. Millett connects these lines to the Old English *Homilies of Wulfstan*, which our text closely parallels: "Ðær is ece bryne grimme gemencged, [and] þær is ece gryre; þær is granung [and] wanung [and] aa singal heof," demonstrating clearly the passage's "distinctively 'native' techniques of rhythm and alliteration" ("Continuity of English Prose," p. 103) [There is eternal burning savagely stirred up, and there is eternal terror; there is groaning and howling and forever everlasting grief]. See also Robertson's discussion of the concretion of the anonymous homilies in connection with the style of these texts (*Early English Devotional Prose*, pp. 144–80).

'Wa beo the!' ant 'Wa beo the!' B has identical "and 'Wa beo the!'," as does T. This looks like an inadvertent repetition, perhaps done in a base text for all three copies that are no longer extant. However, in none of the manuscripts is the repetition marked for deletion. Also, T initially writes the second "the" as "theo" with the *o* marked for deletion (as noted by W, p. 17), which suggests care in the composition of the text. Perhaps, as noted above, the mistake was in the exemplar, or perhaps it is not a mistake at all. Fearlac says earlier that the damned souls in Hell spend far more time cursing each other than they do themselves, so perhaps the repetition of "woe be to you!" attests to this tendency. MWB deals with the repetition by adding emphasis on the second "the" though there is no evidence for this in B.

14.19   *wel were him yef thet he neaver ibore nere.* Compare Matthew 26:24.

15.5   *Ich habbe thervore . . . he hit forswolhe.* Compare 1 Peter 5:8.

16.2   *The apostle seith . . . he flith ananriht.* Compare James 4:7.

16.4–5   *Ye, nis Godd . . . His deore grace.* Compare Ephesians 6:16.

17.2   *foryemeth ham.* MWB glosses this as a passive instance of *foryemen* meaning "are negligent" (p. 181); however, we have chosen to translate the phrase as a reflexive, to "neglect themselves" because of the implication that forgetting God is also a process of forgetting or neglecting the self.

18.2   *onont hireseolven.* See W, p. 49n57, regarding the occurrence of "onont" in the Bodley 34 group. It also occurs at 4.5 of this text. W says it could be related to Old English *on-emn* (which the *MED* records as a preposition meaning "besides, etc."). See *MED anentes* (prep.), sense 5a: "with respect to, as regards, concerning" and *MED anent(es* (adv.): "approximately, about."

18.7   *ne beo we neaver swucche.* MWB translates as "even if we are not" (p. 97); we have chosen a more literal translation.

22.1   *his.* Refers back to the "tidinges" earlier in the same sentence.

26.1   *leor.* See the explanatory note to 5.3 above (*leor*).

28.1   *engles ant to the archangles.* The nine orders of angels are: Angels, Archangels, Virtues, Powers, Principalities, Dominations, Throne, Cherubim, and Seraphim. While the orders of angels are mentioned frequently throughout the Bible, they are organized hierarchically in *De Coelesti Hierarchia* of Dionysius the Pseudo-Aeropagite, and known later in the Middle Ages through the writings of Gregory the Great (see MWB, p. 157n100/23).

29.1–2   *Efter ham Ich iseh . . . . i gasteliche sihthe.* Compare Hebrews 11:13. "Gastelich sihthe" means spiritual visions.

29.3   *alles cunnes ledenes.* According to W, *ledenes* in Old English meant Latin, but by this date meant any foreign language (p. 71n281). See also *BT, Læden* (n.), which indicates that even by the tenth century *Læden* could mean Latin (sense 1) or "any tongue, speech, language" (sense 2). A number of the Bodley 34 texts share a self-consciousness about language; for example, see *SM* 74.1 and the corresponding explanatory note. Both MWB and Savage and Watson translate this line more generally as "nation."

30.1–32.4   *Ich biheolt te . . . . halhen sittende ihereth.* SW omits what Perkins calls the "coenobitic heroes" of its Latin source, *De Custodia*: the "'apostolici et doctores' and 'monachos'" (quoted in Becker, "Literary Treatment," p. 225). Meanwhile, passages of relevance to female religious readers are expanded, further evidence that *SW*, if not intended as reading specifically designed for anchoresses, was almost certainly intended first for the female reader (Perkins, "Reading the Bible," p. 215). See also Eggebroten, "*Sawles Warde*: A Retelling of *De Anima*," and Robertson, *Early English Devotional Prose*, pp. 126–43.

34.1   *The imeane blisse is seovenfald.* On the seven joys of the soul, see MWB p. 157n102/21–23.

37.3   *Ant beoth . . . nebbe to nebbe.* Compare 1 Corinthians 13:12.

37.4   *His domes . . . sea dingle.* Compare Psalm 35:6: "Thy justice is as the mountains of God, thy judgments are a great deep." *Sea dingle* presents difficulties in translation, as *dingle* is of unknown etymology and this is the only recorded instance of the term in Middle English besides in place names. See *MED dingle* (n.), "a deep dell or hollow." According to the *OED*, a dingle is, in the modern dialect of Yorkshire, "the name of a deep narrow cleft between hills," i.e., a valley (*dingle* (n.)). We have chosen to translate *sea dingle* as "sea trench" since "trench" is the term applied to an underwater valley. While the translation is no doubt modern in terminology, the sense remains that the judgments of God reach as physically low as is geographically possible, which, to the medieval writer and audience, would represent the deepest parts of the sea-floor that are therefore closest to Hell. For a detailed explanation as to the possible etymology of "dingle," see W, pp. 74–75n320. Of note is W. H. Auden's use of this line in his poem "Doom is Dark and Deeper than any Sea-Dingle"; see Bloomfield's article of the same name for the implications of this usage.

39.7   *Intra in gaudium.* Compare Matthew 25:21.

39.10   *Beati qui habitant.* Compare Psalm 83:5.

40.1   *ase thin ehe-lid tuneth ant openeth.* Literally, "as your eyelid closes and opens." We translate more idiomatically as "in the blink of an eye." See *OED eye-blink*, sense C4.

43.1–2 *Hwen hit swa is . . . haveth us iyarcket.* Compare Romans 8:35–39.

43.2   *under His wengen.* Refuge under God's wings is a frequent image in the Psalms. See, for example, Vulgate Psalms 16:8, 35:8, 60:5, etc. See also *HM* explanatory note 41.6.

44.1   *Warpeth ut . . . ure fa.* Compare 1 John 4:18. The allegory literalizes John's assertion that "Fear is not in charity: but perfect charity casteth out fear," and serves as the climax to, as Perkins states, "a dramatic enactment of . . . scriptural verse . . . from Fearlac's warnings to Liues Luue's vision of heaven" ("Reading the Bible," p. 214).

48.1   *Nu is Wil thet husewif al stille.* Hassel understands Will's silence as only a temporary victory in "the ongoing work of vigilance" (*Choosing Not to Marry*, p. 96). She compares the ending moment of *SW* to the "tempting but false" moment in *SJ* 34.1–7 where the demon disguised as an angel tries to persuade Juliana that God does not want to see her suffer any more, and will allow her to marry Eleusius, a moment that seems to promise a happy resolution but in reality only poses mortal danger to those who let down their guard.

50.1   *Par seinte charité.* This phrase is the second of two entirely French-derived phrases used in *SW*, in addition to "fol semblant." See also the explanatory note 3.7. See Skaffari, "Lexical Borrowings," p. 92, for more discussion of the implications of "code-switching," i.e., abruptly changing linguistic registers within the text. Skaffari also considers that the entire final note of R, included here, "may not be more than an afterthought" ("Lexical Borrowings," p. 92).

        Johan thet theos boc wrat. This prayer and the brief poem that follows it only appears in R. The John mentioned here is presumably the scribe; his appeal is a conventional envoi that often appears at the end of medieval texts wherein the author or scribe takes his leave and requests readers to pray for his soul.

TEXTUAL NOTES TO *SAWLES WARDE*

ABBREVIATIONS: *AW*: *Ancrene Wisse*, ed. Hasenfratz; **BS**: Bennett and Smithers edition (1968); **BT**: Bosworth and Toller, *Anglo-Saxon Dictionary*; **MED**: Middle English Dictionary; **MS**: Bodleian Library MS Bodley 34 [base text]; **MWB**: Millett and Wogan-Browne edition (1990); **R**: British Library MS Royal 17 A XXVII; **T**: British Library MS Cotton Titus D XVIII; **W**: Wilson edition (1938).

We consulted Wilson's 1938 diplomatic edition of all three manuscripts of *Sawles Warde* over the course of producing our text here. We also consulted Bennett and Smithers and Millett and Wogan-Browne, the two most recent editions of the text. While we turned to the Hall and Morris editions on occasion, we have not collated those readings with the readings below.

1.1	*Si*. MS: capital *S*, two lines high.
2.2	*his*. MS: *his ħ*.
3.1	*Lauerd*. So BS, MWB, R, T. MS: *lauerð*.
3.7	*hwer*. So MS, corrected from *hwet*.
	other. So MWB, R, T. MS: *oðer*, which BS retains.
3.9	*iwiten*. So MS; the word has been inserted in a different hand and is corrected from what looks like *iwelen*. BS and MWB emend to *felen* following R's reading; in BS's case, following W's mis-reading of the inserted word as *iþþlen*. T: *fele*.
	Wit. So BS, MWB, R, T. MS: *hit*.
3.10	*fare*. So BS, MWB, R. T: *fares*. MS omits.
3.11	*tresor*. So BS, MWB, R, T. MS: *tre*. Apparently the MS-scribe finished the line with half of the word then forgot to complete the word at the beginning of the next line.
4.1	*Wit*. MS: capital *Wynn*, three lines high.
4.3	*suster*. So MS, corrected from *þuster*.
	hird. So BS, MWB, T. MS: *hirð*. R: *hinen*.
4.5	*this*. So MWB, R, T. MS: *his*, which BS retains. It should be noted that MS's reading does make sense: "For fear of her his (i.e., Wit's) household . . ." However, we have emended to the R and T reading for greater clarity.
	hird. So BS, MWB, R, T. MS: *hirth*.
	his$_1$. So MWB, R, T. MS omits, which BS retains.
	honden. So BS, MWB, R, T. MS: *hondon*.
5.1	*As*. MS: capital *A*, five lines high, largely due to the flourish on the first ascender.

5.3   *ant leane*. MS: *ant ~~feier~~ leane*.

5.4   *ham*. So MWB, R, T. MS omits, which BS retains.

6.3   *ha*$_1$. So BS, MWB, T. MS, R: *he*. The T scribe is evidently the first to catch this mistake, as the word is corrected from *he*.

7.3   *enbrevet*. MS: *enbrevedt*.

At the bottom of fol. 73v, a later hand has written *Thomas Hauard esquier*. See Ker, *Facsimile of MS Bodley 34*, pp. xiii–xv, for details regarding these additions.

13.1   *tellen*. MS: the word is inserted above the line.

reodien. MS: a decorative mark follows this word to the end of the line.

14.1   *Helle*. MS: capital *H*, three lines high.

wid. So BS, MWB, T. MS and R omit. The Bodley scribe may have omitted the word because of its similarity to the next word, *wiðute*.

14.3   In the left margin of fol. 74v, MS has *Thomas clynton clericus*, along with some scribbles. See Ker, *Facsimile of MS Bodley 34*, pp. xiii–xv, for details regarding these additions.

greot. So MS, BS. MWB, R, T: *grot*. W suggests MS's *greot* is a mistake based on the Old English term *greot* meaning "grit" (*BT greót* (n.)) but goes on to suggest a more probable explanation: "the mechanical transcription of original *o* as *eo* by the B. scribe" (p. 55n101); however, see Millett, Dance, and Dobson who, commenting on *AW* 4.1178, suggest that "it is possible that there was some overlap between the senses of *grot* 'fragment' and *greot* '(particle of) sand, gravel'" (*AW*, vol. 2, p. 181n4.1178). Hence, we have retained MS's reading.

14.6   *hechelunge*. So MS. T: *hechelinge*. See also the corresponding explanatory note.

14.18   *rueth*. So MS, BS, MWB. R: *ruueð*. T *runeð*. The T reading is most likely a mistake. W (p. 61n143) follows Hall in attributing the MS and R readings to a non-extant verb, **ruuen*, meaning "to stiffen, to stand up in disorder." *MED*, which cites only this line under *ruen* (v.), suggests the Middle Dutch *ruderuwen*, "to stand up."

the$_3$. So MS. T: *theo*, with the *o* marked for deletion. See the corresponding explanatory note.

15.1   *Nu*. MS: a space was left for a two-line capital which was never inserted. The indicator letter is faintly visible in the left margin, though part of it has been cropped.

donne. So MS, corrected from *donte*.

15.2   *ha*. So MWB, R, T. MS: *he*, which BS retains.

15.3   *ofdred*. So MS, corrected from *a dred*.

17.4   *we*$_1$. MS: *wei*.

17.5   *middel*. So MWB, R, T. MS: *midel*, which BS retains. We have emended for sense.

18.1   *Rihtwissnesse*. MS: space has been left for a capital *R*, two lines high. A faint *R* is visible but is severely faded, which is the case for all of the capitals that follow.

18.2   *strengthe*. So BS, MWB, T. MS: *strengde*, which W reads as *strengðe*. R: *strencðe*.

to ure alre ehnen — ant. So BS, following R. MS: *ant ure alre ehnen*.

19.1	*Wit*. MS: there is an otiose downstroke between *W* and *i*.
20.1	*The*. MS: space has been left for a capital *T*, two lines high.
	treowliche. So BS, MWB, R. MS: *treowliliche*. T: *treweliche*.
21.1	*swithe*. So BS, MWB, R, T. MS: *swide*.
24.1	*Hercnith*. MS: space has been left for a capital *H*, two lines high.
24.2	*Ich*. So BS, MWB, R, T. MS: *ch*.
25.1	*A*. MS: space has been left for a capital *A*, two lines high.
26.1	*Murhthes*. So BS, MWB, R, T. MS: *murhdes*.
	habbe isehen. MS: *habbe ~~him ofte~~ isehen*.
	mine. So MS, corrected from *meine*.
26.2	*ofte*. MS: the scribe wrote *ofsee*, corrected to *oftee*, then deleted the word. His second attempt was only slightly more successful: having written *ofee*, he corrected to *ofte*.
27.1	*wordes*. So BS, MWB, based on T's *weoredes*. BS also cites *De Anima*'s "super omnes ordines" as a guide for supplying the missing word (Hugh of St Victor, p. 185ff). MS, R omit.
	with. So BS, MWB, R, T. MS: *wid*.
	weoleful. MS: ~~wle~~ *weoleful*.
	therayeinis. So BS, MWB, R. MS: *þe aȝeines*. T: *ther toȝeines*.
27.2	*blitheliche*. So BS, MWB, R, T. MS: *blideliche*.
28.1	*Thet*. MS: space has been left for a capital *T*, two lines high.
	unwerget. MS: corrected from *unwerged*.
28.2	*ha*. So BS, MWB, R, T. MS: *ha ha*. The first *ha* occurs at the end of the line, and the second at the beginning of the next line.
29.1	*Efter*. MS: space has been left for a capital *E*, two lines high.
	makieth. So BS, MWB, R. MS: *makied*. T: *makeð*.
30.1	*Ich*. MS: space has been left for a capital *I*, two lines high.
31.1	*Efter*. MS: space has been left for a capital *E*, two lines high.
	cunfessurs. MS: corrected from *cunfessores*.
	haliliche. So BS, MWB, R, T. MS: *haliche*.
32.1	*Ich*. MS: space has been left for a capital *I*, two lines high.
	ferreden. MS: *fereden*; r_2 is inserted above the line.
32.2	*feierleac*. MS: *feierlac*; e_3 is inserted above the line.
32.4	*smeal*. MS: *smel*; *a* is inserted above the line.
33.1	*Swithe*. MS: space has been left for a capital *S*, two lines high.
34.1	*The*. MS: space has been left for a capital *T*, two lines high.
37.1	*Ha*. MS: space has been left for a capital *H*, two lines high.
	seovevald. MS: the final letter is *d* or *t*, though it is difficult to tell which is the corrected form; we have followed *d* based on R's reading of *seoueuald* and T's reading of *seuefald*.
37.2	*cnawlechunge*. MS: preceded by several partially erased letters, possibly *cwa* with superscript *n*.
37.3	*seoth*. So BS, MWB, R, T. MS: *sod*.
38.1	*Ha*. MS: space has been left for a capital *H*, two lines high.
39.1 ff.	Beginning on fol. 80r (MS's final folio), the manuscript becomes increasingly difficult to read due to staining, water damage, and tearing in the manuscript. Ker advises that this damage is due to the fact that MS

lacked a cover for quite some time (*Facsimile of MS Bodley 34*, p. xii). When text is lacking, we have turned to R and T.

39.1   *Se*. MS: space has been left for a capital *S*, two lines high.

na speche. So BS, MWB, R, T. MS is unreadable.

39.2   *euchan haveth*. So BS, MWB, R, T. MS: *?uch?? ?aveð*.

othres. So BS, MWB, T. MS: *odres*. R: *oðeres*.

39.3   *haveth*. So BS, MWB, T. MS: *h?veð*. R: *haþ*.

39.4   *othre*. So BS, MWB. MS: *odre*. R: *oðer*. T: *þoðre*.

39.6   *undervon*. So BS, MWB. MS: *????rvon*. R, T: *underfon*. A long tear in the page (fol. 80r) obscures this word and affects 41.2, 42.1, and 42.2 (see notes below).

se unimete. So BS, MWB, T. MS: *s?????ete*. R: *so unimete*.

hu is hit thet. So MWB. MS, R, T: *þet*, which BS retains.

nimeth. So BS, MWB, R, T. MS: *nime?*.

hire₃. So BS, MWB, R, T. MS: *hi??*.

39.12   *worlde into worlde*. So BS, MWB, R, T. MS: missing. The bottom corner of the folio is torn off, obliterating this phrase as well as parts of 40.1, and finally ending the text at *sunne-gleam the sch* (40.1).

40.1   *Ha*. MS: space has been left for a capital *H*, two lines high.

lihte . . . sunne. So MWB, R. MS: *lih*. T: *lihte ant ase swifte ase sunne*, which BS retains.

scheot . . . thin. So MWB, R. MS: *sch*. T: *scheot fram est into west as tin*, which BS retains.

41.1   *Sikere*. MS: space has been left for a capital *S*, two lines high.

mei. So BS, MWB. MS: *me*. R omits. T: *mai*.

41.2   *seh₁*. So BS, MWB, T. MS, R: *neh*. Repetition from a previous word.

seh₂. So BS, T. R: *iseh*, which MWB retains. The word is missing from MS because of the tear in the page, although the very top of the *h* is visible (see textual note 39.6 above). We have emended following T since it seems more likely that there is only room for three letters in the lacuna.

42.1   *"Witerliche," quoth*. So BS, MWB, R, T. MS: *iterl*. A space has been left for the capital *wynn* and never filled in; the rest of the phrase is lost due to the tear (see textual note 39.6 above).

42.2   *tu havest*. So BS, MWB, R, T. MS: *t? ?avest*. See textual note 39.6 above.

43.1–2 *halden . . . Ich*. So BS, MWB, T. MS: *hald*, with the rest of the phrase lost due to the torn section of page (see textual note 39.12 above). R: *halden us þeonne ih*.

43.2   *thet₁ . . . wa*. So MWB, R. MS: see textual note 39.12 above. T: *þat ne schal ne lif ne deað ne wa*, which BS retains, omitting *ne₂*.

nowther. MS ends here. From this point forward we have followed R (which BS and MWB also follow).

tresurers. So MWB, R: *tresures*. BS: *etresurers*. T: *tresorers*.

47.1   *quoth Meath*. So BS, M, T. R omits.

49.1   *his₁*. So BS, MWB, T. R omits.

that his. So T. BS, R omit. MWB emends to *thet his*.

drahe. So MWB, T. R: *teach*, which reading BS retains.

the₂. BS omits. R: *þerfore þe.* W (p. 80n394) cites Hall in supposing that *therfore* is a mistaken anticipation of *þe fowre.*

49.2   *ant te . . . ant te.* R: *ant e . . . ant e.* We have emended to the more typical forms for sense.

50.1–59.1   *Par seinte charité . . . sawle yelden. AMEN.* These lines only appear in R; *wrat* in 50.1 refers to the scribe's act of copying.

BIBLIOGRAPHY

Ælred of Rievaulx. *De Institutione Inclusarum*. *Aelred of Rievaulx's De Institutione Inclusarum: Two English Versions*. Ed. John Ayto and Alexandria Barrett. EETS o.s. 287. London: Oxford University Press, 1984.

Aldhelm. *De Virginitate*. In *Aldhelm: The Prose Works*. Trans. Michael Lapidge and Michael Herren. Cambridge: D. S. Brewer, 1979. Pp. 51–132.

Alliterative Morte Arthure. In *King Arthur's Death: The Middle English Stanzaic Morte Arthur and Alliterative Morte Arthure*. Ed. Larry D. Benson. Kalamazoo, MI: Medieval Institute Publications, 1994. Pp. 129–284.

Ancrene Wisse. Ed. Robert Hasenfratz. Kalamazoo, MI: Medieval Institute Publications, 2000.

Ancrene Wisse: A Corrected Edition of the Text in Cambridge: Corpus Christi College, MS 402, with Variants for Other Manuscripts. Ed. Bella Millett. 2 vols. EETS o.s. 325–326. Oxford, Oxford University Press, 2005–06.

Anselm. *Basic Writings*. Trans. T. Williams. Indianapolis: Hackett, 2007.

———. *De Custodia Interioris Hominis*. In *Memorials of St. Anselm*. Ed. R. W. Southern and F. S. Schmitt. London: Oxford University Press, 1969. Pp. 354–60.

Aquinas, Thomas. *Catena aurea: Commentary on the Four Gospels, Collected out of the Works of the Fathers by S. Thomas Aquinas*. Trans. Mark Pattison, J. D. Dalgrins, and T. D. Ryder. 4 vols. Oxford: John Henry Parker, 1841–45.

Astell, Ann W. *The Song of Songs in the Middle Ages*. Ithaca and London: Cornell University Press, 1990.

Augustine. "Confessionum." *Patrologia Latina*. Ed. J. P. Migne. Vol. 32. Paris: Excudebat Migne, 1844–64. Pp. 656–867.

———. *De Sancta Virginitate*. In *Sancti Aureli Augustini*. Ed. Joseph Zycha. Vienna: G. Gerold, 1900. Pp. 234–302.

———. *On Christian Doctrine*. Trans. and intro. D. W. Robertson, Jr. New York: Liberal Arts Press, 1958.

———. *Concerning the City of God Against the Pagans*. Trans. Henry Betterson. Harmondsworth: Penguin Books, 1972.

———. *Confessions*. Trans. and intro. Henry Chadwick. Oxford: Oxford University Press, 1991.

Auslander, Diane. "Clemence and Catherine: The Life of St Catherine in its Norman and Anglo-Norman Context." In *Barking Abbey and Medieval Literary Culture: Authorship and Authority in a Female Community*. Ed. Jennifer N. Brown and Donna Alfano Bussell. Rochester, NY: York Medieval, 2012. Pp. 164–82.

Bartlett, Anne Clark. *Male Authors, Female Readers: Representation and Subjectivity in Middle English Devotional Literature*. Ithaca, NY: Cornell University Press, 1995.

Bately, Janet. "On Some Aspects of the Vocabulary of the West Midlands In the Early Middle Ages: The Language of the Katherine Group." In *Medieval English Studies Presented to George Kane*. Ed. Edward Donald Kennedy, Ronald Waldron, and Joseph S. Wittig. Wolfeboro, NH: D. S. Brewer, 1988. Pp. 67–77.

Becker, Wolfgang. "The Source Text of *Sawles Warde*." *Manuscripta* 24 (1980), 44–48.

———. "The Literary Treatment of the Ps-Anselmian Dialogue *De Custodia Interioris Hominis* in England and in France." *Classica et Medievalia* 35 (1984), 215–33.

281

Bede. *Bede's Ecclesiastical History of the English People*. Ed. Bertram Colgrave and R. A. B. Mynors. Oxford: Oxford University Press, 1969.

———. *Martyrology*. Trans. Felice Lifshitz. In *Medieval Hagiography: An Anthology*. Ed. Thomas Head. London: Routledge, 2001. Pp. 169–98.

Beidler, Peter G., ed. *Geoffrey Chaucer: The Wife of Bath*. Boston: Bedford Books, 1996.

Bennett, J. A. W., and G. V. Smithers, eds. "Prose Allegory: *Sawles Warde*." In *Early Middle English Verse and Prose*. Oxford: Clarendon Press, 1968. Pp. 246–71; 417–26.

Benskin, Michael, and Margaret Laing. "Translations and *Mischsprachen* in Middle English Manuscripts." In *So Meny People, Longages and Tonges: Philological Essays in Scots and Mediaeval English Presented to Angus McIntosh*. Ed Michael Benskin and M. L. Samuels. Edinburgh: Middle English Dialect Project, 1981. Pp. 55–106.

Bernard of Clairvaux. *On the Song of Songs I: The Works of Bernard of Clairvaux*. Trans. Kilian Walsh. Vol. 2. Spencer, MA: Cistercian Publications, 1971–80.

Bernau, Anke. "Virginal Effects: Text and Identity in *Ancrene Wisse*." In Riches and Salih. Pp. 36–48.

———. "A Christian *Corpus*: Virginity, Violence, and Knowledge in the Life of St Katherine of Alexandria." In Jenkins and Lewis. Pp. 109–30.

Bernau, Anke, Ruth Evans, and Sarah Salih, eds. *Medieval Virginities*. Toronto: University of Toronto Press, 2003.

Bethurum, Dorothy. "The Connection of the Katherine Group with Old English Prose." *Journal of English and Germanic Philology* 34 (1935), 553–64.

Blamires, Alcuin. "Women and Preaching in Medieval Orthodoxy, Heresy, and Saints' Lives." *Viator* 26 (1995), 135–52.

Blamires, Alcuin, Karen Pratt, and C. William Marx. *Woman Defamed and Woman Defended: An Anthology of Medieval Texts*. Oxford: Clarendon Press, 1992.

Black, Marja. "AB or Simply A?: Reconsidering the Case for a Standard." *Neuphilologische Mitteilungen* 100 (1999), 155–74.

Blake, N. F. "Rhythmical Alliteration." *Modern Philology* 67 (1969), 118–24.

———. *A History of the English Language*. New York: New York University Press, 1996.

Blesdoe, Jenny C. "The Cult of St. Margaret of Antioch at Tarrant Crawford: The Saint's Didactic Body and its Resonance for Religious Women." *Journal of Medieval Religious Cultures* 39.2 (2013), 173–206.

Bloomfield, M[orton] W. "'Doom is Dark and Deeper Than Any Sea-Dingle.'" *Modern Language Notes* 63.8 (1948), 548–52.

Blumenfeld-Kosinski, Renate, and Timea Szell, eds. *Images of Sainthood in Medieval Europe*. Ithaca, NY: Cornell University Press, 1991.

Boffey, Julia, and A. S. G. Edwards. "Middle English Literary Writings, 1150–1400." In *The Cambridge History of the Book in Britain*. Vol. 2. Ed. Nigel Morgan and Rodney M. Thomson. Cambridge: Cambridge University Press, 2008. Pp. 380–89.

Boethius. *The Consolation of Philosophy*. Trans. Richard Green. New York: The Bobbs-Merrill Company, Inc., 1962.

Bonaventure, St. *The Mind's Road to God*. Trans. George Boas. New York: Liberal Arts Press, 1953.

Bosse, Roberta Bux. *Early Middle English Prose Style: Sawles Warde*. PhD dissertation. St. Louis University, 1971.

———. "Mysticism and Huswifery in *Hali Meiðhad*." *14th-Century English Mystics Newsletter* 2.4 (1976), 8–15.

———. "Female Sexual Behavior in the Late Middle Ages: Ideal and Actual." *Fifteenth-Century Studies* 10 (1984), 15–37.

Bosworth, Joseph, and T. Northcote Toller. *An Anglo-Saxon Dictionary: Based on the Manuscript Collections of Joseph Bosworth*. Oxford: Oxford University Press, 1898. Rpt. 1973. Also available online at http://www.bosworthtoller.com.

Bozon, Nicholas. "La Vie Sein(te) Margaret(e)." In *Three Saints' Lives*. Ed. and trans. Sister M. Amelia Klenke. St. Bonaventure, NY: Franciscan Institute, 1947. Pp. 27–42.

Breeze, Andrew. "Welsh Cais 'Sergeant' and *Sawles Warde*." *Notes and Queries* 40.3 (1993), 297–303.

———. "*Bune* 'Maiden, Beloved' in *Ancrene Wisse*." *Notes and Queries* 53.2 (2006), 152–53.

Bugge, John. *Virginitas: An Essay in the History of a Medieval Ideal*. The Hague: Martinus Nijhoff, 1975.

Burrow, J. A., ed. *Sir Gawain and the Green Knight*. London: Penguin Books, 1972.

Bynum, Caroline Walker. *Holy Feast and Holy Fast: The Religious Significance of Food to Medieval Women*. Berkeley: University of California Press, 1987.

Cadwallader, Robyn. "The Virgin, the Dragon and the Theorist: Readings in the Thirteenth-Century *Seinte Maherete*." PhD dissertation. Flinders University of South Australia, 2002.

Cannon, Christopher. "The Form of the Self: *Ancrene Wisse* and Romance." *Medium Ævum* 70.1 (2001), 47–65.

———. *The Grounds of English Literature*. Oxford: Oxford University Press, 2004.

Capgrave, John. *The Life of Saint Katherine of Alexandria*. Trans. Karen A. Winstead. Notre Dame, IN: University of Notre Dame Press, 1999.

Carlson, Cindy L., and Angela Jane Weisl, eds. *Constructions of Widowhood and Virginity in the Middle Ages*. New York: St. Martin's Press, 1999.

Cartwright, Jane. "*Buchedd Catrin*: A Preliminary Study of the Middle Welsh Life of Katherine of Alexandria and Her Cult in Medieval Wales." In Jenkins and Lewis. Pp. 53–86.

The Castle of Perseverance. In *Medieval Drama*. Ed. David M. Bevington. Boston: Houghton Mifflin, 1987.

Cazelles, Brigitte. "Introduction." In *Images of Sainthood in Medieval Europe*. Ed. Renate Blumenfeld-Kosinski and Timea Szell. Ithaca, NY: Cornell University Press, 1991. Pp. 1–17.

Celletti, M. C. "Marina (Margherita), santa, martire di Antiochia di Pisidia: Iconografia." *Bibliotheca Sanctorum*. Ed. Filippo Caraffa et al., Vol. 8 (1966), cols. 1160–66.

Chambers, R. W. *On the Continuity of English Prose from Alfred to More and his School*. EETS o.s. 191A. London: Oxford University Press, 1957.

Chaucer, Geoffrey. *Riverside Chaucer*. 3rd edition. Gen. ed. Larry D. Benson. Boston: Houghton Mifflin, 1987.

———. *The Wife of Bath*. Ed. Peter G. Beidler. Case Studies in Contemporary Criticism. Boston: Bedford, 1996.

Chewning, Susannah Mary. "The Paradox of Virginity within the Anchoritic Tradition: The Masculine Gaze and the Feminine Body in the *Wohunge* Group." In Carlson and Weisl. Pp. 113–34.

———, ed. *The Milieu and Context of the Wooing Group*. Cardiff: University of Wales Press, 2009.

Christina of Markyate: A twelfth-century holy woman. Ed. Samuel Fanous and Henrietta Leyser. London: Routledge, 2005.

Christina of Markyate. *A Life of Christina of Markyate*. Ed. and trans. C. H. Talbot. Oxford: Oxford University Press, 2008.

Clark, Cecily. "*Ancrene Wisse* and the *Katherine Group*: A Lexical Divergence." *Neophilologus* 50 (1966), 117–23.

Clay, Rotha Mary. *The Hermits and Anchorites of England*. Detroit, MI: Singing Tree Press, 1968.

Clayton, Mary, and Hugh Magennis. *The Old English Lives of St Margaret*. Cambridge: Cambridge University Press, 1994.

The Cloud of Unknowing. Ed. Patrick J. Gallacher. Kalamazoo, MI: Medieval Institute Publications, 1997.

Complaint Against Hope. Ed. Kenneth G. Wilson. Ann Arbor: University of Michigan Press, 1957.

Cursor Mundi. Ed. Richard Morris. 6 vols. EETS o.s. 57, 59, 62, 66, 68, and 101. London: K. Paul, Trench and Trübner, 1874–93. Rpt. Oxford: Oxford University Press, 1966.

d'Ardenne, S. R. T. O., ed. See *Þe Liflade ant te Passiun of Seinte Iuliene*.

d'Ardenne, S. R. T. O., and E. J. Dobson, eds. See *Seinte Katerine*.

Dahood, Roger. "*Ancrene Wisse*, the Katherine Group, and the *Wohunge* Group." In *Middle English Prose: A Critical Guide to Major Authors and Genres*. Ed. A. S. G. Edwards. New Brunswick, NJ: Rutgers University Press, 1984. Pp. 1–33.

Davis, Henry, trans. *St. Gregory the Great: Pastoral Care*. Westminster, MD: Newman Press, 1978.

De Caluwé-Dor, Juliette. "The Chronology of the Scandinavian Loan-Verbs in the *Katherine Group*." *English Studies* 60 (1979), 680–85.

———. "Etymological Convergence in the Katherine Group." In *Current Topics in English Historical Linguistics*. Proceedings of the Second International Conference in English Historical Linguistics, held at Odense University 8–15 April, 1981. Ed. Michael Davenport, Erik Hansen, and Hans Frede Nielsen. Odense: Odense University Press, 1983. Pp. 211–23.

———. "Post-Dating Romance Loan-Words in Middle English: Are the French Words of the *Katherine Group* English?" In *History of Englishes: New Methods and Interpretations in Historical Linguistics*. Ed. Matti Rissanen et al. Berlin: Mouton de Gruyter, 1992. Pp. 483–505.

Dendle, Peter. "Pain and Saint-Making in Andreas, Bede and the Old English Lives of St. Margaret." In *Varieties of Devotion in the Middle Ages and Renaissance*. Ed. Susan C. Karant-Nunn. Turnhout: Brepols, 2003. Pp. 39–52.

The Dicts and Sayings of the Philosophers. Ed. John William Sutton. Kalamazoo, MI: Medieval Institute Publications, 2006.

Dobson, E. J. *The Origins of Ancrene Wisse*. Oxford: Clarendon Press, 1976.

Dor, Juliette. See De Caluwé-Dor, Juliette.

Dresvina, Juliana. "A Note on a Hitherto Unpublished Life of St Margaret of Antioch from MS Eng. th. e 18: Its Scribe and its Source." *Journal of the Early Book Society for the Study of Manuscripts and Printing History* 10 (2007), 217–31.

Earl, James W. "Saint Margaret and the Pearl Maiden." *Modern Philology* 70 (1972), 1–8.

The Early South-English Legendary; or, Lives of Saints. I. MS. Laud, 108, in the Bodleian Library. Ed. Carl Hortsmann. London: N. Trübner & Co., 1887. Rpt. Millwood, NY: Kraus Reprint Co., 1973.

Edsall, Mary Agnes. "'True Anchoresses Are Called Birds': Asceticism as Ascent and the Purgative Mysticism of the *Ancrene Wisse*." *Viator* 34 (2003), 157–86.

Eggebroten, Anne. "*Sawles Warde*: A Retelling of *De Anima* for a Female Audience." *Mediaevalia* 10 (1988 [for 1984]), 27–47.

Einenkel, Eugen. "Eine Englische Schriftstellerin aus dem Anfange des 12. Jahrhunderts." *Anglia-Zeitschrift für engilsche Philologie* 1882.5 (1882), 265–82.

———. *The Life of Saint Katherine: From the Royal MS 17A XXVII*. EETS o.s. 80. London: Trübner & Co., 1884.

Elliott, Dyan. *Spiritual Marriage: Sexual Abstinence in Medieval Wedlock*. Princeton, NJ: Princeton University Press, 1993.

———. "Women and Confession: From Empowerment to Pathology." In Erler and Kowaleski. Pp. 31–51.

English Medieval Lapidaries. Ed. Joan Evans and Mary S. Serjeantson. EETS o.s. 190. London: Oxford University Press, 1933.

Erler, Mary C., and Maryanne Kowaleski, eds. *Gendering the Master Narrative: Women and Power in the Middle Ages*. Ithaca, NY: Cornell University Press, 2003.

Eusebius. *The Church History*. Trans. Paul L. Maier. Grand Rapids: Kregel, 2007.

Evans, Ruth. "The Jew, the Host and the Virgin Martyr: Fantasies of the Sentient Body." In Bernau, Evans, and Salih. Pp. 167–86.

Farmer, David Hugh. *The Oxford Dictionary of Saints*. Oxford: Clarendon Press, 1978.

Fletcher, Alan J. "The Dancing Virgins of *Hali Meiðhad*." *Notes and Queries* 40.4 (1993), 437–39.

Flynn, Rebecca. "Constitutions of Feminine Desire and Sexuality in the Thirteenth-Century *Ancrene Wisse*." In *Proceedings of the 14th Northern Plains Conference on Earlier British Literature*. Ed. Bruce E. Brandt and Michael S. Nagy. Brookings, SD: South Dakota University Press, 2007. Pp. 18–24.

Foster, Edward E., ed. *Three Purgatory Poems: The Gast of Gy, Sir Owain, The Vision of Tundale*. Kalamazoo, MI: Medieval Institute Publications, 2004.

Francomano, Emily C. "'Lady, you are quite a chatterbox': The Legend of St Katherine of Alexandria, Wives' Words, and Women's Wisdom in MS Escorial h–I–13." In Jenkins and Lewis. Pp. 131–52.

Franzen, Christine. "The Tremulous Hand of Worcester and the Nero Scribe of the *Ancrene Wisse*." *Medium Ævum* 72.1 (2003), 13–31.

Frazier, Alison. "Katherine's Place in a Renaissance Collection: Evidence from Antonia degli Agli (c. 1400–1477), *De vitis et gestis sanctorum*." In Jenkins and Lewis. Pp. 221–40.

Fredeman, Jane C. "Style and Characterization in John Capgrave's *Life of St. Katherine*." *Bulletin of the John Rylands University Library of Manchester* 62 (1980), 346–87.

Furuskog, R. "A Collation of the Katherine Group (MS Bodley 34)." *Studia Neophilologica* 19 (1946), 119–66.

Galloway, Andrew. "Middle English as a Foreign Language, to 'Us' and 'Them' (Gower, Langland, and the Author of *The Life of St. Katherine*)." *Studies in Medieval and Renaissance Teaching* 14.1 (2007), 89–102.

Gardiner, Eileen. *Medieval Visions of Heaven and Hell: A Sourcebook*. New York: Garland Publishing, 1993.

Gatch, Milton McC. *Preaching and Theology in Anglo-Saxon England: Ælfric and Wulfstan*. Toronto: University of Toronto Press, 1977.

Gaunt, Simon. *Gender and Genre in Medieval French Literature*. Cambridge and New York: Cambridge University Press, 1995.

Gayk, Shannon. "'Ete this Book': Literary Consumption and Poetic Invention in John Capgrave's *Life of Saint Katherine*." In *Form & Reform: Reading across the Fifteenth Century*. Ed. Shannon Gayk and Kathleen Tonry. Columbus, OH: Ohio State University Press, 2011. Pp. 88–109.

Georgianna, Linda. *The Solitary Self: Individuality in the Ancrene Wisse*. Cambridge, MA: Harvard University Press, 1981.

Gertrude of Helfta (Gertrude the Great). *The Herald of Divine Love*. Trans. and ed. Margaret Winkworth. Intro. Sister Maximilian Marnau. Preface Louis Bouyer. New York: Paulist Press, 1993.

Gilchrist, Roberta. *Gender and Material Culture: The Archaeology of Religious Women*. London: Routledge, 1993.

———. "Medieval Bodies in the Material World: Gender, Stigma and the Body." In Kay and Rubin. 43–61.

Gower, John. *Mirour de l'Omme (The Mirror of Mankind)*. Trans. William Burton Wilson. Rev. Nancy Wilson Van Baak. East Lansing, MI: Colleagues Press, 1992.

———. *Confessio Amantis*. Ed. Russell A. Peck, with Latin translations by Andrew Galloway. 3 vols. 2nd edition. Kalamazoo, MI: Medieval Institute Publications, 2000–06.

Gravdal, Kathryn. *Ravishing Maidens: Writing Rape in Medieval French Literature and Law*. Philadelphia: University of Pennsylvania Press, 1991.

Gray, Douglas, and J. A. W. Bennett. *Middle English Literature*. Oxford: Oxford University Press, 1986.

Guillaume de Lorris, and Jean de Meun. *The Romance of the Rose*. Trans. Charles Dahlberg. Princeton: Princeton University Press, 1995.

Hali Meidenhad: An Alliterative Homily of the Thirteenth Century. Ed. Frederick James Furnivall and Thomas Oswald Cockayne. EETS o.s. 18. London: Oxford University Press, 1922. Rpt. New York: Greenwood Press, 1969.

Hali Meiðhad. Ed. Bella Millett. EETS o.s. 284. London: Oxford University Press, 1982.

Hall, Joseph. *Selections of Early Middle English, 1130-1250*. Oxford: Clarendon Press, 1920.

Hanna, Ralph. "Lambeth Palace Library MS 407: Some Problems of Early Thirteenth-Century Textual Transmission." In *Texts and Traditions of Medieval Pastoral Care: Essays in Honour of Bella Millett*. Ed. Cate Gunn and Catherine Innes-Parker. Cambridge: Boydell and Brewer, 2009. Pp. 78–88.

Harvey, Susan Ashbrook. *Ancient Christianity and the Olfactory Imagination*. Berkeley: University of California Press, 2006.

Hasenfratz, Bob. "The Anchorhold as Symbolic Space in *Ancrene Wisse*." *Philological Quarterly* 84.1 (2005), 1–26.

Hassel, Julie. *Choosing Not to Marry: Women and Autonomy in the Katherine Group*. New York: Routledge, 2002.

Head, Thomas. "The Marriages of Christina of Markyate." *Viator* 21 (1990), 75–95.

Hesketh, Glynn. "An Unpublished Anglo-Norman Life of Saint Katherine of Alexandria from MS. London, BL, Add. 40143." *Romania* 118.1–2 (2000), 33–82.

Hiltunen, Risto and Janne Skaffari, eds. *Discourse Perspectives on English: Medieval to Modern.* Amsterdam and Philadelphia: John Benjamins Publications, 2003.

———. "Telling the Anchorite Code: *Ancrene Wisse* on Language." In Hiltunen and Skaffari.

Hindley, A., Frederick W. Langley, and Brian J. Levy. *Old French-English Dictionary.* Cambridge: Cambridge University Press, 2000.

Hornero Corisco, Ana Maria. "An Analysis of the Object Position in *Ancrene Wisse* and the Katherine Group." *SELIM: Journal of the Spanish Society for Medieval English Language and Literature* 4 (1994), 74–93.

Hostetler, Margaret. "The Characterized Reader in *Hali Meiðhad* and the Resisting Reader of Feminist Discourse." *Journal of Historical Pragmatics* 6.1 (2005), 87–111.

———. "The Politeness of a Disciplining Text: Ideal Readers in *Ancrene Wisse*." *Journal of Historical Pragmatics* 13.1 (2012), 29–49.

Hulbert, James R. "A Thirteenth-Century English Literary Standard." *Journal of English and Germanic Philology* 45 (1946), 411–14.

Innes-Parker, Catherine. "The Lady and the King: *Ancrene Wisse*'s Parable of the Royal Wooing Re-Examined." *English Studies* 75.6 (1994), 509–22.

———. "Fragmentation and Reconstruction: Images of the Female Body in *Ancrene Wisse* and the Katherine Group." *Comitatus* 26 (1995), 27–52.

———. "Sexual Violence and the Female Reader: Symbolic 'Rape' in the Saints' Lives of the Katherine Group." *Women's Studies* 24 (1995), 205–17.

Jacobus de Voragine. *The Golden Legend of Jacobus de Voragine.* Trans. Granger Ryan and Helmut Ripperger. New York: Arno Press, 1969.

James, Montague Rhodes, trans. and ed. *The Apocryphal New Testament: Being the Apocryphal Gospels, Acts, Epistles, and Apocalypses, with Other Narratives and Fragments.* Oxford: Clarendon Press, 1953.

James, Sarah. "'Doctryne and studie': Female Learning and Religious Debate in Capgrave's *Life of St Katharine*." *Leeds Studies in English* 36 (2005), 275–302.

———. "Oculi Carnis, Oculi Mentis: Why Seeing is not Believing in Capgrave's *Life of St. Katherine*." *The Review of English Studies* 65 (2013), 422–27.

Jenkins, Jacqueline. "'This Lyf en Englyssh Tunge': Translation Anxiety in Late Medieval Lives of St. Katherine." In *The Theory and Practice of Translation in the Middle Ages.* Ed. Rosalynn Voaden et al. Turnhout: Brepols, 2003. Pp. 137–48.

Jenkins, Jacqueline, and Katherine H. Lewis, eds. *St. Katherine of Alexandria: Texts and Contexts in Western Medieval Europe.* Turnhout: Brepols, 2003.

Jerome, St. "Letter to Eustochium." In *Selected Letters of Saint Jerome.* Trans. F. A. Wright. Cambridge: Harvard University Press, 1933. Rpt. 1954, 1963. Pp. 53–159.

Jucker, Andreas H. "Between Hypotaxis and Parataxis: Clauses of Reason in *Ancrene Wisse*." In *Historical English Syntax.* Ed. Dieter Kastovsky. Berlin: Mouton de Gruyter, 1991. Pp. 203–20.

Julian of Norwich. *The Shewings of Julian of Norwich.* Ed. Georgia Ronan Crampton. Kalamazoo, MI: Medieval Institute Publications, 1994.

Kalve, Kari. "'The Muthes Wit': Reading, Speaking, and Eating in *Ancrene Wisse*." *Essays in Medieval Studies* 14 (1998), 39–49.

The Katherine Group. A Three-Manuscript Parallel Text: Seinte Katerine, Seinte Marherete, Seinte Iuliene, and Hali Meiðhad, with Wordlists. Ed. Shoko Ono and John Scahill. Frankfurt: Peter Lang, 2011.

Kauth, Jean-Marie. "Book Metaphors in the Textual Community of the *Ancrene Wisse*." In *The Book and the Magic of Reading in the Middle Ages.* Ed. Albrecht Classen. New York: Garland, 1998. Pp. 99–121.

Kay, Sarah, and Miri Rubin, eds. *Framing Medieval Bodies.* Manchester: Manchester University Press, 1994.

Keene, Catherine. "Envisioning a Saint: Visions in the Miracles of Saint Margaret of Scotland." In *Reading Memory and Identity in the Texts of Medieval European Holy Women*. Ed. Margaret Cotter-Lynch and Brad Herzog. New York: Palgrave Macmillan, 2012. Pp. 57–79.

———. *Saint Margaret, Queen of the Scots: A Life in Perspective*. New York: Palgrave Macmillan, 2013.

Kelly, Kathleen Coyne. *Performing Virginity and Testing Chastity in the Middle Ages*. London: Routledge, 2000.

Kempe, Margery. *The Book of Margery Kempe*. Ed. Lynn Staley. Kalamazoo, MI: Medieval Institute Publications, 1996.

Ker, N. R., ed. *Facsimile of MS. Bodley 34: St. Katherine, St. Margaret, St. Juliana, Hali Meiðhad, Sawles Warde*. EETS o.s. 247. London: Oxford University Press, 1960.

Kristensson, Gillis. "On the Origins of the *Ancrene Wisse*." *Studia Neophilologica* 53.2 (1981), 371–76.

Laing, Margaret, and Angus McIntosh. "The Language of *Ancrene Riwle*, the Katherine Group Texts and *Þe Wohunge of Ure Lauerd* in BL Cotton Titus D. xviii." *Neuphilologische Mitteilungen* 96 (1995), 235–63.

Langland, William. *The Vision of Piers Plowman: A Critical Edition of the B-Text Based on Trinity College Cambridge MS B. 15.17*. Ed. A. V. C. Schmidt. London: J. M. Dent, 1995.

Larson, R. Wendy. "The Role of Patronage and Audience in the Cults of Sts Margaret and Marina of Antioch." In Riches and Salih. Pp. 23–35.

———. "Who Is the Master of This Narrative?: Maternal Patronage of the Cult of St. Margaret." In Erler and Kowaleski. Pp. 94–104.

Laȝamon. *Brut*. Ed. G. L. Brook and R. F. Leslie. 2 vols. EETS o.s. 250 and 277. London: Oxford University Press, 1963–78. Also available online at http://quod.lib.umich.edu/cgi/t/text/text-idx?c=cme;idno=LayOtho.

Legenda Aurea. See Jacobus de Voragine.

Lewis, Katherine J. *The Cult of St. Katherine of Alexandria in Late Medieval England*. Woodbridge: Boydell Press, 2000.

———. "'Lete me suffre': Reading the Torture of St Margaret of Antioch in Late Medieval England." In *Medieval Women: Texts and Contexts in Late Medieval Britain: Essays For Felicity Riddy*. Ed. Jocelyn Wogan-Browne et al. Turnhout: Brepols, 2000. Pp. 69–82.

———. "Pilgrimage and the Cult of St Katherine in Late Medieval England." In Jenkins and Lewis. Pp. 37–52.

The Life of Christina of Markyate: A Twelfth-Century Recluse. Ed. and trans. C. H. Talbot. Oxford: Clarendon Press, 1959.

The Life of St. Katherine: From the Royal MS. 17A. XXVII. Ed. Eugen Einenkel. EETS o.s. 80. London: N. Trübner, 1884.

Þe Liflade ant te Passiun of Seinte Iuliene. Ed. S. R. T. O. d'Ardenne. EETS o.s. 248. London: Oxford University Press, 1961.

Þe Liflade of St. Juliana: From Two Old English Manuscripts of 1230 A.D. Ed. Rev. Oswald Cockayne. Trans. Oswald Cockayne and Edmund Brock. EETS o.s. 51. London: N. Trübner, 1872.

Lochrie, Karma. *Margery Kempe and Translations of the Flesh*. Philadelphia: University of Pennsylvania Press, 1991.

Loomis, Richard. *Culhwch and Olwen*. In *The Romance of Arthur: An Anthology of Medieval Texts in Translation*. Ed. James J. Wilhelm. 2nd edition. New York and London: Garland Publishing, Inc., 1994. Pp. 25–48.

Lyall, Sutherland. *The Lady and the Unicorn*. London: Parkstone Press, 2000.

Mack, M. Frances, ed. See *Seinte Marherete*.

Magennis, Hugh. "'Listen Now All and Understand': Adaptation of Hagiographical Material for Vernacular Audiences in the Old English Lives of St. Margaret." *Speculum* 71.1 (1996), 27–42.

Maggioni, Maria Luisa. "Compounding in *Ancrene Wisse*." In *Words in Action: Diachronic and Synchronic Approaches to English Discourse. Studies in Honour of Ermanno Barisone*. Ed. John Douthwaite and Domenico Pezzini. Genoa: Edizioni Culturali Internazionali Genova (ECIG), 2008. Pp. 154–64.

Mandeville, John. *The Book of John Mandeville*. Ed. Tamarah Kohanski and C. David Benson. Kalamazoo, MI: Medieval Institute Publications, 2007.

Margherita, Gayle. "Desiring Narrative: Ideology and the Semiotics of the Gaze in the Middle English Juliana." *Exemplaria* 2 (1990), 355–74.

———. *The Romance of Origins: Language and Sexual Difference in Middle English Literature*. Philadelphia: University of Pennsylvania Press, 1994.

Martyrologium Vetustissimum: S. Hieronymi Presbyteri Nomine Insignatum. In *Patrologia Latina*. Ed. J. P. Migne. Vol. 30. Paris: Venit Apud Editorum, 1846. Pp. 435–86.

McCarthy, Conor. *Marriage in Medieval England: Law, Literature, and Practice*. Woodbridge and Rochester: Boydell Press, 2004.

McCoy, Janice. "Wheels and Wycliffites: The Role of Sacred Images in Capgrave's 'The Life of Saint Katherine'." *Fifteenth-Century Studies* 37 (2012), 97–112.

McFadden, Brian. "'The Books of Life': Theotimus as Narrator of Identity in the Old English Lives of St. Margaret." *English Studies* 86.6 (2005), 473–92.

McSheffrey, Shannon. *Marriage, Sex and Civic Culture in Late Medieval London*. Philadelphia: University of Pennsylvania Press, 2006.

Mews, Constant J., ed. *Listen Daughter: The* Speculum Virginum *and the Formation of Religious Women in the Middle Ages*. New York: Palgrave, 2001.

Middle English Dictionary. Gen. eds. Hans Kurath and Sherman M. Kuhn. Ann Arbor, MI: University of Michigan Press, 1952–2003. Online at http://quod.lib.umich.edu/m/med/.

Millett, Bella. "*Hali Meiðhad, Sawles Warde*, and the Continuity of English Prose." In *Five Hundred Years of Words and Sounds: A Festschrift for Eric Dobson*. Ed. E. G. Stanley and Douglas Gray. Cambridge: D. S. Brewer, 1983. Pp. 100–08.

———. "The Saints' Lives of the Katherine Group and the Alliterative Tradition." *Journal of English and Germanic Philology* 87 (1988), 16–34.

———. "The Audience of the Saints' Lives of the Katherine Group." *Reading Medieval Studies* 16 (1990), 127–56.

———. "The Origins of *Ancrene Wisse*: New Answers, New Questions." *Medium Ævum* 61 (1992), 206–28.

———. "Woman in No Man's Land: English Recluses and the Development of Vernacular Literature in the Twelfth and Thirteenth Centuries." In *Women and Literature in Britain, 1150–1500*. Ed. Carol M. Meale. Cambridge: Cambridge University Press, 1993. Pp. 86–103.

———. "*Ancrene Wisse* and the Conditions of Confession." *English Studies* 80.3 (1999), 193–214.

———. "*Ancrene Wisse* and the Life of Perfection." *Leeds Studies in English* 33 (2002), 53–76.

Millett, Bella, and Jocelyn Wogan-Browne, eds. *Medieval English Prose for Women: Selections from the Katherine Group and* Ancrene Wisse. Oxford: Clarendon Press, 1990.

Millet, Bella, George B. Jack, and Yoko Wada. *Annotated Bibliographies of Old and Middle English Literature. Vol. 2: Ancrene Wisse, the Katherine Group, and the Wooing Group*. Cambridge: D. S. Brewer, 1996.

Millett, Bella, Richard Dance, and E. J. Dobson, eds. *A Corrected Edition of the Text in Cambridge, Corpus Christi, MS 402, With Variants from Other Manuscripts*. Oxford: Oxford University Press, 2005.

Mills, Robert. "Can the Virgin Martyr Speak?" In Bernau, Evans, and Salih. Pp. 187–213.

Mockridge, Diane. "The Order of the Texts in the Bodley 34 Manuscript: The Function of Repetition and Recall in a Manuscript Addressed to Nuns." *Essays in Medieval Studies* 3 (1986), 207–18.

Morris, Richard, ed. *Old English Homilies and Homiletic Treatises: (Sawles warde, and þe wohunge of Ure Lauerd: Ureisuns of Ure Louerd and of Ure Lefdi, &c.) of the Twelfth and Thirteenth Centuries*. London: Trübner for the Early English Text Society, 1868.

Morton, James, ed. *The Legend of St. Katherine of Alexandria, Edited from a Manuscript in the Cottonian Library*. London: Samuel Bentley, 1841.

Mynors, R. A. B., and R. M. Thomson. *Catalogue of the Manuscripts of Hereford Cathedral Library*. Cambridge: D. S. Brewer, 1993.

The N-Town Plays. Ed. Douglas Sugano with assistance by Victor I. Scherb. Kalamazoo, MI: Medieval Institute Publications, 2006.

Newman, Barbara. *From Virile Woman to WomanChrist: Studies in Medieval Religion and Literature.* Philadelphia: University of Pennsylvania Press, 1995.

———. "*Speculum Virginum*: Selected Excerpts." In Mews. Pp. 269–96.

Newhauser, Richard. *The Early History of Greed: The Sin of Avarice in Early Medieval Thought and Literature.* Cambridge: Cambridge University Press, 2000.

Noonan, John. "Power to Choose." *Viator* 4 (1973), 419–34.

O'Keefe, Katherine O'Brien. *Visible Song: Transitional Literacy in Old English Verse.* New York: Cambridge University Press, 1990.

Origen. *Homilies on Numbers.* Trans. Thomas P. Scheck. Ed. Christopher A. Hall. Downers Grove, IL: InterVarsity Press, 2009.

Original Catholic Encyclopedia. Ed. Charles George Herbermann et al. New York: Robert Appleton Co., 1907–1912. Also available online at http://oce.catholic.com/index.php?title=Home.

The Owl and the Nightingale. Ed. J. H. G. Grattan and G. F. H. Sykes. EETS e.s. 119. London: Oxford University Press, 1935.

Owst, G. R. *Literature and Pulpit in Medieval England: A Neglected Chapter in the History of English Letters & of the English People.* Cambridge: Cambridge University Press, 1933.

Oxford Classical Dictionary. Ed. Simon Hornblower and Antony Spawforth. 3rd edition. Oxford: Oxford University Press, 1996. 4th edition available online at http://www.oxfordreference.com/view/10.1093/acref/9780199545568.001.0001/acref-9780199545568.

The Oxford English Dictionary. Ed. J. A. Simpson and E. S. C. Weiner. 2nd edition. Oxford: Clarendon Press, 1989. Online at www.oed.com.

Patch, Howard R. *The Goddess Fortuna in Mediaeval Literature.* London: Frank Cass, 1967.

Payer, Pierre J. *Sex and the Penitentials: The Development of a Sexual Code, 550–1150.* Toronto: University of Toronto Press, 1984.

Pearl. Ed. Sarah Stanbury. Kalamazoo, MI: Medieval Institute Publications, 2001.

Perkins, Nicholas. "Reading the Bible in *Sawles Warde* and *Ancrene Wisse*." *Medium Ævum* 72.2 (2003), 207–37.

Petersen, Zina. "Institution and Individual in Conflict: The Early Middle English *Ancrene Wisse* and the Authority of Speech Acts." *Journal of Historical Pragmatics* 6.1 (2005), 69–85.

Pickering, Oliver. "Two Pynson Editions of the Life of St Katherine of Alexandria." *Library* 9.4 (2008), 471–78.

Postlewate, Laurie. "Vernacular Hagiography and Lay Piety: Two Old French Adaptations of the Life of Saint Margaret of Antioch." In *Saints: Studies in Hagiography.* Ed. Sandro Sticca. Binghamton, NY: Medieval and Renaissance Texts and Studies, 1996. Pp. 115–30.

Price, Jocelyn. See Jocelyn Wogan-Browne.

Price, Paul. "I Want to Be Alone: The Single Woman in Fifteenth-Century Legends of St. Katherine of Alexandria." In *The Single Woman in Medieval and Early Modern England: Her Life and Representation.* Ed. Laurel Amtower and Dorothea Kehler. Tempe, AZ: Arizona Center for Medieval and Renaissance Studies, 2003. Pp. 21–39.

Quatrefoil of Love (Middle English Poem): The Quatrefoil of Love, Edited from Brit. Mus. MS. Add. 31042 with Collations from Bodl. MS. Add. A 106. Ed. Sir Israel Gollancz and Magdalene M. Weale. EETS o.s. 195. London: H. Milford, 1935. Pp. 1–18.

Queen Mary's Psalter: Miniatures and Drawings by an English Artist of the 14th Century Reproduced from Royal MS.2 b. VII in the British Museum. Intro. Sir George Warner. London: Trustees, British Museum, 1912.

Raskolnikov, Masha. *Body Against Soul: Gender and Sowlehele in Middle English Allegory.* Columbus: Ohio State University Press, 2009.

Reames, Sherry L. "St Katherine and the Late Medieval Clergy: Evidence from English Breviaries." In Jenkins and Lewis. Pp. 201–20.

Renevey, Denis. "Figuring Household Space in *Ancrene Wisse* and *The Doctrine of the Hert*." In *The Space of English.* Ed. David Spurr and Cornelia Tschichold. Tübingen: Narr Francke Attempto, 2005. Pp. 69–84.

Riches, Samantha J. E., and Sarah Salih, eds. *Gender and Holiness: Men, Women and Saints in Late Medieval Europe*. London: Routledge, 2002.

Robertson, Elizabeth. *Early English Devotional Prose and the Female Audience*. Knoxville: University of Tennessee Press, 1990.

———. "The Corporeality of Female Sanctity in the Life of Saint Margaret." In *Images of Sainthood in Medieval Europe*. Ed. Renate Blumenfield-Kosinski and Timea Szell. Intro. by Brigitte Cazelles. Ithaca, NY: Cornell University Press, 1991. Pp. 268–87.

———. "'This Living Hand': Thirteenth-Century Female Literacy, Materialist Immanence, and the Reader of the *Ancrene Wisse*." *Speculum* 78 (2003), 1–36.

Roman, Christopher. "Anchoritism and the Everyday: The Sacred-Domestic Discourse in the *Ancrene Wisse*." *Florilegium* 23.2 (2006), 99–122.

Russell-Smith, Joy. "*Keis* in *Sawles Warde*." *Medium Ævum* 22 (1953), 104–10.

Salih, Sarah. "Performing Virginity: Sex and Violence in the *Katherine* Group." In Carlson and Weisl. Pp. 95–112.

———. *Versions of Virginity in Late Medieval England*. Cambridge: Boydell and Brewer, 2001.

———, ed. *A Companion to Middle English Hagiography*. Cambridge: D. S. Brewer, 2006.

Savage, Anne. "The Translation of the Feminine: Untranslatable Dimensions of the Anchoritic Works." In *The Medieval Translator*. Vol. 4. Ed. Roger Ellis and Ruth Evans. Binghamton, NY: Medieval & Renaissance Texts & Studies, 1994. Pp. 181–99.

———. "The Communal Authorship of *Ancrene Wisse*." In Wada, *A Companion*. Pp. 45–56.

Savage, Anne, and Nicholas Watson, eds. *Anchoritic Spirituality*. New York: Paulist Press, 1991.

Sawles Warde: An Early Middle English Homily Edited from the Bodley Royal and Cotton MSS. Ed. R. M. Wilson. Titus Wilson: Kendal, 1938.

Sawles Warde: Kritische Textausgabe auf Grund Aller Handschriften mit Einleitung, Anmerkungen und Glossar. Ed. Wilhelm Wagner. Bonn: P. Hanstein, 1908.

Scahill, John. "More Central than Deviant: The Gonville and Caius Manuscript of *Ancrene Wisse*." *Neuphilologische Mittelungen* 110.1 (2009), 85–104.

Schaefer, Ursula. "Twin Collocations in the Early Middle English Lives of the Katherine Group." In *Orality and Literacy in Early Middle English*. Ed. Herbert Pilch. Tübingen: G. Narr, 1996. Pp. 179–98.

Seinte Iuliene. See *Þe Liflade ant te Passiun of Seinte Iuliene*.

Seinte Katerine: Re-Edited from MS Bodley 34 and the other Manuscripts. Ed. S. R. T. O. d'Ardenne and E. J. Dobson. EETS s.s. 7. Oxford: Oxford University Press, 1981.

Seinte Marherete: Þe Meiden ant Martyr. Ed. Frances M. Mack. EETS o.s. 193. London: Oxford University Press, 1934. Rpt. 1958.

Seyfarth, Jutta, ed. *Speculum virginum*. Turnhout: Brepolis, 1990.

Sheehan, Michael M. *Marriage, Family, and Law in Medieval Europe: Collected Studies*. Ed. James K. Farge. Buffalo and Toronto: University of Toronto Press, 1996.

Sigurdsson, Lotta. "Death Becomes Her: Writing and Reading the Mortified and Dead Body in the *Ancrene Wisse* and Related Works." In *Fleshly Things and Spiritual Matters: Studies on the Medieval Body in Honour of Margaret Bridges*. Ed. Nicole Nyffenegger and Katrin Rupp. Newcastle upon Tyne: Cambridge Scholars Publishing, 2011. Pp. 142–63.

Simpson, James. "Moving Images." In *Reform and Cultural Revolution*. Oxford: Oxford University Press, 2002. Pp. 383–458.

Skaffari, Janne. "Lexical Borrowings in Early Middle English Religious Discourse: A Case Study of Sawles Warde." In Hiltunen and Skaffari.

Smith, Jeremy. "Standard Language in Early Middle English." In *Placing Middle English in Context*. Ed. Irma Taavitsainen et al. Berlin and New York: Mouton de Gruyter, 2000. Pp. 125–39.

Smith, Karen. "Snake-Maiden Transformation Narratives in Hagiography and Folklore." *Fabula* 43 (2002), 251–63.

The South English Legendary: Edited from Corpus Christi College Cambridge MS. 145 and British Museum MS. Harley 2277 with Variants from Bodley MS. Ashmole 43 and British Museum MS. Cotton Julius D.

IX. Ed. Charlotte D'Evelyn and Anna J. Mill. 2 vols. EETS o.s. 235 and 236. London: Oxford University Press, 1956.

Southern, R. W. and F. S. Schmidt, eds. *Memorials of St. Anselm*. London: Oxford University Press, 1969.

Spencer, Frederic. "The Legend of St. Margaret." *Modern Language Notes* 4 (1889), 197–201.

St. Victor, Hugh of. *De Anima*. *Patrologia Latina*. Vol. 176. Paris: Garnier Frères, 1880.

Stevens, William J. "The Titles of 'MSS AB'." *Modern Language Notes* 76.5 (1961), 443–44.

Stevenson, Lorna, and Jocelyn Wogan-Browne, ed. *Concordances to the Katherine Group, MS Bodley 34 and The Wooing Group, MSS Nero A.xiv and Titus D.xviii*. Cambridge: D. S. Brewer, 2000.

Tennyson, Alfred. *The Works of Alfred Lord Tennyson, Poet Laureate*. New York: Grosset and Dunlap, 1892.

The Testament of Solomon. Trans. F. C. Conybeare. *Jewish Quarterly Review* 11.1 (1898), 1–45.

Tertullian. *Index verborum omnium quae sunt in Q. Septimii Florentis Tertulliani tracatu De praescriptione haereticorum, addita lucubratione de praepositionibus in tractatu De praescriptione haereticorum occurentibus*. Ed. Aemilius Michiels. Steenbrugis: Hagae Comitis, 1959.

Thompson, Sally. *Women Religious: The Founding of English Nunneries after the Norman Conquest*. Oxford: Clarendon Press, 1991.

Tolkien, J. R. R. "The Devil's Coach-Horses." *The Review of English Studies* 1.3 (1925), 331–36.

———. "*Ancrene Wisse* and *Hali Meiðhad*." *Essays and Studies* 14 (1929), 104–26.

Traver, Hope. *The Four Daughters of God: A Study of the Versions of this Allegory with Special Reference to those in Latin, French, and English*. Bryn Mawr, PA: Bryn Mawr College, 1907.

———. "The Four Daughters of God: A Mirror of Changing Doctrine." *PMLA* 40 (1925), 44–92.

Treharne, Elaine. "'They Should Not Worship Devils . . . Which Neither Can See, Nor Hear, Nor Walk': The Sensibility of the Virtuous and the *Life of St. Margaret*." *Proceedings of the PMR Conference* 15 (1990), 221–36.

———. *Living Through Conquest: The Politics of Early English, 1020-1220*. Oxford: Oxford University Press, 2012.

———. "A Note on the Sensational Old English *Life of St. Margaret*." In *Saints and Scholars: New Perspectives on Anglo-Saxon Literature and Culture in Honour of Hugh Magennis*. Ed. Stuart McWilliams. Woodbridge: D. S. Brewer, 2012. Pp. 5–13.

Uselmann, Susan. "Women Reading and Reading Women: Early Scribal Notions of Literacy in the *Ancrene Wisse*." *Exemplaria* 16.2 (2004), 369–404.

Vernon Manuscript. The Minor Poems of the Vernon MS. (with a Few from the Digby MSS. 2 and 86). Ed. C. Hortsmann and F. J. Furnivall. 2 vols. EETS o.s. 98, 117. London: K. Paul, Trench, Trübner & Co., 1892–1901. Pp. 756–76.

Wada, Yoko, ed. *A Companion to* Ancrene Wisse. Cambridge: D. S. Brewer, 2003.

———. "What is *Ancrene Wisse*?" In Wada, *A Companion*. Pp. 1–28.

Walsh, Christine. "The Role of the Normans in the Development of the Cult of St Katherine." In Jenkins and Lewis. Pp. 19–35.

———. *The Cult of St Katherine of Alexandria in Early Medieval Europe*. Aldershot: Ashgate, 2007.

Warner, Rubie D. N., ed. *Early English Homilies from the Twelfth Century MS Vespasian. D. XIV*. EETS o.s. 152. London: K. Paul, Trench, Trübner & Co., 1917. Rpt. New York: Kraus, 1971.

The Wars of Alexander. Ed. Hoyt N. Duggan and Thorlac Turville-Petre. EETS s.s. 10. Oxford: Oxford University Press, 1989.

Watson, Nicholas. See Anne Savage.

Weitzmann-Fiedler, Josepha. "Zur Illustration der Margaretenlegende." *Münchner Jahrbuch der bildenden Kunst* 3.17 (1966), 17–48.

White, T. H., ed. and trans. *The Bestiary: A Book of Beasts*. New York: G. P. Putnam's Sons, 1960.

Whitehead, Christina. *Castles of the Mind: A Study in Medieval Architectural Allegory*. Cardiff: University of Wales Press, 2003.

Whiting, Bartlett Jere, with the collaboration of Helen Wescott Whiting. *Proverbs, Sentences, and Proverbial Phrases from English Writings Mainly before 1500*. Cambridge, MA: The Belknap Press of Harvard University Press, 1968.

Wiggins, Alison, ed. *The Stanzaic Guy of Warwick*. Kalamazoo, MI: Medieval Institute Publications, 2004.

Winstead, Karen A. "Capgrave's Saint Katherine and the Perils of Gynecocracy." *Viator* 25 (1994), 361–76.

———. *Virgin Martyrs: Legends of Sainthood in Late Medieval England*. Ithaca, NY: Cornell University Press, 1997.

———, ed. *Chaste Passions: Medieval English Virgin Martyr Legends*. Ithaca, NY: Cornell University Press, 2000.

———. "St Katherine's Hair." In Jenkins and Lewis. Pp. 171–99.

Wogan-Browne, Jocelyn. "The Virgin and the Dragon: The Demonology of Seinte Margarete." *Leeds Studies in English* 16 (1985), 337–57.

———. "Moderation in *Sawles Warde*." In *KM 80: A Birthday Album for Kenneth Muir, Tuesday 5 May 1987*. Liverpool: Liverpool University Press, 1987. Pp. 116–18.

———. "Chaste Bodies: Frames and Experiences." In *Framing Medieval Bodies*. Ed. Sarah Kay and Miri Rubin. Manchester: Manchester University Press, 1994. Pp. 24–42.

———. "The Virgin's Tale." In *Feminist Readings in Middle English Literature: The Wife of Bath and All Her Sect*. Ed. Ruth Evans and Lesley Johnson. London: Routledge, 1994. Pp. 165–94.

———. *Saints' Lives and Women's Literary Culture c.1150–1300: Virginity and Its Authorizations*. Oxford and New York: Oxford University Press, 2001.

———. "Powers of Record, Powers of Example: Hagiography and Women's History." In Erler and Kowaleski. Pp. 71–93.

Þe Wohunge of ure Lauerd. Ed. W. Meredith Thompson. EETS o.s. 241. London: Oxford University Press, 1958.

Wolf, Kristen. "The Severed Breast: A Topos in the Legends of Female Virgin Martyr Saints." *Arkiv för Nordisk Filologi* 112 (1997), 97–112.

Woolf, Rosemary. "The Fall of Man in *Genesis B* and the *Mystère d'Adam*." In *Studies in Old English in Honor of Arthur G. Brodeur*. Ed. S. B. Greenfield. Eugene: University of Oregon Books, 1963. Pp. 187–99.

Wulfstan. *The Homilies of Wulfstan*. Ed. Dorothy Betherum. Oxford: Clarendon Press, 1957.

Zettersten, Arne. *Studies in the Dialect and Vocabulary of the Ancrene Riwle*. Lund: C. W. K. Gleerup, 1965.

GLOSSARY

a (prep.) in, on

a, an(e) (adj./num.) one; single. (indef. art.) a, an (gen. sing. *anes*). used in emphatic phrases in gen. form: **thes feondes an foster**, the very child of the devil; **the an**, one of them; **his anes**, of himself alone; **hire anes**, of herself alone; **anes weis**, one way; indef. pron. meaning some: **ane wlonke wordes**, some haughty words; **an efter an**, one after another

áá (adv.) always, forever; ever; **áá on ec(h)nesse**, forever into eternity, forever and ever

abad (v.) see **abide**

abade (n.) delay

abeoren (v.) endure, bear (past 3rd sing. *aber*)

aber see **abeoren**

abide (v. pres. 1st sing.) abide, wait (pres. 3rd sing. *abit, abideth*; imper. sing. *abid*)

abideth; abit see **abide**

ablindeth (v. pres. 3rd pl.) become blind

aboht see **abuggen**

abufen (adv./prep.) above

abuggen (v.) pay for, buy, purchase (past 3rd sing. *aboht*)

abute(n) (adv./prep.) around; about; nearby

acangin (v.) to be demented, insane (pres. 2nd sing. *acangest*; past part. *acanget*)

acast see **akeasten**

acoveret see **acovrin**

acoverunge (n.) recovering, recovery

acovrin (v.) recover (past part. *acoveret*)

acursede, acurset (v. past part.) accursed

acwalde(st) see **acwellen**

acwelle(n) (v.) to kill (past 2nd sing. *acwaldest*)

acwenct see **acwente**

acwente (v. past 3rd sing.) quenched (past part. *acwenct*)

acwiketh (v. pres. 3rd sing.) revives, returns to life, is resurrected (pres. pl. *acwikieth*; past part. *acwiket*)

acwikieth see **acwiketh**

ad (n.) funeral pyre

adamantines (n. gen. sing.) of adamant

adedet (v. past part.) dampened, mortified

adrede (v. past part.) afraid

adrenchet (v. past part.) drowned

adun (adv.) down

adunewart (adv.) downward

adweschen (v.) cast down, overwhelm (past 3rd sing. *adweschte*)

afeallen, avellen (v.) cast down, fell (pres. 3rd sing. *avealleth, aveallet*; imper. sing. *aval*)

aflei (v. imper.) drive out

afluht (n.) downward flight, swoop

ageasteth (v. pres. 3rd sing.) makes aghast, frightens (past 3rd sing. *agaste*)

agelwede (v. past 3rd sing.) frightened, terrified

agras see **agrisen**

agrisen (v.) terrify, frighten; become terrified or frightened; shudder (past 3rd sing. *agras*; past part. *agrisen*)

agulten see **agulteth**

agulteth (v. pres. pl.) sin, do wrong, be guilty of sin (past pl. *agulten*)

ah (conj.) but; and

ah (v.) ought to, should; own (pres. 1st sing. *ah, hah*; pres. 2nd sing. *ahest*; pres. 3rd sing. *ah,*; pres. pl. *ahen*; past 2nd sing. *ahtest*; past 3rd sing. *ahte, hahte, oht*; past pl. *ahten*; past forms often used in present sense)

ahef (v. past 3rd sing.) lifted up (past part. *aheven(e)*)

ahen, ahest see **ah** (v.)

aheven(e) see **ahef**

ahne (adj./pron.) own

ahon see **ahongeden**

ahongeden (v. pa. 3rd pl.) hanged (past part. *ahon*)

ahte, hahte (n. pl.) cattle; goods, property

ahten, ahtest see **ah**

akast, akeast, akeasten, akeasteth see **akeasten**

akeasten (v.) to cast down, overthrow (pres. 3rd sing. *akeasteth*; past 3rd sing. *akast, acast*; past pl. *akeasten*; past part. *akeast, akest*)

aken (v.) aches, hurts (pres. pl. *aketh*)

akennesse (n.) incarnation; conception (of Christ)

akennet (v. past part.) born, descended

akest see **akeasten**

aketh see **aken**

al, alle, al(l)(e) (adj. sing./pl.) all, every (gen. sing. *alles*; gen. pl. *alre*); **ye alles**, you out of everyone; **the alre least**, the remotest, furthest; **alre meast**, most of all; **alre thing**, of all things, of everything). (n.) everyone; everything. (adv.) all, completely, entirely, thoroughly; **al up** completely . (conj.) although

alde (adj.) old (superl. *ealdeste*)

aldren (n. pl.) elders, parents, ancestors

aleast (adv.) finally, at last

alei see **aliggen**

aleid (v. past part.) subdued

ales see **alesen**

alesde see **alesen**

alesen (v.) redeem, deliver, free (past 3rd sing. *aleset, alesde*; imper. sing. *ales*)

alesendnesse (n.) redemption

alesent (n.) redeemer

aleset see **alesen**

alesunge (n.) redemption

aliggen (v.) fail, cease; fade, subside (pres. 3rd sing. *alith*; past 3rd sing. *alei*)

alith see **aliggen**

alleweldinde, alweldende, alwealdinde (adj./pres. part.) all-ruling, almighty, omnipotent; (as subst.) **Alwealdent**, All-Ruler, the Almighty, God

allunge (adv.) wholly, entirely; **allunge swuch . . . as**, completely like

almihti (adj.) almighty; (prop. n.) the Almighty, God

alre see **alle**

alse see **alswa**

alswa (conj.) also, so, likewise; **alswa as**, just as; **alswa as . . . alswa as**, just as . . . so

alwealdinde see **alleweldinde**

am see **beon**

amanset (v. past part.) damned, accursed

amead (adj.) mad, insane

amid(d)e, amit (prep.) in the middle of, amid

amidheppes (adv.) in the midst of it

amonc (prep.) among

amurthrin (v.) murder

an see **a**

anan (adv.) immediately, at once

ananriht (adv.) immediately, at once

ane (adj.) alone, only. (indef. art.) see **a**

anesweis (adv.) one way, the same way; **wenden alle anesweis**, to turn the same way (i.e., to convert)

angoise (n.) anguish

anhad (n.) unity, oneness

an-hwet (pron.) one thing

an-ihurnde (adj.) one-horned, i.e., unicorn

anlepi (adj.) only, single

another (adj./pron.) another

ant (conj.) and

anvald (adj.) one alone

apostel (n.) apostle (pl. *apostles*)

araht see **areachen**

aras see **arisen**

are (n.) honor, glory

areachen (v.) interpret, describe (past 3rd sing. *araht*)

areare see **arerde**

aren see **beon**

areoweth (v. pres. 3rd sing.) pities; grieves (past 3rd sing. *arew*; imper. sing. *areow*)

arerde (v. past 3rd sing.) raised up (subj. pres sing. areare)

arew, areow (v.) see **areoweth**

arewe (n.) arrow

ariht (adv.) aright, rightly

arise, ariseth see **arisen**

arise(n) (v.) to arise; ascend (pres. 3rd sing. *ariseth*; past 2nd sing. *arise*; past 3rd sing. *aras*; past subj. 3rd sing. *arise*; imper. pl. *ariseth*)

ariste (n.) resurrection, arising

aromaz (n. pl.) aromatic spices

art see **beon**

arudde(n) (v.) rescue, deliver (past 3rd sing. *arudde*; imper. sing., *arude*; past part. *arudd*)

arude see **arudden**

asaileth (v. pres. 3rd. sing.) assails, attacks, assaults

as(e) (adv./conj.) as, like; just as; such as; since; while; how

asenchtest (v. past 2nd sing.) drowned

astearde (v. past 3rd sing.) stirred up, raised

astenche (v.) to assail with stench

astorven (v. past. part.) destroyed

aswiketh (v. pres. 3rd sing.) ceases

aswinden (v.) perish, fade away (pres. 3rd sing. *aswint*)

aswint see **aswinden**

athet (conj.) until

athrusmeth (v. pres. 3rd sing.) smothers, suffocates

atine (n.) dispute, debate

atter (n.) poison

attri (adj.) poisonous

aturn (n.) appearance

atwa see **otwa**

aval see **afeallen**

aveallet, avealleth see **afeallen**

avellen see **afeallen**

awahte (v. past 3rd sing.) awoke

awakeneth see **awakenin**

awakenin (v.) arise (pres. 3rd sing. *awakeneth*; pres. pl. *awakenith*)

awarpen (v.) to cast down, overthrow, destroy (past 3rd sing. *aweorp*; past part. *awarpen*)

aw(e)ariede see **awariede**

awealden (v.) overcome, overrule, master (imper. awelt; past part. *awelt, awealt*)

awealt see **awealdan**

awariede, awariet, aw(e)ariede (v. past part.) accursed

awed (v. past part.) maddened

awei (adv.) away

aweiwart (adv.) away

aweld see **awealden**

aweorp see **awarpen**

awundrede (v. past 3rd sing. refl.) to be surprised or astonished (past pl. *awundreden*; past part. *awundret*)

ax-treo (n.) axle

ayef see **ayeoven**

ayein, ayeines (adv.) against; back; in reply (with regard to speech); in exchange for, in place of; about; **yef ye ayein wulleth**, if you wish to return (go back). (prep.) against

ayeinwart (adv.) back, backwards

ayeove(n) (v.) give up (imper. sing. *ayef*)

ba (adj./pron.) both (gen. *beire*)

balde see **bealden**

baldeliche (adv.) boldly, bravely

bale (n.) bale, misery, suffering; scorn; **to balewe ant to bismere**, abusively and scornfully; (adj.) sorrowful, woeful

baleful (adj.) baleful, fierce; foul, awful

balesith (n.) suffering

balewe see **bale**

bali (adj.) evil one

ban (n.) bone (pl. *banes*)

banes see **ban**

banles (adj.) boneless

bar (n.) boar

barren (n. pl.) gates, bars

bascins (n. pl.) basins

basme (n.) balm, an embalming ointment

bat (n.) boat

bathe (adj.) both. (adv.) too

beah see **buhe**

bealden (v.) encourage, embolden (past 3rd sing. *balde*)

be(a)re (adj.) bare, naked; lacking, barren; intensifier, as in **the beare unhwiht**, the very Devil, the Devil himself

bearmes (gen. sing.) lap, breast; (n. pl.) bosoms

be(a)rn (n.) child; man

bearnde see **bearneth**

bearneth (v. pres. 3rd sing.) burns (past 3rd sing. *bearnde*; pres. part. *bearnninde, berninde, beornind*)

bearnninde see **bearneth**

bearn-team (n.) offspring, child

bearst see **bersten**

beast, beste (n.) beast (pl. *beastes*; gen. sing. *beastes, bestes*)

be(a)steliche (adj.) brutish, beastly

beaten (v.) beat (pres. 2nd sing. *beatest*; pres. 3rd sing. *beateth*; past 3rd sing. *beoten*; imper. pl. *beteth*; pres. part. as n. *beattunge*; past part. *ibeaten*)

beatest see **beaten**

beatewil (adj.) tasty

beath (n.) bath

beathien (v.) bathe

beattunge (n.) beating; see also **beaten**

bed(de) (n.) bed

beddin (v.) live together

bed(e) (v.) see **bidde(n)**

begon see **biginnen**

bei, beide see **beieth**

bei(e)th (v. pres. 3rd sing.) bend, bow; pay homage (past 3rd sing. *beide*; subj. pres. sing., *beie*; imper. sing. *bei*)

beire see **ba**

beisume (adv.) humbly, obediently

bendes see **bondes**

bene (n.) prayer, request (pl. *benen*)

benen see **bene**

beo see **beon**

beodefule (adj.) spiritual, prayerful

beoden (n. pl.) prayers

beoden (v.) to announce

beon (v.) be, exist (pres. 1st sing. *am*; pres. 2nd sing. *art*; pres. 3rd sing. *is, bith*; pres. pl. *aren, beoth, beon*; past 3rd sing. *wes*; past pl. *weren*; imper. *beoth*); negative forms (pres. 1st sing. *nam*; pres. 2nd sing. *nart*; pres. 3rd sing. *nis*; past 3rd sing. *nes*; past 3rd pl. *neren*);

subj. forms (pres. sing. *beo*; pres. pl. *beon*, past sing. *were* (were; would be); past pl. *weren*; neg. past 3rd sing. *nere*); **beo . . . to seggen**, means; **aren sikere of . . . to**, are certain that . . . will

beore(n) (v.) bear, carry; give birth to; bear witness; impress; urge, incite (pres. 2nd sing. *berest*; pres. 3rd sing. *bereth*; past 1st sing. *ber*; past 3rd sing. *ber, beren*; subj. pres. sing., pl. *beore*; imper. pl. *beoreth*; past part. *ibore(n)(e)*); **on ehe bereth ham**, as it impresses them in the eye (i.e., as it appears to them); **beore/bereth forth**, project, stick out, distend; **beoreth me genge**, accompany me; **beore to**, be inclined to

beoreth see **beoren**

beorninde (adj.) burning; see also **bearnde**

beoten see **beaten**

beoth see **beon**

ber see **beoren**

berde (n.) beard

berde (v. past 3rd sing.) cried aloud

bere see **beare**

bere (n.) outcry, uproar

beren, berest, bereth see **beoren**

bern see **bearn**

berninde see **bearneth**

bersten (v.) burst; shatter (past 3rd sing. *bearst*; past pl. *bursten*)

besmen (n. pl.) rods

best see **betere**

beste see **beast**

bestelich see **beastelich**

bet see **bidden**

beten (v.) to make good, atone (past 3rd sing. *bette*; past part. *ibet*)

betere (adj. compar.) better (superl. *best*)

beteth see **beaten**

bette see **beten**

bi (prep.) by; near; to, according to; about; in (**bi westen**, in the west)

biblodeget (v. past part.) stained with blood, bloodied; defiled

biburiede, biburieden, biburiet see **biburien**

biburien (v.) bury (past 3rd sing. *biburiede*; past pl. *biburieden*; past part. *biburiet, iburiet*)

bicapede (v. past 3rd sing.) stared at

bichearreth (v. pres. pl.) dupe, deceive (past 3rd sing. *bicherde*)

bicherde see **bichearreth**

bicluppeth (v. pres. 3rd sing.) embraces; **bicluppeth abuten**, contains, encompasses

bicluset (v. past part.) locked up

bicorven (v. past part.) cut off; in **hefdes bicorven**, beheaded

bicume(n) (v.) to become, be appropriate or fitting (pres. 3rd sing. *bikimeth*; past 3rd sing. *bicom*); **bicom to thet**, it happened that

bidde(n) (v.) to pray; command, order (pres. 1st sing. *bidde*; pres. 2nd sing. *biddest*; pres. 3rd sing. bit; pres. pl. *biddeth*; past 3rd sing. *bed(e), bet*; pres. 3rd sing. subj. *bidde*; pres. part. *biddinde*; past part. *ibeden*)

biddest, biddeth see **bidde(n)**

biddinde see **bidden**

bidweolet (v. past part.) confounded, bewildered

bieoden (v. past pl.) treated

bifunden (v. past part.) filled; in **fulthe bifunden**, filled with filth (or, characterized by filthiness) see also **finden**

bigan see **bigath**

bigath (v. pres. pl.) pass by; cover; bespatter (past 3rd sing. *bigan*; past part. *bigan*)

biget (v. past)

biginnen (v.) to begin; to come into existence or be created (pres. 2nd sing. *biginnest*; past 3rd sing. *begon, bigon*; past pl. *bigunnen*;

imper. *biginneth*; pres. part.
biginunge; past part. *bigunne*,
bigunnen)

biginnest, biginneth see **biginnen**

biginnunge (n.) beginning

bigon see **biginnen**

bigoten (v. past part.) drenched

bigulith (v. pres. pl.) beguile, deceive

bigunne, bigunnen see **biginnen**

bihalden (v.) to look at, gaze, behold
(pres. 2nd sing. *bihaldest*; pres. 3rd
sing. *bihald, bihalde, bihalt*; pres.
3rd pl. *bihaldeth*; past 3rd sing.
biheold, biheolt, past 3rd pl.
biheolden; imper. sing. *bihald,
bihalt*; pres. part. (as n.) *behaldunge*)

bihalt see **bihalden**

bihate(n) (v.) to promise (pres. 1st
sing. *bihate*; pres. 3rd sing. *bihat*;
past 2nd sing. *bihete*; past 3rd
sing. *bihet*; past pl. *biheten*; imper.
sing. *bihat*; past part. *bihaten*)

bihe(a)fdin (v.) behead (past part.
bihefdet)

bihealden (v.) sprinkle (with); pour
over; bathe

bihe(a)ste (n.) promise, behest

bihefden, bihefdet see **bihe(a)fdin**

biheold(en), biheten see **bihalden**

biheste see **bihe(a)ste**

bihete, biheten see **bihaten**

biheve (n.) benefit, profit; advantage

bihofde see **bihoveth**

bihoveth (v. pres. 3rd sing.) behooves,
is appropriate for; is necessary
(past 3rd sing. *bihofde*);
impersonal as in **as ham bihofde**,
as they should have; **thet hire
bihoveth**, what she needs; **hwas
help the bihoveth**, whose help
you need; **ne bihoveth**, must not

bikeorven (v.) cut off

bikimeth see **bicume(n)**

bile(a)ve (n.) belief, faith; **habbe to
bileve**, have faith in (lit. hold as
belief)

bilefden (v. past pl.) believed

bilehwit (adj.) innocent

bilimeth (v. pres. 3rd sing.) mutilate

bilive (adj.) quickly, immediately

biluketh (v. pres. 3rd sing.) expresses

biluvede (v. past 3rd sing.) pleased;
yef me swa biluvede, if I were so
inclined;

bimong (prep.) among, in the midst of

bind, bindest, bindeth see **binden**

binden (v.) bind, tie up (pres. 2nd
sing. *bindest*; pres. pl. *bindeth*; past
3rd pl. *bunden*; imper. sing. *bind*;
past part. *ibunden*)

bineome see **bineometh**

bineometh (v. pres. pl.) deprive, take
away (subj. pres. sing. *bineome*;
past part. *binumen*)

bineothen (prep.) beneath

binumen see **bineometh**

bireadde (v. past 3rd sing.) planned,
decided

bireavet see **bireavin**

bireavin (v.) bereave, deprive, rob
(past part. *bireavet*)

biremen (v.) lament, mourn, bewail

bireowe (v.) regret

bireowsin (v.) to repent (pres. pl.
bireowsith; imper. pl. *bireowsith*;
pres. part. *birewsinde*)

bireowsith, birewsinde see **bireowsin**

bireowsunge (n.) repentance. See also
bireowsin

bisech, biseche see **bisechen**

bisechen (v.) to beseech, ask for (pres.
1st sing. *biseche*; past 3rd sing.
bisohte; past pl. *bisohten*; imper.
sing. *bisech*)

biseh see **biseon**

bisemeth (v. pres. 3rd sing.) it is
fitting, it suits

biseon(n)e (v.) to look at, see (pres.
3rd sing. *bisith*; past 3rd sing.
biseh; imper. sing. *bisih*)

biseonne see **biseon**

biset (v. past part.) seated;
surrounded; provided for;
fashion; **abute biset**, surrounded;

bisetten hire wordes, express herself

bisih see **biseon**

bisiliche (adv.) busily, diligently

bisith see **biseon**

bismere (n.) scorn; see **bale**

bisne (n.) parable; example

bisohte(n) (v.) see **bisechen**

bistearede (v. past 3rd sing.) to stare at

bisteathet (v. past part.) oppressed

bisteken (v. past part.) shut out, excluded

bistepped (v. past part.) beset, surrounded

bistonden (v. past part.) beset

bisuncken (v. past part.) sunk

bit see **bidde(n)**

bitacnet see **bitacneth**

bitacneth (v. pres. 3rd sing.) betokens, signifies (past part. *bitacnet*)

bitaht(e) see **biteche(n)**

bite (n.) bite

bite (v. pres. subj. sing.) may it bite

biteache see **bitechen**

biteche(n) (v.) commit, deliver; surrender; grant, entrust (with a task) (pres. 1st sing. *biteache*; past 3rd sing. *bitaht(e)*); **as thet is bitaht the** as it is granted/ entrusted to you (i.e., as is your right).

bitel (adj.) sharp, keen

bitevelet (n. past part.) defeated, out-argued

bith see **beon**

bithench see **bithenchen**

bithenchen (on) (v.) think of, contrive; as reflexive, consider (pres. 3rd sing. *bithencheth*; pres. pl. *bithencheth*; past. part. *bithoht*; imper. sing. *bithench*);

bithencheth see **bithencheth**

bitimde (v. past 3rd sing.) it befell, happened

bitrumme (v.) to surround (past part. *bitrum(m)et*)

bitter(e), bittre (adj.) bitter, cruel, sharp (gen. sing. *bittres*). (as subst.) bitterness

bitterliche (adv.) cruelly, bitterly (superl. *bitterlukest*)

bitterlukest see **bitterliche**

bitternesse (n.) bitterness, cruelty, torment

bittre(s) see **bitter**

bituh(h)e(n) (prep.) between; among

bitunde (v. past 3rd sing.) confined, sealed; swallowed up

biturde (v. past 3rd sing.) turned around

bitweonen (prep.) between

bivore(n) (prep.) before; in front of; above; more than (adv.) before; **bivoren ham**, in their presence (lit., in front of them)

biwende (v. past 3rd sing.) turned

biwihelin (v.) bewitch, beguile

biwinneth (v. pres. pl.) win, obtain, achieve

biwistest, biwit see **biwite**

biwite(n) (v.) to protect, defend; keep watch, guard (pres. 3rd sing. *biwit*; pres. pl. *biwiteth*; past 2nd sing. *biwistest*; pres. pl. *biwiteth*; imper. sing. *biwite*; infl. infin. *biwitene*)

biwiteth see **biwite**

biwopen (n. past pl.) bewailed

biwunden (v. past part.) wrapped

biyeote(ne) (v.) get, obtain, become; beget (pres. pl. *biyeoteth*; past 3rd sing. *biyet, biyeted*; past part. *biyetene*)

biyet (n.) profit, gain

biyet, biyeted, biyetene see **biyeote**

blac, blake (adj.) black; pale, pallid (compar. *blackre*)

blakede see **blakien**

blakien (v.) to become pale; to become black (past 3rd sing. *blakede*)

blamon (n.) black-skinned person

bleinin (n. pl.) blisters

blencte (v. past 3rd sing.) flinched, jerked

blent (v. past 3rd sing.) blinded (past part. *iblend*, *iblent*)

bleo (n.) face

blescede(st) see **blesci**

blesceunge (n.) blessing

blesci (v. pres. 1st sing.) bless; make the sign of the cross (past 2nd sing. *blescedest*; past 3rd sing. *blescede*; pres. 3rd sing. subj; *blesci*; past part. *iblescet*, *iblescede*); **Ich blesci me**, I make the sign of the cross on myself

blikede (v. past 3rd sing.) glittered (past 3rd pl. *blikeden*; pres. part. *blikinde*)

blikeden, blikinde see **blikede**

blinde (adj., subst.) blind

blindlunge (adv.) blindly

blisfule (adj.) blissful

blisse (n.) bliss (pl. *blissen*)

blissen see **blisse**

blissith (v. pres. pl.) rejoice, are happy

blithe (adj.) blithe, happy

blitheliche (adv.) blithely, happily; gladly, willingly (compar. *blitheluker*)

blitheluker see **blitheliche**

blod(e) (n.) blood; gore (gen. sing. *blodes*)

blodi (adj.) bloody

blodles (adj.) bloodless (i.e., nonliving); cowardly

blostme (n.) blossom

blowinde (v. pres. part.) blooming, blossoming (past part. *iblowen*)

boc (n.) book (pl. *bokes*)

boc-felle (n.) parchment

bode (n.) command

bodi (n.) body (pl. *bodies*)

bodien (v.) to proclaim, command

bokes see **boc**

bolt (n.) dwelling

bondes, bendes (n. pl.) bonds

bone (n.1) prayer, boon (pl. *bonen*)

bone (n.2) bane, destroyer; doom

bonen see **bone** (n.1)

bordes (n. pl.) boards

borh (n.) repayment

borien (v.) bore, pierce

bosum (n.) womb

bote (n.) amends; remedy; **eode on bote**, did penance, expiated sin; **o bote geath**, does penance

botneth (v. pres. 3rd sing.) cures; (past 3rd sing. *bot(t)nede*)

brade (adj.) broad

breades see **bread**

brec see **br(e)oken**

bred (n.) bread (gen. sing. *breades*)

bredest (n. pres. 2nd sing.) breed (pres. 3rd sing. *brede*; pres. pl. *bredeth*)

breid (v. past 3rd sing.) sprang, started

breines (n. gen. sing.) brain's; **breines turnunge**, brain's turning (i.e., head spinning, dizziness)

breken, brekest, breoke(th) see **br(e)oken**

br(e)oken (v.) break; be wounded (in torture); commit (a sin); burst forth; break into (a house); (pres. 2nd sing. *brekest*; past 3rd sing. *brec*; past 3rd pl. *breken*; subj. pres. sing. *breoke*; imper. sing. *brec*; imper. pl. *breoketh*; past part. *ibroken*) **breoketh on**, open up; **brec on**, burst out

breoste (n.) breast; chest; heart or mind (pl. *breosten*; gen. pl. *breostes*); **breoste reste**, peace of mind; **breoste-holke**, breast-hollow (i.e., ribcage)

bres (n.) brass

brethren see **brother**

brides (n.pl.) birds

briht(e) (adj.) bright (compar. *briht(t)re*; super. *brihtest*)

brihtest see **briht**

briht(t)re see **briht**

bringe(n), bringin (v.) bring, take (pres. 2nd sing.; past 1st sing.

brohte; past 2nd sing. *brohtest*; past 3rd sing. *brohte*; past 3rd pl. *brohten*; past part. *ibroht(e)*)

brohte(n), brohtest see **bringen**

broken see **bruken**

broke-rugget (adj.) bent-backed, bow-backed, hunchbacked

brond, bront (n.) sword

brother (n.) brother (pl. *brethren*)

bruche (n.) breach, transgression, sin; wound, cut (pl. *bruchen*); **bruche of hire bodi**, loss of her virginity

bruchel(e) (adj.) breakable, fragile, brittle (brickle)

bruchen see **bruche**

brud(e) see **burde**

brudgume (n.) bridegroom

brudlac (n.) wedlock, marriage (gen. *brudlakes*)

brudlakes see **brudlac**

brugge (n.) bridge

bruken (v.) get, have; enjoy

brune (n.) fire, burning; **bringen o brune**, set on fire

brune-wallinde (adj.) boiling hot

buc (n.) trunk (of the body)

budel (n.) messenger, beadle

buest see **buhest**

buggen (v.) buy (pres. pl. *buggeth*; *iboht*)

buhe (v.) to bow, submit; obey (pres. 2nd sing. buest *buhest*; pres. 3rd pl. *buheth*; past 3rd sing. *beah*; pres. subj. pl. *buhe*; past 3rd subj. sing. *buhe*; imper. sing. *buh*; past part. *ibuhe*)

buhest, buheth see **buhe**

buhsume (adj.) buxom, obedient. (adv.) buxomly, obediently

buhsumnesse (n.) obedience, submissiveness

bulden (v.) build (imper. pl. *buldeth*)

buldeth see **bulden**

bule (n.) bull

bunden see **binden**

bur see **bur(h)**

burde, brud(e) (n.) lady; bride see also **burthe**

burdeboldes, buriboldes (n.) family houses, dwellings; castles, palaces

bur(e) (n.) room, chamber (bower)

bur(h) (n.) city (gen. sing. *burhes*, *burhene*)

burh-domes (n. pl.) court judgments

burhe (v.) save, protect (past part. *iborhen*)

burhene see **bur(h)**

burhmen (n. pl.) citizens, townspeople (gen. pl. *burhmenne*)

burh-reve (n.) magistrate, chief citizen

buriboldes see **burdeboldes**

burnes (n. gen. sing.) of a spring

bursten see **bersten**

burthe, burde (n.) birth; original nature

burtherne (n.) burden, carrying (of a child in pregnancy); heavy burden

buste see **busteth**

busteth (v. pres. 3rd sing.) buffet, beat (subj. pres. sing. *buste*)

bute(n) (conj./adv./prep/adj.) but, except; unless; apart from, without; scarcely, hardly; only (*bute* usually precedes consonants and *buten* precedes vowels, though there are often exceptions); **bute as**, except as; **nis buten an**, there is only one; **nis bute**, [it] is only; **ne . . . bute**, nothing but, no one but; **nefde ha bute iseid**, she had scarcely said; **bute yef**, unless; **ne thearf thu bute**, you need only

butte (n.) belly, uterus

buve(n) (prep.) above

cader (n.) cradle; **cader-clutes**, cradle-clothes, baby clothes

caisere see **keiser**

cake (n.) cake, loaf

calde (n./adj.) cold

callen (v.) call

cang (adj.) foolish

care (n.) care, worry (pl. *care*)

carie(n) (v.) grieve; **carien for**, take
   care of, provide for, see to
carless (adj.) careless, fearless
castel (n.) castle
cendals (n. pl.) coverings of fine linen
chaffere see **ch(e)affere**
changede see **changin**
changin (v.) change; replace,
   substitute, exchange (past 3rd
   sing. *changede*)
chapele (n.) chapel
chapi (v.) to sell, trade
charbucle (n.) carbuncle
charden (v. past 3rd pl.) turned;
   charden ayein, returned
chaste (adj.) chaste
chasti see **chastieth**
chastieth (v. pres. 3rd sing.) control,
   restrain; correct, chastise (subj.
   pres. sing. *chasti*)
ch(e)affere (n.) bargain, deal;
   exchange
chear see **chearre**
chearre (v.) turn back, change [one's]
   mind (imper. sing. *chear*; pres.
   subj. pl. *chearren*)
cheas see **cheosen**
chef (n.) chaff
chele (n.) chill, cold
cheorl (n.) churl (husband)
cheosen (v.) choose (pres. 1st sing.
   cheose; pres. 3rd sing. *cheoseth*;
   past 2nd sing. *chure*; past 3rd
   sing. *ches*, *cheas*; past part. *ichosen*,
   icoren(e), *icore*; superl. *icorenest*
   (choicest, best); imper. *cheos*)
cheowest (v. pres. 2nd sing.) chew;
   nag ("chew out") (pres. 3rd sing.
   cheoweth)
cheping (v. pres. part.) marketing,
   trading
chepmenne (n. gen. pl.) of the
   merchants
chere (n.) expression, countenance
cherre (n.) time, occasion; **ed en
   cherre**, at one time
ches see **cheosen**

chevese (n.) concubine, paramour
chideth (v. pres. 3rd sing.) chides,
   scolds
childe (n.) child; childbed, labor (pl.
   children)
childhade (n.) childhood
children see **childe**
chirche (n.) church
chit (v. pres. 3rd sing.) chides, scolds
chule, chulle see **wulle**
chure see **cheosen**
ciclatuns (n. pl.) silk cloth of scarlet
   interwoven with gold
clane (adv.) completely, entirely
clath (n.) clothing; cloth (pl. *clathes*)
clathes see **clath**
cleane (adj.) clean, pure; chaste
   (superl. *cleaneste*). (adv.)
   completely, entirely
cleannesse (n.) cleanness, chastity,
   purity
cleanschipe (n.) cleanness, chastity
clearc (n.) clerk, scholar (pl. clerkes)
cleargesse (n.) female scholar
cleaterin (v.) shatter
**cleopede, cleopest, cleopeth,
   cleopie, cleopieth** see **cleopien**
cle(o)pien (v.) name, to be called
   (pres. 1st sing. *cleopie*; pres. 2nd
   sing. *cleopest*; pres. 3rd sing.
   cleopeth; pres. pl. *cleopieth*; past 3rd
   sing. *cleopede*; past part. *icleopet*)
cleopieth, clepien see **cleopien**
clergies (n. pl.) branches of learning,
   scholarship
clerkes see **clearc**
cluppunge (n.) embrace
cnawe(n) (v.) to know, be familiar
   with; acknowledge (pres. 1st sing.
   cnawe; pres. pl. *cnaweth*; past sing.
   subj. *cneowe*; past part. *icnawen*);
   we beoth . . . icnawen, we
   acknowledge; see also **icnawen**
cnawes, icnawes (adv.)
   acknowledging, admitting; **beo
   soth cnawes**, be honest, admit the
   truth

cnaweth see cnawen

cnawlechith (v. pres. pl.)
acknowledge

cnawlechunge (n.) knowledge;
acknowledging

cneolin (v.) kneel (pres. part.
cneolinde)

cneolinde see cneolin

cneon (v. pl.) knees

cneowe see cnawe(n)

cnif (n.) knife

cnihtene see cnihtes

cnihtes (n. pl.) knights (gen. pl.
cnihtene)

cnotte (n.) knots (pl. *cnotten*)

cnottede (v. past part.) knotted

cnotti (adj.) knotty; difficult, intricate

cnurnede (adj.) gnarled

colede (v. past 3rd sing.) cooled

colen (n. pl.) coals

colt (n.) colt (as a term of contempt)

com, comen, comme see cume(n)

con see cunnen

confort (n.) comfort

const, constu see cunnen

copni (v. pres. 1st sing.) await; long
for (pres. pl. *copnith*)

copnith see copni

corn (n.) grain, seed (as opposed to
chaff)

cost see cunnen

coss (n.) kiss

coste (n.) cost; **bi lives coste**, at the
cost of life (i.e., on pain of death)

coverunge (n.) recovery; **bute
coverunge**, irrecoverably, without
hope of recovery or redemption

crahien (v.) to stretch out the neck

cravant (adj.) defeated

creap (v. past 3rd sing.) crept (pres.
part. *creopinde*)

crechen (v. pres. subj. pl.) catch, hook

creft (n.) craft, skill; one of the
branches of knowledge known as
the seven liberal arts (pl. *creftes*)

crefti (adj.) crafty, skilled,
knowledgeable

creftiluker (compar. adv.) more craftily

crenge (v.) in **crenge with swire**, to
arch the neck

creopinde see creap

Crist (n.) Christ (gen. *Cristes*)

Cristen (adj.) Christian (pl. *Cristene*);
often as subst.: Christian people

crohe (n.) pot, crock

crokes (n. pl.) wiles, tricks, hooks

crokinde (adj.) crooked, misleading,
astray

Cros (n.) the cross

Cruche (n.) the Cross

cruchede (v. past 3rd sing.) crossed
herself (in **cruchede hire**)

crune (n.) crown (gen. pl. *crunene*)

crunene see crune

cruneth (v. pres. 3rd sing.) crowns
(pres. 3rd sing. subj. *cruni*)

cruni see cruneth

cud(de), cuddest see cuthen

culvre (n.) dove (gen. sing. *culvres*;
gen. pl. *culvrene*)

culvrene see culvre

culvres see culvre

cume (n.) coming, approach; return

cume, cumest, cumme (v.) see
cume(n)

cumeliche (adj.) comely

cume(n) (v.) to come (pres. 1st sing.
cume; pres. 2nd sing. *kimest*,
cumest; pres. 3rd sing. *kimeth*; past
1st sing. *com*; past 3rd sing. *com*;
past 3rd pl. *comen*; pres. 3rd sing.
subj. *cume*, *cumme*; pres. part.
cuminde; past part. *icumen*,
icumene, *icume*, *ikumen*); **me com**,
it happened; **kimeth forth**, comes
forth, happens

cuminde see cumen

cun (n.) kin, family, relations; kind,
type (pl. *cunne*; pl. gen. *cunnes*),
nanes cunnes wise, in no kind of
way

cunde (n.) nature, natural processes;
breed, stock (pl. *cundes*); **doth
hare cunde**, follow their instinct

cundelich (adj.) natural

cundeliche (adv.) naturally

cunestable (n.) constable, chief household office

cunne see **cun**

cunnen (v.) know; have mastery of; be able to, can (pres. 2nd sing. *const, cost, constu*; pres. 3rd sing. *con*; past 3rd sing. *cuthe*; past 2nd sing. subj. *cuthest*; past 3rd subj. pl. *cuthen*)

cunnes see **cun**

cunnith (v. pres. pl.) try, attempt

conqueari (v. pres. 3rd sing.) conquers

cunredden (n.) kindred, tribe

cuntasses (n. pl.) countesses

cure (n.) car, chariot

curen (n. pl.) choices

curseth (v. pres. 3rd sing.) curses

curte (n.) court

cus (n.) kiss

custe (v. past 3rd sing.) kissed

cuth (adj.) well-known, renowned (pl. *cuthe*)

cuth see **cuthen**

cuthe see **cunnen** or **cuthen**

cuthen (v.) make known, reveal, show; tell (pres. 3rd sing. *cutheth*; pres. pl. *cutheth*; past 2nd sing. *cuddest*; past 3rd sing. *cudde*; subj. 3rd sing. *cuthe*; imper. sing. *cuth*; past part. *cud, icud(de)*, renowned, famous, important; as superl. adj. *cuddest*); **cuthe throf**, let him show it

cwakede see **cwakien**

cwakien (v.) quake, tremble (past 3rd sing. *cwakede*; pres. pl. *cwakieth*)

cwakieth see **cwakien**

cwalm (n.) death caused by pestilence

cwal(m)hus(e) (n.) literally, "death-house;" a jail for condemned prisoners

cwarterne (n.) prison

cwavien (v.) tremble, quiver

cweden see **cwethen**

cwellere (n.) killer; torturer (pl. *cwelleres*)

cwemen (v.) please

cwemest (adj. superl.) most pleasing

cwen (n.) queen (pl. *cwenes*)

cwenctest (v. past 2nd sing.) killed

cwenes see **cwen**

cwethen (v.) to say, speak; renounce (pres. 1st sing. *cwethe*; pres. 3rd sing. *cwetheth*; past 3rd sing. *cweth, quoth, quod*; past 3rd pl. *quethen, cweden*)

cwic see **cwike**

cwich (n.) sound, utterance

cwiddest (v. pres. 2nd sing.) say, tell

cwike (adj., often as subst.) quick, living

cwikede (v. past 3rd sing.) quickened, came to life

cwite (adj.) free to go; **cwetheth . . . cwite him**, declares you free to go to him

dahene, dahes see **dei**

dahethes see **dahene**

dale (n.) part, portion, share; **ane dale**, i.e., partly, in part (lit., a part, one part); **half dale**, a half share; **muchel deale**, a great deal

darede see **dearien**

darkest see **dorc**

dead (adj./subst.) dead (pl. *deade*)

deadbote (n.) penance

de(a)dlich(e) (adj.) mortal (deadly); (adv.) mortally, severely

deale see **dale**

dear see **der**

dearie, dearieth see **dearien**

dearien (v.) lurk, lie hidden; cower (pres. 1st sing. *dearie*; pres. pl. *dearieth*; past 3rd pl. *darede*)

de(a)rne (adj. pl.) secret, confidential, private

dearnliche (adv.) secretly

deathbote see **deadbote**

de(a)th(e) (n.) death (gen. sing., *deathes*); **deathes dunt**, deathblow

deathes see **de(a)the(e)**

deathlich (adj.) death-like, deathly (in appearance)

deave (adj./subst.) deaf

dede (n.) deed, matter; business (pl. *deden*)

deden see **dede**

dedlich(e) see **de(a)dlich(e)**

def see **defde**

defde (v. past 3rd sing.) sank in; dive (imper. sing. def)

degré (n.) degree, rank (pl. *degréz*)

degréz see **degré**

deh (v. pres. 3rd sing.) is proper for, is fitting for; **deh to beonne**, is fitting to be, should be

dehtren see **dohter**

dei (n.) day (pl. *deies, dahes, dahene*; gen. sing. *dahethes*, in **euche dahethes dei**, every day at dawn); **to dei**, today

deide, deidest, deie see **deien**

deien (v.) die (pres. 1st sing. *deie*; past 2nd sing. *deidest*; past 3rd sing. *deide*; pres. 2nd sing. subj. *deie*)

delit (n.) delight

dem, demde(n) see **demen**

deme (n.) judge

deme(n) (v.) judge, deem, pass or give judgment; condemn (pres. 3rd sing. *demeth*; past 3rd sing. *demde*; past 3rd pl. *demden*; imper. sing. *dem*; past part. *idemet*)

demeth see **demen**

deofel, deovel (n.) devil, fiend (pl. *deoflen*; dat. pl. *deovele, deofle*; gen. sing. *deofles*)

deofle, deofles see **deofel**

deop (adj.) deep

deop(e) (adv.) deeply

deopliche (adv.) deeply, seriously

deopnesse (n.) deepness, depth; wisdom

deor (n. pl.) beasts

deore (adj.) dear, precious (compar. *deorre*; superl. *deorest*)

deor(e)wurthe (adj.) precious, beloved; excellent, worthy

deorliche (adv.) tenderly

deorling (adj.) darling

deorre see **deore**

deorwurthe see **deorewurthe**

deovel, deovele see **deofel**

der, dear (v. pres. 1st, 3rd sing.) dare (pres. 2nd sing. *derst*; pres. pl. *durre(n)*; past 3rd sing. *durste*)

derf (adj.) dreadful, cruel; difficult (pl. *derve*; comp. *derfre, dervre*; superl. *derveste*)

derf (n.) pain; difficulty, hardship

derfliche (adv.) dreadfully, cruelly

derfre see **derf** (adj.)

derfschipe (n.) boldness, audacity

derne see **de(a)rne**

derst see **der**

derve (adj.) see **derf**

derve (v.) see **derveth**

derveste see **derf** (adj.)

derveth (v. pres. 3rd sing.) hurts; afflicts, torments (pres. 2nd sing. subj. *derve*; past part. *idorven*)

dervre see **derf**

desireth (v. pres. 3rd pl.) desires

desputunge (n.) argument, debate, disputation

dest see **don**

deth (n.) see **de(a)th(e)**

deth (v.) see **don**

diche (n.) ditch

digneté (n.) honor

dihelnesse (n.) mystery, secrecy

diht, dihte see **dihten**

dihten (v.) ordain; order; bring (pres. 3rd sing. *diht*; past 3rd sing. *dihte*; subj. pres. sing. *diht*; past part. *idiht*); **dihten hus**, manage a household

diveri see **diverin**

diverin (v.) to shake, quiver (pres. 1st sing. diveri)

do see **don**

dohter (n.) daughter (pl. *dehtren*)

dom(e) (n.) judgment, doom; trial (dat. sing. *dome*; pl. *domes*)

Domesdei (n.) doomsday, Judgment Day

Domesmon (n.) Judge (referring to God)

don (v.) do; put, place, set; make, cause (something to happen); treat; join; concern (pres. 2nd sing. *dest*; pres. 3rd sing. *deth*; pres. pl. *doth*; past 2nd sing. *dudest*; past 3rd sing. *dude*; past 3rd pl. *duden*; pres. subj. sing. *do*; past part. *ido, idon*, "finished"; imper. *do*; infl. inf. *to donne*); **do ham wurthschipe**, worship them; **don to death**, put to death, condemn; **nave thu nawt to donne**, do not be concerned; **do thet me do the**, let be done what may be done to you; **dude adun**, came down, descended; **do ham ba togederes**, reunites them (lit. put them both together); **dude . . . awei**, sent away; **don hire . . . ut of dahene**, put her days to an end; **don o rode**, crucify; **do . . . awei**, throw away; **don hire scheome**, do her shame, put her to shame; **doth hare cunde**, follow their instinct (nature); **hwet ham beo to donne**, what they should do; **idon . . . ut of**, escaped from

donne see **don**

dorc (adj.) dark (superl. *darkest*)

doskin (v.) to become dim

dotest (v. pres. 2nd sing.) to be mad, foolish

doth see **don**

draf see **driven**

drahen, dreaien (v.) suffer; drag, pull, draw; trace (pres. pl. *dreaieth*; past 2nd sing. *drohe*; past 3rd sing. *droh(e)*; past pl. *drohen*; past 3rd pl. *drohen*; pres. subj. sing. *dreaie*; past part. *idrahen*); **me droh to**

deathe, was put to death; **droh endelong hire**, traced on herself downwards (in making the sign of the Cross)

drake (n.) dragon (gen. sing. *drakes*; pl. *draken*); **on ane drakes liche**, in the likeness of a dragon

draken, drakes see **drake**

dreaie, dreaien, dreaieth see **drahen**

dre(a)m (n.) song, singing (pl. *dreames*)

dreccheth (v. pres. pl.) torments; distresses, harrass, afflict (past part. *idrechet*)

drechunge (n.) misery, grief

dred, dret (n.) dread, fear, terror

dred(e) (v.) see **dreden**

dreden (v.) dread, fear (pres. 1st sing. *drede*; pres. 3rd sing. *dredeth*; pres. pl. *dredeth*; imper. *dred(e), dret*)

drednesse (n.) dread, fear

drehdest, drehe, dreheth, drehest see **drehen**

drehe(n) (v.) endure, tolerate; to suffer, experience (hardship) (pres. 1st sing. *drehe*; pres. 2nd sing. *drehest*; pres. 3rd sing. *dreheth*; past 2nd sing. *drehdest*; past pl. *drehheden, drehden*; past part. *idrohe, idrohen*)

drehheden see **drehe(n)**

drem see **dre(a)m**

dreori (adj.) sorrowful, dreary; grievous

dreoriliche (adv.) dreadfully (drearily)

dret (n.) see **dred**

dret (v.) see **dreden**

drihtfere (n.) procession of attendants

drihtfule (adj.) noble

Drihtin (n.) God, Judge (gen. *Drihtines*)

drihtnesse (n.) divine nature, majesty

drinken (v.) drink

drivel (n.) drudge, slave (pl. *driveles*)

driveles see **drivel**

driven (v.) practice, perform, engage in; drive; fall (pres. 3rd sing.

driveth; pres. pl. *driveth*; past 3rd sing. *draf, drof*, past 3rd pl. *driven*, past part. *idriven*)

driveth see **driven**

drof see **driven**

droh(e), drohen see **drahen**

drue (adj.) dry

dru-fot (adj.) dry-footed

druicninde (v. pres. part.) in the state of dejection; swooning

drunch (n.) drink

druncnede see **druncnith**

druncnith (v. pres. 3rd sing.) drown, be swallowed up (past 3rd sing. subj. *druncnede*)

drupest (adj. superl.) most downcast

dude(n), dudest see **don**

duhethe (n.) company of retainers

duhti (adj.) worthy, valid

dult (v. past part.) dulled, stupefied

dumbe (adj./subst.) dumb, mute

dun (adv.) down

dune (n.) din

dunede (v. past 3rd sing.) resounded

dunewardes, dunewart (adv.) downwards

dunewart see **dunewardes**

dunge (n.) dung

dunriht (adv.) straight down

dunt (n.) dint, blow (pl. *duntes*)

dure (n.) door

durewart (n.) porter, door-keeper

durre(n) see **der**

durste see **der**

dusi (adj.) foolish (pl. subst. *dusie*)

dusilec (n.) foolishness, folly

dusischipes (n. pl.) follies, foolishness

duste (n.) dust, ash

duste (v.) see **dusten**

dusten (v.) to cast, fling; strike (pres. 2nd sing. *dustest*; pres. 3rd sing. *duste*; past 3rd sing. *duste*; past part. *idust*); **dustest adun**, you reject

dusti (adj.) dusty

dustlunges (n. pl.) flinging, tossing

dute (n.) doubt; fear

duvelrihtes (adv.) face-down, headlong

duvelunge (v. pres. part.) headlong

eadi(e) (adj.) blessed, holy (compar. *eadiure*; superl. *eadiest(e)*

eadinesse (n.) blessedness, holiness

eadwat see **edwiteth**

eahte (num.) eight

ealdeste see **alde**

ealdren (n. pl.) parents; elders (gen. pl. *ealdrene*)

ealmesdeden (n. pl.) almsdeeds, charitable acts

eanes (adv.) once

e(a)ni (adj.) any (pl. *eanies*); **eanies weis**, in any way

ear (adv.) previously, earlier, ere, before; until then; **earre** (compar. earre, i.e., former), former; **ear thene**, earlier than, until; **ear thon**, before that time, before then

eard (n.) land, homeland

eardin (v.) dwell (pres. 3rd sing. *eardith*; pres. part. *eardinde*; past part. *ieardet*)

eare (n.) ear (pl. *earen*)

earen see **eare**

eareste (adj. superl.) first

earest(e), erest, earst (adv.) first; **on alre erst, on earst** at first, to begin with

earewen (n. pl.) arrows

earliche (adv.) early; at a young age

earm(e) (adj.) wretched; poor (superl. *earmest*); **earm-hwile**, weary hour

earmes (n. pl.) arms

earmest see **earme**

earmthe (n.) misery, grief (pl. *earmthen*)

earmthen see **earmthe**

earneth (v. pres. 3rd sing.) earns

earnnesse see **ernesse**

earst see **earest(e)**

easkede, easkest, easketh see **easki**

easki (v. pres. 1st sing.) ask (pres. 2nd sing. *e(a)skest*; pres. 3rd sing. *easketh*; past 3rd sing. *easkede*)

easkunge (n.) asking, inquiry

eateliche (adj.) hateful, horrible (compar. *eateluker*; superl. *eatelukest*)

eateluker, eatelukest see **eateliche**

eaver (adv.) ever, always, forever; **hwuch se . . . eaver**, whosoever; **eaver ihwer**, everywhere; **eaver eu(i)ch**, every single

eaveres (n. pl.) boars; beasts, or alternatively, draft-horses or carthorses (See explanatory note to *HM* 8.21.)

eaveryete (adv.) ever yet, up to now; as ever

eavroskes (n. pl.) water-frogs

eawbruche (n.) adultery

eawiht, eawt, ewt (adv.) in any way, at all. (n.) anything, aught; anyone

e(a)wles (n. pl.) awls; hooks

eawt see **eawiht**

ec (adv.) also, as well as

eche (n.) eternity; (adj.) eternal; aching

echeliche (adv.) eternally

echen (v.) increase, enhance; aggravate

ecnesse, echesse (n.) eternity

ed, et (prep.) at; from; through; **et ten ende**, in the end

edbroken (v. past part.) escaped from

edene (n.) threshing floor

edhalt (v. past 3rd pl.) retain, preserve, keep or hold back

edstonden, etstonden (v.) withstand, resist; stop (pres. 3rd sing. *edstont*; subj. pres. sing. *etstonde*; subj. past sing. *edstode*)

edstont see **edstonden**

edwiteth (v. pres. pl.) blame, reproach (past 3rd sing. *eadwat*)

edwrenchen see **etwrenchen**

efne (adv.) exactly

eft (adv.) again; afterwards; moreover

efter (adv.) after, afterwards; in pursuit; according to, for. (conj.) **efter thet**, after the time that, according as, insofar as, to the extent that; **efter thet hit is**, according as it is (i.e., what it is truly like). (prep.) after; for (in **biheolt efter**, looking for).

Efterlithe (subst. adj.) July (lit. "after June")

efterwart (prep.) after, in **beon . . . efterwart**, i.e., seek, desire

egede (n.) foolish, silly

egge (n.) edge

eggeth, eggith (v. pres. pl.) egg on, urge, incite (pres. part. (as n.) *eggunge*)

ehe (n.) eye (pl. *ehnen, hehnen*)

ehnen see **ehe**

ehsihthe (n.) eyesight

ei, eie (pron.) any. See also **e(a)ni**

eie (n.) fear, terror; anger, wrath

eil (adj.) loathsome, disgusting

eileth (v. pres. 3rd sing.) afflicts, troubles, ails (pres., 3rd sing. subj. *eili*)

eilthurl (n.) window

eise (n.) ease, leisure; comfort; opportunity

eisfule (adj.) terrible; lit. "full of anger"; fearful, terrifying

either (adj.) each (of two); either

elheowet (adj.) ill-hued, off-color; ghastly, eerie-looking

elleshwer (adv.) elsewhere

elne (n.) strength; comfort

elnede (v. past 3rd sing.) strengthened (past 2nd sing. *elnedest*)

empti (adj.) empty, vacant; devoid of

enbrevet (v. past part.) recorded, inscribed

ende (n.) end; **on ende**, finally, in the end

endele(a)se (adj.) endless

endelese see **endele(a)se**

endelong (prep.) along (in a downward motion)

endi see **endin**

endin (v.) end, make an end; die; bring about, complete (pres 1st sing. *endi*)

endunge (n.) ending (of life), death; see also **endln**

engel (n.) angel (pl. *engles*; gen. pl. *englene*)

englene, engles see **engel**

Englis, Englisch (n.) English, the English language

eni see **e(a)ni**

eode see **gan**

eoile, eoli (n.) oil

eoli see **eoile**

eorles (n. pl.) earls, lords

eorne, eorneth see **eornen**

eornen (v.) run, flow (pres. 3rd sing. *eorneth*; past 3rd sing. *urne*; pres. 3rd sing. subj. *eorne*)

eorthe (n.) earth

eorthlich(e), heorthliche (adj.) earthly, mortal

eoten (v.) eat (pres. 3rd sing. et; past 3rd sing. *ete*)

ereste see **earst**

eritage (n.) inheritance, heritage

ernde see **erndi**

erndi (v. pres. subj. 3rd sing.) intercede; obtain through intercession or pleading (imper. sing. *ernde*)

erndunge (n.) intercession

ernesse, earnnesse (n.) in **as on ernesse/earnnesse**, as a foretaste or pledge

erveth (adj.) difficult, hard

eskest see **easki**

est (n.) east

estat (n.) state, condition; rank, status

este (n.) joy, pleasure; luxury

estlonde (n.) the east; the Orient

et (prep.) see **ed**

et (v.) see **eoten**

ete see **eoten**

eth (adj.) easy

ethalden (v.) to keep, detain, hold captive (past 3rd sing. *etheold*)

ethele (adj.) native, born

ethelich, ethlich (adj.) inconsiderable; cheap, worthless (compar. *etheluker*)

etheluker see **ethelich**

etheold see **ethalden**

ethie (v.) to breathe

ethlich see **ethelich**

ethluke (adj.) easily dragged

ethsene (adj.) evident, easily seen

etlunge (n.) in **withuten ei etlunge**, beyond calculation, inestimably

etsterten (v.) escape (from)

etstonde, etstonden see **edstonden**

etstutte see **etstutten**

etstutten (v.) remain (past 3rd sing. *etstutte*)

etwrenchen, edwrenchen (v.) to escape

euch, euich (adj.) every; each; any

euchan (pron.) each one; every one

evenald (adj.) equally old, the same age

evene (n.) capacity, means, resources; nature, kind; quality

eveneche (adj.) coeternal

eveneth see **evenin**

evenin (v.) compare; put on the same level (pres. 3rd sing. *eveneth*)

evening, evenunge (n./adj.) equal; **withuten evenunge**, without comparison

ever (adv.) ever, always

ewangliste (n.) evangelist

ewles see **e(a)wles**

ewt see **eawiht**

fa, va (n.) foe, enemy (pl. *fan, van*)

fan see **fa**

fal, val (n.) fall

fale see **fallen**

falewi (v. subj. pres. 3rd sing.) wither, fade

fallen (v.) fall; befall (pres. 3rd sing. *falleth*; past 3rd sing. *feol*; past pl. *feollen*; subj. pres. sing. *fale, feole*; past part. *ifallen*); **falleth to**, belongs or pertains to (something); **falle thet falle**, fall what may befall (i.e., come what may)

fals(e) (adj.) false

false (v. imper. sing.) prove false, deny

fal(s)schipe (n.) falsehood, dishonesty

famon (n.) enemy, foe (pl. *famen, vamen*)

famplin (v.) stuff (full of food), fumble (?) sense unclear; see explanatory note to *HM* 31.1 for further references to food

fare (n.) fortune

fare (v.) see **feare(n)**

fatte (v. 3rd sing. pres.) brought, fetched (past part. *ifat, ifatte*)

fax, vax (n.) hair

feader (n.) father; God the father (gen. sing. *fe(a)dres*)

feaderles (adj.) fatherless

feahe, feahi (v. imper. sing.) adorn

feaht see **fehte(n)**

feahunge (n.) adornment

feamin (v.) foam (at the mouth)

feare(n) (v.) go, fare, travel; depart (from life); to do (pres. 1st sing. *feare*; pres. 2nd sing. *fearest*; pres. 3rd sing. *feareth*; pres. pl. *feareth*; past 3rd sing. *ferde*; past pl. *verden, ferden*; subj. pres. sing. *fare*; subj. pres. pl. *fearen*); **feare with**, be treated (OE]

fearest, feareth see **feare(n)**

fearlac, fearleac (n.) terror, fear

feat see **veat**

feble (adj.) feeble

feche (v. imper. sing.) fetch

feden, veden (v.) feed; nourish (past 1st sing. *fedde*; past 2nd sing. *feddest*; past 3rd sing. *fedde, fed*)

feder, fedres see **feader**

feh (n.) treasure, riches; a precious object, e.g., gold or a jewel

fehere, feherest see **fei(e)r(e)**

feht (n.) struggle, battle, a fight

fehte(n) (v.) fight, attack (pres. pl. *fehteth*; past 3rd sing. *fe(a)ht*)

feier(e), feir(e) (adj.) fair, beautiful, lovely (compar. *fehere*; superl. *feherest*); (adv.) fairly, pleasantly

feierlec (n.) fairness, beauty, loveliness

feinre (adj. compar.) gladder

fel (n.) skin

feld (n.) field

felen (v.) feel (pres. 1st sing. *fele*; pres. 2nd sing. *felest*; past 1st, 3rd sing. *felde*; past part. *ifelet*)

felien, velien (n. pl.) rims

felunge (n.) feeling, touching; touch, one of the five senses

feng(en) see **fon**

fenniliche (adv.) miserably, vilely

feol see **fallen**

feolahe (n.) fellows (pl. *feolahes*)

feolahschipe (n.) fellowship, friendship

feole (adj.) many, numerous

feol(e), feollen (v.) see **fallen**

feonden, feondes see **feont**

feont, veont (n.) fiend, devil; the Devil (gen. sing. *feondes, veondes*; pl. *feonden*)

feor (adv.) far (compar. *fir*; superl. *firreste*); **of feor**, from afar

feorene, feorren (adv.) afar; **feorren to bihinden**, from far behind

feorlich (n.) wonder, marvelous thing

feorthe (adj.) fourth

Feoverreres (n. gen.) February's

ferde (n.) host, army

ferde(n) (v.) see **fearen**

feren (n. pl.) companions, fellows

ferliche (adj.) terrible, fearsome; formidable; rapid, unexpected

ferliche (adv.) terribly; unexpectedly; wonderfully; quickly

ferredene, verredene (n.) fellowship

feste (adv.) hard

festnin (v.) fasten, make firm, fortify (imper. sing. *festne*; subj. pres. sing. *festni*; past part. *ivestnet*)

fet see **fot**

fetles see **veat**

fewe (adj.) few

fif, five (adj.) fifth; (n.) five

fiftene (adj.) fifteenth; (num.) fifteen

fifti, vifty (adj.) fiftieth; (num.) fifty

fikest (v. pres. 2nd sing.) flatter, deceive

finden (v.) find, discover; invent (pres. 3rd sing. *findeth*; past 1st sing. *font*; past 2nd sing. *fundest*; past 3rd sing. *font*; past 3rd pl. *funde*; past part. *ifunden*)

fingres (n. pl.) fingers

finnes (n. pl.) fins

fir, firreste see **feor**

firsen (v.) take away, separate

firsti (v. pres. subj. sing.) delay (pres. pl. subj. *firstin*; past 3rd subj. sing. *fristede*)

firstin see **firsti**

fisc (n.) fish (pl. *fisches*)

fisches see **fisc**

fisch-hal (adj.) fish-whole (i.e., unharmed)

fiten (v.) revile, quarrel with

five see **fif**

fla (n.) arrow (pl. *flan*)

flea (v. pres. sing. subj.) flay

fleah see **fleon**

flede (v.) to flow

fleide (v. past 3rd sing.) put to flight

fleon (v.) to flee; fly; hurry (pres. 1st sing. *fleo*; pres. pl. *fleoth*; past 3rd sing. *fleah*; past 3rd pl. *flue*; imper. sing. *flih*; pres. part. *fleoninde, flihinde*)

fleoteth (v. pres. pl.) swim

fleoth see **fleon**

flesch (n.) flesh (gen. sing. *flesches*)

flesches see **flesch**

flesch-fulet (adj.) flesh-fouled, defiled in body

flesc(h)liche (adv.) in the flesh; mortally; see also **flesliche**

flesch-timber (n.) corporeal matter, fleshly matter

flesliche (adj.) fleshly

fliche (n.) flitch (a salted or cured side of beef or pork)

flih, flihinde see **fleon**

flit (n.) argument, flyting (pl. *flites*)

fliten (v.) argue, contend, dispute, flyte

flod (n.) flood; sea (pl. *flodes*)

floweth (v. pres. 3rd sing.) flows (pres. part. *flowinde*)

flue see **fleon**

fluhte (n.) flight

flum (n.) river

flurs (n. pl.) flowers

flutteth (v. pres. pl.) flit

flut(t)unge (n.) sustenance

fode (n.) food; child (gen. sing. *fode*)

fol (adj.) sinful; foolish

folc, volc (n.) folk, people (gen. pl. *folkene*)

folhin (v.) follow (pres. 1st sing. *folhi*; pres. pl. *folhith, folheth, fulieth*; past part. *ifolhet*)

folkene see **folc**

folliche (adv.) foolishly

fon, von (v.) begin; catch (past 3rd sing. *feng, veng*; past pl. *fengen*; past part. *ivon*); **von on towart**, reproach

fondin (v.) to try, test; experience (pres. 3rd sing. *fondeth*; pres. pl. *fondith*; past 2nd sing. *fondedest*; past 3rd pl. *fondeden*; pres sing. subj. *fondi*; past part. *ifondet*)

fondunge (n.) temptation

fonstan (n.) font-stone (i.e., baptismal font). See also **font**.

font (n.) baptismal font

font (v.) see **finden**

for (prep.) for; because of; in exchange for; for fear of (**forte, forto** in order to [followed by infinitive]).

forbearnen (v.) burn up (pres. 3rd sing., pl. *forberneth*; past. part. *forbearnd, forbernde*)

forbeod see **forbude**

forberest (v. pres. 2nd sing.) forbear; shun, ignore

forbisne (n.) example

forbude (v. past 3rd sing.) forbid (subj. pres. sing. *forbeod*)

forbuh (v. imper. sing.) shun, flee from

forbod (n.) prohibition, command

forcorven (v. past part.) cut off or out; cut down

forcuthest (adj. superl.) most infamous; most wicked, hateful, or terrible

forcwethest (v. pres. 2nd sing.) renounce, repudiate

fordemest (v. pres. 2nd sing.) condemn (past 3rd sing. *fordemde*; past pl. *fordemden*; imper. sing. *fordem*; past part. (often as n.) *fordemed, fordemet*)

fordo(n) (v.) to destroy; kill, put to death (past 3rd sing. *fordude*; past part. *fordon*)

fordrenct (adj.) drunk; see **fordrencte**

fordrencte (v. past 3rd sing.) drowned; *fordrenct* (past part. as adj. *fordrenct*)

fordude see **fordo(n)**

for(e) (adv.) in advance, beforehand; first; (conj.) for, because

foreseide (v. past 3rd sing.) previously told, stated earlier

forewart (n.) promise; agreement; pact, bargain

forfeare (v. pres. sing. subj.) pass away; perish, destroy (past part. *forfaren*)

forgan (v.) forgo (subj. pres. sing. *forga*)

forgulten (v.) fell into sin (past 3rd sing. *forgulte*)

forheccheth (v. pres. 3rd sing.) shuts out, rejects

forhohien (v.) to scorn, disdain (imper. sing. *forhohe*)

forhorest (v. pres. 2nd sing.) whore (yourself), whore around, prostitute

forhwi (adv.) why, for what/which reason

forleaf (v. imper. sing.) forsake, abandon

forleosen, vorleosen (v.) to damn (someone), to destroy, be destroyed; lose (pres. pl. *forleoseth*; past 3rd sing. *forleas*; past part. *forlore(n)*, as subst. adj. *forlorene*)

forle(o)te(n) (v.) relinquish, give up; lose (pres. 2nd sing. *forletest*; pres. pl. *forleteth*; pres. subj. pl. *forlete*; imper. *forlet*)

forlith (v. pres. 3rd sing.) has intercourse with, lies with

forlore(n), forlorene see **forleosen**

forme (adj.) first

formealte (v. past part.) melted up, melted away

forneh (adv.) almost

forreaden (v.) lead to destruction (pres. pl. *forreadeth*)

forrotieth (v. pres. pl.) rot, become filthy or defiled (past pl. *forroteden*; past part. *forrotet*)

forsaken (v.) to forsake (pres. 1st sing. *forsake*; pres. 2nd sing. *forsakes*; past pl. *forsoken*; imper. sing. *forsac*)

forschaldede (v. past 3rd sing.) scalded (them) to death

forschuptest (v. pres. 2nd sing.) misshape, pervert (one's soul); deform (physically) (past part. *forschuppet*)

forsenctest (v. past 2nd sing.) drowned

forseoth (v. pres. 3rd pl.) disregard, forsake

forsoken see **forsaken**

forswelhe see **forswolhe(n)**

forswelten (v.) destroy; die in agony

forswolhe(n) (v.) devour, swallow up (past 3rd sing. *forswelhe*; pres. pl. *forswolheth*)

forte, forto (prep. precedes inf.) in order to; to

forth, vorth (adv.) forward; far; fully; on (compar. *forthre*)

forthest (v. pres. 2nd sing.) carry out

forthfe(a)dres (n. pl.) forefathers

forthi (adv./conj.) therefore, and so; because; **forthi thet** for the reason that, because, so that

forthlich (adj.) thriving, vigorous

forthre see **forth**

forthwardes (adv.) in **heonne forthwardes**, henceforth

forto see **forte**

fortruste (v. subj. pres. sing.) trusts too much, is overconfident or complacent

forwalleth (v. pres. 3rd sing.) boil up, torture by boiling

forwerede (v. past part.) worn out, worn away

forwreie (v.) denounce

forwurthe(n) (v.) perish, die; degenerate (pres. 2nd sing. *forwurthest*; pres. subj. sing. *forwurthe*)

foryelt (v. pres. 3rd sing.) repays (past part. *foryolden*)

foryeme see **foryemeth**

foryemeth (v. pres. pl.) neglect (subj. pres. sing. *foryeme*)

foryeoteth (v. pres. pl.) forget (pres. and past 3rd sing., imper. sing. *foryet*)

foryevene (v. past part.) forgiven

foryevenesse (n.) forgiveness

foryolden see **foryelt**

foster (n.) child, offspring, foster-child

fostrunge (n.) fostering; **fostrunge forth**, raising, upbringing

fot (n.) foot (pl. *fet, vet*), **euch fot**, every one

fow(e)r (num.) four

fowrti (num.) forty

fowrtuthe (adj.) fourteenth

frakele (adj.) foul, vile

fre(a)mien (v.) help, aid, benefit (pres. pl. *freameth*; past 3rd subj. sing. *fremede*)

freinen (v.) to ask (pres. 3rd sing. *freineth*; past pl. *freineden*)

freineth see **freinen**

freken (n. pl.) fighters, warriors

freo (adj.) free

freodom (n.) freedom

freohin (v.) free

freo-iboren (adj.) of noble birth

freolec (n.) kindness, nobility; freedom

freolich(e) (adj.) lovely, beautiful

freomon (n.) free man, i.e., not a serf; men of noble birth (gen. pl. *freomonne*)

freond (n.) friend

freondschipe, freontschipe (n.) friendship

fret (v. pres. 3rd sing.) eats up, devours; gnaws (pres. pl. *freoteth*)

Fridei (n.) Friday

fristede see **firsti**

frithe see **frithedest**

frithedest (v. past 2nd sing.) spared, protected (imper. sing. *frithe*)

froggen (n. pl.) frogs

frovre (n.) comfort

frovrin (v.) to comfort, encourage; to help (past 3rd sing. *frovrede*)

frumscheft (n.) creation

frumthe (n.) beginning

frut (n.) fruit, reward

fuhel (n.) bird, fowl (pl. *fuheles*)

fuheleres (n. gen. sing.) fowler's, bird-catcher's

ful (n.) cup

ful, fulle (adj.) full; utter, absolute; **fulle to bihalden**, weary of looking

fulden see **fullen**

fule (adj.) foul

fule (adv.) foully

fulen (v.) to pollute, befoul (pres. 3rd sing. *fuleth*)

fulhet (v. past part.) baptized

fulieth see **folhin**

fulitohe (adj.) unruly, undisciplined; foolish; ill-bred

fulitohchipes (n. pl.) foulnesses

fullen (v.) fill; fulfill (past pl. *fulden*; past part. *ifullet*)

fulliche (adv.) fully, completely
fulluht (n.) baptism
fulst (n.) help, aid
fulth(e) (n.) filth, filthiness, nastiness (pl. *fulthen*)
funde, fundest see **finden**
fundeth (v. pres. 3rd sing.) tries, attempts
fur(e) (n.) fire
fure (v. imper. sing.) inflame, fire up
furene (adj.) fiery, flaming
furneise (n.) furnace

ga see **gan**
gabbes (n. pl.) taunts, gibes
gadien (n. pl.) metal spikes
gan (v.) go (pres. 1st sing. *ga*; pres. 2nd sing. *geast*; pres. 3rd sing. *geath*; pres. 3rd pl. *gath*; past 3rd sing. *eode*; subj. pres. sing., pl. *ga*; imper. sing. *ga*; infl. inf. *ganne*; past part. *igan*); **o bote geath**, does penance; **ga . . . o grene**, live on the earth; **ga . . . efter hire**, follow her (will); **ayein . . . ga**, disobey
gast (n.) spirit, soul, ghost (pl. *gastes*, *gasttes*)
gasteliche (adj.) spiritual, ghostly
gath see **gan**
gealde (adj.) barren, sterile
geapede (v. past 3rd sing.) gaped, opened (a mouth)
geas, geast, geath see **gan**
gederin (v.) gather, bring together, join (past part. *igederet*); **wel igederet**, well-matched
gederunge (n.) gathering, joining; sexual union
gein (n.) gain, advantage
geinin (v.) to gain; benefit, help (pres. 3rd sing. *geineth*)
genge see **beoren**
genow (n.) mouth
gerlondesche (n.) aureole, saint's crown, diadem
gersum (n.) treasure, gifts

gete (n.) gate (pl. *geten*)
gimmes (n. pl.) gems
gimstan (n.) gemstone (pl. *gimstanes*)
gimstanes see **gimstan**
gin (n.) device, structure
Giw(e)s (n.) Jews
glead (adj.) glad
gleadeth, gleadie see **gleadien**
gleadien (v.) rejoice, be glad (pres. 1st sing. *gleadie*; pres. 3rd sing. *gleadeth*; imper. sing. *glede*; imper. pl. *gleadieth*); **me . . . gleadeth**, I rejoice
gleadliche (adv.) gladly, happily
gleadschipe (n.) gladness, mirth, joy
gle(a)m (n.) gleam, beam of light
gleaminde (v. pres. part.) gleaming
glede see **gleadien**
gleden (n. pl.) coals
gledread (adj.) red-hot, burning hot
gledunge (n.) gladness, pleasure
gleo (n.) instrument; joy, mirth
gleowinde (v. pres. part.) rejoicing, merry-making
gles (n.) glass
glideth see **glit**
glistinde, glistende see **glistnede**
glistnede (v. past 3rd sing.) glistened, glittered (pres. part. *glistinde*, *glistende*)
glit, glideth (v. pres. 3rd sing.) proceeds
God(d) (n.) God (pl. *godes*, i.e., the pagan gods; gen. sing. *Godes*, *God's*)
goddede (n.) goodness, good work/deed
goddnesse (n.) goodness, divinity
god(d)lec (n.) goodness, virtue
god(e) (adj./subst. n.) good (the moral quality); (n.pl.) goods, property; **na thing godes**, no good thing (comp. *goder*; superl. best); **to goder heale**, for your benefit, for your own good; **god lust**, full attention
godlese (adj.) worthless, useless

Godspel (n.) Gospel

gold, golt (n.) gold

golthord (n.) goldhoard

gomeful (adj.) joyful

gomenes (n. pl.) amorous games or play

gomenin, gominen (v.) rejoice (pres. 1st sing. *gomeni*; pres. 3rd sing. *gomeneth*); **me gomeneth**, I rejoice (refl.)

gra (n.) devil, evil spirit

grace (n.) grace

grandame (n. gen. sing.) grandmother's

granin (v.) groan, wail

grap see **grapin**

grapes (n. pl.) gropings

grapin (v.) grasp, take hold of, grab (past 3rd sing. *grap*)

gras see **grisen**

grave-stane (n.) stone coffin

great (adj.) great, important, splendid

gredde (v. past 3rd sing.) cried out

greden (v.) cry out, scream in pain

grei (adj.) gray cloth

greithith, greitheth (v. pres. pl.) make ready, prepare (past 3rd sing. *greithede*; imper. sing. *greithe*)

gremie(n) (v.) anger, provoke, enrage (pres. 2nd sing. *gremest*; pres. pl. *gremieth*; past pl. *gremeden*; past part. *igremet*)

grene (n.) green ground; green cloth

grenin (v.) green, grow or become green; flourish

greot (n.) piece, chunk, fragment

gres (n.) grass

gret (adj.) great, large

greten (v.) greet, salute; pay respects to, honor, glorify; reward (past 3rd sing. *grette*; pres. subj. sing. *grete*; past part. *igret(t)e*; imper. *gret*)

gretunge (n.) greeting, salutation

grevin (v.) grieve, mourn; upset (pres. 3rd sing. *greveth*)

grimfule (adj.) fierce, furious; cruel; terrible

grimliche (adv.) grimly, cruelly

grisen (v.) terrify (past 3rd sing. *gras*) in **ham gras**, they were horrified

grisle (n.) horror, dread

grislich(e) (adj.) terrible, dreadful; hideous, grisly (compar. *grisluker*); (adv.) terrifyingly, fearsomely

grisluker see **grislich(e)**

gristbeatien (v.) grind the teeth (past 3rd sing. *gristbetede*)

gristles (n. pl.) gristles, cartilage

grith (n.) peace, protection

grome (n.) rage, anger; disgrace (pl. *gromen*)

grometh (v. pres. pl.) angers, enrages (past 3rd sing. *gromede*); **him gromede**, he was angry (refl.)

gromful (adj.) fierce, full of anger

gront (v. past 3rd sing.) grounded (subj. past 3rd sing. *grunde*)

grunde (n.) ground; bottom

grunde (v.) see **gront**

grundliche (adv.) deeply

grund-wal (n.) ground-wall, foundation

grune (n.) trap, snare

grure (n.) terror, horror

grurefule (adj.) terrible, horrible

guldene (adj.) golden

gultelese (adj.) guiltless

gultes (n. pl.) sins, failures (guilts)

gultest (v. pres. 2nd sing.) sin; are guilty (pres. pl. *gulteth*)

gume (n.) man; bridegroom; **in alre gume Lauerd**, Lord of all men

gure-blode (n.) gory blood, gore

ha (pron.) she; it; they

hab(b)e(n) (v.) have; keep; also auxiliary denoting perfect aspect (as in Mod. English) with past part. (pres. 1st sing. *habbe*; pres. 2nd sing. *havest*; pres. 3rd sing. *haveth*; pres. 3rd pl. *habbet(h)*; past 2nd sing. *hefdest*; past 3rd sing. *hefde*; past 3rd pl. *hefden*; past part. *ihaved, ihavet*; imper. have;

negative forms: pres. 1st sing.
nabbe; pres. 2nd sing. *navest*; pres.
3rd sing., pl. *naveth*; past 3rd sing.
nefde; subj. past pl. *nefden*; imper.
sing. *nave*); **nave thu nawt to
donne**, do not be concerned with
(lit., have nothing to do with)

hades (n. pl.) persons

hafeth see **habben**

hah(te) (v.) see **ah**

hahte (n. pl.) see **ahte**

hal (adj.) whole, uninjured, intact;
complete (pl. *hale*)

halde(n) (v.) hold, keep; guard; hold
with, stand with/by (i.e., be loyal
to, be allies with) (pres. 2nd sing.
haldest; pres. 3rd sing. *halde*, *halt*;
pres. pl. *haldeth*; past 3rd sing.
heolt; past 3rd pl. *heolden*; imper.
halt, *hald*; imper. pl. *haldeth*; past
part. *ihalden*); **halden on** to
persist, continue; **halden ham**,
consider themselves; **halt on**,
continues to

hal(e)winde, halwunde (adj.)
sanctifying, sacred

half, halve (n.) side, half; behalf; **O
Godes half**, in God's name, for
God's sake; **half dale**, a half share

halhe (n.) saint (pl. *halhen*)

halhunge (adj.) hallowing,
consecration

hali (adj.) holy

halinesse (n.) holiness, blessedness

halle (n.) hall, court

halschipe (n.) wholeness (whole-ship),
integrity

halsi (v. pres. 1st sing.) entreat, beg

halsum (adj.) healing

halt see **halde(n)**

halt(e) (adj.) crippled, lame

halve see **half**

ham (pron.) them

hame (n.) home

hamseolf, hamseolfen, hamseolven
(pron.) themselves; **bi hamseolf**,
by themselves, when by themselves

hantith (v. pres. pl.) engage in, practice

hap (n.) luck

har (poss. pron.) their

hardi (adj.) hardy, bold

hardiliche (adv.) boldly

hare (pron.) their; of them

hat (adj.) hot

haten (v.) in active form: command,
bid, order; in passive: call, name
(pres. 1st sing. *hate*, *hatte*; pres.
2nd sing. *hete*; pres. 3rd sing. *hat*,
hateth, *hatte*; past 2nd sing. *hatest*;
past 3rd sing. *het*, *hehte*; past part.
ihaten; imper. *hat*).

hatien (v.) hate

have, havest, haveth see **hab(b)e(n)**

havene (n.) harbor, haven

he (pron.) he

heafden, heafdes see **heave(a)d**

healde, healdest see **healeth**

healden (v.) pour see also **healeth**

heale (n.) salvation; Savior

heale (v.) see **healeth**

He(a)lent (n.) healer, healing one
(epithet for God), savior (gen.
sing. *Helendes*)

healeth (v. pres. 3rd sing.) heals (past
2nd sing. *healdest*; past 3rd sing.
healde; past pl. *healden*; subj. pres.
sing. *heale*); **healdest . . . te deade**,
raised the dead

healewi (n.) healing liquid or balm;
medicine; ointment

heame (n.) churl (pl. *heamen*)

heande see **heanin**

heane (adj.) hateful, wretched

heanewart (adv.) from here, hence

heanin, heanen (v.) scoff at, disdain;
afflict, oppress (pres. 2nd sing.
heane; pres. 3rd sing. *heaneth*; past
3rd sing. *heande*)

heard(e) (adj.) hard, severe. (adv.)
hard, tight; severely, bitterly

heardeste-iheortet see **heardre-
iheortet**

heardi (v. pres. subj. sing.)
strengthen, harden

heardre-iheortet (adj. compar.) harder hearted (superl. *heardeste iheortet*)

hearm (n.) harm; **mare hearm is**, even worse (lit., more is the harm)

hearmi (v.) harm, hurt (pres. 2nd, 3rd sing. *hearmeth, hearmith*)

hearmith see **hearmi**

heascede (v. past 3rd sing.) persecuted; be angry with (subj. pres. sing. *heasci*)

heast(e) (n.) order, commandment (pl. *heastes*)

heate (n.) heat

heaten (v.) heat (past part. *iheat*)

heatele (adj.) hateful (superl. *hetelest*)

heateliche (adj.) cruel

heathendom (n.) heathendom, paganism

he(a)thene (n./adj.) heathen, pagan

heatien (v.) hate (pres. 3rd sing. *heateth*; pres. pl. *heatieth*)

heatterliche see **het(t)erliche**

heave(a)d, heavet (n.) head; chief, leader; first (pl. *heafdes*; gen. pl. *heafden*); **heaved of the heste**, first among the highest (most distinguished)

hechelunge (n.) gnashing, chattering

heden (v.) to attend to

hef see **he(o)ven**

hefde (n.) see **heave(a)d**

hefde, hefden, hefdest (v.) see **habben**

heh(e) (adj.) high, great, lofty, exalted (also as subst.) (compar. *herre*; superl. *hehest, hest*, pl. *heste*, most distinguished, foremost); **heh-engel**, archangel; **on heh**, out loud

Hehede, hehede see **heien**

heh(e)liche (adv.) richly, highly; solemnly

hehe(n) see **heien**

hehest, heheth (v.) see **heien**

Heh-Feader (n.) the High Father, God

hehliche see **heheliche**

hehnen see **ehe**

hehnesse (n.) high-ness, high rank, exalted state; royalty; dignity; **in hehnesse**, on high

hehschipe (n.) high-ship, eminence

hehte see **haten**

hei (interj.) ha!; well!; usually implying rebuttal or anger

heien, hehen (v.) carry out, support; honor, exalt (pres. 1st sing. *heie, hehe*; pres. 2nd sing. *hehest*; pres. 3rd sing. *heheth*; pres. 3rd pl. *hei(e)th*; past 3rd sing. *hehede*; past 3rd pl. *heheden*; pres. 2nd sing. subj. *heie*; pres. part. *heiunge* (as subst.) past part. *iheiet, iheiyet, ihehet*; imper. pl. *heieth*)

heiunge see **heien**

helde (n.) eld, age

hele (n.) heel (pl. *helen*)

Helendes, Helent see **He(a)lent**

helest (v. pres. 2nd sing.) conceal, hide (pres. 3rd sing. *heleth*)

Helle (n.) Hell

hellene (adj.) hellish, infernal

help (n.) help

helpen (v.) help (pres. 3rd sing. *helpeth*; imper. sing. *help*)

helplese (adj.) helpless; (subst.) the helpless (gen. sing. *helpleses*)

hende (adj.) gracious, courteous

henlunges (n. pl.) vile, contemptible people

heo (pron.) she; they

heold(en) see **halde(n)**

heolen (v.) conceal

heolt see **halde(n)**

heonne (adv.) hence, (away) from here

heonevorth, heonneforth (adv.) henceforth

heore(n) (pron. 3rd pl. gen.) their, theirs, their own; of them

heorte (n.) heart (pl. *heorten*); **on hat heorte**, with a hot heart, angrily

heorteliche (adv.) heartily, devoutly

heorthliche see **eorthlich(e)**

he(o)ven (v.) lift, raise, lit. to heave (past 3rd sing. *hef*)

heovene (n.) Heaven

heovene-getes (n. pl.) Heaven-gates, gates of heaven

heovenlich(e) (adj.) heavenly

heoveriche (n.) the heaven-kingdom (gen. *heoveriches*)

heowe (n.) hue, color; shape, form (pl. *heowes*)

her (adv.) here; **her . . . on**, in here

her (n.) hair

her (v.) see **heren**

herbi (adv.) hereby, by this, from this

hercnin (v.) hearken, listen (past 3rd sing. *hercnede*; past 2nd pl. *hercneden*; imper. sing. *hercne*; imper. pl. *hercneth*; pres. part. *hercnende*)

here (n.) army

herede(n) see **herien**

here(n) (v.) hear (pres. 3rd sing. *hereth*; past 1st, 3rd sing. *herde*; imper. sing. *her*); **herestu**, you hear

herewurthe (adj.) praiseworthy

herhede see **herhedest**

herhedest (v. past 2nd sing.) harrowed (past 3rd sing. *herhede*)

herie(n) (v.) praise, worship (pres. 2nd sing. *herestu*; pres. 3rd sing. *herieth*; pres. 3rd pl. *herieth*; past 3rd sing. *herede*; past pl. *hereden*; imper. pl. *herieth*; pres. part. *heriende*; past part. *iheret*); often used in **heien ant herien**, to honor and praise; **to herien**, to be praised, worthy of praise

her-of (adv.) about it

her-on (adv.) to this

her-onont (adv.) with regard to this

herre see **heh(e)**

hersumin (v.) worship; obey, serve (pres. 3rd sing. *hersumeth*)

herto (adv.) to this

hertowart (adv.) compared with this, in comparison

herthurh (adv.) through this

herunge (n.) hearing, one of the five senses

hervore (adv.) for this reason, on account of this

hest, heste see **heh(e)**

het, hete (v.) see **haten**

hete (n.) hate, hatred

hetelest see **heatele**

heteveste (adv.) cruelly tight

hethene see **he(a)thene**

het(t)erliche, heatterliche (adv.) sternly, fiercely

hevel (n.) in **hevel bedd**, woven bed

heven see **he(o)ven**

hevinesse (n.) heaviness

hider(e) (adv.) hither, here

hiderto (adv.) hitherto, until now, up to this point

hihendliche, hihentliche (adv.) quickly, rapidly

hihin (v.) to hasten, go quickly, hie; urge (past 3rd sing. *hihede*; pres. pl. *hihi*; imper. sing. *hihe*)

hihthe (n.) in **for hihthe**, hurriedly, hastily

him (pron.) him

himseolven (pron.) himself (as refl.); him (emphatic)

hine (n.) servant; shepherd (pl. *hinen*)

hird, hirt (n.) household; company (of retainers or servants), court; military host; shepherd (pl. *hirden*)

hirdmen (n. pl.) retainers, company

hire (pron.) her; to her; (under) her (often as obj. of prep.); (refl.) herself

hireseolf (pron.) herself

hirt see **hird**

his(e) (pron.) his

hit (pron.) it

hofles (adj.) unreasonable, senseless

hoke (n.) hook

hokede (adj.) hooked

hoker (n.) mockery, derision, contempt; insult (pl. *hokeres*);

holden hare hoker of me, i.e., hold me in contempt. (as adj.) contemptible

hokeren (v.) to mock, deride, insult

hokeres see **hoker**

hokerest (v. pres. 2nd sing.) mock, slander

hokerlich (adj.) disgraceful, shameful (compar. *hokerluker*)

hokerliche (adv.) scornfully, disdainfully; with nausea, grudgingly

hokerluker see **hokerlich**

hole (n.) hole, pit

hon (v.) hang

honde(n) see **hont**

hondhwile, honthwile (n.) moment

hondiwerc (n.) handiwork (i.e., God's creation)

hondlin (v.) handle; treat (pres. pl. *hondlith*; past part. *ihondlet*)

hongin (v.) hang (past 3rd sing. *hongede*; past 3rd pl. *hongeden*; pres. 2nd, 3rd sing. subj. *hongi*; imper. pl. *hongeth*)

honi (n.) honey

hont, hond (n.) hand; grasp (pl. *honden*); **herre hont**, upper hand; **beaten honden**, clap the hands

honthwile see **hondhwile**

hope (n.) hope

hopien (v.) hope

hoppin (v.) hop, leap about, dance

hore (n.) whore

horedom (n.) whoredom, prostitution; adultery

horlinges (n. pl.) whores, lechers, fornicators

hornes (n. pl.) horns

hot (adj.) hot; angry

hoverede, hoveret (adj.) hump-backed

hu (adv.) how

hudde (v. past 3rd sing.) hid (past pl. *hudden*; past part. *ihudde, ihud*)

hude (n.) skin, hide

hul (n.) hill

huler (n.) lecher, fornicator

hund, hunt (n.) hound, dog (pl. *hundes*)

hundret (num.) hundred

hundretfald (adj.) hundred-fold, one hundred times over

hunger (n.) hunger

hunt see **hund**

hure (adv.) least of all; especially, most of all

hure (n.) wages; reward

hurne (n) corner

hurten (v.) hurt (past part. *ihurt*)

hurtes (n. pl.) hurts, injuries

hus(e) (n.) house; household

husebonde (n.) husband

hut (v. pres. 3rd sing.) hides

hutung, huting (n.) scorn, mockery, an object of contempt

hwa (pron.) who; **hwa se** who so, whoever, anyone who

hwam (pron.) whom

hwas (pron.) whose

hweat see **hwet**

hweate (n.) wheat

hwen(e) (adv.) when

hweol (n.) wheel (pl. *hweoles*)

hweonne, hweonene (adv.) whence, from where

hwer (adv.) where; **hwer se . . . eaver**, wheresoever, wherever

hwerin (adv.) in what

hwerwith (n.) wherewith, with which the means by which

hwerthurh (prep.) see **thurh**

hwerto (adv.) why, to what end

hwervore (adv.) wherefor, why, for which reason; **beo hit hwervore se hit eaver**, for whatever reason it may be

hwet, hweat (pron.) what; **an hwet**, one thing; **hwet se**, whatever

hwi (adv.) why

hwider (adv.) whither, to what place; **hwider se . . . eaver**, wherever

hwil(e) (n.) time, while, a portion of time; **ane hwile** a while; **summe**

hwile for a while; **the hwile,**
  meanwhile, in the meantime.
  (conj.) while, during the time that
hwilinde (adj.) temporary, transitory,
  passing
hwit(e) (adj.) white
hwon (pron.) what; in **to hwon schal
  Ich iwurthen,** i.e., what shall
  become of me. (conj.) in **for hwon
  thet,** at the time when, when
hwuc(c)h(e) (pron./adj.) which, who,
  what; whichever; **hwuch se** or
  hwuch se . . . eaver, whosoever,
  whoever (one or ones)

ibeaten see **beaten**
ibeden see **bidde(n)**
ibidde (refl. v. past 3rd sing.) pray;
  ibidde me, I pray (imper. sing.
  ibide)
ibet see **beten**
iblend, iblent see **blent**
iblesceden see **blesci**
iblescet see **blesci**
iblowen see **blowinde**
iboht see **buggen**
ibore(n)(e) see **beoren**
iborenesse (n.) birth
iborhen see **burhe**
ibrevet (v. past part.) recorded, set
  down in writing
ibroht(e) (v.) see **bringen**
ibroken see **br(e)oken**
ibrowden (v. past part.) in **ibrowden
  on,** modeled on, resembling
ibuhe see **buhe**
ibunden see **binden**
iburiet see **biburien**
iburst (adj.) bristled
ich (pron.) I
ichosen see **cheosen**
icleopet see **cleopien**
icluhte (v. past part.) clenched
icnawen (v.) to know, recognize (past
  3rd pl. *icneowen*; subj. pres. sing.
  icnawe) see also **cnawe(n)**
icnawes see **cnawes**

icnawlecheth (v. pres. pl.) confess
icnut (v. past part.) knotted
icore, icoren(e), icorenest see
  cheosen
icrunet (v. past part) crowned
icud(de) see **cuthen**
icume(n), icumene see **cume(n)**
icuplet (v. past part.) coupled, joined
icuret (v. past part.) chosen
icweme (adj.) pleasing
icwemet (v. past part.) pleased
idealet (v. past part.) arranged;
  matched (dealt)
idel (adj.) worthless, ineffective; idle
  (pl. *idele*)
idemet see **demen**
idervet (v. past. part.) injured;
  troubled
idiht see **dihten**
ido(n) see **don**
idorven see **derveth**
idrahe, idrahen see **drahen**
idrechet see **dreccheth**
idrehen (v.) to endure
idrencte (v. past part.) dipped
idriven see **driven**
idrohe(n) see **drehe(n)**
idust see **dusten**
ieardet see **eardin**
ifallen see **fallen**
ifat(te) see **fatte**
ifelet see **felen**
iferen (n. pl.) friends, comrades
ifinden (v.) find, obtain; meet (pres.
  3rd sing. *ifint*; pres. pl. *ifindeth*;
  past 3rd sing. *ifont*; past part.
  ifunden)
iflut (v. past part.) traveled; **beoth . . .
  iflut,** have traveled
ifolhet see **folhin**
ifondet see **fondin**
ifont see **ifinden**
ifulhet (v. past part.) baptized
ifullet see **fullen**
ifunden see **finden** or **ifinden**
igabbet (v. past part.) mocked
igan see **gan**

igederet see **gederin**

iginet (v. past part.) devised

ignahene (v. past part.) ruined, destroyed, gnawed or eaten (by worry, anxiety)

igoten (v. past part.) cast (from gold) (pl. *igotene*)

igreithet (v. past part.) built, constructed

igremet see **gremie(n)**

igret(t)e see **greten**

igripe (v. pres. subj. 3rd sing.) grasps

igurd (v. past part.) girded, clothed

ihal (adj.) whole, intact

ihalden see **halde(n)**

ihaten see **haten**

ihaved, ihavet see **hab(b)e(ne)**

iheat see **heaten**

ihehet, iheiet, iheiyet see **heien**

ihente (v. subj. past sing.) catch

iheren (v.) to hear, listen (pres. 3rd sing. *ihereth*; past 3rd sing. *iherd(e)*; imper. *iher*)

iheret, ihereth see **herien**

ihole (v. past part.) concealed

ihondlet see **hondlin**

ihondsald (v. past part.) betrothed

ihud(de) see **hudde**

ihurnde (adj.) horned

ihuret (v. past part.) hired

ihurt see **hurten**

ihwer, iwer (adv.) everywhere

ikelet (v. past part.) quenched, satisfied

iken(nen), ken (adj.) willing to know or acknowledge

ikennet (v. past part.) born

ikepen, ikepte (v.) accept; take; save (past part. *ikepte*) see also **kepe**

ikepunge (n.) saving

ikudd see **cunnen**

ikumen see **cumen**

ilahet (v. past part.) lowered, brought low, humbled. See also **lahede**

ilaht, ilahte see **ilecche**

ilatet (adj.) having manners or appearance, in **lutherly ilatet**, wickedly mannered; **ilatet se luthere**, so wicked looking

ile (n.) calloused sole or underside of the feet

ilead see **leaden**

ileanet (v. past part.) lent

ilearet see **learen**

ileathet (v. past part.) summoned

ileave (n.) belief

ilecche (v. subj. pres. 3rd sing.) seizes, catches (past 3rd sing. *ilahte*; past part. *ilaht*)

ilefde see **ileve(n)**

ileid see **legge(n)**

ilened, ilenet see **lenen**

ilered see **learen**

ileve(n) (v.) to believe (pres. 1st sing. *ileve*; subj. past sing. *ilefde*)

ilevet see **leve(n)**

ilich (adj.) like, similar

iliche (adv.) equally, alike; unceasingly

iliche (n.) likeness

ilicnesse (n.) likeness

iliht see **lihten**

ilimpeth (v. pres. 3rd sing.) happens, occurs

ilitet (v. past part.) colored

ilke (adj.) same; **in the ilke time**, at the same time; **mid tis ilke word**, at these very words

iloket see **loki(n)**

ilome (adv.) often, frequently

iloset (v. past part.) lost

iloten (v. past part.) allotted, assigned, bestowed

iluvet see **luvien**

imakede, imaket see **mak(i)e(n)**

imeane (n.) fellowship, company. (adj.) shared. (adv.) together

imelt see **me(a)lten**

imenget (v. past part.) dismayed, disturbed; confused; mixed

imet (v. past part.) dreamt

imong (prep.) among

imotet see **motin**

imuneget see **munegin, munien**

i(n) (prep.) in; to. (n.) house, dwelling place

in, ine, i (adv./prep.) in, into; within, inside; **ine marhen** in the morning; **in a time**, at one time

inc (dual pron.) you two (gen. sing. *inker*)

inempnet, inemed see **nempnede**

inhinen (n. pl.) household members

inker see **inc**

inoh(e) (adj./adv.) enough, plenty (pl. *inohe*); sufficiently, enough

inohreathe (adv.) easily, readily enough

in-seil (n.) seal

into (prep.) into, unto, to

inumen see **neomen**

inwarde (adj.) inward, innermost

inwardliche (adj.) heartfelt, earnestly

inwardluker (adv. compar.) more earnestly, fervently, deeply, ardently

inwith (adv.) internally; (prep.) within; during the course of

inyong (n.) entry, admission, entrance

ioffret (v. past part.) offered

iopenet (v. past part.) opened

Iordanes (n. gen.) in **Iordanes flum**, river Jordan

ipaiet (v. past part.) pleased, content, satisfied; **is . . . wel ipaiet of**, is happy with, content with

iprud (v. past part.) made proud

iput (v. past part.) put

iredd see **reden**

iriht see **rihte**

irikenet see **rikenin**

irn(e) (n.) iron

irnen(n)e (adj.) iron

irobbet see **robbith**

is see **beon**

isahet (v. past part.) sawed

ischapen, ischapet see **schuppen**

is(c)hawet see **schawin**

ischeapen see **schuppen**

ischend see **schendest**

ischeomet see **scheomien**

ischepene see **schuppen**

ischrud(de) see **schrudde**

iscrippet (v. past part.) scratched, scraped (from a page); in **iscrippet ut of**, i.e., erased; see also **toschrapede**

iselede, iseilet, iseiled (v. past part.) sealed

iseh, isehe, isehen see **iseon, seo(n)**

iseid, iseide, iseit [et al.] see **seg(g)en**

iseilet, iseiled see **seileth**

isent see **senden**

iseo(n) (v.) see; perceive; see to, provide for (pres. 1st sing. *iseo*; pres. 2nd sing. *isist*; pres. 3rd sing. *isith*; pres. pl. *iseoth*; past 1st sing. *iseh, isehe*; past part. *isehen*)

iset, isette see **sette(n)**

iset(te) (v. past part.) see **setten**

iseten see **sitten**

ishawet see **is(c)hawet**

isihen (v. past part.) in **weren isihen**, had come

isist, isith see **iseo(n)**

islein see **slean**

isliket (v. past part.) polished

ismaket (v. past part.) glossed

ismethet (v. past part.) smoothed over, glossed over

ismiret see **smirede**

isoht see **sechen**

istalde (v. past part.) placed, set up, established

isteanet (v. past part.) paved; stoned

istelede (v. past part.) made hard as steel; made of steel

istewet see **stewen**

istihe see **stihen**

istirrede (adj.) starry

istopen see **stepe**

istraht see **strecche(n)**

istrenget see **strenge(n)**

isturet see **sturien**

isuled see **sulen**

isundret see **sundri**

isweamet see **sweameth**

isweche see **swenchest**

iswiken (v.) abandon, forsake

isworen see **swerien**

itaht see **tahte**

itake see **taken**

itald(e) see **telle(n)**

itei(e)t (v. past part.) tied, bound together

iteilede (v. past part.) tailed, having tails

itemet (v. past part.) tamed

itend, itent, iteonet see **teonen**

itholet see **tholien**

ithonket see **thonki**

itiden (v.) happen

itimbret (v. past part.) built, constructed

itimeth (v. pres. 3rd sing.) happens, comes to pass. See also **timeth**

itohe (v. past part.) taught; in **wel itohe**, well-taught, well-mannered, respectable

itohen see **teo(n)**

itu(i)net (v. past part.) enclosed

ituket see **tuken**

iturnd, iturnt see **turne(n)**

ituthet (v. past part.) granted

Iuhan in **Sein Iuhan**, Saint John

iunne(n) (v. past part.) given

ivestnet see **festnin**

ivon see **fon**

ivorthet (v. past part.) carried out

ivostret see **vostrin**

iwaket see **wakien**

iwedded(e), iweddet see **weddest**

iweld see **iwelden**

iwelden (v.) rule, govern, control (past part. *iweld*)

iwemmet (v. past part.) harmed

iwend see **wende(n)**

iwende (v.) turn, change. See also **wenden**

iwenet (v. past part.) weaned

iwepnet see **wepnen**

iwer see **ihwer**

iwiket (v. past part.) lodged, stayed

iwilnet see **wilni(n)**

iwis(s) (adv.) certainly, indeed

iwisset, iwist see **witen**

iwiten (v.) notice, perceive

iwlaht (v. past part.) warmed up

iworthen see **iwurthen**

iwrahte see **wurchen**

iwreathet see **wreathen**

iwriten see **writen**

iwundet (past part.) wounded

iwunet see **wunien**

iwur(d)get see **wurthgin**

iwurthen (v.) become; befall, happen; be (pres. pl. *iwurtheth*; past 3rd pl. *iworthen*; pres. 3rd sing. subj. *iwurthe*); **lette . . . iwurthen**, ignored; **wel schal . . . iwurthen**, it will go well; **iwurthe to**, becomes, turns into. See also **wurthen**

iyarket see **yarki(n)**

iyettet see **yetti**

iyeve, iyeven see **yeoven**

iyotten (v. past part.) melted down for refinement (metallurgy); cast, molded

jacinct (n.) jacinth

kahten see **kecheth**

kalende (n. pl.) calends, the first day of a month

k(e)asten (v.) cast (past 3rd sing. *keste*, *keaste*)

kecheth (v. pres. 3rd sing.) catches, seizes (past 3rd pl. *kahten*)

keis (n. pl.) officers, henchmen

keiser, caisere (n.) caesar, emperor; **keiseres** (gen. sg.) of the emperor

kelf (n.) calf

keli (v.) cool; quench, satisfy

kempe (n.) champion, warrior (pl. *kempen*; gen. pl. *kempene*)

ken see **iken(nen)**

kenchen (v.) jeer, laugh loudly (pres. part. *kenchinde*)

kene (adj.) cruel, fierce; mighty; sharp (compar. *kenre*; superl. *kenest*)

keneliche (adv.) fiercely, bravely

kenne(n) (v.) declare, make known (pres. pl. *kennith*; pres. subj. sing. *kenne*)

kenre see **kene**

kenschipe (n.) fierceness

keorven (v.) carve

kepe (v.) keep, hold, have; care, regard; await; wait to find out; catch; **ikepen**, to receive (pres. 1st sing. *kepe*; pres. 3rd pl. *kepeth*; past 3rd sing. *kepte*; past part. *ikepte*)

keste see **k(e)asten**

kimest, kimeth see **cumen**

kine (adj.) royal, kingly

Kine-bern (n.) royal prince

kineburh (n.) capital city

kinedom (n.) kingdom

kinemotes (n.) royal council

kineriche (n.) royal kingdom

kineseotle (n.) royal seat, throne

kinewurdliche (adj.) royally

kinewurthe (adj.) royal, kingly

king (n.) king; secular ruler or God (pl. *kinges*; gen. sing. *kinges*; gen. pl. *kingene*)

kumelich (adj./n.) decent, seemly, appropriate

lac, lak (n.) offering, gift (pl. *lakes*)

ladli, lad(d)lich(e) (adj.) loathsome, horrible (compar. *ladluker*; superl. *ladlukeste*)

ladliche (adv.) horribly

ladluker, ladlukeste see **ladli**

lah, lahe (adj./subst.) low, lowly (compar. *lahre*; superl. *laheste*); lawful, legitimate

lahe (n.) law (pl. *lahen, la(g)hen*); **lahe of wedlac**, bond of wedlock

lahen see **lahe** (n.)

lahede (v. past 3rd sing.) ordained, established (by or as) law; allowed (past part. *ilahet*)

lahelese (adj.) lawless

laheliche (adv.) lawfully

laheste see **lah**

lahhe (v.) laugh (pres. part. *lahinde*)

lahinde see **lahhe**

lahre see **lah**

lahte (v. past 3rd sing.) darted

lahtre (n.) laughter

lak, lakes see **lac**

lake (n.) lake

lam (n.) loam, earth, clay, dirt; flesh

lampe (n.) lamp, light

lan (n.) reward; loan

lanhure (adv.) at least

lare (n.) lore, learning, teaching

largeliche (adv.) generously

larspel (n.) teaching; Scripture

lastin (v.) curse, revile

late (adv.) recently

late (n.) behavior, bearing; look, expression (pl. *lates*)

lates see **late** (n.)

lath(e) (adj) loathsome, hateful (superl. *lathest*); (n.) malice, hatred

lathi(n) (v.) loathe, become hateful

lathlese (adj.) innocent

laththe (n.) loathing, hatred

lattow (n.) leader

Lauerd, Lauert (n.) lord (gen. sing. *Lauerdes*)

lauerdom (n.) lordship; dominance, control

leac see **luken**

lead(d)en (v.) lead; carry off; set, place (pres. 1st sing. *leade*; pres. 2nd sing. *lead(d)est*; pres. 3rd sing. *lead, leadeth*; pres. pl. *leadeth*; past 2nd sing. *leddest*; past 3rd sing. *leaded*; past 3rd pl. *ledden*; pres. subj. sing. *leade*; imper. *lead*; past part. *ilead*)

leaf, leafed, leafeth (v.) see **leaven**

leaf, leave (n.) leaf (a page of a book), i.e., book or text

le(a)fdi (n.) lady, noblewoman (pl. *leafdis*)

leafdischipe (n.) ladyship

leafful(e) (adj.) loyal, faithful; (subst.) believer, faithful one

leane (adj.) lean, thin

leanin (v.) become lean

leapen (v.) leap (pres. 3rd sing. *leapeth*; past 3rd sing. *leop*; subj. past sing. *leope*; pres. part. *leapinde*

learen (v.) teach, instruct; exhort (pres. 1st sing. *leare*; pres. 2nd sing. *learst*; pres. 3rd sing., pres. pl. *leareth*; past 3rd pl. *learden*; subj. pres. sing. *leare*; past part. *ilearet, ilered*)

leas(e) (adj.) false, deceptive; (n.) falsehood

leasse (adj. comp.) less

leassith (v. pres. 3rd sing.) lessen

least (adj.) last; furthest, most remote; most recently, last; **the alre least**, the most distant (lit. the furthest of all)

least (n.) sin, fault

leastelese (adj.) blameless, faultless

leasten (v.) last, continue; carry out, fulfill (pres. 3rd sing. *lest, lesteth, leasteth*; pres. part. *leastinde*)

leasunges (n. pl.) lies

leat (v. past 3rd sing.) bowed

leatere (adv. compar.) latter; later; **neaver the leatere**, nevertheless

leathieth (v. pres. pl.) invite; incite (subj. pres. sing. *leathie*)

leattres (n. pl.) letters (of the alphabet)

leave (n.) belief; authority; permission. See also **leaf** (n.)

leave, leavest, leaveth (v.) see **leaven**

leaven (v.) leave, abandon, reject, renounce, give up; depart; linger, remain (pres. 2nd sing. *leavest*; pres. 3rd sing. *leafeth*; pres. pl. *leaveth*; past 1st sing. *leafed*; past 3rd sing. *leafed*; imper. sing. *le(a)f*; imper. pl. *leaveth*; subj. pres. sing. *leave*; past part. *ileavet*)

leawede (adj.) unlearned, lay

lec(c)herie (n.) lechery

leche (n.) help, rescue

lechnunge (n.) medicine, healing

ledden, leddest see **lea(d)den**

ledene (n.) language

lef see **leaven, leven**

lefde, lefden, lefdest see **leven**

lefdi see **le(a)fdi**

lefmon see **le(o)fmon**

legge(n) (v.) lay; lay on (i.e., to strike) (pres. 2nd sing. *leist*; pres. pl. *leith*; pres. 3rd sing. subj., *legge*; past pl. *leiden*; past part. *ileid*); **leggen ... adun**, overcome, put down; **leist lac**, offer sacrifice; **leith me se lahe**, lays me so low, humbles me

lei (n) law; religion

lei, leien (v.) see **liggen**

leiden see **leggen**

lei(e) (n) flame, fire, light

leifen, leiven (n.) bog, swamp

leirwite (n.) fine or punishment in hell for fornication

leist see **leggen**

leitede see **leiten**

leiten, leiti(n) (v.) blaze, gleam (pres. 3rd sing. *leiteth*; past 3rd sing. *leitede*; pres. part. *leitinde*)

leith see **leggen**

lenden(e) (n. pl.) loins

lenen (v.) give, grant (past part. *ilened, ilenet*)

lengre see **long(e)**

leod (n.) song, lay

leode (n.) people, nation; language (pl. *leoden*; gen. pl. *leodes*)

leof(e)/leov(e) (adj.) dear, beloved; pleasing (compar. *leovere, levere*; superl. *leovest*); **leovere** a dearer one; **this me were leovere**, I would rather

leofliche (adj.) lovely, beautiful (superl. *leoflukest*)

leofliche (adv.) lovingly, tenderly

leoflukest see **leofliche** (adj.)

le(o)fmon (n.) lover (gen. sing. *leofmones*)

leoftede (v. past 3rd sing.) cajoled, flattered

leohe (n.) den, lair

leome (n.) light, flame (pl. *leomen*)

leomen (n. pl.) limbs. See also **leome**

leometh (v. pres. 3rd sing.) gleams, shines

leop, leope see **leapen**

leor (n.) face (pl. *leores*)

leornin (v.) learn (pres. 1st sing. *leorni*; past 3rd sing. *leornede*; past part. *ileornet*)

leosen (v.) lose (pres. 1st sing. *leose*; pres. 2nd sing. *leosest*; pres. 3rd sing. *leoseth*; pres. pl. *leoteth*; pres. sing. subj. *leose*)

le(o)te(n) (v.) consider, think, regard; to let, allow; give up, relinquish; cause (followed by infinitive); to abandon; stop, cease (imper.) (pres. 1st sing. *leote*; pres. 2nd sing. *letest*; pres. 3rd sing. *let, leote*; pres. pl. *leoteth, letteth*; past 1st sing. *lette*; past 2nd sing. *lettest*; past 3rd sing. *lette*; subj. pres. 2nd sing. *lete*; subj. pres. 3rd sing. *lette*; imper. sing. *let*; imper. pl. *leoteth*); **let bringen hire**, have her brought; **let(te) . . . iwurthen**, let be, ignore; **leoteth se lihtliche of**, take so lightly; **lette don**, had put; **lette . . . setten**, founded, established

leothebeie (adj.) supple

leothien (v.) undo, loosen (past 3rd sing. *leothede*; imper. sing. *leothe*)

leove(re), leovest(e) see **leof(e)**

leovie (adj.) loving, affectionate

leowse see **lowsin**

lest (v.) see **leasten**

lest, leste (conj.) lest; for fear that

lest, lesteth (v.) see **leasten**

let(e), leten, lette, let(t)est, let(t)e(th) see **le(o)te(n)**

leve(n) (v.) believe; grant, allow (pres. 1st sing. *leve*; pres. 2nd sing. *levestu*; pres. 3rd sing. *leveth*; pres. pl. *leveth*; past 3rd sing. *lefde*; past 3rd pl. *lefden*; pres. 2nd sing. subj. *lefdest*; past 1st sing. subj. *livede*;

imper. sing. *lef*; imper. pl. *leve*; past part. *ilevet*)

levere see **leof**

libbe(n) (v.) live (pres. 1st pl. *libbe*; pres. pl. *libbet, libbeth, liveth, livieth*; past 3rd sing. *livede*; imper. pl. *livieth*; pres. part. *liviende*); **al . . . thet we livieth**, all that we experience

lich (n.) body; corpse (pl. *liches*)

liche (n.) likeness, appearance

lickith (v. pres. pl.) lick

licnesse (n.) likeness, similarity

licome (n.) body (gen. sing. *licomes*; pl. *licomes*)

licomliche (adj.) bodily, physical

licunge (n.) pleasure

licwurthe (adj.) praiseworthy, pleasing

lif (n.) life (pl. *lives*; gen. sing. *lives*); **lives writ**, the book of life

liffule (adj.) life-giving

liflade (n.) life; way of life

lif-leovi (adj. pl. as subst.) life-long friends

liflese (adj.) lifeless

lifsithe (n. pl.) lifetime (pl. *lifsithen*)

liggen (v.) lie; to be subject; to pertain to; to remain; to be proper (pres. 2nd sing. *list*; pres. 3rd sing. *lith*; pres. pl. *liggeth*; past 3rd sing. *lei*; past pl. *leien*)

lihe(n) (v.) lie, be deceitful; be false (pres. pl. *liheth*; subj. pres. sing. *lihe*; pres. part. *lihinde*)

liht (n.) light

liht (v.) see **lihten**

lihte (adj.) light; frivolous, faint; **of lihte bileave**, credulous

lihte (adv.) brightly, brilliantly

lihte (v. subj. pres. sing.) enlighten. See also **lihten**

lihten (v.) descend, alight; proceed; fall (spiritually), drop; arrive, come (pres. 3rd sing. *lihteth*; past 2nd sing. *lihtest*; past 3rd sing. *lihte*; past 3rd pl. *lihten*; subj. pres. 2nd sing. *lihte, liht*; pres. part. *lihtinde*; past part. *iliht*); **lihte to**, settle on, adopt; **lihteth i**, comes into

lihtlich(e) (adv.) lightly; **leoteth se lihtliche**, take so lightly, disregard; (adj.) trivial

liketh (v. pres. 3rd sing.) pleases, gives pleasure; **the god liketh**, pleases you well

lilie (n.) lily (gen. sing. *lilies*)

lim (n.) limb; part of the body; follower, agent (pl. *limen*, gen. sing. *limes*)

limeth (v. pres. 3rd sing.) joins, unites

limmel (adv.) limb from limb

limpeth (v., pres. 3rd sing.) pertains, belongs; is fitting, proper (past 3rd sing. *lomp*); **thet te limpet to the**, that which is proper for you, i.e., what your job is

linneth (v. pres. 3rd sing.) cease (pres. part. as n. *lin(n)unge*)

lire (n.) flesh, countenance

list, lith (v.) see **liggen**

liste (n.) skill, cunning

lith (n.) joint, limb

lith (v.) see **liggen**

litheri (v.) become lathered (past part. *litherede*)

litheth (v. imper. pl.) listen to, hear

liun (n.) lion (pl. *liuns*; gen. sing. *liunes*)

live see **lif**

livede see **leven, libben**

liveneth (n.) support, sustenance

liveth, liviende, livieth see **libben**

lo, lowr (interj.) lo, ah, oh, look (used for emphasis)

lockes (n. pl.) locks (of hair)

loft-song (n.) praise-song

loke, lokede, loketh see **lokin**

loki(n) (v.) look, see; consider; determine, decree, ordain; protect, keep; ensure (past 3rd sing. *lokede*; imper. sing. *loke, loki*; imper. pl. *loketh, lokith*; subj. pres. pl. *loki*; pres. part. *lokinde*; past

part. *iloket*); **lokin/lokith . . . hwenne**, anticipate

lokunge (n.) gaze, attention

lomb (n.) lamb

lomp see **limpeth**

lonc (adj.) lank, skinny

londe, lont (n.) land

long(e) (adj.) long, of great duration (comp. *lengre*); **swa lengre swa levere**, the longer the more dear (i.e., more dear with more time). (adv.) a long while, a long time; **haldeth longe**, i.e., keep it up for a while

longede (v. past 3rd sing.) longed, desired (pres. 3rd sing. *longeth*; pres. part. *longunge*); **me longeth**, I long

lonke (n.) side, flank

lont see **londe**

losede (v. past 3rd sing.) lost

lothest (adj. superl.) most loathsome

low(e) (interj.) lo, behold

lowinde (pres. part./n.) lowing

lowr see **lo**

lowsin, lowse (v.) loosen; release (past 3rd sing. *lowsede*; imper. sing. *lowse, leowse*)

lude (adv.) loudly

ludere (adj. compar.) louder

ludinge (pres. part. as n.) shouting, clamor

lud-stevene (adj.) loud-voiced

lufsum(e) (adj.) lovely, beautiful (compar. *lufsumre*)

lufte (n.) air; sky

luft-fuheles (n. pl.) birds of the sky

lufsumlec (n.) beauty

luken (v.) tear out; drag (past 3rd sing. *leac*); **leac him ayeinwart**, jerked himself backward

lupe (n.) leap, jump

lure (n.) loss (pl. *luren*)

lust (n.) lust, desire; pleasure (pl. *lustes*); **god lust**, full attention

luste (v. past 3rd sing.) desired; impersonal as in **hire luste**, she desired

lusten (v.) listen (to) (pres. 3rd sing. *lusteth*; pres. pl. subj. *lusten*; imper. sing. *lustu*; imper. pl. *lusteth*)

lusti (adj.) joyful; eager

lustiliche (adv.) eagerly

lustnin (v.) listen, hear (pres. subj. sing. *lustni*; imper. sing. *lustne*; imper. pl., *lustnith*)

lustu see **lusten**

lut (pron.) few; (adj.) short

lutede (v. past 3rd sing.) lay hidden

luten (v. 1) bow down; worship (pres. pl. *luteth*). (v. 2) lurk, lie hidden, hide (pres. pl. *luteth*)

luther(e) (adj.) terrible; wicked; fierce; as subst. wicked one, wickedness; **luther strencthe**, brute force

luthere (adv.) wickedly

lutherliche (adv.) wickedly; cruelly

lutlen (adv.) gradually; **lutlen ant lutlen**, little by little

lutli(n) (v.) lessen, diminish, grow little

lut-stevene (adj.) loud-voiced

lut(t)el, lutle (adj.) little

luve (n.) love

luvede, luvedest, luveden see **luvien**

luvefule (adj.) lustful

luveliche (adj.) loving, dear

luve-runes (n. pl.) love-stories

luvewende (adj.) beloved

luvien (v.) love (pres. 1st sing. *luvie*; pres. 2nd sing. *luvest*; pres. 3rd sing. *luv(i)eth*; pres. pl. *luvieth*; past 2nd sing. *luvedest*; past 3rd sing. *luvede*; past pl. *luveden*; pres. subj. sing. *luvie*; pres. part. *luviende*; past part. *iluvet*); **as me luvede**, as it was practiced, as was the custom

ma (n.) more

mahe (n.) stomach, belly

mahe(n), maht, mahte(n) (v.) see **mei**

mahte (n.) might, strength

make (n.) mate

makelese (adj.) matchless

mak(i)e(n) (v.) make, create; cause; often as auxiliary (pres. 2nd sing. *makest*; pres. 3rd sing. *maketh*, *makith*; pres. pl. *makieth*; past 1st and 3rd sing. *maked*, *makede*; past 2nd sing. *makedest*; subj. pres. sing. *makie*; imper. sing. *make*; past part. *imaket*, *imakede*)

makunge (n.) making, cause

man (n.) fellowship; sexual intercourse

mantles (n. pl.) mantles, cloaks

marbrestan (n.) marble

mare (adj./adv.) more; greater; still (superl. *mest*, *meast*); as subst. in **meast con**, knows the most; **áá mare**, forever; **al thet measte deal**, for the most part; **meast alle**, almost all

marhen (n.) morning; **to marhen**, tomorrow

marhe-yeve (n.) morning-gift, given by the husband to his wife the morning after they have consummated their marriage

Marie (prop. n.) the Virgin Mary

martir (n.) martyr

martyrdom (n.) martyrdom

mate (adj.) vanquished, defeated

maumetes, maumez (n. pl.) maumets, idols; pagan gods

me (adv.) yet, but, moreover; even

me (pron.) me; one, someone, person, people; often used in forming passive, e.g., **me foreseide**, it was predicted; **me droh ham**, they were dragged; **me dude**, it was done

meadliche (adv.) madly

meadschipe (n.) madness, insanity

meale (v.) speak; declare (pres. 3rd sing. *mealeth*; past 3rd sing. *mealde*)

mealles (n. pl.) mauls, sledgehammers

meallith (v. pres. pl.) beat

me(a)lten (v.) melt; dissolve (pres. 3rd sing. *mealteth*; subj. past sing. *mealte*; past part. *imelt*)

meanen (v.) say; complain, lament (past pl. *meanden*)

Mearch (n.) March

meare (adj.) noble

mearminnes (n. gen. sing.) mermaid

meari (n.) marrow

me(a)rrin (v.) mar; harm, damage (pres. 2nd sing. *merrest*; pres. 3rd sing. *merreth*; pres. pl. *mearreth*; past pl. *merden*)

meast see **mare**

meastling (n.) copper, brass

meath (n.) moderation, measure, temperance

meatheluker (adv. compar.) more moderately

meathen (n.) maggots

mede (n.) reward (pl. *meden*)

medi(n) (v.) reward; **medi with**, traffic with

mehes (n. pl.) kinswomen

mei (v.) auxiliary verb usually followed by infinitive; be able, can, might, may (pres. 2nd sing. *maht*; pres. 3rd sing. *mei*; pres. pl. *mahen, muhen, muhe*; past 3rd sing. *mahte*; past 3rd pl. *mahten*; pres. 1st sing. subj. *mahe*; past subj. 1st sing. *mahte*)

meide (n.) maid

meiden (n.) maiden, virgin; young woman (pl. *meidnes*, gen. sing. *meidnes*; gen. pl. *meidene*)

meies (n. pl.) kinsmen

mein (n.) might, power

meinful(e) (adj.) strong, mighty

meister (n.) master, scholar, teacher (pl. *meistres*); **to meistres**, as teachers

meistrie (n.) mastery, authority; victory

meistrin (v.) master, defeat; rule (pres. 3rd sing. *meistreth*; imper. *mestre*)

meithhad (n.) maidenhood, virginity (gen. sing. *meithhades*)

mekelec see **me(o)kelec**

mel (n.) meal, food, nourishment

mel-seotel (n.) meal seat

men see **mon**

mene (v. pres. 1st sing.) mean

mennes see **mon**

mennesse (n.) humanity, lit. man-ness

menske (n.) honor

menskin (v.) glorify, honor (pres. 3rd sing. *mensketh*; imper. sing. *menske*)

meoke (adj.) meek, modest (superl. *meokest*)

me(o)kelec (n.) meekness

meokeliche (adv.) meekly

meokeschipe (n.) meekness, humility

meosure see **mesure**

merden see **me(a)rren**

merke (n.) mark, sign

merkest (v. pres. 2nd sing.) mark, lay out, design (past 2nd sing. *merkedest*)

merren, merrest, merreth see **me(a)rrin**

mest see **mare**

mestre see **meistrin**

mesure, meosure (n.) measure, moderation

met(e) (n.) measure, moderation, temperance. See also **mete** (n.)

mete (n.) food

meten (v.) measure out; fashion (past 2nd sing. *mete*)

mi (pron.) my, mine

mid (prep.) with; **mid tet ilke**, at that moment, with that; **mid alle**

middel (adj.) middle

midniht (n.) midnight

mihte (n.) might, power; virtue

mihti (adj.) mighty

milc (n.) milk; **milc strunden**, streams of milk

milce (n.) mercy, pity

milce (v. imper.) pity, have mercy on

milde (adj.) mild, gentle (superl. *mildest*)

mildheortfule (adj.) mild-hearted

mildschipe, miltschipe (n.) mildness, gentleness

milen (n. pl.) miles

miltschipe see **mildschipe**

milzfule (adj.) merciful

mine see **mi**

miracle (n) miracle (pl. *miracles*)

mis (n.) in **on mis**, amiss

misbileave (n.) misbelief, heresy, false belief

misbilevede (adj. from past part.) heathen, wrongly believing; **misbilevede men**, heathen people, false believers

misboren (v. past part.) misborn, deformed at birth

misdude (v. past 3rd sing.) did wrong

misfeare (n.) misfortune

misfearen (v.) go astray, go wrong; come to harm (past 3rd pl. *misferden*; subj. pres. sing. *misfeare*)

misliche (adj.) various, diverse; separate; erratic, wandering; improper, sinful

misliche (adv.) wrongly

mislimet (adj.) misshapen, deformed

misnome (v.) to be in error; be mistaken

misseist (v. pres. 2nd sing.) slander, abuse

misthuncheth (v. pres. 3rd sing.) displeases, seems wrong to

mix (adj.) filthy, foul

mixne (n.) midden-heap, dunghill

mixschipes (n. pl.) filthy things, villainies

mod (n.) mind, mood, spirit

moder (n.) mother (pl. *modres*)

moder-bern (n.) mother-children, person

moder-burh (n.) mother-city

moderles (adj.) motherless

modgeste see **modi**

modi (adj.) proud, obstinate (moody) (superl. *modgeste*)

modres see **moder**

mohthe (n.) moth

mon (n.) a person, human; one, someone; a man; human; humankind, humanity (more gender neutral than today's "man"); (pl. *men*; gen. sing. *monnes*; gen. pl. *mennes, monne*); **mon drem**, human joy; **seolf the mon**, the human being, the human self; **monnes sawle**, the soul of humanity, the human soul

moncun (n.) humankind, humanity

mone (n.) moon

moneth (n.) month

mong (n.) mingling, mixture; confusion; conflict

monhad (n.) personhood, humanity

moni (adj./pron.) many (pl. *monie*)

monifalde (adj.) manyfold

monlich (adj.) human

monne, monnes see **mon**

monslahe (n.) man-slayer, killer

most, moste see **moten**

mot (n.) argumentation, reasoning; assembly, meeting, moot (pl. *motes*); **haveth mot**, holds debate

mot(e) (v.) see **moten**

motede see **moti(n)**

moten (v.) auxiliary verb followed by infinitive expressing necessity, obligation, or compulsion, must; may, shall; (pres. 1st sing. *mot*; pres. 2nd sing. *most*; pres. pl. *moten*; past 3rd sing. *moste*; subj. pres. sing. *mote*; past 3rd sing. subj. *moste, mote*); idiomatically in curses: **Theo thet ham makieth mote beon ilich ham**, may those who make them be like them; **Ich mot nede**, I must needs (i.e., I am compelled)

moteres (n. pl.) orators, debaters

motild (n.) female debater or orator, female lawyer

moti(n) (v.) debate, argue, dispute; speak (pres. 1st sing. *moti*; pres. 2nd sing. *motest*; pres. 3rd sing.

moteth; past 3rd sing. *motede*; past part. *imotet*)

muche(le) (adj.) great, powerful, much; **muchel deale**, a great deal. (adv.) much, greatly; **ase muchel . . . ase**, as much as, the same as

muchelin, mucli (v.) increase

muhe, muhen see **mei**

munde (adj.) present in (one's) mind

munegeth see **munegin**

munegin (v.) admonish, remind, call to mind (pres. 3rd sing. *munegeth*; past part. *imuneget*)

munegunge (n.) remembrance, memory, reminder. See also **munegin**

munien, munnen (v.) remember, have in mind; imagine; relate, tell (pres. 1st sing. *munie*; pres. 3rd sing. *munneth*; pres. 3nd sing. *munnest*; pres. pl. *munneth*, *munieth*; past 1st sing. *munne*; imper. pl. *munneth*; past part. *imuneget*)

munt (n.) mount

murie (adj.) merry, joyful

murne (v.) mourn

murthe, murhthe (n.) mirth, joy (pl. *murhthen*)

muth (n.) mouth

nabbe see **hab(b)e(n)**

naht (n.) night

nahtes (adv.) at night

nai (interj.) no (as response)

nakede (adj.) naked

nalde (v.) see **wulle**

nam see **beon**

nameliche (adv.) namely, especially

nan(e) (adj./n./pron.) none, not any; nothing; **ne for na**, nor for any

nanesweis (adv.) in no way, by no means

nart see **beon**

nat see **wite(n)**

nathing (n.) nothing; anything

naut see **nawt**

nave, navest, naveth see **hab(b)e(n)**

nawt, nawiht, naut, noht (adv.) not, by no means, not at all; often used as repeated negative for emphasis (i.e., **nes . . . nawiht**, was not at all; **ne beo thu nawiht**, be not at all); (pron.) naught, nothing; no one

ne (adv./conj.) not; nor ("*ne/nowther . . . ne*," neither . . . nor)

nearewe, nearowe (adj.) narrow

nease (n.) nose

nease-gristles (n. pl.) nose-gristle (i.e., the cartilage of the nose)

nease-thurles (n. pl.) nostrils

neavele (n.) navel

neaver, neavre (adv.) never; ever (with neg.) (often doubled with other negatives for emphasis); **neaver mare**, nevermore, never again

neb, nebbe (n.) face; snout (pl. *nebbes*)

nebscheft, nebschaft (n.) face; countenance, expression

necke (n.) neck

neddren (n. pl.) adders, snakes, vipers

nede (adv.) by need, necessarily; **ich mot nede**, i.e., I am compelled

nede (n.) see **neode**

ned(l)unge (adv.) necessarily; against one's will

nefde, nefden see **hab(b)e(n)**

neh (adv.) nearly (compar. *neor*; superl. *nest*); **ga nu neor**, go closer now; **nower neh**, nowhere near (i.e., not by any means)

neil (n.) fingernail (pl. *neil(l)es*)

neil-cnives (n. pl.) razors

nemeth see **neomen**

nempnede (v. past 3rd sing.) named; mentioned (past part. *inempnet*, *inemed*)

ne(o)de (n.) need; time of need; difficulty

neodefule (adj./subst.) needy

neodeles (adv.) needlessly

neodelukest (adv. superl.) most diligently

neolechin (v.) approach, come near

neomen (v.) take; seize; commit; undertake (pres. 2nd sing. *nimest*; pres. 3rd sing. *nimeth*; past 2nd sing. *nome*; past 3rd sing. *nom*; past pl. *nomen*; pres. subj. sing. *neome*; imper. sing. *nim*; imper. pl. *ne(o)meth*; past part. *inumen*); **nom yeme**, took care of; **neomen ow**, visit (lit., betake yourselves); **nim the to**, turn to

neor see **neh**

neother (adv.) down, downward; lower

neowcin see **nowcin**

neowe (adj.) new

nere, neren see **beon**

nes see **beon**

nest see **neh**

nestfalde (adj.) closest

nette (n.) net

newcin see **nowcin**

Nichomedesse (gen.) in **Nichomedesse burh**, the city of Nicomedia

nihtes (n. pl.) nights

nim, nimest, nimeth see **neomen**

nis see **beon**

no (adv.) not

Noees (gen. sing.) Noah's

noht (adj.) evil

noht (pron.) see **nawt**

nohtunge (n.) scorn, insult; trifle; (pron.) nothing

nohwer (adv.) anywhere; nowhere; never; ever; in any respect

nohwider (adv.) to nowhere

nom, nome, nomen (v.) see **neomen**

nome (n.) name (pl. nomen)

nomecuthe (adj.) well-known, famous; **mest nomecuthe icud**, most widely known (superl. *nomecuthest*)

nomeliche (adv.) namely, especially

nomen see **nome**

noteth (v. pres. 3rd sing.) partakes of

notheles (adv.) nevertheless

notheletere (adv.) nevertheless

nother see **nowther**

nowcin, ne(o)wcin (n.) hardship, distress

nower (adv.) nowhere

nowther (adj., conj., pron., adv.) neither; **nowther . . . ne**, neither . . . nor

Novembres (n. gen. sing.) of November

nu (adv.) now; since

nule, nulle, nullen, nulli, nult, nultu see **wulle**

nunan (adv.) soon

nurhth see **nurth**

nurrice (n.) nurse (gen. sing. *nurrices*)

nurth, nurhth (n.) noise

nuste, nusten, nuten see **wite(n)**

nuten see **witen**

nuthe (adv.) now

nutteth (v. pres. pl.) make use of, profit by

o see **on**

o(f) (prep./adv.) of; from, out of; (away) from; by; for, about; in, with respect to; by means of; full of, filled with

ofdret (v. past part.) afraid

offeare see **offearen**

offearen (v.) frighten, be afraid, terrify (past 3rd sing. *offearet*; pres. sing. subj. *offeare*; past part. *offert, offearet*)

ofearnest (v. pres. 2nd sing.) deserve; earn

offert see **offearet**

offrin (v.) offer (past 3rd sing. *offrede*)

offruht(e) (v. past part.) frightened, terrified

ofhungret (v. past part.) ahungered, very hungry

ofrahte (v. past 3rd sing.) came upon

ofservet see **ofservin**

ofservin (v.) to earn (past part. *ofservet*)

ofsloh (v. past 3rd sing.) slew, killed

ofte (adv.) oft, often, frequently (superl. *oftest*)

ofthuncheth (v. pres. 3rd sing.)
   displeases
ofthunchunge (n.) displeasure; grief,
   regret (pl. *ofthunchunges*)
oht (adj.) good
oht (v.) see **ah**
ohwider (adv.) anywhere, elsewhere
olhnede (v. past 3rd sing.) cajole
olhnung(e) (n.) flattery
omidhepes (adv.) in the middle
o(n) (prep.) on, upon; on top of; **o**
   least at last
on (v. pres. 1st sing.) grant; wish
   (pres. pl. *unneth*)
onde(n) (n.) jealousy, envy
ondswere see **onsware**
ongon (v. past 3rd sing.) began; tried
onont (prep.) in/with respect to, with
   regard to, about; of the same rank
   as; by, by means of; **onont thet**,
   insofar as; **onont him**, on his part
onsware, ondswere (n.) answer
ontend, ontende see **ontenden**
ontenden (v.) inflame, set afire (pres.
   3rd sing. *ontent*; past 3rd sing.
   ontende; imper. sing. *ontend*)
ontfule (adj.) envious; malicious
ontswere, ontswerede, ontswerest,
   ontsereth see **on(t)swerien**
on(t)swerien, ondswerien (v.) answer,
   reply (pres. 1st sing. *ondswerie*,
   ontswerie; pres. 2nd sing.
   ontswerest; pres. 3rd sing.
   ontswereth; past 3rd sing.
   onswerede, ontswerede; imper. sing.
   ontswere; pres. subj. sing. *ontswerie*)
onuven (adv.) after
opene, openede see **openeth**
openeth (v. pres. 3rd sing.) opens
   (past 3rd sing. *openede*; imper.
   sing. *opene*)
openliche (adv.) openly, clearly;
   publicly
orcost (n.) wealth
ord (n.) beginning, point of origin;
   point (of a sword)
ordfrume (n.) beginning

orhel (n.) pride
ort (n.) beginning, in **ort and ende**,
   the beginning and the end
other, othre (adj.) other; second (pl.
   othre; gen. sing. *othres*); (conj.) or;
   (subst. n.) rest, remainder; **al thet**
   other, all the rest; **other . . .**
   other, one . . . the other, either . .
   . or; **hare othres**, each other's
otherhwile(s) (adv.) sometimes; at
   other times
otherweis (adv.) otherwise
otwa, atwa (adv.) in two, asunder
over (adv./prep.) over, above; upon;
   beyond, too much
overal (adv.) all over, everywhere;
   entirely
overcume(n) (v.) overcome, defeat
   (past 3rd sing. *overcom*; past 3rd
   pl. *overcomen*; past part.
   overcumen)
overeorninde (v. pres. part.)
   overflowing
overfullet (v. past part.) overfull
   (filled over), overflowing
overgan (v.) go over, traverse, travel
   through; pass by; surpass, exceed,
   outdo (pres. 3rd sing. *overgeath*)
overgart (n.) arrogance
overguld (v. past part.) gilded over
   with gold
overhardi (adj.) overconfident,
   reckless, too bold
overherren (n. pl.) overlords,
   superiors
overhohe (n.) arrogance, disdain
overkim see **overcumen**
overstihen (v.) surpass
overtild (v. past part.) canopied,
   covered over
overtoke (past 3rd sing.) extended,
   reached
overwarpen (v. past part.) ruined,
   destroyed
ow (pron.) you, to you; yourselves
ower (pron.) your; **ower an**, one of
   you

pappes (n. pl.) paps, breasts

Paraise (n.) paradise (gen. *Paraises*)

passeth (v. pres. 3rd sing.) surpasses (pres. pl. *passith*)

Passiun (n.) passion, suffering

patriarche (n.) patriarch

pe(i)s (n.) peace

pel (n.) fine purple cloth (pl. *pelles*); in collacative **with pel and with purpre**, i.e., with rich and purple (clothes)

pelles see **pel**

pes see **peis**

Pharaones (gen.) Pharaoh's

pich (n.) pitch

pikes (n. pl.) points

pilche-clut (n.) a ragged or tattered cloak

pilegrimes (n. pl.) pilgrims

pine (n.) pain, torment (pl. *pinen*)

pine (v.) see **pineth**

pineth (v. pres. 3rd sing.) tortures; troubles; suffers pain (imper. sing. *pine*); **ne pine thu**, do not trouble yourself; **pineth o childe**, suffers pain in labor, suffers in childbirth

pinfule (adj.) painful; **pineful gin**, instrument of torture

pinunge (n.) pain; **pinunge thraen**, labor pains

place (n.) place, public place; **come i place**, appeared in public

pleien (v.) play (pres. part. *pleinde*)

plohen (n. pl.) games, playing; **plohe-speche**, playful or flirtatious speech

ploiveren (n. pl.) playfellows

poisun (n.) poison

postles (n. pl.) pillars

povre (adj.) poor; (as subst.) the poor (people)

preones (n. pl.) pins

preovin (v.) prove; demonstrate; convict (pres. 3rd sing. *preoveth*)

prince (n.) commander; prince

prisun (n.) prison (gen. sing. *prisunes*)

privileges (n. pl.) privileges

procunges (n. pl.) prickings, proddings

prokie (v.) incite, spur on (prick); (pres. 2nd sing. *prokest*; pres. pl. *prokieth*)

prophete (n.) prophet

prud (adj.) proud

prude (n.) pride

prudeliche (adv.) proudly; bravely

psalmwruhte (n.) psalm-writer, psalmist

puissun (n.) poison

purpre (n.) purple cloth (pl. *purpres*)

put(te) (n.) pit

quethen, quod, quoth see **cwethen**

ra (n.) roe

rad (v.) see **rit**

rade (n.) riding; **o rade**, on horseback

rahte(n) see **reache**

rake (n.) jaws

raketehe (n.) chain, fetter (pl. *raketehen*)

ran (v. past 3rd sing.) touched

rarin (v.) roar, howl (pres. part. *rarinde*)

rarunge (n.) roaring, howling

rawe (n.) row

rawen (n. pl.) rays

reache (v.) stretch; reach (past 3rd sing. rahte; past 3rd pl. *rahten*)

read (n.) advice, counsel; meeting, council; plot; **toc read**, considered

reade (adj.) red

reade (v. pres. 1st sing.) advise (pres. 3rd sing. *read*, *reat*; past 2nd sing. *readdest*; past 3rd sing. *readde*; imper. sing. *read*)

readesmen (n. pl.) advisors, counselors

readliche (adv.) swiftly, speedily; readily

readwisest (adj. superl.) wisest of counsel

reaf, reafde see **reavin**

ream (n.) cry, clamor, lamentation (pl. *reames*)

reasde (v. past 3rd sing.) rushed

reat (v. past 3rd sing.) threw, flung, rushed at (with great force). See also **reade** (v.)

reavers (n. pl.) reavers, raiders, robbers

reavin (v.) seize, take, rob; rescue (pres. pl. *reaveth*; past 3rd sing. *reavede*, *reafde*; imper. sing. *reaf*)

reccheth (v. pres. 3rd sing.) proceeds

rechelese (adj.) reckless

redden (v.) read (pres. 3rd sing. *redeth*; past part. *iredd*)

reden (v.) estimate

redere (n.) reader

redeth see **redden**

redunge (n.) legend

refschip(e) (n.) reeveship, governorship (position of governor)

rehest (adj. superl.) boldest

reisun (n.) reason, answer; **yelde reisun**, give an answer

remen (v.) mourn; cry out, lament (past pl. *remden*)

remunge (n.) lamentation, crying out, screaming

rende (v.) rend, rip (past 3rd sing. *rende*)

reng see **ring**

rente (n.) rent, property revenue

reodien (v.) strive

reopen (v.) reap

reotheren (n. pl.) cattle

reoweth (v. pres. 3rd sing.) repent, rue; **us reoweth ure sith**, we rue/regret

reowfule (adj.) merciful; pitiful

reowfulnesse (n.) mercy, pity; compassion, sympathy

reowliche (adv.) wretchedly, cruelly

reowthe, reothe, rewthe (n.) sorrow, pity, ruth

reowthfule (adj.) pitiable, sorrowful

reowthfulliche (adv.) piteously, sorrowfully

reschte (v. past 3rd sing.) crackled

reste (n.) rest; peace

resten (v.) rest (pres. 2nd sing. *restest*; pres. 3rd sing. *resteth*; past 3rd sing. *reste*)

reufulliche (adv.) ruefully, pitiably

reuliche (adv.) miserably, piteously

reve (n.) reeve, magistrate, governor (pl. *reven*; gen. pl. *revene*)

riche (n.) kingdom; (adj.) rich, wealthy; (as subst.) the rich (people) (superl. *richest*)

richedom (n.) riches

richesce (n.) riches, wealth, abundance

riht (adj.) right (directional); true

riht (adv.) rightly, truly

riht(e) (n.) right; truth; justice; deserts, merit; **with rihte**, justly; **efter his rihte**, according to his deserts (what he deserves)

rihte (v. past 3rd sing.) raised, erected; righted, corrected; directed (pres. sing. subj. *rihte*; past part. *iriht*; imper. sing. *riht*)

rihtwise (adj./n.) righteous, just (gen. *rihtwises*)

rihtwisliche (adv.) righteously; fairly, equitably

rihtwis(s)nesse (n.) righteousness, justice

rikenin (v.) reckon, count; describe (past part. *irikenet*)

rinen (v. past pl.) touch; strike

ring, reng (n.) ring; circle

rinneth (v. pres. 3rd sing.) flows, runs

ripe (n.) fruit, harvest

rit (v. pres. 3rd sing.) rides (past 3rd sing. *rad*)

rive (adj.) plentiful, abundant

rixlen (v.) rule, reign (pres. 3rd sing. *rixleth*; pres. 3rd pl. *rixlith*)

rixlinge (n.) reign (lit. ruling)

ro (n.) repose, rest

robbith (v. pres. pl.) rob, steal (past part. *irobbet*)

Rode (n.) rood, cross; **Rode-merk**, sign of the Cross

Rome (n.) Rome (city); the Roman Empire

ron (v. past 3rd sing.) ran, flowed

ronnes (n. pl.) love-songs

rose (n.) rose

roten (n. pl.) roots

rotunge (n.) rotting, putrefaction

rowen (v.) row

ruddest (v. past 2nd sing.) rescued

rudie (adj.) flushed, rosy; red

rudnin (v.) redden (past 3rd sing. *rudnede*; subj. pres. 3rd sing. *rudni*)

rug (n.) back

ruglunge (adv.) backwards

ruhe (adj.) shaggy, bristly

run (n.) mystery (pl. *runes*); consultations, meetings

rune (n.) running, flowing; movement, course (of the sun); violence

ruten (v. past 3rd pl.) in **ruten forth**, burst forth, exploded

sahe (n.) words, saying (pl. *sahen*)

sahte (n.) accord, agreement

sake (n.) sake

salve (n.) salve

salve, salvi (v.) see **salvin**

salvin (v.) heal (pres. 1st sing. *salvi*; imper. sing. *salve*; imper. pl. *salvith*)

samblant see **semblant**

sar (n.) pain, discomfort; trouble

sar, sore (adj.) bitter, grievous

sare (adv.) sorely, painfully; terribly, sore, very (compar. *sarre*)

sari (adj.) sad, sorry

sariliche (adj.) horrible, foul

sariliche (adv.) grievously; painfully

Sathanesse (n. gen. sing.) Satan's

savour (n.) savor, smell

savure (adj.) delicious, savory (compar. *savurure*)

savurure see **savure**

sawl(e) (n.) soul (pl. *sawlen*; gen. pl. *saw(u)lene*)

schad (n.) discernment or discrimination; **tweire schad**, the ability to tell the difference between two things

schadewe (n.) shadow; reflection

schafte (n.) creature (a living creature created by God); idol (pl. *schaftes*)

schal (v.) auxiliary and modal verb always followed by an infinitive (occasionally implied infinitive is dropped) should, ought to, must (obligation, often with past tense); shall, will (futurity); would, should (condition); were accustomed to (consuetudinal); (pres. 2nd sing. *schalt, schald*; pres. 3rd sing. *schal*; pres. pl. *schule, schu(l)len*; past 2nd sing. *schuldest*; past 3rd sing. *sculde, schulde*; past 3rd pl. *schulden*; pres. 1st sing. subj. *schule*)

schan see **schinest**

schape (n.) shape, figure, form

scharp, scherpe (adj.) sharp

scharpe (adv.) sharply

schaw, schawde, schawdest, schawest, schaweth see **schawin**

schawi, schawith see **schawin**

schawin (v.) show, demonstrate (pres. 2nd sing. *schawest*; pres. 3rd sing. *schaweth*; pres. pl. *schawith*; past 2nd sing. *schawdest*; past 3rd sing. *schawde*; subj. pres. pl. *schawi*; imper. sing. *schaw*; past part. *ischawet*); **schawith . . . forth**, demonstrate, put forward

scheaftes (n. pl.) creatures (gen. pl. *schefte*)

scheat(e) see **scheote**

schefte see **scheaftes**

schelde (n.) shield

schendest (v. pres. 2nd sing.) shame, disgrace, humiliate (pres. 3rd sing. *schent*; imper. pl. *schendeth*; past part. *ischend*)

schendeth see **schendest**

schendlac, schenthlac (n.) shame, humiliation; insult; **to schendlac,** disgracefully

schene (adj.) beautiful, fair, bright, sheen (compar. *schenre*)

schenre see **schene**

schent see **schendest**

schenthlac see **schendlac**

sch(e)ome (n.) shame, humiliation (pl. *scheomen*; gen. pl. *scheomene*); **to scheome,** shamefully; **scheome creft,** shameful or humiliating craft (i.e., midwifery)

scheomelese (adj.) shameless

scheomeliche (adv.) shamefully

scheomen, scheomene see **sch(e)ome**

scheometh, scheomie see **scheomien**

scheomien (v.) shame; be ashamed (pres. 3rd sing. *scheometh*; subj. pres. 3rd sing. *scheomie*; past part. *ischeomet*)

sch(e)op see **schuppen**

scheote (v. pres. 1st sing.) shoot (pres. 3rd sing. *scheoteth*; past 3rd sing. *scheat(e)*; imper. pl. *scheoteth*; past part. *schoten*)

scheoteth see **scheote**

schep (n. pl.) sheep

scher (adv.) completely

scher (v. past 3rd sing.) shear, cut

scherpe see **scharp**

schilde (v. subj. pres. sing.) shield, guard, protect (against doing something); **schilde . . . to freinin,** prevent or protect from asking

schilinde (v. pres. part.) resounding, ringing

schim(m)ede (v. past 3rd sing.) shimmered, glistened (pres. part. *schim(m)inde*)

schim(m)minde see **schimmede**

schine see **schinest**

schinest (v. pres. 2nd sing.) shine (pres. 3rd sing. *schineth*; subj. pres. sing. *schine*; pres. part. *schininde*)

schir (adj.) pure, complete

schireve (n.) sheriff, reeve, governor

schonken (n. pl.) shanks, legs

schop see **schuppen**

schoten see **scheote**

schreamen (v.) scream, shriek

schrenchen (v.) deceive (past 3rd sing. *schrencte*)

schrencte see **schrenchen**

schrift(e) (n.) shrift, confession; penance

schrud (n.) shroud; clothes (pl. *schrudes*)

schrudde (v. past 3rd sing.) shrouded, clothed (past part. *ischrud, ischrudde*)

schu(c)ke (n.) devil (gen. sing. *shukes, schuken*)

schuderin (v.) shudder (pres. part. *schuderinde*)

schuderinde see **schuderin**

schuldi (adj.) guilty, responsible

schuldren (n. pl.) shoulders

schule, schulen, schullen see **schal**

schunchen (v.) terrify, frighten (away)

schunien (v.) shun, refuse (to do something) (subj. pres. sing. *schunie*)

schuppen (v.) create, shape, make (past 2nd sing. *schuptest*; past 3rd sing. *schupte, scheop*; *schop*; past part. *ischapen, ischapet, ischeapen, ischepen(e)*)

Schup(p)ent (n.) lit. "the creating/shaping one"; the Maker/Creator (God)

schupte, schuptest see **schuppen**

schurgen (n. pl.) scourges

schome see **scheome**

sclein see **slean**

sclepinde see **slepten**

scolmeistres (n. pl.) schoolmasters, wise men

se (adv.) so, such; **se . . . se,** as . . . as; **sone se,** as soon as; in compar. **se lengre se mare,** the longer the greater; **beaten se ye beaten,**

however hard you beat; **ne (. . .)
se, neaver (. . .) se, neaver se,**
however; **se mare (or other
comp.) . . . se mare (or other
compar.)**, the more . . . the more

se (n.) see **se(a)**

se(a) (n.) sea

sea-strem (n.) sea-stream, ocean
current

sechen (v.) attack; come; seek;
advance (as in battle) (pres. 1st
sing. *seche*; pres. 3rd sing. *secheth*;
past 3rd sing. *sohte*; subj. pres. sing.
seche; imper. pl. *secheth*; past part.
isoht); **forte sechen**, looking to

sed (n.) seed

seg(g)en (v.) say, speak, tell; (pres. 1st
sing. *segge, seh*; pres. 2nd sing.
seist, seggeth; pres. 3rd sing. *seith*;
past 1st, 3rd sing. *seide*; past 2nd
sing. *seidest*; past pl. *seiden*; imper.
sing. *sei*; past part. *iseid, iseit*); **beo
. . . to seggen/iseide**, means

seheliche (adj.) visible

sei, seide, seiden, seist, seith (v.) see
seggen

seil (n.) seal

seileth (v. pres. 3rd sing.) binds, seals,
joins (past. part. *isledede, iseilet,
iseiled*)

seith see **seggen**

seke (adj.) sick. (n.) the sick, sick
people

selcuthe (adj.) wondrous

selhthe (n.) joy; grace (pl. *selhthen*)

seli (adj.) holy, blessed; innocent;
lucky, fortunate (pl. *selie*)

seltscene (adj.) seldom seen, rarely
seen

semblant, samblant (n.) appearance;
expression, countenance; conduct,
manner, behavior; **na semblant
ne makien**, give no outward sign,
do not express or show

semden (v. past 3rd pl.) seem, appear
(past 3rd sing. *semde*; pres. 3rd
sing. subj. *seme*)

semliche (adj.) seemly, attractive

senchen (v.) sink (past 3rd sing.
sencte)

senden (v.) send; send a message (to
find out); inquire (pres. 1st sing.
sende; pres. 3rd sing. *sent, send*;
past 1st and 3rd sing. *sende*; past
part. *isent*)

seolf, seolve (n.) self; same; (pl.
seolven) (ref. pron.) himself;
herself; themselves; **seolf the ilke**,
the very same; **seolf the mon**, the
human being, the human self

seolver (n.) silver

seo(n), to seonne (v.) see, look at,
behold (pres. 2nd sing. *sist*; pres.
3rd sing. *sith*; pres. pl. *seoth*; past
3rd sing. *seh*; past 3rd pl. *sehen*;
past part. *isehen*)

seonewwen (n. pl.) sinews

seorfule see **sorhful(e)**

seorhfuliche (adv.) sorrowfully,
wretchedly

seoth(th)en (adv.) after, afterwards

seotel, seotle (n.) seat

seove (num.) seven

seovethe (adj.) seventh

seovevalt (adj.) seven-fold, seven
times

seowen (v. past 3rd pl.) sowed

serve, servi see **servin**

servise (n.) service

servin (v.) serve (pres. pl. *servith*; subj.
pres. sing. *servi*; imper. sing. *serve*)

set, seten see **sitten**

sete, sette see **sette(n)**

sette(n) (v.) set, place, put; (of speech)
to express (past 2nd sing. *settest*;
past 3rd sing. *sette*; imper. *sete*;
past part. *iset*; pl. *isette*); **lette . . .
setten**, founded, established

sic (n.) sigh

siden (n. pl.) sides

sihen (v. past pl.) made their way

sihinde (v. pres. part.) descending

sihthe (n.) sight, vision; sight, one of
the five senses (pl. *sihthen*)

sikel (n.) sickle; **sette sikel forth**, put forth the sickle (i.e., start the debate)

siken (v.) sigh (pres. 3rd sing. *siketh*)

siker(e) (adj.) sure, certain; safe (compar. *sikerure*)

sikere (adv.) surely, certainly

sikerlec (n.) security, certainty

sikerliche (adv.) certainly, truly (superl. *sikerlukest*)

simplete (n.) modesty, humility; simplicity

singe(n) (v.) sing (pres. pl. *singeth*; past 3rd sing. *song*; past pl. *sungen*; pres. part. *singinde*)

sinken (v.) sink (past pl. *sunken*)

sist see **seo(n)**

sith (n. 1) actions, behavior; way of life. (n. 2 pl.) **sithe,** times (in expressions of multiplication)

sith (v.) see **seo(n)**

sitten (v.) sit; suit (pres. 3rd sing. *sit*; past 3rd sing. *set*; past 3rd pl. *seten*; pres. sing. subj. *sitte*; pres. pl. subj. *sitten*; past part. *iseten*); **sitte . . . uvele,** sits badly (i.e., grieves)

sixtenthe (adj. num.) sixteenth

sixtifald (adj.) sixty-fold, sixty times over

sker (adj.) free, clear

slahte (n.) slaughter

slakien (v.) slacken, relax, fail (pres. 1st sing. *slakie*)

slean, sclein (v.) slay, kill (past 3rd sing. *sloh*; pres. 2nd sing. subj. *slea*; past part. *islein*)

sleatten (v. past 3rd pl.) set; in **sleatten on him hundes,** set dogs on him

slec (n.) mire, ooze

sleheste (adj.) slyest

slepe (n.) sleep (gen. sing. *slepe*); **o slepe,** asleep

slepten (v. past 3rd pl.) slept (pres. part. *sclepinde*)

sloh (n.) mud, mire, slough

sloh (v.) see **slean**

slong (v. past 3rd sing.) slung, threw

smat (v. past 3rd sing.) smote; surged, dashed; **smat hire cneon,** fell on her knees

smeale (adj.) small

smeal (n.) smell (gen. pl. *smelle*)

smealleth see **smellen**

smeallunge see **smellunge**

smeate (adj.) pure (superl. *smeatest*)

smeche, smecche (n.) odor, stink

smecheth (v. pres. 3rd pl.) tastes

smechunge (n.) taste, one of the five senses

smelle see **smeal**

smellen (v.) smell (pres. 3rd sing. *smealleth*; pres. part. as adj. *smellinde*)

smellunge, smeallunge (n.) smell, the sense of smell

smeorteth (v. pres. 3rd sing.) smarts, hurts

smeortliche (adv.) smartly, sharply, hard

smetheliche (adv.) sweetly

smetheste (adj. superl.) smoothest

smirede (v. past pl.) anointed, smeared (with balm), embalmed (past part. *ismiret*)

smirkinde (v. pres. part.) smiling

smirles (n. pl.) ointments

smit (v. pres. 3rd sing.) strike, smite (imper. sing. *smit*)

smoke (n.) smoke

smorthrinde (v. pres. part.) smoldering; suffocating, smothering

snahwit(e) (adj.) snow-white

snawi (adj.) snowy, icy, freezing

snercte (v. past 3rd sing.) scorched

sniketh (v. pres. pl.) creep, crawl

so see **se**

soffte (adv.) softly

softe (adj.) soft, pleasing (superl. *softest*)

softe (v. imper. sing.) soften, alleviate

softeliche (adv.) softly, quietly

sohte (v. past 3rd sing.) sought; deliberated

somet (adv.) together

sompnin (v.) meet together

som(p)nunge (n.) meeting, union; sexual union

sond(e) (n.) messenger

sondesmon (n.) messenger

sone (adv.) soon; **sone se** as soon as

song (n.) song (pl. *songes*)

song (v.) see **singe(n)**

so(o)th(e) (adj.) true, right; **beo soth cnawes**, be honest, admit the truth. See also **sothe** (n.)

sore see **sar**

sorfulest see **sorhful(e)**

sorhe (n.) pain; sorrow, pain (pl. *sorhen*; gen. pl. *sorhene*)

sorhful(e), seorfule (adj.) sorrowful, painful, pitiful, terrible (superl. *sorhfulest*)

sorhin (v.) be sorrowful or sad; lament, mourn, grieve (pres. 3rd sing. *sorheth*)

sothe (n.) truth

sothes (adv.) truly

sothliche (adv.) truly

sotschipe (n.) foolishness, folly (pl. *sotschipes*)

sotte (adj.) stupid, foolish

sottliche (adv.) stupidly, foolishly

spaken (n. pl.) spokes

spearieth (v. pres. pl.) spare (imper. pl. *spearie*)

speatewile (adj.) disgusting (compar. *speatewilre*)

speatewilliche (adv.) horribly; disgustingly

spec, speken, speketh see **speoke(n)**

speche (n.) speech

speden (v.) achieve; succeed (at something), prosper (pres. 2nd sing. *spedest*; pres. pl. *spedeth*; subj. pres. 3rd sing. *spede*)

spedest, spedeth see **speden**

speken, speketh see **speoke(n)**

spende (v. past 3rd sing.) spent

speoke(n), speokene (v.) speak (pres. 3rd sing. *speketh*; pres. pl. *speoketh*; past 1st, 3rd sing. *spec*; past pl. *speken*)

speokene, speoketh see **speoke(n)**

speowen (v.) spew, vomit; defecate (pres. pl. *speoweth*); **speoweth . . . ut bivoren ant bihinden**, spews out from in front and behind (i.e., vomits and defecates simultaneously)

sperclede see **sperken**

sperke, sperki (n.) spark, fire

sperken (v.) sparkle; kindle (past 3rd sing. *sperclede*)

spillen (v.) waste (pres. 2nd sing. *spillest*)

spitten (v.) spit (pres. 3rd sing. *spit*)

springeth (v. pres 3rd sing.) spring, spring up; arise (past 3rd pl. *sprong*)

sprong see **springeth**

sprung (n.) source, origin (pl. *sprunges*)

spruteth (v. pres. 3rd sing.) sprouts, flowers, blooms, grows

spureth (v. pres. 3rd sing.) spur, incite (past 3rd sing. *spurede*)

spus (n.) spouse

sputi (adj.) eloquent

sputi (v.) dispute, debate

sputte (v. pres. 1st sing.) urge, incite

stal (n.) theft; stealth, secrecy. See also **steal**

stalewurthe see **stealewurh(th)e**

stalle see **steal**

stan (n.) stone (pl. *stanes*)

stanene (adj.) made of stone

stani (adj.) stony

steah (v. past 3rd sing.) ascended

steal, stal (n.) place; state, condition (pl. *stalle*); **i stude ant it stalle**, in all places

stealewurh(th)e, stalewurthe (adj.) stalwart

steap see **stepe**

steape (adj.) bright, gleaming, glaring; passionate, amorous (compar. *steapre*)

steap(p)re see **steape** (adj.)

stearc (adj.) severe, intense; foul

steareden (v. past 3rd pl.) stared

steathelvest (adj.) steadfast

ste(a)vene, stefne (n.) voice, speech; utterance

stefne see **ste(a)vene**

stele (n.) steel

stench (n.) stench, stink, foul smell

steoleth (v. pres. pl.) steal

steoren, steorin (v.) steer, govern (pres. 2nd sing. *steorest*; pres. pl. *steorith*; past 3rd sing. *steorede*; imper. sing. *steor*)

steoresmon (n.) steersman

steorliche (adv.) severely, greatly

steorre (n.) star (pl. *steoren, steorren*)

steort-naket (adj.) completely naked

steorve (n.) pestilent creature

steorven (v.) kill, destroy

stepe (v. past 2nd sing.) advance, proceed (past 3rd sing. *ste(a)p*; past part. *istopen*); **stepe adun**, descended, went downward; **step up**, ascended

stercliche (adv.) strongly, stoutly

sterclukest see **sterke**

sterke (adj.) stark, strong. (adv.) starkly, strongly (superl. *sterclukest*)

steu see **stewen**

stevene (n.) delay. See also **ste(a)vene**

steventith (v. pres. pl.) stand

stew see **stewen**

stewen (v.) stop, restrain, check; stop talking (imper. sing. *stew, steu*; past part. *istewet*); **stew the**, shut up, hold your tongue

stich(e) (n.) sharp or stabbing pain, birthing pain (pl. *stiches*)

sticheth (v. pres. pl.) causes sharp pain, pricks

stihen (v.) arise, ascend (pres. 3rd sing. *stiheth*; past 2nd sing. *stuhe*; past pl. *stuhen*; imper. sing. *stih*; past part. *istihe*)

stikelunge (adv.) intently

stikinde (v. pres. part.) stabbing, piercing

stille (adj.) quiet, silent, still (**beo stille**, be quiet).

stille (adv.) silently

stille (v. imper.) be still, be silent

stilthe (n.) stillness, silence

stinkinde (v. pres. part.) stinking

stockes (n. pl.) logs, planks of wood

stod, stoden, stonde see **stonden**

stonden (v.) stand, stand up; be situated, positioned, placed (pres. 2nd sing. *stondest*; pres. 3rd sing. *stont, stonde*; pres. pl. *stondeth*; past 3rd sing. *stot, stod*; past 3rd pl. *stoden*; subj. pres. sing. *stonde*; imper. *stont*; pres. part. *stondinde*); **hu thet wif stonde**, how that wife is situated (i.e., how it goes for that wife)

stormes (n. pl.) storms

storvene (v. past part.) the dead

stot see **stonden**

strac see **striketh**

strahte see **strecche(n)**

stream, streem (n.) stream

strecche(n) (v.) stretch; move (past 3rd sing. *strahte*; imper. sing. *streche*; past part. *strahte, istrahte*); **strahte him . . . toward**, made his way towards

streem see **stream**

strencthe see **strengthe**

strengeluker (adv. compar.) more strongly

strenge(n) (v.) strengthen (pres. pl. *strengeth*; imper. sing. *streng*; pres. 3rd subj. sing. *strenge*; past part. *istrenget*)

strengre see **strong(e)**

strengthe, strencthe (n.) strength, force; violence

streon (n.) offspring, line; progeny, child

streoneth (v. pres. 3rd sing.) begets, conceives offspring; (in contempt) spawn; copulates, makes love

(past 3rd sing. *streonede*; pres. part. *streonunge*)

streonunge (n.) copulation, intercourse; begetting

strete (n.) street

strif (n.) strife, contest, struggle

striketh (v. pres. 3rd sing. and pl.) run, flow; move, make (one's) way (past 3rd sing. *strac*; past pl. *striken*; pres. part. *strikinde, striding*)

strong(e) (adj.) strong, powerful; severe; fierce (compar. *strengre*; superl. *strengest*)

stronglich (adv.) strongly, stalwartly

strund (n. 1) race, lineage. (n. 2) stream; streak (pl. *strunden*)

strunden see **strund**

strupen (v.) strip (pres. 3rd sing. *strupeth*; past 2nd sing. *struptest*; imper. pl. *strupeth*)

stucches (n. pl.) fragments

stude (n.) place

studegith see **studgi**

studevest (adj.) steadfast

studgi, studegith (v. pres. pl.) stop, hesitate

stuhe, stuhen see **stihen**

stunde (n.) opportunity, turn; time; **umbe stunde**, sometimes

stupin (v.) stoop

sturien (v.) stir, move, incite (pres. pl. *sturieth*; past 3rd sing. *sturede*; past part. *isturet*)

stutten (v.) stop, pause; remain, not escape (pres. 3rd pl. *stutteth*; past 3rd sing. *stutte*; imper. *stute*)

suken (v.) suckle, suck

sulen (v.) sully, pollute, become filthy (pres. 2nd sing. *sulest*; pres. 3rd sing. *suleth*; past part. *isuled*)

sullen (v.) to sell

sulli, sulliche (adj.) strange; remarkable, wondrous

sum(me) (adj.) some, someone (as pron.); certain; **him on his thrituthe sum**, him and some thirty of his [men]

sumchearre, sumchere (adv.) once, formerly

sumdel (adv.) somewhat, a little

sumerlich (adj.) summerlike

sumhwet (adv.) somewhat

sumhwet (n.) something

sumhwile (adv.) at one time, formerly

sunken see **sinken**

sunderliche (adv.) specially; separately

sundri (v.) sunder, separate (pres. pl. *sundrith*; past part. *isundret*)

sune (n.) son (pl. *sunen*)

sunegede (v. past 3rd sing.) sinned

sunegilt (n.) sinner

sunfule (adj./n.) sinful (gen. *sunfules*)

sungen see **singe(n)**

sunne (n.) sin (pl. *sunnen*)

suster (n.) sister (pl. *sustren*)

sut (n.) grief, sorrow

sutel (adj.) clear, evident

sutelen (v.) make clear, manifest (pres. 3rd sing. *suteleth*; past 3rd sing. *sutelede*)

sutelin (v.) seem, appear (pres. sing. subj. *suteli*)

sutel(l)iche (adv.) clearly

suti (adj.) foul, filthy

swa (adv.) so, thus, in this way; **swa thet**, so that; for this reason; because of this; **swa . . . swa** (with compar. adj.), the more . . . the more; **swa as he cuthe**, as best he could. See also **se**

swart(e) (adj.) dark, black

swartede (v. past 3rd sing.) blackened

sweameth (v. pres. 3rd sing.) grieves, laments (past part. *isweamet*)

swearf (v. past 3rd sing.) departed, made off (swerve)

swelleth (v. pres. 3rd sing.) swells

swelten (v.) suffer, die (pres. 3rd sing. *swelteth*)

swenchest (v. pres. 2nd sing.) trouble; labor, suffer in childbirth (past part. *iswech*); **thu swenchest t(h)e**, you trouble yourself

swengde see **swingen**

swenges (n. pl.) tricks, strokes

sweoke (n.) traitor, deceiver

sweort, swerd (n.) sword (gen. sing. *sweordes*)

sweovete (n.) sleep

swerien (v.) swear (pres. 1st sing. *swerie*; pres. pl. *swerieth*; past 3rd sing. *swor*; past part. *isworen*)

swete (adj.) sweet; fragrant (compar. *swottre, swetture*; superl. *swotest, sweteste*); (as subst.) sweetness

sweteliche, swoteliche (adv.) sweetly

swettnesse, swotnesse (n.) sweetness, gentleness

swetture see **swete**

swevene (n.) dream

swic see **swiken**

swifte (adj.) transitory, fleeting (swift)

swift(e)liche (adv.) swiftly, quickly

swikel(e) (adj.) deceitful

swikelliche (adv.) treacherously

swiken (v.) cease (subj. pres. 2nd sing. *swike*; imper. sing. *swic*)

swinc (n.) work, labor (gen. *swinkes*)

swinketh (v. pres. sing. and pl.) work, labor

swingen (v.) swing, turn (past 3rd sing. *swengde*)

swipten (v. past pl.) struck

swire (n.) neck

swireforth, swirevorth (adv.) head first, headlong

swithe (adv.) intensifier: very; quickly; greatly (compar. *swithere, swithre*; superl. *swithest*); **swithe open**, wide open

swuch (adj.) such; like this, similar (pl. *swucche*); **swucches**, of such things; **al swuch**, just so

swong (v. past 3rd sing.) flung

swor see **swerien**

swote, swotest, swottre see **swete**

sy (n.) victory, triumph

tac see **taken**

tadden (n. pl.) toads

tah see **thah**

tahte (v. past 3rd sing.) taught, directed, guided, led (past 2nd sing. *tahtest*; past 3rd pl. *tahten*; past part. *itaht*)

taken (n.) token, sign; **taken of the deore Rode**, the sign of the dear Cross

taken (v.) take; commit (past 1st sing. *toc*; past 3rd sing. *toc*; past 3rd pl. *token*; sub. 3rd sing. pres. *take*; past part. *itake*; imper. *tac*); **toc me Him to Lauerd**, adopted him as my Lord (lit., took me to Him as Lord); **toc on**, began

talde, talden see **telle(n)**

tale (n.) tale, speech; number (pl. *tales*); account, worth; **ne telest na tale of**, hold no account of, consider worthless

talede see **talien**

talien (v.) speak to, talk; argue (past 3rd sing. *talede*)

talkin (v.) talk (pres. pl. *talkith*)

tan (n. pl.) toes; **from the top to the tan**, from the top to the toes (i.e., from head to toe)

tat see **t(h)et**

tavelin see **tevelin**

te see **the**

teacheth (v. pres. 3rd sing.) teaches

tealen see **telle(n)**

team (n.) progeny, offspring; family (pl. *teames*)

teapers (n. pl.) tapers

teares (n. pl.) tears

teke (prep.) in addition to, also, besides [elision from *to-eke*]. See also **to-eche**

tele, telest see **telle(n)**

telle(n), tealen (v.) tell; reckon, count; consider; judge (pres. 2nd sing. *telest*; pres. 3rd sing. *telleth*; past 3rd sing. *talde*; imper. sing. *tele*; past pl. *talden*; past part. *italde, itald*); **ne tele . . . to widewen ne**

to iweddede, do not consider widows or the wedded

teluken, toluki (v.) rip, tear (past 3rd sing. *tole(a)c*; past part. *toluken*, *toloken*)

temen (v.) become pregnant, conceive, beget; be pregnant, breed; bear (children) (pres. 2nd sing. *temest*; pres. 3rd sing. and pres. pl. *temeth*; subj. pres. sing. *temi*)

temest, temeth, temi see **temen**

temple (n.) temple

ten see **the**

tendrin (v.) to grow inflamed, burn (pres. 3rd sing. *tendreth*)

tene (num.) ten

tenne see **thenne**

teo(n) (v.) tug, tear away; draw, pull (past pl. *tuhen*; past part. *itohen*)

teone (n.) torment, pain; wrath; suffering, adversity (pl. *teonen*) frequently in collocative **na teone ne tintreohe**, no torment or torture

teonen (v.) to anger, enrage; (pres. 3rd sing. *teoneth*, *teonith*; past part. *itend, itent, iteonet*); **me teoneth**, it angers me

teos see **this**

ter see **ther**

terin see **thrin**

terof see **th(e)rof**

tes see **this**

tet see **t(h)et**

teth (n. pl.) teeth (gen. sing. *tothes*, trans. as pl.)

tevelin, tavelin (v.) debate, argue (pres. sing. subj. *teveli*)

tha (adv.) then, at that time; when

thah (adv.) yet, nevertheless, still; even if

thah, tah (conj.) though, although

the, te (def. art.) the (gen. *thes*; acc./dat. *thene, then, ten*), (rel. pron.) who, that, which, what; whoever; (pers. pron. 2nd pers. sing.) you; you who (objective form); **the an**, one of them

thear see **t(h)er**

thearas (adv.) where

the(a)rf (v. pres. 2nd sing.) should; need; used as auxiliary to express necessity (pres. 3rd sing. *thearf*); **ne thearf thu bute**, you need only

thearmes (n. gen. pl.) bowels

theavien (v.) allow, permit (pres. 3rd sing. *theaveth*; pres. pl. *theavieth*)

theaw (n. pl.) moral quality (virtuous or wicked) (pl. *theawes*)

theawfule (adj.) virtuous

theines (n. pl.) men

the-hwethere (adv.) nevertheless

then(e) (adv.) then; when; **then thet** than if

then(e) (conj.) than; **then thet**, than if

then(e) (def. art.) see **the**

thenchen (v.) think; think about, consider; intend (pres. 2nd sing. *thencheth, thenchest*; past 3rd sing. *thohte*; imper. sing. *thench*; imper. pl. *thence, thenche, thencheth*)

thenne, tenne (adv.) then, when

theo (pron.) they, those

theodom see **theo(w)dom**

theof (n.) thief

theonewart (adv.) from there, away from there, from that place

theonne (adv.) thence, from there, out of there

theos, theosse see **this**

theosternesse (n.) darkness

theostri (adj.) dark

theoten (v.) cry out, howl (pres. part. *theotinde*)

theoves (n. pl.) thieves

theowdom, theodom (n.) servitude, slavery

the(o)we (n.) servant; slave; **theowe-wummon**, slave woman, bondwoman

t(h)er, thear (adv.) there; where; **thear as, ther ase,** thereas, where

therabuten (adv.) around there

ther-ayeines (adv.) towards it, before it

therbi (adv.) thereby, by that, from that; near that

therbivoren (adv.) before that time

therefter (adv.) thereafter

therf see **the(a)rf**

therfore see **thervore**

therfrommart (adv.) away from there

therin(ne) (adv.) therein, in it

th(e)rof, terof (adv.) thereof, of/from it; **cuthe throf**, let him show it

ther-onont (adv. comp. with prep. *onont*) in that regard, concerning that, about that

therto (adv.) thereto, in addition; to it, to that

thertowart, thertoward (adv.) towards that/it

ther-toyeines (adv.) to the contrary, in opposition to (something)

therunder (adv.) thereunder, under it

therupon (adv.) thereupon, on that

thervore (adv.) therefore, for that/this reason

therwith (adv.) with that

therwithinnen (adv.) inside it

thes see **this**, **the**

theseolven (pron.) thyself, yourself

t(h)et, tat (conj.) that, so that, in order that; because (in clause of reason); until; often used in result clause **se/swa . . . thet** ("so much . . . that"); in (dem./rel. pron.) that, who(m), which, what; **mid tet ilke** lit. "with that same," i.e., at that moment; **with thon thet**, provided that; so that

thewe see **the(o)we**

theyet (adv.) still, even then

thicke (adj.) thick (superl. *thickest*)

thider (adv.) thither, to that place

thideward(es), thiderwart (adv.) in that direction

thiderwart see **thideward(es)**

thin(e), ti, tine (poss. pron.) your (gen. sing. *tines*)

thing (n.) creature; thing, something, anything, matter, reason (gen. pl. *thinge*)

t(h)is, t(h)eos, t(h)es (dem. pron.) this (pl. *theos, theose*; dat. sing. *thisse*)

thoht (n.) thought; **i thi thoht**, mentally, in your mind (pl. *thohtes*)

thohte (v.) see **thenchen**

thole, tholede, tholeden, tholedest see **tholien**

tholemod(e) (adj.) patient; meek

tholemodnesse (n.) patience; meekness

tholien (v.) suffer, endure, bear; undergo; be patient, abide (pres. 1st, 3rd sing. *tholie*; pres. 3rd pl. *tholieth, tholeth*; past 2nd sing. *tholedest*; past 3rd sing., pl. *tholede*; past pl. *tholeden*; imper. sing. *thole*; past part. *itholet*); **to tholien**, to be endured, suffered

thon see **t(h)et**

thonc (n.) mind; thought (pl. *thonkes, thonckes*)

thonki (v.) thank (pres. 1st sing. *thon(c)ki*; past 3rd pl. *thonkede*; past part. *ithonket*)

thornes (n. pl.) thorns

thraen (n. pl.) throes, pains, pangs; **pinunge thraen**, labor pains, contractions during labor

thralunge (n.) discomfort, pain

threalles see **threl**

threat (n.) threat (pl. *threates*)

threat (v.) see **threatin**

threatin (v.) threaten (pres. 2nd sing. *threatest*; pres. 3rd sing. *threat, threateth*; pres. subj. sing. *threate*; imper. *threat*)

threfter (adv.) afterwards, thereafter; according to (something)

threl (n.) servant; thrall, slave (pl. *threalles*)

threo, thrie (num.) three

threofalt see **threovald**

threohad (n.) trinity (lit. three-hood)

threotuthe (adj.) thirteenth

threovald, threofalt (adj.) threefold

threpeth (v. pres. 3rd sing.) scold, rebuke (imper. *threp*)

threste (v. past 3rd sing.) pressed out

thridde (adj.) third

thrie see **threo**

thriftre (n.) thriving, vigorous growth

thrile (adj.) threefold

thrin, thrinne, terin (adv.) in it, therein; inside, within; in that thing

thrinwith (prep.) inside it

thritti (num.) thirty

thrittifald (adj.) thirty-fold, thirty times over

thrit(t)uthe (adj.) thirtieth; **on his thrituthe sum**, and some thirty of his

throf see **th(e)rof**

thron (adv.) thereon; on/at it; **thron thet**, about the fact that

throwin (v.) suffer, endure (past 3rd sing. *throwede*)

thruh (n.) coffin

thrumnesse (n.) Trinity (three-ness)

thrungen (v. past 3rd pl.) thronged

thruppe (adv.) above (there-up); earlier

thrute (adv.) outside (lit. there-out)

t(h)u (pron.) thou, you

thudde (v. pres. 3rd sing.) stamp, push forcefully; thrust (past 3rd sing. *thudded*)

thuftenes (n. gen. sing.) handmaiden

thuhte see **thunc(h)en**

thuldeliche (adv.) patiently

thuldi (adj.) patient, long-suffering

thulli, thullich, thulliche (adj.) such, of such a kind, like this

thunc(h)en (v. imper.) to seem (to someone). (pres. 3rd sing. *thunceth*, as in **thunceth ow**, "it seems to you"; past 3rd sing. *thuhte*; pres. sing. subj. *thunche*); almost always accompanied by dative pronoun

thunre (n.) thunder; a thunder-clap (gen. sing. *thunres*)

thurh (prep.) through; with; because of; by means of; with the help of; **thurh thet** (conj.) because, because of the fact that; **hwethurh** (prep.) where-through, through which

thurh-driven (v.) drive through, pierce

thurh-ferde (v. past 3rd sing.) underwent, passed through

thurh-soht (v. past part.) searched through, searched from end to end

thurh-spitien (v.) fit with spikes, stud (past part. *thurhspitet*)

thurh-thurli (v.) pierce through

thurh-wunest (v. pres. sing.) lasts forever (pres. part. *thurh-wuniende*)

thurs (n.) demon, monster

thurst (n.) thirst

thurve (v. pres. subj. pl.) need; **ne thurve**, need not, have no cause

thus (adv.) thus, in this way, like this; so; with these words

thusent (num.) thousand

thusentfalt (adj.) thousandfold, a thousand times

thwertover (prep.) cross-wise

ti see **thin(e)**

tide (n.) tide, time

tidinge (n.) tidings, news

tidliche (adv.) quickly

timbrin (v.) to bring about

time (n.) time

timeth (v. pres. 3rd sing.) happens, occurs. See also **itimeth**

timliche (adv.) soon (compar. *timluker*)

tine, tines see **thin(e)**

tintr(e)ohe (n.) torture, torment (pl. *tintreohen*)

tis see **t(h)is**

tittes (n. pl.) nipples

to (adv./prep.) to, towards, at; as (also functions as inf. marker, as in to *habbe*); **to His ilicnesse**, in his likeness, **to help**, as a help

tobearst see **tobursten**

tobeoreth (v. pres. pl.) quarrel

tobreken (v. past pl.) broke up, tore up (past part. *tobroken*)

tobroken see **tobreken**

tobursten (v.) burst up, burst apart, explode; break apart (past 3rd sing. *tobearst*)

toc see **taken** (v.)

tocheoweth (v. pres. pl.) chew up, chew to pieces

tocleaven (v.) split apart, cleave

todei (adv.) today

todrif (v. imper. sing.) drive apart, destroy (past part. *todriven*)

todreaven (v.) drive apart, scatter (past 3rd pl. *todreavet*)

todriven see **todrif**

to-eche, to-eke (prep.) in addition to, also; see also **teke**

tofeol (v. past 3rd sing.) fell apart

togedere(s) (adv.) together

toggith (v. pres. pl.) tussle, wrestle amorously

tohwitheret (v. past part.) whirled apart; shatter (pres. subj. pl. *tohwitherin*)

token see **taken** (v.)

toleac, tolec see **teluken**

tole(a)c see **teluken**

tolimede (v. past 3rd sing.) dismembered, tore apart (past pl. *tolimeden*; past part. *tolimet*)

tollith (v. pres. pl.) tug, wrestle playfully

toloken, toluki, toluken see **teluken**

tom (adj.) tame

top (n.) top of the head, hair; **bi thet top**, by the hair (on his head); **from the top to the tan**, from the top to the toes (i.e., from head to toe)

toreafde see **toreven**

torenden (v.) tear apart, tear to pieces (pres. pl. *torendeth*)

toreven (v.) shatter, break apart. (past 3rd sing. *toreafde*)

torondin (v.) tear up

toschrapede (v. past 3rd sing.) scraped up, lacerated; fig., robbed, lacerated; robbed, duped; **toschrapede his hefde**, scraped up his head (fig., robbed him blind)

toswelleth (v. pres. 3rd sing.) swells up, puffs up (past part. *toswollen*)

toteore (v.) tear apart, tear to pieces (past part. *totoren*)

tothes see **teth**

totoren see **toteore**

toturn (n.) refuge

totweamde (v. past 3rd sing.) yawned open; severed, separated (subj. sing. pres. *totweame*)

towart (prep.) to, toward, in the direction of; before; upon

toyein (prep.) in opposition to

toyein(es) (adv.) in reply, against

treitres (n. pl.) traitors

treo (n.) tree, wood; the Cross

treow(e) (adj.) true, right; faithful, loyal

tre(o)w(e)liche (adv.) truly

tresor (n.) treasure

trewliche see **tre(o)w(e)liche**

troden (n. pl.) steps, footsteps

trondlin (v.) roll

trubuil (n.) trouble, turmoil, distress

trukien (v.) spare; be insufficient, fail; leave, abandon; cease, stop (pres. pl. *truketh*; past 3rd sing. *truked*)

trume (n.) company, host

trusten (v.) trust (pres. 1st and 3rd sing. *truste*; pres. 3rd pl. *trusteth*; past 3rd sing. *truste*)

trusti (adj.) trusting, confident

tu see **t(h)u**

tuhen see **teo(n)**

tuht (n.) discipline, behavior, conduct

tuhte (v. pres. 3rd sing.) discipline; teach, instruct

tuken (v.) to abuse (physically or verbally), ill-treat; revile (pres.

2nd sing. *tukest*; pres. 3rd sing.
tuketh; past part. *ituket*)

tun (n.) town

tung(e) (n.) tongue (pl. *tungen*)

tunne (n.) barrel, cask

tur (n.) tower

turnde(n) see **turne(n)**

turne (n.) turn; trick, subtlety (pl.
turnes). See also **turne(n)** (v.)

turne(n) (v.) turn, change, alter;
convert; translate (pres. pl. *turneth*;
past 3rd sing. *turnde*; past 3rd pl.
turnden; past pl. *turnden*; past part.
iturnd, *iturnt*); **turne/turneth to
gode**, turn out well

turnunge (n.) turning; movement

tus see **thus**

tuskes (n. pl.) tusks

twa (adj./num.) two (gen. sing. *tweire*)

tweamen, twemen (v.) divide,
separate

tweien (num.) twain, two

tweire see **twa**

twemen see **tweamen**

twenti, twenty (adj./num.) twenty

twentuthe (adj.) twentieth

twenty see **twenti**

tweolf, tweolve (num.) twelve

twinnen (v.) separate into two, part
(subj. pres. sing. *twinni*)

twinni see **twinnen**

twinnunge (n.) separation, parting

ufel (n.) see **uvel(e)**

uleth (v. pres. 3rd sing.) flatters

umbe (prep.) after (a period of time);
umbe forte, aim to, intent on;
umbe hwil, after a while; **eaver
umbe hwil**, always; **umbe long**,
after a time, in due course; **umbe
stunde**, sometimes; **eaver umbe
stunde**, always. (adj.) with forms
of **beon**, eager to, busy to,
aiming/seeking to; **beo umbe me
to helpen**, be busy to help me; **is
umbe forte leaden**, is aiming/aims
to lead

unaginninde (v. pres. part.) without
beginning

unbileave (n.) unbelief, lack of faith

unblescet (adj.) unblessed

unbotelich (adv.) irremediable,
irrecoverable

unbruche (n.) lack of sin or moral
breach, integrity; **with unbruche
of thi bodi**, cleanness or chastity
of body, physically a virgin

unburiet (v. past part.) unburied

unc (pron. dual) us two. See also **wit**

uncnut (v. past part.) unknotted,
untied

uncoverlich (adj.) irrecoverable

uncumelecheth (v. pres. 3rd sing.)
mars, disfigures

uncumelich (adj.) unseemly, indecent

**undead(de)lich(e), undeathlich,
undedlich(e)** (adj.) immortal

undedlichnesse (n.) immortality

under (n.) undern, the third hour of
the day (around 9am)

under (prep.) under, beneath; with;
in, in a state of; **nawiht under al**,
i.e., nothing at all

underneomen (v.) to undertake; trick,
trap; receive (pres. 1st sing.
underneome; past 3rd sing.
undernom(e); subj. pres. sing.
underneome; past part. *undernume*)

underneothe (prep.) underneath

undernume see **underneomen**

understonden (v.) understand (pres.
3rd sing. *understont*; past 3rd sing.
understode, *understot*; pres. subj.
sing. *understonde*; imper. sing.
understont)

underveng, underveth see **undervon**

undervo(n) (v.) receive, accept; take
on (pres. 1st and 2nd sing.; pres.
2nd sing. *undervest*; pres. 3rd sing.
underveth; past 3rd sing.
underveng; imper. sing. *underveng*;
subj. pres. sing. *undervoth*; past
part. *undervon*, *undervo*; infl. inf.
undervonne)

unduhtie (adj.) worthless

undutte (v. past 3rd sing.) revealed

unevenlich (adj.) incomparable

unforgult (adj.) innocent, guiltless

ungeinliche (adv.) threateningly

unhale (adj.) unwhole, sick

unhap (n.) misfortune, bad luck

unheale (n.) disease

unhende (adj.) indecent, improper

unhendeliche (adv.) roughly, unkindly

unhope (n.) despair, wanhope, lack of hope

unhurt (adj.) unhurt

unhwiht see **unwiht**

unilich see **unlich**

unimete, unimeath (adv.) immeasurably

unirude, unrude (adj.) cruel; huge

unkumelich (adj./n.) indecent, inappropriate, unseemly

unlahan (n. pl.) evil laws or customs

unlaheliche (adv.) unlawfully

unlefliche (adj.) unbelievable, false

unlich, unilich (adj.) unlike, different

unlicnesse (n.) unlikeness, dissimilarity

unlust (n.) distaste, lack of appetite

unlusti (adj.) without passion, listless, apathetic; lazy, slothful

unmeath (n.) immoderation, excess

unmeathlich(e) (adv.) immensely, immoderately

unmenskith (v. pres. pl.) dishonor, disgrace

unmerret (adj.) unmarred, unspoiled

unmihte (n.) weakness

unmuclin (v.) to diminish

unmundlunge (adv.) unexpectedly, without warning

unneathe (adv.) hardly, scarcely

unnen (v. pres. pl.) wish

unneomelich (adj.) unseizable

unneth see **on** (v.)

unnett(e) (adj.) vain, foolish; (as n.) foolish or trivial matters

unofservet (adj.) undeserved

unroles (adj.) nonstop, unresting

unrude see **unirude**

unrudeliche (adv.) roughly

unseh(e)lich (adj.) invisible, unseen

unsehen(e) (adj.) unseen, invisible; strange

unseli (adj.) unhappy; unlucky, wretched; foolish; wicked, evil, unholy; (as n.) wicked people

unselhthe (n.) evil thing

unsperliche (adv.) unsparingly

unstrencthe (n.) lack of strength, weakness

unstrenget (v. pres. pl.) weaken (past part. *unstrenget*)

unstrong (adj./n.) weak; weak people

unsulet (adj.) unsoiled

untalelich (adj.) untellable, indescribable, unspeakable

untheaw (n.) wantonness, immorality; vice (gen. sing. *untheawes*)

untholelich (adj.) unbearable, intolerable

unthonkes, unthonc (n.) in **hare unthonkes**, unwillingly; **unthonc in his teth**, damn his teeth

unthrowlich (adj.) incapable of suffering

unthuldeliche (adv.) impatiently; complainingly

untidi (adj.) untimely, unseasonable

untodealet (adj.) undivided

untohe (adj.) wanton; unruly (pl. *untohene*)

untoheliche (adv.) rudely

untrumme (adj.) sick, infirm

untuliche (adv.) indecently, improperly; wrongly

untweamet (v. past part.) undivided

unwarre (adj.) unwary

unwedde (adj.) unwedded

unwemmet (adj.) untouched, unblemished

unweoten (n. pl.) ignorant people, fools

unwerste see **unwre(a)ste**

unwiht, unhwiht (n.) lit., un-creature or anti-being; the Devil; demon

unwil (n.) displeasure; (adverbially) unwillingly, against one's will (pl. *unwilles*); **min unwilles hit is**, it is against my will/wishes; **hit hire unwil were**, she was unwilling; **muchel hire unwil**, greatly against her will

unwine (n.) foe, enemy

unwit (n.) lack of reason

unwit(e)lese (adj.) witless, without sentience or consciousness

unwitti (adj.) unwise, foolish

unwreah (v. past 3rd sing.) revealed, made clear

unwre(a)ste, unwerste (adj.) miserable, wicked

unwurdgeth (v. pres. 3rd sing.) degrades, dishonors

unwurth (adj.) worthless

up (adv.) up, upwards

up-aheve (v. past part.) uplifted

upastihunge (pres. part. as n.) ascension

upbredeth (v. pres. pl.) upbraid, blame

upbrud (n.) scorn, reproach, upbraiding

upo(n) (prep.) upon; over

uppart (adv.) upwards

ure (pron.) our; ours; (gen.) of us; in **hwuch ure**, which of us

urne see **eornen**

us (pron.) us

ut (adv.) out

utcumene (n. pl.) foreigners, (lit., out-comers)

utewith (prep.) outside

utlahe (n.) exile; outlaw

utnume (adv.) exceedingly

uvel(e), ufel (n.) evil (also as adj.); misfortune, suffering; disease; pain (pl. *uveles*)

uvele (adv.) evilly, badly

va see **fa**

val see **fal**

vamen see **famon**

vanité (n.) vanity

veat see **feat**

velien see **felien**

van see **fa**

vax see **fax**

veat, feat (n.) vat, vessel (pl. *vetles, fetles*)

veden see **feden**

velien see **felien**

veng see **fon**

veont, veondes see **feont**

verden see **feare(n)**

verredene see **ferredene**

vertu (n.) virtue (pl. *vertuz*)

vertuz see **vertu**

vet see **fot**

vetles see **veat**

vifti see **fifti**

virgines (n. pl.) virgins

volc see **folc**

von see **fon**

vore see **for(e)**

vorleosen see **forleosen**

vorth see **forth**

vorthriht (adv.) at once, right away

vostermoder (n.) foster-mother (gen. sing. *fostermodres*)

vostrin (v.) foster, nourish (past part. *ivostret*)

wa (n.) woe, misfortune, pain. (adj.) woeful, painful; **me is wa fore**, unfortunately (lit., it is ill for me); **wa me mine lives**, woe is me (lit., woe to me of my life); **wa wes him o live**, he was sorry to be alive

wac, wake (adj.) weak; poor (compar. *wacre*); (as subst.) weak person

wacliche (adv.) poorly, unworthily

wahes (n. pl.) walls

wake see **wac**

wakenin (v.) arise, appear; spring, be born (past 3rd sing. *wakenede*)

waker (adj.) watchful, vigilant, alert (compar. *wakere*)

waketh see **wakien**

wakien (n.) be, lie, or stay awake; be vigilant; awaken (pres. 3rd sing. *waketh*)

wala see **weila**

wal (n.) wall

wal-hat (adj.) boiling hot

wald (n.) forest

wald (n.) keeping, possession

waldes (adv.) willingly, voluntarily

walde, waldest (v.) see **wulle**

waleweth (v. pres. pl.) wallow

walh (adj.) nauseating

walketh (n. pres. 3rd pl.) move, pursue (a course)

wallen (v.) boil (past 3rd sing. *weolle*; pres. part. *wallinde*)

walm-hat (adj.) boiling hot

wan (n.) dwelling (pl. *wanes*)

wandrethe see **wontreathe**

wani (v. pres. sing. subj.) lament

wanunge (n.) wailing, weeping

war (adj.) aware; wary

warant (n.) protector

warde (n.) wardship, keeping; guardianship, protection; ward (person under guardianship); **nimeth . . . his warde to witene**, takes up watch over his ward

ware (n. pl.) inhabitants

wari (n.) felon, villain, outlaw

waried (v. past part.) accursed

warliche, wearliche (adv.) warily, cautiously, prudently

warnedest, warneth see **warnin**

warni(n) (v.) warn, defend (pres. 1st sing. *warni*; pres. 3rd sing. *warneth*; past 2nd sing. *warnedest*)

warpe(n) (v.) throw, cast; attack; drive (pres. 1st sing. *warpe*; pres. 2nd sing. *warpest*; pres. 3rd sing. *warpeth*; past 1st, 3rd sing. *weorp*; past 2nd sing. *wurpe*; imper. sing. *warp*); **warpen . . . theonne**, cast out; **warpen honden**, lay hands on, seize; **warpeth . . . ut**, vomit

warschip (n.) caution, wariness, vigilance, watchfulness; discretion, discernment, prudence (gen. sing. *warschipes*)

warth see **wurthen**

wa-sith (n.) state of distress or wretchedness, woeful or wretched time (pl. *wa-sithes*)

wast see **witen**

wastith (v. pres. pl.) lay waste to, destroy; consume (pres. part. *wastinde*)

wat see **witen**

wat (v. past 3rd sing.) went away

waxen (v.) wax, grow (pres. 3rd sing. *waxeth*; past 3rd sing. *weox*)

wealde, wealden see **welden**

We(a)ldent (n.) Ruler, Lord (God)

wealt see **welden**

weane (n.) wretchedness, misery, woe (pl. *weanen*)

wearne (v.) deny, refuse

wearth see **wurthen**

weattre, weater (n.) water (pl. *weattres*); **weater-bulge**, water-skin

wecchen, wecches (n. pl.) watches, vigils

wecchinde (v. pres. part.) watching

wed(de) (adj.) mad, insane

weddest (v. pres. 2nd sing.) wed, marry (past part. *iweddet, weddede*). (as n.) spouse, wedded people

weden (n. pl.) clothes (weeds)

weden (v.) rage, rave, go insane (pres. 3rd sing. *wed*; pres. part. *wedinde*)

wedere (n.) weather (pl. *wederes*)

wedlac (n.) wedlock (gen. sing. *wedlackes*)

wedlackes see **wedlac**

wei(e) (n.) way; **anes weis**, one way, the same way; **eanis weis**, in any way; **summes weies**, in some ways, to some extent

wei, weila, weilawe (interj.) alas, wellaway; come now, look here; **wei ower wurthes**, alas for your fates

weimeres (n. gen. sing.) of mourning, woe

wel (adv.) well; clearly, easily

welden, wealde(n) (v.) rule, reign; control; possess (pres. 1st sing. *welde*; pres. 3rd sing. *we(a)lt*, weld, *wealdeth*; pres. pl. *weldeth*; pres. part. *weldinde*)

welle (n.) well, spring

wem (n.) spot, blemish

wemmunge (n.) defilement, corruption

wen, wende, wenden, wendest see **wenen**

wende(n) (v.) turn, change, turn back, return; direct; go; come; turn into, transform (pres. 3rd sing. *went*; pres. pl. *wendeth*; past 3rd sing. *wende*; past 3rd pl. *wenden*; imper. pl. *wendeth*; past part. *iwend*); **iwend uppon Him**, modeled after. (as refl.) to make one's way, proceed, travel; **wende hire**, made her way; **wenden anes weis**, turned one way (converted)

wene(n) (v.) believe, think, expect; intend (pres. 2nd sing., *wenest*; pres. 3rd sing. *weneth*; pres. 3rd pl. *weneth*; past 2nd sing. *wendest*; past 3rd sing. *wende*; past 3rd pl. *wenden*; imper. *wen*)

weneth see **wene**

Weodnesdei (n.) Wednesday

weol (v. past 3rd sing.) boiled

weolc (v. past 3rd sing.) walked

weol(e) (n.) wealth, riches; joy (pl. *weolen*)

weolefule (adj.) joyful; well-off, prosperous

weolewede (v. past part.) wallowed

weolewunge (n.) wilting, withering

weolle see **wallen**

weordes see **word**

weordes (n. pl.) hosts

weorlde/weorlt see **world**

weorp, weorpth see **warpen**

weorre (n.) war; attack

weorredest see **weorrin**

weorreth, weorrith see **weorrin**

weorri(n) (v.) wage war on (pres. 1st sing. *weorri*; pres. 2nd sing. *weorrith*; pres. 3rd sing. *weorreth*, *woreth*; pres. pl. *weor(r)ith*; past 2nd sing. *weorredest*; pres. subj. sing. *wori*)

weoved (n.) pagan altar

weox, weoxe see **waxen**

wepen (v. pres. subj. pl.) weep (pres. part. *wepinde*)

wepme(n) (n. pl.) men

wepnen (n. pl.) weapons

wepnen (v. refl.) arm oneself (for combat, for spiritual battle), to prepare oneself (past 3rd sing. *wepnede*)

wepunge (n.) weeping, crying

werc see **werke**

were (n.) husband (pl., gen. sing. *weres*)

were, weren (v.) see **beon, werie**

weres see **were** (n.)

wergest (v. pres. 2nd sing.) grow weary, become tired (pres. 3rd sing. *wergeth*; past 3rd sing. *wergede*)

weri (adj.) weary

werie(n) (v.) defend (subj. pres. 3rd pl. *werien*; imper. sing. *were*)

werke, werc (n.) deed, work, action (pl. *werkes*); **ibroht to werke**, brought to action, acted upon

werlahen (n. pl.) scoundrels, villains

wes see **beon**

wes (v. past 3rd sing.) pastured, tended (livestock)

wesch (v. imper. sing.) wash

west (n.) west

westen (adv.) in **bi westen**, in the west

westi (adj.) bare, empty, desolate

westum(e) (n.) form, body

wicche(n) (n.) witch, male or female (pl.) witches

wicchecrefte (n.) witchcraft (pl. *wicchecreftes*)

wid (adj.) wide

wide (adv.) widely; (adj.) wide, broad; big; **wide yont**, everywhere throughout

widewen (n. pl.) widows (gen. pl. *widewene*)

widewehad (n.) widowhood

widnesse (n.) wideness

wif (n.) wife; woman

wiheles (n. pl.) wiles, tricks

wiht (n. pl.) being, creature; demon (pl. *wihtes*)

wike (n.) office

wilcweme (adj.) well-pleased

wilde (adj.) wild

wildernesse (n.) wilderness

wil, wille (n.) will, wish, volition, desire; the function of the will

wilcweme (adj.) pleased

willes (adv.) willingly

willesfule (adj.) willful, unruly, obstinate, headstrong (lit., full of will)

willre (adj.) preferable

wilni(n) (v.) desire, wish (pres. 1st sing. *wil(l)ni*; pres. 2nd sing., *wilnest*; pres. 3rd sing. *wilneth*; pres. pl. *wilnith*; past 3rd sing. *wilnede*; past part. *iwilnet*)

wilnunge (n.) desire, wish

wilyeove (n.) voluntary gift, present

wimmen see **wummon**

wind, wint (n.) wind (pl. *windes*)

windi (adj.) devoid of, set free from, quit of

windweth (v. pres. 3rd sing.) winnows

wint see **wind**

wis(e) (adj.) wise (superl. *wisest*, *wiseste*). (n.) way, manner

wise (n.) way, manner

wisent (n.) guide

wisdom (n.) wisdom, good judgment, soundness of mind

wisliche (adv.) wisely

wisse (n.) in **to wisse**, for certain

wissen (n.) guide, govern (pres. 3rd sing. *wisseth*; past 3rd sing. subj.

wissede; imper. *wise*; pres. part. *wissinde*)

wissunge (n.) guidance; ordination

wiste see **witen**

wit (n.) wit, reason; mind; sense (dat. sing. *witte*, as in **ut of his witte**, out of his mind; pl. *wittes*); **fif wittes**, the five senses

wit (pron. dual) we two

witege (n.) prophet (pl. *witegen*)

wite(n) (v. 1) know; find out. (pres. 2nd sing. *wast, wastu* [*wast + tu*, do you know]; pres. 3rd sing. *wat*; pres. 1st pl. *witen*; imper. sing. *wite*) (negative forms: pres. 1st sing. *nat*; pres. pl. *nuten*; past 3rd sing. *nuste*; past pl. *nusten*). (v. 2) keep, guard, protect; keep watch over (past 3rd sing. *wiste*; pres. 2nd sing. subj. *wite*; imper. *wite*; past part. *iwist, iwisset*). (v. 3) blame; punish (pres. pl. *witith*); **to witen**, to be blamed, worthy of blame; **nimeth . . . his warde to witene**, takes up watch over his warde (lit., undertakes to guard his ward)

witerliche (adv.) certainly, truly (compar. *witerluker*)

witerluker see **witerliche**

with (prep.) with; against; from; by means of. (adv.) with; **with thet ilke**, at that moment

withbreide (v. pres. sing. subj.) withdraw

withbuhe (v.) avoid

withdreiest (v. pres. 2nd sing.) restrain; cease; withdraw

witherin (v.) struggle

witherwine (n.) enemy, adversary (pl. *witherwines*)

withinne (prep.) inside, within

withinnen (adv.) within

withseist (v. pres. 2nd sing.) refuse

withstonden (v.) withstand, resist

withute(n) (prep.) without; outside

withward (adv.) side by side

witith see **witen** (v. 3)

wit(t)i (adj.) witty, clever, wise (superl. *witiest*)

wit(t)lese (adj.) witless, foolish

wit(t)nes(s)e (n.) witness; **beore . . . witnesse,** bear witness, reveal

wive (n.) wife; **to wive,** as a wife

wiven (v.) to marry, take as a wife

wleateful (adj.) disgusting

wleatewile (adj.) disgusting

wlech (adj.) lukewarm (fig. for passionless, indifference) (pl. *wlecche*)

wlecheunge (n.) lukewarm state (i.e., indifference)

wlenchest (v. pres. 2nd sing.) pride yourself (in **wlenchest te**)

wlite (n.) face; beauty, loveliness

wlonke (adj.) haughty, proud

wod(e) (adj.) mad, insane (dat. *wodi*), **o wodi wise,** madly, frantically

wodeliche (adv.) insanely, savagely; fiercely (compar. *wodeluker*; superl. *wodelukest*)

wodelukest see **wodeliche**

wodi see **wod**

woh (n.) error in judgment; injustice (dat. *wohe*); **withuten woh,** truly, without a doubt; **mid woh,** wrongfully

wolden see **wulle**

wombe (n.) belly; womb

won (adj.) wan, dull, without brilliance or luster

wondrethe see **wontreathe**

wondrinde (n./pres. part.) wandering, spiritually lost; erratic or intermittent

wone (adv.) less, lacking

wone (n.) want, poverty

wonie see **wonieth**

wonieth (v. pres. pl.) wane, diminish, lessen (pres. subj. sing. *wonie*)

wonlese (subst. adj.) the hopeless

wonnin (v.) become dark or dim, darken

wonteth see **wontin**

wonti(n) (v.) to lack, be lacking (pres. 3rd sing. *wonteth*)

wontre(a)the, wondrethe, wandrethe (n.) hardship, misery

wonunge (n.) waning, diminishing, failing

wop (n.) weeping (pl. *wopes*)

word (n. sing./pl.) word, words (pl. *w(e)ordes*)

woreth see **weorrin**

wori see **weorrin**

world(e), worlt (n.) world (gen. sing. *worldes*; gen. pl. *worldene*); **world buten ende,** world without end (i.e., forever)

worldene see **worlde**

worldlich(e), worltlich(e) (adj.) worldly, material, corporeal

world-men (n. pl.) worldly ones, men of the world

world-witti (n. pl.) worldly wisemen, secular wisemen, clever fellows

worlt see **worlde**

worltlich(e) see **worldlich(e)**

wracfulliche (adv.) vengefully

wraht, wrahte, wrahtest, wrahtte see **wurchen**

wrake (n.) vengeance

wrakeliche (adv.) vengefully

wrat see **writen**

wrath (adj.) angry

wrathe (adj.) evil, terrible

wrather heale (n.) ruin, destruction; in **him to wrather heale,** to his destruction

wraththe (v.) see **wreathen**

wreastlin (v.) wrestle

wreathede see **wreathen**

wreath(th)(e) (n.) wrath, anger

wreathen, wreaththin, wreth(th)en (v.) anger, enrage; annoy; become angry or enraged (pres. 2nd sing. *wreathest*; pres. 3rd sing. *wreatheth*; pres. pl. *wreatheth*; pres. 2nd subj. sing. *wreathe*; past 3rd sing. *wreathede*; imper. sing. (as refl.) *wraththe . . . the*; past part.

iwreathet); **wreathe se thu wreathe**, angry as you may be

wrecche (n.) wretch, caitiff, miserable person or thing (pl. *wrecches*)

wrecchedom (n.) wretchedness, misery

wrenchen (v.) to wrench; turn aside (past 1st sing. *wrencte*)

wrenches (n. pl.) tricks, wiles

wrenchfule (adj.) crafty, deceitful

wrencte see **wrenchen**

wreoken (v.) wreak vengeance, avenge

wreothieth (v. pres. pl.) lean, rely (pres. 3rd sing. *wreotheth*)

wreththe see **wreaththe**

wreth(th)en see **wreathen**

wringinde see **wrong**

writ (n.) writ, writing (gen. sing. *writes*); book; **Hali Writ**, Holy Scripture; **lives writ**, the book of life

writ (v.) see **writen**

writeres (n. pl.) writers (gen. pl. writers)

writen (v.) write; trace (a sign); copy (a text) (pres. 3rd sing. *writ*; past 1st sing. *wrat*; past 3rd sing. *wrat*; past part. *iwriten*)

wrong (v. past 3rd sing.) wrung, twisted; caused pain; writhed (past subj. pl. *wrungen*; pres. part. *wringinde*)

wruhte (n.) maker

wrungen see **wrong**

wude (n.) wood (pl. *wudes*)

wulf (n.) wolf (pl. *wulves*)

wulle (v.) will, wish; often used as auxiliary to mark future tense or desire (pres. 1st sing. *wul(l)e*, *chulle*; pres. 2nd sing. *wult*; pres. 3rd sing. *wule*; pres. pl. *wulleth*; past 3rd sing. *walde*; past 3rd pl. *wolden*; negative forms: pres. 1st sing. *nulle*, *nulli*; pres. 2nd sing. *nult(u)*; pres. 3rd sing. *nule*; pres. pl. *nullen*; past 3rd sing. *nalde*; past subj. 2nd sing. *waldest*); **wulle**

ha, nulle ha, will she, nill she (i.e., whether she wishes to or not); **wullen ha nullen ha**, will they, nill they

wult see **wulle**

wulves see **wulf**

wumme (interj.) woe is me, alas!

wummen see **wummon**

wummon (n.) woman (pl. *wimmen*, *wummen*; gen. sing. *wummone*)

wunde (n.) wound (pl. *wunden*)

wunden see **wunde**

wundeth see **wundi**

wundi (v. pres. 1st sing.) wound (pres. 3rd sing. and pl. *wundeth*)

wunder (n.) wonder, strange thing; ruin (pl. *wundres*); **to wundre**, shamefully, scandalously

wunderlich (adj.) dreadful, terrifying; wondrous, marvellous

wundrede (v. 3rd sing. past and refl.) wondered, was surprised or astonished (**wundrede him . . . of**, wondered at, marveled at; **wundrede hire**, was surprised)

wundri (adj.) marvelous, wondrous

wune (n.) custom, habit

wunie(n) (v.) dwell, stay (pres. 2nd sing. *wunest*; pres. 3rd sing. *wuneth*; pres. pl. *wunieth*; past 3rd sing. *wunede*; subj. pres. sing. *wunie*; pres. part. *wuniende*; past part. *iwunet*; imper. *wune*)

wunne (n.) joy, pleasure (pl. *wunnen*); (as adj.) happy, joyful

wunsum (adj.) pleasant

wununge (n.) dwelling

wurchen (v.) work, perform, do; make, create (pres. 2nd sing. *wurchest*; pres. 3rd sing. *wurcheth*; past 2nd sing. *wrahtest*; past 3rd sing. *wrahte*, *wrahtte*; pres. 2nd sing. subj. *wurche*; imper. sing. *wurch*; past part. *iwrahte*)

wurdgin see **wurthgin**

wurhte (n.) creator

wurm (n.) dragon, serpent, snake; worm (pl. *wurmes*; gen. pl. *wurmene*)

wurpe see **warpen**

wurse (adj. compar.) worse, more evil or cruel; (as n.) fiend, devil

wursi (v. pres. subj. sing.) weaken, undermine

wurst (adv. superl.) worst; **theo thet wurst is throf**, the one who has the worst of it

wurth (n. 1) worth, merit; a thing of value (pl. *wurthes*); **withute mine wurthes**, without merits of mine (i.e., though I do not deserve it). (n. 2) fate, lot in life

wurth(e) (adj.) valuable, worthy, esteemed; **ha wurthe is**, she deserves; **beo wurthe**, deserves

wurth(e)munt, wurthmund (n.) worship, honor

wurthe(n) (v.) become; happen; come to (past 3rd sing. *warth, wearth*; pres. sing. subj. *wurthe*; past pl. *worthen*); **wa wurthe**, cursed be, may misfortune come from/happen to (something)

wurthful (adj.) worthy

wurthgin (v.) worship; respect (pres. 3rd sing. *wurthgith, wurthgeth*; past 3rd sing. *wurdgede*; pres. 3rd sing. subj. *wurthgi*; imper. *wurge*; past part. *iwur(d)get*)

wurthinc, wurthinge (n.) mire, filth

wurthliche (adj.) worthy, honorable

wurthschipe (n.) worship; **do ham worthschipe**, worship them

yare (adv.) before, already

yarki(n) (v.) prepare; ordain (past part. *iyarket*)

yarow (adj.) prepared, ready (pl. *yarowe*)

ye, yea (adv.) yes, yea

ye (pers. pron. 2nd pl. nom.) you

ye (interj.) on the contrary, indeed

yeat (v. past 3rd sing.) poured

yelden (v.) to repay (subj. 2nd sing. *yulde*; past 3rd sing. *yeald*)

yef, yif (conj.) if; whether; **bute yef**, unless

yef (v.) see **yeoven**

yeien (v.) wail, howl, shout; announce, cry out (i.e., speak in a loud voice) (pres. 3rd sing. *yeiyeth*; past 3rd sing. *yeide*; past 3rd pl. *yeiden*; imper. pl. *yeieth*; pres. part. *yeinde*)

yeinclappes (n. pl.) counterstrokes

yeinturn (n.) turning around, reversal; **do the i the yeinturn**, turn yourself around

yeiyeth see **yeien**

yeld (n.) sacrifice, tribute (to devils); yield (from crops)

yelde(n) (v.) give, yield; repay, give in exchange (pres. 3rd sing. *yelt*; imper. pl. *yeldeth*)

yellen (v.) yell

yelp (n.) boasting, arrogant speaking (yelp)

yelpen (v.) to boast, brag (pres. 1st sing. *yelpe*)

yelt see **yelden**

yeme (n.) heed, care

yemelese (adj.) careless, negligent

yeomere (adj.) wretched

yeomerliche (adv.) cruelly, piteously

yeomerunge (n.) wailing, crying out

yeont(e) (prep.) through; throughout, everywhere in

yeorliche (adv.) eagerly; carefully

yeorn(n)e (adv.) eagerly, earnestly, carefully

yeohthe (n.) itch; craving

yeove (n.) gifts (pl. *yeoven, yeoves*)

yeove(n) (v.) give; give in marriage (pres. 1st sing. *yeove*; pres. 3rd sing. *yeveth*; pres. pl. *yeoveth*; past 3rd sing. *yef*; pres. subj. 2nd sing. *yeve*; pres. subj. 3rd sing. *yeve, yeove*; past part. *iyeve, iyeven*); **nawiht ne yeove ich**, I care nothing for

yeoves see **yeoven**

yer (n.) year (pl. *yeres*)

yerde (n.) scepter; rod (pl. *yerden*)

yerdede (v. past 3rd sing.) beat with a stick or rod

yet (adv.) yet, still; even now, as of now; moreover

yetti (v. pres. 1st sing.) grant; allow (past 3rd sing. *yet(t)ede*; pres. 3rd sing. subj. *yette*; imper. sing. *yette*; past part. *iyettet*)

yetten (adv.) still, yet; moreover, even further

yif see **yef**

yirnde see **yirne**

yirne (v. pres. 1st sing.) yearn for; ask for (past 3rd sing. *yirnde*)

yisceunge (n.) covetousness, avarice, greed

yiscith (v. pres. 3rd sing.) long for, desire, covet (something wrongly)

ymage (n.) statue, image

yong (n.) going, journey; course, path; **bute yonge**, without movement. See also **gan**

yont (prep.) through, throughout

yuhelunge (v. pres. part.) yowling

yuhethe (n.) youth

yung (adj.) young (superl. *yungeste*)

yunglich (adj.) youthful, appearing young; **yunglich on yeres**, young in age

yuren (v.) to yell, yowl, shout (pres. part. *yurinde*)

Sentimental and Humorous Romances: Floris and Blancheflour, Sir Degrevant, The Squire of Low Degree, The Tournament of Tottenham, and The Feast of Tottenham, edited by Erik Kooper (2006)

The Dicts and Sayings of the Philosophers, edited by John William Sutton (2006)

Everyman and Its Dutch Original, Elckerlijc, edited by Clifford Davidson, Martin W. Walsh, and Ton J. Broos (2007)

The N-Town Plays, edited by Douglas Sugano, with assistance by Victor I. Scherb (2007)

The Book of John Mandeville, edited by Tamarah Kohanski and C. David Benson (2007)

John Lydgate, *The Temple of Glas*, edited by J. Allan Mitchell (2007)

The Northern Homily Cycle, edited by Anne B. Thompson (2008)

Codex Ashmole 61: A Compilation of Popular Middle English Verse, edited by George Shuffelton (2008)

Chaucer and the Poems of "Ch," edited by James I. Wimsatt (revised edition 2009)

William Caxton, *The Game and Playe of the Chesse*, edited by Jenny Adams (2009)

John the Blind Audelay, *Poems and Carols*, edited by Susanna Fein (2009)

Two Moral Interludes: The Pride of Life and Wisdom, edited by David Klausner (2009)

John Lydgate, *Mummings and Entertainments*, edited by Claire Sponsler (2010)

Mankind, edited by Kathleen M. Ashley and Gerard NeCastro (2010)

The Castle of Perseverance, edited by David N. Klausner (2010)

Robert Henryson, *The Complete Works*, edited by David J. Parkinson (2010)

John Gower, *The French Balades*, edited and translated by R. F. Yeager (2011)

The Middle English Metrical Paraphrase of the Old Testament, edited by Michael Livingston (2011)

The York Corpus Christi Plays, edited by Clifford Davidson (2011)

Prik of Conscience, edited by James H. Morey (2012)

The Dialogue of Solomon and Marcolf: A Dual-Language Edition from Latin and Middle English Printed Editions, edited by Nancy Mason Bradbury and Scott Bradbury (2012)

Croxton Play of the Sacrament, edited by John T. Sebastian (2012)

Ten Bourdes, edited by Melissa M. Furrow (2013)

Lybeaus Desconus, edited by Eve Salisbury and James Weldon (2013)

The Complete Harley 2253 Manuscript, Vol. 2, edited and translated by Susanna Fein with David Raybin and Jan Ziolkowski (2014); Vol. 3 (2015); Vol. 1 (2015)

Oton de Granson Poems, edited and translated by Peter Nicholson and Joan Grenier-Winther (2015)

The King of Tars, edited by John H. Chandler (2015)

John Hardyng Chronicle, edited by James Simpson and Sarah Peverley (2015)

Richard Coer de Lyon, edited by Peter Larkin (2015)

Guillaume de Machaut, The Complete Poetry and Music, Volume 1: The Debate Poems, edited and translated by R. Barton Palmer (2016)

Lydgate's Fabula Duorum Mercatorum and Guy of Warwyk, edited by Pamela Farvolden (2016)

COMMENTARY SERIES

Haimo of Auxerre, *Commentary on the Book of Jonah*, translated with an introduction and notes by Deborah Everhart (1993)

Medieval Exegesis in Translation: Commentaries on the Book of Ruth, translated with an introduction and notes by Lesley Smith (1996)

Nicholas of Lyra's Apocalypse Commentary, translated with an introduction and notes by Philip D. W. Krey (1997)

Rabbi Ezra Ben Solomon of Gerona, *Commentary on the Song of Songs and Other Kabbalistic Commentaries*, selected, translated, and annotated by Seth Brody (1999)

John Wyclif, *On the Truth of Holy Scripture*, translated with an introduction and notes by Ian Christopher Levy (2001)

Second Thessalonians: Two Early Medieval Apocalyptic Commentaries, introduced and translated by Steven R. Cartwright and Kevin L. Hughes (2001)

The "Glossa Ordinaria" on the Song of Songs, translated with an introduction and notes by Mary Dove (2004)

The Seven Seals of the Apocalypse: Medieval Texts in Translation, translated with an introduction and notes by Francis X. Gumerlock (2009)

The "Glossa Ordinaria" on Romans, translated with an introduction and notes by Michael Scott Woodward (2011)

Nicholas of Lyra, Literal Commentary on Galatians, translated with an introduction and notes by Edward Arthur Naumann (2015)

Early Latin Commentaries on the Apocalypse, edited by Francis X. Gumerlock (2016)

Secular Commentary Series

Accessus ad auctores: Medieval Introduction to the Authors, edited and translated by Stephen M. Wheeler (2015)
The Vulgate Commentary on Ovid's Metamorphoses, *Book 1*, edited and translated by Frank Coulson (2015)
Brunetto Latini, La rettorica, edited and translated by Stefania D'Agata D'Ottavi (2016)

Documents of Practice Series

Love and Marriage in Late Medieval London, selected, translated, and introduced by Shannon McSheffrey (1995)
Sources for the History of Medicine in Late Medieval England, selected, introduced, and translated by Carole Rawcliffe (1995)
A Slice of Life: Selected Documents of Medieval English Peasant Experience, edited, translated, and with an introduction by Edwin Brezette DeWindt (1996)
Regular Life: Monastic, Canonical, and Mendicant "Rules," selected and introduced by Douglas J. McMillan and Kathryn Smith Fladenmuller (1997); second edition, selected and introduced by Daniel Marcel La Corte and Douglas J. McMillan (2004)
Women and Monasticism in Medieval Europe: Sisters and Patrons of the Cistercian Reform, selected, translated, and with an introduction by Constance H. Berman (2002)
Medieval Notaries and Their Acts: The 1327–1328 Register of Jean Holanie, introduced, edited, and translated by Kathryn L. Reyerson and Debra A. Salata (2004)
John Stone's Chronicle: Christ Church Priory, Canterbury, 1417–1472, selected, translated, and introduced by Meriel Connor (2010)

Medieval German Texts in Bilingual Editions Series

Sovereignty and Salvation in the Vernacular, 1050–1150, introduction, translations, and notes by James A. Schultz (2000)
Ava's New Testament Narratives: "When the Old Law Passed Away," introduction, translation, and notes by James A. Rushing, Jr. (2003)
History as Literature: German World Chronicles of the Thirteenth Century in Verse, introduction, translation, and notes by R. Graeme Dunphy (2003)
Thomasin von Zirclaria, Der Welsche Gast (The Italian Guest), translated by Marion Gibbs and Winder McConnell (2009)
Ladies, Whores, and Holy Women: A Sourcebook in Courtly, Religious, and Urban Cultures of Late Medieval Germany, introductions, translations, and notes by Ann Marie Rasmussen and Sarah Westphal-Wihl (2010)

Varia

The Study of Chivalry: Resources and Approaches, edited by Howell Chickering and Thomas H. Seiler (1988)
Studies in the Harley Manuscript: The Scribes, Contents, and Social Contexts of British Library MS Harley 2253, edited by Susanna Fein (2000)
The Liturgy of the Medieval Church, edited by Thomas J. Heffernan and E. Ann Matter (2001; second edition 2005)
Johannes de Grocheio, Ars musice, edited and translated by Constant J. Mews, John N. Crossley, Catherine Jeffreys, Leigh McKinnon, and Carol J. Williams (2011)
Aribo, De musica *and* Sententiae, edited and translated by T.J.H. McCarthy (2015)

To Order Please Contact:

Medieval Institute Publications
Western Michigan University • Kalamazoo, MI 49008-5432
Phone (269) 387-8755 • FAX (269) 387-8750
http://www.wmich.edu/medievalpublications

Typeset in 10/13 New Baskerville
and Golden Cockerel Ornaments display

Medieval Institute Publications
College of Arts and Sciences
Western Michigan University
1903 W. Michigan Avenue
Kalamazoo, MI 49008-5432
http://www.wmich.edu/medievalpublications

 WESTERN MICHIGAN UNIVERSITY